DISCARD

Volume **4**

Hebrews to Revelation

Zondervan Illustrated Bible Backgrounds Commentary

Clinton E. Arnold

GENERAL EDITOR

ZONDERVAN™

GRAND RAPIDS, MICHIGAN 49530

ZONDERVAN™

Zondervan Illustrated Bible Backgrounds Commentary: Volume 4, *Hebrews to Revelation*
    Hebrews—Copyright © 2002 by George H. Guthrie
    James, 2 Peter, Jude—Copyright © 2002 by Douglas J. Moo
    1 Peter—Copyright © 2002 by Peter H. Davids
    1, 2, 3 John—Copyright © 2002 by Robert Yarbrough
    Revelation—Copyright © 2002 by Mark Wilson

Requests for information should be addressed to:

Zondervan, *Grand Rapids, Michigan 49530*

Library of Congress Cataloging-in-Publication Data
        Zondervan illustrated Bible backgrounds commentary / Clinton E. Arnold, general editor.
            p.cm.
        Includes bibliographical references.
        Contents: v. 1. Matthew, Mark, Luke—v. 2. John, Acts—v. 3. Romans to Philemon—
    v. 4. Hebrews to Revelation.
        ISBN 0–310–21806–3 (v. 1)—ISBN 0–310–21807–1 (v. 2)—ISBN 0–310–21808–X (v. 3)—
    ISBN 0–310–21809–8 (v. 4)
        1. Bible. N.T.—Commentaries.   I. Arnold, Clinton E.
        BS2341.52.Z66 2001
        225.7—dc21   2001046801
                                                                        CIP

Printed in China

Interior design by Sherri L. Hoffman

---

02 03 04 05 06 07 08 /❖HK/ 10 9 8 7 6 5 4 3 2 1

ABOUT THE AUTHORS

General editor:

Clinton E. Arnold (Ph.D., University of Aberdeen), professor and chairman, department of New Testament, Talbot School of Theology, Biola University, Los Angeles, California

Hebrews:

George H. Guthrie (Ph.D., Southwestern Baptist Theological Seminary), Benjamin W. Perry professor of Bible school of Christian studies, Union University, Memphis, Tennessee

James:

Douglas J. Moo (Ph.D., University of St. Andrews), Blanchard professor of New Testament, Wheaton College Graduate School, Wheaton, Illinois

1 Peter:

Peter H. Davids (Ph.D. University of Manchester), adjunct professor of New Testament/educational missionary, Tyndale Theological Seminary, Amsterdam, the Netherlands, and International Teams, Innsbruck, Austria

2 Peter:

Douglas J. Moo (Ph.D., University of St. Andrews), Blanchard professor of New Testament, Wheaton College Graduate School, Wheaton, Illinois

1, 2, 3 John:

Robert W. Yarbrough (Ph.D., University of Aberdeen), associate professor of New Testament and department chair, Trinity Evangelical Divinity School, Trinity International University, Deerfield, Illinois

Jude:

Douglas J. Moo (Ph.D., University of St. Andrews), Blanchard professor of New Testament, Wheaton College Graduate School, Wheaton, Illinois

Revelation:

Mark W. Wilson (D.Litt. et Phil., University of South Africa), adjunct professor of New Testament, Regent University, Virginia Beach, Virginia

Zondervan Illustrated Bible Backgrounds Commentary

CONTENTS

INTRODUCTION

All readers of the Bible have a tendency to view what it says it through their own culture and life circumstances. This can happen almost subconsiously as we read the pages of the text.

When most people in the church read about the thief on the cross, for instance, they immediately think of a burglar that held up a store or broke into a home. They may be rather shocked to find out that the guy was actually a Jewish revolutionary figure who was part of a growing movement in Palestine eager to throw off Roman rule.

It also comes as something of a surprise to contemporary Christians that "cursing" in the New Testament era had little or nothing to do with cussing somebody out. It had far more to do with the invocation of spirits to cause someone harm.

No doubt there is a need in the church for learning more about the world of the New Testament to avoid erroneous interpretations of the text of Scripture. But relevant historical and cultural insights also provide an added dimension of perspective to the words of the Bible. This kind of information often functions in the same way as watching a movie in color rather than in black and white. Finding out, for instance, how Paul compared Christ's victory on the cross to a joyous celebration parade in honor of a Roman general after winning an extraordinary battle brings does indeed magnify the profundity and implications of Jesus' work on the cross. Discovering that the factions at Corinth ("I follow Paul . . . I follow Apollos . . .") had plenty of precedent in the local cults ("I follow Aphrodite; I follow Apollo . . .") helps us understand the "why" of a particular problem. Learning about the water supply from the springs of Hierapolis that flowed into Laodicea as "lukewarm" water enables us to appreciate the relevance of the metaphor Jesus used when he addressed the spiritual laxity of this church.

My sense is that most Christians are eager to learn more about the real life setting of the New Testament. In the preaching and teaching of the Bible in the church, congregants are always grateful when they learn something of the background and historical context of the text. It not only helps them understand the text more accurately, but often enables them to identify with the people and circumstances of the Bible. I have been asked on countless occasions by Christians, "Where can I get access to good historical background information about this passage?" Earnest Christians are hungry for information that makes their Bibles come alive.

The stimulus for this commentary came from the church and the aim is to serve the church. The contributors to this series have sought to provide illuminating and interesting historical/cultural background information. The intent was to draw upon relevant papyri, inscriptions, archaeological discoveries, and the numerous studies of Judaism, Roman culture, Hellenism, and other features of the world of the New Testament and to make the results accessible to people in the church. We recognize that some readers of the commentary will want to go further, and so the sources of the information have been carefully documented in endnotes.

The written information has been supplemented with hundreds of photographs, maps, charts, artwork, and other graphics that help the reader better understand the world of the New Testament. Each of the writers was given an opportunity to dream up a "wish list" of illustrations that he thought would help to illustrate the passages in the New Testament book for which he was writing commentary. Although we were not able to obtain everything they were looking for, we came close.

The team of commentators are writing for the benefit of the broad array of Christians who simply want to better understand their Bibles from the vantage point of the historical context. This is an installment in a new genre of "Bible background" commentaries that was kicked off by Craig Keener's fine volume. Consequently, this is not an "exegetical" commentary that provides linguistic insight and background into Greek constructions and verb tenses. Neither is this work an "expository" commentary that provides a verse-by-verse exposition of the text; for in-depth philo-

logical or theological insight, readers will need to have other more specialized or comprehensive commentaries available. Nor is this an "historical-critical" commentary, although the contributors are all scholars and have already made substantial academic contributions on the New Testament books they are writing on for this set. The team intentionally does not engage all of the issues that are discussed in the scholarly guild.

Rather, our goal is to offer a reading and interpretation of the text informed by what we regard as the most relevant historical information. For many in the church, this commentary will serve as an important entry point into the interpretation and appreciation of the text. For other more serious students of the Word, these volumes will provide an important supplement to many of the fine exegetical, expository, and critical available.

The contributors represent a group of scholars who embrace the Bible as the Word of God and believe that the message of its pages has life-changing relevance for faith and practice today. Accordingly, we offer "Reflections" on the relevance of the Scripture to life for every chapter of the New Testament.

I pray that this commentary brings you both delight and insight in digging deeper into the Word of God.

Clinton E. Arnold
General Editor

LIST OF SIDEBARS

2 Peter

1 John

2 John

3 John

Jude

LIST OF CHARTS

INDEX OF PHOTOS AND MAPS

ABBREVIATIONS

1. Books of the Bible and Apocrypha

1 Chron.	1 Chronicles
2 Chron.	2 Chronicles
1 Cor.	1 Corinthians
2 Cor.	2 Corinthians
1 Esd.	1 Esdras
2 Esd.	2 Esdras
1 John	1 John
2 John	2 John
3 John	3 John
1 Kings	1 Kings
2 Kings	2 Kings
1 Macc.	1 Maccabees
2 Macc.	2 Maccabees
1 Peter	1 Peter
2 Peter	2 Peter
1 Sam.	1 Samuel
2 Sam.	2 Samuel
1 Thess.	1 Thessalonians
2 Thess.	2 Thessalonians
1 Tim.	1 Timothy
2 Tim.	2 Timothy
Acts	Acts
Amos	Amos
Bar.	Baruch
Bel	Bel and the Dragon
Col.	Colossians
Dan.	Daniel
Deut.	Deuteronomy
Eccl.	Ecclesiastes
Ep. Jer.	Epistle of Jeremiah
Eph.	Ephesians
Est.	Esther
Ezek.	Ezekiel
Ex.	Exodus
Ezra	Ezra
Gal.	Galatians
Gen.	Genesis
Hab.	Habakkuk
Hag.	Haggai
Heb.	Hebrews
Hos.	Hosea
Isa.	Isaiah
James	James
Jer.	Jeremiah
Job	Job
Joel	Joel
John	John
Jonah	Jonah
Josh.	Joshua
Jude	Jude
Judg.	Judges
Judith	Judith
Lam.	Lamentations
Lev.	Leviticus
Luke	Luke
Mal.	Malachi
Mark	Mark
Matt.	Matthew
Mic.	Micah
Nah.	Nahum
Neh.	Nehemiah
Num.	Numbers
Obad.	Obadiah
Phil.	Philippians
Philem.	Philemon
Pr. Man.	Prayer of Manassah
Prov.	Proverbs
Ps.	Psalm
Rest. of Est.	The Rest of Esther
Rev.	Revelation
Rom.	Romans
Ruth	Ruth
S. of III Ch.	The Song of the Three Holy Children
Sir.	Sirach/Ecclesiasticus
Song	Song of Songs

Sus.	Susanna
Titus	Titus
Tobit	Tobit
Wisd. Sol.	The Wisdom of Solomon
Zech.	Zechariah
Zeph.	Zephaniah

2. Old and New Testament Pseudepigrapha and Rabbinic Literature

Individual tractates of rabbinic literature follow the abbreviations of the *SBL Handbook of Style*, pp. 79–80. Qumran documents follow standard Dead Sea Scroll conventions.

2 Bar.	2 Baruch
3 Bar.	3 Baruch
4 Bar.	4 Baruch
1 En.	1 Enoch
2 En.	2 Enoch
3 En.	3 Enoch
4 Ezra	4 Ezra
3 Macc.	3 Maccabees
4 Macc.	4 Maccabees
5 Macc.	5 Maccabees
Acts Phil.	Acts of Philip
Acts Pet.	Acts of Peter and the 12 Apostles
Apoc. Elijah	Apocalypse of Elijah
As. Mos.	Assumption of Moses
b.	Babylonian Talmud (+ tractate)
Gos. Thom.	Gospel of Thomas
Jos. Asen.	Joseph and Aseneth
Jub.	Jubilees
Let. Aris.	Letter of Aristeas
m.	Mishnah (+ tractate)
Mek.	Mekilta
Midr.	Midrash I (+ biblical book)
Odes Sol.	Odes of Solomon
Pesiq. Rab.	Pesiqta Rabbati
Pirqe R. El.	Pirqe Rabbi Eliezer
Pss. Sol.	Psalms of Solomon
Rab.	Rabbah (+biblical book); (e.g., Gen. Rab.=Genesis Rabbah)

S. ʿOlam Rab.	Seder ʿOlam Rabbah
Sem.	Semahot
Sib. Or.	Sibylline Oracles
T. Ab.	Testament of Abraham
T. Adam	Testament of Adam
T. Ash.	Testament of Asher
T. Benj.	Testament of Benjamin
T. Dan	Testament of Dan
T. Gad	Testament of Gad
T. Hez.	Testament of Hezekiah
T. Isaac	Testament of Isaac
T. Iss.	Testament of Issachar
T. Jac.	Testament of Jacob
T. Job	Testament of Job
T. Jos.	Testament of Joseph
T. Jud.	Testament of Judah
T. Levi	Testament of Levi
T. Mos.	Testament of Moses
T. Naph.	Testament of Naphtali
T. Reu.	Testament of Reuben
T. Sim.	Testament of Simeon
T. Sol.	Testament of Solomon
T. Zeb.	Testament of Zebulum
Tanh.	Tanhuma
Tg. Isa.	Targum of Isaiah
Tg. Lam.	Targum of Lamentations
Tg. Neof.	Targum Neofiti
Tg. Onq.	Targum Onqelos
Tg. Ps.-J	Targum Pseudo-Jonathan
y.	Jerusalem Talmud (+ tractate)

3. Classical Historians

For an extended list of classical historians and church fathers, see *SBL Handbook of Style*, pp. 84–87. For many works of classical antiquity, the abbreviations have been subjected to the author's discretion; the names of these works should be obvious upon consulting entries of the classical writers in classical dictionaries or encyclopedias.

Eusebius

| Eccl. Hist. | Ecclesiastical History |

Josephus

Ag. Ap.	*Against Apion*
Ant.	*Jewish Antiquities*
J.W.	*Jewish War*
Life	*The Life*

Philo

Abraham	On the Life of Abraham
Agriculture	On Agriculture
Alleg. Interp	Allegorical Interpretation
Animals	Whether Animals Have Reason
Cherubim	On the Cherubim
Confusion	On the Confusion of Thomas
Contempl. Life	On the Contemplative Life
Creation	On the Creation of the World
Curses	On Curses
Decalogue	On the Decalogue
Dreams	On Dreams
Drunkenness	On Drunkenness
Embassy	On the Embassy to Gaius
Eternity	On the Eternity of the World
Flaccus	Against Flaccus
Flight	On Flight and Finding
Giants	On Giants
God	On God
Heir	Who Is the Heir?
Hypothetica	Hypothetica
Joseph	On the Life of Joseph
Migration	On the Migration of Abraham
Moses	On the Life of Moses
Names	On the Change of Names
Person	That Every Good Person Is Free
Planting	On Planting
Posterity	On the Posterity of Cain
Prelim. Studies	On the Preliminary Studies
Providence	On Providence
QE	Questions and Answers on Exodus
QG	Questions and Answers on Genesis
Rewards	On Rewards and Punishments
Sacrifices	On the Sacrifices of Cain and Abel
Sobriety	On Sobriety
Spec. Laws	On the Special Laws
Unchangeable	That God Is Unchangeable
Virtues	On the Virtues
Worse	That the Worse Attacks the Better

Apostolic Fathers

1 Clem.	*First Letter of Clement*
Barn.	*Epistle of Barnabas*
Clem. Hom.	*Ancient Homily of Clement (also called 2 Clement)*
Did.	*Didache*
Herm. Vis.; Sim.	*Shepherd of Hermas, Visions; Similitudes*
Ignatius	*Epistles of Ignatius (followed by the letter's name)*
Mart. Pol.	*Martyrdom of Polycarp*

4. Modern Abbreviations

AASOR	Annual of the American Schools of Oriental Research
AB	Anchor Bible
ABD	*Anchor Bible Dictionary*
ABRL	Anchor Bible Reference Library
AGJU	Arbeiten zur Geschichte des antiken Judentums und des Urchristentums
AH	*Agricultural History*
ALGHJ	Arbeiten zur Literatur und Geschichte des Hellenistischen Judentums
AnBib	Analecta biblica
ANRW	*Aufstieg und Niedergang der römischen Welt*

ANTC	Abingdon New Testament Commentaries
BAGD	Bauer, W., W. F. Arndt, F. W. Gingrich, and F. W. Danker. *Greek-English Lexicon of the New Testament and Other Early Christina Literature* (2d. ed.)
BA	*Biblical Archaeologist*
BAFCS	Book of Acts in Its First Century Setting
BAR	*Biblical Archaeology Review*
BASOR	*Bulletin of the American Schools of Oriental Research*
BBC	*Bible Background Commentary*
BBR	*Bulletin for Biblical Research*
BDB	Brown, F., S. R. Driver, and C. A. Briggs. *A Hebrew and English Lexicon of the Old Testament*
BDF	Blass, F., A. Debrunner, and R. W. Funk. *A Greek Grammar of the New Testament and Other Early Christian Literature*
BECNT	Baker Exegetical Commentary on the New Testament
BI	*Biblical Illustrator*
Bib	*Biblica*
BibSac	*Bibliotheca Sacra*
BLT	Brethren Life and Thought
BNTC	Black's New Testament Commentary
BRev	*Bible Review*
BSHJ	Baltimore Studies in the History of Judaism
BST	The Bible Speaks Today

BSV	Biblical Social Values
BT	*The Bible Translator*
BTB	*Biblical Theology Bulletin*
BZ	*Biblische Zeitschrift*
CBQ	*Catholic Biblical Quarterly*
CBTJ	*Calvary Baptist Theological Journal*
CGTC	Cambridge Greek Testament Commentary
CH	*Church History*
CIL	*Corpus inscriptionum latinarum*
CPJ	*Corpus papyrorum judaicorum*
CRINT	*Compendia rerum iudaicarum ad Novum Testamentum*
CTJ	*Calvin Theological Journal*
CTM	*Concordia Theological Monthly*
CTT	Contours of Christian Theology
DBI	*Dictionary of Biblical Imagery*
DCM	*Dictionary of Classical Mythology.*
DDD	*Dictionary of Deities and Demons in the Bible*
DJBP	*Dictionary of Judaism in the Biblical Period*
DJG	*Dictionary of Jesus and the Gospels*
DLNT	*Dictionary of the Later New Testament and Its Developments*
DNTB	*Dictionary of New Testament Background*
DPL	*Dictionary of Paul and His Letters*
EBC	*Expositor's Bible Commentary*
EDBT	*Evangelical Dictionary of Biblical Theology*
EDNT	*Exegetical Dictionary of the New Testament*

EJR	Encyclopedia of the Jewish Religion	JAC	Jahrbuch fur Antike und Christentum
EPRO	Études préliminaires aux religions orientales dans l'empire romain	JBL	Journal of Biblical Literature
EvQ	Evangelical Quarterly	JETS	Journal of the Evangelical Theological Society
ExpTim	Expository Times	JHS	Journal of Hellenic Studies
FRLANT	Forsuchungen zur Religion und Literatur des Alten und Neuen Testament	JJS	Journal of Jewish Studies
		JOAIW	Jahreshefte des Osterreeichischen Archaologischen Instites in Wien
GNC	Good News Commentary		
GNS	Good News Studies	JSJ	Journal for the Study of Judaism in the Persian, Hellenistic, and Roman Periods
HCNT	Hellenistic Commentary to the New Testament		
HDB	Hastings Dictionary of the Bible		
		JRS	Journal of Roman Studies
HJP	History of the Jewish People in the Age of Jesus Christ, by E. Schürer	JSNT	Journal for the Study of the New Testament
		JSNTSup	Journal for the Study of the New Testament: Supplement Series
HTR	Harvard Theological Review		
HTS	Harvard Theological Studies	JSOT	Journal for the Study of the Old Testament
HUCA	Hebrew Union College Annual	JSOTSup	Journal for the Study of the Old Testament: Supplement Series
IBD	Illustrated Bible Dictionary		
IBS	Irish Biblical Studies	JTS	Journal of Theological Studies
ICC	International Critical Commentary		
		KTR	Kings Theological Review
IDB	The Interpreter's Dictionary of the Bible	LCL	Loeb Classical Library
		LEC	Library of Early Christianity
IEJ	Israel Exploration Journal		
IG	Inscriptiones graecae	LSJ	Liddell, H. G., R. Scott, H. S. Jones. A Greek-English Lexicon
IGRR	Inscriptiones graecae ad res romanas pertinentes		
ILS	Inscriptiones Latinae Selectae	MM	Moulton, J. H., and G. Milligan. The Vocabulary of the Greek Testament
Imm	Immanuel		
ISBE	International Standard Bible Encyclopedia	MNTC	Moffatt New Testament Commentary
Int	Interpretation	NBD	New Bible Dictionary
IvE	Inschriften von Ephesos	NC	Narrative Commentaries
IVPNTC	InterVarsity Press New Testament Commentary	NCBC	New Century Bible Commentary Eerdmans

NEAE	*New Encyclopedia of Archaeological Excavations in the Holy Land*
NEASB	*Near East Archaeological Society Bulletin*
New Docs	*New Documents Illustrating Early Christianity*
NIBC	New International Biblical Commentary
NICNT	New International Commentary on the New Testament
NIDNTT	*New International Dictionary of New Testament Theology*
NIGTC	New International Greek Testament Commentary
NIVAC	NIV Application Commentary
NorTT	*Norsk Teologisk Tidsskrift*
NoT	*Notes on Translation*
NovT	*Novum Testamentum*
NovTSup	Novum Testamentum Supplements
NTAbh	Neutestamentliche Abhandlungen
NTS	*New Testament Studies*
NTT	New Testament Theology
NTTS	New Testament Tools and Studies
OAG	*Oxford Archaeological Guides*
OCCC	*Oxford Companion to Classical Civilization*
OCD	*Oxford Classical Dictionary*
ODCC	*The Oxford Dictionary of the Christian Church*
OGIS	*Orientis graeci inscriptiones selectae*
OHCW	*The Oxford History of the Classical World*
OHRW	*Oxford History of the Roman World*

OTP	*Old Testament Pseudepigrapha*, ed. by J. H. Charlesworth
PEQ	*Palestine Exploration Quarterly*
PG	*Patrologia graeca*
PGM	*Papyri graecae magicae: Die griechischen Zauberpapyri*
PL	*Patrologia latina*
PNTC	Pelican New Testament Commentaries
Rb	*Revista biblica*
RB	*Revue biblique*
RivB	*Rivista biblica italiana*
RTR	*Reformed Theological Review*
SB	Sources bibliques
SBL	Society of Biblical Literature
SBLDS	Society of Biblical Literature Dissertation Series
SBLMS	Society of Biblical Literature Monograph Series
SBLSP	*Society of Biblical Literature Seminar Papers*
SBS	Stuttgarter Bibelstudien
SBT	Studies in Biblical Theology
SCJ	*Stone-Campbell Journal*
Scr	*Scripture*
SE	*Studia Evangelica*
SEG	*Supplementum epigraphicum graecum*
SJLA	Studies in Judaism in Late Antiquity
SJT	*Scottish Journal of Theology*
SNTSMS	Society for New Testament Studies Monograph Series
SSC	Social Science Commentary

SSCSSG	Social-Science Commentary on the Synoptic Gospels
Str-B	Strack, H. L., and P. Billerbeck. *Kommentar zum Neuen Testament aus Talmud und Midrasch*
TC	Thornapple Commentaries
TDNT	*Theological Dictionary of the New Testament*
TDOT	*Theological Dictionary of the Old Testament*
TLNT	*Theological Lexicon of the New Testament*
TLZ	*Theologische Literaturzeitung*
TNTC	Tyndale New Testament Commentary
TrinJ	*Trinity Journal*
TS	*Theological Studies*
TSAJ	Texte und Studien zum antiken Judentum
TWNT	*Theologische Wörterbuch zum Neuen Testament*
TynBul	*Tyndale Bulletin*
WBC	Word Biblical Commentary Waco: Word, 1982
WMANT	Wissenschaftliche Monographien zum Alten und Neuen Testament
WUNT	Wissenschaftliche Untersuchungen zum Neuen Testament
YJS	Yale Judaica Series
ZNW	*Zeitschrift fur die neutestamentliche Wissenschaft und die Junde der alteren Kirche*
ZPE	*Zeischrift der Papyrolgie und Epigraphkik*
ZPEB	*Zondervan Pictorial Encyclopedia of the Bible*

5. General Abbreviations

ad. loc.	in the place cited
b.	born
c., ca.	circa
cf.	compare
d.	died
ed(s).	editors(s), edited by
e.g.	for example
ET	English translation
frg.	fragment
i.e.	that is
ibid.	in the same place
idem	the same (author)
lit.	literally
l(1)	line(s)
MSS	manuscripts
n.d.	no date
NS	New Series
par.	parallel
passim	here and there
repr.	reprint
ser.	series
s.v.	*sub verbo*, under the word
trans.	translator, translated by; transitive

Zondervan Illustrated Bible Backgrounds Commentary

HEBREWS

by George H. Guthrie

Who Wrote Hebrews?

Unlike most other New Testament works, the book of Hebrews does not reveal the identity of its author. Since the second century, people have loved to speculate concerning that identity. The early church fathers were mixed in their opinion on the matter. Scholars of the eastern part of the Mediterranean world often suggested that the apostle Paul wrote the book. Scholars in the West, focused in Rome, argued against that opinion. Even those who held to Pauline authorship, such as Clement of Alexandria and Origen, recognized that the style of the book differs sharply from Paul's writings.

ROME

The Tiber River.

▶ **Hebrews**
IMPORTANT FACTS:

- **AUTHOR:** Unknown, but someone like Apollos.
- **DATE:** Approximately A.D. 64–66.
- **OCCASION:**
  - To address the problem of apostasy among the recipients.
  - To bolster the resolve of Christians facing persecution.
  - To challenge the believers to move on to maturity, in terms of theological understanding and practical obedience.
  - To address friction between the members of the church and their leaders.
- **THEMES:**
  1. God has spoken and we should obey him.
  2. God has spoken ultimately in the person and work of his Son.
  3. The Son is incarnate and exalted.
  4. The high-priestly ministry of the Son is manifested through his death and exaltation.
  5. The Son's person and work form a superior basis for perseverance in the face of trial.
  6. There are terrible consequences for those who reject the salvation provided by the Son's person and work.

Today few scholars of any theological tradition hold to Pauline authorship for the following reasons. (1) Many of the book's images, theological motifs, and terms are not found in the Pauline literature. For instance, the image of Christ as high priest is unique to Hebrews, and 169 words used in Hebrews are not used anywhere else in the New Testament. (2) The author introduces his quotations of the Old Testament in a different manner from what Paul normally does. Paul usually uses the phrase, "It is written"; Hebrews, following the style of sermons in the Greek-speaking, Jewish synagogues of the Mediterranean world, introduces scriptural quotations with some form of God speaking (e.g., "he says"). (3) Finally, the author of Hebrews depicts himself as having received the gospel from the original witnesses commissioned by the Lord (2:3), and, in light of his often-made assertions to the contrary, it is difficult to imagine Paul making such a statement![1]

Through the centuries other names have been put forward, such as Luke, Clement of Rome, Barnabas, Jude, Apollos, Philip, Silvanus, and Priscilla. What do we know about the author who wrote this intriguing book?

First, the author is a dynamic preacher who really knows his Old Testament and has been trained in the forms of interpretation common in Jewish synagogues. The synagogue was the center of social and religious life for the Jews, and the worship service was at the center of the synagogue service. Focal to the worship service was an exposition of what we now call the Old Testament Scriptures. Hebrews exhibits a number of characteristics of a first-century sermon. The author uses techniques and patterns in his expositions of the Old Testament that were common sermonic features, and he uses these techniques and patterns with great skill and eloquence. Moreover, the book is packed with references to the Old Testament. There are some thirty-

five quotations, thirty-four allusions, and numerous summaries of material and references to names and topics given. What is clear is that the author has a broad grasp of Scripture and a heart committed to its authority.

Second, the person who wrote Hebrews is obviously highly educated, which means that he has advanced training in rhetoric. At the heart of ancient rhetorical training was education in the art of expression and argumentation, and numerous stylistic forms were learned as tools to these ends. Such forms are found throughout Hebrews, so the author brings a wealth of education to bear on his task of communicating his message.

Third, the author serves as a Christian leader of the church and exhibits a deep concern for the spiritual state of the book's recipients. All of his background in the synagogue forms of preaching, his copious understanding of the Old Testament, and his training in the art of rhetoric are brought to bear on the task of challenging this group of Christians to stay the course of commitment to Christ. He shows a detailed understanding of the congregation's past and present situations and demonstrates great urgency about their condition.

Although any suggestion as to the authorship of Hebrews must remain in the category of a "best guess," a number of scholars since the time of Martin Luther have followed the Reformer in putting forth Apollos as the best guess on who penned the work. In Acts 18:24–26 Luke describes Apollos as follows:

Meanwhile a Jew named Apollos, a native of Alexandria, came to Ephesus. He was a learned man, with a thorough knowledge of the Scriptures. He had been instructed in the way of the Lord, and he spoke with great fervor and

taught about Jesus accurately, though he knew only the baptism of John. He began to speak boldly in the synagogue.

Several of the descriptors used by Luke of this early Christian leader seem to fit the author of Hebrews. (1) Apollos was from Alexandria, and numerous terms used in Hebrews are also found in the works of Philo of Alexandria and Wisdom of Solomon, a book also associated with that city. We should not overstate the significance of the verbal parallels here since these literary achievements enjoyed wide readership in the Mediterranean world, but the vocabulary shared by these works from Alexandria and Hebrews does provide a possible connection with Apollos. (2) Luke refers to Apollos as "a learned man." The Greek term can also be translated as "eloquent" and was used of those with rhetorical

ITALY

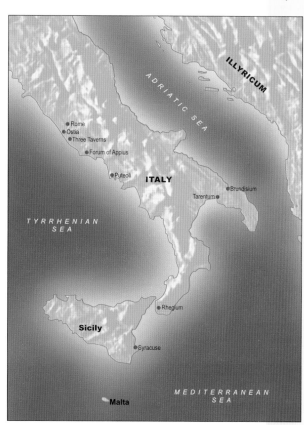

training. Alexandria was a major center for such training. (3) Luke writes that Apollos had a thorough grasp of the Scriptures (i.e., the Old Testament) and spoke with great fervor in the synagogue. Hebrews demonstrates a broad understanding of the Old Testament and a great fervor, and it exhibits characteristics of a synagogue homily in Greek-speaking synagogues of that time. While with Origen we must confess that only God knows who wrote Hebrews, we can also reasonably say that "someone like Apollos" wrote the book.[2]

▶

ROME

(right) The Arch of Constantine.

(bottom) The Via Sacra leading to the Colosseum.

▼

To Whom Was Hebrews Written and Why?

The Recipients. As is the case with authorship, the first recipients of Hebrews are not explicitly identified in the book. What the interpreter is left to, therefore, is sorting through clues to their identity. Fortunately, a number of such clues exist.

First, the author seems to address a group of people who have some background in the Jewish synagogue. His use of the Old Testament seems to assume a fairly broad understanding of the Scriptures. Also, theological concepts popular in the Greek-speaking synagogues of the day are found in the book—such as a special veneration of Moses, the mediatorial role of angels in relation to the old covenant law, and interest in the role of the divine Wisdom in creation.

Second, some associated with this Christian community seem to have abandoned the Christian faith and, perhaps, returned to Judaism proper, and others are struggling with the temptation to do so.

Third, the church addressed is likely located in the city of Rome. Among the over one million inhabitants of Rome in the first Christian century, some forty to sixty thousand were Jews. Many of these were Roman citizens, had Greek or Latin names, and spoke Greek. Acts 2 tells us that there were Jews from Rome at the Pentecost event, and it may be that some of these converted to Christianity, returning to the capital to establish a church there. In Hebrews 13:24 the author writes, "Those from Italy send you their greetings." Although the phrase "from Italy" is ambiguous, the same phrase is used of Aquila and Priscilla in Acts 18:2. In context it refers to those from Rome who then reside somewhere other than

Rome. Therefore, it seems that the author is writing back to Rome while associated with some who are from there.

A second point in favor of a Roman destination is that the earliest documented use of Hebrews in the early church is in a pastoral letter known as *First Clement*, a letter written by Clement of Rome to the church at Corinth. Hebrews' influence is seen throughout the work.

Finally, only Hebrews among the New Testament documents refers to those who govern the church as "leaders" (*hegoumenoi*, a participle used as a noun), although Acts 15:22 (RSV) uses the same Greek term adjectively to describe the delegation, "leading men," sent to Antioch with the decision of the Jerusalem council. This designation for church leadership is also found in the books of *First Clement* and *The Shepherd of Hermas*, both of which are associated with the church in Rome.

Therefore, in all likelihood the first recipients of Hebrews are a Jewish Christian community in the city of Rome that has members struggling with enduring in their Christian commitment.

What Was the Author Attempting to Accomplish?

Consequently, the author of the book has a specific goal in view—to encourage those who are faltering spiritually to endure in the faith. He attempts to accomplish this goal by an interworking of theology and exhortation. In fact, the book is structured around a movement back and forth between teachings about Jesus as Son of God and great high priest, and strong exhortations to be faithful to him.[3] The main expositional sections about Christ deal with his superiority to the angels (1:5–14), the necessity of his incarnation (2:10–18), his appointment as superior high priest (5:1–10; 7:1–28), and the superiority of his heavenly offering for sins (8:3–10:18). Woven throughout the rest of the book are exhortation sections made up of positive and negative examples, warnings and promises, general encouragement and expressions of deep concern. These two great streams of theology and exhortation are masterfully woven together to communicate a central message: *Jesus provides a superior basis for relating to God and enduring in that relationship, and those who reject him are in deep trouble!*

When Was Hebrews Written?

If we have assessed rightly the destination of Hebrews as the city of Rome, several facts gleaned from the book help to narrow the date of writing. The recipients have been Christians for a while (5:11–6:3) and at some time in the past have faced rather severe persecution for the faith (10:32–34). Yet, it seems that although they are facing an increasing intensity of persecution at present, at the time of writing they have yet to face martyrdom (12:4). These facts point to sometime in the mid–60s A.D., just before an escalating and severe time of persecution instigated by Emperor Nero. In the mid–60s the church had existed for some three decades. In A.D. 49 the

NERO

A coin depicting the emperor (A.D. 54–68).

Christian community seems to have had harsh conflicts with the Jewish community, resulting in a general expulsion of all Jews by the emperor Claudius. This could be the persecution referred to in 10:32–34. Also, the rise of Nero's terrible persecution of Christians in Rome in the mid–60s would account for the faltering of some in the church.

How Is Hebrews Relevant for Today?

The Gospels and Paul's letters have overshadowed the study and teaching of Hebrews for a number of reasons, not the least of which is the complexity of the book. However, Hebrews is a rich mine of theological insight and pastoral encouragement, and it has much to say to the modern-day church. Foremost of all, Hebrews speaks to the challenge of perseverance in the Christian life over

against "falling away" from God. In a day in which thousands every year abandon the church, either in overt rejection or quiet separation, the church needs to address the problem and what to do about it. Thousands more worldwide are caught in the crucible of persecution and put under pressure to leave the faith. In relation to these matters, Hebrews demonstrates the foundational nature of theology for Christian life and practice.

The author uses his extensive exposition on the Son of God as the *basis* for his exhortation material in the book. Right thinking, Hebrews suggests, leads to right choices in life. Thus, this Jewish-Christian sermon champions a clear view of Christ and his superiority to other ways of approaching God as mandatory for perseverance in true Christianity. Further, the book challenges Christians to choose a path of drawing near to God and to the Christian community as the

▶

ROMAN EMPERORS

(left) Nero (A.D. 54–68).

(right) Claudius (A.D. 41–54)

◀

ROMAN COLOSSEUM

The photo shows the interior of the structure and the labyrinth beneath the stadium floor.

relational bases of endurance. Christianity at heart is a relational religion, and Hebrews presents a clear picture of community as vital for correct living. Therefore, once the modern reader begins to sort through the twists and turns of Hebrews' argument and the background of its thought world, a rich depository of encouragement and spiritual nourishment is tapped. If, as a Christian community, we can see Jesus more clearly (3:1; 12:1–2), draw near to God more consistently (4:14–16; 10:19–23), and encourage one another more readily (3:13; 10:24–25), Hebrews will have served us well.

Introduction (1:1–4)

As noted above, it is a widely held opinion that Hebrews constitutes a first-century sermon rather than a letter. In both the contexts of the Jewish synagogue and the forums in which speeches were delivered in the broader Greco-Roman culture, much emphasis was placed on an address beginning with a powerful and appropriate introduction, also referred to as a *proem* or *exordium*. Jewish sermons often started with a reference to the text to be expounded. Greek rhetoricians saw the introduction as well-crafted if it accomplished two goals. (1) The introduction should sum up the primary topic or topics to be discussed in the speech. Aristotle, whose work on rhetoric was used in rhetorical training in the first century, likened the introduction to a prelude in a performance on the flute because it paves the way for what follows.[4] (2) The word-crafters of the day suggested that an introduction should capture the attention of the audience rather than allow the hearers to drift into disinterest. Philo of Alexandria, a contemporary of the author of Hebrews, writes concerning Moses' introduction to the book of Genesis: "His exordium . . . is one that excites our admiration in the highest degree."[5] This compliment can also be applied to Hebrews. Here in the introduction to the book the author presents the primary topics that will be detailed in the sermon (e.g., God, God's Word, the Son, the Son's superiority and sacrifice) and does so with flair, using such stylistic devices as parallelism and alliteration (five words in 1:1 begin with the Greek letter *p*).

God spoke (1:1). The concept of "God speaking" must be understood against the backdrop of the author's orientation to what we know as the Old Testament. In the sermons and writings of Greek-speaking synagogues of the Greco-Roman era, Old Testament quotations most often were introduced as being spoken by God. In this tradition Hebrews almost always utilizes forms of the Greek word *legō* ("to say"), with God as the speaker. Thus the author of Hebrews utilizes the Old Testament text extensively as a basis of proclamation and exhortation. One of his main presuppositions is that God has spoken his authoritative word, and people should hear and obey it.

REFLECTIONS

THE NEED TO HEAR GOD'S VOICE through his Word has not changed. You and I need to hear it today both for its encouragement and correction. What avenues are providing you with that opportunity? Are you hearing the Word preached consistently? Do you have habits of Bible reading and reflection? If you are studying, are you also "hearing" in the sense of applying the Word obediently? God has spoken; we should listen.

To our forefathers (1:1). The reference to "forefathers" is a generic designation meaning "ancestors," rather than a specific reference to the patriarchs of the Jewish faith. The term refers to all the people of God to whom the prophets spoke, who are considered by the author to be spiritual ancestors of those addressed by Hebrews (cf. 1 Cor. 10:1, which was written to a primarily Gentile audience).[6] The practice of noting God's relationship with past generations has a rich tradition in the biblical and extra-biblical Jewish literature; it presupposes God's consistency through the centuries in dealing with his people. For example, Tobit 8:5 proclaims in part, "Blessed are you, O God of our ancestors, and blessed is your name in all generations forever."

Through the prophets (1:1). Prophets were known in broader Greek culture—for example, in connection with the oracle of Delphi.[7] Yet, Hebrews' reference here points directly to the prophets of Jewish history. The noun *nambî*, is found 309 times in the Old Testament, 92 of these occurring in the book of Jeremiah. The designation must not be seen as restricted to the so-called "writing prophets," such as Isaiah and Amos, nor even to other bearers of the prophetic mantel such as Samuel and Elijah. In the Old Testament, figures such as Abraham (Gen. 20:7), Moses (Deut. 34:10), Aaron (Ex. 7:1), and Miriam (Ex. 15:20) were called "prophet/prophetess."[8] In Hebrews 1:1 the author probably has in mind all those through whom God delivered divine revelation (cf. David referred to as such in 4:7). That revelation came "at various times," meaning it varied temporally, and "in various ways," referring to the diversity of forms it took. To name a few, God spoke through dreams, visions, mighty acts, appearances, commands, and promises.

In these last days (1:2). Old Testament prophets spoke of a "day" or "days" in which the Lord would judge his enemies and redeem his people.[9] In some New Testament passages the reference to the "last days" is forward-looking, emphasizing the consummation of the ages and the final judgment.[10] Yet, it is clear that both Peter's use of the phrase at Pentecost, attached as it is to the quotation of Joel 2:28 (Acts 2:17), and the use here in Hebrews speak of "the last days" as having been inaugurated in the person and ministry of Christ. These references follow a classic Jewish apocalyptic conception of history as divided into two stages, the former times and the end times. The Qumran community also understood itself as living in the last days of human history.[11] In Hebrews' Christian conception, the "former times" constitute the era prior to the coming of the Christ, and the "last days" the era of Christ's kingdom.

By his Son, whom he appointed heir of all things (1:2). In Greco-Roman cultures the exact laws of inheritance varied from the fifth century B.C. to the second century A.D. Sons were the primary heirs in earlier times, but later on, in certain circumstances, wives, daughters, and mistresses could also be heirs.[12] Nevertheless, the practice of inheritance had great social import throughout the cultures of the Mediterranean, and the concept was undoubtedly an important one to the first hearers of Hebrews. In biblical literature, the land was the Lord's, and as a privilege and blessing he gave it as an inheritance to Israel. Thus the concept of inheritance was tied to possession of the land and the importance of land to a family. Thus in the ancient world an heir was one with authority to utilize or administer some possession.[13]

When having to do with royal families, however, the inheritance often was expansive, involving the transfer of a kingdom. The reference to the Son as "heir" in 1:2 alludes to a royal psalm (Ps. 2:8), which the author of Hebrews also quotes at Hebrews 1:5: "Ask of me, and I will make the nations your inheritance, the ends of the earth your possession." In context, this psalm addresses the rebellion of the nations against God and God's rebuke of them. The content of that rebuke largely has to do with the enthronement of his Son, who will rule the nations with strength and crush any form of insurrection with his "iron scepter." Those nations that are wise, however, will submit themselves to the Anointed One (Ps. 2:11–12) and will find cause for rejoicing. Regardless of the nations' response, however, the extent of the Son's rule comes through clearly as "the ends of the earth." All are subject to his will. The author expands this idea to "all things," meaning the whole created order.

Radiance of God's glory (1:3). In the biblical literature "glory" when used in relation to God speaks of the radiant manifestation of his presence.[14] To see God's glory, therefore, was to witness the presence of God. The term *apaugasma*, rendered here as "radiance," indicates intense brightness or splendor.[15] Philo, commenting on humanity's legacy from Adam, suggests that, in their minds, people are connected to the divine logos, or reason, because they come into being as a "ray" of that "blessed nature."[16] Philo's main point in the context is identification or kinship with Adam, the first father of humanity, in his connection to God as creator. In Wisdom of Solomon 7:26 divine wisdom is praised as follows: "For she is a reflection [*apaugasma*] of eternal light, a spotless mirror of the working of God, and an image of his goodness." Again, close association is the emphasis here. Hebrews' point is related but framed from a Christian point of view. The author wishes to proclaim the close relationship between the Father and the Son. Just as one cannot separate the brightness of light from the light itself, one cannot separate seeing the Son from witnessing the presence of God, since the Son manifests the person of God.[17]

The exact representation of his being (1:3). The word translated "representation" (*charaktēr*), used only here in the New Testament, originally was used for an engraving tool or an engraver, a stamp, or even a branding iron. It also came to be used of the image, impress, or mark made, for example on coins or seals. Metaphorically the word developed the meaning of a distinguishing mark on a person or thing by which it is distinguished from other persons or things.[18] Thus, the term denotes features of an object or person by which one is able to identify it.[19] Philo of

Alexandria uses the word fifty-one times in his works, and it is possible that the author of Hebrews has picked up the term in interaction with Philo's works. Yet, as William Lane points out, our author employs the word to make his point for Christian theology.[20] The idea that the Son is the "exact representation of [God's] being" means that he gives a clear picture of the nature of God. This echoes other New Testament texts that speak of Jesus as the "form," "likeness," or "image" of the Father.[21]

Sustaining all things by his powerful word (1:3). In the ancient Orient a word was often conceived of as a powerful force, for instance in the use of blessings or spells. Gods especially were understood to have words of dynamic power that could create, sustain, or destroy. The words of God in the Old Testament have such force, of course. The heavens were made by his dynamic word,[22] and God's voice is heard in the booming of the storm as well as other aspects of nature. God interacts with the world he has made (Ps. 29). More significantly, the creative word of God is tied to the governing word of God in Psalm 33. The God of nature is also the God who works out his plans among the nations and people. This is the sense of the Son "sustaining all things by his powerful word" in Hebrews 1:3. This is not an echo of the mighty Atlas holding the weight of the world on his shoulders. Rather, it speaks of the Son's governmental power to bring all of the created order, including people, to his desired ends. Under the Son's direction history is progressing according to his plan.

He sat down at the right hand (1:3). The imagery of "sitting at the right hand," con-

tained in this allusion to Psalm 110:1, has a rich background in the Old Testament as well as pagan and extrabiblical Jewish literature. For instance, Athena is depicted by Pindar of Cynoscephalae as sitting at the right hand of Zeus.[23] In the Canaanite *Poem of Baal* the architect, Koshar, sits at the right hand of Baal as they discuss plans for Baal's temple.[24] Egyptian art often portrays the pharaoh as sitting on a throne to the right of a god.[25] The concept of the "right hand" was primarily used in the Old Testament to represent either superior power, rank, or honor. In Psalm 80:17 a person whom Yahweh uses for the accomplishment of his purposes is described as "at [his] right hand." Bathsheba was given the honor of sitting on Solomon's right hand (1 Kings 2:19), and the right hand position was occupied by the bride at the marriage ceremony of an unnamed monarch (Ps. 45:9). At Yahweh's right hand are an abundance of pleasures (16:11), learning (45:4), and righteousness (48:10). Psalm 110:1 is a royal psalm that speaks of the "Lord" being seated at Yahweh's right hand in a rank of power, as demonstrated by the subjugation of his enemies. The New Testament utilizes this psalm more than any other Old Testament text, heralding its fulfillment in the exaltation of Jesus.[26]

The name (1:4). The word rendered here as "name" (*onoma*) was used variously to mean name, status, rank, fame, or person. A papyrus of the third century A.D., for example, speaks of questionable officials who have devised "offices" (*onomata*) for themselves.[27] Richard Longenecker points out that "the Name," initially used as a pious reference to God, came to be employed among first-century Jewish Christians as a title for Jesus.[28] In Ephesians 1:21 and Philippians 2:9, as well as Hebrews 1:4, Jesus' "name" is above every name. What the Son has inherited, therefore, is a rank or title of power and divinity that formerly was used of God alone.

Angels (1:5). Angels serve many roles in the biblical story, including that of messengers (e.g., Matt. 1:18–25), providers of practical help (e.g., 1 Kings 19:5–7),

---

> ## ▶ A String of Old Testament Passages Bearing Witness to Christ's Superiority (1:5–14)

Jewish interpreters of the New Testament era, including the rabbis, early Christians, and scholars of the Qumran community, produced what have been called "chain quotations" or "a string of pearls." Such strings of quotations were brought together on the basis of common words and served to support an argument by virtue of the quantity of scriptural evidence brought to bear. The idea was to document so much scriptural material on a given topic that the audience would be persuaded to agree with the scholar's conclusion. Hebrews 1:5–14 contains such a string of quotations, consisting of three pairs of passages proclaiming the superiority of the Son over the angels, followed by a climactic quotation of Psalm 110:1. The first pair (2 Sam. 7:14; Ps. 2:7) asserts the Son's superiority by virtue of his unique relationship with God the Father (Heb. 1:5). The Son's superiority may be seen vis-à-vis the inferior status of the angels through the second pair of Old Testament passages.[A-1] In 1:8–12 the Son's eternal nature and enthronement over the universe provide the focus of the third pair of texts.[A-2]

deliverers (Dan. 3; Acts 5:17–24), and guides (Gen. 24:7). They also serve God as those who carry out his wrath (e.g., Ps. 78:49) and sometimes act as interpreters of divine revelation (Rev. 22:6).[29] Their role largely has to do with ministering to people on God's behalf.

For to which of the angels did God ever say (1:5)? Rhetorical questions formed a common feature of sermons in the Greek-speaking synagogues of the first century. The question amounts to an assertion that God has never said any-thing of the sort to an angel.

You are my Son; today I have become your Father (1:5). Here the author quotes Psalm 2:7. In its original context Psalm 2 addresses the rebellion of the nations against God and his Anointed One (see comments on Heb. 1:2). Such insurrec-tion will be annihilated by the enthroned king's great power. The concept of the Messiah as God's Son seems to have existed in Judaism prior to the advent of Christianity. A manuscript from Qumran (4Q246), says that the Messiah "will be called son of God; they will call him son of the Most High."[30] The early Christians applied Psalm 2 to Jesus, understanding the victory heralded as God's victory over the earthly forces opposed to the church.[31] Specifically, this psalm is under-stood as God's open proclamation of his relationship with the Son.

I will be his Father, and he will be my Son (1:5). Second Samuel 7:14 presents the words of Nathan the prophet to David, promising him that one of his descen-dants will have an eternal kingdom. The author of Hebrews understands that promise as fulfilled in the person of Christ. He ties this passage to Psalm 2:7 by virtue of the term "son" that the two passages have in common. Interpreters of the era would interpret one passage in light of another with a common term or phrase, or present two together in an argument. This practice, used extensively throughout Hebrews, is called "verbal analogy."

Firstborn (1:6). In the ancient world the term *prōtotokos* most often referred to the firstborn offspring of either a human or an animal. The concept's background in Jewish history and literature is rich, espe-cially in relation to the consecration of the firstborn to Yahweh.[32] In the Old Tes-tament era a firstborn son had a special place in his father's heart, shared in the authority of the father, and inherited the larger share of his property.[33] In the New Testament the word most often serves as a title for Christ and is an expression of his preeminence in both the church and the cosmos. It is especially used in rela-tion to the resurrection.[34]

He makes his angels winds, his servants flames of fire (1:7). The original context of Psalm 104:4 has to do with God's lordship over nature, and in the Hebrew suggests that the winds are God's mes-sengers and flames of fire his servants. Old Testament scholars point out, how-ever, the strong strand of tradition in the Old Testament in which the natural phe-nomena of wind and fire are associated with angels.[35] This tradition is picked up in a wide range of Jewish literature, including the targums and literature from Qumran, and is probably why the Sep-tuagint translates the Hebrew text so overtly as a reference to the angels. The point for the author of Hebrews is that the angels are *servants*, serving in a role inferior to that of the Son.

Anointing you with the oil of joy (1:9). Olive oil had a wide variety of uses in the ancient world, including cooking, lighting, skin conditioning, and medical treatments.[36] Significantly for the use of Psalm 45:6–7 in Hebrews 1:8–9, oil also was used to anoint Israelite kings, priests, and prophets upon their installation into their office (e.g., 1 Sam. 10:1; 1 Kings 19:15–16).[37] By his anointing the king was shown to be above his companions. By his exaltation Christ has been enthroned as king of the universe and shown to be superior.

Laid the foundations of the earth (1:10). Cities and buildings of the biblical era were only as structurally stable as their foundations. A bed of rock often was used. Solomon's temple, for example, used large, expensive blocks of stone for the foundation, and the foundations of ancient buildings often are the only remaining part of an ancient building today.[38] The image of a foundation can be used to point out the devastating circumstances of a life not built on God's Word and will over against the stability

of a life grounded in truth, as in Jesus' treatment of the two foundations (Matt. 7:24–27). Yet in Hebrews 1:10 the imagery directs our attention elsewhere. As creator of the cosmos, the Lord has "built" the earth as a master architect. That he laid its "foundations" means he is the one who has given the earth its structural integrity. The earth has endured the test of time because it has been well crafted in the beginning. Hebrews 1:10 praises the Son as the creator of the world.

They will all wear out like a garment. You will roll them up like a robe; like a garment they will be changed (1:11–12). Although some variety in clothing existed throughout the biblical times, people generally wore some type of tunic, normally extending from the shoulders to at least the knees. A cloak was worn over the tunic at times, especially in cooler weather. As perishable items, pieces of clothing wore out over time, as they do today. The imagery used in 1:10–11 is that of taking off and putting away an old article of clothing. Although the earth has been made by the Son and given a sure foundation (1:10), it is not eternal; it will eventually "wear out" like an old article of clothing. By contrast, the Son, who laid its foundation in the beginning, will be there to pack it away in the end. He "is the same" (13:8), the eternal one who is superior by virtue of his eternal nature.

A Warning About Rejecting the Word of Salvation (2:1–4)

One of the key roles of ancient speakers, rhetoricians and rabbis alike, was to motivate people to take specific courses of action, and they utilized a wide variety of

◀ *left*

FOUNDATION

Herodian-era foundation stones in Jerusalem.

oratorical and literary tools to accomplish that end. One such tool was the "argument from lesser to greater," also known as an a fortiori argument. This device lies at the heart of 2:1–4. This type of argument reasoned that if some principle is true in a less important situation, then it certainly is true—and has greater implications—in a more important situation. The author of Hebrews dynamically follows this logic by making first an assertion with which his audience certainly would agree: The law of the old covenant was binding and the breaking of that law had very negative consequences (2:2). This, for the author, is the "lesser" situation. The "greater" situation surrounds the giving of the word of salvation through the Lord Jesus, this message of salvation being confirmed by the apostles and God himself. His reasoning is that if punishment followed rejection of the law, it certainly will follow rejection of the word of salvation.

So that we do not drift away (2:1). The concept of drifting provides a powerful image for the spiritual state against which the audience is warned. The term translated "drift" (*pararyomai*) could be used of something that slipped from

REFLECTIONS

THE CULTURE OF THE MODERN, Western world is increasingly uncomfortable with the concept of punishment being attached to religion. Yet the concept constitutes a cornerstone of biblical revelation and relates directly to the problems of sin and human beings' desire for self-legislation. It must be insisted from a biblical worldview that modern opposition to the concept of punishment also fails to deal adequately with the problem of sin. How do you respond to this conflict in worldviews? Do you take the consequences of sin seriously?

one's person, such as a ring that accidentally slipped off a finger. It also could be employed to indicate something or someone heading in the wrong direction. For instance, if someone choked on a piece of food—the morsel going down the windpipe instead of to the stomach—this word could be used to describe the misdirection.[39] A nautical image, however, comes closer to the concept of drifting and may reflect more nearly the author's concern since the word translated "pay . . . attention" in 2:1 was used as a technical term for bringing a ship into port.[40] The wind or oars powered ancient ships. A test of a captain's skill in controlling a large, wind-driven vessel came upon entering a harbor and approaching a dock, since there were no "reverse engines" to slow the ship's progress. To carry too much speed would result in crashing into the docks; to carry too little speed resulted in falling short. A ship in the latter instance would "drift" by the place at which it was supposed to land, perhaps being impeded or driven

DRIFT AWAY

A column in Rome in honor of the emperor Marcus Aurelius (A.D. 161–180) depicting Roman merchant ships.

▼

off course by strong currents or prevailing winds. Thus, the author of Hebrews expresses concern over the spiritual state of his readers, whom he fears may be drifting off course from a clear focus on the gospel of salvation.

The message spoken by angels was binding (2:2). The idea that God gave the law on Sinai through angels was commonly held among Jews of the Greek-speaking synagogues in the first-century Mediterranean world and matches the broader witness of the Old Testament that God often delivered messages through angels. Josephus writes, "And for ourselves, we have learned from God the most excellent of our teachings, and the most holy part of our law by angels."[41] In the New Testament both Acts 7:38 and Galatians 3:19 echo this belief. As pointed out with reference to Hebrews 1:7, angels were often associated with natural elements such as wind and lightning, and it may be that the manifestation of these elements at Sinai came to be associated with angelic beings. Also, Psalm 68:17 notes that the chariots of God were with the Lord at Sinai, which implies for some interpreters that angels were with the Lord on the holy mountain.

The old covenant law was "binding" (*bebaios*), a legal term, in that it was so sure and durable as to be unchanging. In legal contexts of the first century this word and its relatives referred to a legal guarantee.[42] Philo wrote that the law of Moses is "firm" (*bebaios*), unshakable, and unchangeable, being planted firmly so as to endure forever.[43] Thus, a person under that law was obligated legally to follow it or face punishment. For example, punishment was handed out for the sins of murder (Num. 35:16–21), adultery, incest, bestiality, and sodomy.[44] The guilty party received from God in accordance with his sin, and there was no escaping God's judgment.[45]

Which was first announced . . . confirmed . . . God also testified (2:3–4). This message of salvation announced by

---

▶ Salvation

In Greco-Roman culture "salvation" connoted deliverance from especially perilous situations such as war, shipwrecks, or desert crossings. Plutarch, for instance, tells of one young woman who was "saved" at sea by a dolphin. The most common usage, however, comes in medical contexts. People are "saved" from severe illness, and both medicines and doctors are referred to as "saviors."[A-3]

Broadly speaking, in biblical literature the word, when used theologically, communicates what God has done, is doing, and will do on behalf of people. In the Old Testament God saves from oppression or disaster, preeminently seen in the Exodus from Egypt (Deut. 26:5–9). In the New Testament one may be saved from spiritual or physical dangers, especially from the wrath of God and the coming day of judgment.[A-4] The message of salvation in the New Testament focuses on the deliverance from the consequences of sin by Christ's work, his "announcement" (Heb. 2:3) of the good news of salvation characterizing his ministry (Matt. 9:35). In Hebrews this word of deliverance is played out in high-priestly imagery with Christ as both high priest and sacrifice.

the Lord has been validated to humanity via impressive means, and the author of Hebrews continues with terminology common to the courts of the first century to drive home its legitimacy. The message was "confirmed" by those who first heard the message. Here we find the verb form of the word translated "binding" in 2:2 (see comments). In a court of law or business deal the term referred to something that was guaranteed or legally authenticated to the point of being beyond question. Thus the first hearers of the Lord's message, rather than offering mere hearsay, "confirmed" the word of salvation's veracity in a way that could be counted on absolutely.

Moreover, "God also testified to it by signs, wonders and various miracles, and gifts of the Holy Spirit." God entered the courtroom of history with miraculous works as a joint witness with the first witnesses. Thus he added his stamp of validation on the preaching of the first Christians. The triple expression "signs, wonders and miracles" was used in early Christianity of God's works among his people that attended the preaching of the gospel.[46]

A Transition From a Discussion of Exaltation to One Concerning Incarnation (2:5–9)

Hebrews 2:5–9, by its use of Psalm 8:4–6, serves to move the focus from the exalted status of Christ above the angels to his incarnation, the Psalm having both elements of exaltation ("crowned with glory and honor") and elements of incarnation ("a little lower than the angels"). The author uses this psalm in proximity to Psalm 110:1 (Heb. 1:13),

center ▶

CROWN

the capstone on his discussion of the Son's exaltation, because both Old Testament passages refer to the act of subjecting someone or something under Christ's "feet." Such use of "verbal analogy" was common among the rabbis, who interpreted one passage in light of another that had the same or similar wording. These two psalms are used together elsewhere in the New Testament at 1 Corinthians 15:25–27 to speak of Christ's authority.

It is not to angels that he has subjected the world to come (2:5). The teachers of ancient Judaism believed that angels had been assigned positions of authority over the nations, an interpretation associated with the Greek form of Deuteronomy 32:8, which suggests the boundaries of the earth were established according to the number of God's angels. In Daniel 10:20–21 and 12:1 angels are referred to as "princes" of Persia and Greece and Michael as the "great prince" over God's people. In his exaltation, however, Christ has been positioned over all principalities and powers (e.g., Eph. 1:20–23), an authoritative rule that will be fully known at the end of the age. Thus, it is to him that "the world to come" (an allusion to the phrase "until I make your enemies a footstool for your feet" in Ps. 110:1/Heb. 1:13) has been subjected.

Crowned him with glory and honor (2:7). A crown in the ancient Mediterranean world symbolized royal authority, and both literature and art, spanning the cultures of that world, witness to its significance. The image of the crown used in Psalm 8 originally referred to the dignity of humanity and the unique role of people in God's creation. The early Christians, however, in conjunction with Psalm 110:1, adopted this psalm as a witness to the exaltation of Christ and, consequently, emphasized the royal overtones inherent in it. A ruler being crowned for a position of authority was familiar to the first hearers of Hebrews. For example, the coinage they used as citizens of the Roman empire often carried the image of the Caesar with a crown on his head. Coins from the reign of Nero, who probably ruled at the time of Hebrews' writing, show him wearing radiant crowns, identifying him with gods such as Apollo and Hercules.[47]

We do not see everything subject to him (2:8). Psalms 8 and 110 each witness to the exaltation of Christ, but the reader notices that the *timing* of subjugation of things or people to Christ is different in these two texts. Psalm 110:1 puts the subjection of Christ's enemies in the future ("until"), and Psalm 8 states the subjection of all things as an accom-

plished fact ("and put everything under his feet"). The author of Hebrews addresses the potential confusion posed by the two passages in fine rabbinic style. The rabbis often sought to dispel confusion and to clarify a point of interpretation when two such texts presented a seeming contradiction. The writer of Hebrews suggests, in light of Psalm 8, that all things have indeed been placed under the feet of Christ (2:8). What Psalm 110:1 means, according to the author, is that we do not yet see all things subject to him at present (2:8–9). Thus, the subjugation of all things to Christ is an accomplished fact that has yet to be consummated. The enemies have been defeated, but the total realization of that victory will be seen in the future. This explanation would have been especially meaningful to the readers of Hebrews, who were facing persecution at the hands of an evil government.

The Purpose of the Incarnation (2:10–18)

Author of their salvation perfect (2:10). The term rendered "author" had a range of meanings as used by ancient authors, including founder (of a family, city, people, nation, or even creation or humanity as a whole), hero or heroine, prince, chief, captain, leader, or scout. Several of these meanings are possible in the given context. Jesus certainly is the founder or originator of salvation, but also can be considered the leader or trailblazer, since he paves the way to glory. Another possibility is hero or champion in this context, since Jesus wins freedom for those who have been held in bondage (2:14–15). For instance, Hercules is often called champion (*archēgos*) and savior in inscriptions, coins, and literature.[48]

REFLECTIONS

IT CAN BE DISCOURAGING WHEN we face trials that appear to be outside of God's concern or control. Prayers for healing or deliverance may seem to get no higher than the ceiling. Yet we must base our beliefs and confidence on what God has shown us to be true through the Scriptures—he alone has perfect perspective on all the dynamics surrounding our present circumstances. Thus, we should remember Jesus, who also suffered when he was here on earth, and look to him as our exalted Lord, who will put things right in his own timing.

Being "perfect" does not mean without flaw—although that certainly is true of Jesus (4:15); rather, it has to do with bringing to completion or being fully equipped. Especially relevant for 2:10 is the use in the LXX of both the noun and verb forms of the term translated "perfection" when referring to the preparation of the Levitical priests for service.[49] Therefore, the word rendered "author" in Hebrews 2:10 may best be understood as having to do with Jesus being the founder or originator of the new covenant religion, since this idea provides a fitting complement to the concept of his being perfected for his high-priestly ministry. Jesus is the founder of our salvation because he has been fully prepared, through suffering on the cross, to serve as our high priest.

▶

HERCULES

A Roman-era bronze statue of the god.

I will declare your name (2:12). The writer to the Hebrews utilizes two Old Testament texts to support the theme of Christ's solidarity with believers—Psalm 22 and Isaiah 8. Sensitivity to the context of each is vital for an understanding of why the passages are used at this point in the book.

The early church received Psalm 22 as a profound prophecy concerning the sufferings of Christ. Psalm 22:1 is the origin of the Son's words of anguish on the cross, "My God, my God, why have you forsaken me?" (Matt. 27:46). Verses 7–8 of the same psalm constitute a taunt by wicked people against the righteous sufferer: "He trusts in God. Let God rescue him," words that echo taunts around the cross (Matt. 27:43). Psalm 22:16–18 tell of the piercing of the sufferer's hands and feet, the wholeness of his bones, and the game played for his clothing.[50] Thus Psalm 22 foreshadows the crucifixion and depicts the excruciating suffering of a righteous person. With Psalm 22:22 (the passage quoted at Heb. 2:12) one finds a shift in mood. Here the righteous one praises God for his help. The psalm supports the author's discussion of the solidarity between Jesus and believers with its reference to "brothers" (i.e., Christians are a part of the Son's family) and the phrase "in the presence of the congregation," which for the author alludes to the incarnation. Thus Psalm 22:22, when understood in light of its Old Testament backdrop, encapsulates a rich statement of Jesus' humanity, suffering, and solidarity with believers.

I will put my trust in him (2:13). Isaiah 8:17–18 also has strong messianic overtones. In 8:14, three verses earlier, the prophet refers to "a stone that causes men to stumble and a rock that makes them fall," words that New Testament authors appropriate as referring to the Messiah (Rom. 9:33; 1 Peter 2:8). The first part of the Isaiah passage quoted in Hebrews states, "I will put my trust in him." Originally this expression of faith stated the prophet's trust in God in the face of the Assyrian crisis. Hebrews applies it to Jesus' trust in the Father. The next phrase, "Here am I, and the children God has given me," points both to the Son's location as among people and his being in a familial relationship with God's children.

The devil (2:14). The Old Testament (e.g., Gen. 3:1–7), and Jewish traditions generally, associate the devil with death. For example, Wisdom of Solomon 2:24 states, "but through the devil's envy death entered the world, and those who belong to his company experience it" (NRSV). Yet, the New Testament is clear that Christ's work has destroyed the devil and his work (1 John 3:8).

Held in slavery by their fear of death (2:15). Specifically, Christ's provision of the forgiveness of sins through his death on the cross has freed those who were slaves to the fear of death. Greco-Roman authors such as Euripides, Cicero, Seneca, and Epictetus speak of the powerful effect the fear of death has on people. Epictetus states, "And where can I go to escape death? Show me the country, show me the people to whom I may go, upon whom death does not come; show me a magic charm against it. If I have none, what do you wish me to do? I cannot avoid death."[51]

Lucretius, a contemporary of Cicero, wrote a long didactic poem entitled *On The Nature of Things* (*De Rerum Natura*) from an Epicurean perspective. The Epicureans taught that all of reality is material, thus denying an afterlife. Lucretius sought to free people from the fear of death by proclaiming that people cease to exist after death and need not worry about eternal punishment (1.102–26). Thus, the fear of death was associated with the ideas of judgment and consequent punishment both in the Greek and Roman writings.

Although holding a different worldview, Philo, a Jewish writer of the first century, echoes the sentiment, "Nothing is so calculated to enslave the mind as fearing death through desire to live" (*Good Person* 22). Christ, however, by his death that destroyed the work of the devil, has delivered those of the new covenant from such paralyzing fear. His death provides forgiveness of sins and removes the threat of punishment.

The Faithfulness of Jesus, God's Son (3:1–6)

In this section the author utilizes "synkrisis," or comparison, a rhetorical device common in both Greco-Roman literature and Jewish writings. In certain forms of rhetoric the point of such a comparison, rather than to disparage the comparable person (in this case Moses), is to

◀ *left*

RECEIPT FOR DELIVERY OF A SLAVE

This receipt is written on a pottery shard (*ostracon*) discovered in Egypt.

highlight the special status of the speech's main figure (in this case Christ).

Holy brothers, who share in the heavenly calling (3:1). At several points in Hebrews the author uses a noun (*metochos*) that the NIV translates here as a verb, "share" (1:9; 3:14; 6:4; 12:8). In the plural this word can be rendered companions, partakers, associates, or sharers. Ancient authors used the word to refer to a person in an especially close relationship or association. For instance, it could refer to a companion on a journey or a housemate. The Greek form of Ecclesiastes uses the word to translate 4:10: "If one falls down, his friend can help him up." The word is used widely to speak of business associates or those banded together by a common profession, and it also occurs in the context of persons sharing a meal or some form of instruction.[52] Hebrews uses the word to connote the close association formed around spiritual realities. The "heavenly calling" the hearers share gives them a firm basis for closeness of relationships in their community of faith.

Just as the builder of a house has greater honor (3:3). The construction of build-

▶ MICHELANGELO'S STATUE OF MOSES

▶ Moses

Moses was specially venerated in the Judaism of the first century A.D. In particular strands of Jewish tradition he is considered the greatest person of history, and a wealth of literature focuses on him as the main figure. Some teachings suggest that Moses held a greater status before God than the angels because of his special intimacy with God, seen in passages like Exodus 33:11: "The LORD would speak to Moses face to face, as a man speaks with his friend."[A-5] Sirach, a book in the Apocrypha, which dates from about 180 B.C., calls Moses:

> a godly man, who found favor in the sight of all and was beloved by God and people . . . [his] memory is blessed. He made him equal in glory to the holy ones, and made him great, to the terror of his enemies. By his words he performed swift miracles; the Lord glorified him in the presence of kings. He gave him commandments for his people, and revealed to him his glory. For his faithfulness and meekness he consecrated him, choosing him out of all humankind. He allowed him to hear his voice, and led him into the dark cloud, and gave him the commandments face to face, the law of life and knowledge, so that he might teach Jacob the covenant, and Israel his decrees. (44:23–45:5)

Thus Moses' faithfulness to God was recognized and appreciated, as it is in Hebrews. Some interpreters expected the Messiah to come as a "new Moses," who would deliver his people. Note Deuteronomy 18:15–18, "The LORD your God will raise up for you a prophet like me from among your own brothers. . . ." The comparison in Hebrews 3, therefore, utilizes the great respect people had for Moses and makes a powerful case for an even greater honor as appropriate for Jesus.

ings and houses had reached the level of an art form in first-century Rome. The Romans started importing marble on a large scale at the beginning of the first century B.C. and, by the rise of Augustus, buildings such as the temple of Mars Ultor and the temple of Apollo Sosianus boasted marble walls or veneers. Builders also used stone, concrete, terra-cottas, wood, and bronze.

The housing industry thrived in the private sector as the emperors of the first century A.D. carried out impressive building campaigns in the public sector. Roman townhouses could be elaborate with dining rooms, a reception hall, and rooms for relaxation. The writer Vitruvius, in *The Ten Books on Architecture* (6.5.2), states that different types of houses were appropriate to persons of different classes:

> . . . for advocates and public speakers, handsomer and more roomy [houses], to accommodate meetings; for men of rank who, from holding offices and magistracies, have social obligations to their fellow-citizens, lofty entrance courts in regal style, and most spacious atria and peristyles, with plantations and walks of some extent in them, appropriate to their dignity. They need also libraries, picture galleries, and basilicas, finished in a style similar to that of great public buildings. . . .

At the apex of grand mansions was Nero's "Golden House," built after the great fire in Rome, which was a large villa in the middle of the city. His architect and engineer, Severus and Celer, are remembered for creating the triumph in a short span of time. These builders were famous for their work. As Hebrews notes, the builder of such a house has greater honor than the house itself.[53]

Hold on to our courage (3:6). The word translated "hold on to" (*katechō*) was used at times to mean "hold to, keep, detain, contain, occupy, or possess." Students of the era could be said to "hold to" a body of teaching. Hebrews uses the word to speak of holding to an identification with Christ, his teachings, and his community. The word translated "courage" (*parēssia*) communicates public boldness or the taking of a stand openly.

The Example of the Faithless Desert Wanderers (3:7–19)

The Exodus, in which faithful Moses led the Israelites from Egypt, and the subsequent desert wanderings constitute the most important era in the religious memory of the Jewish people. In a broad band of the Old Testament as well as in extrabiblical texts, the desert experience of the Israelites represents a paradigmatic symbol for disobedience to God.[54] Paul follows in this tradition:

> Now these things occurred as examples to keep us from setting our hearts on evil things as they did. Do not be idolaters, as some of them were. . . . We should not commit sexual immorality, as some of them did—and in one day twenty-three thousand of them died. We should not test the Lord, as some of them did—and were killed by snakes. And do not grumble, as some of them did—and were killed by the destroying angel.
>
> These things happened to them as examples and were written down as warnings for us, on whom the fulfillment of the ages has come. So, if you think you are standing firm, be careful that you don't fall![55]

Here in Hebrews 3 the author issues a stark warning to the hearers by quoting Psalm 95:7c–11. This passage was used liturgically as a preamble to synagogue services on Friday evenings and Sabbath mornings; thus the first hearers of Hebrews probably were familiar with the text. Some have suggested the psalm itself is a meditation on the desert rebellion recounted in Numbers 14.[56] In that chapter the Israelite spies have returned from their reconnaissance mission and, with the exception of Joshua and Caleb, have given their bad report to the people. The people weep and grumble against Moses and Aaron, insisting it would have been better to die in Egypt than to face the mighty enemies in the land of promise. They reject the godly men as leaders and threaten to stone them. The Lord takes this rebellion as an affront, a rejection and disbelief in himself. The tandem acts of disbelief and disobedience are especially egregious since God had worked mighty miracles in the congrega-

tion's midst. The Lord says they have not listened to his voice (Num. 14:22) and, consequently, will not enter the Promised Land (14:30).

The methodology the author uses in this section is a form of *midrash* or running exposition on the Old Testament text. In midrash a rabbi cites and then explains a text on the basis of certain interpretative principles, often highlighting certain words as especially significant for his audience. Note how the author of Hebrews does this, taking the concepts "heart," "day," "today," "hear," "enter," "test," "rest," "unbelief," and "swear" from Psalm 95 and weaving them in a dynamic expositional exhortation.

A sinful, unbelieving heart (3:12). In biblical literature the "heart" is used metaphorically to refer to personality, intellect, memory, emotions, desires, or the will. On the negative side, the heart can be evil (1 Sam. 17:28), misguided (Jer. 17:9), or uncircumcised (Deut. 10:16; Jer. 9:26).

Hardness of heart refers to those who have set their wills against the will of the Lord.[57] Hebrews 3:12 makes this clear in that the hard heart is sinful and unbelieving (which the author practically equates with disobedience) and, consequently, turns away from the living God.

We have come to share in Christ if . . . (3:14). At a number of places in Paul's writings the apostle makes a statement of fact concerning the spiritual condition of his readers but then qualifies it. Romans 8:9, for instance, says, "You, however, are controlled not by the sinful nature but by the Spirit, if the Spirit of God lives in you." Similarly, Colossians 1:22–23 reads, "But now he has reconciled you by Christ's physical body through death to present you holy in his sight, without blemish and free from accusation—if you continue in your faith, established and firm, not moved from the hope held out in the gospel."[58] Our author does something similar in Hebrews 3:6, 14. He may have been influenced by Paul's writings or by the apostle himself in the use of this device.

Notice that in every case the author is dealing with a person's relationship with God. One explanation for this phenomenon is as follows. Paul and the author of Hebrews cannot look into a person's heart to see if faith is valid. Thus they are dependent on outward manifestations of inner spiritual realities.[59] The author of Hebrews cannot give unqualified assurance to those who may be turning away from God. Thus, he addresses the Christian community as a whole as those who "have come to share in Christ" but then qualifies that description as depending on one's perseverance in the faith. Such perseverance does not save but manifests the reality of one's salvation.

Who were they who heard and rebelled? (3:16). The question and answer format of 3:16–19 was a common rhetorical technique known as *subiectio*, in which an author or orator developed his message by asking and then answering a series of questions in rapid-fire succession.[60] In this passage the questions are taken from Psalm 95 and the answers from other Old Testament passages having to do with the desert rebellion.[61] It was a common feature of midrashic commentary to begin with a focal text and supplement a commentary on that text by referring to other, related texts. Thus the author draws on a broad range of Old Testament passages having to do with the rebellion in the desert to drive home the terrible

REFLECTIONS

THE HARDNESS OF HEART WITH which the author deals in Hebrews 3 stems from a pattern of life that turns a deaf ear to God's Word. The hardness may be thought of in terms of a spiritual callous that is built up by an action done time and again. A life characterized by disobedience, by neglect of one's relationship with God, becomes desensitized to God's voice. The actions we do day to day—even those that seem small infractions or slight aberrations on our moral landscape—compound over time when not dealt with appropriately. Thus, one of our most important spiritual exercises—indeed one that may determine the course of our very lives—is the practice of "hearing" God's voice daily through his Word, seeking to apply the truth consistently and repenting of sin.

price of disobedience to God. The format of question and answer provides a stylistic summary presenting the desert deserters as paradigmatic of that disobedience.

The Promise of God's Rest (4:1–11)

As is clear in the first three chapters of Hebrews, the author was a master of rabbinic techniques of interpretation and exposition, and one of the techniques he uses liberally is "verbal analogy." When using this method an ancient interpreter would bring two Scripture passages together that shared a common word or phrase, with the intention of elucidating one or both texts. In Hebrews 3:7–19 the focus is on Psalm 95, and the author concentrates on God's judgment for the wanderers' disobedience. In short, they were not allowed to enter God's rest. In 4:1–11 the author turns to a positive side of his exhortation—the promise of God's rest, which still stands for those who believe.

In commenting on God's "rest" the author introduces Genesis 2:2: "And on the seventh day God rested from all his work" (Heb. 4:4). Both Psalm 95 and Genesis 2:2 refer to God's rest, and, therefore, the writer of Hebrews brings these two passages together for consideration. From the word "today" in the psalm he concludes that God's rest is still available for his people (Heb. 4:1, 9). After all, David wrote the psalm years after the desert wanderers had passed from the scene and Joshua had led their children into the Promised Land (4:7–8). From the Genesis passage he reasons that God's rest involves ceasing from one's own works as God did from his (4:10), so it is a spiritual reality. Therefore, the writer encourages the hearers to make every effort to cease from their own works (i.e., enter God's rest) and not fall by following the example of the desert wanderers.

We who have believed enter that rest (4:3). The verb translated as "we who have believed" (*pisteuō*) occurs over two hundred times in the New Testament and is found in every book of the new covenant canon except Colossians, Philemon, 2 Peter, 2 and 3 John, and Revelation. The verb only occurs in Hebrews here and at 11:6, which is interesting given the author's emphasis on faith (esp. in ch. 11). In both the biblical literature generally and the secular literature of the Greco-Roman world the term can mean to be convinced of something or to believe someone. In religious contexts especially the word connotes trust. God or Christ is often the object, though the object may not be expressed at all, as here; rather, it is to be understood from the context. The exposition of Psalm 95 clearly shows that God is the object of belief or, in the case of the desert wanderers, the object of unbelief (Heb. 3:12, 19). Therefore, "we who have believed" refers to those who have placed their confidence in God, throwing their lot in with him.

Enter that rest . . . seventh day . . . Sabbath-rest (4:3–11). The concept of "rest" in Hebrews 4 has stimulated a good deal of discussion, with little consensus as the result. This concept forms an important motif in the Old Testament with various nuances. As is clear in Psalm 95, the "rest" can refer to entrance into the Promised Land of Canaan as the place of "resting" from bondage and wandering.[62] In Deuteronomy 12:9 this rest is coupled with the concept of inheritance of the land.

Genesis 2:2, which the author of Hebrews adds to his exposition at Hebrews 4:4, speaks of rest in terms of God's rest on the seventh day of creation. Both this verse from the Pentateuch and Psalm 95 speak of the rest as *God's* rest, and for our author this constitutes the connection between the two passages. Philo interpreted God's rest not as meaning that God ceased from his activity, but that God needed no effort for his continual work on the created order. Rather, he worked with such ease and skill as to continually be at rest.[63] Some rabbis also considered God's day of rest as open-ended—an eternal rest—since the creation account of the seventh day does not carry the refrain "and there was evening, and there was morning. . . ." For the author of Hebrews the emphasis is on the fact that God ceased from his works (Heb. 4:10).

Related directly to God's rest on the seventh day, the rest motif is also attached to the Sabbath Day and Sabbath festivals in the Old Testament.[64] The seventh day, grounded both in creation (Ex. 20:11) and in the deliverance from Egypt (Deut. 5:15), was to be a day of renewal as the devout Jew entered into God's rest. Festivals also could be referred to as "Sabbaths." Perhaps of significance for Hebrews 4, the Day of Atonement is said to be a "sabbath of rest."[65] The people were commanded to cease from work because the Lord made atonement for them. Hebrews 4 does not speak of the sacrifice of Christ specifically, but the author does mention the "gospel," which is to be heard with faith (4:1–2). Perhaps the ceasing from one's own works in Hebrews 4 is akin to Paul's concept of trusting God for covenant relationship.

"Rest" also could refer to the eternal or "eschatological" rest found at the end of one's life. This theme finds expression widely in extrabiblical Jewish literature. For instance, *Testament of Daniel* 5.12 speaks of the saints' rest they will find in Eden, which the author equates with the new Jerusalem, and *4 Ezra* 8:52 tells of a city that is built in paradise for the purpose of giving rest.

It may be suggested for Hebrews that the "rest" that those who believe have entered constitutes blessings of the "now" and the "not yet" of new covenant experience. We enter into a covenant Sabbath in which we, by faith, cease from our own works and persevere in trusting Christ's sufficiency for all our needs. Unlike the wanderers in the desert, we do not fall through unbelief. Yet, the concept of "rest" also seems to have a "not yet" component that focuses on our inheritance at the end of our pilgrimage. Thus we enter into the rest now, but will experience the consummation of full rest at the end of the age.

He spoke through David (4:7). The LXX, which is the author's translation of choice, specifically attributes Psalm 95 to

REFLECTIONS

WE LIVE IN A CULTURE DESPERATE FOR "REST." IT may be suggested that the root of the problem, rather than simply being physical exhaustion—a real issue in modern, Western culture—is a spiritual issue. We, as a culture, are much more oriented to human accomplishment than God's accomplishment on our behalf. Most turn away from God's works and God's ways, preferring, instead, life in the desert. As a believer, are you benefiting from God's promised rest today? Are you experiencing the peace and forgiveness provided for you under the new covenant, or is your life a spiritual frazzle? It may be that the lack of focus and the physical fatigue we experience has more to do with the state of our spirits than the fullness of our schedules.

David, the second king of Israel. That David penned the Psalm long after the passing of the deserters in the desert is significant for the author's argument (Heb. 4:7). Through David God implies that God's people may enter his rest by not following the example of disobedience recounted in the psalm. Even the fact that Joshua and the children entered the Promised Land does not mean that the promise of rest was thus fulfilled (4:8). Rather, as indicated by the word "today" in Psalm 95, God still offers an invitation to rest (Heb. 4:9). What Genesis 2 adds to the equation is that the rest offered constitutes ceasing from one's own works. For Hebrews this seems to be both a present and future reality.

A Warning Concerning God's Word (4:12–13)

The word of God is living and active (4:12). The beautifully crafted prose on God's word should be understood as echoing the reference to God's voice in the quotation of Psalm 95 (Heb. 3:7). First-century Judaism and Christianity both understood the word of God to be a force in creation, administration of the world, and judgment. The word, as indicated by the words "living and active," must not be thought of as static speech-act. Rather, it is a dynamic power that has the ability to effect change, both in the created order and in individual lives.

Sharper than any double-edged sword (4:12). The sword, ranging in size from sixteen inches to three feet, was the most basic weapon used in battle in the Greco-Roman world. For the first recipients of Hebrews the sight of a Roman soldier fully armored would have been common. As his primary weapon a Roman legionnaire would carry a *gladius*, a double-edged sword about twenty inches long, strapped to his right side. This weapon was designed for slashing and thrusting in close, hand-to-hand combat.[66]

Although the vast majority of the over four hundred references to a sword in Scripture refer to the literal weapon, it is used to symbolize war (e.g., Jer. 19:7; Hos. 2:18), bloodshed and conflict (e.g., 2 Sam. 12:10), and judgment, either human (Rom. 13:4) or divine (Ps. 7:12; Rev. 1:16). Negatively, the sword symbolizes anything that causes harm to people, such as destructive words (Ps. 57:4; Prov. 12:18), a false witness (Prov. 25:18), a sexually immoral woman (5:4), and the character of those who exploit the poor (30:14). Here in Hebrews 4:12 the author uses the image positively to speak of the power and effectiveness of God's Word (cf. Isa. 49:2; Eph. 6:17).[67] This "sword's" ability to cut deeply is seen in its penetration to a person's inner life. We might say that God's Word "gets to the heart" of any matter. In this sense it can be a powerful force of judgment when thoughts and intentions of the

◀ *left*

**DOUBLE-EDGED
ROMAN SWORDS**

Models of a Roman
gladius.

heart are not what they should be. Thus the author of Hebrews uses this image to warn against neglecting God's Word by failing to obey him.

Nothing in all creation is hidden from God's sight. Everything is uncovered and laid bare (4:13). The idea that the guilty were not able to hide from God's intense, penetrating judgment was common in Jewish theology of the era. In Revelation 6:16–17 those who face God's judgment wish to hide: "They called to the mountains and the rocks, 'Fall on us and hide us from the face of him who sits on the throne and from the wrath of the Lamb! For the great day of their wrath has come, and who can stand?'" Yet, of course, there is nowhere to hide from God. No one can stand. The term translated in Hebrews 4:13 as "uncovered" (*gymnos*) normally connotes nakedness or lack of adequate clothing, but figuratively speaks of being vulnerable or helpless. Similarly, things that are "laid bare" are exposed and unprotected. So those who are disobedient to God, not attending to his voice, are vulnerable before his penetrating, judging Word.

A Capsule of the Author's Main Message (4:14–16)

Packed in these three verses we find the main elements of the author's message. We have a superior basis for holding onto our confession of Christ and drawing near to God. That superior basis is a relationship with Jesus, the Son of God, who functions as our great high priest. The passage forms the opening of an *inclusio* that the author closes at 10:19–25. An *inclusio* functioned to bracket a unit of text by marking its beginning and ending with an introduction and conclusion that were worded similarly. In this case the author marks the great central section on the Son's appointment to (5:1–10; 7:1–28), and ministry as (8:3–10:18), a superior high priest.

▶ Great High Priest

Under the old covenant the high priest was the chief leader in the worship of God and was the primary mediator between God and the nation. He is referred to variously as simply "the priest" (Ex. 31:10), "the anointed priest" (Lev. 4:3), "the chief priest" (2 Chron. 26:20), and the "high priest" (2 Kings 12:10). In the Pentateuch this last designation only occurs at Numbers 35:25–32; it also appears in Joshua 20:6. The appointment to high priesthood was hereditary and usually was an appointment for life.[A-6] The high priest had certain duties in common with other priests, but only he entered God's presence in the Most Holy Place on the Day of Atonement (Lev. 16:1–25).

Gone through the heavens (4:14). That Jesus has "gone through the heavens" simply means that he has entered God's presence. In the biblical literature "the heavens" can refer to the physical cosmos as distinct from the earth: "In the beginning God created the heavens and the earth" (Gen. 1:1). Biblical writers joined other peoples of the ancient world in describing the universe phenomenologically, that is, as they observed it. The heavens were above, the earth below. The physical heavens could be described as having a partition that God had "spread out" (Ps. 136:6; Isa. 42:5). Yet, the author of Hebrews is not primarily interested in Christ's physical journey through the cosmos but rather his going into the presence of the Father, and the imagery here has much to do with the exaltation theme already raised in the book (Heb. 1:3, 13). That he has "gone through the heavens" makes his passage into God's presence distinct from the earthly high priest, who entered God's presence through the earthly tabernacle (8:1–6; 9:1–10).

Jesus the Son of God (4:14). In the first chapters of Hebrews the author focused on Jesus as the "Son" of God. The designation of "son" or "sons of God" has a varied background in the Old Testament and Jewish literature. It could be used, for instance, of angels (e.g., Gen. 6:2; Job 1:6), the nation of Israel (Ex. 4:23), or the Davidic king (2 Sam. 7:12–14; 1 Chron. 17:13). *Wisdom of Solomon* 2:18 and *Sirach* 4:10, both Jewish writings of the Apocrypha, speak of the righteous person as "God's son." The latter reads: "Be a father to orphans, and be like a husband to their mother; you will then be like a son of the Most High, and he will love you more than does your mother."

The Dead Sea Scrolls, in a text from Cave 4 (4Q246), specifically refer to the Davidic Messiah, whose rule will be an eternal rule, as God's son:

All the peoples will serve him, and he shall become great upon the earth. . . . All will make peace, and all will serve him. He will be called son of the Great God; by His Name he shall be designated. He will be called the son of God; they will call him son of the Most High. . . . His Kingdom will be an Eternal Kingdom, and he will be Righteous in all his Ways.

Outside of Judaism, the title "son of God" is rare in the ancient Mediterranean world, and, "with one exception, is never used as a title."[68] That one exception is Augustus's adoption of the title *divi filius*, a Latin phrase translated on Greek inscriptions as *theou huios*, "son of God." But in no way should this be seen as the backdrop of the Christian use of the title, which takes its cues from the Old Testament and, especially, the title as used in Jesus' life and ministry.[69] For the author of Hebrews the title "Son of God" speaks of Jesus' unique relationship to God the Father, a relationship in which he reigns as Messiah and functions as our sinless, heavenly high priest.

Tempted in every way . . . yet was without sin (4:15). The confession that Jesus never sinned was common teaching in early Christian circles.[70] Matthew 4 and Luke 4 tell of the temptation of Jesus by the devil upon the launch of Jesus' ministry. The Lord answered those temptations with Scripture and won the day. That Jesus was tempted "in every way" and "was without sin" are important to the author's argument. The experience of temptation gives Jesus, as our high priest, a basis for sympathizing with us as human beings (a requirement of a

REFLECTIONS

DO YOU HAVE A SENSE OF CONFI- dence or boldness as you approach God in prayer? The clearer your picture of Jesus as high priest, the greater the confidence you will have. His sacrifice has opened the way completely for our access to God. What, then, are your needs for grace today? Bring those boldly to him now.

high priest, Heb. 5:1–3). Yet, his being without sin shows that Jesus is a high priest who is superior to the earthly priests, who had to offer sacrifices for themselves as well as the people (5:1–3; 7:26–28).

Let us then approach the throne of grace with confidence (4:16). Monarchs of the ancient world sat on thrones as symbols of their power and authority. Consequently, to approach a monarch's throne could be a fearsome act, for one was at the mercy of the ruler, who had the power of life and death in hand. The throne imagery also carried over into religious beliefs. For instance, a fresco from Pompeii depicts Bacchus (called Dionysus by the Greeks) sitting on a throne nude, with a wine cup in his right hand. When used with reference to the gods, a throne also was a symbol of power and authority. In Christian belief God's throne is a seat of authority and power, but, as Hebrews points out, it too is a seat of grace. Thus, the believer who has Christ as his high priest can approach the throne with "confidence" or boldness. In Hellenistic Judaism and early Christianity the concept of drawing near to God with confidence refers especially to approaching God in prayer.

An Introduction on Christ's Appointment as High Priest (5:1–10)

Hebrews 5:1–10 offers an introduction to a section running from 5:1 to 7:28 (with the exception of the strategic exhortation at 5:11–6:20). The author marks the section with a detailed *inclusio* (see introductory comments on 4:14–16), the opening of which occurs in 5:1–3 and the closing at 7:27–28. The content of 5:1–3 and 7:27–28, which demonstrate the contrast between Levitical priests and the priesthood of Christ, expresses the author's main concern. Specifically he addresses the theme of a high priest's appointment and shows that Jesus has been appointed in a superior fashion as a superior high priest. At the heart of this agenda lies Psalm 110:4: "You are a priest forever, in the order of Melchizedek."

Every high priest (5:1). Both the Greeks and Romans had organizations of priests who had various functions, including the offering of sacrifices to the gods. For example, the Romans had The College of

HIGH PRIEST

An artistic representation of the Jewish high priest in his vestments.

Priests, a group of sixteen who controlled the ritual practices of the religious calendar. Other Roman groups were the flamines, the Vestal Virgins, and the augurs, all of which had different functions.[71] But Hebrews' orientation is strictly to the Old Testament and the priesthood as described in its pages. The first four verses of Hebrews 5 delineate universal principles on high priesthood gleaned from that source.

First, the high priest has a relationship of solidarity with the people because he is appointed "from among" them (5:1). It may be that this principle derives from Exodus 28:1, which says that Aaron was brought to Moses "from among the Israelites."

Second, the high priest represents people by joining the other priests in offering sacrifices to God (Heb. 5:1). Yet, the high priest alone offers the sacrifice on the Day of Atonement (Ex. 29:1–46; Lev. 16:1–25). The Day of Atonement sacrifice involved two goats and a ram. One of the goats was slaughtered as a sin offering, and the other was the "scapegoat," which the high priest, having laid hands on its head and confessing the sins of the people, sent into the desert (Lev. 16:15, 20–22).

Third, on the Day of Atonement the high priest also was required to offer a sacrifice for himself and his household before he offered the sacrifice for the people (5:3; cf. Lev. 16:11). The reason for this sacrifice was to deal with his own weakness (Heb. 5:2). His weaknesses, however, play a significant role in his ministry since they enable him to "deal gently with those who are ignorant and are going astray" (5:2).

A fourth general principle concerns how one becomes a high priest. It is not by enlisting, but rather by being appointed by God (5:1, 4)[72]. Thus the basis for the position of high priest rests in the authority of God, not people. These four principles lay the foundation for the author's understanding of Jesus' unique service as high priest.

Gifts and sacrifices for sins (5:1). Neighbors who participated in religious sacrifices to various degrees certainly surrounded the first recipients of Hebrews. Sacrifices were made primarily to get what one wanted or to protect one from some harm. Thus the sacrifices were expressions of self-centered superstition. Also, in Greek and Roman religion there was a great emphasis on the exact performance of such rituals. In fact, if a ceremony or sacrifice was not executed in exactly the right manner, the process had to be started again. The gods were the strictest sort of legalists in the Greco-Roman understanding of things.

The gifts and sacrifices Hebrews 5:1 mentions are quite different because they center on relationship with God. The sacrifices of the old covenant system included the burnt offering, the sin offering, the guilt offering, and the thank offering (Lev. 1–7), each in its own way addressing one's relationship with God. The Day of Atonement sacrifice, offered on the tenth day of the seventh month (September/October), was the most important sacrifice and is the primary sacrifice in mind here. This sacrifice covered all of the sins not covered in the previous year by other sacrifices. On this day the people drew near to God by the high priest's entering the Most Holy Place. The temple sacrifices continued through most of the New Testament era but ceased after the destruction of the temple by the Romans in A.D. 70.

A priest forever, in the order of Melchizedek (5:6). The quotation of Psalm 110:4 here introduces the discussion of Jesus' superior appointment as a priest, a topic that will govern the author's arguments in Hebrews 7:1–28. The proclamation of the Davidic king as "a priest forever, in the order of Melchizedek" has its background in David's conquest of Jerusalem about a thousand years before the birth of Christ. As a consequence of that victory, David and his descendants became heirs of Melchizedek's dynasty of priest-kings.[73] Jesus and his first followers understood this psalm to be a prophecy concerning the Messiah, and the author of Hebrews is especially focused on the fact that Psalm 100 shows that Jesus, as Messiah, was appointed priest by a divine proclamation.

Prayers and petitions with loud cries and tears (5:7). The wording of Hebrews 5:7 seems to echo Jesus' agonizing submission to his Father in Gethsemane.[74] Yet, it should be noted that the Gospel accounts do not mention "cries and tears," and, consequently, scholars have sought to ascertain the background of the author's reflections on these expressions of grief. The early Christians meditated on the psalms as predictive of the life, suffering, and exaltation of Jesus. The psalms of "righteous suffering" probably form the backdrop of the "cries and tears" of Hebrews 5:7.

Although he was a son, he learned obedience from what he suffered and, once made perfect (5:8–9). Paul noted that the crucifixion of Jesus was a stumbling block to the Jews and foolishness to the Gentiles (1 Cor. 1:23). That God's Son should die a shameful death by the most base form of execution was outside the bounds of all expectation in both Jewish

---

▶ Psalms of Righteous Suffering

Psalm 116:1–8 declares:

> I love the LORD, for he heard my voice;
> he heard my cry for mercy....
>
> The cords of death entangled me,
> the anguish of the grave came upon me;
> I was overcome by trouble and sorrow....
>
> You, O LORD, have delivered my soul from death,
> my eyes from tears,
> my feet from stumbling.

Psalm 22, a messianic psalm of suffering (cf. the author's quote of Ps. 22:22 at Heb. 2:12), reads:

> My God, my God, why have you forsaken me?
> Why are you so far from saving me,
> so far from the words of my groaning?
> O my God, I cry out by day, but you do not answer,
> by night, and am not silent. (2:1–2)

> My strength is dried up like a potsherd,
> and my tongue sticks to the roof of my mouth;
> you lay me in the dust of death. (2:15)
> Revere him, all you descendants of Israel!
> For he has not despised or disdained
> the suffering of the afflicted one;
> he has not hidden his face from him
> but has listened to his cry for help. (2:23b–24)

When Hebrews says that the Father heard the Son's cry because of his reverent submission, it reflects a key value of Jewish piety, that is, humble submission to God's will. Also, that God the Father affirms Jesus in his suffering ultimately is seen in the resurrection and exaltation, twin events that vindicate Jesus as the Messiah.

and Greek cultures. Sons of high position in the ancient world were honored and advanced on the basis of their status. Yet Jesus' relationship with the Father did not make for an easy appointment to high priesthood.

That Jesus "learned obedience" does not mean that he was disobedient and then became obedient. Rather, it means that Jesus followed fully and obediently the path of suffering the Father had designed for him. He experienced fully what it meant to be in complete submission to the Father. Also, his being "made perfect" relates to the completion of his course of suffering—not that he was imperfect before, but he "ran the full course" of his sufferings and thus became fully qualified as our high priest.

The Spiritual Immaturity of the Recipients (5:11–14)

In ancient rhetoric a sudden shift of topic could be used strategically to rivet the audience's attention. This is what the author of Hebrews does at 5:11. He departs momentarily from a discussion of Jesus' appointment as a priest like Melchizedek to confront the hearers with their spiritual lethargy. The language used in this passage was common in educational circles of the Mediterranean.

Slow to learn (5:11). The Greek expression here means "dull of hearing." The first word in the phrase, *nōthroi*, can mean "sluggish, dull, dimwit, negligent," or "lazy." For instance, Plutarch notes that Parmenion was sluggish and lazy in battle; the term could also be used of an athlete who was slow because he was out of shape physically.[75] In both the Wisdom literature and Greek literature generally,

the word connotes the failure to follow through with work or a responsibility because of being dull or slow in some aspect of life.[76] Specifically the author links the laziness of the recipients of Hebrews to "hearing," since he is concerned that they are failing to give full attention to God's Word.

Elementary truths of God's word (5:12). The word rendered "elementary truths" (*stoicheia*) means "basic principles" and can refer to spiritual beings of the universe in more metaphysical contexts.[77] But another use of the word in ancient literature comes closer to the author's use here. Writers used *stoicheia* to refer to basic elements of the alphabet or the most basic, fundamental concepts in education.[78] Thus, we might, with the NEB translation, think of the term as used in Hebrews 5:12 as meaning "the ABCs of God's Word." The author of Hebrews is concerned that the hearers, who have been believers long enough to be advanced in the faith, have stagnated at, or even digressed to, a point of gross immaturity.

You need milk, not solid food (5:12). In educational contexts the imagery of "milk and solid food" was a common means of delineating basic from ad-

vanced teachings. The rabbis sometimes called their young students "sucklings."[79] Epictetus, a crippled Greek slave during the reign of Nero, uses the milk/meat imagery to comment on the immaturity of the person who demands life be a certain way in order to be happy. He states, "Are you not willing, at this late date, like children, to be weaned and to partake of more solid food, and not to cry for mammies and nurses—old wives' lamentations?" Having challenged the young man to get out into the world and taste widely of the challenges God brings in life, he laments, "Nay, you will not; sit rather in the house as girls do and wait for your mammy until she feeds you!"[80] Speaking of education, Philo of Alexandria writes that milk is the food of babies and suited for the time of childhood (i.e., the beginning stages of education), but grown men should partake of more substantial fare that leads to wisdom, self-control, and virtue.[81]

The concern expressed by the writer of Hebrews is that this community of believers evidences a staggering lack of maturity. They should be much farther down the road of faith and should be assimilating advanced teachings of the Christian life (e.g., the high priesthood of Christ), but they rather need to have their attention refocused on the most basic teachings of Christ (cf. 2:1).

By constant use (5:14). By contrast, those who are mature can handle "solid food," because of their spiritual condition. The term translated by the NIV with "constant use" (*hexis*) has been widely mistranslated and misinterpreted as referring to "exercise" or "practice" of one's spiritual faculties. The term refers rather to the "condition" or "state" of the mature person. It is because of their

DO YOU SEE A PATTERN OF GROWTH in your own life by which you are moving from the need of "milk" to the spiritual intake of "meat"? Would you say that the past year of your Christian life has been characterized by progression in understanding Christian teachings or by stagnation? Notice that growth in this passage is tied to *teachings* about Christ. Theology, in a real sense, lays the foundation for living. In other words, right thinking leads to right living. As we grow in character, however, we grow in our ability to grasp deeper truths of the faith.

mature condition that the mature have the faculties to discern good and evil.

A Challenge to Move on in the Faith (6:1–3)

Let us leave the elementary teachings about Christ (6:1). In 5:11–14 the author has pointed out that there are those in the church he addresses who have stagnated spiritually, needing remedial work on Christian teachings. But he does not accede to their infantile appetites; rather, he challenges them to move on in the faith. Early Christianity seems to have borrowed from Judaism the practice of using catechisms for instructing new converts or young believers. Most foundational materials certainly pointed to the Old Testament Scriptures as providing the basics of Christian faith. Therefore, the items that follow, although cornerstones of basic Jewish teaching in the era, had been assimilated as basics of Christian belief and could only be seen as foundational. To stay at the level of those most basic beliefs constituted immaturity. Nevertheless, the author's listing of these basic theological concepts shows their importance in the basic teachings of the first-century church.

The foundation of repentance from acts that lead to death, and of faith in God (6:1). Repentance and faith are two of the most basic elements of Jewish and Christian teachings of the first century. Some commentators have suggested that this first pair of concepts in the author's list of 6:1–3 lays the foundation for the other two pairs. Those two pairs, baptisms and laying on of hands, and resurrection from the dead and eternal judgment, relate to the beginning and end, respectively, of the life of faith. Yet, the beginning point of everything is to repent of sins and to have faith in God. The *Didache*, a collection of Christian teachings written after Hebrews, tells of the "way of death," which involves sins such as murder, adultery, lust, fornication, robbery, idolatry, magic, hypocrisy,

and arrogance. In Romans 6:21 Paul notes that the outcome of slavery to the life of sin is death.[82] Death, however, can be avoided by genuine repentance. What corresponds to genuine repentance is faith in God, and the relationship between repentance and faith can be seen readily in the preaching both of Jesus and Paul. Jesus called people to "repent and believe the good news" (Mark 1:15), and Paul gave these twin concepts as the essence of his gospel (Acts 20:21).

Instruction about baptisms (6:2). The term "baptisms," as indicated by the NIV translation, is plural, and thus challenges the interpretation that the author simply has in mind Christian baptism. The act of religious washings was prevalent in first-century Judaism. The Qumran community (the writers of the Dead Sea Scrolls), for instance, had "baptisms" for those who were joining their group; they also had subsequent washings so that ritual purity could be maintained. Excavations near the caves where the Dead Sea Scrolls were found include pools and containers that may have been used for such washings. Some wealthy, devout Jews in the city of Jerusalem had pools in their home for ritual cleansing. The Pharisees took the hand washings done by the Levitical priests and applied them generally to ritual purity before eating.

Yet it may be that the author's primary reference point is the Old Testament writings. In 9:13 and 10:22 the author refers to the cleansing ceremonies of the old covenant. These washings are presented as inadequate from a Christian perspective, though they do have significance in foreshadowing the cleansing offered by Christ's superior new covenant offering.

BAPTISMAL POOL

A *miqveh* from the southern wall excavations just south of the Temple Mount in Jerusalem.

The laying on of hands (6:2). In the New Testament the laying on of hands is associated with ritual blessing (e.g., Matt. 19:13, 15), healing of the sick (e.g., Mark 5:22–23; Luke 4:40; 13:13), the initial ministry of the Holy Spirit in a new convert's life (e.g., Acts 8:17–19), and the authorization or, perhaps, the acknowledgement of a particular ministry (e.g., 6:6; 13:3). In line with the context of Hebrews 6:2, the book of Acts shows that the laying on of hands sometimes accompanied baptism in early Christian circles (Acts 8:16–17; 19:5–6). Significantly for the broader context of Hebrews, the practice of the laying on of hands also relates to the old covenant sacrificial system, most notably the act of the high priest, who laid his hands on the scapegoat on the Day of Atonement.

The resurrection from the dead, and eternal judgment (6:2). Resurrection from the dead and eternal judgment are linked together in the biblical literature and extrabiblical, Jewish writings. The raising of the dead results in new life and reward for those who are righteous and judgment for the wicked. Isaiah 26:19 tells of the resurrection of the righteous, for instance, and Daniel 12:2 includes resurrection for the righteous and the wicked. Sources such as 2 Maccabees 7 and *2 Baruch* 49–51 speak of physical resurrection to a bodily existence. In the rabbinic writings resurrection refers to God's bringing all the dead, righteous and unrighteous, back to life on the Day of Judgment. With the decline of the sect of the Sadducees and the firm control of Pharisaic Judaism after the destruction of the temple in A.D. 70, the doctrine was fixed in broader Jewish thought. In *m. Sanhedrin* 10:1 those who do not believe that the doctrine of the resurrection has

its origin in the Torah have no place in the coming age.[83] Jesus himself chastised the Sadducees for their lack of understanding of the resurrection, doing so by pointing to the Torah (Luke 20:37–38): "But in the account of the bush, even Moses showed that the dead rise, for he calls the Lord 'the God of Abraham, and the God of Isaac, and the God of Jacob.' He is not the God of the dead, but of the living, for to him all are alive."

A Harsh Warning Against Falling Away (6:4–6)

It is impossible for those who have once been enlightened (6:4). The word "impossible" is positioned at the beginning of the Greek sentence beginning with 6:4, and, based on a principle from Greek grammar, the author wishes to place emphasis on this term. Elsewhere in Hebrews the word is used to refer to something that cannot happen. In 6:18 we are told that God cannot lie, in 10:4 that the blood of bulls and goats cannot take away sins, and in 11:6 that it is impossible to please God apart from faith.

Broadly in the writings of the ancient world, the word translated "enlightened" served as a metaphor for making known what was previously unknown. In writers such as Plato, Plutarch, Aristotle, and Sophocles, those who gained some form of knowledge are called "enlightened." More specifically "light" is connected to the world of the gods; in the Old Testament it is associated with the one true God (Ps. 4:6; 89:15; Dan. 2:22). Philo describes right teaching or thought as "the light of thought," the "light of the spirit," or "the light of truth."[84]

Who have tasted the goodness of the word of God (6:5). The concept of "tasting" here has at times been misinterpreted to mean "partially ingested," but this understanding cannot hold up to scrutiny. Rather, as in Jesus' tasting death in 2:9, to taste something means to experience it. To "taste the goodness of the word of God" perhaps follows from the "spiritual food" imagery of 5:11–14 and recalls the exhortation of Psalm 34:8, "Taste and see that the LORD is good," and the exultation of 119:103, "How sweet are your words to my taste!"

And the powers of the coming age (6:5). In Jewish thought "this age" constitutes the period from creation to the Day of Judgment. The "coming age" follows the final judgment of God and will see God's total rule consummated. For Paul, the present age is evil and ruled by the evil powers (1 Cor. 2:6; Gal. 1:4). That those spoken of in Hebrews 6:5 have tasted "the powers of the coming age" means that in some way they have experienced the effects of God's rule, which will be experienced ultimately in the age to come—his powerful intervention in humanity, his breaking the evil powers of this evil age.

If they fall away (6:6). The word rendered "fall away" recalls the "drifting" of 2:1 and the warning against a heart that "turns away" in 3:12. The image draws most, however, from the desert wanderers who "fell" and were not able to enter the Promised Land (3:17; 4:11). Telling of God's judgment on the wanderers, Numbers 14:29–30 reads, "In this desert your bodies will fall—every one of you twenty years old or more who was counted in the census and who has grumbled against me. Not one of you will enter the land I swore with uplifted hand to make your home, except Caleb son of

Jephunneh and Joshua son of Nun" (cf. Ps. 106). The verb used in Hebrews 6:6, used only here in the New Testament, occurs in contexts in the LXX in which unfaithfulness is in view (e.g., Ezek. 14:13; 15:8).

They are crucifying the Son of God all over again and subjecting him to public disgrace (6:6). In 13:13 the author notes the proper stance of a Christian, a stance that constitutes standing with Christ, bearing his disgrace. Thus believers are challenged to follow the example of the Lord, who "scorned [the] shame" of the cross (12:2). The apostates used as a negative example in Hebrews 6:4–8, however, have reversed this position, instead standing with those who used the cross, the ultimate instrument of public shame in the Greco-Roman world, to crucify Christ. Crosses often were placed on main thoroughfares so that the victim would be publicly humiliated. Matthew 27:39–44 vividly recounts the shaming of Christ:

> Those who passed by hurled insults at him, shaking their heads and saying, "You who are going to destroy the temple and build it in three days, save yourself! Come down from the cross, if you are the Son of God!"
> In the same way the chief priests, the teachers of the law and the elders mocked him. "He saved others," they said, "but he can't save himself! He's the King of Israel! Let him come down now from the cross, and we will believe in him. He trusts in God. Let God rescue him now if he wants him, for he said, 'I am the Son of God.'" In the same way the robbers who were crucified with him also heaped insults on him.

An Agricultural Image of Blessing and Judgment (6:7–8)

The agricultural image contrasting good ground and poor ground was common in the ancient world. Many ancient societies were oriented to agriculture, and ground that failed to produce was seen as a curse. Such ground often was burned off. The image forms the backdrop, for example, of the Song of the Vineyard in Isaiah 5:1–7 and of Jesus' parable of the sower (Matt. 13:1–9; Mark 4:3–9). Those who have rejected Christ, failing to bear the fruit of faith, correspond to ground that has failed to produce anything worthwhile, in spite of favorable conditions. The inevitable outcome of such people is devastation.

In Greek culture curses were hostile prayers that at times were scratched on tablets called *defixiones*, addressed to the gods of the underworld and placed in the ground, in wells, or in graves.[85] In biblical literature blessings and curses for the most part, rather than referring to a magical incantation, refer to the good gifts of God over against tragic circumstances that result from unfaithfulness. Blessings and curses, therefore, can be formal statements of good or ill fortune, visited on people in response to their actions. For example, in Deuteronomy 27:15–29:1 the Lord gives the Israelites the terms of the covenant. If they follow the Lord's commandments, faithfully fulfilling the covenant, a whole host of blessings will be lavished on them. However, if they forsake the Lord's commands, rejecting the terms of the covenant, they will be cursed with a long list of curses. The agricultural image of Hebrews 6:7–8 is analogous to this concept. The land that produces good fruit receives God's blessing or favor. The land that does not produce (failing to be faithful to the covenant?) faces an inevitable curse.

Further Encouragement (6:9–12)

Dear friends (6:9). The author softens the harshness of the previous negative example (6:4–6) and agricultural figure (6:7–8) with a reference to his hearers as "dear friends." The verb form of this word, *agapaō*, was used at times in Greek literature to mean "greet with affection," and the use of the word *agapētos* in 6:9, as indicated by the NIV, is meant to be an affectionate greeting.

We are confident of better things in your case (6:9). Expressing confidence in an audience or recipients of a letter was a rhetorical device used to create a sense of obligation or to persuade those addressed to take a certain course of action. Paul uses the device to good effect, for instance, at Romans 15:14: "I myself am convinced, my brothers, that you yourselves are full of goodness, complete in knowledge and competent to instruct one another."

HARVEST

A modern harvest of vegetables in Jordan near the Dead Sea.

He will not forget your work (6:10). God is a God who remembers. In the Old Testament God "remembers his covenant" he made with his people.[86] In an interesting contrast to Hebrews 6:10, Ezekiel 18:24 states, "But if a righteous man turns from his righteousness and commits sin and does the same detestable things the wicked man does, will he live? None of the righteous things he has done will be remembered. Because of the unfaithfulness he is guilty of and because of the sins he has committed, he will die." This is not the situation under the new covenant, however. The faith of the hearers of Hebrews has been lived out in "work," a manifestation of love for God expressed through ministry to others. The description points to genuine relationship with God, a relationship manifested by good works and ministry to the saints.[87] Thus, unlike the negative examples of Hebrews 6:4–8, they have been fruitful, good "ground."

Imitate those who through faith and patience inherit what has been promised (6:12). The theme of imitation is one that occurs consistently in Paul's writings and anticipates both the treatment of Abraham in the next few verses and, especially, the great list of the faithful in chapter 11.[88] The pattern common to those whom the author has in mind, is a life of faith, exercised in patience, that leads ultimately to God's fulfillment of his promises. This is the great story of the Bible. God has promised; his people must wait for the answer; the answer, in accordance with the character of God, follows the life of faith.

The Power of God's Promises (6:13–20)

The whole of 6:13–20 is transitional, leading back to the discussion on Melchizedek

from which the author temporarily departed at 5:11. God's oath, or promise, constitutes the author's main topic for discussion. The passage progresses along the lines of an illustration (6:13–15), followed by a truism (6:16) and then the main point (6:17–18).

When God made his promise to Abraham (6:13). In Jewish culture of the first century, Abraham was the example par excellence of faithful perseverance since he persevered in believing God for a son and then was willing to sacrifice that son in obedience to God. The key here is that God swore an oath to Abraham, saying, "I will surely bless you and make your descendants . . . numerous" (Gen. 22:17); the context of this verse recounts the near sacrifice of Isaac. In an obedient response to God's oath Abraham waited on God's timing and received the promise (Heb. 6:15). The author wishes to stress that Abraham did well because he believed God's oath. This is the point of the illustration.

Men swear by someone greater than themselves (6:16). The writer of Hebrews here offers a truism, or universal truth; the language used in this passage is taken right out of the legal contexts of the day. The author points out that oaths taken in a court of law or a legal situation have two characteristics. First, they require that the oath-giver appeal to a superior. The superior lends the oath-giver credibility, a credibility founded in the character of the superior. Second, witnesses swear an oath as a means of giving a legal guarantee of the truthfulness of their words. This is a "confirmation" that what they are saying is true. When the testimony of the witness comes to this point, room for dispute no longer exists.

Another area in which an oath gave assurance was that of contractual relationships, especially verbal ones. The *Ius iurandum liberti*, for example, was an oath given by a recently freed slave. The new freedman swore an oath to render services to his patron promised prior to his liberation.[89] Thus, the oath served as a guarantee that such services would be forthcoming. Philo comments on such oath-giving in human relationships, "Matters that are in doubt are decided by an oath, insecure things made secure, assurance given to that which lacked it."[90] The author of Hebrews reasons in Hebrews 6:17 that if oaths give assurance in courts of law or legal situations where human beings are involved, God's oath can be counted on as an even greater confirmation of truth.

By two unchangeable things in which it is impossible for God to lie (6:18). The "two unchangeable things" of 6:18 are the two parts of Psalm 110:4, to which the author alludes: "You are a priest forever" and "in the order of Melchizedek." The allusion as used here begins a transition back to a discussion of Melchizedek in chapter 7. In that chapter the author expounds the two parts of Psalm 110:4 in inverse order:

"You are a priest forever" (Heb. 7:15–28).
"In the order of Melchizedek" (Heb. 7:11–14).

Why are these two proclamations by God "unchangeable"? In the words of Psalm 110:4, "The LORD has sworn and will not change his mind." God cannot lie (Heb. 6:18).

Fled to take hold of the hope (6:18). Although the concept of fleeing to a refuge has parallels in Greek literature (e.g., Plato, *Theaet.* 176A-B), the motif is a common one in the Old Testament. Generally speaking, God is the believer's refuge, to whom the believer can go in times of trouble (e.g. Ps. 144:2), and those who take refuge in God will inherit the land (Isa. 57:13). The "cities of refuge" were for those who had accidentally killed someone; such cities provided a safe place from revenge taken by the victim's family.[91]

It seems that the author combines two Old Testament themes in his imagery here, themes related to the horns of the altar. First, at the end of God's instructions concerning the altar of incense (Ex. 30:1–10), the horns of the altar are said to have a special role in the Day of Atonement. Speaking of the altar, the writer says, "Once a year Aaron shall make atonement on its horns. This annual atonement must be made with the blood of the atoning sin offering for the generations to come. It is most holy to the LORD." Exodus 30:6, moreover, makes it clear that the altar was to be located in front of the veil separating the outer room of the sanctuary from the inner room (the author of Hebrews understands the altar to be inside the Most Holy Place; see 9:3–4). Second, in 1 Kings 1:50–53 Adonijah fled to take hold of the horns of the altar as a place of safety from Solomon's wrath and was spared (Joab, whom Solomon deemed guilty, attempted the same but was not so fortunate; 1 Kings 2:28–35). Thus, believers have fled to take hold of the hope—the "horns of the altar" where atonement has been made for sins through Jesus' high priestly offering (see also Lev. 16:18). This hope, therefore, enters "behind the curtain" (6:19) and gives us a place of refuge.

An anchor for the soul, firm and secure (6:19). Plato said the cities of Greece were clustered on the shores of the Mediterranean "like frogs on a pond," and the Romans referred to that body of water as "our Sea."[92] The strong orientation to this large, central body of water was due to the importance of shipping as a primary mode of transportation for both Greeks and Romans. Ships served mainly to carry grain, oil, and wine, but people could buy passage to different locations at certain times of the year. Therefore, ancient peoples were familiar with nautical imagery, and the anchor was a common philosophical metaphor representing stability. For instance, the Greek philosopher Plutarch, who lived in the first Christian century, criticizes those who cannot control their desires, saying, "The spirit yields and can resist no more, like an anchor-hook in sand amid the surge."[93] In other words, a person who gives in to passions is no more stable than an anchor in sand. Philo uses the image of an anchor when speaking of virtue as a stabilizer in life. To have virtue is like being anchored in a safe place.[94]

Hebrews uses the anchor imagery to emphasize that believers have a firm basis for spiritual security. The word translated "secure" refers to something that is reliable, well-founded, or confirmed. So our hope in Christ, rather than based on emotions or wishful thinking, provides a firm basis for a life of stability.

The inner sanctuary behind the curtain (6:19). The tabernacle of the Israelites was a network of curtains made in part of fine twisted linen (Ex. 26:1) and a series of boards made of acacia wood (26:15–30). The tabernacle was divided into two rooms, an outer room (the Holy Place) that contained the lampstand and the table holding the bread of the Presence (25:23–40), and the Most Holy Place or inner room, which contained the ark of the covenant (25:10–22). Separating the two rooms was a "curtain," and God commanded the following concerning this curtain:

> Make a curtain of blue, purple and scarlet yarn and finely twisted linen, with cherubim worked into it by a skilled craftsman. Hang it with gold hooks on four posts of acacia wood overlaid with gold and standing on four silver bases. Hang the curtain from the clasps and place the ark of the Testimony behind the curtain. The curtain will separate the Holy Place from the Most Holy Place (Ex. 26:31–33).

For the author of Hebrews, the Christian's hope is to enter the inner sanctuary behind the curtain because that is where Jesus has gone as our high priest.

STONE ANCHOR

In the old covenant religion, only the high priest could enter the inner sanctuary, and he could do so only once a year on the Day of Atonement. Jesus, however, has entered the true Most Holy Place, heaven, and there intercedes always for us (Heb. 7:25). Thus our hope is made as sure as it could be, Jesus providing a superior, lasting covenant that guarantees our permanent audience with the living God.

He has become a high priest forever, in the order of Melchizedek (6:20). In 6:20 the author now cites overtly what he has alluded to in 6:17–18, restating the content of Psalm 110:4 (Heb. 5:6). These two parts of this Psalm verse, that Jesus is a priest forever and is in the order of Melchizedek, constitute the two main themes of 7:11–28.

The Superiority of Melchizedek (7:1–10)

Hebrews 7 picks up on the topic introduced in 5:1–10—Jesus' appointment as high priest—and presents a tightly woven argument built around the enigmatic, Old Testament figure Melchizedek. There are only two references in the Old Testament to this "priest of God": Genesis 14:17–20 and Psalm 110:4. The first gives the narrative recounting Abraham's meeting with Melchizedek after the patriarch's return from battle and is the focal text for Hebrews 7:1–10. Psalm 110:4, on the other hand, offers a reflection on the Davidic monarch, whose priesthood is enduring (see comments on Heb. 6:18).

The type of commentary found in 7:1–10 is known as *midrash* (see comments on 3:7–19). J. A. Fitzmyer has noted that Hebrews 7 has features in common with a midrash: The Old Testament text is the point of departure, the exposition is homiletical, the author stresses details of the scriptural passage, the text is shown to be relevant to the contemporary audience, and the focus is on the narrative of the Old Testament situation, not just the individual characters.[95]

This Melchizedek (7:1). The author of Hebrews may have been familiar with

---

▶ **What Jews in the Greco-Roman Era Thought About Melchizedek**

Extrabiblical literature prior to, during, and following the advent of Christianity shows an interest in the figure of Melchizedek. Philo mentions him at several places, mostly using him as a symbol, for instance, of the Logos.[A-7]

The Qumran community had an interest in the priest as a heavenly figure, as shown by a Dead Sea scroll fragment on Melchizedek found in Cave 11, which dates from around the time of Christ's birth. The fragment interprets, among other texts, Leviticus 25:9–13, a passage dealing with the Jubilee Year. In the Qumran fragment the last Jubilee is called the "Year of Melchizedek," in which Melchizedek is said to bring deliverance and salva-

tion to the people of God by defeating Belial and his evil spirits. 11QMel ii.13 states, "And Melchizedek will exact the ven[geance] of E[l's] judgments [and he will protect all the sons of light from the power] of Belial and from the power of all [the spirits of] his [lot]." Melchizedek is apparently some type of heavenly figure in this scroll fragment, perhaps an exalted angel.[A-8]

In the first-century work *2 Enoch* Melchizedek also is a heavenly figure. Here Melchizedek is saved from the flood so he can continue a line of priests started with Seth. Michael takes the child Melchizedek to paradise, where he is to be a priest forever.[A-9]

speculations about Melchizedek in various religious communities of his day. Yet, the author's treatment of this priest can be explained wholly on his treatment of the two Old Testament texts in which Melchizedek is named. His treatment of Melchizedek in 7:1–10 can be explained as an exposition of Genesis 14:17–20 with Psalm 110:4 in mind.

He met Abraham returning from the defeat of the kings (7:1). Melchizedek was a priest-king from the city of Salem. He met Abraham as the patriarch was returning from an important victory over a confederation of four kings from the east: Kedorlaomer of Elam, Tidal of Goiim, Amraphel of Shinar, and Arioch of Ellasar. These four kings had attacked the kings of Sodom, Gomorrah, Admah, Zeboiim, and Bela, defeating them at the Valley of Siddim and plundering their cities. Abraham's nephew Lot was taken captive from Sodom. Upon hearing of his nephew's plight, Abraham pursued the invaders to the city of Dan, where he won the victory in a nighttime attack. On his way back home, the king of Sodom and Melchizedek met the patriarch, at which time Abraham gave the latter a tenth of his spoils and Melchizedek blessed him. Genesis 14:17–20 says this about Melchizedek:

> After Abram returned from defeating Kedorlaomer and the kings allied with him, the king of Sodom came out to meet him in the Valley of Shaveh (that is, the King's Valley).
> Then Melchizedek king of Salem brought out bread and wine. He was priest of God Most High, and he blessed Abram, saying,
>
> "Blessed be Abram by God Most High,
>   Creator of heaven and earth.
> And blessed be God Most High,
>   who delivered your enemies into your hand."
>
> Then Abram gave him a tenth of everything.

His name means (7:2). In dealing with Melchizedek's name the author of Hebrews alludes to words from the Hebrew language. When he suggests his name means "king of righteousness," the reference is to the Hebrew words *melek*, which means "king," and *sedeq*, which may be rendered "righteousness." The city name "Salem," furthermore, he interprets to mean "peace," drawing an association between the city's name and the Hebrew word *shalom*.

Without father or mother, without genealogy, without beginning of days or end of life (7:3). A common exegetical practice from the era may be called "an argument from silence"; the author uses this technique, pointing out what the Old Testament passage *does not* say about Melchizedek. He uses this technique both in anticipation of his treatment of the Levitical priests and in reflecting on Ps. 110:4. The Levites were appointed to priesthood by virtue of their ancestry as descendants of Aaron. From the historical context of the Genesis passage we know that Melchizedek met Abraham long before God gave the guidelines for the old covenant priesthood. The lack of any reference to Melchizedek's parents or ancestors shows that considerations important for the Levites were not attached to Melchizedek's service as priest. Furthermore, the service of the Levites ended upon death, as the author points out in Hebrews 7:8, 23. Psalm

110:4, however, makes clear that Melchizedek holds his priesthood forever, a fact not contradicted by Genesis 14:17–20.

He collected a tenth from Abraham (7:6). The concept of the "tithe" was practiced across numerous societies of the ancient Mediterranean. Success in war or in one's profession could result in giving a tenth part to the gods. As with other places in Hebrews, however, the author draws on material for his discussion from the biblical text, specifically the laws concerning the tithe paid to the Levitical priests. In Numbers 18:20–32 the Lord instructs Aaron and Moses that the Levites, who would not receive a portion of the Promised Land as their inheritance, would receive the tithe from the rest of the Israelites as their inheritance in return for their work of serving in the Tent of Meeting. In turn, the Levites were to give as an offering to the Lord a tenth of what they received, the best and holiest part, as the Lord's portion.

The author's logic follows that the great patriarch Abraham, whose descendants, the Levites, would receive tithes from their fellow Israelites, gave a tithe to Melchizedek. This man was not a Levite, but Abraham tithed to him—and thus Levi, a future descendant of Abraham, who was still in Abraham's body, played a part in giving that tithe. This shows that Melchizedek was superior to the Levitical priests. It should be remembered that, in the case of the Levites, they were instructed to pay a tenth to the Lord through Aaron. They tithed to the Lord through a superior, who was the Lord's chief representative.

And blessed him who had the promises (7:6). As seen in the agricultural image of 6:7–8 the twin concepts of blessing and cursing are important motifs in the biblical literature. Individuals might bless God (e.g., Gen. 9:26; 14:20) or be blessed by God (e.g., Gen. 12:3; Num. 23:20). A blessing could be used informally as a greeting or in the event of a departure. Yet, a blessing could be a formal pronouncement of goodwill that was seen as having a positive impact on the blessed person's future. In the book of Genesis, the broader context for Melchizedek's meeting with Abram, the concept occurs over sixty times, many of the occurrences following the line of formal proclamations of goodwill.

The Superiority of Our Melchizedekan High Priest (7:11–28)

Now in inverse order the author probes two parts of God's "oath" in Psalm 110:4. Jesus as a priest "in the order of Melchizedek" constitutes the discussion of Hebrews 7:11–14, and the balance of the chapter concerns the phrase, "you are a priest forever." This section continues the author's use of *midrash* or running commentary on the Old Testament texts

BURNT OFFERINGS

A model of the courtyard of the tabernacle with the altar of burnt offering.

▼

(see comments on 7:1–10), but now the emphasis has shifted from the Genesis passage on Melchizedek to the Psalm passage.

For on the basis of it (7:11). In the NIV translation, "for on the basis of it the law was given to the people," the pronoun "it" seems to refer to the Levitical priesthood. Yet the translation might better be rendered "for concerning it" or "in the case of it." What the author has in mind are the directions given in the law concerning the establishment and function of the old covenant Levitical priesthood. During the time of the desert wanderings the Levites conducted worship in the tabernacle and took care of that structure (Num. 1:47–54; 3:14–39). The author points out that perfection was not attained through this priesthood.

There must also be a change of law (7:12). Insofar as Jesus has been appointed a priest apart from the normal guidelines for appointment detailed in the law, it is clear, in the author's view, that God has changed the law in some way. In other words, God has instituted a new basis for dealing with sin and sacrifice, as is also indicated by the change in covenant (8:7–13).

A different tribe (7:13). At the heart of this change in the law's requirement stands the primary basis for appointment as priest. In the old covenant system, appointment as priest was based on heredity—priests were taken from the tribe of Levi. That Jesus hailed from the tribe of Judah demonstrates this requirement has been set aside.

Our Lord descended from Judah (7:14). The tribe of Judah was, of course, one of the twelve tribes of the nation Israel, named for the sons of the man Israel. The man Judah was the one who interceded for his brother Joseph's life when his other brothers were about to kill him (Gen. 37:12–26) and then suggested they sell him into slavery instead (37:26–27). Significantly, his father's prophetic benediction concerning Judah included a statement about his descendants as rulers not only of the nation of Israel, but of the nations generally. This prophecy focused on a future ruler who would rule the nations: "The scepter will not depart from Judah, nor the ruler's staff from between his feet, until he comes to whom it belongs and the obedience of the nations is his" (49:10). The tribe of Judah historically was tied to the royal house of David, the archetypal ruler of God's people; in Revelation 5:5 Jesus is called the "Lion of the tribe of Judah, the Root of David."

The former regulation is set aside because it was weak and useless (7:18). Among the various first-century movements within Judaism, the view that certain aspects of past revelation have been overturned is seen especially in Christianity. The reason for this—illustrated preeminently by Hebrews—is that Christ, the Messiah, has become the reference point by which all of God's revelation should be understood. The author of Hebrews locates grounds in the Old Testament Scriptures for his assertion that the old covenant systems of priesthood and sacrifice have been superseded. According to Psalm 110:4 God has decided to appoint a priest by a means other than those found in the law.

The author goes on, however, to suggest the reason God "set aside" a regulation that, in the past, was binding. The old covenant law concerning appointment had its purpose in its time, but ultimately it was too weak and ineffective to accomplish the greater purposes of God. It was weak in that the priests of that system were mortal and limited by death, and the sacrifices were unable to cleanse permanently.

And it was not without an oath (7:20). The author alludes to the phrase in Psalm 110:4 that says, "The LORD has sworn and will not change his mind." No such oath can be found in relation to the Levitical priests. For the author of Hebrews this oath, made doubly strong by the assertion that the Lord will not change his mind, gives strong encouragement because it indicates a permanent provision for God's people.

Jesus has become the guarantee (7:22). Because God's oath must be seen as permanent, the threat of our change in status before God must be understood as having been dealt with decisively. Jesus has become the "guarantee" of a covenant that is "better." The word translated "guarantee" (*engyos*), which could also be

translated "guarantor," was common in legal contexts, but was not normally used in the ancient world to discuss covenants or testaments. In legal contexts the word indicated a person who guarantees the position or endeavors of another person by putting himself or herself at risk. In 7:22 the author pictures Jesus as the guarantee for God's covenant promises. As the originator of that covenant, through his sacrifice of himself, and his permanent position as the high priest of our new covenant with God, Jesus gives firm assurance that this relationship with God will last.

Such a high priest meets our need (7:26). The author now brings us back around to the place at which the section started in 5:1–3. In giving the general guidelines for high priesthood at the beginning of chapter 5, the author points out that the high priest under the old covenant served to meet the needs of God's people in a specific context. In that context, however, the high priest also had to deal with his own weaknesses. His sacrifices too had to be offered over and over again. Jesus, by contrast, has been appointed by different means (an oath) and has a superior basis for meeting our needs. He does not die and, thus, always lives to intercede for us. His sacrifice for sins was offered once for all. Therefore, he meets our needs in a superior way because he serves as the ever-present high priest whose sacrifice for sins does not need to be repeated.

A Key Transition (8:1–2)

With Hebrews 8 the author makes a major transition to the next great section of this book, a section dealing with Christ's superior sacrifice for sins. These

REFLECTIONS

THE PERMANENCE OF CHRIST'S priesthood and his ever-occurring intercession on our behalf should be causes of great peace and stability. This system of the new covenant, by definition, cannot be replaced with another system. Jesus is a priest "forever" and can save us completely. Therefore, we do not have to worry about our status before God. Jesus is the guarantee of covenant life lived in spiritual stability.

first two verses are a special form of transition that bridges the gap between two larger sections. Then 8:3–6 introduces the ministry of Christ as high priest and rivets our attention on the heavenly sphere of that ministry. This passage might be titled, "Introduction: The More Excellent Ministry of the Heavenly High Priest." The balance of the chapter (8:7–13) presents Jeremiah 31:31–34, the longest Old Testament quotation in the New Testament. By virtue of this quotation the author focuses attention on the superiority of the new covenant vis-à-vis the old covenant, using a rabbinic method of commentary by which the commentator draws out the implications of the passage.

One of the ways an ancient author could tie blocks of material together was by utilizing what have been called "hook words." In ancient Greek rhetoric this literary device was called *hysteron proteron*, literally "latter-former." The device "hooked" one literary unit to the next by presenting a key word (or words) used at the end of the first unit, at the beginning of the new unit. Thus a verbal bridge tied the two units together. The author of Hebrews does this by using the words "heavens" and "high priests" in Hebrews 7:26–28, words that correspond to "high priest" and "heaven" in 8:1. He also ties 8:1–2 to 8:4–6 by use of the word translated "high priest."

Who sat down at the right hand of the throne of the Majesty in heaven (8:1). The author has already drawn attention to Psalm 110:1 twice in the book, once with an allusion in Hebrews 1:3 and then with the quotation at 1:13. As with the allusion to that psalm verse in 1:3, the writer now adds to the words of the psalm the phrase "in heaven," which would have been understood as the location of the Son's exalted position at the "right hand."

The concept of "heaven" or "the heavens" meant different things to different philosophical and theological orientations of the first century world. Philo understood heaven more in Platonic

▶ The Heavenly Tabernacle in Judaism

A number of texts from the Dead Sea Scrolls speak of the new Jerusalem with a new temple (e.g., 2QNew Jerusalem; 5QNew Jerusalem). *Fourth Ezra*, a book from about 100 A.D. states, "For indeed the time will come, when the signs that I have foretold to you will come to pass, that the city that now is not seen shall appear, and the land that now is hidden shall be disclosed."[A-10] The "city that now is not seen" is the heavenly Jerusalem. In *Second Baruch*, from the first half of the second Christian century, the prophet looks into heaven and sees a vision of "the likeness of Zion, with its measurements, which was to be made after the likeness of the present sanctuary."[A-11] Finally, Wisdom of Solomon 9:8

states, "You have given command to build a temple on your holy mountain, and an altar in the city of your habitation, a copy of the holy tent that you prepared from the beginning." So the holy tent has been in heaven with God all along.

In Christian literature, Galatians 4:26 speaks of "the Jerusalem that is above," and Revelation 21:1–22:5, in describing the new heaven and new earth, describes the holy city, the new Jerusalem, coming down out of heaven. It is interesting that in this new city described in Revelation there is no temple building because "the Lord God Almighty and the Lamb are its temple."

terms as the sphere of the ideal reality. In the past the weight of scholarly opinion placed Hebrews in a philonic conceptual framework, but studies in the past forty years have taken a decided turn against this position. Most scholars on Hebrews are now convinced the author understands the concept of heaven in the tradition of first-century Jewish apocalyptic thought. In the Old Testament and post-biblical Judaism, heaven is seen as the dwelling place of God par excellence (e.g., 1 Kings 8:30–39). In the rabbinic literature specifically, heaven is the seat of God and is the focus of human prayer.[96]

The true tabernacle set up by the Lord, not by man (8:2). The tabernacle was the old covenant worship center where God met with his people (Ex. 25:1–27:21). It contained several items of importance, including the ark of the covenant, the table for the bread of the Presence, and the golden lampstand. In 25:9, 40 God tells Moses to make the tabernacle according to the pattern he would be shown on the mountain; this instruction lies behind an important theological vein of thought in early Judaism and early Christianity that held there were heavenly counterparts (either present or future) to the earthly Jerusalem and the earthly tabernacle or temple.

Introduction: The More Excellent Ministry of the Heavenly High Priest (8:3–13)

So it was necessary for this one also to have something to offer (8:3). In 5:1–10; 7:1–28, the author presented the appointment of the Son as a superior high priest. That section started with the statement, "Every high priest is selected from among men and is appointed to represent them in matters related to God, to offer gifts and sacrifices for sins" (5:1). Now the author provides a parallel introduction to the corresponding section running from 8:3 to 10:18, which deals with the superior high priest's heavenly offering: "Every high priest is appointed to offer both gifts and sacrifices, and so it was necessary for this one also to have something to offer."

Note that the proclamation of 5:1 places the statement concerning appointment before the statement concerning sacrifices for sins. This was done for emphasis, since the section beginning with 5:1 focuses on the Son's appointment to the office of high priest. At 8:3 the focus shifts to the necessity of a high priest having an offering to offer. This statement introduces the focus of 8:3–10:18: The Son, who has been appointed as a superior high priest (5:1–10; 7:1–28), has a superior, new covenant offering he has offered.

HIGH PRIEST

An artistic representation of the Jewish high priest in his vestments including the breastplate with twelve stones representing the tribes of Israel.

If he were on earth, he would not be a priest (8:4). The author alludes here to the argument he has made in 7:11–25. The earthly priesthood was one limited to tribal descent and limited by death. Psalm 110:4 shows that Christ is not a priest according to the earthly guidelines of the law. His priesthood involves rather a heavenly sacrifice offered in the heavenly sanctuary (Heb. 9:24).

A sanctuary that is a copy and shadow of what is in heaven (8:5). The word translated "copy" could be used variously to mean a sample, suggestion, symbol, outline, or example—something, in other words, that forms the basis for further instruction or imitation.[97] Thus, the word here means that Moses made the tabernacle as a sketch or shadow when compared to the real thing in heaven. The old covenant place of worship, as important as it was for that era, can only be conceived as an imperfect sketch of the heavenly reality, since human hands made it (cf. 9:11). As a "shadow" it imitates the heavenly original sufficiently to point to it. Yet as part of the earthly realm of existence, it is passing off the scene and ultimately is insufficient for the overarching purposes of God.

The time is coming, declares the Lord, when I will make a new covenant (8:8–13). Jeremiah 31:31–34 is part of a larger section of the prophetic book that has

▶ How the "New Covenant" Was Understood at Qumran

Among the Qumran sectarians, the "new covenant" passage from Jeremiah was interpreted to herald their eschatological community. Yet the contexts in which that community commented on the new covenant indicate a legalistic understanding of the covenant's implications:

But all those who have been brought into the covenant shall not enter the temple to kindle his altar in vain. . . . Unless they are careful to act in accordance with the exact interpretation of the law for the age of wickedness: to separate themselves from the sons of the pit; to abstain from wicked wealth which defiles, either by promise or by vow, and from the wealth of the temple and from stealing from the poor of the people, from making their widows their spoils and from murdering orphans; to separate unclean from clean and differentiate between the holy and the common; to keep the Sabbath day according to the exact interpretation, and the festivals and the day of fasting, according to what they had discovered, those who entered the new covenant in the land of Damascus. . . . (CD 6:11b–19)

For the earliest Christians the implications of the new covenant were very different from those drawn by Jews at Qumran. Rather than a legalistic approach that focuses on a believer's shortcomings in relation to the covenant, the early Christians understood the covenant to be a proclamation of God's grace brought through the sacrificial death of Christ and celebrated in the Lord's Supper (Luke 22:20; 1 Cor. 11:25). The new covenant does not have to do with a legalistic approach to the law, the letter that kills, but is a covenant of the life-giving Spirit (2 Cor. 3:6).

The author of Hebrews does not provide a detailed commentary on aspects of the Jeremiah passage. It might be argued that the primary characteristics of the covenant are self-evident when one simply reads the passage. The covenant involves the laws of God internalized, placed in the minds and written on the hearts of God's people. In truth God will be their God (they will not bow before idols), and each and every one will know God. Finally, the new covenant involves forgiveness from sins.

◀

THE TABERNACLE

A model of the
tabernacle and its
courtyard.

been titled "The Book of Consolation" (30:1–33:26). Whereas the earlier chapters of Jeremiah focus on judgment, these chapters offer hope for the future of God's people.[98]

By calling this covenant "new" (8:13). In 8:13 one encounters a rabbinic technique of commentary used to bring into focus a key reason the author has quoted the passage from Jeremiah at this point in the book. Rabbis sometimes quoted a text

and then commented on the implications of a single word or phrase. The author of Hebrews focuses attention on the word "new" in the Jeremiah passage. He stresses that the designation "new" covenant means there was an "old" covenant that is now obsolete. His greater purpose is to show that the new covenant established by the heavenly, Day of Atonement sacrifice of Christ has been proclaimed superior to the old covenant in which the levitical priests were involved.

The Old Covenant Structure and Regulations for Worship (9:1–10)

In 9:1–10:18 the author addresses the specific ways in which Christ's new covenant ministry of sacrifice should be seen as superior to the sacrificial ministry of the priests under the old covenant. In order to highlight the contrasts, he begins by explaining aspects of the worship

◀ left

THE ARK OF THE
COVENANT

A bas-relief of
the ark from the
synagogue at
Capernaum.

under the old covenant in 9:1–10. Three characteristics form the focus of attention: (1) the *place* of the offerings in the earthly tabernacle (9:1–6); (2) the *blood* of the offerings (9:7); and (3) the perpetual *nature* of the offerings (9:6–7, 9–10). Then in 9:11–10:18 he shows how Christ's sacrifice is superior at every turn: (1) the *place* of his offering was in heaven rather than on earth (9:11, 23–25; 10:12–13); (2) the *blood* of the offering was Christ's own rather than the blood of mere animals (9:12–28); and (3) the offering of Christ was *eternally* effective, eradicating a need for continual offerings (9:25–26; 10:1–18).

THE TABERNACLE

A life-size model set up in the Timnah.

▼

Regulations for worship (9:1). The word translated "regulations" refers to requirements or commandments and is related to a whole family of Greek words associated with the concept of justice or righteousness. What the author has in mind are those guidelines, "God's just directives," concerning how the sacrificial worship practices were to be conducted by the priests under the old covenant. These regulations are explained in 9:6–7.

In its first room were the lampstand, the table and the consecrated bread (9:2). Being especially concerned with movement of the priests and high priest into the tabernacle, the author of Hebrews explains that there was a "first" or outer room called the Holy Place (9:2) and an "inner" room designated the "Most Holy Place" (9:3). These two rooms were separated by a curtain, behind which only the high priest could go once per year, on the Day of Atonement.

The lampstand, made of pure gold, had six flowered branches protruding from its sides, three to a side. There were

▶ The Tabernacle

The tabernacle was the tent, or moveable worship center, erected under the leadership of Moses during the desert wanderings. The Hebrew term we render as "tabernacle" relates to the concept of dwelling, and it was the physical structure identified with the presence of God. The structure also was called the "sanctuary," the "tent of meeting" (e.g., Ex. 33:7; Num. 11:16), simply "the tent," and "the tabernacle of the testimony" (Ex. 38:21), among other designations. The instructions concerning the building of the tabernacle are found in Exodus 25–31; 35–40. Gifts freely given by the Israelites were to supply the materials needed for construction—among them gold, silver, bronze, fine linen, yarn colored blue, purple, and scarlet, goat hair, ram skins dyed red and sea cow hides, and acacia wood (25:1–5).

In structure the tabernacle was a tent made up of a series of curtains. Ten curtains, all the same size, made from the finely twisted linen, formed the inner part of the tabernacle (Ex. 26:1–2), which was covered with eleven curtains of goat hair (26:7–13), which in turn were covered with red ram skins and the hides of sea cows (26:14). All of these curtains were supported by frames made of acacia wood, overlaid with gold, and by various kinds of clasps and loops (26:15–29).

seven lamps on the stand, and the lamp-stand was situated on the south side of the Holy Place (Ex. 25:31–40; 26:35). Also called the *menorah* (a Hebrew word) in Jewish history, the lampstand was the most popular image in ancient Jewish art, appearing on coins, ceramic lamps, and the walls of synagogues and tombs. The earliest known picture of the lampstand occurs on a coin from the reign of Antigonus Mattathias (40–37 B.C.).[99]

The table for the bread of the Presence, like the frames of the tabernacle, was made of acacia wood overlaid with gold. It was two cubits long, a cubit wide, and one and a half cubits high (Ex. 25:23–30). It is difficult to determine the exact measurements by today's reckoning, since a "cubit" varied between seventeen and twenty-one inches and had its basis in the distance between a person's elbow and the tip of the middle finger.[100] The four corners of the table had four gold rings through which acacia poles were placed to carry the table. In addition, the plates and utensils for the table were also made of pure gold. The consecrated bread, called the "showbread" or "bread of the Presence," consisted of

twelve loaves of unleavened bread that symbolized God's covenant with the Israelites. These were arranged on the table in two rows of six loaves, and were to be eaten only by Aaron and his sons (Lev. 24:5–9). The table itself was consecrated by sacred oil and placed on the north side of the Holy Place (Ex. 26:35).

Behind the second curtain was a room called the Most Holy Place (9:3). Two curtains, or veils, served as sacred barriers for the tabernacle. The first served as the covering for the entrance to the tent. This curtain was made of "blue, purple and scarlet yarn and finely twisted linen." Five posts, made of acacia wood and overlaid with gold, held up the curtain, and bronze bases stabilized these posts (Ex. 26:36–37).

The second and more significant curtain separated the outer room from the inner—the "Most Holy Place." This second curtain also was made of "blue, purple and scarlet yarn and finely twisted linen," but Exodus adds that a skilled craftsman embroidered cherubim on the curtain. Gold hooks were attached to four acacia posts overlaid with gold, and the posts sat on silver bases (rather than

---

ITEMS FROM THE HOLY PLACE

(left) A model of the golden table of showbread with two stacks of bread and two golden bowls of incense.

(right) The golden lampstand (*menorah*).

▼

bases of bronze as with the first curtain) (Ex. 26:31–32).

In various strands of Jewish interpretation in the ancient world the curtain separating the Holy Place from the Most Holy Place was understood as symbolic of various realities. For instance, the veil could be understood as symbolic of the separation of heaven and earth, or perhaps two parts of heaven. Regardless, the key point for all interpretations focused on the veil as a separator from the presence of God.[101] For the author of Hebrews the "second curtain" is that through which the high priest passed into that presence. Christ as high priest takes the new covenant believer with him through the curtain into the very presence of God (Heb. 10:19–20).

The golden altar of incense (9:4). The golden altar of incense was another item of the tabernacle made of acacia wood and overlaid with gold. The altar was a cubit long and a cubit wide, standing two cubits high. Like the table for the consecrated bread, the altar had rings through which poles of acacia wood could be placed for carrying it. The purpose of the altar, as its name suggests, was to burn incense before the Lord. Aaron was instructed to burn incense on the altar every morning and every evening at twilight, both times corresponding to his tending of the lamps in the tabernacle. Significantly, the altar of incense also played a role in the Day of Atonement ritual. Blood from the atoning sin offering was to be placed on the horns of the altar (Ex. 30:1–10).

Hebrews places the altar of incense in the Most Holy Place, yet in the Old Testament and in the history of interpretation, the location of the altar is ambiguous. However, the altar is closely associated with the ark in many Old Testament passages.

The gold-covered ark of the covenant (9:4). The ark of the covenant has numerous designations in the Old Testament, among them, "the ark," "the ark of God," "the ark of the testimony," and "the ark of the Lord." It was the most important item of furniture in the tabernacle since it represented the presence of God. The ark was a chest made of acacia wood and overlaid with gold both inside and out. The chest was two and a half cubits long, one and a half cubits wide, and one and a half cubits high; it had four gold rings through which acacia poles would be placed for carrying it. The cover for the ark was made of pure gold and had a golden cherub on each end, the two facing each other, with their wings spread upward (Ex. 25:10–22). The "testimony" (i.e., the tablets of the Ten Commandments) was placed in the ark. In all of ancient literature, Hebrews alone adds that the jar of manna and Aaron's staff were also in the ark.

The manna was from God's provision of food for the desert wanderers recounted in Exodus 16. The jar of manna was kept as a memorial for future generations, Aaron placing the jar in front of the ark (16:34). Numbers 17 provides the

ALTAR OF INCENSE

▼

THE ARK OF THE COVENANT AND ITS CONTENTS

A model of the ark, Aaron's rod, the two stone tablets, and the golden pot of manna.

account of Aaron's staff budding. In response to rebellion against the leadership of Moses and Aaron, God had Moses gather twelve staffs, one to represent the leader of each of the twelve tribes. These staffs were placed in the Tent of Meeting for God to single out his chosen leader. Aaron's staff evidenced God's choice by budding, blossoming, and producing almonds. The Lord then instructed Moses to put Aaron's staff back in front of the Testimony as a reminder to those who would rebel against the Lord's chosen leaders (17:1–13).

The cherubim of the Glory (9:5). Rather than human in form, the cherubim are winged angels of composite animal form, sometimes having human characteristics as well, being one category of angels found in the Old Testament and extra-biblical, Jewish literature.[102] The designation "cherubim" may be derived from a word meaning "intercessor," and in the biblical witness, these angelic beings are associated especially with the presence of God. They guard the tree of life (Gen. 3:24), flank God's throne (Ps. 80:1; 99:1;

Isa. 37:16), and carry Yahweh through the heavens (Ps. 18:10). Images of cherubim were crafted as part of the ark's cover and were embroidered on the curtain leading into the Most Holy Place (Ex. 25:18–20; 26:31–32).

REFLECTIONS

THE DETAILS OF THE OLD COVENANT WORSHIP EXPE-riences related to the tabernacle must seem tedious and monotonous to most modern readers. Yet, we should not miss key points of the Christian faith to which they speak. First, God is a holy God from whom people are separated because of sin. The "sacred barrier" of the Holy Place, the necessity of sacrifices, and the unapproachable nature of the Most Holy Place all speak to humanity's foundational problem in relation to God. Yet, and this is a second key point, God's initiative in the construction of the tabernacle whispers his desire for more in relation to us. He wants to be approached; he wants to relate to his people. While the existence of the Holy Place shows that the way into God's presence for his people had not yet been revealed, the sacrifices and high priesthood demonstrate God's desire that sin not have the final word. The sacrifice and high priesthood of Jesus gave the ultimate answer to the problem and to God's desire that we come near to him.

The Tabernacle
A portable temple for the wilderness journey

The new religious observances taught by Moses in the desert centered on rituals connected with the tabernacle, and amplified Israel's sense of separateness, purity, and oneness under the Lordship of Yahweh.

A few desert shrines have been found in Sinai, notably at Serabit el-Khadem and at Timnah in the Negev, and show marked Egyptian influence.

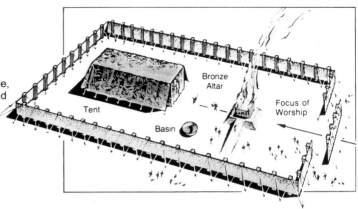

Tent

Bronze Altar

Basin

Focus of Worship

Specific cultural antecedents to portable shrines carried on poles and covered with thin sheets of gold can be found in ancient Egypt as early as the Old Kingdom (2800–2250 B.C.), but were especially prominent in the 18th and 19th dynasties (1570–1180). The best examples come from the fabulous tomb of Tutankhamun, c. 1350.

Comparisons of construction in the text of Ex. 25–40 with the frames, shrines, poles, sheathing, draped fabric covers, gilt rosettes, and winged protective figures from the shrine of Tutankhamun are instructive. The period, the Late Bronze Age, is equivalent in all dating systems to the era of Moses and the Exodus.

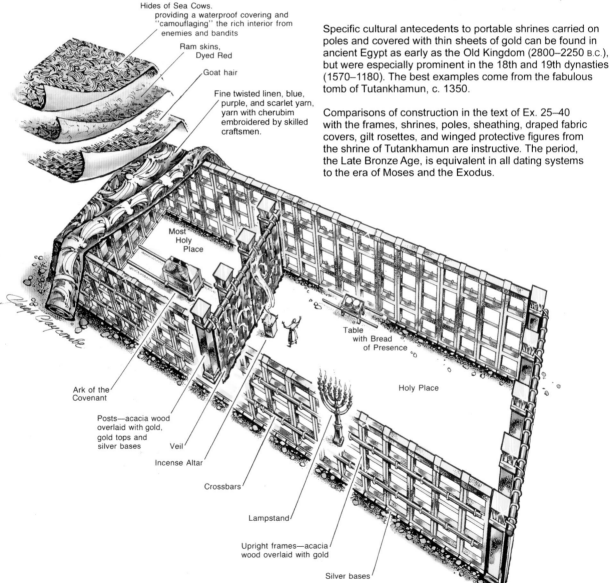

Hides of Sea Cows, providing a waterproof covering and "camouflaging" the rich interior from enemies and bandits

Ram skins, Dyed Red

Goat hair

Fine twisted linen, blue, purple, and scarlet yarn, yarn with cherubim embroidered by skilled craftsmen.

Most Holy Place

Table with Bread of Presence

Holy Place

Ark of the Covenant

Posts—acacia wood overlaid with gold, gold tops and silver bases

Veil

Incense Altar

Crossbars

Lampstand

Upright frames—acacia wood overlaid with gold

Silver bases

© Hugh Claycombe 1997

The priests entered regularly into the outer room (9:6). Ministry in the Holy Place, the outer room of the tabernacle, was the priests' responsibility. They entered to keep the lamps lit and to change the bread of the Presence (Ex. 27:20–21; Lev. 24:8).

But only the high priest entered the inner room (9:7). The Day of Atonement sacrifice, offered on the tenth day of the seventh month (September/October), was the most important sacrifice of the year for the Israelites. This sacrifice covered all of the sins not covered in the previous year by other sacrifices. On this one day of the year the people drew near to God by the high priest's entering the Most Holy Place with the Day of Atonement sacrifice (Lev. 16:1–25). Two animals were sacrificed in the ceremony, a bull as a sin offering for Aaron and his household, and a goat for the sins of the people. The blood of these two animals was sprinkled in the Most Holy Place (16:11–17).

The first tabernacle was still standing (9:8). The phrase rendered "first tabernacle" by the NIV is a reference to the outer room of the old covenant tabernacle. The author's point here is that the existence of the Holy Place, a sacred space separating God's people from his presence in the Most Holy Place, was indicative of the old covenant era. The way into that presence for his people in general had not yet been revealed.

Christ's Superior Ministry As Priest (9:11–28)

The greater and more perfect tabernacle (9:11). As with 8:2, the author understands that there exists a heavenly tabernacle in the heavenly city of God (cf. 12:22), a

▶ The Jerusalem Temple

What about the Jerusalem temple? Given that the temple in Jerusalem was at the very center of Jewish life until its destruction in A.D. 70, it is reasonable to ask why the author of Hebrews focuses on the Old Testament tabernacle rather than the first-century temple. The question is especially pertinent if, as argued in our introduction, Hebrews was written in the 60s just prior to the Jewish war with Rome, when the temple was still a glorious symbol of contemporary Judaism. Would not the author have found in the temple a ready target for his statements concerning the ineffectual nature of the older covenant? Indeed, some commentators have suggested that the uses of the present tense to speak of old covenant worship activity are an indication that the contemporary temple activities were in mind and demonstrate that the temple in Jerusalem was still standing when Hebrews was written. However,

this argument falters upon further research, for texts such as Josephus' *Antiquities*, *1 Clement* 31:2, and *Barnabas* 7–8, all of which were written after the destruction of the Jerusalem temple, similarly speak of old covenant worship in the present tense.[A-12]

There probably are two main, interrelated reasons why the author focuses on the tabernacle rather than the temple. First, he is interested in the dynamics surrounding the establishment of the old covenant (see esp. 8:4–6; 9:18–22), so he can contrast it with the establishment of the new covenant sacrifice of Christ. Second, the author grounds his entire sermon in the Old Testament Scriptures. He is interested in demonstrating the superiority of Christ's new covenant from the authoritative Word of God, and it is the tabernacle, not the temple of the first century, to which the Scriptures bear witness.

concept common in Jewish apocalyptic of his era. The writers of Qumran, *4 Ezra, 2 Baruch*, and Wisdom of Solomon, for instance, all mention the heavenly Jerusalem with its heavenly place of worship.

The blood of goats and calves (9:12). Leviticus 16 gives the details of the Day of Atonement sacrifices, which included the sacrifice of a goat and a young bull (Lev. 16:6–10). As with the broader context, this specific sacrifice is in view here.

The ashes of a heifer sprinkled (9:13). In Numbers 19 we find instructions concerning the "red heifer." The Israelites were commanded to bring Moses and Aaron a perfect heifer that had never been under a yoke. It was taken outside the camp and killed, and its blood was sprinkled seven times toward the front of the Tent of Meeting. The animal was burned then and its ashes collected for ceremonial cleansing. These ashes could be mixed with water and sprinkled on an unclean person. The tabernacle also had to be sprinkled when an Israelite had defiled the worship center by touching a dead body (Num. 19:1–21).

Cleanse our consciences (9:14). The term translated as "conscience(s)" in 9:9, 14 was used rarely in Greek literature prior to 200 B.C., but is found in first-century A.D. writers such as Plutarch, Philo, and Josephus. In A.D 59 a papyrus tells of a former soldier named Lucius Pamiseus, who met a procession of donkeys carrying stones and led by a slave. Lucius suffered a violent kick by one of the donkeys, and the frightened slave, because of his bad "conscience," ran away.[103] The term connotes a personal knowledge of something, or more specifically, the moral "consciousness" of good and evil. The problem with the old covenant system of sacrifice was its inability to deal with a worshiper's awareness of personal guilt.

Christ is the mediator (9:15). The word translated "mediator" was used widely in the Greco-Roman period, often with legal overtones. It was used for an arbiter in a political dispute or to one who settled an argument over a business deal. It also connoted a "guarantor" of an oath given in a legal situation. In religious contexts the word referred to someone who represented the people before God. Philo calls both Moses and angels mediators between God and his people.[104] In the New Testament, Jesus is the supreme mediator between God and people (1 Tim. 2:5; Heb. 8:6; 12:24).

He has died as a ransom to set them free (9:15). The word rendered "ransom" by the NIV does not occur often outside the New Testament, and then found especially in Paul's letters. It refers to the liberation effected by God on behalf of his

GOATS
▼

people, by his dealing with sin (Rom. 3:24; 1 Cor. 1:30).

In the case of a will, it is necessary to prove the death (9:16). The translation of the Greek term *diathēkē* here as "will" is out of step with the context, which has to do with the ratification of a covenant. In the context the author is concerned with the establishment of the older covenant through sacrifice (9:12–14, 18–22). The sense of 9:16–17 is that the covenant was established by a death. In the death of the sacrificial animal the ratifier's death was symbolically realized. Such a death is necessary for the establishment of the covenant.

Blood (9:18). For the past century at least, commentators have misunderstood the blood motif in the New Testament to represent "life."[105] Instead, the concept of blood in the Scriptures represents death. In Hebrews specifically the author, when referring to the shedding of Christ's blood, is speaking of his sacrificial death

that effects our cleansing (9:14), brings us freedom (9:15), and establishes the new covenant.

He took the blood of calves, together with water, scarlet wool and . . . hyssop (9:19). Exodus 24:8 recounts that Moses ratified the first covenant between God and his people by the sprinkling of blood: "Moses then took the blood, sprinkled it on the people and said, 'This is the blood of the covenant that the LORD has made with you in accordance with all these words.'"

He sprinkled with the blood both the tabernacle and everything used in its ceremonies (9:21). The assertion that Moses sprinkled the tabernacle and vessels used in worship may seem problematic, since Exodus does not tell us this. Yet, often interpreters of the ancient world, by verbal analogy, considered related passages of Scripture, with similar language, together. For instance, the Day of Atonement ritual in Leviticus 16 and the ceremony of the

SACRIFICE AT THE TABERNACLE

red heifer in Numbers 19 both involved sprinkling the Tent of Meeting (Num. 19:4; Lev. 16:14–19), and the former also included sprinkling of the altar and the cover of the ark.

But the heavenly things themselves [purified] with better sacrifices (9:23). Why would the heavenly things need to be purified? The answer is found in the instructions concerning the Day of Atonement sacrifice:

> In this way he will make atonement for the Most Holy Place because of *the uncleanness and rebellion of the Israelites*, whatever their sins have been. He is to do the same for the Tent of Meeting, which is among them *in the midst of their uncleanness*. No one is to be in the Tent of Meeting from the time Aaron goes in to make atonement in the Most Holy Place until he comes out, having made atonement for himself, his household and the whole community of Israel.
> Then he shall come out to the altar that is before the LORD and make atonement for it. He shall take some of the bull's blood and some of the goat's blood and put it on all the horns of the altar. He shall sprinkle some of the blood on it with his finger seven times *to cleanse it and to consecrate it from the uncleanness of the Israelites* (Lev. 16:16–19; italics added).

In other words, the need for cleansing the earthly worship center and its furniture had nothing to do with the uncleanness of the center or its furniture, but rather related to the uncleanness of the people. Therefore, the "heavenly things" would need to be cleansed, in the author's conception, for the same reason.

To bring salvation (9:28). In secular Greek the word translated "salvation" speaks of deliverance from a perilous situation, such as war, an enemy, a storm, or a difficult trip. In a medical context it speaks of good health. The New Testament also uses the word for such secular meanings, but the theological sense predominates. Salvation is deliverance from sin and God's coming wrath (Luke 1:68; Rom. 5:9), and it may be seen as already experienced (Rom. 8:24), a continuing process (1 Cor. 1:18), and a reality consummated in the future, as here in Hebrews 9:28.[106]

The Provisional Nature of the Old Covenant Worship Laws (10:1–18)

Hebrews 10:1–18 serves as the crowning point in the author's treatment of Christ's superior appointment as a high priest, who offers a superior offering. In 9:11–28 the focus has been on the offering's superiority based on (1) Christ's blood being superior to the blood of the Day of Atonement sacrifices, and (2) its location in the heavenly tabernacle. The author now focuses attention on a third point in favor of the Son's offering as superior: It was made just one time, which was sufficient for the permanent cleansing of God's people.

A shadow (10:1). In 8:5 the author makes the point that the tabernacle was a "shadow" of God's heavenly dwelling, merely mimicking the greater reality. He now points out that the law, providing instructions for approaching God through animal sacrifices in an earthly tent, is of the same nature, being only the "shadow . . . not the realities themselves." The word rendered "shadow" also can be translated as a "foreshadowing," a "sketch," or a "faint outline." The point is that it does not embody the greater reality of which it hints. In Plato's allegory of the cave the philosopher also contrasts the shadows from the images casting the shadows.[107] Cicero used the imagery to contrast natural and civil law, suggesting that humans do not possess a firm and clear model of true law and real justice, but rather utilize a shadow of the real thing.[108] Harold Attridge rightly notes that Hebrews uses Platonic terms, but applies them to a horizontal or temporal relationship between two time periods.[109] Those things of the past are mere shadows of the greater realities that have now been manifested. In Colossians 2:16–17 Paul uses a phrase similar to "a shadow of the good things that are coming," found here in Hebrews 10:1:

> Therefore do not let anyone judge you by what you eat or drink, or with regard to a religious festival, a New Moon celebration or a Sabbath day. These are a shadow of the things that were to come; the reality, however, is found in Christ.

Reminder of sin (10:3). In Numbers 5:15 the offering for a woman suspected of adultery is called "a reminder offering." The man who suspected his wife of adultery, with his wife, was to take an offering of barley flour to the priest. The priest mixed holy water and dust from the floor of the tabernacle, and if the woman was guilty and drank the mixture of water and dust, while holding in her hands the grain offering, it was a curse to her, causing tremendous suffering. The point is that the barley offering was a reminder of sin that brought sin to light. Commenting on this passage from Num-

bers, Philo remarks that God does not take delight in the sacrifices of people who are not virtuous. If a group of persons has a blazing altar fire that is not accompanied by good hearts, those persons' sacrifices only remind God of their ignorance and sinfulness.

Hebrews' point applies to the whole of the old covenant sacrificial system, as it is epitomized in the Day of Atonement sacrifice. Since the sacrifices really cannot cleanse the worshipers, as is shown by the offerings' repetition, all they really serve to do is affirm the perpetual state of sin in which the worshipers suffer. The offerings, thus, in their inability to remove sin, remind of sin.

"Sacrifice and offering you did not desire" [Ps. 40:6–8] (10:5–10). Psalm 40, a psalm of David, falls roughly into two movements, the first (40:1–11) praising God for his good gifts and proclaiming the psalmist's desire to do God's will, and the second (40:12–17) seeking God's help in a time of great need. Our author focuses on two points from the first half of the psalm that together convey the message that submission to God's will is more important than the offering of sacrifices. First, he highlights the

ANIMALS
APPOINTED FOR
SACRIFICE
▼

proclamation of God: "Sacrifice and offering you did not desire," and the parallel, "with burnt offerings and sin offerings you were not pleased." Tucked between these parallel statements is the statement, "but a body you prepared for me." Hebrews takes this statement from the LXX. The Hebrew behind the Greek text reads obscurely, "you have dug ears for me," perhaps meaning that God has prepared the psalmist's body for a posture of obedience, ready to hear and obey God's command. The main point concerning sacrifices, however, fits the broader context in which the author shows that God ultimately is not interested in sacrifices as an end in themselves.

The second part of the quotation finds the psalmist quoting himself, "Here I am—it is written about me in the scroll—I have come to do your will, O God." Prior to about the second century A.D. books existed in the scroll form. Sheets of papyrus or other materials, such as leather or even metal, were attached end on end and rolled up in a scroll. The scroll spoken of here may have originally been the laws of God concerning the king. For the author of Hebrews, who takes the psalm as Christological, the scroll probably speaks of the whole witness of the Scriptures. Nevertheless, the psalm confesses a willingness to do the will of God.

In interpreting the psalm Christologically, Hebrews takes the order of the material in this section as significant. The first part concerning sacrifices and offerings, for the author, alludes to the sacrificial system of the old covenant. The fact that Christ, through the Old Testament Scripture, follows with "Then I said, 'Here I am . . . I have come to do your will,'" demonstrates that there is a temporal sequence to the psalm, showing that "he sets aside the first to establish the second" (10:9). In fine rabbinic style, the author interprets the "then" in the text as indicative of that sequence. The words translated "sets aside" and "establish" in 10:9 are legal terms from the era for

A SCROLL

The "Temple Scroll" from Qumran.

annulment and institution. Christ's willingness to submit obediently to his Father's will and to be a sacrifice for sins has legally annulled the old covenant sacrificial system and instituted the new covenant of Jeremiah 31. So, "by that will, we have been made holy through the sacrifice of the body of Jesus Christ once for all" (Heb. 10:10).

But when this priest had offered for all time one sacrifice for sins (10:12). Rhetorical arguments often used contrasts to show the relative strengths and weaknesses of various positions, people, or institutions. Here the author highlights four comparisons between the old and new covenant offerings. First, the old covenant offerings were presented daily, whereas Christ's offering was made but once. Second, the priests stood when presenting their offerings, but Christ's offering climaxed in his sitting down at the right hand of God. Third, under the old covenant system numerous sacrifices were made, whereas Christ made but one. Finally, the old covenant offerings could never take away sins, but Christ's sacrifice has accomplished that feat for those for whom the sacrifice was offered.

Hebrews 10:12 alludes to Psalm 110:1, the fourth reference to that verse in this book (see comments on Heb. 1:3). As used here in 10:12 the psalm verse emphasizes the finality and decisive nature of Christ's sacrifice for sins. For Hebrews, that the Son has sat down in his place of authority until the end of the age when all his enemies will be dealt their final blow shows that his sacrifice was completely sufficient for the forgiveness of sins. He is not a priest who must stand time and again to offer ineffectual sacrifices. His one sacrifice is enough. The new covenant people have

been made whole, complete, and perfectly suited for entrance into the presence of the Father.

"This is the covenant I will make with them" [Jer. 31:33–34] (10:15–18). The author now quotes a portion of Jeremiah 31:31–34, which he quoted in full at Hebrews 8:8–12. The quotation here, which highlights parts of Jeremiah 31:33–34, has two purposes, one literary and the other theological. Literarily, the quotation works with the longer quotation of the same passage in chapter 8 to form brackets around this section of Hebrews dealing with Christ's new covenant offering. The use of same or similar material at the beginning and ending of a section was called an *inclusio* and functions somewhat like paragraph or section headings function today, marking larger sections of a text or discourse. Theologically the author understands Jeremiah 31 to affirm what he has been arguing since chapter 8. Sin has been completely forgiven because of the decisive, new covenant sacrifice of Christ. This fact is in the warp and woof

R E F L E C T I O N S

THE BOOK OF HEBREWS DEALS EXTENSIVELY WITH how decisively the Son of God has dealt with our sin. His one sacrifice has provided complete forgiveness for all our sins for all time. Since we continue to deal with sin—alas, it still is a power against which we struggle—it is easy to forget the decisiveness with which our sin has been addressed. Hebrews proclaims that new covenant believers no longer have a "consciousness of sin," meaning an awareness of sin as prohibitive of our relationship with God. Rather, we have free entrance into the Most Holy Place by virtue of our high priest, Jesus. This is a cause for great celebration. Our sins past and present have already been paid for by one sacrifice, a sacrifice so effective that it never needs to be repeated.

of the new covenant. To be a person of the new covenant is to be a person completely forgiven.

Where these have been forgiven, there is no longer any sacrifice for sin (10:18). A rabbi at times would quote a passage and then state an obvious implication of that quotation, as the author does here. Since Christ has made a once-for-all sacrifice, every system of sacrifice has been outdated or annulled. Sacrifice for sin has been rendered a thing of the past.

Strong Encouragement for Christian Commitment (10:19–25)

Hebrews 10:19–25 forms the closing of an *inclusio* that the author started at 4:14–16. In this case the author marks the great central section on the Son's appointment to (5:1–10; 7:1–28) and ministry as a superior high priest (8:3–10:18) by including no fewer than eight parallel elements in 4:14–16 and 10:19–25.[110] Packed in these five verses we find the main points of the author's message. We have a superior basis for drawing near to God and holding fast to our confession, namely, our new covenant relationship with Jesus, the Son of God, who functions as our great high priest.

Since we have confidence (10:19). A rare word in ancient Greek literature, the word translated "confidence" connotes a freedom of expression and openness of conduct.[111] In ancient Jewish thought the concept relates at points to approaching God in prayer. Therefore, on the basis of Jesus' ministry as our high priest, we have courage, a reasonable boldness to approach God in his heavenly Most Holy Place.

A new and living way opened for us through the curtain (10:20). The imagery of 10:20 has its basis in the Day of Atonement ritual of the older covenant. Christ not only passes through the curtain as our high priest, but blazes a trail for us to follow. That this way is "new" may mean that it was previously unavailable, and its description as "living" suggests that we take it by association with the Living One.

In Greek and Roman heroic traditions, of which the author of Hebrews certainly was aware, the champion of the trail, someone who paved the way for others at great personal sacrifice, constituted an important theme. For instance, in the *Epitome* (1.14.3) of Lucius Annaeus Florus one finds this comment on the valor of the consul Decius Mus:

> . . . while the other consul, as though acting upon a warning from heaven, with veiled head devoted himself to the infernal gods in front of the army, in order that, by hurling himself where the enemy's weapons

right ▶

THE CURTAIN

A representation of the Most Holy Place with a priest before the Ark of the Covenant.

were thickest, he *might open up a new path to victory along the track of his own lifeblood.*[112]

Having our hearts sprinkled . . . and having our bodies washed with pure water (10:22). Commentators often have found in the references to sprinkling and washing in 10:22 references to Christian baptism. However, the backdrop of the old covenant purification rituals is in play here. The author has already referred to those rituals, for example, in 9:13–14, where they parallel Christ's cleansing of our consciences, and 9:19–23, where they occur in the inauguration of covenants. Our hearts are sprinkled and our bodies washed by the sacrifice of Christ.

Love and good deeds (10:24). To "spur . . . on" translates a noun that can be used either positively, in the sense of encouragement, or negatively with the meaning "irritation" or "sharp disagreement" (cf. Acts 15:39, where Paul and Barnabas had such a conflict). Here it is used positively. Christians are to relate to one another in such a way that encouragement in love and good deeds results. Authentic Christian love expresses itself in good works, and the challenge to such a love forms a cornerstone of a basic Christian ethic.[113]

The Day approaching (10:25). Old Testament prophets spoke of a "day" or "days" that would result in judgment for the Lord's enemies and redemption for his people.[114] The Israelites of Amos's day called for the day of the Lord, expecting it to be a day of light; but the prophet warned that for them, the unrighteous, it would be a day of darkness (Amos 5:18). In apocalyptic literature, the day often is called the "day of judgment."[115] "The Day"

for Hebrews, and the New Testament generally, is the day of Christ's return.[116]

Further Warnings and Encouragement (10:26–39)

These verses may be divided into two main movements. The first constitutes a harsh warning—perhaps the harshest in the book (10:26–31). The author crafts this warning around a technique used both among the rabbis and the rhetoricians of the day. This technique, "an argument from lesser to greater," suggests that if something is true in a lesser situation, it is more certainly true in a greater situation and normally carries greater implications. The author of Hebrews argues that if those who rejected the law of Moses died without mercy upon the testimony of two or three witnesses, those who have trampled the Son of God under foot, treated the blood of the covenant as unholy, and insulted the Spirit of grace deserve an even greater punishment. The second movement hands out encouragement in large doses, especially by instructing the readers to remember their past faithfulness (10:32–39). This pattern of harsh warning followed by a softened word of encouragement is found also at 6:4–12.

Deliberately keep on sinning (10:26). The Old Testament addresses what is called "sinning with a high hand," a rebellion against the laws of the Lord that was considered equivalent to blasphemy. Note Numbers 15:30–31: "But anyone who sins defiantly, whether native-born or alien, blasphemes the LORD, and that person must be cut off from his people. Because he has despised the LORD's word and broken his commands, that person must surely be cut off . . . his guilt remains on him." In Hebrews 10:26 the person who remains in a state of rebellion after receiving a knowledge of the gospel has nowhere else to go for forgiveness. "No sacrifice for sins is left" because Jesus has annulled all other sacrifices as a means of dealing with sin and relating to God.

Raging fire that will consume the enemies of God (10:27). An allusion to Isaiah 26:10–11, this fire constitutes a judgment of the wicked and a vindication of those who truly are God's people:

> *Though grace is shown to the wicked,*
> *they do not learn righteousness;*
> *even in a land of uprightness they go*
> *on doing evil*
> *and regard not the majesty of the*
> *LORD.*
> *O LORD, your hand is lifted high,*
> *but they do not see it.*
> *Let them see your zeal for your people*
> *and be put to shame;*
> *let the fire reserved for your*
> *enemies consume them.*

The wicked will be put to shame, God's fire consuming them.

Anyone who rejected the law of Moses died without mercy (10:28). Deuteronomy 17:2–7 commands that those who violate God's covenant by worshiping other gods must be put to death by stoning. This is only done if there is more than one witness to the breaking of the covenant, and the witnesses are to cast the first stones. According to Deuteronomy 13:8 the worshiper of false gods is to be stoned without mercy.

Trampled the Son of God under foot, who has treated as an unholy thing the blood of the covenant (10:29). To reject

the new covenant high priest, Jesus, and his offering for sin is a greater travesty than those who turned to other gods under the old covenant. The image of trampling someone under foot was used both in classical literature and the Old Testament as an image of utter contempt. Further, those familiar with the ceremonial laws of sacrifice knew the requirements for a fit offering. The word translated as "unholy" means common, defiled, or unclean; in the context of the Levitical purity laws of the LXX, it referred to that which was ceremonially impure, not worthy of sacrifice to God. Thus, those who have rejected Christ have considered his sacrifice as unworthy, unclean, or inappropriate as an offering for sin.

For we know him who said (10:30). The seriousness of the situation for those who have turned away from Christ finds further expression with words from the Song of Moses in Deuteronomy 32. This eloquent song, offered by the lawgiver at the end of his life, speaks of God's judgment toward a faithless people who have rejected the covenant. They had rejected God in spite of his great works of love on their behalf. Judgment resulted. The author of Hebrews draws his quotations from two parts of Deuteronomy 32:35–36:

> *It is mine to avenge; I will repay.*
> *In due time their foot will slip;*
> *their day of disaster is near*
> *and their doom rushes upon them.*
> *The LORD will judge his people*
> *and have compassion on his*
> *servants*
> *when he sees their strength is gone*
> *and no one is left, slave or free.*

The first statement, "It is mine to avenge; I will repay," speaks of God's judgment on the wicked. The second, "The Lord will judge his people," sounds like a statement of vindication, but it too is given in the context of judgment. In Hebrews 10:31 the author speaks of the dreadfulness of falling into God's hands. The Song of Moses speaks further of the Lord's hand. No one can deliver out of his hand (Deut. 32:39); when his hand grasps the flashing sword for judgment, vengeance on his enemies is a sure thing (32:41).

Remember those earlier days (10:32). An important aspect of Greek rhetoric and ancient preaching was to use examples effectively. In 10:32–39 the author uses the hearers themselves as an example for endurance. That they had "stood [their] ground in a great contest in the face of suffering" suggests they had been persecuted severely.

A great contest in the face of suffering (10:32). The word translated "contest" (*athlēsis*) speaks of a difficult struggle, and commentators have pointed to the expulsion of Jews from Rome by the emperor Claudius in A.D. 49 as a possible backdrop for the experience mentioned here. At various points in the first century Jews were abused publicly as a group. Eviction from their homes was accompanied by looting of their possessions. It may be that the Christians, caught up in the conflict of Claudius's eviction, experienced various forms of persecution.

The author mentions in 10:32–34 that (1) they were "publicly exposed" to ridicule. The word translated "publicly exposed" (*theatrizō*) originally was associated with public performance, meaning to bring up on stage. As the language developed it took on the negative, figurative meaning evidenced here. Evidently these Christians had suffered both verbal and physical abuse. (2) Even when members were not being abused themselves, they suffered the emotional trauma of standing with those who were mistreated. (3) Their identification extended to those in prison, as members of the group sympathized with them. (4) Some of the believers had their property confiscated. The happy response to these persecutions, however, was joy. They celebrated the greater realities of God rather than focusing on the material problems of the moment. Such a perspective provides a solid foundation for Christian endurance.

He who is coming will come (10:37–38). The quotation in these two verses juxtaposes Isaiah 26:20–21 and Habakkuk 2:3–4, contrasting the righteous who live by faith in God and the wicked who reject him. Both Old Testament texts mention the "coming"—Isaiah says the Lord is coming, and Habakkuk proclaims the revelation of judgment is coming. In line with dominant twin motifs in Jewish thought, the righteous will be rewarded and the wicked punished. The author interprets these texts to refer to Christ's coming, an event for which the hearers must wait, demonstrating perseverance in the meantime. In the face of difficulties as they now stand with the community of faith, the author challenges them to choose faith and perseverance so they will receive the promises of God.

Overture (11:1–3)

Hebrews 11 constitutes one of the church's most loved portions of Scripture. The author sets before the reader a panoramic view of Old Testament history, highlighting significant events of that history involving faith. Much more than simply reminding his readers of interesting stories, he has a specific aim in the way he packages these narratives. For Hebrews 11 has the form of an ancient "example list," a rhetorical and preaching tool used to exhort listeners to take a specific course of action.[117] For example, the Jewish writer Philo has a similar list extolling the virtues of hope.[118] The aim is to give example after example of people who have taken the desired course of behavior, impressing the hearers with the positive outcome of their actions. Specifically in Hebrews 11, by providing those addressed with copious examples, the author challenges them to grasp that God's people must live by faith, and having grasped that truth, to live a life of persevering faith. Since the examples used in Hebrews 11 constitute great personages of the Old Testament, it is not surprising that these persons get press in the Jewish literature of our author's era.

By faith we understand that the universe was formed at God's command (11:3). One modern Jewish commentator calls creation "the fundamental affirmation of

heirs of the biblical tradition."[119] In his *Antiquities* Josephus notes that Moses, in laying out the laws for humankind, does not start, like most lawgivers, with contracts and questions concerning rights, but rather with God and his creation of the world (1:21), thus laying a firm foundation for the giving of the law. This is the place to begin when discussing any subject worth discussing. *Joseph and Aseneth*, an ancient Jewish book of the Greco-Roman world, states that God is he "who brought the invisible (things) out into the light, who made the (things that) are and the (ones that) have an appearance from the non-appearing and non-being" (12:1–2). Faith grasps that the created order has resulted from the command of God and that what is seen, at times, relates directly to what is unseen.

Movement 1: First Examples of Faith (11:4–12)

By faith Abel (11:4). Abel, Adam and Eve's second son, was murdered by Cain, his brother, because his sacrifice was better than Cain's (Gen. 4:4–12). It may be that Abel's sacrifice was better because that sacrifice, "fat portions from some of

---

▶ What Is Faith?

Faith was a foundational component of Judaism in both Old Testament and postbiblical Judaism. Faith had to do with a posture of obedience (i.e., faithfulness to the covenant with God), and, closely related, trust in God. Greek philosophers often understood faith to be an inferior way of thinking, that is, "mere belief."[A-13] Yet, for the Jews of ancient Greco-Roman society, faith continued to be a key to relationship with God and was even called "the queen of virtues."[A-14] In Hebrews the author defines faith as "being sure of what we hope for and certain of what we do not see" (1:1). The term *hypostasis*, translated by the NIV as a participle ("being sure"), is in fact a noun with a range of meanings, including substance, firmness, confidence, guarantee, or proof. Given the examples of chapter 11, the definition can be translated as "faith is the firm confidence . . . ," since the exemplars listed have a resolute confidence in the unseen God.

the firstborn of his flock," reflected an attitude of Abel's heart. In line with this interpretation, Genesis 4:4 reports "the LORD looked in favor on Abel and his offering." Hebrews also proclaims "by faith" Abel "still speaks, even though he is dead." There is a strand of Jewish tradition that heralds Abel as one who continues to plead for vengeance on the descendants of Cain. *First Enoch*, a pre-Christian book, has Abel's spirit pleading with heaven to exterminate all of Cain's seed (22:5–7). In the *Testament of Abraham* 13:1–6 Abel sits as judge of all creation. At Hebrews 12:24 the author celebrates the fact that Jesus' blood speaks better than Abel's, proclaiming forgiveness rather than vengeance.

By faith Enoch (11:5). Genesis 5:24 reports Enoch's transportation from this life without experiencing death. That he was "commended as one who pleased God" is reflected in the Old Testament text as he "walked with God"—and he is the only one in that genealogy to receive such a description.

Without faith it is impossible to please God (11:6). This statement consists of a further reflection on the conflated quotation of Isaiah 26:20–21 and Habakkuk 2:3–4 in Hebrews 10:37–38. God is pleased with the one who exhibits faith and does not shrink back.

By faith Noah (11:7). Noah was the first to respond in faith to the Word of God (Gen. 6:1–9:17). The author of Hebrews places great emphasis on faith as acting in the face of what is not seen, and so he points out how Noah acted though the Flood was not yet seen. Consequently, by faith he became "[an] heir of . . . righteousness" and condemned those who

did not believe. Josephus comments that God loved Noah because of his righteousness, and *1 Enoch* 65–66 sees him as a prophet of cosmic judgment.[120]

By faith Abraham (11:8–12). Given the prominence of Abraham as a stellar example of faith in Jewish and early Christian traditions,[121] it is not surprising that the author of Hebrews gives extensive space to this patriarch as exemplar. Genesis 12:1–9 tells how Abraham obediently left his country and his father's house in order to pursue God's call to a new life. Hebrews again emphasizes that this act of obedience involved an unseen element since he went, "even though he did not know where he was going" (11:8). Furthermore, Abraham was a foreigner, who, as heir to God's promise, was looking for a city built by God himself (11:10). The fulfillment of God's promise not only involved a place but also a progeny. An old man and woman having a son demonstrates God's faithful response to faith (11:11–12).

Interlude: A Faith of Pilgrims (11:13–16)

Aliens and strangers on earth (11:13). The view that God's people are aliens and strangers in this world, who are looking for a heavenly city, has at its core an apocalyptic understanding of reality, yet it is based on an Old Testament motif. Passages like Genesis 23:4, 1 Chronicles 29:15, and Psalm 39:12 have the Old Testament faithful confessing that they are "aliens and strangers" on the earth. In both Jewish theology and early Christianity this concept developed to the idea that earthly passions are to be denied and the heavenly home is the believer's object of true affection.[122] Jewish apocalyptic emphasized the heavenly Jerusalem as the only true city, the only city that is eternal, since God is its builder.

Movement 2: More Examples of Faith (11:17–31)

By faith Abraham . . . offered Isaac (11:17–18). Among Abraham's acts of faith, the offering of Isaac, also known as the *akedah* and recounted in Genesis 22:1–8, shines as the example of faith par excellence. This act is celebrated in Jewish tradition. For instance, *Jubilees*, a Jewish writing from the second century B.C., shares the story from the vantage point of the angel Mastema and concludes with the Lord saying to Abraham, "I have made known to all that you are faithful to me in everything which I say to you" (17:15–18:19). In a catalogue of Old Testament "famous men," Sirach 44:20 comments of Abraham: "When he was tested he proved faithful." Hebrews points out that Abraham's obedience

came in the face of an excruciating juxtaposition of the promises of God concerning his heir and the command of God to kill that heir. All the patriarch could do was trust God, and Hebrews states "Abraham reasoned that God could raise the dead." This is the only way that both the command and God's promises could be fulfilled.

By faith Isaac blessed Jacob and Esau (11:20). Hebrews deals briefly with the next three generations of the faithful. Why does the author not go into more detail? Remember that the "example list" form of exhortation is effective because of the quantity of evidence or the number of examples brought to bear. At this point the author is not interested in the details of each example but rather that each may be said to have exemplified faith in a specific, dynamic way. The blessing of Jacob and Esau by Isaac is found in Genesis 27:27–40. The ritual of blessing was considered a powerful act of bestowing or foretelling good and is at times contrasted with the concept of curse in the Old Testament. Jacob continued the ritual by blessing Joseph's sons, Ephraim and Manasseh (48:8–22). By faith Joseph, the great leader of Egypt, prophesied about the Exodus of the Israelites from the land of Egypt and instructed his descendants concerning the care of his bones (50:24–25). All of these acted in faith because they were speaking of as-yet unseen events.

By faith Moses (11:23–24). Moses held a special place in the hearts of first-century Jews, many of whom considered him to be the greatest person of history. He was understood to have achieved a unique intimacy with God, and some thought that the Messiah, when he came,

▶

ROSETTA STONE

An Egyptian monument inscription dating to 196 B.C. written in hieroglyphic Egyptian, demotic Egyptian, and Greek.

would be a "new Moses."[123] Sirach 45:4–5, a book that dates from about 180 B.C., points out Moses' character as one who was faithful:

> For his faithfulness and meekness he
>   consecrated him,
>   choosing him out of all humankind.
> He allowed him to hear his voice,
>   and led him into the dark cloud,
>   and gave him the commandments face
>   to face,
>   the law of life and knowledge,
> so that he might teach Jacob the
>   covenant,
>   and Israel his decrees.

Thus Moses' faithfulness to God was recognized in Judaism and lauded, as in Hebrews. The account of Moses in Hebrews 11 begins with the faith of his parents, who hid him from Pharaoh (Ex. 2:1–4).

Second, the faith of Moses himself is celebrated (Heb. 11:24–26) in that he rejected his adoptive mother, Pharaoh's daughter, in favor of solidarity with the people of God: "He regarded disgrace for the sake of Christ as of greater value than the treasures of Egypt" (11:26). The so-called "New Kingdom" of Egypt, which began in about 1552 B.C. and ended in 1069 B.C., saw the height of Egypt's political power and considerable wealth. It was a time of splendor and opulence. Yet, Moses rejected the Egyptian culture for the sake of suffering with God's people. So he left Egypt and "persevered because he saw him who is invisible" (11:27). Once again the author emphasizes perseverance based on the invisible God.

Finally, Moses kept the Passover, with its sprinkling of blood. Those in the congregation addressed by Hebrews who were of Jewish heritage undoubtedly grew up celebrating the Passover festival with its *haggadah*, or narrative, of the events surrounding the Exodus, focused on the Passover itself—the passing over of the houses of the Israelites who had placed blood on their doorposts.

By faith the people passed through the Red Sea (11:29). Recounted in Exodus 13:17–14:21, the crossing of the Red Sea does not seem at first glance to be illustrative of the faith of the people, who were often timid grumblers lacking trust in God (Heb. 3:7–19). Yet, the author considers acts of obedience carried out on God's command to be acts of faith, and the people did go forward when told to do so.

By faith the walls of Jericho fell (11:30). Joshua 5:13–6:27 records the conquering of Jericho. Obedience to the odd command to march around the city for seven days resulted in its walls falling down. The Old Testament city of Jericho normally is identified with the mound of Tell es-Sultan, northwest of the mouth of the Jordan River at the Dead Sea. The city was ancient even in Joshua's time and owed its location to a perennial spring. Walls were especially significant in ancient warfare, because they both gave a good defensive position (i.e., the top of the walls) and protection to those in the city. Thus the falling of Jericho's walls heralded God's act against the city and its inhabitants. The Israelites manifested faith by acting in obedience to a promise from the Lord, "See, I have delivered Jericho into your hands" (Josh. 6:2).

By faith the prostitute Rahab (11:31). Rahab plays a big part in the Jericho narrative. The prostitute had hidden the two spies during their reconnaissance of the land (Josh 2:1–24), and in return the spies had given an oath of protection to her and her family. When Jericho was destroyed, she and her family were saved. Prostitutes of the Old Testament era, either male or female, might be common prostitutes or sacred prostitutes of a pagan cult. Rahab seems to have been the former. The Joshua story demonstrates her belief in the power of Israel's God. She is noted as an ancestor of Jesus in Matthew 1:5, and James 2:25 points to the activeness of her faith as commendable and an illustration of true faith.

Crescendo and Conclusion (11:32–40)

What more shall I say? (11:32). This stylized question is found widely in classical oratorical literature of the period, as well as being used extensively by Philo of Alexandria.[124] It is a way of the author turning a corner from his methodical example list offered thus far and moving toward a conclusion.

I do not have time to tell about ... (11:32). The author of Hebrews now gives a concise summary of Old Testament and, perhaps, intertestament acts of faith. Six heroes from the era of the judges and united monarchy begin the summary, with the general designation "the prophets" tacked on. The six names are not in chronological order, but each brings to mind a history of valor lived out in faith under the rule of the unseen God. Gideon and his three hundred routed the Midianites with torches and jars (Judg. 7:7–25). A military leader under the judge Deborah, Barak defeated Sisera and the Canaanites (4:8–16). Samson championed the Israelites' cause during the Philistine crisis (13:1–16:31), and Jephthah, who made a horrific vow of

sacrifice, defeated the Amorites and Ammonites (10:6–12:7). Samuel, the bridge figure between the time of the judges and the united monarchy, discerned God's voice, and David, the only king mentioned here, lived a life of devotion to God and did great acts of faith. "The prophets" covers numerous figures who lived faithfully for God, mostly in the face of hostile cultures.

Shut the mouths of lions ... (11:33–35). The great heroes of faith at times saw positive outcomes of their faith. An obvious reference to Daniel, the author states that some of them "shut the mouths of lions." Daniel 6:23 says that "no wound was found on him, because he had trusted in his God." Shadrach, Meshach, and Abednego probably are in view as those who "quenched the fury of the flames" (cf. 3:16–30). Other prophets such as Elijah, Elisha, and Jeremiah "escaped the edge of the sword" by their faith. In the Old Testament women such as the widow of Zarephath and the woman of Shunem had sons who were resuscitated from death by Elijah and Elisha respectively (1 Kings 17:17–24; 2 Kings 4:17–37).

Others were tortured ... (11:35b–38). The outcomes of faith were not always positive by this world's values. Some in faith "were tortured and refused to be released, so that they might gain a better resurrection." During the first century, Jews who suffered under Roman oppression held heroes from the Maccabean era in high esteem because of their opposition to Greek rule in the first half of the second century B.C. Perhaps the author of Hebrews has some of these heroes in mind at this point. Second Maccabees 6 tells of a horrible time during which the

Greeks attempted to force pagan religion on the Jewish people, defiling the temple and forcing the Jews to disobey divine law. Eleazar, a ninety-year-old scribe, in the face of a death penalty, refused to eat pork, even as friends encouraged him to "fake it" by using another type of meat. At his death he stated, "It is clear to the Lord in his holy knowledge that, though I might have been saved from death, I am enduring terrible sufferings in my body under this beating, but in my soul I am glad to suffer these things because I fear him" (2 Macc. 6:30).

In 2 Maccabees 7, a mother and her seven sons die nobly under horrible torture. The first son, before the eyes of his family, has his tongue cut out, is scalped, and has his hands and feet cut off. Finally, he is fried in a pan until he dies. The second son dies in the same way, but with his last breath says, "You accursed wretch, you dismiss us from this present life, but the King of the universe will raise us up to an everlasting renewal of life, because we have died for his laws" (2 Macc. 7:9).

According to tradition, the prophet Jeremiah was "stoned" and Isaiah was "sawed in two."[125] Clement of Rome, in *1 Clement* 17:1, points to Elijah, Elisha, and Ezekiel as those who wore "sheepskins and goatskins," who were "destitute, persecuted and mistreated," wandering "in deserts and mountains, and in caves and holes in the ground." These words are also descriptive of the Jews of the Maccabean revolt who were persecuted under Antiochus IV Epiphanes.

The author of Hebrews points out that the world was not worthy of these great people of faith, who lived out their commitment to the unseen God in the face of hostility. God commended them for their faith, meaning he bore witness to their faith. The conclusion the author of Hebrews wishes the reader to draw is that faith is the only way to live for God.

Enduring Under Trial (12:1–17)

The author of Hebrews has already shown the connection between faith and endurance under adverse circumstances in 10:32–39 and given numerous examples of faithful endurance in chapter 11. Now the author adds a metaphor (the race imagery of 12:1–2, 12–13), an analogy (parental discipline in 12:3–11), and a negative example (Esau in 12:14–17), all of which extend his treatment of endurance as a Christian virtue.

Cloud of witnesses (12:1). The "cloud of witnesses" refers to the exemplars of Hebrews 11. Writers of classical literature used cloud imagery to describe a large throng of people. That they are a "cloud of witnesses" has prompted some to envision the faithful of Hebrews 11 as sitting in the stands of eternity, observing contemporary Christians in their struggle. The word we translate "witness" can connote "spectator" (e.g., 1 Tim. 6:12), and *perikeimenon*, translated as "surrounded," perhaps brings to mind the ancient amphitheater. Yet, it is doubtful

---

R E F L E C T I O N S

IN MODERN, WESTERN CHRISTIANITY FAITH OFTEN is tied to positive outcomes. In the so-called "health and wealth" gospel, negative outcomes only happen to those who do not have sufficient faith. Hebrews 11 dispels this theological myth. Yes, God does answer immediately in certain situations, but the faithful may also face severe persecution for which there seems no immediate answer. Is your concept of faith big enough to encompass both the triumphs and tragedies of life?

that the author sees the ancient faithful as passive spectators. Rather, as a "cloud of witnesses" they bear witness to God's faithfulness to the faithful. As such they offer great encouragement to Christians struggling to endure in faith.

Throw off everything that hinders ... and let us run (12:1). The use of athletic imagery to speak to the need for endurance in suffering or virtue is widespread in both Greco-Roman and Jewish literature.[126] For instance, extolling the virtues of piety and faith for the virtuous person, Philo, the Alexandrian Jew of the first century, states:

> If, however, as he goes on his way, he neither becomes weary, so that he gives in and collapses, nor grows remiss, so that he turns aside, now in this direction, now in that, and goes astray missing the central road that never diverges; but, taking the good runners as his example, finishes the race of life without stumbling, when he has reached the end he shall obtain crowns and prizes as a fitting guerdon [reward].[127]

In another place Philo proclaims that physical contests, such as foot races, are laughable, because most small or large beasts would be able to defeat a human. He suggests that the only contest that is worth the effort is

> the contest for the winning of the virtues which are divine and really

▶ The Discipline of a Father in the Ancient World

The Jews, Greeks, and Romans of the ancient world embraced the concept of paternal authority, yet this authority often was wielded in a context of love and nurture. From literary sources we know that fathers often were involved in the day-to-day aspects of raising their children. For example, Aeschylus writes of the challenge one faces in determining what a young child wants, Horace acknowledges the balkiness of two-year-olds, and Euripides speaks of a child's fear of being abandoned.[A-15] Early childhood was seen as a significant stage of development in which the child was moldable. Children were seen as needing to play, eat well, be clothed adequately, loved, protected, and disciplined.

The father had the ultimate responsibility of training his son. Although in wealthier families a tutor might be used in the care and training of a boy after age six or seven, the continued role of the father was paramount (cf. 1 Cor. 4:15). The father trained his son so as to prepare him for adult life, and this training often involved correction and punishment. In Jewish literature this picture of the father who disciplines for the good of the child can be seen in the Wisdom tradition,[A-16] and the image is extended to the Lord as the one who corrects his children out of love.[A-17] Thus Hebrews is heir to this tradition.

Olympian. For this contest those who are very weaklings in their bodies but stalwarts in their souls all enter, and proceed to strip and rub dust over them and do everything that skill and strength enables them to do, omitting nothing that can help them to victory.[128]

So too the author of Hebrews challenges his readers to "strip" off everything that hinders them in the race of endurance. An ancient writer could use the term *onkos*, translated in 12:1 as [something] "that hinders," to refer to a mass, weight, or bodily fat. In the context of running, it could refer to burdensome clothing or excess bodily weight. There-fore, believers are to run the Christian race with endurance, laying aside those things that bind or weigh us down.

Scorning its shame (12:2). The Greek word *kataphroneō*, rendered as "scorning" by the NIV, means to treat someone or something as though he or it had little value. Jesus uses the word when he speaks to the impossibility of serving two masters (Matt. 6:24): One master will be loved and the other "scorned." When the author of Hebrews says that Jesus "endured the cross, scorning its shame," he uses powerful imagery to which hearers of the first century would have been attuned. Crucifixion was the lowest form of capital punishment in the ancient world, reserved for slaves and criminals and consisting of a perverse mix of humiliation and torture. As such, it was a most intense form of scorning. In crucifixion the Roman and Jewish officials treated Jesus as valueless. What Jesus did was to "scorn this shame" by looking beyond it to the joy at the Father's right hand. He, therefore, serves as the ultimate example for those who suffer under persecution.

You have forgotten that word of encouragement that addresses you as sons (12:5). In 12:5–6 the author quotes Proverbs 3:11–12, which puts "discipline" in a positive framework. The Lord's discipline and rebuke are indications of his love and commitment to believers as "sons." Hebrews 12:7 makes clear that the author understands the hardship the hearers are facing to be synonymous with the Lord's discipline. They are to endure it and perceive it as a mark of their legitimacy as God's children (12:8).

Strengthen your feeble arms and weak knees (12:12). Hebrews picks up once

REFLECTIONS

IT DOES NOT TAKE LONG EXPERI-ence in the Christian faith to learn that maintaining a resolute commitment to Christ is not easy and demands endurance. We can find help, however, from several directions. The "cloud of witnesses" reminds us that God's people of the past have walked similar paths as the ones we are walking presently and have done so keeping faith. The exhortation of Scripture to put off those things that hinder us reminds us that the weights we embrace in life—whether unwholesome activities or attitudes of questionable value—can impede our progress in the faith. Finally, we must look to Jesus as the ultimate example of endurance. His attitude of scorning shame gives us a powerful reference point from which to evaluate the difficulties of life, especially those that come because we are committed to God's path.

again on the athletic imagery used earlier in the chapter, this time drawing from Isaiah 35:3 and Proverbs 4:26. The phrase "feeble arms and weak knees" serves as a metaphor for emotional and spiritual fatigue, which the persecuted first hearers of Hebrews must have been feeling.

According to Isaiah 35:3–8, the imagery of strengthening weak knees and hands is connected to the idea of hope in the Lord, who will come with retribution on Israel's enemies and salvation for his people. The message, therefore, is one of encouragement and consideration of God's holy way—to continue to walk in the Lord's path and to endure until he brings deliverance.

Drawing a connection in Hebrews 12:13 to the concept of the right path, the author quotes Proverbs 4:26: "Make level paths for your feet." The straight and level path serves as a common image for God's way of right living. Paths that are full of holes and bumps are dangerous, especially for a person who already is lame. The verb *ektrepō* is often translated "turn aside, go astray," but "disabled" is appropriate. Writers of the ancient world sometimes used the word to refer to dislocation.[129] All paths other than the Lord's path are dangerous; only his path leads to health.

Bitter root (12:15). Continuing with a theme of right living, the author alludes to the "bitter root" of Deuteronomy 29:18: "Make sure there is no man or woman, clan or tribe among you today whose heart turns away from the LORD our God to go and worship the gods of those nations; make sure there is no root among you that produces such bitter poison." The Old Testament context holds great significance for understanding the author's concerns at this point in Hebrews. In Deuteronomy, Moses is renewing the covenant prior to the crossing into the Promised Land. He challenges the Israelites not to turn away from the covenant. In the larger context of Hebrews the concern is that the hearers not turn away from the superior covenant offered by Christ.

Godless like Esau (12:16). Although the biblical text does not say specifically that Esau was "sexually immoral," some strands of Jewish interpretation describe him as sexually questionable because of his marriage to the Hittites Judith and Basemath (Gen. 26:34).[130] The word translated "godless" describes something that is unholy or base. Esau was godless because of his misplaced values, shown by his emphasis on food; in this Old Testament incident Esau betrays a heart that does not value the greater values of God.

Inheritance rights as the oldest son (12:16). The receiving of an inheritance from one's father was a socio-legal practice throughout the ancient world. Deuteronomy 21:16–17 says that a firstborn son receives a double portion of the father's inheritance, and this is what Esau treated so lightly (Gen. 25:29–34).

Inherit this blessing (12:17). Adding insult to injury, Jacob not only garnered Esau's birthright, but also took his blessing by deceiving their father (27:30–40). At their heart, Old Testament blessings, such as the one found in this narrative, are words of power, meant to impact the future of the child blessed. Isaac's blessing of Jacob was so comprehensive that he could not similarly bless Esau (27:36–38). The author of Hebrews wishes to point out by analogy that once an inheritance and blessing have been rejected, only tears and rejection result. Believers, rather, should value their inheritance.

A Contrast of Two Covenants (12:18–29)

A rich tradition of biblical imagery lies behind the contrast of Mount Sinai and Mount Zion at 12:18–24. Mountains often are significant sacred sites where people meet God.[131] The author of Hebrews has already dealt with the ratification of the covenant at Mount Sinai, and that experience of the Israelites, with Moses going up into the cloud to meet with God, is symbolic of the old covenant. As biblical history developed, with the movement of God's people into the Promised Land, Mount Zion, on which the temple stood in Jerusalem, displaced Mount Sinai as God's residence on earth.[132] In keeping with his orientation to apocalyptic Judaism, however, the author of Hebrews contrasts the earthly Sinai with the heavenly Mount Zion.

A mountain that can be touched (12:18). Though the author of Hebrews never mentions Mount Sinai by name, he clearly has this significant Old Testament mountain in view and draws his descriptive language in this passage from the desert wanderers' encounter with God as told in Exodus and Deuteronomy.[133] The event is Israel's drawing near to God in solemn assembly to covenant with him (Deut. 4:10–14). Strikingly visual and aural, the language in Hebrews 12:18–21 (fire, darkness, gloom, storm, trumpet blast, and the voice) is at the same time impersonal and terrible.

The auditory manifestations—the "trumpet blast" and the "voice speaking words"—were especially terrifying. The sound of the trumpet filled the air around Mount Sinai on the morning of the third day at the mountain, and it grew louder and louder, causing the Israelites to tremble with fear (Ex. 19:16, 19; 20:18). The "voice speaking words" came from the fire (Deut. 4:12), and the people, not seeing God but hearing the

disembodied voice, begged that God would be quiet (Ex. 20:18–19; Deut. 5:23–27). The message of Hebrews 12:18–21, therefore, is that one must keep one's distance and not come near to God. After all, this is a mountain that "can be touched," but the consequences for doing so are disastrous: "Whoever touches the mountain shall surely be put to death" (Ex. 19:12).

But you have come to Mount Zion (12:22). By contrast, the participants in the new covenant have come to Mount Zion, the dwelling place of God, a place of relationships. Mount Zion and the city of Jerusalem are so closely related in biblical literature that the two at times are practically synonymous, representing the dwelling place of God. Notice the poetic parallelism in passages like Joel 2:32 and Micah 4:2. Amos 1:2 states, "The LORD roars from Zion and thunders from Jerusalem." In keeping with the author's apocalyptic framework, the city to which new covenanters have come is the heavenly Jerusalem, the "heavenly . . . city" mentioned in Hebrews 11:16 and the "city that is to come" of 13:14.

Thousands of angels in joyful assembly (12:22). Believers also have come to a host of angels. The term *panēgyris*, translated in 12:22 as "in joyful assembly" and only found here in the New Testament, was used in secular literature of parties or the atmosphere of celebration at the annual athletic competitions. In the LXX, the term connotes a gathering, often at festival time, to celebrate with joy and delight.[134]

The sprinkled blood that speaks a better word than the blood of Abel (12:24). Having gone to great lengths to demonstrate that the blood of Christ cleanses completely and forever from sin (8:7–13; 9:11–14; 10:15–18), the author makes a striking statement that Jesus' blood "speaks." What does he mean that it speaks better than Abel's blood? After Cain had killed Abel, Abel's blood "cried out" to God from the ground for judgment (Gen. 4:10), a figurative way of saying that the murder must be met with justice. Furthermore, *1 Enoch* 22:5–7 says Abel continued to plead for vengeance on the descendants of Cain, wishing all of his brother's seed to be exterminated. Based on the Old Testament text's confession of Abel's blood as speaking, the author of Hebrews proclaims that Jesus' blood speaks a "better word." Whereas Abel's blood cries out for justice, Christ's blood cries out that justice has been met by his sacrifice for sins. His blood, in other words, says, "forgiven."

Once more I will shake not only the earth but also the heavens (12:26). The "time" in view here is again the manifestation of God's awesomeness at Mount Sinai.[135] Now the author turns attention to a time in the future, quoting Haggai 2:6 and weaving elements of interpretation into his quotation. The Old Testament text reads, "In a little while I will shake the heavens and the earth." This passage includes both the shaking of earth, a manifestation that occurred in relation to Mount Sinai, and the shaking of heaven. Thus, to emphasize the point, the author of Hebrews reverses the words "heaven" and "earth" and inserts the connectives "not only . . . but also": "Once more I will shake not only the earth but also the heavens." This cosmic shaking speaks of the eschatological judgment brought on the earth at the end of the age, when the material universe will pass from the scene.[136]

General Guidelines for Christian Living (13:1–6)

Keep on loving each other as brothers (13:1). The word *philadelphia*, translated by the NIV as "loving . . . as brothers" was a common ethical term in early Christianity.[137] As the word is used in its various contexts it speaks to the meeting of one another's needs and is part of a larger theological complex that understands love as the foundational Christian posture.[138]

Remember those in prison (13:3). In ancient Rome there were both public prisons and private homes used as jails. While the latter were used primarily for holding slaves, the former had various uses, including the detainment of those awaiting trial and those awaiting execution.[139] An infamous part of the prison system in Rome was the *Tullianum*, which consisted of an upper and a lower vault. The lower vault could be reached only through a hole in the ceiling. Sallust describes the *Tullianum* as follows:

> There is in the prison a chamber named the Tullianum, about twelve feet below the surface of the earth. It is surrounded by walls, and covered by a vaulted roof of stone; but its appearance is repulsive and fearful, because of the neglect, the darkness, and the stench.[140]

This chamber is the traditional site of the imprisonments of Paul and Peter. If Hebrews was originally addressed to Christians in Rome, as we have suggested, the readers would have been familiar with the harshness of the prisons. Prisoners were not treated well in the first century and often had to depend on family and friends for basic needs.[141] Consolation, gifts such as food, and

---

▶ Hospitality in the Ancient World

One of the foremost rules of brotherly love in the Christian churches was to show hospitality, especially perhaps to traveling preachers of the gospel.[A-18] Hospitality constitutes the act of making strangers welcome in one's home, caring for their needs as one would a friend. In the ancient world the cost of staying at an inn was prohibitive for most, and such establishments usually had poor reputations as hangouts for prostitutes and thieves. Thus hospitality became highly valued in Greco-Roman as well as Jewish society, and these form the backdrop of the Christian ethic.

Junia Theodora, for instance, a Roman citizen living in Corinth in mid-first-century A.D., was honored by the Lycian confederation and by the people of Telmessos because of her hospitality. The decree states that she "tirelessly showed zeal and generosity toward the Lycian nation and was kind to all travelers, private individuals as well as ambassadors, sent by the nation or the various cities."[A-19] The value placed on hospitality in Jewish society can be seen in passages such as *Test. Job* 10, which probably was written in the first century B.C. or A.D.:

> And I established in my house thirty tables spread at all hours, for strangers only. I also used to maintain twelve other tables set for the widows. When any stranger approached to ask alms, he was required to be fed at my table before he would receive his need. Neither did I allow anyone to go out of my door with an empty pocket.

Many Jews regarded Abraham as the paradigm par excellence for hospitality. Writers such as Philo and Josephus lauded his hospitality shown to the angelic visitors (Gen. 18:2–15), to which the writer of Hebrews seems to allude in 13:2.

prayers all would have been greatly valued.[142] Therefore, the author of Hebrews challenges this congregation to "remember those in prison as if you were their fellow prisoners."

Marriage should be honored by all (13:4). The Jewish and Christian ethic of fidelity in marriage was attacked from two sides in the ancient world. On the one hand, some social commentators of the day felt chastity in marriage was unreasonable. Men, for instance, were expected to take mistresses as confidants and sexual partners. On the other hand, there were those holding to asceticism. To "honor" marriage means to "hold it as especially valuable." Correspondingly, the marriage bed is to be kept pure from sexual immorality and adultery. The latter concept refers to those who break their marriage vows by having sexual relations with someone other than their spouse. The former word, *pornoi*, addresses any sexual activity outside the context of marriage.

Keep your lives free from the love of money (13:5). The New Testament links sexual impurity and the love of money in several places, perhaps because the topics are addressed side by side as the seventh

right ▶

ROMAN GOLD COINS

and eighth of the Ten Commandments.[143] To abstain from the love of money was extolled as a virtue in the broader Greco-Roman culture. Money was thought to corrupt government officials, for example, so one who was not a lover of money was seen as having the ability to manage objectively. The author of Hebrews challenges his hearers to "be content." Part of the background here may be the seizing of the believers' properties, which the author mentions at Hebrews 10:32–34.

Guidelines on Church Leadership and Doctrine (13:7–19)

Remember the leaders (13:7). Among the books of the New Testament, Hebrews alone refers to the church's officials as "leaders" (*hoi hegoumenoi*), although Acts 15:22 uses the same Greek word as an adjective to describe the "men" sent as a delegation to Antioch. The term was used in the broader culture of state officials and in the LXX for religious, political, and military leaders. The word also is used in the *Shepherd of Hermas* and *1 Clement*, early Christian documents associated with the city of Rome.

Ceremonial foods . . . an altar (13:9–10). Special cultic meals were practiced in some branches of first-century Judaism,

REFLECTIONS

NOTICE THAT THE ETHIC REFLECTED IN HEBREWS 13:1–6 begins with a focus on the needs of others. What are ways in which you are expressing "brotherly love?" The need for hospitality, perhaps, takes different forms in modern contexts, but the foundational need to minister to God's people with our resources remains the principle of concern. Furthermore, there are many places in the world today in which brothers and sisters in Christ are suffering for the faith, many being put in prison. How might we apply 13:3 to their situation?

especially the fellowship meal, which was understood as communicating the grace of God. Giving God blessing, thanksgiving for his grace, and prayers of petition were all involved in such a meal. Jewish meals in general were understood to give the participants spiritual strength through the joy experienced at the table (Ps. 104:14–15). Meals gave faithful Jews the opportunity to reflect on God's goodness and provision and were meant to remind the faithful that the ultimate expression of thanks to God for redemption must be made in the thank offering and the fellowship meal at the Jerusalem altar. It may be, therefore, that some addressed by Hebrews were tempted to abandon the Christian meals, in which the grace of God through Christ was celebrated, in favor of Jewish meals that celebrated the altar in Jerusalem.[144]

The bodies are burned outside the camp . . . Jesus also suffered outside the city gate (13:11–12). The author has dealt extensively with the Day of Atonement sacrifices under the old covenant and Christ's superior atoning offering on the cross (9:11–14, 24–28; 10:1–4). The reference to "bodies . . . burned outside the camp" alludes to Leviticus 16:27, part of the instructions for the Day of Atonement offerings: "The bull and the goat for the sin offerings, whose blood was brought into the Most Holy Place to make atonement, must be taken outside the camp; their hides, flesh and offal are to be burned up." Drawing a parallel between the old covenant sacrifices and Jesus' experience, the writer notes that Jesus "suffered outside the city gate." The image is one of rejection. Crucifixion was a means of killing through torture and humiliation (Heb. 6:6; 12:2). Therefore, believers are to reject the comfort of

associating with the world, particularly the religion of Judaism, and embrace the disgrace of Christ.

Sacrifice of praise (13:15). This phrase occurs in the LXX at Leviticus 7:12, referring to the highest form of peace offering under the old covenant.[145] The thank offering, as the name implies, was given to express gratitude to God; it was voluntary and could only be made after the worshiper had been made ritually clean. As Christians we give this offering "through Jesus" and "continually" since he has cleansed us once for all time. The phrase "fruit of lips" also is associated with thanksgiving, especially in Psalms (e.g., Ps. 50:14, 23; 107:22).

Closing (13:20–25)

Hebrews generally has the form of a first-century sermon rather than a letter (see the Introduction); yet an epistolary ending was attached to this sermon, perhaps so it could be sent to the congregation by courier. Early Christian letters follow the general form of letters in the broader Greco-Roman culture, often containing a postscript meant to maintain the relationship between the sender and the recipient.[146] The Christian expression of the form includes some or all of the following elements: requests, a benediction, doxology, comments on the work's contents, personal news, greetings, and a farewell wish.[147] Hebrews includes all of these but the first.

May the God of peace (13:20). Benedictions were important both to letters and to other forms of address such as sermons, and in Jewish contexts were considered an act of worship.[148] An author could form his benediction to express specific needs of his hearers, as the author of Hebrews does in 13:20–21. The themes of the blood, the eternal covenant, and doing God's will are all important for Hebrews. The benediction, therefore, expresses the author's deep prayers for his hearers, especially that they may have a dynamic relationship with the great Shepherd, Jesus.

Shepherd of the sheep (13:20). The image of the shepherd has its roots in the pastoral setting of the Old Testament and is expressed poignantly with passages such as Psalm 23. The image developed in broader Jewish contexts of the Greco-

Roman world, for instance, expressing hopes concerning the coming Messiah: "And the blessing of the Lord will be with him in strength, and he will not weaken; His hope (will be) in the Lord. Then who will succeed against him, mighty in his actions and strong in the fear of God? Faithfully and righteously shepherding the Lord's flock, he will not let any of them stumble in their pasture" (*Ps. Sol.* 17.40). Philo, moreover, applied the image to the divine Logos (*Agric.* 51). In the New Testament the Gospel of John picks up the image in 10:11–18, and 1 Peter 2:25 calls Jesus the "Shepherd and Overseer of your souls."

ANNOTATED BIBLIOGRAPHY

Attridge, Harold. *To the Hebrews.* Hermeneia. Philadelphia: Fortress, 1989.

A technical but clearly written commentary, which offers a wealth of information and a balanced treatment of the text at most points. After Lane, this is the best English-language commentary available.

Bruce, F. F. *The Epistle to the Hebrews,* revised ed. NICNT. Grand Rapids: Eerdmans, 1990.

Prior to the publication of the technical commentaries by Lane and Attridge, this volume, originally published in 1963, was the best English-language work available, with that by Hughes running a close second. As usual, Bruce offers outstanding, evangelical scholarship in the task of elucidating the New Testament.

Ellingworth, Paul. *Commentary on Hebrews.* NIGTC. Grand Rapids: Eerdmans, 1993.

An outstanding source of information, which, with the technical commentaries of Lane and Attridge, should be consulted. However, Ellingworth's treatment often misses important contextual concerns and shows too little sensitivity to the overall structure of Hebrews.

Guthrie, George H. *Hebrews.* NIVAC. Grand Rapids: Zondervan, 1998.

My own attempt at commenting on Hebrews. The approach follows the pattern for the series, addressing original meaning, bridging the contexts of the ancient and modern world, and application. Evangelical in orientation, the book seeks to be accessible by pastors and laypeople while addressing more technical issues such as structure and word meanings.

Hagner, Donald A. *Hebrews.* NIBC. Peabody, Mass.: Hendrickson, 1990.

This is a solid, evangelical, medium-level commentary that offers consistently helpful insights to the book.

Hughes, Philip E. *A Commentary on the Epistle to the Hebrews.* Grand Rapids: Eerdmans, 1977.

Not as detailed as Bruce in some respects but more inclined to deal with wide-ranging theological issues in the course of commentary. Prior to Lane and Attridge, with the exception of Bruce, Hughes offers the most helpful English-language commentary on the text of Hebrews.

Lane, William L. *Hebrews: Call to Commitment.* Peabody, Mass.: Hendrickson, 1985.

A popular treatment from one of the foremost scholars on Hebrews.

_____. *Hebrews 1–8* and *Hebrews 9–13.* WBC. Dallas: Word, 1991.

These two volumes are the best detailed exegetical commentary available today. Lane offers the most extensive and helpful introduction on the book available.

Main Text Notes

1. E.g., Rom. 1:1; 1 Cor. 15:8; Gal. 1:11–16.
2. Eusebius, *Eccl. Hist.* 6.25.14
3. For more on the structure of the book see George H. Guthrie, *Hebrews* (NIVAC; 1998), 27–31.
4. Aristotle, *The "Art" of Rhetoric*, trans. John Henry Freese (LCL; Cambridge, Mass.: Harvard Univ. Press, 1982), 427.
5. Philo, *On the Account of the World's Creation Given by Moses*, trans. F. H. Colson and G. H. Whitaker (LCL; Cambridge, Mass.: Harvard Univ. Press, 1981), 7.
6. Cf. Luke 1:55; Acts 3:13; 7:38–39; Harold W. Attridge, *The Epistle to the Hebrews* (Hermeneia; Philadelphia: Fortress, 1989), 38.
7. See, e.g., Plato, *Timaeus* 71e–72b.
8. C. H. Peisker, "Prophet," *NIDNTT*, 3:84–85.
9. E.g., Isa. 2:2–21; Joel 1–3; Amos 8:9–11; 9:9–12.
10. E.g., 2 Tim. 3:1; James 5:3; 2 Peter 3:3.
11. E.g., 4QFlor. 1:12.
12. Michael Grant and Rachel Kitzinger, eds., *Civilization of the Ancient Mediterranean: Greece and Rome* (New York: Charles Scribner's Sons, 1988), 3:1349.
13. B. F. Westcott, *The Epistle to the Hebrews: The Greek Text with Notes and Essays* (London: MacMillan, 1892), 168.
14. E.g., Ex. 16:7; 33:18; Isa. 40:5.
15. Donald Hagner, *Hebrews* (NIBC; Peabody, Mass.: Hendrickson, 1990), 23.
16. Philo, *Creation* 146.
17. E.g., Luke 9:32; John 1:14; 2:11; 17:5; Rom. 8:17; Phil. 3:21.
18. James Hope Moulton and George Milligan, *The Vocabulary of the Greek New Testament Illustrated from the Papyri and Other Non-Literary Sources* (London: Hodder and Stoughton, 1949), 683; Henry George Liddell and Robert Scott, *A Greek-English Lexicon*, revised by Henry Stuart Jones (Oxford: Clarendon, 1996, 1977).
19. Westcott, *Hebrews*, 12.
20. William Lane, *Hebrews 1–8* (WBC; Dallas: Word, 1991), 13.
21. E.g., John 1:14; Phil. 2:6; Col. 1:15.
22. Ps. 33:6; Isa. 40:26; 48:13.
23. Pindar, *Hymn 2, to Apollo*, line 29.
24. Theodor Herzl Gaster, *Myth, Legend, and Custom in the Old Testament: A Comparative Study with Chapters from Sir James Frazier's Folklore in the Old Testament* (New York: Harper & Row, 1969), 773–80.
25. Sigmund Mowinckel, "General Oriental and Specific Israelite Elements in the Israelite Conception of the Sacral Kingdom," in *The Sacral Kingship*, ed. G. Widengren (Leiden: Brill, 1959), 287.
26. E.g., Matt. 22:44; Acts 2:33; 5:31; Rom. 8:34; 1 Cor. 15:25.
27. P. Oxy. 1.58, MM, 451.
28. Richard Longenecker, *The Christology of Early Jewish Christianity* (Grand Rapids: Baker, 1981), 41–46.
29. Duane A. Garrett, *Angels and the New Spirituality* (Nashville, Tenn.: Broadman and Holman, 1995), 12–17.
30. Longenecker, *Christology*, 95. See Robert H. Eisenman and Michael Wise, *The Dead Sea Scrolls Uncovered* (Rockport, Mass.: Element, 1992), 70.
31. E.g., Acts 4:23–31; 13:33–34.
32. E.g., Ex. 13:2; 22:29; Lev. 27:26; Num. 3:13.
33. Ceslas Spicq, *Theological Lexicon of the New Testament*, trans. James D. Ernest, 3 vols. (Peabody, Mass.: Hendrickson, 1994), 3:210; e.g., 2 Sam. 13:36–37; 1 Chron. 3:1.
34. Rom. 8:29; Col. 1:15, 18; Heb. 12:23; Rev. 1:5.
35. A. A. Anderson, *Psalms (73–150)* (NCBC; Grand Rapids: Eerdmans, 1972), 719; Hans-Joachim Kraus, *Psalms 60–150: A Continental Commentary*, trans. Hilton C. Oswald (Minneapolis, Minn.: Fortress, 1993), 299–300; Franz Delitzsch, *Biblical Commentary on the Psalms*, trans. Francis Bolton (Grand Rapids, Mich.: Eerdmans, 1959), 3:129–30.
36. J. A. Thompson, *Handbook of Life in Bible Times* (Downers Grove, Ill.: InterVarsity, 1986), 274.
37. Attridge, *Hebrews*, 60.
38. J. Douglas et al., eds., *New Bible Dictionary*, 2d ed. (Downers Grove, Ill.: InterVarsity, 1982), 394; 1 Kings 5:17; 6:37; 7:10.
39. Westcott, *Hebrews*, 36–37; Aristotle, *De partibus animalium* 3.3; R. C. H. Lenski, *The Interpretation of the Epistle to the Hebrews and the Epistle of James* (Columbus, Ohio: Wartburg, 1946), 64.
40. So Lane, *Hebrews 1–8*, 35, 37, who follows P. Teodrico, "Metafore nautiche in *Ebr.* 2, 1 e 6, 19," *RB* 6 (1958): 33–49. Herodotus (e.g., 2.150; 6.20) and Strabo (9.2.31) speak of the flow of a body of water past some point.
41. Josephus, *Ant.* 15.5.5 §136.
42. Deissmann, *Bible Studies*, 107–9.
43. Philo, *Moses* 2.14.
44. Num. 35:16–21; Lev. 20:10; Deut. 22:24; Lev. 20:11–14; Ex. 22:19; Lev. 18:22; 20:13.

45. Job 34:11; Ps. 62:12; Prov. 24:12; Ezek. 7:3, 27; Job 11:20; Prov. 1:24–31; Jer. 11:11.
46. E.g., Acts 2:22; Rom. 15:19; 2 Cor. 12:12.
47. Stephens, *The New Testament World in Pictures*, 24.
48. Attridge, *Hebrews*, 87–88; Lane, *Hebrews 1–8*, 56–57.
49. Ex. 29:9, 29, 33, 35; Lev. 8:33; 16:32; Num. 3:3.
50. Matt. 27:35; John 19:23, 31–36.
51. Epictetus, *Diss.* 1.27.9–10
52. Spicq, *TLNT*, 2:478–781.
53. Grant and Kitzinger, *Civilization of the Ancient Mediterranean*, 1:299–308; 3:1373–76.
54. E.g., Num. 32:7–11; Deut. 1:19–35; Neh. 9:15–17; Ps. 106:24–26; *4 Ezra* 7:106.
55. 1 Cor. 10:6–12.
56. Lane, *Hebrews 1–8*, 84–85.
57. Cf. Ex. 4:14; 7:3; 8:15; Ezek. 11:19.
58. Cf. also Rom. 8:17; 11:22; 2 Cor. 13:5b.
59. Cf. Matt. 7:15–23; James 2:14–26.
60. Ibid., 84.
61. Num. 14:1–38; Deut. 9; Ps. 78:22, 32; 106.
62. E.g., Deut. 3:20; 12:9; Josh. 1:13, 15; Isa. 63:14.
63. Ronald Williamson, *Philo and the Epistle to the Hebrews* (ALGHJ; 1970), 547–48.
64. E.g., Ex. 16:23, 30; 31:15; 34:21; 35:2.
65. Lev. 16:29–31; 23:26–28, 32.
66. Garland Young, "A Soldier's Armor," *BI* 21 (Fall 1994): 38.
67. Leland Ryken et al., *DBI* (1998), 835.
68. Martin Hengel, *The Son of God* (Philadelphia: Fortress), 30. Hengel's work devastated earlier suggestions that Christianity borrowed its concept of Jesus as God's dying and rising son from broader Greek mythology.
69. E.g., Matt. 11:27; Mark 1:11; 9:7; 13:32; 14:36.
70. E.g., John 7:18; 8:46; 2 Cor. 5:21; 1 Peter 1:19; 2:22; 3:18; 1 John 3:5, 7.
71. Grant and Kitzinger, *Civilization of the Ancient Mediterranean*, 2:910–11.
72. Cf. Ex. 28:1; Lev. 8:1; Num. 16:5.
73. F. F. Bruce, "Melchizedek," *NBD*, 759.
74. Matt. 26:36–46; Mark 14:32–42; Luke 22:40–46.
75. Plutarch, *Alexander* 33.10; Philostratus, *De Gymnastica* 46.
76. Spicq, *TLNT*, 2:552–54.
77. E.g., Gal. 4:3, 9; Col. 2:8, 20; 2 Peter 3:10, 12.
78. Philo, *Prelim. Studies* 149–50.
79. Westcott, *Hebrews*, 134.
80. Epictetus, *Diss.* 2.16.39, 44.
81. Philo, *Agriculture* 9.
82. F. F. Bruce, *Hebrews*, 140.
83. Jacob Neusner and William Scott Green, eds., *Dictionary of Judaism in the Biblical Period: 450 B.C.E. to 600 C.E.* (New York: Simon and Schuster and Prentice Hall International, 1996), 2:526–27.
84. Spicq, *TLNT*, 3:477–78.
85. Grant and Kitzinger, *Civilization of the Ancient Mediterranean*, 2:963.
86. 1 Chron. 16:15; Ps. 105:8; 111:5.
87. Cf. Rom. 2:6–7; 1 Cor. 3:13–15; James 2:15–16; 1 John 3:16–20.
88. E.g., 1 Cor. 11:1; Eph. 5:1; Phil. 3:17; 1 Thess. 1:6; 2:14.
89. Grant and Kitzinger, *Civilization of the Ancient Mediterranean*, 1:622.
90. Philo, *Dreams* 1.12.
91. Num. 35:9–34; Deut. 4:41–43; Josh. 20:1–9.
92. Grant and Kitzinger, *Civilization of the Ancient Mediterranean*, 1:353.
93. Plutarch, *Moralia*, 446A.
94. Philo, *Sacrifices* 90.
95. J. A. Fitzmyer, "'Now This Melchizedek' (Heb. 7:1)," *CBQ* 25 (1963): 305–21.
96. Neusner and Green, eds., *Dictionary of Judaism in the Biblical Period*, 1:278–79.
97. Hurst, *The Epistle to the Hebrews*, 13.
98. J. A. Thompson, *The Book of Jeremiah* (NICOT; Grand Rapids, Mich.: Eerdmans, 1980), 551.
99. Neusner and Green, *Dictionary of Judaism in the Biblical Period*, 2:423.
100. F. B. Huey, *Bible Study Commentary: Exodus* (Grand Rapids, Mich.: Zondervan, 1977), 107.
101. Attridge, *Hebrews*, 184–85.
102. E.g., Ezek. 1:4–14; *1 En.* 61:10; 71:7.
103. Spicq, *TLNT*, 3:332–33.
104. *Dreams* 1.142–43; *Moses* 2.1.66.
105. E.g. Westcott, *Hebrews*, 266. For the correct interpretation see Alan M. Stibbs, *The Meaning of the Word "Blood" in Scripture* (reprint, Leicester, Eng.: Theological Students' Fellowship, 1978).
106. Spicq, *TLNT*, 3:344–50.
107. Plato, *Rep.* 7.514A–517A.
108. Cicero, *De off.* 3.17.69.
109. Attridge, *Hebrews*, 271.
110. Guthrie, *Hebrews*, 341.
111. Spicq, *TLNT*, 3:56–62.
112. As quoted in Attridge, *Hebrews*, 285.
113. E.g., Gal. 5:13; 1 Thess. 1:3; James 2:8; 1 Peter 1:22; 1 John 3:10–18; Rev. 2:19.
114. E.g., Isa. 2:2–21; Joel 1–3; Amos 8:9–11; 9:9–12.
115. E.g., *1 En.* 94:9; *4 Ezra* 7:26–44.
116. E.g., 1 Cor. 5:5; 1 Thess. 5:2; 2 Peter 3:10.

117. Michael R. Cosby, "The Rhetorical Composition of Hebrews 11," *JBL* 107 (1988): 250–70.
118. *Praem. poen.* 11–15.
119. Neusner and Green, eds., *Dictionary of Judaism in the Biblical Period*, 1:137.
120. Josephus, *Ant.* 1.3.2 §75.
121. E.g., *Jubilees* 10–12; *Apoc. Ab.* 1–8; *Gen. Rabbah* 38:13; Rom. 4:16–25; Gal. 3:6–14; 4:21–31.
122. Ellingworth, *Hebrews*, 594; see also 1 Peter 2:11.
123. Mary Rose D'Angelo, *Moses in the Letter to the Hebrews* (SBLDS; Chico, Calif.: Scholars, 1979), 91–131.
124. Bruce, *Hebrews*, 320.
125. On Jeremiah, who tradition says was stoned in Egypt, see Tertullian, *Scorpiace* 8; Jerome *Contra Jovinianum* 2:37. On the martyrdom of Isaiah see *Mart. Isa.* 5:11–14; Jutin, *Dial.*, 120; Jerome, *Comm. in Isa.*, 57:2.
126. See, e.g., 1 Cor. 9:24–27; Gal. 2:2; 2 Tim. 4:7; *4 Ezra* 7:127.
127. Philo, *Migration* 133.
128. Philo, *Agriculture* 119.
129. Attridge, *Hebrews*, 365.
130. Philo is typical of those who see Esau as a representative of wicked living. See. e.g., *De virtutibus* 208; *Legum allegoriae* 3.139–40.
131. Gen. 22:1–14; Ex. 3:1–2; Ezek. 28:13–15.
132. Leland Ryken et al., *DBI*, 573.
133. E.g., Ex. 19:16–22; 20:18–21; Deut. 4:11–12; 5:23–27.
134. Ezek. 46:11; Hos. 2:11; 9:5; Amos 5:21.
135. Ex. 19:18; Judg. 5:5; Ps. 68:8; 77:18.
136. 1 Cor. 7:31; 2 Peter 3:10–12; Rev. 21:1.
137. Rom. 12:10; 1 Thess. 4:9; 1 Peter 1:22; 2 Peter 1:7.
138. E.g., John 13:34–35; 1 Cor. 13:1, 13.
139. A. Berger, "Prison," *OCD*, 879.
140. As quoted in Harry T. Peck, *Harper's Dictionary of Classical Literature, and Antiquities* (New York: Harper & Brothers, 1898), 278.
141. Leon Morris, "Hebrews," *EBC*, 146.
142. E.g., Matt. 25:36; 1 Cor. 4:17–18; 2 Tim. 1:16; Heb. 13:18–19.
143. E.g. 1 Cor. 5:10–11; Eph. 4:19; 1 Thess. 4:3–6.
144. Lane, *Hebrews 9–13*, 533–35.
145. Westcott, *Hebrews*, 445.
146. D. F. Watson, "Letter, Letter Form," *DLNT*, 651.
147. Attridge, *Hebrews*, 404–5.
148. J. L. Wu, "Liturgical Elements," *DLNT*, 660.

Sidebar and Chart Notes

A-1. Ps. 97:7; 104:4; see Heb. 1:6–7.
A-2. Ps. 45:6–7; 102:25–27.
A-3. Spicq, *Theological Lexicon of the New Testament*, 3:344–46.
A-4. Leland Ryken et al., eds., *Dictionary of Biblical Imagery*, 752–54; e.g., Matt. 8:25; Mark 3:23–27; 5:28; James 5:15; Rom. 5:9–10; Rom. 2:5; 1 Thess. 2:16.
A-5. D'Angelo, *Moses*, 91–131.
A-6. Ex. 29:29–30; Lev. 16:32; Num. 18:7; 25:11–13; 35:25, 28; Neh. 12:10–11.
A-7. See esp. Philo, *Alleg. Interp.* 3.79–82.
A-8. Lane (*Hebrews 1–8*, 160–61) points out the differences between this conception of Melchizedek and that given by Hebrews.
A-9. For a detailed look at Melchizedek outside the biblical literature see Attridge, *Hebrews*, 192–95.
A-10. *4 Ezra* 7:26.
A-11. *2 Bar.* 59:4.
A-12. Josephus, *Ant.* 4.8.17–23 §§224–57.
A-13. Attridge, *Hebrews*, 311–14.
A-14. Philo, *Abraham* 270.
A-15. Grant and Kitzinger, eds., *Civilization of the Ancient Mediterranean*, 3:1359.
A-16. E.g. Prov. 13:24; Sir. 30:1.
A-17. See comments on Heb. 12:5–6; see also Deut. 8:5; Jer. 2:30; 5:3.
A-18. James 4:13; 1 Peter 4:9; Matt. 10:11; Acts 16:15; Titus 3:13; Philem. 22; 3 John 5–8.
A-19. As quoted in Spicq, *TLNT*, 3:455–56.

JAMES

by Douglas J. Moo

James

We meet several men in the New Testament who have the name James (see "Men Named 'James' in the New Testament"). Only two of them were prominent enough to write a letter to Christians and identify themselves simply as "James": James the brother of John, one of the twelve apostles; and James "the brother of the Lord." The former James, as Luke tells us, was executed by Herod Agrippa I in A.D. 44 (Acts 12:2); and this letter was probably not written this early. So we are left with James the brother of the Lord as the most likely author. This James did not at first believe in his brother's messianic claims (see John 7:5), but was apparently converted as a result of a resurrection appearance (cf. 1 Cor. 15:7). He became the leader of the early Christian church in Jerusalem.[1]

JORDAN NEAR
THE DEAD SEA

James
IMPORTANT FACTS:

- **AUTHOR:** James, the brother of the Lord.
- **DATE:** A.D. 44–48.
- **OCCASION:** James, leader of the Jerusalem church, writes to former parishioners who have had to leave Jerusalem to take up lives elsewhere.
- **THEMES:** The overall theme is expressed in 4:4–5: Believers must commit themselves wholeheartedly to their God, who demands absolute allegiance. Subordinate themes are:
  1. Encouragement for believers who are suffering trials.
  2. God's perspective on wealth and poverty.
  3. The need for biblical faith always to show itself in good works.

The New Testament tells us little about James's own background. Some Christians in the patristic period picture James as a radical Jewish-Christian who insisted on observance of Torah for Christians.[2] But the letter of James itself paints a different picture. To be sure, the letter is thoroughly Jewish—so Jewish that a few scholars have thought that it might be a Jewish book with the name of Jesus added later. But the Greek of the letter reveals that the author is well acquainted with good Greek style and with certain Greek religious and philosophical concepts. In fact, the letter uses words and concepts in ways similar to certain other Greek-influenced Jewish writings of the time: the book of Sirach, the *Testaments of the Twelve Patriarchs* in the Pseudepigrapha, and (less strikingly) the works of the Alexandrian philosopher Philo. We can surmise, therefore, that James, though raised in Galilee, had at some point become acquainted with the particular Hellenistic trajectory of Jewish moral thinking. God used that background to prepare him to write a letter of moral exhortation to struggling and tempted believers.

One other element in James's background deserves brief comment: his exact physical relationship to Jesus. Powerful ascetic tendencies in the church of the second and third centuries led to the view that Mary remained perpetually a virgin. New Testament references to "brothers" of the Lord constituted an obvious challenge to this view. Hence, Jerome and other fathers argued that the Greek word (*adelphos*) in these texts meant "cousin." But evidence for this meaning of the word in the New Testament is lacking. If James was an *adelphos* of the Lord, he and Jesus must have shared at least one blood parent. Some scholars think that this common parent was Joseph, and that James was older than Jesus, born to Joseph and a wife before Mary (this is called the Epiphanian view). But the close relationship between Mary and the brothers of Jesus (e.g., Mark 3:32; 6:3) suggests that Mary was the mother of Jesus' brothers also. In this case, James would have been a younger brother of Jesus (the so-called Helvidian view). If James was, then, born to the same parents as Jesus and raised in the same home, we may surmise that

Men Named "James" in the New Testament	
James, the father of Judas	• his son, Judas, was one of the twelve apostles • see Luke 6:16; Acts 1:13
James, the son of Alphaeus	• one of the twelve apostles • see Luke 6:15; Acts 1:13
James, the brother of John	• the son of Zebedee • one of the twelve apostles • killed by Herod Agrippa I (Acts 12:2) • see Luke 5:10; 9:28, 54; Acts 1:13
James, the brother of the Lord	• half-brother of the Lord Jesus; son of Mary and Joseph (cf. Mark 6:3) • see Acts 12:17; 15:13; 21:18; Gal. 1:19; 2:9, 12; 1 Cor. 15:7; letter of James; Jude 1

this background influenced his views of Christianity. In fact, however, we have little evidence that this was the case. Physical relationship to Jesus did not, apparently, lead to much spiritual benefit for James.[3]

The Recipients of the Letter

James describes the people he is writing to very generally: "the twelve tribes scattered among the nations" (1:1). "Twelve tribes" might suggest that James is writing to Jewish Christians, or even to Jews. But the language had become symbolic of the people of God and may have been transferred to Christians in general. Nevertheless, the content of the letter certainly suggests a Jewish-Christian audience.

Where did these Jewish Christians live? "Scattered among the nations" indicates that they were living outside of Palestine. The verb James uses here is cognate to the word "Diaspora," the name given to the Jewish community outside of Israel.

But since we think James is writing at an early date (A.D. 44–48), his recipients probably do not live far from Palestine. In fact, Acts 11:19 suggests the circumstances of the readers that James addresses in the letter: "Those who had been scattered by the persecution in connection with Stephen traveled as far as Phonecia, Cyprus and Antioch, telling the message only to Jews." On this scenario, then, the Jewish Christians James addresses are living as exiles in areas near Palestine because of their faith in Jesus. Their status as exiles explains why they are experiencing some of the trials James mentions. They are poor (cf. James 5:1–11), they are hauled into court by wealthy people (2:4–6), and they are oppressed by large landowners (5:5–6).

These are typical difficulties faced by exiles, accentuated in the case of these particular exiles by the hostility stemming from Jews who are unhappy with their commitment to Jesus as Messiah.

Some scholars are persuaded that this background data provides the key socioeconomic criterion by which James must be interpreted. Such interpreters think that James defends the poor, who are righteous, against the rich, who are evil. The letter of James has therefore become a favorite among liberation theologians.[4] But the situation in James is not as simple as that. The most natural interpretation of 1:10 suggests that there were "brothers" in the churches James addresses who were themselves rich. His reference to traveling business people in 4:13–17 suggests the same scenario. Ultimately, therefore, while James has a lot to say about poverty and wealth, we are prevented by the letter itself from any such simplistic equations as "rich=evil" or "poor=righteous." James's concern is not ultimately with economics or social status, although these play their role in the situation of the readers. His concern is with the spiritual problems created, in part, by these circumstances.

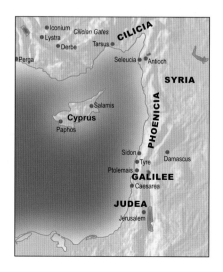

JUDEA, SYRIA, AND CILICIA

The Letter

James clearly belongs in the genre of *letter*. But on the wide spectrum of ancient letter types, it falls more toward the literary end than the personal end. Absent from James are the greetings, personal references, specific situations, and so on, that mark a more personal type of letter. The lack of these features, along with the vague address, has led some to categorize James as a *general* letter, written to the whole church rather than to a single church. But James has a definite audience in view; it is just that the audience is scattered across a large area and that he writes to that audience as a whole.

Other genres, or literary styles, are also thought to influence James. One of the most influential commentaries on James in the twentieth century was written by Martin Dibelius.[5] He argued that

THE DISPERSION OF THE JEWS

The Jewish dispersion extended as far east as Media and Parthia and west to Italy and beyond.

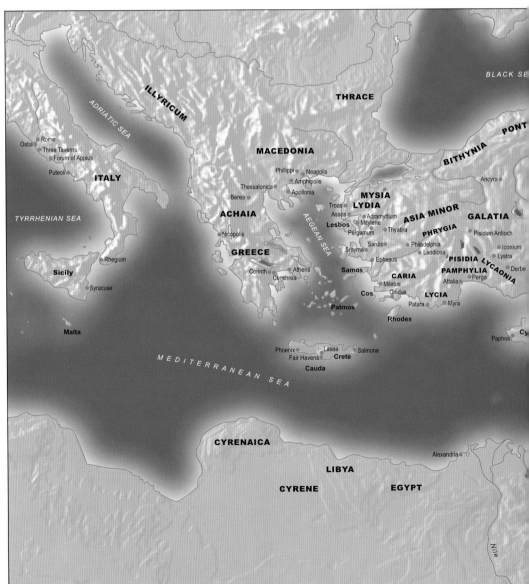

James belonged in the genre called *paraenesis*. This genre was characterized, according to Dibelius, by four features: (1) a focus on moral exhortation; (2) attention to a general rather than specific situations; (3) the use of traditional material; and (4) loose organization. Each of these characteristics is, indeed, typical of James—although most interpreters now find a lot more organization in James than Dibelius did. But modern scholars are less certain that *paraenesis* was an identifiable genre. The most we can say is that James makes some use of a paraenetic style.

A second genre in which many scholars place James is wisdom literature.[6] James refers to wisdom twice (1:5; 3:13–18), and the brief, direct, and practical admonitions of the letter remind us of the style of Proverbs and similar books from the intertestamental period (Sirach,

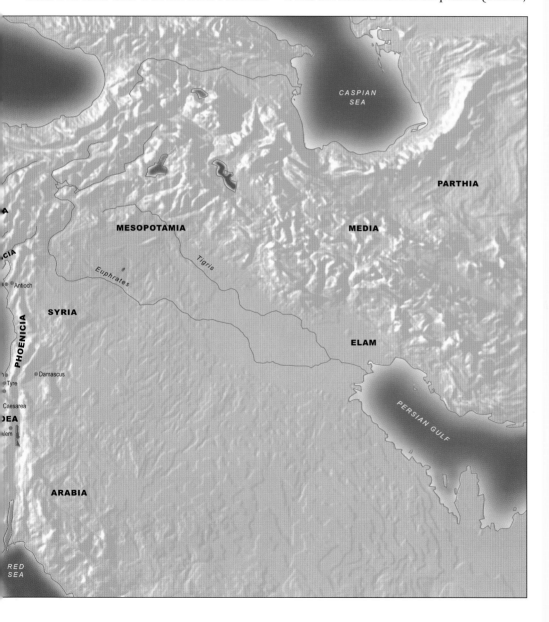

Wisdom of Solomon). However, James develops his topics at greater length than is typical of these books. The most we can say, again, is that James adopts certain conventions and emphases typical of wisdom books.

Introduction to the Letter (1:1)

James, a servant of God and of the Lord Jesus Christ (1:1). By calling himself a "servant" or "slave" (*doulos*) of God, James expresses his sense of being totally committed to the Lord. But the title also reveals his dignity, for it was used in the Old Testament of great leaders of Israel, such as Moses (Deut. 34:5; Dan. 9:11) and David (Jer. 33:21; Ezek. 37:25). James reveals his exalted view of Christ by associating him with God in this introduction to his letter.

To the twelve tribes scattered among the nations (1:1). Old Testament Israel, of course, was divided into twelve tribes, each headed by a patriarch, one of the sons of Jacob (or Israel). After the Israelites were "scattered among the nations" or "dispersed" in exile, hopes for a restoration of the nation were often expressed in terms of a reunification of the twelve tribes.[7] James is probably following the early Christian custom of referring to the church as the renewed Israel of the last days.

The Purpose and Benefit of Trials (1:2–12)

The topic of "trials" frames this section (1:2–4 and 1:12). James knows that his readers are experiencing tough times, including, as the letter indicates, poverty and persecution. So he begins by encouraging them to recognize that God has a purpose in trials: When we respond to them in wholehearted faith, they can bring us to a new level of spiritual maturity.

Consider it pure joy (1:2). James is not saying that we should pretend that trials are easy to take but that we should look beyond the difficulty to the spiritual benefit.

Because you know (1:3–4). The crescendo of virtues in these verses reminds us of two other passages in the New Testament where we find similar "stair-step" lists of virtues: Romans 5:3–4 and 2 Peter 1:5–7. These passages use an ancient literary device called *sorites*. The last virtue in the list is especially important, the goal toward which all the others lead. For James, this supreme virtue is being "mature and complete." Christian maturity is a big concern of James, a thread that runs through the fabric of his many exhortations.

If any of you lacks wisdom (1:5). Wisdom is a prominent idea in the Old Testament and in intertestamental Judaism. It is a practical idea: the ability to understand God's ways and to live in light of his purposes and values. James knows that genuine Christian maturity will be possible only if believers possess this wisdom from God.[8]

He must believe and not doubt (1:6–7). Since God is willing and able to give us the wisdom we need, any lack of wisdom must be our fault. The problem is that we do not always have the same kind of consistent attitude toward God that he has toward us. "Doubt" here refers to a conflict of loyalties that disturbs the purity of faith. James often refers to the teaching of Jesus in his letter, and he may be doing so here. For Jesus taught the disciples to expect answers to their prayers if they would only "have faith" and "not doubt" (Matt. 21:21).

A double-minded man (1:8). The word James uses here, *dipsychos*, means, literally, "double-souled." James may have been the first to use this word (see also 4:8), which expresses one of his central concerns. Hindering maturity in Christ, James suggests, is this fundamental duality in attitude and spirit. The importance of a single, focused affection for God is highlighted throughout the Old Testament, where sinners are described in terms similar to James as having a "divided heart."9

The brother in humble circumstances . . . the one who is rich (1:9–10). The ancient world, like ours, featured great extremes of wealth and status. The problems that these conflicting situations in life created for Christians is an important theme in James. Many commentators think James here contrasts a Christian, who is poor (1:9), with a non-Christian, who is rich and arrogant (1:10–11). But the syntax suggests that the word "brother" in 1:9 should also be applied to the "one who is rich" in 1:10. On this reading, James is contrasting two kinds of Christians. Each kind of Christian, James suggests, has a particular kind of challenge, or "trial," to face. The poor Christian can become downhearted because of his or her low value on the world's socioeconomic scale. That Christian needs to rejoice in his or her identification with Christ, the "high position" he or she enjoys in Christ. But the rich Christian can become arrogant and self-satisfied. That kind of believer needs to remember that he or she is identified with one who is meek and lowly, despised by the world.

The rich man will fade away (1:11). On our reading of 1:9–10, these words refer not to condemnation at the judgment but to the transitory nature of all worldly wealth and status. The rich believer must remember that wealth cannot be brought into the eternal kingdom of Jesus Christ.

Blessed is the man who perseveres under trial (1:12). James wraps up this first paragraph of his letter by returning to where he began: trials. He encourages us to adopt the right attitude toward the problems that life brings our way by reminding us of the reward that God has for us when we "persevere," namely, "the crown of life."

The crown of life (1:12). The Greek word for "crown" here (*stephanos*) probably refers not to a royal crown but to the laurel wreath given to victorious athletes. Paul uses the word in just this way in 1 Corinthians 9:25: "Everyone who competes in the games goes into strict training.

REFLECTIONS

IN CALLING ON POOR CHRISTIANS TO BOAST IN THEIR exaltation with Christ and rich Christians to boast in their humility as they identify with Christ, James suggests that the church should be an institution in which the usual worldly markers of status are left behind. For in Christ all are equal—alike in needing to be saved by grace and alike in depending daily on that same grace for spiritual vigor and hope for the future. Yet the equality James pictures is often absent in the modern church. We fawn over the rich and powerful and ignore the poor and insignificant. We perpetuate the world's distinctions by the way we dress and the way we act. We need to work hard at becoming the kind of church that focuses only on spiritual distinctions.

They do it to get a crown that will not last; but we do it to get a crown that will last forever." Since James, like Paul, is thinking of a metaphorical crown, "life" is probably the reward denoted by the crown. A similar idea appears in Revelation 2:10, a word from Jesus to suffering Christians: "Be faithful, even to the point of death, and I will give you the crown of life."

Trials and Temptations (1:13–18)

The transition from 1:2–12 to 1:13–18 is easier to spot in Greek, because the word for "trial" and "temptation" is the same in Greek (*peirasmos*). But beyond the play on words, James undoubtedly sees an important connection in content. One of the gravest challenges Christians under trial face is temptation: temptation to question God's goodness or even his very existence. James therefore reminds us that, however difficult the circumstances, God is always working for our good.

No one should say, "God is tempting me" (1:13). The Scriptures make clear that God does bring trials to his people, as when he "tested" Abraham (Gen. 22:1). But God never "tempts" his people; he never entices them to commit an evil act. This whole issue of God's providence in trials was one that many Jews in the first century were debating.[10] Some were apparently excusing evil actions by claiming that God was himself leading them to do such acts. James does not want any of his readers to suffer under this blasphemous error. God, by his very nature, can never desire that his people sin.

Each one is tempted . . . by his own evil desire (1:14). Temptation, James makes clear, comes not from God but from within, from each person's "evil desire." Here James may be reflecting Jewish teaching about conflicting "desires" within people. Some rabbis taught that each person has within him or her two "desires" or "tendencies": the *yetzer ha-ra*, "the tendency toward evil," and the *yetzer ha-tov*, "the tendency toward good."[11] Sin arises when the *yetzer ha-ra* drags away and entices people.

The language of "drag away" and "entice" reflects the activities of hunting and fishing: Like bait on a hook, sin tempts people and then drags them away. But the Jewish philosopher Philo had already used such language to describe the process of temptation: "There is no single thing that does not yield to the enticement of pleasure, and get caught and dragged along in her entangling nets."[12]

Desire . . . gives birth to death (1:15). Switching metaphors, James now describes the continuing effects of sin in terms of conception. Temptation comes to all of us, but it is when we listen to the voice of desire that sin begins. If sin is not checked, it will ultimately result in eternal, spiritual death. Persevering under trials brings life (1:12), but succumbing to the temptation that accompanies trials brings death.

Every good and perfect gift is from above (1:17). To reinforce his teaching that God does not tempt people, James reminds us of what God does do: He gives his people good and perfect gifts. The Greek of 1:17 is carefully structured in an almost poetic rhythm, suggesting that James might be quoting from an early saying about God. Philo, for instance, makes a point similar to James, contrasting God's unchanging nature with the variations that are an inevitable part of the created world.[13]

The Father of the heavenly lights (1:17). "Heavenly lights" is a good interpretive rendering of the Greek, which has simply "lights." James is referring to the "lights" that appear in the sky: sun, moon, planets, stars (cf. Ps. 136:7–9; Jer. 31:35). "Father" connotes God's creative power. As the creator of the heavenly bodies, God, unlike them, is without change. Philo makes a similar point: "Every created thing must necessarily undergo change, for this is its property, even as unchangeableness is the property of God."[14]

He chose to give us birth through the word of truth (1:18). God's supreme gift to us is the new birth. In using this imagery, James both continues the metaphor of 1:15 and picks up a popular early Christian way of describing conversion. Jesus, of course, spoke of the need for such a new birth to Nicodemus (John 3:3); Peter also writes to Christians that "you have been born again, not of

perishable seed, but of imperishable, through the living and enduring word of God" (1 Peter 1:23).

True Religion (1:19–27)

With this paragraph, James begins to develop one of his greatest themes: the indispensability of works for any genuine Christian experience. James develops this point in three paragraphs. In 1:19–27, he introduces it by contrasting true and false religion. In 2:1–13 he illustrates the point with reference to the issue of discrimination in the church. And in 2:14–26 he takes a more theological tack, showing that works are necessary to secure a positive verdict from God in the judgment.

Quick to listen, slow to speak and slow to become angry (1:19–20). These verses are a kind of "aside" in James's argument, not directly related to what came before or what comes after. Passages like this remind us of books like Proverbs, in which various topics are treated in quick succession. The theme of careful speech is also prominent in Proverbs. Jewish wisdom teaching stressed the importance of speaking deliberately and carefully.[15] These sources also connect looseness in speech with unrestrained anger, explaining James's quick move from speech to anger in these verses.

The righteous life that God desires (1:20). The NIV is an interpretive rendering of a Greek phrase that literally translated is "the righteousness of God." But the interpretation seems to be justified here, since the Old Testament and Jewish writers often used this language to describe the moral righteousness that met God's own standard of righteousness.[16]

Therefore . . . accept the word planted in you (1:21). With this verse, James turns to the key idea in this paragraph: the right response to God's word. "Accepting" the word often refers to conversion in the New Testament, but this meaning does not work here, where James is writing to Christians. Rather, "accepting" the word here means to allow it to have its intended impact on our lives. James has told us (1:18) that this word was used by God to bring us into his family. When that happens, he now notes, this word becomes "planted" in us. He probably is thinking of the famous prophecy of Jeremiah 31:31–34, where God promised to make a new covenant with his people and to write his law on the hearts of his people. Christians have God's word planted within them and now need to let it grow and flourish.

Do what it says (1:22). Lest we fail to understand what James means by "accepting" the word, he now spells it out: We must "do" it. People who only listen to the word are deceiving themselves, convinced that they are acceptable to God when they are not. This point is one that is made often by Jewish teachers also: "Not the expounding [of the law] is the chief thing, but the doing [of it]."[17]

Like a man who looks at his face in a mirror (1:23). James reinforces his point with an illustration. The "mirror" in the ancient world was composed of polished metal, usually bronze. How foolish it would be for a person to look at himself or herself in such a mirror and then do nothing about it—to see in a mirror that one's hair is all ahoo and not comb it afterwards! But just as foolish, James implies, are people who hear God's spoken message but then do nothing about it.

BRONZE MIRROR

A mirror discovered in Canaanite excavations.

The man who looks intently into the perfect law . . . doing it . . . will be blessed (1:25). Some commentators think that the contrast between the man of 1:23–24 and the man of 1:25 is the intensity with which they look—an interpretation perhaps reflected in the NIV rendering "looks intently" in 1:25. But the contrast is probably simpler than that. The person in 1:25 is blessed for one reason: because, in contrast to the person described in 1:23–24, this person responds to what he or she sees or hears. It is the _doing_ that brings blessing.

The sequence of words to describe the message of God in these verses is striking. James began with "the word of truth" as an instrument of conversion (1:18). Then he spoke of the importance of doing the "word" (1:22). Now he calls for Christians to look intently into, and respond to, "the perfect law that gives freedom." What James is implicitly saying is that God's word is one single entity, and we cannot pick and choose from it. If we want the benefit of the "gospel," the word that brings us into God's family, we must also respond to the "law," the word that commands and instructs us.

If anyone considers himself religious (1:26–27). The words "religion" and "religious" do not occur often in the New Testament. But they occur widely in the ancient Greek world, where they connote especially outward acts of worship. See, for instance, Philo's reference to "the worship of the gods in the different cities."[18] James perhaps uses the term here to reinforce his stress on outward works. He wants to leave no doubt about the practical nature of doing the word.

The "religion" God accepts will reveal itself in three activities: care in speech, concern for the helpless in society, and the avoidance of worldly attitudes and values. James has already mentioned care in speech (1:19), and he will return to the subject again (3:1–11). "Widows and orphans" are often singled out in the Old Testament as people of special concern to God (Ps. 68:5) and therefore as people who deserve kindness and help from God's people (cf. Isa. 1:10–17). Lest we think that doing the word involves only outward acts, James reminds us that obedience to God also includes and, indeed, is often the product of, an inner mind-set that avoids the contagion of the world's false ideas and values.

Condemnation of Discrimination (2:1–13)

James now applies the general principle of 1:19–27 to a specific situation. The person who is truly religious will not discriminate against the poor. For such discrimination violates the kingdom law of love. In other words, the person who discriminates is not doing the word.

Our glorious Lord Jesus Christ (2:1). This rendering, found in most English Bibles, is probably correct. But it is worth noting that the phrase could also be translated "our Lord Jesus Christ, the glorious one." The basis for this rendering is the Old Testament use of "glory" (Heb. *kabōd*) to signify God's own presence (cf. 1 Sam. 4:22). On this view, James is transferring the title "glory" to Jesus Christ.

Favoritism (2:1). The Greek word behind "favoritism" is, literally, "receiving the face" (*prosōpolēmpsia*). The word was apparently invented by the New Testament writers as a literal rendering of the Hebrew word for partiality.[19] "Receiving the face" vividly portrays the essence of partiality: making judgments about people on the basis of outward appearance.

Your meeting (2:2). The Greek word is *synagōgē*, which everywhere else in the New Testament refers to the Jewish house of study and worship. The Jewish Christians to whom James writes, then, may still be worshiping regularly in the synagogue. But the qualification "your" *synagōgē* may imply that the Christian believers are already gathering for worship in their own assembly (the word is used this way in Hermas, *Mandates* 11.9). Another possibility is that *synagōgē* refers more generally to a "meeting" or "gathering" of Christians to sit in judgment over a dispute between two believers. James uses a lot of judicial language in this context, and the situation he depicts in 2:2–3 is somewhat similar to community judicial settings described by the rabbis. See *b. Shebuot* 31a: "How do we know that, if two come to court, one clothed in rags and the other in fine raiment worth a hundred manehs, they should say to him, 'Either dress like him, or dress him like you'"; and *Sifre 4.4* (on Lev. 19:15): "You must not let one litigant speak as much as he wants, and then say to the other, 'Shorten thy speech.' You must not let one stand and the other sit."

Wearing a gold ring (2:2). The gold ring was an emblem of the upper-level Roman "equestrian" class.

Have you not discriminated among yourselves (2:4). These words can also be translated, "Are you not divided in yourselves?" The Greek verb James uses here (*diakrinō*) occurs in 1:6 with this sense of "doubt, be divided."[20] James's point may be, then, that the believers' discrimination against the poor is an indication of the deeply divided nature of their spiritual allegiance, which is at the heart of James's concern throughout the letter.

Listen, my dear brothers (2:5). The call to "listen" reminds us of similar appeals from the Old Testament; see, e.g., Deuteronomy 6:3: "Hear, O Israel, and be careful to obey so that it may go well with you and that you may increase greatly in a land flowing with milk and honey, just as the LORD, the God of your fathers, promised you."

Has not God chosen those who are poor in the eyes of the world to be rich in faith? (2:5). James's teaching about poverty and wealth can be accurately appraised only if we read what he says against the background of biblical teaching. In the Old Testament, the Hebrew word *'anaw* (plural *'anawim*) sometimes refers to people who are "poor" in a spiritual sense: humble and meek, recognizing their own weakness and utter dependence on God for deliverance.[21] It is this biblical usage of the word that explains the variation in Jesus' beatitude: "Blessed are you who are poor" (Luke 6:20) / "Blessed are the poor in spirit" (Matt. 5:3).

In James 2:5, the word "poor" has mainly an economic sense. James reminds his readers that God delights to choose those who are of no account in this world to inherit great blessing in the world to come. But the spiritual sense of the word is also hinted at. Indeed, James may well have in mind Jesus' beatitude as he writes, for he is permeated with influence from the teaching of Jesus.

Is it not the rich who are exploiting you? (2:6). James reflects accurately here (and in 5:1–6) the class divisions that wracked the first-century Middle East. Wealthy landholders were constantly increasing their land holdings at the expense of the poor. The poor, in turn, were forced to work for the rich on their own terms, a situation the rich took advantage of by suppressing wages and other unjust activities. Of course, such a situation was noth-

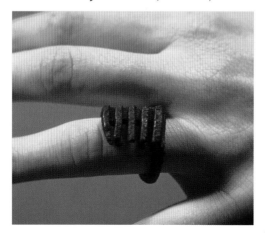

RING

A key worn on the finger as a ring found in excavations of Herodian-era Jerusalem.

ing new; the Old Testament prophets often denounced just such practices. See, for example, Amos 4:1: "Hear this word, you cows of Bashan on Mount Samaria, you women who oppress the poor and crush the needy and say to your husbands, 'Bring us some drinks!'"

The noble name of him to whom you belong (2:7). The NIV is a fair paraphrase of a cumbersome Greek construction, which, literally translated, reads: "the good name that has been called over you." The Greek itself is awkward because it is a rather literal translation of a Semitic phrase. To have a name "called" over one means to be owned by that person. A good example of this usage is found in Amos 9:12, which is quoted in Acts 15:17: "so that they may possess the remnant of Edom and all the nations that bear my name [lit., that are called by my name]."

The royal law found in Scripture (2:8). The NIV suggests that the love command from Leviticus 19:18 *is* the "royal law." But the preposition "in" can also be translated "according to" (Gk. *kata*), in which case James may be referring to a royal law that is based on, or similar to, Leviticus 19:18. That law may then be Jesus' own ratification of the love command. When asked what the greatest commandment was, Jesus cited the command to love God and love one's neighbor as oneself (cf. Matt. 22:34–40). On this interpretation the word "royal" means "coming from the king," a meaning well established in intertestamental Judaism. Philo, for instance, uses the same word James uses here (*basilikos*) to refer to the law of God, claiming that it is "royal" because it both belongs to God and leads to him.[22] Jesus established the law of love as a central demand of the kingdom he

inaugurated. It is to this "law" that James probably refers.

Love your neighbor as yourself (2:8). James quotes Leviticus 19:18 because Jesus himself highlighted this command as basic to God's moral demand. But its appropriateness in this context is accentuated by the fact that a prohibition of partiality occurs in this same context (19:15). Indeed, James appears to mine the immediate context of 19:18 for a number of key moral exhortations that he passes on to his readers.[23]

Whoever keeps the whole law (2:10). The conviction that the law is a unity and that a person is therefore obliged to keep every part of it without exception was commonplace in James's day. The Stoics in particular emphasized the unity of vices and virtues. Augustine reflects this attitude: "Whoever has one virtue has all of them, and whoever does not have a particular one has none."[24] Jewish teachers claimed the same is true of God's law. For instance, when the pious Eleazar is commanded by a pagan king to eat forbidden food, he responds: "Do not suppose that it would be a petty sin if we were to eat defiling food; to transgress the law in matters either small or great is of equal seriousness, for in either case the law is equally despised" (*4 Macc.* 5:19–21).[25] Paul reflects the same strand of teaching in Galatians 5:3: "I declare to every man who lets himself be circumcised that he is obligated to obey the whole law." But critical for James, as usually is the case, may be Jesus' affirmation of the continuing relevance of every detail of the law:

> I tell you the truth, until heaven and earth disappear, not the smallest

letter, not the least stroke of a pen, will by any means disappear from the Law until everything is accomplished. Anyone who breaks one of the least of these commandments and teaches others to do the same will be called least in the kingdom of heaven, but whoever practices and teaches these commands will be called great in the kingdom of heaven. (Matt. 5:18–19)

"Do not commit adultery" . . . "Do not commit murder" (2:11). The order of the commandments does not, of course, follow the order of the commandments in their original context (Ex. 20:13–14; Deut. 5:17–18). But this order is found in one important manuscript of the LXX.[26]

Judgment without mercy will be shown to anyone who has not been merciful (2:13). The importance of mercy is highlighted in many Old Testament passages. Particularly noteworthy, because of the

connection between mercy and concern for the poor and powerless, is Zechariah 7:9–10: "This is what the LORD Almighty says: 'Administer true justice; show mercy and compassion to one another. Do not oppress the widow or the fatherless, the alien or the poor. In your hearts do not think evil of each other.'" See also *Testament of Zebulun* 8:1: "You also, my children, have compassion toward every person with mercy, in order that the Lord may be compassionate and merciful to you." Closest to home is Jesus' own promise: "Blessed are the merciful, for they will be shown mercy" (Matt. 5:7; cf. 18:21–35).

True Religion Manifested in Works (2:14–26)

James has insisted that our actions (mercy) will be taken into account in the judgment (2:12–13). But he has no wish to minimize the importance of faith. Thus, he argues that an unbreakable connection exists between saving faith and works.

Such faith (2:14). The NIV recognizes the importance of the article before the word "faith" in Greek by translating "such." This is vitally important. James is not contesting the saving ability of true faith; he claims that the faith "a man claims to have" but is without "deeds" cannot save.

If one of you says to him, "Go, I wish you well" (2:16). The pious wish expressed by the person claiming to have faith echoes a common biblical blessing. The Greek is more literally translated, "Depart in peace"; similar language occurs in both the Old Testament and New Testament.[27]

Faith by itself (2:17). A better rendering might be "in itself." What James is argu-

---

REFLECTIONS

WHAT JAMES SAYS IN 2:8–13 MAY SEEM TO IMPLY that believers continue to be obliged to keep every single Old Testament commandment, including those pertaining to food, sacrifices, and civil affairs. But James hints at a broader perspective. He calls the law Christians are to obey the "royal law" (2:8), a reference, we have argued, to the law of the kingdom established by Jesus. He also calls it a "law that gives freedom," again suggesting that more than the Old Testament law itself may be in mind. In fact, we think James shares the perspective of Jesus, who both affirms the permanent validity of the Old Testament law and claims to be the One who now, as its fulfiller (Matt. 5:17), has the right to determine what its ultimate meaning and application are. In other words, James is not insisting that we will be judged by the law of the Old Testament but by the law, based on the Old Testament, set down by Jesus for our guidance.

▶ Was James Writing Against Paul's Teaching on Justification By Faith Alone?

Just why James puts so much emphasis on the relationship between faith and works is not certain. But one likely historical scenario goes like this. After his conversion, Paul preached in Damascus, Jerusalem (briefly), and in Tarsus (from perhaps about A.D. 36–45). Certainly during this time he would have developed his characteristic emphasis on faith alone as a means of justification. But Paul used justification in a peculiarly Christian sense, not always recognized by his opponents or his listeners.

We can surmise that Paul's emphasis has been misunderstood by some who have heard him preach and turned the doctrine into an excuse for not bothering any more with "works." James hears of this perverted form of Paul's teaching and attacks it in these verses. So we do not have to assume that James is directly attacking Paul. They have probably not yet had opportunity to learn about each other's theology; and, when they did, shortly after this at the Jerusalem Council (Acts 15), they would have had ample time to compare notes on this matter.

---

ing is that a faith unaccompanied by deeds is intrinsically unable to save. James's wording (*kath' heautēn*) has a parallel in a statement about the law in Josephus: "The greatest miracle of all is that our Law holds out no seductive bait of sensual pleasure, but has exercised this influence *through its own inherent merits*."[28]

But someone will say (2:18). The sequence of thought in 2:18–19 is difficult to unravel. Who is James quoting? Is the person arguing against James or is he an ally of James? One factor in answering these questions is the literary background of the language James uses. He is employing at this point an ancient style called the "diatribe," which features a lively question-and-answer format to convince people of a certain viewpoint (see comments on this style in the introduction to Romans). The opening phrase "but someone will say" reflects this style and makes it quite certain that the person James is quoting is an opponent

rather than an ally. The closest New Testament parallel comes in 1 Corinthians 15:35: "But someone may ask, 'How are the dead raised?'"

You believe that there is one God (2:19). The monotheism maintained by these people who have faith without deeds is perhaps the most fundamental of all Jewish beliefs. It is enshrined in the *Shema*, a standard Jewish confession based on Deuteronomy 6:4: "Hear, O Israel: The LORD our God, the LORD is one" (it is called the *Shema* after the first Heb. word, "Hear"). The early Christians took over without question this Jewish monotheism.[29] James has no problem with this verbal profession; he is concerned that it is no more than an intellectual assent.

The demons believe that—and shudder (2:19). The Greek verb behind "shudder" (*phrissō*) occurs only here in the New Testament. But it is used in the papyri to describe the effect that a sorcerer aims to produce in his hearers.[30] Ancient people often thought that pronouncing a god's name had power to provoke fear and terror. Moreover, Philo uses this verb to describe the dread experienced by sinful people who know they deserve judgment.[31] James may then also be suggesting that the demons shudder in fear and trembling, recognizing in this truth about God the doom to which they are destined. In this respect the demons are better off than the so-called Christians James is attacking, for at least the demons have *some* reaction to their "orthodox" confession!

Our ancestor Abraham (2:21). James's appeal to Abraham as a key test case for

his insistence on a faith that works is entirely natural. For it was God's promise to Abraham that formed the starting point for God's creation of his own people, Israel. "Descendants of Abraham" became a standard designation of God's people.[32]

Considered righteous (2:21). This expression translates one Greek verb (*dikaioō*, "to justify"). One key in reconciling the teaching of James and Paul on this matter is to recognize that they use this verb in different ways (see "Two Ways of Understanding 'Justify': Paul and James").

When he offered his son Isaac on the altar (2:21). Abraham was celebrated in Jewish tradition for his great moral virtue. "Abraham was perfect in all his deeds with the Lord, and well-pleasing in righteousness all the days of his life" (*Jub.* 23:10); Abraham "did not sin against thee" (Pr. Man. 8); "no one has been found like him in glory" (Sir. 44:19). Abraham's willingness to sacrifice his son Isaac (Gen. 22) is naturally highlighted as the pinnacle of his devout obedience. Philo claims that Abraham's offering of Isaac was the greatest of Abraham's "works" (*Abraham* 167).

▶
A SORCERER'S PAPYRUS

A third-century magical text (*PGM* LXX).

▶ Two Ways of Understanding "Justify": Paul and James

Paul, in a creative move borne of his Christian convictions, uses the verb *dikaioō* ("to justify") to refer to the establishment of a right relationship with God in this life. But this was not the typical Old Testament and Jewish meaning of the verb. "Justification" usually referred to the ultimate verdict of God over a person in the time of judgment.[A-1] Jesus' own words express this perspective clearly: "By your words you will be acquitted [*dikaioō*], and by your words you will be condemned" (Matt. 12:37).

James, therefore, uses the language of justification in the typical Old Testament/Jewish manner to refer to what we would call the judgment. Against those who are suggesting that a person can be saved by faith apart from deeds, James cites Abraham to show that true faith is always revealed in deeds, and that these deeds are taken into consideration by God in the judgment.

Even more pertinent is the tradition reflected in 1 Maccabees 2:51–52: "Remember the deeds of the ancestors, which they did in their generations; and you will receive great honor and an everlasting name. Was not Abraham found faithful when tested, and it was reckoned to him as righteousness?" "When tested" almost certainly refers to the offering of Isaac, and the author of 1 Maccabees uses the language of Genesis 15:6 ("reckoned to him as righteousness") to interpret the significance of that event. This, of course, is precisely the text James quotes in 2:23. Paul also uses this text, but to make a different point.

Abraham believed God (2:23). James may be reacting also against some Jewish interpreters who viewed Abraham's faith in more or less intellectual terms, as his turning from idolatry to worship of the one God.[33]

God's friend (2:23). The Old Testament never uses this exact language about Abraham, although a few texts come close (cf. 2 Chron. 20:7; Isa. 41:8).[34] But Abraham was called the "friend of God" in Jewish tradition.[35]

Rahab the prostitute (2:25). Why does James choose the examples of Abraham and Rahab to illustrate his point about faith and works? Perhaps simply because they represent polar opposites: the patriarch and the prostitute, the revered founder of the Israelite nation and the pagan, immoral woman. But some scholars note a tradition that surfaces in the early Christian book *1 Clement*. In this book, Abraham and Rahab are cited together as examples of hospitality— Rahab, of course, because she welcomed and hid the Jewish spies and Abraham because he received the three "men" who brought him news of God's promise (Gen. 18).[36] But it is not clear that his tradition predates James; and he makes no point of hospitality in this context.

Controlling the Tongue (3:1–12)

Having shown that "true religion" is rooted in a faith that infallibly produces works, James now turns to some of those deeds that believers particularly need to exhibit. The first of these is the control of one's speech. James echoes Old Testament wisdom teaching in his concern about personal speech habits. Our speech, James makes clear, reveals the attitude of the heart. A "divided" heart will lead to inconsistent habits of speech, while the person with a wholehearted allegiance to the Lord will be marked by godliness in speech.

If anyone is never at fault in what he says, he is a perfect man (3:2). The tongue, James argues here, is one of the hardest of all parts of the body to bring into full subjection to the Lord. The difficulty of avoiding sins of speech is acknowledged by Jewish authors who have apparently influenced James. Note, for example, Sirach 19:16: "A person may make a slip without intending it. Who has never sinned with his tongue?" See also Philo: "But if a man succeeded, as if handling a lyre, in bringing all the notes of the thing that is good into tune, bringing speech into harmony with intent, and intent with deed, such a one would be considered perfect and of a truly harmonious character."[37]

When we put bits into the mouths of horses to make them obey us, we can turn the whole animal (3:3). Appeal to

wishes. . . . A ship, again, keeps to her straight course, when the helmsman grasping the tiller steers accordingly. . . . Just so, when Mind, the charioteer or helmsman of the soul, rules the whole living being as a governor does a city, the life holds a straight course. . . . But when irrational sense gains the chief place . . . the mind is set on fire and is all ablaze, and that fire is kindled by the objects of sense which Sense-perception supplies.[42]

a horse to illustrate how a small object can control a large one was widespread in the ancient world. The fifth-century B.C. playwright Sophocles has one of his characters say, "I know that spirited horses are broken by the use of a small bit."[38]

Or take ships as an example (3:4). James adds a second illustration of the way in which a small object controls a much larger one. Great ships, driven by strong winds, are steered by a relatively small rudder. This imagery is again common in James's day. Aristotle contrasted the small size of the rudder with the "huge mass" of the ship it controls.[39] But especially helpful in illuminating James are ancient texts that use the same combination of images found in these verses. A number of ancient writers, for instance, compare the rule of God over the world to the charioteer's guidance of the horse by reins and bit and to the pilot's steering of a ship.[40] We also find texts that combine references to charioteer, helmsman, and the taming of the animal world (cf. 3:7).[41] The best example comes from Philo:

> Mind is superior to Sense-perception. When the charioteer is in command and guides the horses with the reins, the chariot goes the way he

The moralist Plutarch even uses the imagery of a runaway ship and a fire to illustrate the destructive nature of loose speech. What these parallels reveal is that James is tapping into a widespread series of images from his culture to get his points across to his Christian readers.

Consider what a great forest is set on fire by a small spark (3:5). The Old Testament and Jewish authors had applied the imagery of the destructive and rapid spread of a fire to the damage caused by unrestrained speech. See, for example, Proverbs 16:27: "A scoundrel plots evil, and his speech is like a scorching fire"; Sirach 28:22: ["The tongue] has no power over the godly; they will not be burned in its flame."

The Greek word behind the NIV's "forest" is *hylē*, which means "wood." Forests being somewhat rare in the Middle East of James's day, the word may here refer to the brush on the hillsides of Palestine—easily consumed by fire in hot, dry weather.[43]

Is itself set on fire by hell (3:6). "Hell" translates the Greek *gehenna*, a transliteration of a Hebrew phrase that means "Valley of Hinnom." This valley, just outside of Jerusalem, had an evil reputation because trash was burned in it and pagan child sacrifices had been carried out there in earlier times (cf. Jer. 32:35). James again reveals his dependence on the teaching of Jesus, because this word occurs elsewhere in the New Testament only on his lips.

All kinds of animals, birds, reptiles and creatures of the sea (3:7). Although the words are not identical, James's reference to the creation account of Genesis 1 cannot be missed. See, for example, Genesis 1:26: "Then God said, 'Let us make man in our image, in our likeness, and let them rule over the fish of the sea and the birds of the air, over the livestock, over all the earth, and over all the creatures that move along the ground.'" Jewish and Christian writers reflect this same tradition.[44]

A restless evil (3:8). James has described the "double-minded" man as "unstable" in 1:8 (same Gk. word as translated "restless" here). This word was also occasionally applied to the tongue.[45]

Men, who have been made in God's likeness (3:9). Cursing other people is all the more terrible because these people bear God's own likeness. James again alludes to the creation account and is probably reflecting common Jewish teaching. The rabbis, for instance, taught that one should not say, "'Let my neighbor be put to shame'—for then you put to shame one who is in the image of God."[46]

My brothers, this should not be (3:10). James here rebukes Christians whose use of the tongue is "double"—blessing or praising God and cursing other human beings—acting unnaturally like a spring that gives forth both fresh and salty water (3:11). Certain Jewish moral teachings that James seems to know well emphasize the same problem of "doubleness" with the tongue. See, for instance, *Testament of Benjamin* 6:5: "The good set of mind does not talk from both sides of its mouth: praises and curses, abuse and honor, calm and strife, hypocrisy and truth, poverty and wealth, but it has one disposition, uncontaminated and pure, towards all men." Sirach 6:1 condemns "the double-tongued sinner."

Can a fig tree bear olives, or a grapevine bear figs? (3:12). The commonplace truth of the natural world, that plants bear according to their kind, was often

GRAPE VINES AND A BRANCH WITH FIGS

employed in the ancient world to illustrate consistency. Epictetus, a second-century writer, asked, "How can a vine be moved to act, not like a vine, but like an olive, or again an olive to act, not like an olive, but like a vine? It is impossible, inconceivable."[47]

Peaceful Relations Through Wisdom (3:13–4:3)

Most Bibles and commentaries divide these verses into two separate paragraphs, but they have a lot in common. Both focus on the need for community reconciliation and make clear that such peace is the product only of the right mind-set.

Let him show it by his good life (3:13). James's insistence that wisdom is revealed in a godly lifestyle picks up a key theme of the letter (see 2:14–26) and reflects the common Jewish focus on the practical dimensions of wisdom. Wisdom, Proverbs reminds us, leads us to "walk in the ways of good men and keep to the paths of the righteous" (Prov. 2:20).

Selfish ambition (3:14). The sense of the word James uses here (*eritheia*) can be gleaned from its one pre-New Testament occurrence, in Aristotle, where it refers to the selfish party spirit that governed too many politicians in his day.[48]

Wisdom . . . is . . . peace-loving (3:17). In a text that reminds us of Paul's famous "fruit of the Spirit" passage, James lists the fruit of wisdom. Outstanding among this fruit is peace, which James emphasizes again in 3:18. Proverbs had already made the connection between wisdom and peace: "Her [wisdom's] ways are pleasant ways, and all her paths are peace" (Prov. 3:17).

Fights and quarrels (4:1). The Greek word behind "quarrels" (*machai*) means "battles" or "strife" of any kind. When we add the evidence of 4:2, where James refers to "killing," therefore, we may conclude that James is rebuking believers for engaging in violence of some kind in these verses. While at first sight it might seem impossible that Christians would be engaged in such violence with one

▶ First-Century Jewish Moral Teaching

The ideas found in these verses are also found together in several writings from the time of James. The best examples come from the intertestamental Jewish book *The Testaments of the Twelve Patriarchs*. Modeled on the speech of the dying Jacob to his twelve sons from Genesis 48–49, this book contains a "testament" from each of the twelve patriarchs to his children. In each testament, the patriarch recounts some of the key experiences of his life and uses them as a basis for moral instruction. The book was probably written in Greek sometime in the second century B.C., although it is widely thought that Christian scribes may have added

some material to the book as it was transmitted over time. The book has never been accepted as canonical by any part of the Christian church and appears in the collection called the "Pseudepigrapha."[A-2]

This book traces slander (*katalalia*, T. Gad 3:3), violence (*polemos*), and murder (T. Sim. 4:5) to jealousy. It also frequently condemns "double-mindedness." These are the themes that bind together James's argument in this part of the book. He is therefore adapting a literary theme about jealousy and its terrible effects that was apparently well known in certain Hellenistic Jewish circles.[A-3]

REFLECTIONS

JAMES IS NOT EXPLICITLY ADDRESS-
ing church leaders in this paragraph. But he has mentioned "teachers" in 3:1, and especially prominent Christians may tend to think of themselves as "wise and understanding" (3:13). Leadership of God's church requires many gifts, some of them intellectual in nature. But the leader who brings lasting good to the church, fostering unity rather than division, will above all possess wisdom and the humility that comes from true biblical wisdom. Too many leaders are motivated, perhaps unconsciously, by the "party spirit" that is the mark of the wrong kind of wisdom (3:16). They make the mistake of confusing their own agendas with God's. The wise leader will have the humility to see the difference.

another (cf. "among you" in 4:1), certain elements in the religious and political atmosphere of the mid-first century make it at least possible, for the Jewish Zealot movement was becoming prominent at just this time.

This movement advocated violence in defense of Israel's right to be a theocracy. Some of the believers to whom James writes have been (former) Zealots and so brought their violence in defense of God and his kingdom into the church.[49] But surely James would have said more about the matter if the Christians are actually resorting to such violence. The words James uses in 4:1 are commonly applied to verbal "battles." Particularly applicable, in light of James's concern with speech in the context, is *Psalms of Solomon* 12:3, which warns that slanderous lips "kindle strife" (*polemos*, the word translated "fights" in 4:1).

They come from your desires (4:1). Behind the NIV "desires" is the Greek *hēdonē*, "pleasure." This word often refers to an attitude of sinful self-indulgence; we get our word "hedonistic" from it. James is not the first to trace sinful conduct to sinful desire; note, for instance, *4 Maccabees* 1:25–27: "In pleasure [*hēdonē*] there exists even a malevolent tendency, which is the most complex of all the emotions. In the soul it is boastfulness, covetousness, thirst for honor, rivalry, and malice; in the body, indiscriminate eating, gluttony, and solitary gormandizing."

You want something but don't get it. You kill and covet, but you cannot have what you want. You quarrel and fight (4:2). English versions differ over the punctuation of this verse (the original manuscripts, for the most part, had no punctuation). But the background of James's teaching strongly points to a punctuation different from what the NIV adopts. We may set it out as follows:

> You want something but you can't get it; so you kill.
> You covet and you cannot have what you want; so you quarrel and fight.

This arrangement preserves the parallelism of the verse. In each sentence, frustrated desire leads to a violent attitude. This is just the sequence we find in the theme about "envy" or "jealousy" that James depends on in these verses (see the introduction to 3:13–4:3). An excellent example is the *Testament of Simeon*. A substantial portion of this book deals with the problem of envy and describes how it led Simeon to seize and attempt to murder his brother Joseph. Simeon is portrayed as reflecting on his motivations and attitudes. He says, "Envy dominates the whole of man's mind" and "keeps prodding him to destroy the one whom he envies" (*T. Sim.* 3:2–3). A similar connection between envy and violence is implied by Epictetus, who notes that Caesar can free people from "wars and fightings" but not from "envy."[50] "Kill," then, is probably James's way of warning his readers about the ultimate outcome of the attitude they have adopted.

A Call to Wholehearted Commitment (4:4–10)

This paragraph is the heart of James's letter. In it he brings to a climax the underlying theme of the letter: the need for wholehearted, unreserved allegiance to God.

You adulterous people (4:4). The Greek is actually feminine: you "adulteresses." The use of the feminine form reinforces the biblical imagery that James depends on here. The Old Testament frequently portrays the relationship between God and his people in terms of marriage. See, for instance, Isaiah 54:4–6:

> "Do not be afraid; you will not suffer
>   shame.
>   Do not fear disgrace; you will not
>   be humiliated.
> You will forget the shame of your
>   youth
>   and remember no more the
>   reproach of your widowhood.
> For your Maker is your husband—
>   the LORD Almighty is his name—
> the Holy One of Israel is your
>   Redeemer;
>   he is called the God of all the earth.
> The LORD will call you back
>   as if you were a wife deserted and
>   distressed in spirit—

> a wife who married young,
>   only to be rejected," says your God.

This text is typical of Old Testament texts presenting the Lord as the husband and his people as the bride. When his people go astray after other gods, they can be said to be committing adultery against the Lord. Jeremiah compares unfaithful Israel to "a woman unfaithful to her husband" (Jer. 3:20). But the climax of this imagery comes in Hosea, who is commanded by the Lord to marry a faithless prostitute to illustrate the spiritual waywardness of Israel. In this abrupt and startling address of his readers, therefore, James reminds them of this broad biblical teaching about God's demand for unswerving faithfulness in his people's relationship to him.

REFLECTIONS

JAMES'S USE OF THE OLD TESTAMENT marital imagery to depict the relationship between the Lord and his people is vivid and convicting. As a jealous lover, God demands that we return to him an exclusive and unwavering love. No flirtation with the world is to be tolerated. Our allegiance to God must be wholehearted and consistent. This call for spiritual "oneness" lies at the heart of James's message to us today. The opposite of this "oneness" is the double-mindedness that he condemns in 1:8 and 4:8—thinking we can be friends with the world and be committed believers at the same time (see 4:4). James's strong and eloquent plea should stimulate each of us to look carefully at ourselves, seeking to uncover any hint of love for the world that is competing with our love for God.

Or do you think Scripture says without reason that the spirit he caused to live in us envies intensely? (4:5). Interpreters go in two radically different directions in this verse. The NIV represents one alternative: James reminds his readers that the Scripture itself warns about a proneness to sinful envy in the human spirit. But note the translation in the NIV note: "God jealously longs for the spirit that he made to live in us." This interpretation assumes that James is reminding his readers of the Old Testament emphasis on God's jealousy for his people.

Each interpretation fits well in the context, with its focus on both human envy (3:16; 4:2) and on God's demand for total allegiance from his people (4:4). But the latter theme is both closer in context and more striking. A reminder of God's jealousy for his people fits nicely in a context where James uses the imagery of faithfulness in marriage to make a spiritual point. If, then, we adopt the NIV alternative rendering, what is the "Scripture" to which James refers? A few interpreters think James may be referring to a noncanonical source, such as the *Apocalypse of Moses* or the lost *Book of Eldad and Modad*. But a more likely reference is the general Old Testament teaching about God's jealousy.[51] The singular "Scripture" (*graphē*) can sometimes refer in this manner to the Old Testament in general (cf. John 7:37–39).

God opposes the proud but gives grace to the humble (4:6). With this quotation of Proverbs 3:34, James sets the agenda for the next verses, in which he calls on his readers to humble themselves so that they can experience God's grace to them. Peter quotes this same text in a similar context in his first letter (1 Peter 5:5), one of the many points of contact between the letters. Probably both James and Peter rely on widespread early Christian moral tradition.

Come near to God and he will come near to you (4:8). The language of "come near" often refers to worship.[52] But this meaning does not fit this verse well, since it promises that God will also "come near" us. Probably, then, James uses the verb in a way similar to Hosea 12:6: "But you must return to your God; maintain love and justice, and wait for [LXX *engize*, come near] your God always." See also *Testament of Dan* 6:2, where the command to "draw near to God" is preceded by the exhortation to "be on your guard against Satan and his spirits" (cf. James 4:7).

Wash your hands, you sinners, and purify your hearts, you double-minded (4:8). James calls on his readers to transform both their outward behavior ("hands") and their inner attitude ("hearts"). The combination of "washing" and "purifying" stems from Old Testament requirements for priestly purity when administering the things of the Lord. The verbs have this sense the three times they occur together in the Old Testament.[53] Note also Psalm 24:3–4, which requires "clean hands and a pure heart" for those who would stand before the Lord.

Grieve, mourn and wail (4:9). James shifts from priestly to prophetic imagery. "Grieve," "mourn," and "wail" are all verbs used by the prophets to connote the radical and heartfelt repentance from sin that God calls for from his people. Joel, warning of the imminent Day of the Lord, pictures the Lord's inviting his people to "return to me with all your heart, with fasting and weeping and mourning" (Joel 2:12).

Change your laughter to mourning (4:9). James is no killjoy, wanting Christians to walk around with long faces and somber expressions. Key to understanding his exhortation here is to recognize that "laughter" is often associated with the "fool" in biblical wisdom. This is the person who scorns the Lord and any moral standards, delighting in sinful behavior and mocking any idea of judgment to come.[54] Jesus reflects this same tradition when he said, "Woe to you who laugh now, for you will mourn and weep" (Luke 6:25b).

Condemnation of Critical Speech (4:11–12)

In these verses James returns briefly to the theme of 3:1–12: the danger of sinful speech. He again reflects the moral theme that lies behind much of his teaching in chapters 3–4, for this theme

frequently linked "speaking evil" to jealousy, selfishness, quarrels, and pride.[55] The early Christian writer Hermas even claims that evil speech is the product of "double-mindedness."[56]

Anyone who speaks against his brother or judges him speaks against the law and judges it (4:11). James's reference to the "neighbor" in 4:12 suggests that the "law" he has in mind is again the love command—that is, Leviticus 19:18 (see James 2:8). The likelihood of this allusion is heightened when we note that Leviticus 19:16 prohibits slander. James may again be raising issues that are prominent in the Old Testament passage where the love command is given.

Condemnation of Arrogant Planning (4:13–17)

This paragraph and the next (5:1–6) resemble each other. Each begins with the formula "now listen" and each focuses on sins having to do with wealth.

RELIEF OF A BATTLE SCENE

Trajan's column in Rome decorated with a spiral of series of battle reliefs.

The people James chastises in this paragraph appear to be well-to-do merchants who can afford to travel and look forward to earning a healthy profit. Some interpreters think these people might be non-Christians. But James's call on them to acknowledge the will of the Lord in what they do (4:15) suggests rather that they are believers who are becoming too self-sufficient and proud.

Now listen, you who say (4:13). This form of address is typical of the diatribe style James uses elsewhere in the letter (see comments on 2:18–21).

We will go to this or that city, spend a year there, carry on business and make money (4:13). The picture James paints with these words would have been familiar to his first-century readers. The first century was marked by growing commercial activity, which was especially true in the Hellenistic cities of Palestine (such as those in the Decapolis). Jews were especially prominent in these commercial ventures; many left Palestine to pursue their business interests.

You are a mist that appears for a little while and then vanishes (4:14). The Old Testament and Jewish literature is permeated with reminders of the transitory nature of human life. Proverbs 27:1 warns, "Do not boast about tomorrow, for you do not know what a day may bring forth." Life is compared to a "breath" in Job 7:7, 9; Psalm 39:5–6.

Anyone, then, who knows the good he ought to do and doesn't do it, sins (4:17). This reminder about "sins of omission" comes somewhat unexpectedly at the end of this paragraph. One commentator suggests, however, that

James may be including this saying because of some Old Testament texts that he had in mind. Proverbs 3:27–28 prohibits any delay in doing good to a neighbor; and in the LXX this prohibition is grounded in the warning that "you do not know what the next day will bring forth." James has already quoted from Proverbs 3 in James 4:6, so his attention may still be on this passage.[57]

Condemnation of the Wicked Rich (5:1–6)

The "rich people" that James addresses in this paragraph are not Christians. They manifest a selfish lifestyle inconsistent with Christian values, and James holds out no hope for their repentance. He simply condemns them. James thus imitates the prophets, who often pronounced doom on sinful pagan nations in prophecies directed to Israel. Their purpose is to reveal the seriousness of sin and to encourage the people of God who suffer from such sin to endure until the certain Day of Judgment to come.

You rich people (5:1). James can simply address these people as "rich" without explicitly saying that they are the "wicked" rich because of the biblical and Jewish tradition that tends to associate the rich and the wicked. "Rich" is sometimes a synonym for "the unrighteous" (e.g., Prov. 10:15–16; 14:20); and both Old Testament prophets and intertestamental Jewish writers regularly denounce the rich for their luxurious lifestyles and oppression of the poor.[58]

Weep and wail (5:1). Both these words (*klaiō* and *ololyzō*) occur frequently in the prophets to depict the reaction of wicked people when they are faced with the judgment of the Day of the Lord. See, for instance, Isaiah 13:6: "Wail, for the day of the LORD is near; it will come like destruction from the Almighty" (see also Isa. 15:3; Amos 8:3). The "misery" that is coming to the rich, therefore, is not earthly disaster but divine judgment.

Your wealth has rotted (5:2). Not all forms of wealth can "rot," literally. But this verb (*sēpō*) is applied metaphorically to anything that is transitory. "Every work decays and ceases to exist, and the one who made it will pass away with it" (Sir. 14:19).[59]

Your gold and silver are corroded (5:3). Again, gold and silver cannot become corroded. But this language was commonly applied to all kinds of metals, including gold and silver (e.g., Sir. 29:10; Ep. Jer. 10) with the general sense "decay" (cf. Ezek. 24:6, 11, 12). Verses 2b–3a therefore characterize wealth as transitory and in process of decay.

Eat your flesh like fire (5:3). The same language is used to describe the judgment of God in Judith 16:17: "Woe to the nations that rise up against my people! The Lord Almighty will take vengeance on them in the day of judgment; he will send fire and worms into their flesh; they shall weep in pain forever."

You have hoarded wealth in the last days (5:3). We could also translate "for the last days"; some interpreters think that James may simply be describing the way the

---

▶ The Problem With Wealth

James does not make clear why the transitory nature of wealth will bring judgment to these rich people. But Old Testament and Jewish teaching can fill in the gap. (1) The hoarding of wealth was often thought to manifest a sinful tendency to focus on this world instead of the world to come. See, for example, Ezekiel 7:19: "They will throw their silver into the streets, and their gold will be an unclean thing. Their silver and gold will not be able to save them in the day of the LORD's wrath. They will not satisfy their hunger or fill their stomachs with it, for it has made them stumble into sin." Jesus, reflecting this tradition, warns people about focusing on "earthly treasures" at the expense of "heavenly treasure," thereby indicating the tendency of the heart (cf. Matt. 6:19–21).

(2) James may also be implying a more specific condemnation. Sirach, a book that has many parallels with the teaching of James, suggests a connection between wealth and a failure to help the poor in language similar to what we find here in James: "Help the poor for the commandment's sake, and in their need do not send them away empty-handed. Lose your silver for the sake of a brother or a friend, and do not let it rust under a stone and be lost. Lay up your treasure according to the commandments of the Most High, and it will profit you more than gold" (Sir. 29:9–11). So James might think that the rich are to be condemned because they have hoarded wealth for themselves while others have gone without the basic necessities of life.

wealthy are saving money for the future. But the "last days" is a phrase that New Testament writers use against the background of Jewish apocalyptic to denote the age of salvation. The "last days" begin with the coming of Messiah and, in a twist on the Jewish apocalyptic scheme, will be climaxed in a second coming of the Messiah. Thus, the period of the church is "the last days."[60] What James suggests is that the hoarding of wealth is all the more culpable because it is occurring in the age of salvation, with the Day of Judgment imminent.

The wages you failed to pay the workmen (5:4). The Greek text for the verb translated "failed to pay" in the NIV is uncertain. Some manuscripts have a form of the verb *apostereō* ("defraud") while others have *aphysstereō*, "withhold." But the former is more likely because the verb occurs elsewhere in the Bible in just this sense. See especially Malachi 3:5: "'So I will come near to you for judgment. I will be quick to testify against sorcerers, adulterers and perjurers, against those who defraud laborers of their wages, who oppress the widows and the fatherless, and deprive aliens of justice, but do not fear me,' says the LORD Almighty." James might again be influenced by Leviticus 19 in his selection of this particular example, for 19:13 reads, "Do not defraud your neighbor or rob him. Do not hold back the wages of a hired man overnight."

Are crying out against you (5:4). We are reminded of Cain's blood, "crying out" for justice (Gen. 4:10). But even more pertinent may be Deuteronomy 24:14–15: "Do not take advantage of a hired man who is poor and needy, whether he is a brother Israelite or an alien living in one of your towns. Pay him his wages each day before sunset, because he is poor and is counting on it. Otherwise he may cry to the LORD against you, and you will be guilty of sin." The language of "crying out" is often used in the Bible when God's people plead with God for deliverance from their oppressors.[61]

The Lord Almighty (5:4). "Almighty" translates a word that means "armies" (*sabaōth*). The language pictures God as the powerful leader of a great army, usually the heavenly hosts. It may not be coincidence that Isaiah uses this title of God when he describes the judgment God will bring on his people for their oppression of the poor (Isa. 5:9).

The day of slaughter (5:5). The Greek of this phrase does not occur in the LXX, but the Hebrew equivalent is found as a reference to the Day of the Lord in Isaiah 30:25. It also occurs in a similar way in *1 Enoch* 90:4. Almost certainly, then, James refers to the time of final judgment.

You have condemned and murdered innocent men (5:6). James's accusation reflects a widespread Old Testament/Jewish tradition about the sinfulness of rich people in using their wealth and influence to defraud the poor and to deprive them of their living. In Wisdom of Solomon 2:6–20, for instance, the rich are pictured as living luxuriously with no thought of tomorrow, oppressing "the righteous man" (2:12) and condemning them "to a shameful death" (2:20).[62] To withhold wages from a working man is, in effect, to murder him, as Sirach says: "To take away a neighbor's living is to commit murder" (Sir. 34:22).

The Need for Patient Endurance (5:7–11)

The contribution of this paragraph to the argument of the letter is debated. Some interpreters note parallels between this paragraph and 1:2–12 (notably God's blessing on those who "endure") and think that James here begins the conclusion of the letter. But the biblical background suggests a closer relationship with 5:1–6. Several Old Testament texts—Psalm 37 is perhaps the best example—exhort the oppressed people of God to take comfort from the fact that God will judge the wicked. So James turns from portraying the terrible fate that the wicked rich, who are oppressing the righteous, will face on the Day of the Lord to encouraging God's people to endure faithfully in light of the nearness of that Day.

The Lord's coming (5:7). "Coming" translates *parousia*, a word that is applied throughout the New Testament to the appearance of Christ in glory at the end of history. *Parousia* basically means "presence" and was used in secular Greek to depict the "arrival" of a king or dignitary.[63]

The farmer waits for the land to yield its valuable crop and how patient he is for the autumn and spring rains (5:7). In Palestine, the growth of crops was particularly dependent on the rain that came in late autumn and early spring.[64] Note, for example, Deuteronomy 11:14, where God, in response to his people's obedience, promises: "Then I will send rain on your land in its season, both autumn and spring rains, so that you may gather in your grain, new wine and oil." Every passage in which the language of "early and late rains" appears in the Old Testament affirms God's faithfulness to his people.[65] James's readers may well have detected an "echo" of this faithfulness theme in the illustration here.

Don't grumble against each other (5:9).
The word "grumble" translates a word (*stenazō*) that often connotes the frustration of God's people at the oppression that they are suffering. Exodus 2:23 is a classic example: "During that long period, the king of Egypt died. The Israelites groaned in their slavery and cried out, and their cry for help because of their slavery went up to God." James, of course, here prohibits believers from grumbling against each other. But his use of this word may hint at the fact that their impatience with one another is the product of the persecution they are enduring.

As an example of patience in the face of suffering (5:10). Citing examples of endurance under the pressure of persecution became a standard Jewish means of encouragement in the wake of the Maccabean revolt in the early second century B.C. The Seleucid king of that era, Antiochus IV Epiphanes, sought to eradicate the Jewish faith by prohibiting circumcision, possession of the Torah, and other Jewish customs. Many Jews refused to abandon their faith and were severely persecuted as a result. Books such as 2 Maccabees celebrate the faithfulness and endurance of these martyrs as means of encouraging God's people. The word translated "example" (*hypodeigma*) occurs in some of these traditions (cf. 2 Macc. 6:28; 4 Macc. 17:23). Note especially *4 Maccabees* 9:8: "For we, through this severe suffering and endurance, shall have the prize of virtue and be with God." Hebrews 11:35–37 refers to some of these same martyrs, and James here alludes briefly to this same tradition.

We consider blessed those who have persevered (5:11). James may again be reflecting a dependence on the Maccabean martyr tradition. At the opening of his book, after introducing Eleazar, his seven brothers, and their mother as model martyrs, the author of *4 Maccabees* says, "It is fitting for me to praise for their virtues those who, with their mother, died for the sake of nobility and goodness, but I would call them blessed for the honor in which they are held" (*4 Macc.* 1:10).

You have heard of Job's perseverance (5:11). The canonical book of Job does not put much emphasis on the heroic perseverance of Job; although he does tenaciously cling to his faith in God despite the best efforts of his "friends." But the noncanonical *Testament of Job* puts much greater stress on this element of Job's response, praising him for his "endurance" (*T. Job* 1:5) and having him remind his children that "patience is better than anything." The date of this book is uncertain and may even have been redacted by Christian scribes.[66] But the tradition found in the book may predate James.

What the Lord finally brought about (5:11). The NIV suggests that James refers at this point to the blessings God eventually restored to Job at the end of the book. But the Greek is ambiguous, referring more vaguely to "the end [or purpose] of the Lord." Nevertheless the NIV translation is probably justified, for the closest parallels to James's wording in intertestamental literature have a similar reference.[67]

Concluding Exhortations (5:12–20)

New Testament letters often end with a focus on prayer. James is no exception. The power of prayer in all circumstances, but especially in times of illness, is the focus of these verses. But James begins with a brief prohibition of oaths (5:12) and ends with a fitting encouragement to believers to bring back fellow Christians who may be leaving the straight path of the faith (5:19–20).

Do not swear (5:12). James does not refer to uncouth speech but to invoking God's name as the guarantee of truth or a future course of action. Such oaths are apparently being abused in James's day. Intertestamental writers warn against taking oaths too often.[68] James has apparently modeled his prohibition on the similar teaching of Jesus that we find in Matthew 5:34–37. Perhaps Leviticus 19 is also exerting some influence on James, for verse 12 in that chapter reads, "Do not swear falsely by my name and so profane the name of your God. I am the LORD."

Is any one of you sick? (5:14). "Sick" translates a Greek word (*astheneō*) that means "to be weak." Some interpreters think the weakness to which James refers is perhaps spiritual rather than physical. But, as we have seen throughout the letter, James is strongly influenced by the teaching of Jesus. In the Gospels, *astheneō* consistently refers to physical weakness, such as an illness.

The elders of the church (5:14). The office of elder in the early church may well have been modeled on the elders of the synagogue. They were the spiritual leaders of the local congregations of believers.[69]

right ▶

JARS FOR OIL

Small jars discovered at Masada.

Anoint him with oil (5:14). Why does James encourage the elders to anoint the sick person with oil? One possibility is

that the oil will have had a medicinal value. Oil was widely used in the ancient world in cases of illness. Galen, the most famous ancient physician, recommended oil as "the best of all remedies for paralysis."[70] Note that the good Samaritan, when he came across the injured man, "bandaged his wounds, pouring on oil and wine" (Luke 10:34). Yet we have no evidence that oil was considered a panacea (note that Galen stipulates its usefulness in cases of paralysis). So it seems unlikely that James recommends oil as the natural remedy for illness in general.

The anointing is more likely, then, to have a symbolic value. In the Old Testament anointing especially often symbolizes the setting apart of a thing or person for God's special attention or use. Typical is Exodus 28:41: "After you put these clothes on your brother Aaron and his sons, anoint and ordain them. Consecrate them so that they might serve me as priests." To be sure, the Greek verb in the LXX of many of these passages is *chriō* rather than the *aleiphō*, which James uses

here. But *aleiphō* can be used in this same way (see Ex. 40:15; Num. 3:3), and James probably avoids *chriō* because in the New Testament it has ceased to refer clearly to a physical action. James wants the elders to perform an actual physical anointing as a means of assuring the person who is ill that he or she is being held up in a special way for God's attention in prayer.

And the prayer offered in faith will make the sick person well (5:15). A few zealous Christians insist that God wants to heal his people through prayer and that any recourse to medicine betrays a lack of faith in God's power. But James almost certainly shares the view enunciated by Sirach:

> *Honor physicians for their services,*
> *for the Lord created them;*
> *for their gift of healing comes from the*
> *Most High,*
> *and they are rewarded by the king.*
> *The skill of physicians makes them*
> *distinguished,*
> *and the sensible will not despise*
> *them.*
> *The Lord created medicines out of*
> *the earth,*
> *and the sensible do not despise*
> *them.*[71]

He prayed earnestly that it would not rain (5:17). Elijah's prayer is found in 1 Kings 17–18. This text does not explicitly claim that Elijah prayed for the drought. But 1 Kings 18:42 does picture him praying for the drought to end, and it is a legitimate inference that he prayed for its onset as well. Note also that a few Jewish texts associate the drought with Elijah's praying.[72]

Cover over a multitude of sins (5:20). James alludes to Proverbs 10:12: "Hatred stirs up dissension, but love covers over all wrongs." In Proverbs, "cover" refers to the overlooking of the sins that people commit against us. But, since "cover" here in James is parallel with "save from death," it seems to refer to God's forgiveness. There is some evidence, based on the use of this same text in 1 Peter 4:8, that this language had become a proverbial way of referring to divine forgiveness.

REFLECTIONS

A SACRAMENTAL UNDERSTANDING OF THE "ANOINTING with oil" that James refers to here arose early in the history of the church. On the basis of this text, the early Greek church practiced what they called the *euchlaion* (a combination of the words *euchē*, [prayer] and *elaion* [oil], both used in this text), which had the purpose of strengthening the body and soul of the sick. The Western church continued this practice for many centuries. Later, the Roman church gave to the priest the exclusive right to perform this ceremony and developed the sacrament of extreme unction (in A.D. 852). This sacrament has the purpose of removing any remnant of sin and of strengthening the soul of the dying (healing is considered only a possibility). The Council of Trent (14.1) found this sacrament "insinuated" in Mark 6:13 and "promulgated" in James 5:14. Since Vatican II, the rite has been called "the anointing of the sick." Clearly this developed sacrament has little basis in James's text; he recommends anointing for any illness and associates it with healing rather than with preparation for death.

ANNOTATED BIBLIOGRAPHY

Davids, Peter. *The Epistle of James.* NIGTC. Grand Rapids: Eerdmans, 1982.
Excellent commentary on the Greek text, particularly strong on Jewish backgrounds.

Dibelius, Martin. *A Commentary on the Epistle of James*, rev. by H. Greeven. Philadelphia: Fortress, 1976.
Classic work, very good on backgrounds but weak on literary structure.

Johnson, L. T. *The Letter of James.* AB. Garden City, N.Y.: Doubleday, 1995.
The best recent commentary, with excellent material on Greco-Roman background and structure.

Laws, Sophie. *A Commentary on the Epistle of James.* New York: Harper & Row, 1980.
Classic exposition of the English text.

Martin, R. P. *James.* WBC. Waco, Tex.: Word, 1988.
Detailed commentary on the Greek text, with a particular slant on the Jewish background.

Moo, D. J. *The Letter of James.* Pillar. Grand Rapids: Eerdmans, 2000.
Exposition of the English text.

CHAPTER NOTES

Main Text Notes

1. Acts 12:17; 15:13; 21:18; cf. Gal. 1:19; 2:9, 12.
2. See esp. Hegesippus (and cf. R. B. Ward, "James of Jerusalem in the First Two Centuries," *ANRW* 2.26.1 [1992]: 799–810).
3. On the issue of James's family background, see esp. R. Bauckham, *Jude and the Relatives of Jesus in the Early Church* (Edinburgh: T. & T. Clark, 1990), 125–30.
4. See, e.g., Elsa Tamez, *The Scandalous Message of James: Faith Without Works Is Dead* (New York: Crossroad, 1990).
5. *A Commentary on the Epistle of James*, ed. H. Greeven (Hermeneia; Philadelphia: Fortress, 1976).
6. See, e.g., W. R. Baker, *Personal Speech-Ethics in the Epistle of James* (Tubingen: Mohr, 1995), 7–12.
7. Ezek. 47:13; *Pss. Sol.* 17:26–28; see also Matt. 19:28; Rev. 7:4–8; 21:12.
8. For further information on "wisdom," see esp. Ben Witherington, III, *Jesus the Sage: The Pilgrimage of Wisdom* (Minneapolis: Fortress, 1994), 3–116.
9. Ps. 12:2 (LXX, where it is 11:3); Hos. 10:2 (LXX).
10. See, e.g., Sir. 15:11–20; *b. Men.* 99b; *b. Sanh.* 59b.
11. See *Gen. Rab.* 9:7; *b. Yoma* 69b.
12. Philo, *Husbandry* 103.
13. Philo, *Alleg. Interp.* 2.33.
14. Ibid., 2.33.
15. Prov. 10:19; 15:1; 17:27–28; Sir. 5:9–6:1.
16. See, e.g., Prov. 8:20; Isa. 1:21; Jer. 9:24; Tobit 1:3.
17. Simeon b. Gamaliel, *m. Abot.* 1:17.
18. Philo, *Spec. Laws* 1.315.
19. See Rom. 2:11; Eph. 6:9; Col. 3:25; related words are found in Acts 10:34; James 2:9; 1 Peter 1:17; on the Hebrew idea of partiality, see, e.g., Lev. 19:15; Deut. 1:17; Ps. 82:2; Prov. 28:21; Mal. 1:8.
20. See also Matt. 21:21; Mark 11:23; Acts 10:20; Rom. 4:20; 14:23; Jude 22.
21. E.g., Ps. 69:32; Isa. 29:19; 61:1; Amos 2:7.
22. Philo, *Posterity* 101–2.
23. See esp. L. T. Johnson, "The Use of Leviticus 19 in the Letter of James," *JBL* 101 (1982): 391–401.
24. Augustine, *Letter to Heironymum* 4.
25. See also *b. Hor.* 8b; *b. Shab.* 70b; 1QS 8:16; *T. Asher* 2:5–10; Philo, *Alleg. Interp.* 3.241.
26. Vaticanus, B; see also Luke 18:20; Rom. 13:9.
27. Judg. 6:23; 1 Sam. 25:35; 2 Kings 5:19; Mark 5:34; Luke 7:50; 8:48; 24:36; John 20:19; Acts 16:36.
28. Josephus, *Ag. Ap.* 2.40 §284.
29. Cf. 1 Cor. 8:4–6; Gal. 3:20; Eph. 4:6; 1 Tim. 2:5.
30. MM, 676.
31. Philo, *Worse* 140.
32. Cf., e.g., Ps. 105:6; Jer. 33:26; cf. Gal. 3:16; Heb. 2:16.
33. Cf. Philo, *Virtues* 216; Josephus, *Ant.* 1.154–57; *Jub.* 11–12.

34. The translation "friend" in many English translations of these verses is a paraphrase of a Hebrew construction that means "one loved."

35. *Jub.* 19:9; 20:20; Philo, *Sobriety* 56; *Abraham* 273; *T. Ab.*, passim.

36. See esp. R. B. Ward, "The Works of Abraham: James 2:14–26," *HTR* 61 (1968): 283–90.

37. Philo, *Posterity* 88.

38. Sophocles, *Antigone* 477.

39. Aristotle, *Questiones Mechanica* 5.

40. E.g., Pseudo-Aristotle, *De mundo* 6; frequently in Philo.

41. Philo, *Creation* 83–86.

42. Philo, *Alleg. Interp.* 3.224.

43. L. E. Elliott-Binns, "The Meaning of 'YLH in Jas. III.5," *NTS* 2 (1995): 48–50.

44. E.g., Philo, *Spec. Laws* 4.110–16; Acts 11:6.

45. Prov. 26:28; cf. Hermas, *Mandates* 2:3.

46. *Gen. Rab.* 24 (on Gen. 5:1).

47. Epictetus, *Diss.* 2.20.18–19.

48. Aristotle, *Politics* 5.3.

49. See esp. R. P. Martin, *James* (WBC; Waco, Tex.: Word, 1988), 144.

50. Epictetus, *Diss.* 3.13.9.

51. E.g., Ex. 20:5; 34:14; Zech. 8:2.

52. E.g., Lev. 21:17, 21, 23; Isa. 29:13; 58:2; Ezek. 40:46; Heb. 7:19.

53. Num. 31:23; 2 Chron. 29:15; Isa. 66:17.

54. Cf. Prov. 10:23; Eccl. 7:6; cf. Sir. 27:13.

55. See, e.g., *Pss. Sol.* 12:3; *T. Gad* 3:3; cf. also 2 Cor. 12:20; 1 Peter 2:1.

56. Hermas, *Mandates* 2; cf. James 4:8.

57. See Sophie Laws, *A Commentary on the Epistle of James* (New York: Harper & Row, 1980), 194.

58. See esp. *1 En.* 94–105.

59. See also Job 16:7; 19:20; 33:21; 40:12; Ps. 37:36; Ezek. 17:9; Ep. Jer. 71.

60. See, e.g., Acts 2:17; 2 Tim. 3:1; Heb. 1:2; 2 Peter 3:3.

61. Ex. 2:23; 1 Sam. 9:16; 2 Chron. 33:13; cf. *3 Macc.* 5:7.

62. See also Ps. 10:8–9; 37:32; Amos 2:6; 5:12; Mic. 2:2, 6–9; 3:1–3, 9–12; 6:9–16.

63. Cf. 1 Cor. 16:7; 2 Cor. 10:10; Phil. 2:12.

64. D. Baly, *The Geography of the Bible* (New York: Harper & Row, 1974), 50–51.

65. Cf. also Jer. 5:24; Hos. 6:3; Joel 2:23; Zech. 10:1.

66. See C. Hass, "Job's Perseverance in the Testament of Job," in *Studies on the Testament of Job*, eds. M. A. Knibb and P. W. van der Horst (SNTSMS 66; Cambridge: Cambridge Univ. Press, 1989), 117–18.

67. Cf. *T. Gad* 7:4; *T. Benj.* 4:1; cf. Heb. 13:7.

68. Sir. 23:9, 11; Philo, *Decalogue* 84–95.

69. Cf. Acts 11:30; 14:23; 15:2; 20:17; 21:18; 1 Tim. 5:17.

70. Galen, *De simplicitate medicamentum* 2.

71. Sir. 38:1–4.

72. Sir. 48:2–3; 2 Esd. 7:109.

Sidebar and Chart Notes

A-1. See, e.g., Isa. 43:9; 45:25; 50:8.

A-2. An introduction and translation can be found in James H. Charlesworth, ed., *The Old Testament Pseudepigrapha*, vol. 1 (Garden City, N.Y.: Doubleday, 1983), while the classic commentary is R. H. Charles, *The Testaments of the Twelve Patriarchs* (2 vols.; Oxford: Clarendon, 1908).

A-3. On this, see esp. L. T. Johnson, "James 3:13–4:10 and the *Topos PERI FQONOU*," *NovT* 25 (1983): 327–47.

1 PETER

by Peter Davids

The Church in Northwest Asia Minor

We do not know when the church started in northwest Asia Minor. Paul planted churches in the southern Galatian region in the late A.D. 40s (Acts 13–14), but when he later tried to extend this work westward into Asia or northwestward into Bithynia, the Spirit prohibited him (16:6–7), apparently because the Lord wanted to use Paul in Macedonia and Achaia (Greece; 16:10). Paul's interest in those areas probably means that he did not know of churches there, for his general procedure was to go where the church did not yet exist (Rom. 15:20; 2 Cor. 10:14). Did the Lord know that some of the people cited in Acts 2:9 had already carried the gospel there, or was it his plan to leave the evangelization of that area to someone else at a later date? What we do know is that about fifteen years later

► 1 Peter
IMPORTANT FACTS:

- ■ **AUTHOR:** Silvanus (Silas) and Simon Peter.
- ■ **DATE:** A.D. 64–68 (shortly before or after Peter's martyrdom).
- ■ **OCCASION:**
  - To encourage believers in northwest Asia Minor experiencing persecution.
  - To instruct believers on how to relate to societal structures.
- ■ **KEY THEMES:**
  1. Believers have a secure home and inheritance with Christ.
  2. Believers should live holy lives following the model of Christ.

1 Peter witnesses to the existence of churches throughout this area. We should probably think of house churches scattered throughout the area, the larger ones consisting of thirty to forty members—sometimes several in one city (collectively forming the church in that city) and sometimes only one. They would be loosely connected as Christians traveled through the area for one reason or another, bringing news about other Christian groups as they went.

One thing that we do know about the churches of this area is that they were largely Gentile in makeup. First Peter frequently refers to these Christians in terms that would not be appropriate for Jews.[1] There is also none of the Jew-Gentile or circumcision-uncircumcision tension in this letter that is so common in Paul's writings. While Jews probably lived in these areas, as Acts 2:9 indicates, most of the church came from people native to the region. This made rejection by their neighbors as a result of their commitment to Christ so much more painful, since they had gone from being completely at home in the culture to being social outcasts.

Despite the problems mentioned in 1 Peter, these churches survived. When Trajan sent Pliny to Bithynia as Senatorial governor about A.D. 112, Pliny discovered, as he wrote to Trajan, "The contagion of that superstition [i.e., Christianity] has penetrated not the cities only, but the villages and the country."[2] Pliny himself thought he could still stamp Christianity out, but he would fail and the area would remain a strong Christian center for centuries.

A Portrait of the Situation

When missionaries arrived in these provinces, people listened to the gospel and believed. As a result their lifestyle changed. First and foremost, they stopped worshiping the various gods of their empire, city, trade guild, or family, and instead worshiped only "the God and Father of our Lord Jesus Christ" (1:3). This change in behavior meant that they were now viewed as unpatriotic (worship of the genius of the emperor was equivalent to flag worship in modern America), disloyal to their city (since they would not take part in civic ceremonies involving worship), unprofessional in their trade (since guild meetings usually took place in pagan temples), and haters of their families (family gatherings and ceremonies also took place in temples, and household worship was thought to hold the family together). After all, no one was asking these Christians to

ITALY
▼

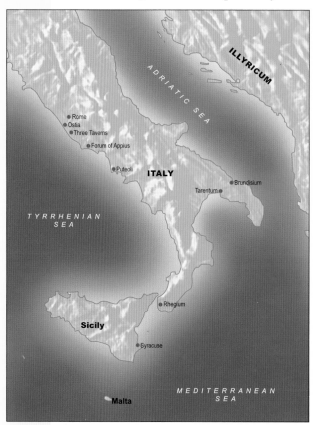

ILLYRICUM

ADRIATIC SEA

● Rome
● Ostia
● Three Taverns
  ● Forum of Appius

● Puteoli   **ITALY**

  ● Brundisium
 Tarentum ●

*T Y R R H E N I A N
S E A*

● Rhegium

Sicily

● Syracuse

*M E D I T E R R A N E A N
S E A*

Malta

believe in the gods (many of their neighbors did not really believe in them), but only to offer token worship as a sign of their familial or civic allegiance. People who were so obstinate as to refuse this simple duty surely had to be "haters of humankind," as many in the Roman Empire considered them.

Second, they now followed a morality different from that of their fellow citizens. Previously they had enjoyed drunken parties and loose sexual morals, but now they demonstrated self-control in their drinking, eating, and sexual habits. This different behavior cut them off from their former friends, who thought that they had become weird (4:4).

The result of these changes in their lives was social ostracism: insults, abuse, rejection, shame, and likely economic persecution with the resulting loss of property. There is no evidence in this letter of official persecution, such as imprisonment or execution, but rejection, abuse, punishment by family leaders (owners of slaves; husbands of women) and perhaps occasional mob violence had certainly taken their toll. (Official persecution would come in the time of Pliny.) Their fellow citizens thought that these believers in Jesus no longer belonged in their city or family and were communicating that message loud and clear.

This is the situation that has come to the attention of our writer. He apparently does not know these Christians personally (the letter lacks the personal greetings found in many of Paul's letters), but he is concerned about their situation. He will write to them, citing the general Christian teachings he is sure they know. He follows a threefold strategy in his letter: (1) to exhort them to stand firm in the light of the return of Christ, (2) to advise them on how to minimize persecution through wise behavior, and (3) to encourage them to consider where they do belong and what property they do own because they belong to Christ.

These strategies should be kept in mind as one reads the letter.

Letter Opening (1:1–2)

Peter, an apostle of Jesus Christ (1:1). It was standard practice in the ancient world to begin a letter by identifying the sender. Normally the sender was viewed as the person who either dictated the letter or requested someone to write it for him, not the secretary who wrote down the dictated words or, if trusted, composed the letter on behalf of the sender. Our letter is from Peter (meaning "Rock"), and since that was a common name, he identifies which Peter is writing, namely, the one who was sent or commissioned (the meaning of "apostle") by Jesus Christ.

To God's elect, strangers in the world, scattered throughout Pontus, Galatia, Cappadocia, Asia and Bithynia (1:1). After identifying the sender, ancient letters identified the recipients. Peter is sensitive to the situation of his readers. Their society may reject them, but they are chosen (elect) by God (which idea is underlined in the next verse). They may be technically citizens of their various cities, but the way their fellow citizens treat them and the reality of their new life in Christ make them feel like temporary residents, noncitizens (both better translations than "strangers"). We will later discover where they really belong. At present they are scattered, which term would remind any Jews among them of the scattering of the Jewish people among the nations (called the "Diaspora," a word from the same root as the term "scattered") at the time of the Exile (586 B.C.) and the hope of their eventual regathering in Palestine.

The sanctifying work of the Spirit, for obedience to Jesus Christ and sprinkling by his blood (1:2). The idea that the Spirit sanctifies indicates not simply a positional change when God reached out to them, but a practical change in lifestyle for the better, from a less holy lifestyle to one that is set apart for God. This change appeared in their obedience to Jesus Christ. The basic Christian confession was "Jesus is Lord," which contrasted with the assertion of the Roman

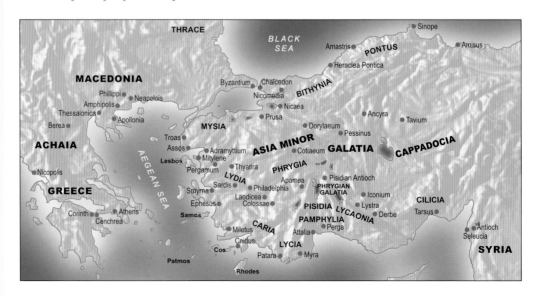

Empire that "Caesar is Lord." In both cases "Lord" implied that the person was someone whom you obeyed. It had practical consequences. This clash in allegiance was one cause of the persecution of the church. In chapter 2, Peter will set this clash of allegiance in perspective.

The image of sprinkling is taken from Old Testament and pagan sacrificial rites, with which the readers were surely familiar. They had all seen animals sacrificed and the blood sprinkled on people or objects for various religious purposes. Peter is probably thinking primarily of the Old Testament. For example, in Exodus 24:7–8 we read that the people respond to the law (which began with announcing God's choice of them to be his people) with obedience, "We will do everything the LORD has said; we will obey." As a result, "Moses . . . took the blood, sprinkled it on the people and said, 'This is the blood of the covenant that the LORD has made with you in accordance with all these words.'" The sprinkled blood sealed the covenant and set the people apart for God.

Grace and peace be yours in abundance (1:2). A Greek letter normally had a greeting. In Christian letters this normal greeting (*chairein*, which in Greek sounds like the word for "grace," *charin*, and so was changed to "grace") was expanded with the Hebrew greeting (*shalom* = peace). However, it still retained its character as a formal greeting and thus functions like the "dear" that is often found at the beginning of English letters.

Thanksgiving 1:3–12

Praise be to the God and Father of our Lord Jesus Christ! (1:3). A normal Greek letter followed the greeting with thanks to one or more of the gods for the benefits that had been given to the letter writer or recipients. Christians tended to expand this rather short, formal thanksgiving into a much longer statement that often introduced some of the significant theological themes of the letter. Peter is no exception to that practice. Naturally, the God he praises is "the God and Father of our Lord Jesus Christ," which fits the New Testament tendency to worship the Father much more than Jesus.

In his great mercy he has given us new birth into a living hope (1:3). Christians were not the only ones who could talk about a new birth. In some of the pagan mystery religions[3] (e.g., Mithraism) one

BITHYNIA

Part of the ornamentation on the city gate at Nicea.

went through initiatory experiences that led to new life or new birth or life on a higher order. Despite the possibility of confusion with pagan beliefs, Peter (like John) prefers birth imagery rather than Paul's usual choice of adoption imagery for describing new life in Christ. The contrast with pagan belief is clear, however. While pagan religion brought about rebirth through instruction and various rites, that is, human activities, the Christian's rebirth had come through the activity of another person, "through the resurrection of Jesus Christ from the dead." The emphasis of the sentence is that of "a living hope," which both fits with the birth imagery and contrasts with the somewhat hopeless situation believers were physically living in.

An inheritance that can never perish, spoil or fade—kept in heaven for you (1:4). The hope is defined in terms of an inheritance. In the Old Testament Abraham was promised an inheritance (Gen. 12:7), which was the land of Canaan. This promise would become central to the Old Testament. Furthermore, each Hebrew family originally had ancestral land, the title to which they carefully guarded (as Naboth did in 1 Kings 21:3, "The LORD forbid that I should give you the inheritance of my fathers"). While, as a result of the Exile, virtually no one in Palestine was living on his or her original ancestral land, many not only in Palestine but also in Asia Minor did have land and other possessions that had been passed down for generations. An inheritance showed that you belonged somewhere, and it was also security for yourself and your offspring. Persecution affected one's inheritance, as hostile neighbors might drive one from ancestral land, possessions might be destroyed by mobs, or the gov-

ernment might confiscate both goods and land (as Jason risked in Acts 17:8–9). First Peter points to an inheritance that cannot be touched by human hostility, for it is stored in a place where human beings cannot reach.

Who through faith are shielded by God's power (1:5). The concept of being shielded by a great power was familiar in the ancient world. Having a powerful patron was one form of protection people sought. The Roman Empire as a whole was viewed as protecting its inhabitants from the chaotic and destructive peoples along the borders of the empire, such as the Parthians to the east. Likewise the Roman peace (*pax Romana*) prevented one province or city-state of the empire from attacking another. Various gods were also viewed as protecting their adherents. In the Old Testament God is often spoken of as a shield.[4] Christians, Peter asserts, do have a shielding power, not one which they can physically see, such as a patron or Roman legions, but (as in the Old Testament) God himself. Because they cannot see the power, faith is necessary.

Until the coming of the salvation that is ready to be revealed in the last time (1:5). Salvation was also a common idea in the ancient world. It could mean physical deliverance, political deliverance (such as that through Roman armies), or spiritual deliverance. For non-Christians the latter might be enlightenment achieved through a pagan cult or deliverance from some curse or problem, achieved through magic. For pagans deliverance, even when future, was normally thought of as within this lifetime or world. Christians could similarly speak of salvation (which for them was ultimately physical and political as well as spiritual)[5] in three tenses. At times, although rarely, they spoke of salvation in the past, "I was saved."[6] Somewhat more frequently they spoke of it in the present, "I am being saved."[7] Peter focuses on the most frequent tense, the future, "I will be saved," for the Christians to whom he was writing certainly did not feel delivered in their present circumstances.[8] (Nor might Peter, if he wrote this during imprisonment in Rome.) The full deliverance does already exist, but it will only be revealed "in the last time."

The idea of deliverance at the very end of this age was deeply embedded in Jewish and Christian literature, especially apocalyptic literature like Daniel and Revelation in the Bible and *1 Enoch* or some of the *Testaments of the Twelve Patriarchs* outside of the Bible. Likewise the Dead Sea Scrolls spoke of such an expectation. For instance, the War Scroll presents a final battle during which the deliverance of God appears as the faithful fight a final battle. Thus anyone who had read Jewish or Christian literature would have been familiar with this idea.

In this you greatly rejoice, though now for a little while you may have had to suffer grief in all kinds of trials (1:6). The contrast of present trials (or tests) and joy is common in New Testament literature, indicating that these were common teachings in the early church. James 1:2 uses exactly the same phrase for "all kinds of trials" ("trials of many kinds" in the NIV) and also contrasts this with joy. Likewise Romans 5:3 says, "We also rejoice in our sufferings," using different wording, but expressing the same idea. Ultimately such teaching went back to Jesus: "Blessed are you when people insult you, persecute you and falsely say all kinds of evil against you because of me. Rejoice and be glad, because great is your reward in heaven, for in the same way they persecuted the prophets who were before you" (Matt. 5:11–12).

◄
"LIKE THE FLOWERS OF THE FIELD..."

A field of wildflowers near Capernaum.

The rejoicing is not because one enjoys persecution or because one denies the reality of pain and suffering (or because one ignores it, as in the *apatheia* of the Stoics); rather, it is because the Christian has an eschatological perspective. That is, he or she understands that at the end of the age God will pay back each person for the evil they have suffered as a result of their allegiance to him; therefore they can rejoice now, in anticipation of the coming heavenly reward.

The tests or trials (Gk. *peirasmos*) mentioned in any of these passages are not those that are the common lot of all humanity, and certainly not illness (which uses a different vocabulary),[9] but those that result from the person's commitment to Jesus. These might be the pains of direct persecution, or they might be the struggles of Christian service (e.g., Paul's list in 2 Cor. 11:23–29). Certainly this was the experience of the Christians to whom our letter is addressed.

Your faith—of greater worth than gold, which perishes even though refined by fire—may be proved genuine (1:7). The believers addressed in this letter are given the hope that their faith (or, better, commitment to Jesus) would be proved genuine, like genuine gold remains when put into a refiner's fire and other things that look like gold are burned up or removed as waste. (The same root in Greek is translated in the NIV "refined" and "proved genuine" here and "testing" in James 1:3.) Not only do James and 1 Peter use similar language and imagery, but so did earlier Jewish literature. *Wisdom of Solomon* 3:5–6 states, "Having been disciplined a little, [the righteous] will receive great good, because God tested them and found them worthy of himself; like gold in the furnace he tried them, and like a sacrificial burnt offering he accepted them" (NRSV). The Christian version of the saying, built on Jewish roots, was apparently popular with early Christian teachers, for 1 Peter, James, and Paul (Rom. 5:3–5) all use differing forms of it.

You are receiving the goal of your faith, the salvation of your souls (1:9). The author is not thinking here of soul as opposed to body, but "soul" in its meaning "life" or "self."[10] The goal of commitment to Jesus is that when he appears, the lives or selves of these believers will be delivered because they belong to him. Again salvation is viewed as future, for in the present they are not experiencing a lot of deliverance, but rather persecution and rejection.

The prophets, who spoke of the grace that was to come to you (1:10). In the ancient world something that was old and deeply rooted in tradition was valued more than something that was new and innovative. In pointing to the prophetic announcement of coming deliverance (we do not know what specific passages Peter has in mind, although the reference to "the sufferings of Christ and the glories that would follow" [1:11] suggests passages such as Ps. 22 and Isa. 53, or perhaps a combination of passages), Peter locates salvation as something old, traditional, and valuable.

The Spirit of Christ (1:11). The Spirit is so named to underline the fact that the Spirit who spoke about Christ had animated the prophets and the same "Holy Spirit sent from heaven" (1:12) had brought the gospel to them. Jews certainly believed that God's Spirit had animated the prophets (although they would not have called him "the Spirit of

Christ"); they were divided as to whether the Spirit departed after the time of Ezra (one part of the proto-rabbinic tradition asserts this) or whether there was a continuing prophetic tradition (most other Jewish traditions, including parts of the proto-rabbinic tradition).[11] Peter places the gospel within this tradition, tracing it back to the ancient prophets.

Even angels long to look into these things (1:12). Angelology was important in the Jewish world, and the names of angels are mentioned in books like *1 Enoch* and the Dead Sea Scroll *4Q Songs of the Sabbath Sacrifice*. The law was exalted because it was given through the mediation of angels (Heb. 2:2, following Jewish thought). Peter indicates that the suffering Christians are privileged above the ancient prophets and holy angels, a teaching also found in Hebrews 1:14 and 2:16.

These Christians have been told by their neighbors that they have abandoned their ancestral traditions, but in fact they stand in a most ancient tradition. They have probably been told that they have abandoned the gods, but in fact the angels above envy them and the Holy Spirit of God is the one who has brought the gospel to them and whom they have experienced at conversion. They are "plugged into" heaven. Throughout the whole thanksgiving Peter has countered their sense of alienation by emphasizing that they belong to heaven, have a reward coming, are related to God, and even stand in an ancient tradition.

The Call to Holiness (1:13–2:10)

Prepare your minds for action; be self-controlled (1:13). This expression depicts a person getting ready for active work by tucking up the skirt of a garment into a belt and tightening it so the legs would be free. "Self-controlled" is the opposite of intoxication; thus Peter means thinking soberly and clearly in the light of the coming revelation of Jesus.

Do not conform to the evil desires (1:14). This means living in contrast to their former pagan lifestyle that was characterized by following their desires (the word "evil" is not in the original text). For Greeks any life controlled by changing desires was less worthy than one directed by sober thought, while for the Jews the inclination towards evil (*yēṣer*) was nothing more than desire without the boundaries set by the law. Thus control by desire is characterized as "ignorance" of either rational thought (Greek, including the Jew Philo) or God's law (most Jews).

As obedient children (1:14). Peter has already implied his readers are God's children when he wrote about being born anew and having an inheritance. Now he suggests the commonplace idea in the Mediterranean world that they should obey and be like the character of the father of the family. This was part of upholding the honor of the family and its father, the opposite of shaming the family.[12]

"Be holy, because I am holy" (1:16). In Leviticus 19:2 this clause appears in the context of regulations related to topics of the Ten Commandments (Lev. 11:45 and 20:7 also contain it in different contexts). Peter is contrasting such moral holiness to a life controlled by desires and so is using it of moral purity, as Jesus did when he used a similar phrase in Matthew 5:48, "Be perfect, therefore, as your heavenly Father is perfect." Jesus, of course, was not referring to absolute perfection, but the type of perfection that Noah had (Gen. 6:9–"blameless" in the NIV translates the same word for "perfect" that is in Matthew). Noah, of course, was a human person who lived a life pleasing to God.

A Father who judges each [person's] work impartially (1:17). We may be God's children, but our "Father" is an impartial judge. Impartiality (as opposed to taking bribes or considering the social standing of the plaintiffs) was a key characteristic of a righteous judge in the Old Testament. Deuteronomy 16:18–20 instructs, "Appoint judges and officials for each of your tribes in every town the LORD your God is giving you, and they shall judge the people fairly. Do not pervert justice or show partiality. Do not accept a bribe, for a bribe blinds the eyes of the wise and twists the words of the righteous. Follow justice and justice alone, so that you may live and possess the land the LORD your God is giving you." As the supreme judge God is supremely impartial. He is indeed Father, but that does not mean that his children can get away with behavior he would condemn in others. This means that even though they are "away from home" (i.e., "strangers here" [1 Peter 1:17]) they should live with "respectful fear." While the term "respectful" is not in the Greek text, what is implied is the fear a child would have of a father if the child were considering some act the father would punish. The analogy was even clearer in that world than in ours, for fathers in that culture were more emotionally distant from the family and wielded more authority over the family.[13]

You were redeemed (1:18). While this verse is another indication that the read-ers were Gentile Christians, the focus is on the idea of redemption. The readers would have been familiar with the concept of purchasing themselves or an enslaved friend or relative out of slavery and the redeeming of prisoners of war by their friends or their country.[14]

The precious blood of Christ (1:19). While sacrifice is common in the Old Testament and was practiced in most Mediterranean cultures, here there is probably a specific reference to the Passover sacrifice, which could be a goat, but was often a lamb. Like most sacrifices, it had to be without "blemish or defect," although this pairing of the two words is New Testament, not Old Testament. Naturally Christ is greater than the Passover since that animal was chosen on the tenth of Nisan (the Jewish month falling in the March–April period) and sacrificed on the fourteenth, while Jesus was "chosen before the creation of the world" and "revealed" a few decades earlier than this letter ("revealed" probably includes the whole complex of events—Jesus' incarnation, life, death, and resurrection). Jesus is thus the greater Passover.

Obeying the truth (1:22) is Peter's concept of turning to Christ. It comes across clearly in the commands in Acts 2:38 ("Peter replied, 'Repent and be baptized, every one of you, in the name of Jesus Christ for the forgiveness of your sins. And you will receive the gift of the Holy Spirit'"); 2:40; and 17:30 ("He [God] commands all people everywhere to repent").

Born again . . . of imperishable [seed] (1:23). This image expands on the idea of "new birth" (1:3) with a reference to the sperm (i.e., seed) of our Father (an image used in John 1:12; James 1:18; and 1 John 3:9). This is identified as "the living and enduring word of God," that is, the gospel message.

All men are like grass . . . but the word of the Lord stands forever (1:24–25). This quotation in 1:24–25 is from the Greek version of Isaiah 40:6b–8, a text that in Isaiah refers to human frailty versus the certainty of God's promise of redemption, using images drawn from the hot desert wind's withering the vegetation in its path. Peter is not the only New Testament writer to use this passage (cf. James 1:10–11), and it fits well in this context. While their experience of life under persecution might be that "the grass withers and the flowers fall," it is really their pagan persecutors who "are like grass," while they have been born of "the word of the Lord [that] stands forever." In an insecure world they have security through the power of the gospel.

Rid yourselves of all malice and all deceit, hypocrisy, envy, and slander of every kind (2:1). The vices listed are similar to the various vice catalogues in the New Testament (e.g., James 3:14–16: "bitter envy and selfish ambition. . . . For where you have envy and selfish ambi-

tion, there you find disorder and every evil practice") that stress anger, envy, and similar sins that destroy Christian community, rather than murder and sexual sins that were presumed to be issues only in their pre-Christian past (1 Cor. 6:9–10 and Gal. 5:19–21 do include sexual sins, because at least in Corinth they were issues for the Christian community). Paul mentions slander in 2 Corinthians 12:20 ("quarreling, jealousy, outbursts of anger, factions, slander, gossip, arrogance and disorder") and in Ephesians 4:31 ("Get rid of all bitterness, rage and anger, brawling and slander, along with every form of malice"), whereas James goes on to reject

REFLECTIONS

IN THE WESTERN WORLD OUR tendency is to look on new birth as an individual affair and salvation as a past possession, rather than viewing new birth as something that places us in a new family with a new Father and new brothers and sisters and salvation as a future goal. Could that be why the vices Peter mentions, which destroy the Christian family, are readily tolerated among us rather than being rejected in favor of sincere love?

▶ The Image of the Temple

The temple as a building appeared firm and unmovable in the New Testament Jewish world. Such a structure provided a picture of security to the persecuted Christians. It appealed to other Jewish groups as well. The Dead Sea Scroll 1QS 8:7 calls the council of the community a "precious cornerstone, whose foundations shall neither rock nor sway in their place," although the Targum on Isaiah 28 referred the cornerstone image to the king or the Messiah.

In our passage, a master mason, God, selects a stone, Jesus, that others have rejected (a reference to the crucifixion) and finds it just the stone for his building project. Jesus is the "cornerstone" (2:6) on which the building rests (thus the quotation is from Isa. 28:16, which Rom. 9:33 and Eph. 2:20 also use—this shows that the church as a whole, not just Peter, used these passages).

hypocrisy and anger by stressing the opposite virtue (James 3:17).

Like newborn babies, crave pure spiritual milk (2:2). The image of newborn babies fits with the references to "new birth" and divine "seed." Notice that "milk" does not mean the same here as it does in 1 Corinthians 3:2 and Hebrews 5:12–13. There it is a metaphor for the basics of the faith that Christians should grow beyond, while here it means spiritual teaching that one should never outgrow. This fact underlines the danger of defining a metaphorical term in one place by its use in another.

The living Stone (2:4). . . . You also, like living stones, are being built into a spiritual house (2:5) . . . a chosen and precious cornerstone (2:6). The image shifts from family to temple. Drawing on the phrase "Come to him" in the Greek version of Psalm 34:5, our author does not entirely leave the realm of people (the stones are living), but does shift the imagery to a temple (see "The Image of the Temple"). Jesus is as solid as the temple and thus security for those who trust in him, but he is a consternation and rock

in the way for those who reject him (using Ps. 118:22, where "cornerstone" may be the better translation than "capstone," and Isa. 8:14). Chaining together of commonly used texts (called *testamonia*) is a typical style of Jewish exegesis.

Jesus as the cornerstone, however, is only one side of the imagery of the temple. The Christians are also chosen by God and built into the walls alongside Jesus. (Such imagery was also used by Jewish groups; for example, the Dead Sea Scroll 1QS 5:6 describes that community as "a house of holiness for Israel.") The process is ongoing, for the church is still being built as more and more people obey Christ.

Holy priesthood, offering spiritual sacrifices (2:5). The imagery shifts from the solid, unmovable walls of the temple to the Christians as the priesthood within the temple. Readers of the Old Testament, whether Jew or Gentile, would be aware of the Aaronic priesthood. Furthermore, all of them had seen pagan priests, even though none may have seen the priests in Jerusalem. The Christians are priests because, unlike a building, people do something. What they do is offer, not physical sacrifices of incense and animals as in the Old Testament, but

FOUNDATION STONES

The foundation of the temple of Apollo at Delphi.

▼

spiritual sacrifices. (Peter does not specify what they are; the analogy of Hebrews 13:15–16 suggests that he is thinking of praise and charitable deeds)

A chosen people, a royal priesthood, a holy nation, a people belonging to God (2:9). This image is more specific than a general reference to Old Testament priesthood. Any of the readers familiar with the Old Testament would recognize the weaving together of Exodus 19:5–6 and Isaiah 43:20–21: ". . . out of all nations you will be my treasured possession. Although the whole earth is mine, you will be for me a kingdom of priests and a holy nation" and, "I provide water in the desert and streams in the wasteland, to give drink to my people, my chosen, the people I formed for myself that they may proclaim my praise." As other New Testament writers also do, Peter is calling these Gentile Christians by the titles God gave to Israel in the desert.[15] For him there are not two covenants, one for the Jews and another for Gentile Christians, but one covenant, which the Gentiles, who once "were not a people," have been brought into and made "the people of God" (1 Peter 2:10), while

---

▶ Household Duties

The phrase "Household Duties" or *Haustafel* (German for "Table of Household Duties") is used to refer to the descriptions of duties or household codes in the letters of Paul and in 1 Peter.[A-1] The bulk of this ethical teaching has to do with relationships within the household: husband–wife; father–children; master–slave. First Peter also includes a section on the relationship of the household to the state, whereas Paul discusses a similar topic in Romans 13 outside of the household duty structure.

The reason the authors include this material is that Christianity was viewed as subversive to the household and therefore to the good order of the city or state. That is, inviting wives, slaves, and children to believe in Christ whether or not the *pater familias* (male head of the household) did was clearly a rejection of his traditional authority to determine the religion of the whole household. These codes, then, make it clear that the traditional cultural submission of wives, slaves, and children is still valid, although it is now "in Christ" (as part of their overriding commitment to him and so limited by what he would approve of).

The codes also had another function insofar as Paul and Peter (1 Peter 3:7) described the ways the male household head should serve his wife, children, and slaves. This was not part of the traditional cultural teaching; it might even shock the male readers to hear that they had a responsibility to serve those whom they had learned should serve them. To hear that their wives were equal heirs of God's grace (3:7) or that they should behave towards them like Christ's giving his life for the good of the church (rather than as Christ ruling in heaven, Eph. 5:25) would have been a novel idea for most converts, one that turned their ideas of what was right order on its head. This, of course, is like what Jesus did to the idea of how a Messiah should behave. Paul and Peter are applying the teaching of Jesus to the household, not as a revolution from below but as a revolution from above. The one with power gives up power in the service of others, just as Jesus did.

So the *Haustafeln* had two roles. First, they reassured the Greco-Roman world that the church was not subversive of good order as defined by the culture. That is, they taught the women, slaves, and children to live out submission without compromising their allegiance to Christ. Second, they taught male heads of families to follow the example of Christ and lay aside their privileges for the good of those who were their underprivileged equals.[A-2]

those Jews and others who do not believe in Jesus stumble and fall from their natural heritage in the covenant.

How to Relate to Society so as to Minimize Persecution (2:11–4:11)

In the previous section Peter has clearly explained the Christians' identity. However, the non-Christian society around them remains a reality they must deal with. This next section, often referred to as an example of a Table of Household Duties, advises them on how to do this so as to minimize conflict.

Aliens and strangers (2:11). This phrase indicated their low status in this world. Foreigners were those who lacked the rights and privileges of citizens. Thus they were only a step above slaves, who lacked freedom and personhood. Yet in practice slaves of socially important masters would have received more respect than a foreigner.

Abstain from sinful desires (2:11). While many Greek philosophers, especially the Stoics, also saw "sinful (Greek "fleshly") desires" as the enemy of true virtue, in their view the body and its emotions and desires were evil *per se*. Peter follows the more Jewish view that human desires will lead one astray if they are not controlled by a higher principle, which for the Jew was the law. The strategy advised is that by controlling desire the pagans would see the Christians leading the lives of virtue that philosophers talked about, but that the people as a whole lacked the power to accomplish.

On the day he visits us (2:12). This clause means when God comes to judge (using the Old Testament image of God "visiting" in judgment and salvation, e.g., Jer. 15:15, "You understand, O LORD; remember me and care for me. Avenge me on my persecutors"). The pagans will have to admit then that God had been honored by his people's virtue.

The king, as the supreme authority (2:13). The first example of the "good deeds" mentioned in 2:12 is that of submitting to the ruling Caesar, or king, and his representatives. Whereas pagan authors often called for absolute obedience to the ruler, Peter conditions this submission by pointing out that it is "for the Lord's sake" and that the ruler is a humanly created authority ("authority instituted among men"), not a divine authority. Rulers often claimed divine appointment and even divine status (for most Roman emperors this was granted after death, although in some provinces the citizens began rites of worship while the emperor still lived).[16] Peter rejects this absolute right and points to an authority above the ruler for whose sake submission is given (and thus submission could not include anything which the Lord would not want) and the human origin of the government.

To punish those who do wrong and to commend those who do right (2:14).

The Roman governor was sent to a province to promote the order of Rome in that place. They usually spent the first part of their day hearing cases in order to punish evildoers (Mark 15:1, 25, are accurate pointers to the practice of dealing with such business early in the day). Peter asserts that this ideal of government is good. Yet everyone in the empire

knew that such justice was the ideal, not the reality of Roman emperors and governors. The emperor at the end of Peter's life was Nero, who, while starting off well enough, was the first emperor to persecute Christians. The governors were the Roman proconsuls (Senatorial provinces) or procurators (imperial provinces) appointed by Rome, whom even some Romans (e.g. the emperor Tiberius) realized enriched themselves through graft.[17] However, whether or not the person's character deserved it, showing proper respect would "silence the ignorant talk of foolish" people, for some non-believers looked on the Christian movement as a seditious movement that was undermining the good order of the empire.

Slaves, submit yourselves to your masters with all respect (2:18). The slaves, the second example Peter gives, was not viewed as a moral person, but rather as one who was simply to obey unquestioningly. Thus even in addressing them

Peter is raising their status. The slaves had few rights and could be treated by their masters arbitrarily. Thus the dichotomy of "good and considerate" and "those who are harsh" was a known part of life. While some slaves were treated well and were educated at the master's expense, a slave could also be abused or beaten for little or no reason. Thus it was quite possible that a slave would "suffer for doing good." Furthermore, the slave, unlike the Roman citizen, could be crucified. Thus Peter urges them to identify with Jesus, who also suffered the extreme penalty, which was so shameful that Roman writers would rarely mention it.[18]

"He committed no sin, and no deceit was found in his mouth" (2:22). The example of Christ is cited from Isaiah 53:9. Peter alludes to this passage in Isaiah several more times: he "bore our sins in his body on the tree" (2:24) = Isaiah 53:5, 12; "he made no threats" (2:23) = Isaiah 53:7; "you were like sheep going astray" (2:25) = Isaiah 53:6. It is identification with Jesus that gives dignity to their suffering.

Shepherd and Overseer (2:25). This image of Christ comes from Ezekiel 34:11–16, which begins, "For this is what the Sovereign LORD says: I myself will search for my sheep and look after them." Peter will pick up the image again in 5:1–4, applying it to church leadership.

Wives, in the same way be submissive to your husbands (3:1). Peter's third example of doing good is addressed to the wives of non-Christian husbands (the whole focus of the passage is evangelistic). Wives in most of the Roman Empire were expected to adhere to the religion of their husbands. Christianity was viewed as subversive in that it invited women to

◀ *left*

"FREEDOM"

A *libertas* coin celebrating freedom in the Roman empire.

commit themselves to Jesus whether or not their husbands approved. By being generally "submissive to [their] husbands" they would be living up to pagan virtue, although their submission was not to extend to disobedience to Christ, such as doing immoral acts or worshiping pagan gods (how would that show either "purity" or "reverence"?). Our author expected that such exemplary behavior would mean that the husbands would "be won over without words by the behavior of their wives." Since husbands were often significantly older than their wives (the Roman ideal was a man of thirty marrying a woman of fifteen), as well as better educated, this nonverbal approach to evangelism was appropriate.

Not . . . from outward adornment, such as braided hair and the wearing of gold jewelry and fine clothes (3:3). Since men often displayed their wealth and social status in the dress of their wives, some "outward adornment" might be the wishes of a husband and thus an expression of submission. Yet both Jewish and pagan writers often advised men to prohibit their wives from dressing up.[19] The Jewish *Testament of Reuben* 5:5 states: ". . .order your wives and your daughters not to adorn their heads and their appearances so as to deceive men's sound minds." With this sentiment the Stoics Seneca and Epictetus agreed.[20] Epictetus said:

> Immediately after they are fourteen [i.e., at puberty, when they were eligible for marriage], women are called "ladies" by men. So when they see that they have nothing else but only to be the bedfellows of men, they begin to beautify themselves, and put all their hopes in that. It is worth while for us to take pains,

therefore, to make them understand that they are honored for nothing else but only for appearing modest and self-respecting.[21]

This same idea was probably a frequent teaching in the churches, as 1 Timothy 2:9 uses almost identical language. What is clear is that such teaching applied only to upper-class women, whose husbands sometimes approved of their attending synagogue or church as a possible morally uplifting, harmless indulgence in a foreign superstition. Lower-class women and slaves often had only a single set of clothing and no jewelry at all. Note that the form of this statement is wisdom teaching, not law. Peter is not saying that women should never wear jewelry, but that virtue rather than adornment should be their focus.

A gentle and quiet spirit (3:4). "Gentle" means an amiable friendliness in contrast to roughness, bad temper, or brusqueness. These virtues were also valued in women by pagan writers.[22] "Quiet" (also appearing in the NT in 1 Tim. 2:2) is the opposite of restless, rebellious, or insubordinate. Thus up to this point Peter has not said

right ▶

BRAIDED HAIR

Julia Domina, the second wife of the emperor Severus (A.D. 193–211).

anything that a pagan moralist might not have said. He is advising women to live up to the best common morality of their day. It is only when he mentions the worth of this virtue "in God's sight" and goes on to refer to "the holy women of the past," meaning Hebrew and Jewish heroines of the faith, that Peter gives a motivation that goes beyond the best of pagan ethics. Christians live up to the best of their culture, but for better reasons.

Sarah, who obeyed Abraham and called him her master (3:6). This refers to Genesis 18:12, "After I am worn out and my master is old, will I now have this pleasure?" The Hebrew word for "master" (*'adonai*) can mean that, but it is also a typical Hebrew word for husband ("husband" is probably the better translation in Genesis). In the Greek version of the Old Testament, *'adonai* was translated by *kyrios*, a word meaning "sir," "master," or "lord," which allows Peter to make his point that Sarah thought of her husband respectfully (even if in Genesis she is laughing at God's promise when she does so).

Do not give way to fear (3:6). The allusion is to Proverbs 3:25–26 ("Have no fear of sudden disaster or of the ruin that overtakes the wicked, for the LORD will be your confidence and will keep your foot from being snared"), which uses two of the same Greek words as 1 Peter 3:6. Husbands then as now might try to intimidate their wives into giving up the faith or otherwise disobeying Jesus. The same Lord for whose sake they were generally submissive is the Lord, whom no threat or intimidation could keep them from obeying.

Be considerate as you live with your wives, and treat them with respect as the weaker partner and as heirs with you of the gracious gift of life (3:7). When he turns briefly to husbands, Peter makes the assumption that their wives are Christians ("heirs with you of the gracious gift of life"), for normally a pagan wife would follow her husband into his new belief. Rather than use his socially sanctioned power, the husband is to "be considerate" (lit., "live knowledgeably") and "treat [her] with respect," which is normally what one did to a person to whom one owed respect and deference. Here "considerate" means to recognize the one who is "weaker" (following both Jewish and pagan observations that women were physically weaker than men and thus vulnerable).[23] Notice that the New Testament never follows the pagan idea that women were weaker in mind or morally inferior to men. One treats her with respect by recognizing her as an equal in every way (lit., "fellow heir with you").

So that nothing will hinder your prayers (3:7). This clause may refer to the Old Testament teaching that God is the protector of the weak.[24] Peter implies that because of this God will not hear the prayers of one who is taking advantage of the vulnerability of his wife.

REFLECTIONS

IN HIS INSTRUCTIONS FOR THE CHRISTIAN HOUSEHOLD, Peter demonstrates a willingness to fit the cultural values of his day (e.g., those of marriage and slavery) insofar as they do not violate allegiance to Christ. Do we have the same willingness today, neither clinging onto values that society used to hold but no longer does, nor separating from society over values that are part of our Christian subculture rather than truly a matter of allegiance to Christ? Would this make it clear to our society what being a Christian really means and thus assist the witness of the church?

137

1 Peter

Live in harmony with one another; be sympathetic, love as brothers, be compassionate and humble (3:8). The summary list of virtues in 3:8 binds the community together, as a similar list bound the people of the Dead Sea Scrolls together: "a spirit of humility, patience, abundant charity, unending goodness . . . great charity towards all the sons of truth" (1QS 4:3ff.). Thus there are Jewish precedents for these virtues.

Do not repay evil with evil or insult with insult, but with blessing, because to this you were called so that you may inherit a blessing (3:9). This teaching of nonretaliation because one is aware of God's coming reward recalls Jesus' teaching: "Blessed are those who are persecuted because of righteousness, for theirs is the kingdom of heaven" (Matt. 5:10). This is amplified in 5:11 (which adds the idea of insult) and then even more in 5:38–48. Peter follows up the allusion to Jesus by quoting Psalm 34:13–17 in the next three verses. He has already cited Psalm 34:8 in 1 Peter 2:3 (Heb. 6:5 cites it as well), so this psalm was clearly a favorite in the early church. The psalmist is concerned with long life on earth, but in Peter's context it refers to the eternal life and heavenly inheritance he mentioned in chapter 1.

But even if you should suffer for what is right, you are blessed (3:14). This too is an allusion to the teaching of Jesus in Matthew 5:10 (see above), for suffering vocabulary usually refers to persecution and "for what is right" is equivalent to "righteousness."

"Do not fear what they fear; do not be frightened" (3:14). Peter cites the Greek version of Isaiah 8:12–13. In the Old Tes-tament this refers to the fear of the Aram-Israel alliance (Kings Rezin and Pekah), who planned to remove Ahaz from the throne of Judah in order to place someone there who would join them in their alliance against Assyria. In 1 Peter the statement refers to fear of persecutors.

In your hearts set apart Christ as Lord (3:15). This instruction also comes from Isaiah 8:13, "The LORD Almighty is the one you are to regard as holy, he is the one you are to fear, he is the one you are to dread." The quotation is shifted from God to Christ by changing two words found in the Greek version of Isaiah.[25] In the Isaiah context it is part of a promise of salvation, and this is implicit in 1 Peter as well. Rather than fear people, Christians are to answer them confidently, although also "with gentleness" (a virtue of wives in 3:4 above, now to be part of every Christian life) "and respect," a point sometimes forgotten by modern apologists.

Be prepared to give an answer (3:15). This instruction likely depends on the teaching of Jesus in places like Luke 12:4–12, but Jews also taught similarly: R. Eleazar said, "Be alert to study the Law and know how to make an answer to the unbeliever" (*m. ᵓAbot* 2:14).

Those who speak maliciously against your good behavior in Christ may be ashamed of their slander (3:16). The shame refers to shame at final judgment. Christians were slandered as "haters of humankind" (because they would not go to pagan festivals and parties), traitors to the state (because they called Christ and not Caesar Lord and also because they refused to worship the genius of the emperor), and immoral (because in pagan eyes their warm love for their "brothers and sisters" was thought to be sexual and it was even rumored that they ate flesh and drank blood at their meals, which was thought to have come from infants they had slaughtered).[26]

Later (A.D.177) Athenagoras states in his *Legatio pro Christianis* 3, "Three things are alleged against us: atheism, Thyestean feasts, Oedipodian intercourse." Atheism came from their not worshiping the various Greco-Roman deities; Thyestean feasts showed a belief that they ate real human flesh and drank human blood; and Oedipodian intercourse indicated the belief that they had sexual intercourse with their "brothers and sisters."

Christ died for sins ... the righteous for the unrighteous (3:18). The idea that something dies for sins is common in the Old Testament in sacrificial contexts, e.g., Leviticus 5:7, "If he cannot afford a lamb, he is to bring two doves or two young pigeons to the LORD as a penalty for his sin—one for a sin offering and the other for a burnt offering" (the "as a penalty for his sin" is the same in the Greek version of the Old Testament as "for sins" in 1 Peter 3:18). In saying "the righteous for the unrighteous" Peter again reminds his readers of Isaiah 53, this time 53:11: "After the suffering of his soul, he will see the light of life and be satisfied; by his knowledge my righteous servant will justify many, and he will bear their iniquities." Peter's point, of course, is not simply that his readers identify with Jesus' suffering, but that they see that he went through suffering to exaltation.

▶ The Spirits and Genesis 6

Who are the "spirits in prison" in 1 Peter 3:19? Some argue that these are human spirits from the people who died in Noah's day. However, in the New Testament "spirit" by itself never refers to a human spirit. When a human being is referred to, the word is always qualified, such as a "man's spirit" in 1 Corinthians 2:11. Normally humans existing apart from the body are called "souls" (as in Rev. 6:9). Therefore it is probable that this passage refers to nonhuman spiritual beings.

According to the text, these spirits existed and "disobeyed ... in the days of Noah." Elsewhere the Bible refers three times to beings who fit this description: Genesis 6:1–2; 2 Peter 2:4–5; Jude 6. The two New Testament passages refer to Genesis 6, "When men began to increase in number on the earth and daughters were born to them, the sons of God saw that the daughters of men were beautiful, and they married any of them they chose." While the Old Testament does not refer to the fate of these beings, both 2 Peter and Jewish tradition do.

For example, *1 Enoch* describes the fall of the angels in chapter 6 and their imprisonment in chapter 10. Then Enoch intercedes for them in chapters 12–13, which intercession is rejected. Then in chapter 21 he says, "And I came to an empty place. And I saw there neither a heaven above nor an earth below, but a chaotic and terrible place. And there I saw seven stars of heaven [angels are called stars, angels, spirits or Watchers in *1 Enoch*] bound together in it ...I said, 'For what sin are they bound ... ?' Then one of the holy angels ... spoke to me and said to me ... 'These are among the stars of heaven which have transgressed the commandments of the Lord and are bound in this place until the completion of ten million years....'" Enoch goes on and sees a worse place and is told, "'This place is the prison house of the angels; they are detained here forever.'" The location of the prison is not always specified in Jewish tradition, but some traditions locate it in the second heaven,[A-3] which would be appropriate for 1 Peter if Jesus' ascension is in view.

Was put to death in the body but made alive by the Spirit (3:18). This is not the best translation. Better would be: "He was put to death from the point of view of the physical world, but made alive from the point of view of the spiritual world." That is, 1 Peter is making a distinction between the present state and the resurrection state, similar to what Paul makes in 1 Corinthians 15:35–57.

Went and preached to the spirits in prison (3:19). It was "in this resurrection state" (a better translation than "through whom") that Jesus "went and preached to the spirits in prison." As to the identity of these spirits, see "The Spirits and Genesis 6." Wherever this prison is located, Peter is referring to Jesus' resurrection proclamation of triumph, vindicating the justice of God and sealing the fate of the fallen angels as he ascends into heaven.

God waited patiently in the days of Noah while the ark was being built. . . . In it only a few people, eight in all, were saved (3:20). This refers to Genesis 5:32; 7:6, which are often interpreted as indicating that the ark took a hundred years to build, and to 6:18; 7:7; 8:15, which all refer to Noah, his wife, his three sons, and their wives. The ark itself was a rectangular box 450 x 75 x 45 feet, containing three decks. There was ventilation at the top under the roof.

This water symbolizes baptism that now saves you also (3:21). The salvation in the ark is compared to baptism as practiced in Peter's day. In baptism the person officially pledged his or her commitment to Christ and therefore was only considered a Christian afterward. It was the official moment of salvation, much as we today consider persons married only after they have publicly pledged their commitment to one another, no matter how much they have pledged their commitment privately. Peter makes it clear that it is the sincere pledge, "the pledge of a good conscience," that saves, not simply the action of the water on the body. Furthermore, the power is found in "the resurrection of Jesus Christ."

He who has suffered in his body is done with sin (4:1). The principle itself is clear in Jesus' life, which forms the background for this whole passage. Once Jesus died, all of his dealings with sin were over. He could no longer be touched by it. It is also true for the Christian, for the choice of the path of suffering for Christ is at the same time a choice against sin.

He does not live the rest of his earthly life for evil human desires, but rather for the will of God (4:2). The word "evil" is not part of the Greek text. It may be implied, or Peter may be noting that even legitimate human desires are no longer primary motivations if one is choosing suffering in the will of God over against possible physical comfort by compromising the faith.

Debauchery, lust, drunkenness, orgies, carousing and detestable idolatry (4:3). Again 1 Peter refers to the fact that his addressees are pagan converts, not Jewish Christians, when he refers to their former life: Jews were known for neither orgies nor idolatry. This list is a stylized list of Jewish and Christian critique of paganism rather than giving specific examples of what these Christians had done in their pagan life. We see this in that (1) many pagan philosophers also condemned these same vices (except idolatry, which was approved, at least when it showed allegiance to family and the state), (2) Jews had long made similar condemnations of pagans and paganizing Jews (e.g., *Testament of Moses* 7:3–10), and (3) only wealthier citizens could indulge in some of these things—the poor lived hand-to-mouth without extra income. Still, popular culture did not condemn such things.

They think it strange that you do not plunge with them into the same flood of dissipation (4:4). The Christian did not show up at the trade guild banquet in the temple of the patron deity, did not celebrate a family festival (also often in a pagan temple), did not celebrate national festivals, and did not attend some parties. Such behavior was considered so "unnatural" that the Christians must be against their family, trade, or city, devoid of human feelings and enjoyment, even a "hater of humanity."

Him who is ready to judge the living and the dead (4:5). This is a Jewish designation of God, as the rabbinic citation in *m. ʾAbot* 4:22 shows, "It is [God] that shall judge. . . . You shall hereafter give account and reckoning before the King of Kings, the Holy One, blessed be he."

The gospel was preached even to those who are now dead (4:6). These dead are not the imprisoned spirits of 3:19, but rather Christians who have died. As Christ was judged, human beings judge them in the physical world (a better translation than "in regard to the body"). They judge them either by killing them, as they did Christ, or by condemning their lifestyle and concluding at their death that their Christianity did not keep them from the common lot of humanity.

Since there is little evidence of martyrdom in 1 Peter, such mockery is more likely what he is talking about, although actual martyrdom was not far off. Yet human beings do not have the last word: God does. As Jesus was resurrected "from the point of view of the spiritual world" (cf. 3:18), so they will "live according to God" in this spiritual world. The final verdict is God's resurrection.

The end of all things is near (4:7). While most Christians of the first generation expected the return of Christ and the end of the age within their lifetime, the clause itself refers to the idea that Jesus inaugurated the last stage of human history. Therefore the next major event on God's timetable was the final end of the age.

Clear minded and self-controlled (4:7). These were virtues that pagans as well as Christians admired. As in Romans 12:3 ("think of yourself with sober judgment, in accordance with the measure of faith God has given you"), this means a proper view of self and an avoidance of intoxication. A good, clear mind is presented as the best foundation for prayer.

DISSIPATION

This *amphoriskos* depicts a Roman orgiastic party.

Love covers over a multitude of sins (4:8). Proper relationships ("Love each other deeply") within the Christian community were important to Peter. Here he cites Proverbs 10:12, which was proverbial in the early church. By love our author is thinking of forgiving one another. He is not concerned about emotional feelings about other Christians, but rather concrete acts of kindness.

Offer hospitality (4:9). Hospitality meant offering food and lodging to traveling Christians. This was an important Jewish virtue centuries before Jesus.[27] In fact, later Jews would point to Abraham's receiving the travelers in Genesis 18:2–5 as evidence of his virtue,[28] and Job protests his virtue by saying, "The stranger has not lodged in the street; I have opened my doors to the traveler" (Job 31:32 NRSV). While there were some practical aspects to this (what inns there were in the Roman world were often associated with immoral behavior), the main idea was that a traveler was away from his or her family and clan and thus vulnerable. Offering food and housing was both an act of charity and an offer of protection in the home of one who belonged in the city.

Gift he [or she] has received . . . God's grace in its various forms (4:10). The early church believed the coming of the Spirit was the mark of the new age. One way one recognized the presence of the Spirit was by his or her gifts. All descriptions of spiritual gifts are *ad hoc* lists, examples given to fit the purpose of the author. So while Paul in 1 Corinthians 12 lists teaching, prophecy, and tongues as verbal gifts and only mentions administration, miracles, and healing as serving gifts, in Romans 12 encouraging appears

as a verbal gift, and serving, contributing, and showing mercy appear in the serving category. Peter never tells us in this letter which gifts he might stress, for he gives only two categories, the one who "speaks" and the one who "serves." In this he divides gifts as Luke says that Peter did in Acts 6:2, where "word of God" is contrasted with "wait[ing] on tables."[29]

To him be the glory and the power for ever and ever. Amen (4:11). Doxologies punctuate 1 Peter (the other one is in 5:11) and occur throughout the New Testament as the closings to sections of letters.[30] They are, of course, also common in Revelation.

How to Live in a Context of Persecution (4:12–5:11)

Dear friends (4:12). This word (*agapētoi*, "beloved") is an indication that a new section of the letter, the closing of the body, is beginning. It is more a formal statement than an expression of a special relationship.

Painful trial (4:12). A more literal translation would be "fiery trial." Some believe that this refers to the burning of some Christians in Rome under Nero:

> Accordingly, an arrest was first made of all who confessed; then, upon their information, an immense multitude was convicted, not so much of the crime of arson [since Nero claimed the Christians were responsible for the great fire in Rome], as of hatred of the human race. Mockery of every sort was added to their deaths. Covered with the skins of beasts, they were torn by dogs and perished, or were nailed to crosses, or were doomed to the flames. These served to illuminate the night

when daylight failed. Nero had thrown open his gardens for the spectacle, and was exhibiting a show in the circus, while he mingled with the people in the dress of a charioteer or drove about in a chariot.[31]

There is no evidence that this persecution extended to the provinces where the recipients of this letter lived. It appears to have been confined to Rome. Moreover, 1 Peter never refers to the death of Christians, but to their suffering.

▶ Persecution in the Early Church Period

In the first decades of the church's existence it quickly became clear that the church differed from the surrounding culture and that the culture did not like it, whether this culture was Jewish or Greco-Roman. This displeasure was expressed in a number of ways: (1) commands and threats (Acts 4:17, 21); (2) physical punishment (5:40); (3) fines and confiscation of goods (17:9; Heb. 10:34); (4) imprisonment (Acts 16:23–24); (5) mob violence and lynching (7:57–58); and (6) judicial execution (12:1–4). Along with these came public shaming and insults (Heb. 10:33; 1 Peter 4:4) and economic discrimination (part of the background of James). Christians did not fit in, and the surrounding culture was prepared to use all of the means at its disposal to force them to return to cultural conformity. While execution, particularly judicial execution, was apparently rare (e.g., Rev. 2:13 names only one martyr and 2:10 mentions prison, not execution) and often localized when it happened (e.g., Nero did execute Christians in the 64–68 period, but we only hear of executions in Rome), the other forms of persecution were certainly painful and at times even worse than execution (e.g., economic discrimination and confiscation of goods and property could lead to slow starvation if other members of the church did not share with those experiencing the loss). Execution became more common in the second and third centuries, but still remained sporadic and localized, affecting relatively small numbers of Christians.

What did the church do to "deserve" such treatment? (1) They refused to take part in the normal worship life of the household, city, or state. To their fellow citizens this implied a lack of loyalty and a rebellious spirit, an undermining of good order.

(2) They refused to take part in family celebrations, guild feasts, and other social events, because of the connection of such events to idolatry or immoral behavior. This led to stigmatizing the Christians as antisocial, "haters of humanity," and the like. (3) There was the Christian critique of their culture: the claim that the Messiah had come and been executed by the Jewish leaders (in the Jewish world) or the claim that the lifestyle of the people was immoral and/or that idols were meaningless (in the Greco-Roman world). (4) There were specific Christian practices (their acceptance of Gentiles, their "stealing" the Gentile "God-fearers," their gathering together in "secret" societies, their treating one another as brother and sister across class, gender, and racial lines). (5) There were false rumors about the Christians (they encouraged Jews not to circumcise their children; they ate the flesh and drank the blood of babies at their ritual meals; they held orgies behind closed doors, calling them "love feasts"; they caused riots everywhere they went). (6) They claimed that Jesus was Lord, while Caesar claimed to be the only Lord. Add to these six elements normal human suspicion, fear of loss of power in the face of a growing movement, and general jealousy, and one gets a ripe climate for all types of persecution.

Christians responded to this treatment with patient endurance, with explanations (both informal and in court situations) of their real beliefs and practices, with flight to other cities, and with communal support for those who were suffering. In doing this they modeled their response on the teaching of Jesus (e.g., "flee to the next city") and the example of Jesus.[A-4]

Therefore he is referring to the sharp persecution that the whole community is experiencing—fierce and painful as fire, but not literally fire.

Something strange were happening (4:12). It is not as if God had lost control or persecution was not supposed to happen to Christians. They agreed with Jewish writers that it is to be expected. Jesus ben Sira taught, for example, "My child, when you come to serve the Lord, prepare yourself for testing. Set your heart right and be steadfast, and do not be impetuous in time of calamity. . . . For gold is tested in the fire, and those found acceptable [to God] in the furnace of humiliation" (Sir. 2:1–5).

Participate in the sufferings of Christ (4:13). This imitation of Christ is frequently cited in the New Testament, whether in terms of personal example (Col. 1:24) or an example to follow (Phil. 2:5–11). It builds on Jesus' frequent command to "follow me." In a Jewish context to follow a rabbi meant not just to travel with him, but also learn his teaching and copy his lifestyle. In fact, the rabbi's lifestyle was an important part of the teaching (*halakah*, which refers to how one lives). It is not a surprise, then, that Paul and Peter would be so insistent that our lives should be patterned on that of Jesus.

Rejoice (4:13). See the comments on 1:6 (cf. James 1:2). One rejoices, not because one enjoys persecution, but because being joined to Christ in persecution is a sign of being joined to him "when his glory is revealed," that is, in his second coming. This is based on Jesus' teaching, such as Luke 6:22–23: "Blessed are you when men hate you, when they exclude you and insult you and reject your name as evil, because of the Son of Man. Rejoice in that day and leap for joy, because great is your reward in heaven. For that is how their fathers treated the prophets."

If you are insulted because of the name of Christ (4:14). Christians were originally called followers of "the Way" or disciples of Jesus of Nazareth. It was only in Antioch that they were called Christians (Acts 11:26)—which is the Jewish term *Messiah* ("anointed one") translated in Greek as "Christ." However, since this term was not a title for Greek-speakers as "Messiah" was for many Jews, it was taken as a proper name and followers of Christ were called Christians, those belonging to Christ. It was therefore under this name that they were persecuted.

The Spirit of glory and of God (4:14). Jesus promised that the Holy Spirit would rest on them, his followers, when they were persecuted: "Whenever you are arrested and brought to trial, do not worry beforehand about what to say. Just say whatever is given you at the time, for it is not you speaking, but the Holy Spirit" (Mark 13:11), or "the Holy Spirit will teach you at that time what you should say" (Luke 12:12). Acts reports that Stephen was full of the Spirit (Acts 6:15; 7:55), so the presence of the Spirit might lead to execution, not deliverance. Peter refers to the "Spirit of glory" in that (1) this contrasts with the insults they are receiving, and (2) it (along with "of God") points to the future that they will experience (cf. 1 Peter 1:7; 5:4; cf. Col. 3:4).

A meddler (4:15). This is a person who sticks her or his nose into other people's affairs (which would include an overzealous witness). The word appears here for the first time in Greek. It is later writers that make its meaning clear.

Suffer as a Christian (4:16). The quotation cited on 4:11 indicated that Christians were accused as criminals, but that the real basis for the accusation was their Christian commitment. Thus Peter is talking about the real basis of the charges, not the actual charge against them.

Do not be ashamed, but praise God that your bear that name (4:16). In that culture any public accusation and punishment

▸ Honor/Shame and Its Meaning

In the world of which the New Testament is a part, honor and shame were the chief motivating values. Honor is a publicly acknowledged claim to value or worth; shame is the diminishing of such public worth. A person would be born into a family with a given level of honor according to the social status of the family and the behavior of the individuals in the family. The child would end up either maintaining that honor against challenges through acts of courage, generosity, or wisdom, or would diminish his own honor and that of his family through cowardice, lack of generosity, foolishness, and the like. For instance, when Paul speaks of his escape from Damascus, he speaks of it in terms of shame or weakness, for he did not display courage or valor, for example, by fighting to the death in the gate of Damascus (2 Cor. 11:30–33). As a Christian, however, Paul had a different value system. His non-Christian social values included racial purity and religious achievement (2 Cor. 11:22; Phil. 3:5–6), as well as courage and strength when suffering (2 Cor. 11:23–29). However, he put such values ("boasting") aside and instead pointed to shameful things ("weakness") as his badge of "honor" (2 Cor. 12:5, 9), for in that Christ's power and Christ's relationship to him were demonstrated (Phil. 3:7–11). In other words, his new sense of honor was drawn from relationship with Christ, who had been shamed in this world but honored by God.

This sense of honor and shame is not only in Paul, but is also apparent in Hebrews, 1 Peter, and elsewhere in the New Testament. In Hebrews, even though Christ was shamed by human beings (Heb. 12:2) he has superior honor to the various aspects of Judaism. Thus by identifying with Jesus, the readers will (1) be associated with the superior honor of Christ and (2) honor the God who so honored Christ (rather than insult or shame God and receive the consequences).

In 1 Peter the readers are being shamed by their neighbors (words like "abuse," "insult," and "slander" are used), but it is these neighbors who will receive shame at the final judgment (1 Peter 3:16). The readers' faith, however, will bring them honor when Christ returns (1:7), not shame (2:6). It is they who have the honorable titles given them by God (2:9).

In both Hebrews and 1 Peter, then, there is an attempt to reverse honor-shame valuations given by the outside culture. In Hebrews Christ is not less honorable than Judaism (which is what a return to Judaism would imply), but more honorable. In 1 Peter the believers are not shameful (as their fellow citizens claim), but honorable, and it is those "honorable" (in the eyes of this world) fellow citizens who are heading toward shame when Christ appears.

Thus, while North American society appears guilt motivated (internal feelings predominate), the society of the early church period was honor–shame motivated (external valuations were most important). The surrounding society used shame as a major weapon of persecution (and especially in the cross, where the shaming was as significant as the execution), and the New Testament writers argued for a reversal of values, showing that Christ and the Christians were in fact the more honorable.[A-5]

would bring shame, so it is significant that Peter reframes the situation and tells the believer to feel proud ("praise God") rather than experience shame.

For it is time for judgment to begin with the family of God (4:17). The suffering the believers are experiencing is a type of purifying fire, a judgment. That God judges his children was well known to Jews: "For the Lord first judges Israel for the wrong she has committed and then he shall do the same for all the nations" (*T. Benj.* 100:8–9). The form of argument used here, "if this is so, how much more will that be so," was frequently used by Jewish writers. It was called qal wᵃhomer or "light and heavy," as early as the time of Jesus (i.e., it is one of the seven hermeneutical rules of Hillel).

If it is hard for the righteous to be saved, what will become of the ungodly and the sinner? (4:18). Peter quotes the Greek translation of Proverbs 11:31 (which differs significantly from the Hebrew) to use Scripture for what he said in the previous verse.

Commit themselves to their faithful Creator (4:19). While this is the only New Testament place in which God is called "Creator" (a central teaching of the Old Testament), Jesus himself viewed God's creative activity as evidence that he could be trusted (Matt. 6:25–33; 10:29–31). More important, this passage in 1 Peter echoes Psalm 31:5: "Into your hands I commit my spirit; redeem me, O LORD, the God of truth." Jesus in his greatest persecution used a phrase from this verse in Luke 23:46.

The elders among you (5:1). The typical Jewish community, whether a village or a synagogue, was led by elders—honorable senior members of the community (one could be an older member of the community but lack honor because of shameful behavior at some time in one's life). Many pagan communities were also led by the senior members, whether one thinks of the *pater familas* (senior adult male, normally the father or elder brother of the other adult males) running the Roman family or village councils. The early church adopted the Jewish structure (e.g., Acts 11:30; 14:23; 15:2). Generally the elders or overseers (an alternative term, indicating function rather than seniority) led a city-wide church, irrespective of the number of house churches within the area. For example, Jerusalem had many house churches to accommodate the large number of believers, but we never read of more than one body of elders. Likewise Philippians 1:1 points to one group of leaders in a mature church. Titus 1:5 instructs Titus to appoint elders in every town, without any indication he should appoint multiple groups if the town was large. This structure is probably the reason the local bishop (in the second century) developed before the local church pastor (in the sixth century).

Peter assumes that the churches he is writing to are led by elders. While in 1:1

R E F L E C T I O N S

FIRST-CENTURY CHRISTIANS COULD "REJOICE" DESPITE persecution because of their strong belief in the return of Christ and coming reward. Christians today appear focused on present happiness and success as a result of being Christian. Therefore there is a reluctance to take risks. What would it take to return to the church, not just a doctrine about the future, but a living expectation of the future strong enough to die for?

he has called himself an apostle, here he terms himself "a fellow elder," that is, a person who like them must lead the church.

Be shepherds of God's flock . . . serving as overseers (5:2). The image of the shepherd for the leaders of God's people goes back to the Old Testament. In Ezekiel 34 it applies to leaders who have failed, when God says, "Prophesy against the shepherds of Israel" (Ezek. 34:2). Yet the Jews always remembered that Moses and David were shepherds before they were chosen to lead Israel. These two became the image of the faithful leader, modeled on that of God ("The LORD is my shepherd" [Ps. 23:1]). The elders are to walk in this tradition, overseeing the "flock" (we notice that the "overseer" function is clearly indicated).

Because you are willing (5:2). The elder could easily feel he had to take up the office because he was the senior person in the community, but he might resent it because of its duties and because it exposed him to greater persecution.

Not greedy for money (5:2). Because the elders normally were not paid but still had oversight over the charity funds, an attitude of service rather than a desire for money was imperative. First Timothy 5:17–18 teaches that some elders should be paid (the Greek term for "honor" can also mean "pay" [cf. the English "honorarium"]; "double" in biblical literature often means "full," thus "full pay"). Yet even if that were sometimes the norm for certain elders throughout the church, the part-time elders in many areas would have continued unpaid.

Not lording it over those entrusted to you (5:3). The models of leadership in the Roman world were those of hierarchical structure in which the leaders gave orders and those under them obeyed (as Jesus notes in Mark 10:42 and the centurion states in Matt. 8:9). Peter rejects this hierarchical model and instead instructs the elders to be "examples to the flock," leading by modeling rather than by commanding. This fits the picture of the Palestinian shepherd walking in front of the flock and calling the sheep to come after him or her.

Chief Shepherd (5:4). This title for Jesus is taken from the picture of God in Psalm 23 as well as from sayings of Jesus, such as those in John 10 (e.g., "I am the good shepherd," 10:11).

SHEPHERD

A modern Syrian shepherd with his sheep.

Crown of glory (5:4). This Chief Shepherd returns as an official with high authority. That is, one would expect the Chief Shepherd to give wages to his undershepherds, and "will receive" *is* the language for receiving wages. But this Chief Shepherd gives for wages what a high official might give, "the crown of glory," such as was given to the victorious general after a battle (e.g., to wear in a triumphal procession, when such an honor was granted to him) or the winning athletes in the games. Those crowns, however, were laurel leaves and would fade. The crown for the elders will never fade, so is perhaps thought of as made of a precious metal.

Young men ... be submissive to those who are older (5:5). Submission was an appropriate cultural virtue that all segments of the culture would have approved of. In this case, however, it fits the situation of persecution, for younger men, especially if unmarried, tend to be more radical and in a tense situation need to listen to the seasoned wisdom of the elders.

Humility toward one another (5:5). This command is based on Proverbs 3:34, which is also quoted in a similar context in James 4:6–10. It broadens the submission to the whole community and not only preserves the internal unity of the church, but it is also the basis for the proper response to persecution.

Cast all your anxiety on him (5:7). This instruction may be based on teachings of Jesus, such as Matthew 6:25–34: If God cares for the birds and clothes the lilies,

what is the Christian worrying about? The teaching is another that fits well in the situation of persecution.

Be self-controlled and alert (5:8). First Peter has twice before called for self-control (1:13; 4:7), a virtue valued in his world. Now he combines it with being "alert," a term referring to a soldier on watch. Jesus used this word for alertness as the end approaches.[32]

Your enemy the devil prowls around like a roaring lion looking for someone to devour (5:8). The term "the devil" is Greek for "accuser" and the equivalent for the Hebrew "Satan." While the Old Testament has relatively little to say about the devil (and only speaks of him by name in the later books), intertestamental Judaism was well aware of him, as is the New Testament.[33] Job 1:7 speaks of the devil roaming around, while the picture of a roaring lion comes from Psalm 22:13. "Devour" refers to swallowing in one gulp, as the fish did to Jonah. Certainly this picture presents a good reason to be alert!

Resist him, standing firm in the faith (5:9). This was apparently a common teaching in the church. In James 4:7, as here, one is to "resist" the devil. In James the means of resistance are not noted, but here they are clearly stated. The devil devours by getting a person to renounce or compromise his or her faith; standing firm in one's commitment is an act of resistance.

Restore you and make you strong, firm and steadfast (5:10). Restoration has to do with the production of character; "strong" means strong in faith, underlined by the rare word "firm." The final word,

▶

"LIKE A ROARING LION..."

"steadfast," means "placed on a solid foundation."

To him be the power for ever and ever. Amen (5:11). This is an abbreviation of the doxology in 4:11. The final "Amen" is an untranslated Aramaic or Hebrew word meaning "sure," which along with other untranslated expressions like "Hallelujah" and "Maranatha" have passed into the church's liturgical language. "Amen" is a response something like "Yes!" or "So be it!"

Letter Closing (5:12–14)

With the help of Silas (5:12). Having finished the letter body, Peter comes to the letter closing. It is equivalent to the salutation and signature of an English letter. It is at this point that a *Greek* author often took the stylus himself, making the last paragraph or two visibly different from the careful scribal hand that preceded it. Even if Silas or someone else wrote the whole letter, stylistically it was important to indicate the closing as if you were writing it yourself. The first item in the closing identifies the letter carrier, who in this case may have been virtually the cowriter. In Romans 16:22 Paul allows the scribe Tertius to identify himself, but here Peter uses the formula that identifies the letter carrier,[34] adding that Silas is a "faithful brother." This should remove any doubts readers might have had about the role Silas has played while with Peter or any questions about the expansion he might give as the person carrying the letter. (The person carrying a letter like this one was expected to give an oral expansion along with reading the letter.) Saying he is a "faithful brother" identifies him as one who shared Peter's ministry.

Briefly (5:12). Saying that he had written "briefly" is more a statement of politeness than one of fact. Ancient letters were supposed to be brief, so even Hebrews claims to be brief (Heb. 13:22).

Encouraging you and testifying that this is the true grace of God. Stand fast in it (5:12). This clause states the purpose of the letter (another part of a proper Greek letter closing).

She who is in Babylon . . . Mark (5:13). This next part of the letter closing is the greetings. In many cultures travelers with letters are expected to bring greetings from friends and relatives in a distant location; it would be impolite not to do so. "She who is in Babylon" and "Mark" could indicate Peter's wife and literal son, since we know that he sometimes traveled with a wife (1 Cor. 9:5) and could easily have had an adult son by this time (Peter was already married in Mark 1:30, around thirty years earlier). However, these two expressions probably indicate the church (the Greek word for "church" is feminine, thus "she") in Rome (Babylon equals Rome in Rev. 17:5, 9) and John Mark of Jerusalem (Acts 12:12). Mark was Paul's companion in travel (Acts 13:5), whom Paul calls for at the end of his life (2 Tim. 4:11). The reason

REFLECTIONS

PETER EXPECTS CHRISTIANS TO DEMONSTRATE BY their lifestyle that they are family. It has fathers (the elders) and youths, family issues and family affection. Today we often contrast family with church rather than finding family in the church. Perhaps we should consider how we might demonstrate in our estranged and divorcing age that the church is a family that will never reject its members and never break up through divorce or death.

for suspecting this is the meaning is not only that the church in 2 John 1 is called "the chosen lady," but also that otherwise the letter would lack a greeting from the church in Peter's location, which would be a strange oversight. Also, there is no other indication that Peter had a physical son named "Mark."

Kiss of love (5:14). The standard Greco-Roman family greeting was a kiss on each cheek, mentioned repeatedly in the New Testament (e.g., Rom. 16:16). While it was sometimes exchanged between rulers and clients, it was normally only used within a family. Thus Christian brothers and sisters were indicating by its use that they considered one another not just members of a club, but family. This practice may well have been the source of the rumor that the love among Christian brothers and sisters was physical, not simply an emotional bond.[35] While the practice was later confined to the Eucharist, in the first century it was probably used for greeting and parting.

Peace (5:14). This final benediction is Greek for the Hebrew *shalom* (see comments on 1:2). It fits the situation of persecution well.

ANNOTATED BIBLIOGRAPHY

Balch, David L. *Let Wives Be Submissive: The Domestic Code in 1 Peter.* SBLMS, 26. Atlanta: Scholars, 1981.
    A specific study of 1 Peter 2–3, which remains a starting point for the study of such codes.

Davids, Peter H. *The First Epistle of Peter.* NICNT. Eerdmans, 1990.
    An expansion of the material found in this commentary, along with extensive introductory materials.

Elliott, John H. *A Home for the Homeless.* Minneapolis: Fortress, 1981.
    The first major work on 1 Peter to set it in the context of the social values of his world. While not perfect, it is a groundbreaking work.

Kelly, J. N. D. *The Epistles of Peter and of Jude.* London: Adam and Charles Black, 1976.
    The major conservative work on 1 Peter between Selwyn and Michaels; still very useful.

Marshall, I. Howard. *1 Peter.* IVPNTC. Downers Grove: InterVarsity, 1991.
    The best of the brief commentaries on 1 Peter; by a leading evangelical scholar.

Michaels, J. Ramsey. *1 Peter.* WBC 49. Waco, Tex.: Word, 1988.
    A major evangelical commentary on 1 Peter based on the Greek text and including exposition.

Selwyn, Edward Gordon. *The First Epistle of St. Peter.* London: Macmillan, 1969.
    A careful study of the Greek text, to which all other commentators refer.

CHAPTER NOTES

Main Text Notes

1. 1 Peter 1:14, 18; 2:9–10, 25; 3:6; 4:3–4.
2. Pliny, *Letters* 10.96.
3. For more information on the mystery religions see E. Ferguson, "Religions, Graeco-Roman," *DLNT*, 1006–11; M. W. Myer, *The Ancient Mysteries: A Sourcebook* (San Francisco: Harper, 1987).
4. E.g., Deut. 33:29; Ps. 3:3; 7:10; 18:2.
5. The resurrection of the dead and the rule of Jesus are the ultimate expressions of physical and political salvation, but the church saw signs of this ultimate salvation in the healing of the sick (physical), the Christian community (political), and the expulsion of demons (spiritual), partial and temporary though they were.
6. Cf. Rom. 8:24; Eph. 2:5, 8.

7. Cf. Acts 2:47; 1 Cor. 1:18; 2 Cor. 2:15.

8. Cf. Matt. 10:22; Rom. 5:9–10; 1 Tim. 4:16.

9. P. H. Davids, "Suffering in 1 Peter and the New Testament," in idem, *The First Epistle of Peter* (NICNT; Grand Rapids: Eerdmans, 1990), 30–44.

10. E.g., Matt. 6:25; 10:39; Acts 27:10.

11. Robert L. Webb, *John the Baptizer and Prophet* (Sheffield: Sheffield Academic Press, 1991), esp. ch. 1.

12. J. M. Reese, "Obedience," in J. J. Pilch and B. J. Malina, *Biblical Social Values and Their Meaning* (Peabody, Mass.: Hendrickson, 1993), 125–26.

13. J. J. Pilch, "Parenting" in Pilch and Malina, ibid., 128–31.

14. A. A. Ruprecht, "Slave, Slavery," *DPL*, 881–83; S. S. Bartchy, "Slave, Slavery," *DLNT*, 1098–1102.

15. See, for example, Rev. 1:6; 5:10; 20:6.

16. M. Reasoner, "Emperor, Emperor Cult," *DLNT*, 321–26.

17. B. Rapske, "Christians and the Roman Empire," *DLNT*, 1059–63.

18. M. Hengel, *Crucifixion* (Philadelphia: Fortress, 1977).

19. Philo, *Virtues* 39; *Moses* 2.243; Plutarch, *Mor.* 1 and 141.

20. For Seneca see *De Ben.* 7.9.

21. Epictetus as quoted in *Encheiridion* 40.

22. For example, see Plutarch, *Praec. Conj.* 45.

23. For example, the Jew Philo, *Drunkenness* 55, and the pagan Plato, *Resp.* 5.455e, both observe that women were physically weaker than men.

24. For example, see Deut. 10:18; Ps. 68:5; 146:9; Jer. 49:11; Mal. 3:5.

25. The Masoretic text has "the Lord Almighty" (*Yahweh Sabaoth*), while the Septuagint has "the Lord himself" (*kyrion auton*). First Peter has "the Lord Christ" (*kyrion ton Christon*).

26. For instance, Tacitus, *Ann.* 15.44.3 calls Christians, "a class hated for their abominations." He notes in 15.44.5 that they were convicted of "hatred of the human race [*odium humani generis*]," the same charge that magicians were charged with.

27. E.g., Gen. 19:1–3; Judg. 19:15–21.

28. For Jewish interpretation see the evidence presented in P. H. Davids, "Tradition and Citation in the Epistle of James," in W. W. Gasque and W. S. LaSor, eds., *Scripture, Tradition and Interpretation* (Grand Rapids: Eerdmans, 1978), 113–16.

29. Barth L. Campbell, *Honor, Shame, and the Rhetoric of 1 Peter* (SBLDS 160; Atlanta: Scholars, 1998), 196–97.

30. E.g., Rom. 11:36; 16:27; 1 Tim. 1:17; 6:16; 2 Tim. 4:18; Heb. 13:21; 2 Peter 3:18, all of which have similar wording to this text in 1 Peter.

31. Tacitus, *An*.15.44.5–7 from J. Stevenson, *A New Eusebius*.

32. Matt. 24:42–43; 25:13; 26:38–41.

33. Two excellent books on this topic are Sydney H. T. Page, *The Powers of Evil: A Biblical Study of Satan and Demons* (Grand Rapids: Baker, 1995); Stephen F. Noll, *Angels of Light, Powers of Darkness* (Downers Grove: InterVarsity, 1998).

34. Randolph Richards, "Theological Bias in Interpreting διὰ Σιλουανοῦ . . . ἔγραψα in 1 Pet. 5:12," a paper read at the 1999 meeting of the Evangelical Theological Society in Danvers, Mass.

35. G. Stählin, "φιλέω," *TDNT*, 9:118–24, 138–46. The erotic kiss is not stressed in Greco-Roman literature, although if one treated an unrelated male or female as if they were family, it might be assumed that one was treating them as husband or wife. See Robert Banks, *Going to Church in the First Century* (Chipping Norton, NSW, Australia), 12–15, 39, for an illustration of this practice.

Sidebar and Chart Notes

A-1. Eph. 5:21–6:9; Col. 3:18–4:1.

A-2. See further Dale W. Brown, "Revolutionary Subordination: A Bible Study of the Haustafeln," *BLT* 20 (1975): 159–64; Eric C. Lovik, "A Look at the Ancient House Codes and Their Contributions to Understanding 1 Peter 3:1–7," *CBTJ* 11 (1995): 49–63; John Howard Yoder, *The Politics of Jesus* (Grand Rapids: Eerdmans, 1994).

A-3. For example, *2 En.* 7:1, "And those men picked me up and brought me up to the second heaven. And they showed me, and I saw a darkness greater than earthly darkness. And there I perceived prisoners under guard. . . ." Later in the chapter the prisoners are identified as the fallen angels.

A-4. See further M. Reasoner, "Persecution," *DLNT*, 907–14.

A-5. See further: Pilch and Malina, *Biblical Social Values and Their Meaning*, and David deSilva, *Despising Shame: Honor Discourse and Community Maintenance in Hebrews* (Atlanta: Scholars, 1995).

2 PETER

by Douglas J. Moo

Authorship

The writer of the letter identifies himself clearly: "Simon Peter, a servant and apostle of Jesus Christ" (1:1). Some scholars doubt the accuracy of this identification, arguing that certain indications from within the letter reveal that Peter the apostle could not have written it. But these arguments are not convincing.[1] If, then, Peter did write the letter, what can we learn about his own situation at the time? In a phrase, not much. Peter, of course, appears as a prominent figure throughout the Gospels and in the early chapters of the book of Acts. He was a key leader in the early church in Jerusalem. Persecution, however, forced him to flee Palestine; Luke tells us vaguely that he "left for another place" (Acts 12:17). What this "other place" may have been has been a topic of lively conjecture.

While we cannot be sure where Peter fled after his release from imprisonment, we do find him back in Jerusalem some years later for the council held there (Acts 15). Paul's references to "Cephas" (= Peter) in

MOUNT TABOR

Traditional site of the transfiguration of Jesus.

◀

2 Peter
IMPORTANT FACTS:

- **AUTHOR:** Peter the apostle.
- **DATE:** A.D. 63–65.
- **OCCASION:** False teachers have invaded the churches to which Peter writes. These teachers are arrogant and immoral and are mocking the idea of the return of Christ.
- **PURPOSE:** Peter warns the believers in these churches about the false teachers and urges them to grow in their knowledge of Christ.

1 Corinthians suggest that he may have ministered in Corinth for a time (1 Cor. 1:12; 9:5). Nothing more is known about Peter until he writes a letter from Rome about A.D. 60 to Christians in northern Asia Minor (see the introduction to 1 Peter). We have only later legends to go by in reconstructing the last years of Peter. Tradition confirms that he spent some time in Rome.[2] Apparently reliable testimony has it that Peter, along with Paul, perished in the persecution of Emperor Nero in Rome in A.D. 64–65.[3] Some traditions hold that he was crucified head downward, but they do not appear to be reliable.[4]

The style and teaching of 2 Peter suggest strongly that it was written toward the end of Peter's life. It must have been written after A.D. 60 or so if 2 Peter 3:1 is a reference to 1 Peter. Peter was in Rome, as we have seen, in A.D. 60, and again at the time of his death in A.D. 64–65. He may have been there also when he wrote 2 Peter, therefore, although we cannot be sure. Nor can we be sure of the location of the Christians Peter addresses. Again, if the earlier letter implied in 2 Peter 3:1 is 1 Peter, then we can also know that 2 Peter is addressed to the same churches in northern Asia Minor. We are left with more questions than answers in our quest for specifics about the situation in which 2 Peter was written.

The False Teachers

Peter tells us little about what the false teachers are actually teaching. His only clear reference is to their "scoffing" about the return of Christ to judge the world (3:3–4). He spends most of the letter

TRAVELS OF PETER

From Judea to Asia Minor to Greece to Rome.
▼

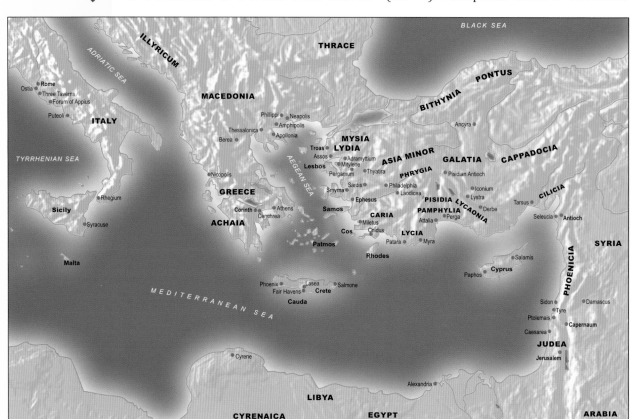

denouncing their lifestyle. They assume that the grace of God gives them the liberty to do just about anything they want (2:19–20). This "libertinism" manifests itself in arrogance toward authority (2:10–11), sexual misconduct (perhaps including homosexuality), excess in drinking and eating, and greed for money (2:13–16, 18–20).

Unfortunately, this profile is not specific enough to enable us to identify the false teachers with any known first-century group. Many scholars think that the teaching may have some relationship to Gnosticism. Although not formally distinguished as a full-blown "ism" until the second century, gnostic-like ideas were in circulation throughout the last half of the first century. Among other things, gnostics tended rigidly to separate the material from the spiritual realm. What people did in the "body," therefore, had little to do with spirituality: Note the libertine lifestyle Peter describes in chapter 2.[5]

But just how difficult it is to pin down these false teachers is revealed in the very different proposal of Jerome Neyrey. He notes that one of the most influential Greco-Roman philosophies of the day was Epicureanism. The Epicureans were known especially for their denial of providence, the afterlife, or any kind of divine judgment—just the view that seems to be taken by the false teachers according to chapter 3. In contrast to the popular picture of Epicureans, they did not foster a licentious lifestyle. But their denial of providence and the activity of the gods in daily life could easily lead among some adherents to such a lifestyle. This is just the point made by the early Christian writer Lactantius:

If any chieftan or pirates or leaders of robbers were exhorting his men to acts of violence, what other language could he employ than to say the same things which Epicurus says: that the gods take no notice; that they are not affected with anger or kind feeling; that the punishment of a future state is not to be dreaded, because the souls die after death, and there is no future state of punishment at all. (*Inst.* 3.17)[6]

These conflicting proposals suggest that we do not have enough evidence to identify the false teachers that lie behind 2 Peter. Indeed, our very quest to identify them with a particular group may be misguided. People in the ancient world, as in our day, were bombarded by viewpoints and ideas from many different perspectives. They could probably not have themselves always distinguished the exact religious or philosophical sources for their ultimate beliefs and habits of life. The false teachers, in other words, may have been influenced both by the broad philosophical climate of Epicureanism as well as incipient Gnosticism—and by other movements as well.

The Letter

Peter writes moral instruction to believers just before his death (1:14). This scenario is similar to that found in a popular Jewish intertestamental genre called a *testament*. Works such as the *Testaments of the Twelve Patriarchs*, the *Testament of Job*, and the *Testament of Moses* illustrate the genre. The original impetus for the form comes from Jacob's words to his sons on his deathbed in Genesis 48:8–49:27. Jewish writers used it as a convenient device to convey moral advice. Many scholars think that 2 Peter is in the form of a testament. Since such testaments are usually pseudonymous (i.e., written in someone else's name), these same scholars also think 2 Peter is pseudonymous.

They suggest that a disciple of Peter has built a letter of moral encouragement on the basis of some genuine fragments of Peter's own teaching.[7] However, while similarities between 2 Peter and the Jewish testaments exist—and Peter may well have adapted it to his own purposes—2 Peter in genre is a letter, not a testament. We do not have evidence that letters were written pseudonymously.

Introduction (1:1–2)

In common with both secular and New Testament letters, Peter identifies himself as the sender of the letter and then identifies his readers. They, however, are described in general, theological terms, leaving us in doubt about where they lived.

A servant . . . of Jesus Christ (1:1). The title, of course, connotes Peter's humble recognition that Jesus Christ is his Lord and that he is obliged to serve him in any way the Lord might decide. This was what it meant to be a "servant" or "slave" (*doulos*). But great figures in Israel's past were also called "servants" of God, especially Moses (e.g., Josh. 14:7; 2 Kings 18:12) and David (e.g., Ps. 18:1; Ezek. 34:23). So the title also conveys a certain honor and authority.

The Need to Grow in Knowledge of Christ (1:3–11)

This paragraph gets right to the heart of Peter's concern for his readers. He reminds them that God has provided all that is needed to become spiritually mature, and that believers thus have the responsibility to use the immense resources at their disposal to grow in relationship to Christ and thus secure their welcome in the kingdom of God.

Knowledge (1:3). Peter highlights the importance of "knowledge" throughout his letter (cf. 1:5, 6, 8; 2:20; 3:18). But especially significant is the way he ends the letter: "Therefore, dear friends, since you already know this, be on your guard so that you may not be carried away by the error of lawless men and fall from your secure position. But grow in the grace and

knowledge of our Lord and Savior Jesus Christ. To him be glory both now and forever! Amen" (3:17–18). By focusing on "knowledge" at both the beginning and the end of the letter, Peter draws special attention to it. The "framing" of material by beginning and ending on the same note is called *inclusio* and is used widely throughout the New Testament.

We are less certain why Peter highlights knowledge in this way. One possibility is that he is implicitly correcting the false teachers by using a term that they themselves put great stock in and setting it in its appropriate Christian context. As we noted in the introduction, many scholars think that Peter may be combating some form of early or incipient "Gnosticism," a religious system that focused on intellectual knowledge (Gk. *gnōsis*). While we cannot be certain that Peter is combatting early gnostics, we can surmise that these teachers are singling out *gnōsis* in a way that the later gnostics also did and that he therefore wants to help his readers understand that useful religious knowledge is always focused on God in Christ and has a thoroughly practical purpose: conformity to the image of Christ.

You may participate in the divine nature and escape the corruption in the world (1:4). The language Peter uses here is unusual in the Bible and is reminiscent of the pantheistic focus of some ancient Near Eastern and Greco-Roman religions. These religions had a mystical bent, promising deliverance from the contagion of the material world through absorption into the person of a god. The mystery religions, for instance, offered initiates the opportunity to become identified with a god and so escape death and corruption.[8] Philo, a Jewish philosopher from Alexandria, uses some of the same language Peter here uses in just this sense:

For how could the soul have conceived of God, had he not breathed into it and mightily laid hold of it? For the mind of man would never have ventured to soar so high so as to grasp the nature of God, had not God himself drawn it up to himself, so far as it was possible that the mind of man should be drawn up, and stamped it with the impress of the powers that are within the scope of its understanding.[9]

However, while Peter probably borrows the language from this cultural context, he applies it to a different conception. "Participating in the divine nature" means not to become absorbed in a mystical union with a god, but to the indwelling of God's Spirit and the consequent holiness of life that arises from that indwelling. We participate in the divine nature by imitating in our thinking and behaving the holy character of God himself.

Add to your faith goodness; and to goodness, knowledge . . . (1:5–7). The series of moral virtues in these verses resembles an ancient literary style called the *sorites*. An example from Jewish writings comes in Wisdom 6:17–20:[10]

> The beginning of wisdom is the most
>   sincere desire for instruction,
> and concern for instruction is love
>   of her,
> and love of her is the keeping
>   of her laws,
> and giving heed to her laws is
>   assurance of immortality,
> and immortality brings one near
>   to God;
> so the desire for wisdom leads to
>   a kingdom.

One implication of recognizing this literary device in 2 Peter 1:5–7 is the possibility that Peter is not suggesting that the virtues he lists must always be acquired in the order in which he lists them. Indeed, it is unlikely that he thinks believers can truly acquire "goodness" before "knowledge," since knowing God is basic to all virtues.

Self-control (1:6). Peter's mention of this virtue (Gk. *enkrateia*) is another example of his "accomodation" to Hellenistic culture. This virtue was prized by Greco-Roman philosophers as a basic necessity for a thoughtful and intelligent person. Aristotle and Philo made a great deal of this virtue.[11]

Holding Fast to the Biblical Promises (1:12–21)

In 1:12–15, Peter focuses on his own situation as a way of giving greater impetus to his exhortations. He then turns to what seems to be the key doctrinal problem with the false teachers: their scorn of the idea of Christ's return in glory. Peter emphasizes the certainty of that return by reminding them of the Transfiguration, a prefigurement of Christ's eschatological glory, and by insisting that the prophecies about that return are certain to be fulfilled.

The tent of this body (1:13). There is no word corresponding to "body" in the Greek text here; the NIV has added it to clarify the meaning of "tent." The relationship between these words is therefore one of definition; we could paraphrase "this tent, that is, my body." Greek authors sometimes use the word "tent" (*skēnōma*) to refer to the physical body, especially when wanting to distinguish it from the soul, or spirit, of a person. Paul uses a related term (*skēnos*) in just this way: "Now we know that if the earthly tent we live in is destroyed, we have a building from God, an eternal house in heaven, not built by human hands. . . . For while we are in this tent, we groan . . ." (2 Cor. 5:1, 4a). The word is appropriate in this context, where Peter is thinking of the day when he will "put . . . aside" this tent.

I will soon put it aside (1:14). The language Peter uses here to describe his death is yet another case of contextualization. His language of "putting aside" the body might suggest that he agrees with the Greek notion of the immortality of the soul. But Peter hints at his belief in the usual biblical teaching about resurrection in his first letter (1 Peter 4:6; cf. 3:18). So we can presume that Peter here adapts a normal Greek way of speaking about death without taking over the Greek notion of immortality.

R E F L E C T I O N S

PETER'S CLAIM THAT BELIEVERS MUST ACTIVELY cultivate spiritual virtues in order "to make your calling and election sure" is controversial, especially for Calvinists, who teach what is called "unconditional election": God chooses from eternity past who will be saved; and his choice is final and irrevocable. How, then, can believers add anything to God's sovereign choice? Arminians, of course, respond that this verse (along with many others) reveals that God's choosing takes place in conjunction with our own choosing to respond to the gospel of Jesus Christ. But the Calvinist view can be maintained if we recognize that God's sovereign choosing of us always demands our response to it. The Bible suggests a careful balance, or tension, between God's sovereignty and our own responsibility. God chooses, but we must choose also. God brings us to final salvation; but we are responsible to act on the basis of his grace in order to reach that final goal.

▶Views of the Afterlife

The Greeks had a variety of views on the afterlife. Adherents to the Orphic religions thought of death as a time when the soul would be released from the body to enjoy an immortal existence. Both Plato and Aristotle held that some part of the human being (whether the "soul" or "reason") was immortal and would live on after death. But probably the dominant view was that found in Homer—that most people (apart from notorious sinners and great heroes) would survive death only as bodiless shades in Hades, without consciousness of personal existence.[A-1]

The biblical perspective is quite different. Hinted at in the Old Testament and made explicit in the New Testament, biblical authors teach that the body will be raised from the dead to live forever. Not all Jews in the intertestamental period, however, agreed; some taught the immortality of the soul.

As the Lord Jesus Christ has made clear to me (1:14). Some scholars who think that an anonymous Christian wrote 2 Peter after his death assert that the author is here referring to the famous *Quo Vadis* legend. This legend is found in the apocryphal *Acts of Peter* and tells how Peter, on leaving Rome to escape arrest, is confronted by Jesus. Peter asks the Lord, "Where are you going" [Lat. *Quo vadis*]; the Lord responds that he is going to Rome to be crucified. Peter then turns back to be crucified in Rome. But we certainly do not need to refer to this legend to explain Peter's reference, for Jesus predicted Peter's death during his postresurrection appearances: "'I tell you the truth, when you were younger you dressed yourself and went where you wanted; but when you are old you will stretch out your hands, and someone else will dress you and lead you where you do not want to go.' Jesus said this to indicate the kind of death by which Peter would glorify God" (John 21:18–19). To be sure, this prophecy gives no indication of timing. But we can surmise that Peter writes 2 Peter in a situation where intense persecution has broken out; he might even be under arrest. So he now realizes that the Lord's prediction of his martyr's death is about to be fulfilled.

We did not follow cleverly invented stories (1:16). "Stories" translates the word *mythoi*, literally, "myths." This word was used in a wide variety of ways in the ancient world, but the meaning that best fits the context is "fictional account, fable."[12] The *mythos* was often viewed as a mechanism to teach religious truth to people who did not have the intellectual capacity to apprehend matters of the spirit directly. Aristotle comments: "The mythical form is chosen to make apprehension possible for the masses, for their religious and ethical instruction."[13] We can assume that the false teachers are claiming that the idea of Jesus' return in glory was just such a *mythos*—a religious story to encourage "ordinary" Christians.

The power and coming of our Lord Jesus Christ (1:16). "Power" and "coming" form a construction that means "powerful coming." The word behind "coming" is the familiar *parousia*, used throughout the New Testament to denote the second "coming" of Jesus. The word has the basic sense of "presence" or "arrival." Some of the Greeks used it to refer to the special "presence" or even "coming" of a god. Jewish writers, accordingly, applied the word to the biblical God: Josephus, for instance, uses it to depict the terrifying appearance of God at Sinai.[14]

"This is my Son, whom I love; with him I am well pleased" (1:17). These words of God himself at the occasion of the Transfiguration allude to two important Old Testament passages. The first is Psalm 2:7, where God addresses the messianic king; the second is Isaiah 42:1, the opening of the first Servant Song in Isaiah. These words, therefore, combine to identify Jesus as the Messiah, whose mission will take the form of the Suffering Servant of Isaiah.

The sacred mountain (1:18). This language is again cited by some who doubt that Peter could have written this letter. They claim that it smacks of a later period in Christian history, when the places where significant events in the life of Jesus took place were being revered as "holy" places. But such skepticism is unwarranted. As R. Bauckham has pointed out, Peter is probably alluding to Psalm 2:6 (note that Ps. 2:7 is alluded to in 2 Peter 1:17): "I have installed my King on Zion, my holy hill."[15]

Until the day dawns (1:19). The rich biblical teaching about the "Day of the Lord" makes it certain that Peter intends here more than a metaphor. The "Day of the Lord" is the day when God visits his people for judgment or salvation (Deut. 30:17–18), and the prophets use the phrase extensively as a way of depicting the final events of human history (e.g., Joel 1:15; Obad. 15).[16]

And the morning star rises in your hearts (1:19). "Morning star" translates a word that means, literally, "light-bringer" (*phōsphoros*). Ancient people thought especially of the planet Venus as the "light-bringer," since it often appears just before the dawn. Peter picks up this pop-

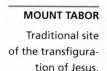

MOUNT TABOR

Traditional site of the transfiguration of Jesus.

ular imagery to describe the effect of the coming of the Day of the Lord on the believer: The "morning star" rises in the heart. Behind Peter's imagery may also lie the biblical use of "star" language to depict the Messiah (Num. 24:17; cf. Rev. 22:16).

By the prophet's own interpretation (1:20). Some interpreters think that the verse should be translated: "No prophecy of Scripture is a matter of one's own interpretation." The focus would thus shift to the current interpretation of prophecy. But the interpretation assumed in the NIV is preferable. That Peter is referring to the prophet's own "interpretation" or "unravelling" (*epilysis*) is probable because the Old Testament uses this same language to speak of the interpretation of dreams sent by the Lord. See especially the story of Joseph's interpretation of the dreams of the baker and butler in Genesis 40–41.

Peter's insistence on this point may have arisen because the false teachers were making a contrary point. At a later date, for instance, the Ebionites (radical Jewish Christians) claimed that the prophets spoke "of their own intelligence and not the truth."[17]

Introduction of the False Teachers (2:1–3)

Peter now turns to the topic that will dominate the rest of the letter: the false teachers who are plaguing these Christians. The key note in these verses is destruction: their heresies are "destructive" (2:1), and the false teachers themselves are destined for "destruction" (2:1, 3).

There were also false prophets among the people (2:1). Peter reminds his read-

ers that the Old Testament is strewn with examples of people who claimed to speak in the name of the Lord but were leading the people astray by propagating their own notions. As Richard Bauckham notes, these false prophets in Israel generally displayed three characteristics: (1) They did not speak with God's authority; (2) their message was usually upbeat, in contrast to the authentic prophets' warning of divine judgment; and (3) they were denounced as worthy of condemnation. Peter applies all three characteristics to the false teachers he denounces.

There will be false teachers among you (2:1). The word "false teachers" (*pseudo-didaskaloi*) is used nowhere else in the New Testament, although Paul does warn about "teachers" who "say what [people's] itching ears want to hear" (2 Tim. 4:3; cf. also 1 Tim. 4:1). We might expect Peter to complete his comparison in verse 1 by announcing the coming of "false prophets" in the church, who were like the false prophets of old. Perhaps, however, the people introducing these doctrines do not claim to be prophets. Another surprising feature of this verse is the future tense Peter uses: "will be." Elsewhere in the letter Peter appears to presuppose that these false teachers have already arrived on the scene. Most likely Peter is thinking of Jesus' own prophecies about the rise of false teachers in the last days (see esp. Jesus' warnings in the Olivet Discourse):

> Jesus answered: "Watch out that no one deceives you. For many will come in my name, claiming, 'I am the Christ,' and will deceive many. . . .
> At that time many will turn away from the faith and will betray and

hate each other, and many false prophets will appear and deceive many people. . . .

At that time if anyone says to you, 'Look, here is the Christ!' or, 'There he is!' do not believe it. For false Christs and false prophets will appear and perform great signs and miracles to deceive even the elect—if that were possible.[18]

Since the early Christians believed they were living in "the last days," they could readily apply such predictions to their own circumstances.

The sovereign Lord (2:1). The Greek here is *despotēs* (from which we get "despot"), a term applied to God or Christ only four other times in the New Testament.[19] It connotes commanding authority, and Peter probably uses it to underscore the false teachers' rebellious attitudes. Their scorn of authority emerges at several points in 2 Peter 2.

Destructive heresies (2:1). The NIV rendering is quite literal; indeed, it is a transliteration—the Greek word is *haire-*

▶

COLOSSEUM IN ROME

Outside and inside view (floor missing).

▼

seis. But this translation may not be entirely accurate. In the New Testament period, this Greek word refers to a "party" or a "sect."[20] Only later did the word take on the sense of deviation from orthodox teaching.

Stories they have made up (2:3). This Greek expression was used in the classical period to denote deceitful speech; note *Testament of Reuben* 3:5, which refers to the person who "handles his affairs smoothly and secretly even with his relatives and household."

The Condemnation of the False Teachers (2:4–10a)

The end of the last paragraph (2:3) announces the theme of this one: "Their condemnation has long been hanging over them, and their destruction has not been sleeping." Peter cites Old Testament examples of God's judgment as warning to these false teachers. But he also encourages faithful Christians by reminding them that God also "knows how to rescue godly men from trials" (2:9).

God did not spare angels when they sinned (2:4). The examples of God's judgment that Peter cites in 2:5–6 are clear allusions to well-known Old Testament events: the flood of Noah and the destruction of Sodom and Gomorrah. But the reference in 2:4 is not so clear. Some interpreters think Peter may have in mind Isaiah 14:12–17 and Ezekiel 28:11–19. These texts may, according to some interpreters, refer to a primeval "fall" of Satan and the angels who followed him in his rebellion.[21] But it is not clear that Isaiah and Ezekiel are referring to such a fall. A more likely background emerges when we consider a prominent

intertestamental Jewish tradition, which took its starting point from the enigmatic Genesis 6:1–4:

> When men began to increase in number on the earth and daughters were born to them, the sons of God saw that the daughters of men were beautiful, and they married any of them they chose. Then the LORD said, "My Spirit will not contend with man forever, for he is mortal; his days will be a hundred and twenty years."
> The Nephilim were on the earth in those days—and also afterward—when the sons of God went to the daughters of men and had children by them. They were the heroes of old, men of renown.

Old Testament scholars debate about whether the "sons of God" were human beings or angels; but the Jewish interpreters of Peter's day left no doubt about the matter. They viewed the "sons of God" as angels and their cohabiting with women as a key moment in the "fall" of the world into sin. The idea is found in several different books, but is most prominent in *1 Enoch*. See, for instance, 6:1–2:[22]

> In those days, when the children of man had multiplied, it happened that there were born unto them handsome and beautiful daughters. And the angels, the children of heaven, saw them and desired them, and they said to one another, "Come, let us choose wives for ourselves from among the daughters of man and beget us children."

Peter cites what was apparently a well-known tradition to illustrate the way in which God judges those who rebel against him.

Sent them to hell (2:4). These words translate a single Greek verb, *tartareō*. From this word comes "Tartarus," a common name for the subterranean abyss to which disobedient gods and rebellious people were consigned. Jewish writers had already adopted this term as a way of communicating in a Greek environment the biblical idea of a place of punishment for sin.[23] The NIV "hell" conveys the idea well enough but may miss one point. Tartarus was often pictured more as a temporary holding-place than a place of final punishment. Peter suggests that the angels who sinned are being "held for judgment."

Putting them into gloomy dungeons (2:4). This phrase continues to use popular Greek notions of the afterlife to convey the sense of judgment. It is not clear whether Peter is speaking of "gloomy dungeons" or "chains of darkness" (see the NIV footnote; the difference is a textual variant). But the idea of gloom and darkness conveys the sense of punishment. Note, for instance, *1 Enoch* 10:4: "Bind Azazel [a disobedient angel] hand and foot and throw him into darkness."

Noah, a preacher of righteousness (2:5). The Old Testament presumes that Noah, by his lifestyle and commitment to God's promise, was an example of righteousness in his generation. But it never calls him a "preacher." Intertestamental Jewish traditions, however, used this language for him.[24]

Condemned the cities of Sodom and Gomorrah (2:6). The destruction of the world through the Flood and the destruction by fire of Sodom and Gomorrah make a natural pair of examples of God's judgment. Nevertheless, Peter may be influenced by Jesus, who alluded to these two Old Testament incidents together:

> Just as it was in the days of Noah, so also will it be in the days of the Son of Man. People were eating, drinking, marrying and being given in marriage up to the day Noah entered the ark. Then the flood came and destroyed them all.
> It was the same in the days of Lot. People were eating and drinking, buying and selling, planting and building. But the day Lot left Sodom, fire and

SODOM

The salt pans south of Lisan—the possible site of Sodom. ▼

sulfur rained down from heaven and destroyed them all. (Luke 17:26–29)

By burning them to ashes (2:6). The same Greek word that Peter uses here to denote the destruction of Sodom and Gomorrah (*tephroō*) was used by Dio Cassius to depict Pompeii after the eruption of Mount Vesuvius in A.D. 79 (Dio Cassius 46). Jewish authors used similar language to describe the fate of Sodom and Gomorrah. Philo claims that God "consumed the impious and their cities, and to the present day the memorials to the awful disaster are shewn in Syria, ruins and cinders and brimstone and smoke" (*Moses* 2.56).

Lot, a righteous man (2:7; cf. 2:8). This description of Lot is not out of keeping with the profile given in Genesis 19. Although vacillating in his faith to some extent, Lot, in the midst of a sinful context, never lost his basic orientation to God. Jewish writers before Peter also called him "righteous" (see, e.g., Wisd. Sol. 10:6: "Wisdom rescued a righteous man when the ungodly were perishing; he escaped the fire that descended on the Five Cities"). However, some other Jewish traditions portray Lot as a notorious sinner.

A Characterization of the False Teachers (2:10b–16)

Peter provides a profile of the false teachers' sinfulness by moving quickly through a list of their evil tendencies.

These men are not afraid to slander celestial beings (2:10). "Celestial beings" translates the Greek word *doxai* (lit., glories). The word could refer to illustrious or honored human beings, such as lead-ers in the early church. But a reference to angelic beings is more likely. To be sure the Old Testament never calls angels "glorious ones," but Jewish writers sometimes did. See, for example, *2 Enoch* 22:6–7: "And Michael, the Lord's leading angel, lifted me up and brought me in front of the face of the Lord. And the Lord said to his servants, sounding them out, 'Let Enoch join in and stand in front of my face forever!' And the Lord's glorious ones did obeisance and said, 'Let Enoch yield in accordance with your word, O Lord!'"[25] Other Jewish traditions also link angels and glory.[26] The context further suggests that Peter refers to evil angels, since the "celestial beings" in this verse appear to be identical to the "beings" in 2 Peter 2:11, which the "angels" (apparently "good" angels) do not slander.

How are these false teachers slandering evil angels? Peter does not tell us; but perhaps their arrogance is manifesting itself in speaking in a disparaging way

REFLECTIONS

IN NO SPIRITUAL MATTER, PERHAPS, are Christians more prone to unfortunate extremes than in our attitude toward spiritual beings. Some believers tend virtually to ignore the entire spiritual realm, acting in practice as if the world of spirits does not exist. When this happens, we are open to the onslaughts of Satan. For his greatest victory, as C. S. Lewis reminds us, comes when people act as if he doesn't exist. But, in an overreaction to such neglect, some Christians go too far the other direction, giving too much credit to spiritual beings and failing to claim the benefits of Christ's victory over them at the cross.

about these beings. They may be dismissing the power and significance of the demons, willfully ignoring the degree to which their own actions are being influenced by them.

Angels . . . do not bring slanderous accusations against such beings (2:11). Nothing in the Old Testament directly supports this assertion; Peter is once again relying on Jewish tradition. Jude, in a roughly parallel text, quotes from a tradition found in *The Assumption of Moses* (cf. Jude 8–9); Peter may have the same text in mind. Or perhaps Peter continues to rely on *1 Enoch*. In chapter 9 of this book, the author describes how good angels, upon hearing the outcry of human

▶

beings as they are being harmed by evil angels, do not directly intervene but bring the matter before the Lord.

They are like brute beasts, creatures of instinct, born only to be caught and destroyed (2:12). Peter alludes to a widespread ancient teaching about certain animals born only to be slaughtered and eaten.[27]

Their idea of pleasure is to carouse in broad daylight (2:13). The Greek for "pleasure" is *hēdonē*, from which we get the word "hedonist." The Greeks numbered this kind of "pleasure" among the four "deadly sins," sometimes contrasting it with "reason" (cf. the "unreasoning animals" of 2:12). Drinking and excessive eating in daylight hours were a standard indication of a degenerate lifestyle.[28]

Reveling in their pleasures while they feast with you (2:13). The allusion is probably to the "love feast," the meal that early Christians ate in conjunction with their celebration of the Lord's Supper. Such a meal is implied in 1 Corinthians 11:17–34 and is mentioned in many early Christian writings.[29]

With eyes full of adultery, they never stop sinning (2:14). Peter may be alluding to a popular ancient proverb, that a shameless man does not have *koras* (a pun, for the word can mean both "pupils" and "young women") in his eyes, but *pornas* ("prostitutes").[30]

They are experts in greed (2:14). "Experts" renders the Greek *gegymnasmenē*, a word that refers to athletic training. These false teachers, Peter implies, have worked hard to become as proficient in greediness as they are.

They have left the straight way and wandered off (2:15). The "way" was a popular means of characterizing a particular religious or philosophical teaching. The imagery is of a path that a true devotee will follow to the end. The Old Testament, therefore, pictures faithfulness to the Lord as a "straight path" to be followed, and the New Testament writers depict Christianity as a "Way."[31] Sin can therefore be described as "wandering" from that path. See, for example, God's warning to the people of Israel: "See, I am setting before you today a blessing and a curse—the blessing if you obey the commands of the LORD your God that I am giving you today; the curse if you disobey the commands of the LORD your God and turn from the way that I command you today by following other gods, which you have not known" (Deut. 11:26–28).

Balaam son of Beor (2:15). Balaam is introduced in Numbers 22–24 as a prophet whom the pagan king Balak pays to prophesy against Israel. Despite Balaam's own reluctance and corruption, God causes him to utter prophecies in favor of his people. Providing a point of connection between Numbers and 2 Peter is the use of the word "way" in the story. The "way of Balaam" in Numbers 22:23 is the road that Balaam is following; and in 22:32 Balaam is rebuked for taking a "reckless [way]." Peter's use of Balaam is undoubtedly influenced by the way he is used in Scripture as a negative example (Deut. 23:4–5).[32] The NIV's "son of Beor" either presumes a variant reading or simply standardizes the biblical names for Balaam's father. The best-attested text has "Bosor." This name may be a play on the Hebrew word for "flesh" (*basar*), reflecting Jewish traditions that characterize Balaam as a "fleshly" person.

Who loved the wages of wickedness (2:15). Hinted at in the Old Testament, Balaam's willingness to curse Israel for profit became a staple in Jewish stories about him.[33]

He was rebuked for his wrongdoing by a donkey . . .restrained the prophet's madness (2:16). Both are highlighted in Jewish traditions about Balaam. The idea of the donkey's "rebuke" of Balaam is found in several of the targums; and Philo calls Balaam "most foolish" of men.[34]

The False Teachers' Impact and Destiny (2:17–22)

If 2:10b–16 have focused on the false teachers' character, 2:17–22 stress their impact on other people. Because of the terrible spiritual effects of their teaching, their judgment will be certain and severe.

Springs without water (2:17). The dry Mediterranean climate, with long stretches of land and little water, rendered fresh water springs essential to life. As useless and dangerous as springs without water is the teaching of these false Christians.

Mists driven by a storm (2:17). Aristotle uses the rare Greek word translated "mist" here (*homichlē*) to refer to the haze left after the condensation of a cloud into rain.[35] Such condensation often dissipates and becomes the harbinger of dry weather.

They are worse off at the end than they were at the beginning (2:20). Peter probably alludes to Jesus' teaching at the end of his story about the evil spirit in Matthew 12:43–45:

> When an evil spirit comes out of a man, it goes through arid places seeking rest and does not find it. Then it says, 'I will return to the house I left.' When it arrives, it finds the house unoccupied, swept clean and put in order. Then it goes and takes with it seven other spirits more wicked than itself, and they go in and live there. And the final condition of that man is worse than the first. That is how it will be with this wicked generation.

"A sow that is washed goes back to her wallowing in the mud" (2:22). The proverb that Peter quotes may go back to a popular seventh- or sixth-century B.C. book of proverbs called *Ahiqar*. The Aramaic version reads, in 8:8: "My son, you have been to me like the pig who went into the hot bath with people of quality, and when it came out of the hot bath, it saw a filthy hole and it went down and wallowed in it."[36]

Remembering the Truth (3:1–7)

After a chapter focused exclusively on the false teachers, Peter turns to his readers again. In contrast to the false teachers, who have forgotten the truth and lapsed into a heretical denial of the Lord's return, Peter wants his readers to "recall" what they have been taught by the prophets and by the Lord himself.

My second letter to you (3:1). With the New Testament canon before us, we naturally assume that Peter here refers to 1 Peter; and this may indeed be the case.[37] But Peter probably wrote more letters than have been included in the canon. Paul, for instance, mentions at least three letters that we do not have: a letter previous to 1 Corinthians (1 Cor. 5:9); a "severe" letter to the Corinthians, written between 1 and 2 Corinthians (2 Cor. 7:8); and a letter to the Laodiceans (Col. 4:16). Peter may, then, be referring to a letter we do not possess.[38]

Wholesome thinking (3:1). "Thinking" translates a noun (*dianoia*) that occurred frequently in certain philosophical circles in ancient Greece; indeed, the exact phrase Peter uses here (*eilikrinē dianoia*) occurs in Plato, though Peter does not use the phrase with the same philosophical associations. Rather, he does here what he has so skillfully done throughout the letter: utilize words and phrases from Greco-Roman philosophy and religion to

REFLECTIONS

AT KEY JUNCTURES IN THIS LETTER, Peter repeatedly calls on his readers to remember or recall the truth of Christ (1:12–13; 3:2; cf. the negative "forget" in 3:5, 8). He wants us not simply to call to mind some facts we may have forgotten but to dwell on biblical truth in such a way that it transforms our thinking and behavior. We may have a solid mental understanding of the "facts" of the faith: that Christ died for me, that he was raised, that I am indwelt by the Holy Spirit, and so on. But do we allow these truths to penetrate our minds and take possession of us? God called on his Old Testament people to "remember" their deliverance from Egypt so that they would always appreciate God's gracious work in their history (Ex. 13:3, 9; Deut. 7:18). Believers need to reflect similarly on the gracious work of God in Christ on our behalf.

communicate Christian truth to an audience apparently familiar with such language.

The words spoken in the past by the holy prophets (3:2). The reference (as in the somewhat parallel 1:20) is to the Old Testament prophets, who predicted that God would bring his plan to its climax through an earth-shaking event at the end of history.

The command given by our Lord and Savior through your apostles (3:2). The singular "command" gathers up the various elements of New Testament ethical teaching into one overall category. The false teachers, as we have seen, combined eschatological skepticism with ethical unconcern. Peter, by contrast, insists that his readers be mindful of the teaching of Jesus about true discipleship—a teaching passed on to them through the apostles.

In the last days scoffers will come (3:3). The future tense has the same explanation as the one in 2:1: Peter cites earlier predictions about what is, in fact, taking place in his own time. The early Christians believed that, with the coming of Messiah and pouring out of the Spirit, the "last days" predicted by the prophets had arrived (see, e.g., Acts 2:17–18; Heb. 1:2). Thus, they could apply predictions about those days to their own situations. Peter may particularly have in mind Matthew 24:5: "Many will come in my name, claiming, 'I am the Christ,' and will deceive many." Note Paul's similar predictions:

> I know that after I leave, savage wolves will come in among you and will not spare the flock. Even from your own number men will arise and distort the truth in order to draw away disciples after them. (Acts 20:29–30)

The Spirit clearly says that in later times some will abandon the truth and follow deceiving spirits and things taught by demons. (1 Tim. 4:1)

However, while the "last days" will be especially marked by "scoffers," the phenomenon is nothing new in the history of God's people. The psalmist pronounced "blessed" the person who does not "sit in the seat of the mockers" (Ps. 1:1). Likewise, Proverbs cautions the righteous to avoid the ways of the "mocker" (Prov. 1:22; 9:7–8; 13:1).

They will say, "Where is this 'coming' he promised?" (3:4). The form of the question reminds us of some Old Testament passages where sinners express their unbelief or mockery. For example:

> You have wearied the LORD with your words. "How have we wearied him?" you ask. By saying, "All who do evil are good in the eyes of the LORD, and he is pleased with them" or "Where is the God of justice?" (Mal. 2:17)

> They keep saying to me, "Where is the word of the LORD? Let it now be fulfilled!" (Jer. 17:15)

Our fathers (3:4). Some scholars seize on this reference as clear evidence that Peter could not have written this letter. The "fathers," they argue, must be the first generation of Christian believers, since the whole issue in the context is about the reality of Christ's returning in glory. But the evidence is by no means clear. There is no "our" in the Greek text, so Peter simply refers to "the fathers."

This word occurs elsewhere in the New Testament as a reference to the patriarchs (cf. Rom. 9:5; 11:28; 15:8). Moreover, as we have seen ("prophets" in 2 Peter 3:2), Peter is concerned to ground the fact of a climactic judgment at the end of history in the teaching of the Old Testament (cf. also the reference to the flood in 3:6).

Died (3:4). The Greek here is actually "fallen asleep" (*ekoimēthēsan*). Some scholars insist that this word is used for death in the New Testament as a reflection of the special Christian perspective on death. "Sleep" connotes the truth that believers are to be raised from their dead state to live again (cf. esp. John 11:11). But the Greeks had used the language of "sleep " to describe death since the time of Homer; note the way the Roman writer Catullus puts it: "The sun can set and rise again, but once our brief light sets, there is one unending night to be slept through" (5.4–6).

By God's word the heavens existed and the earth was formed out of water and by water (3:5). A better translation, recognizing the typical biblical idiom of "heavens and earth," is the REB: "There were heavens and earth long ago, created by God's word out of water and with water." The instrumentality of God's word in creation is, of course, clear enough, attested in many Old Testament texts. In addition to the creation account itself, see, for instance, Psalm 33:6: "By the word of the LORD were the heavens made."

But why does Peter mention "water" as a second instrument of creation? This probably refers to the creation account, where water plays a prominent role. In Genesis 1:2, before God began to organize his creation, we read about the Spirit "hovering over the waters." These waters, which are apparently covering the entire globe, are separated as God makes the "sky" (Gk. *ouranos*, "heaven"; Gen. 1:6–8). Then God forms the dry land by gathering the water together (Gen. 1:9). Peter also introduces "water" here for rhetorical reasons, for he goes on to compare God's creation with his judging of the world through water (2 Peter 3:6).

The world of that time was deluged and destroyed (3:6). Does Peter's remark have any bearing on the vexing debate about the extent of the flood? Jewish sources certainly imply a destruction of the whole physical universe. See, for example, *1 Enoch* 83:3–5:

> I saw in a vision the sky being hurled down and snatched and falling upon the earth. When it fell upon the earth, I saw the earth being swallowed up into the great abyss, the mountains being suspended upon mountains, the hills sinking down upon the hills, and tall trees being uprooted and thrown and sinking into the great abyss. Thereupon a word fell from my mouth; and I began crying aloud, saying, "The earth is being destroyed."[39]

Nevertheless, Peter's shift from "heavens and earth" to a word that often refers to humankind (*kosmos*; NIV "world") might imply a focus on the destruction of people.

The present heavens and earth are reserved for fire (3:7). Only here in the Bible do we find a prediction of the eventual destruction of the universe through fire. The Stoics, an influential school of philosophers in Peter's day, taught just such an end of the universe; and some scholars think that Peter derives his teaching from this background. But the

▶ Jewish Tradition Regarding God's Delay of His Judgment

Jews in the apocalyptic tradition theorized that God was delaying his judgment to give opportunity for people to repent. See, for example, *1 Enoch* 60:4–6:

> And Michael sent another angel from among the holy ones and he raised me up. And when he had raised me up, my spirit returned; for (I had fainted) because I could not withstand the sight of these forces and (because) heaven has stirred up and agitated itself. Then Michael said unto me, "What have you seen that has so disturbed you? This day of mercy has lasted until today; and he has been merciful and long-suffering toward those that dwell upon the earth. And when this day arrives—and the power, the punishment, and the judgment, which the Lord of the Spirits has prepared for those who do not worship the righteous judgment, for those who deny the righteous judgment, and for those who take his name in vain—it will become a day of covenant for the elect and inquisition for the sinners."

Peter essentially endorses this tradition, which had Old Testament roots.A-2

Old Testament often uses "fire" as an image of God's judgment. "See, the LORD is coming with fire, and his chariots are like a whirlwind; he will bring down his anger with fury, and his rebuke with flames of fire. For with fire and with his sword the LORD will execute judgment upon all men, and many will be those slain by the LORD."[40]

Living in Light of the End (3:8–13)

In contrast to the false teachers, who forget or deliberately suppress the truth about the end of the world, believers must not forget that this universe is not permanent, for God has appointed a day when he will judge it and usher in "a new heaven and a new earth." Peter urges his readers to live holy lives in light of this truth.

With the Lord one day is like a thousand years, and a thousand years are like a day (3:8). Peter adopts these words from Psalm 90:4: "For a thousand years in your sight are like a day that has just gone by, or like a watch in the night." God, being eternal, does not experience time as we do. Later Christians built elaborate systems of historical predictions on the basis of this text. They understood Psalm 90:4 as teaching that a biblical "day" would last a thousand years. They furthermore believed that the seven "days" of creation would be matched by seven "days" of world history. The seventh, the day of "rest," would be the Messianic age.[41] Peter betrays no evidence of any such application of the verse.

The Lord is not slow in keeping his promise (3:9). As we pointed out in the introduction, the false teachers may have been influenced by a certain skepticism about judgment that was widespread in the Greco-Roman world of that time. As Plutarch comments, "God's slowness [to judge] undermines our belief in providence."[42] At a later date, we find a rabbi uttering this curse: "Cursed be the bones of those who calculate the end. For they would say, since the predetermined time has arrived, and yet he has not come, he will never come" (*b. Sanh.* 97b).

He is patient with you, not wanting anyone to perish, but everyone to come to repentance (3:9). Theologians debate the significance of this text, questioning why anyone should ever be finally damned if, indeed, God "wills" no one to perish. But our concern must be with the possible background of this assertion. In this respect, we must refer to a widespread Jewish teaching directed to the problem of delay: Why was God waiting so long to vindicate his name and rescue his people from their trials? The answer took its lead from Habakkuk 2:3: "For the revelation awaits an appointed time; it speaks of the end and will not prove false. Though it linger, wait for it; it will certainly come and will not delay." Peter's comments are essentially in accord with Jewish apocalyptic tradition, which viewed God as delaying his judgment as a means of mercifully providing people with time to repent (see "Jewish Tradition Regarding God's Delay of His Judgment").

The elements will be destroyed by fire (3:10). "Elements" translates the Greek word *stoicheia*. Scholars debate its precise reference, especially in the Pauline phrase "the basic principles of the world" (Gal. 4:3; Col. 2:8, 20). Some think Paul refers to spiritual beings. But Peter cannot mean that, since this meaning is unattested in the New Testament outside Paul. Two alternatives are therefore left: the heavenly bodies, or the basic "building blocks" of the world. The former has in its favor the many Old Testament texts that predict a destruction of the heavenly bodies

at the time of the judgment. Note, for instance, Isaiah 34:4: "All the stars of the heavens will be dissolved and the sky rolled up like a scroll; all the starry host will fall like withered leaves from the vine, like shriveled figs from the fig tree." But Peter's focus on the "earth" in this context favors the latter interpretation.

Everything in it will be laid bare (3:10). "Laid bare" translates a difficult word. Many manuscripts have the Greek word *katakaēsetai*, which can be rendered "burned up," an idea that would make perfect sense in a context in which Peter has already claimed that the earth is "reserved for fire" (3:7; cf. NASB). But it is just because this word fits so well that we should be suspicious of it on text-critical grounds. For the early scribes tended to substitute natural readings for what seemed to them more difficult ones. So we should probably accept the Greek word *heurethēsetai*, which means, literally, "will be found." This word can have the connotation "be manifest," with the nuance "before God"; this is the general idea that the NIV has adopted. On the Judgment Day all things will be manifest before God, "laid bare" to his scrutinizing assessment.

As you look forward to the day of God and speed its coming (3:12). How can believers "hasten" the coming of the day of God? Peter's words can be explained by recognizing his dependence on a widespread Jewish teaching to the effect that the repentance of God's people would bring in the final day. This tradition is well attested in a rabbinic text that purports to give a debate between two first-century rabbis. R. Joshua b. Hananiah argued that God had sovereignly determined the time of the end and that nothing could alter that decision. But R. Eliezer b. Hyrcanus maintained that Israel's repentance would trigger the events of the end (*b. Sanh.* 97–98). Peter himself seems to reflect the view of R. Eliezer in his speech in the temple precincts: "Repent, then, and turn to God, so that your sins may be wiped out, that times of refreshing may come from the Lord, and that he may send the Christ, who has been appointed for you—even Jesus" (Acts 3:19–20).

The elements will melt in the heat (3:12). The word "melt" (*tēkō*) is particularly appropriate in this context, since the Old Testament uses the same language to depict the cosmic disasters that accompany the Day of the Lord. See Micah 1:3–4: "Look! The LORD is coming from his dwelling place; he comes down and treads the high places of the earth. The mountains melt beneath him and the valleys split apart, like wax before the fire, like water rushing down a slope" (see also Isa. 63:19–64:1).

A new heaven and a new earth (3:13). The promise of a re-creation of the universe rests especially on Isaiah 65–66, the only Old Testament passage to speak about a "new heaven and new earth." See, for example, 65:17: "Behold, I will create new heavens and a new earth. The former things will not be remembered, nor will they come to mind" (cf. also 66:22; Rev. 21:1).

Concluding Exhortation (3:14–18)

Peter ends his letter on the note with which he began: an exhortation to believers to "grow in the grace and knowledge of our Lord and Savior Jesus Christ"

(3:18; cf. 1:3–4). He underscores this exhortation with a reminder of the Lord's patience (3:14–16) and warns for a last time about the dangerous influence of the false teachers (3:17).

Make every effort to be found spotless (3:14). Peter echoes his command in 1:5 to "make every effort to add to your faith goodness" and the language of judicial scrutiny from 3:10. "To be found spotless" is to appear before God, the Judge, as righteous by virtue of Christ's work on our behalf on the last day.

Our dear brother Paul (3:15). Many believers have concluded from texts such as Galatians 2 that Paul and Peter were constantly at odds in the early church; an influential school of scholarship still assumes basically the same thing. But the New Testament generally portrays Peter and Paul as agreeing over the gospel and other key theological issues.[43] In addition, Silvanus, the scribe of 1 Peter, was a member of Paul's circle too.[44]

In all his letters (3:16). This need not mean that Peter was familiar with all the letters we now have in the New Testament. All Peter notes is that he has read some of Paul's letters and he finds them to focus on the same kind of matters Peter is writing about. We have no way to know what letters they may have been.

Hard to understand (3:16). The flavor of the Greek word here (*dysnoētos*) may be gauged from its application to Greek oracles. These oracles were often completely ambiguous, the most famous being the response of the Delphi oracle to a king asking if he should go to war: "If you go to war, you will destroy a great nation."[45] Whether the nation was his own or the one against which he fought was not clear.

The other Scriptures (3:16). The word *graphai* as used here and everywhere else in the New Testament refers to canonical books of the Old Testament. Peter there-fore implicitly places the letters of Paul in the category of "biblical books"—an important early indication of the way some New Testament letters were being viewed. Somewhat similar is Paul's cita-tion of a saying of Jesus as "Scripture" in 1 Timothy 5:18.

ANNOTATED BIBLIOGRAPHY

Bauckham, Richard. *Jude, 2 Peter*. WBC. Waco, Tex.: Word, 1983.

The most important conservative commen-tary on these letters in decades; arguably the best technical commentary now available. Rich in ref-erences to extrabiblical materials and marred only by its assumption of pseudonymity for 2 Peter.

Bigg, Charles. *A Critical and Exegetical Commentary on the Epistles of St. Peter and St. Jude*. ICC. New York: Scribners, 1903.

Classic treatment, oriented to historical and grammatical issues.

Kelly, J. N. D. *A Commentary on the Epistles of Peter and of Jude*. HNTC. New York: Harper & Row, 1969.

Careful treatment of the text.

Mayor, Joseph B. *The Epistle of St. Jude and the Second Epistle of St. Peter: Greek Text with Introduction, Notes and Comments*. Grand Rapids: Baker, 1979 (= 1907).

Lengthy treatment, focusing especially on his-torical and linguistic matters.

Moo, Douglas J. *2 Peter and Jude*. NIVAC. Grand Rapids: Zondervan, 1996.

Exposition of the English text with focus on contemporary application.

Neyrey, Jerome H. *2 Peter, Jude: A New Translation with Introduction and Commentary*. AB. Garden City, N.Y.: Doubleday, 1993.

The most recent English language technical commentary, incorporating social-critical and lit-erary approaches.

CHAPTER NOTES

Main Text Notes

1. See, for instance, Donald Guthrie, *New Testament Introduction* (Downers Grove: Inter-Varsity, 1990), 805–42.
2. Eusebius, *HE* 2.25.8 .
3. *1 Clement* 5–6; Tacitus, *Ann.* 15.44.
4. See R. P. Martin, "Peter," in *ISBE*, 3.802–7.
5. See, e.g., J. N. D. Kelly, *A Commentary on the Epistles of Peter and of Jude* (HNTC; San Fran-cisco: Harper & Row, 1969), 227–31.
6. See Jerome Neyrey, *2 Peter, Jude* (AB; New York: Doubleday, 1993), 123–24.
7. See esp. R. Bauckham, *2 Peter, Jude* (WBC; Waco, Tex.: Word, 1983), 131–35.
8. See further in D. E. Aune, "Religions, Greco-Roman," *DPL*, 792–93.
9. Philo, *Alleg. Interp.* 1.38.
10. See also Hermas, *Mandates* 5.2.4; *Visions* 3.8.7; *m. Sotah* 9:5. New Testament examples are found in Rom. 5:3–4 and James 1:2–4.
11. Aristotle, *Nicomachean Ethics* 7.1–11; Philo, *Spec. Laws* 2.195. See W. Grundmann, "ἐγράτεια," *TDNT*, 2.339–42, for additional references and discussion.
12. See, e.g., Philo, *Creation* 1; Josephus, *Ant.* 1.22.
13. Aristotle, *Metaphysics* 11.8.
14. Josephus, *Ant.* 3.5.2 §80.
15. Bauckham, *Jude, 2 Peter*, 221.
16. See also Isa. 11:11; 13:6, 9; 22:5; 34:8; Jer. 46:10; Ezek. 7:10; 13:5; 30:3; Joel 2:1–11; Amos 5:18–20; Zeph. 1:7–8, 14–18; Zech. 14:1.
17. Epiphanius, *Pamarion* 30.1.5.
18. Matt. 24:4–5, 10–11, 23–24.
19. Luke 2:29; Acts 4:24; Jude 4; Rev. 6:10.
20. Acts 5:17; 15:5; 24:5, 14; 26:5; 28:22; 1 Cor. 11:19; Gal. 5:20.
21. See, e.g., J. Calvin, *The Epistle of Paul the Apostle to the Hebrews and First and Second Epis-*

tles of St. Peter (reprint; Grand Rapids: Eerdmans, 1963), 348.

22. See also *Jub.* 5:1; 10:1–6; Josephus, *Ant.* 1.73; Philo, *Giants* 6; QG 1.92; CD 2:18.

23. See *1 En.* 20:2; *Sib. Or.* 4.186; Philo, *Moses* 2.433; *Rewards and Punishments* 152.

24. See, for example, Josephus, *Ant.* 1.3.1 §74; *Sib. Or.* 1.148–98, esp. 1.129.

25. Cf. also 1QH 10:8; *Ascen. Isa.* 9:32.

26. See, e.g., the LXX rendering of Ex. 15:11; Philo, *Spec. Laws* 1.45; *T. Judah* 25.2.

27. E.g., Juvenal 1.141; Pliny, *Natural History* 8.81.

28. Eccl. 10:16; Isa. 5:11; *T. Mos.* 7:4; Juvenal 1.103.

29. See G. Wainwright, "Lord's Supper, Love Feast," *DLNT*, 686–94.

30. Cf. Plutarch, *Moralia* 528E.

31. 1 Sam. 12:23; Ps. 107:7; Prov. 2:13; Isa. 33:15; Acts 9:2; 19:9, 23; 22:4; 24:14, 22.

32. See also Josh. 13:22; 24:9–10; Neh. 13:1–2; Mic. 6:5; Jude 11; Rev. 2:14.

33. See, e.g., Philo, *Moses* 1.266–68.

34. Philo, *Moses* 2.193.

35. Aristotle, *Meteor.* 1.346B.

36. See Bauckham, *Jude, 2 Peter,* 279.

37. Most commentators agree; see, e.g., C. Bigg, *A Critical and Exegetical Commentary on the Epistles of St. Peter and St. Jude* (ICC; New York: Scribners, 1903), 288–89.

38. See, e.g., E. M. B. Green, *The Second Epistle General of Peter and the General Epistle of Jude* (TNTC; Grand Rapids: Eerdmans, 1968), 123–24.

39. See also Philo, *Moses* 2.63–65.

40. Isa. 66:15–16; cf. also 30:30; Nah. 1:6; Zeph. 1:18; 3:8.

41. See, e.g., Justin, *Dialogue* 81; *Barn.* 15.4.

42. Plutarch, *Moralia* 549b.

43. See, e.g., Acts 11:2–18; 15:7–11.

44. See 1 Peter 5:12; cf. Acts 15:40; 1 Thess. 1:1.

45. Aristotle, *Rhetoric* 3.5.

Sidebar and Chart Notes

A-1. See the survey in M. J. Harris, *From Grave to Glory: Resurrection in the New Testament* (Grand Rapids: Zondervan, 1990), 36–40.

A-2. See also Wisd. Sol. 11:23; *4 Ezra* 3:30; 7:33, 134; *2 Apoc. Bar.* 89:12.; Joel 2:12–13.

1 JOHN

by Robert Yarbrough

The Setting of 1 John

First John was apparently quoted as early as the end of the first century A.D. by Papias of Hierapolis, whose writings we may place at about A.D. 95–110.[1] Polycarp's letter to the Philippians (early second century) likewise shows knowledge of 1 John (*Phil.* 7:1). John's first letter is one of the best attested letters in the New Testament.

Now both Papias and Polycarp of Smyrna were residents of western Asia Minor, not far from the major cultural center of Ephesus. This may be the reason they knew John's letter, for late in life John was a spiritual leader in that part of the Mediterranean world. He apparently lived in Ephesus and helped administer church affairs in the surrounding region.[2] He lived to a great old age and was still active at the beginning of the reign of the Roman emperor Trajan (A.D. 98–117).

This is probably the best tangible clue to the geographical setting of this letter. Although 1 John lacks explicit reference to city or region, it

177

1 John

REMAINS OF THE FOURTH-CENTURY A.D. CHURCH OF ST. JOHN NEAR EPHESUS

▶ 1 John
IMPORTANT FACTS:

■ **AUTHOR:** John the son of Zebedee, one of the Twelve chosen as apostles (Matt. 10:2).

■ **DATE:** Last third of the first century A.D.

■ **OCCASION:**
- To reaffirm apostolic teaching about Jesus Christ and the Christian life.
- To confront false beliefs and practices that were harming churches.
- To furnish a diagnostic tool for assessing the validity of people's claim to know Christ.

■ **KEY THEMES:**
1. The person of Christ.
2. The work of Christ.
3. The importance of both right belief and right practice in the Christian life.
4. Christlike love as a hallmark of true knowledge of God.

is most likely that John is speaking to problems that have arisen in the churches over which he has some jurisdiction. These may well include those congregations to whom he addressed part of the book of Revelation—Ephesus, Smyrna, Pergamum, Thyatira, Sardis, Philadelphia, and Laodicea (Rev. 2–3).[3]

Problems in the Churches

Since 1 John is not addressed to any specific leader or location, we can assume it was meant for a group of churches facing similar challenges. If their general location was the Roman province of Asia, we

WESTERN ASIA MINOR

WESTERN ASIA MINOR

EPHESUS

Remains of the city council building (the *prytaneion*).

are on firmest historical ground if we infer first of all from Revelation (which addresses churches in Asian cities) features of local belief or practice known to be at work in the churches that might well have created confusion about the gospel.

Influence of false teachers. First John (e.g., 2:18–19; 4:6) addresses a cultural setting in which key leaders are seeking to lead churches in a direction different from that laid out by Jesus Christ through hand-picked disciples like John. At Ephesus there are "wicked men . . . who claim to be apostles but are not" (Rev. 2:2). Among these are the Nicolaitans (2:6), a group that apparently rose within the church and promoted pagan sexual morals. They are also making their presence felt at Smyrna (2:15). At Thyatira a similar crisis has arisen. A woman whom John calls Jezebel[4] claims to have prophetic gifts. She teaches people "deep secrets" of Satan (2:24). Like the Nicolaitans she lures followers toward immoral sexual expression (2:20). This seems to have been a widespread problem in certain segments of the early church (2 Peter 2:15; Jude 11).

Influence of lax practice. From earliest times the God of the Bible called for a faith that expressed itself in loving obedience (Deut. 6:4ff.). Jesus, Paul, and other New Testament writers (e.g., James) preached a faith that was to be rich in works.[5] First John addresses readers who seem to have lost sight of the active nature of biblical faith.[6] This is known to have become a problem at Ephesus, where the church has forsaken its "first love" and has to be told, "Repent and do the things you did at first" (Rev. 2:5). At Thyatira and Philadelphia believers are told to "hold on" to what they have until Christ comes (2:25; 3:11).

More gravely, Christ warns the church at Sardis: "I have not found your deeds complete in the sight of my God" (3:2). There are only "a few people" there "who have not soiled their clothes," that is, not fallen prey to sub-Christian behavior patterns. Laodicea's level of active commitment is revoltingly tepid in Christ's sight (3:16). If these historic churches are in any way similar to the situation 1 John addresses, then the letter's numerous references to lax practice make good sense.

Influence of hostile rival religions and the threat of persecution. Whatever the situation of the churches that receive 1 John, it is not a religious vacuum. John has to encourage readers to stand their ground and not be intimidated by forces arrayed against them (e.g., 4:4–5). Religious leaders (see above) hostile to gospel belief and practice preside over quasi-Christian splinter groups or non-Christian currents that defy and even persecute the fledgling apostolic churches.

The Nicolaitans have already been mentioned. At Smyrna are self-proclaimed Jews on the verge of imprisoning Christians and even hastening their deaths (Rev. 2:9–10). At Philadelphia is a "synagogue of Satan," whom Christ promises to bring to its knees in recognition of his presence among the true people of God (3:9). Rival groups at Pergamum teach idolatrous and immoral doctrines that appear to have been worked out in practice (2:14). Christ warns that he will strike dead those pseudo-Christians at Thyatira who have been seduced by the Jezebel movement (2:23). At Sardis the majority of the visible church is charged with having "a reputation of being alive, but you are dead" (3:1). Things are no better at Laodicea, a church denounced by Christ as lukewarm and so blind that it cannot see its own poverty (3:17–18). First John likely addresses a situation where aberrant religious views and even persecution threaten to jeopardize the integrity of many churches in God's sight.

Challenges Confronting the Churches

The problems cropping up in churches have points of contact, if not their origin, on the outside. There are numerous possibilities here but few sure facts. If 1 John is written as late as the A.D. 90s, then one

EPHESUS

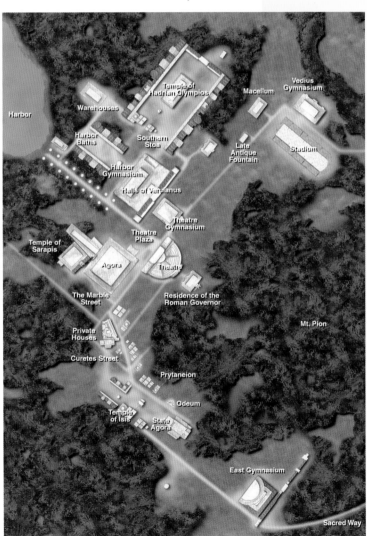

challenge to faith may be imperial persecution. The emperor Domitian (ruled A.D. 81–96) is thought to have made things hard for a number of groups, including Christians (see "Imperial Persecution of Christians," below).[7]

A second challenge may have been the first phase of the later well-known movement called Gnosticism. The views of groups known by this name are varied, and they never formed a unified body of faith and practice in the same way that the apostolic churches did. But as a whole, and in confusingly varied ways, they taught that salvation was by esoteric knowledge, not by Christ's atoning death and bodily resurrection. For gnostics, created matter (including the human body, and therefore even Jesus' body) was inherently evil, so salvation involved a flight from bodily existence, not resurrection of the body to eternal life. This flight sometimes resulted in asceticism, harsh treatment of the body—as if punishing it would demonstrate that the flesh was nothing. In other cases the gnostics' low view of the body resulted in moral license—if the body is nothing, why not indulge it as a means of expressing the irrelevance of bodily deeds and the transcendence of the redeemed spirit over fleshly constraints?

Gnostic views of Christ varied. Some were docetic, believing that Christ was divine but did not really become fully human (cf. 4:2). A group following a leader called Cerinthus (see "Irenaeus and Cerinthus") taught that a divine spirit came on Jesus, making him divine in a sense—while denying Jesus' full and essential deity. "Jesus" and "Christ" were ultimately two different beings (see John's response in 2:22).

We cannot be sure that John addresses the problem of Gnosticism in its technical sense, which dates to the time after he wrote. But even if he does not, there are features of religious thought and practice that his first letter seeks to correct that later came to be associated with Gnostic religion.

The errors that 1 John decries may also have points of contact with more generic pagan or Jewish belief. The commentary below will explore these possibilities at the appropriate junctures.

Structure of the Letter

Numerous outlines of 1 John have been proposed. None has won universal agreement.[8] John seems to proceed in a topical rather than logical fashion. He "has no intention of producing a systematic treatment like that of Romans or Galatians."[9] He mentions a topic, elaborates on it, then drops it and goes to another, only to return to the first one at some later point. Some topics he touches on repeatedly; others he mentions but once or twice. The power of his counsel lies in its concentrated focus and cumulative effect, not its logically compelling systematic development.

In comments below we follow the paragraph divisions used by ancient Greek copyists.[10] They divided the letter into seven sections (see chart "Structure of 1 John"). The chart's divisions are more rhetorical than material in nature. They have the advantage of not imposing a material structure on a letter that tends to proceed by digressions rather than by closely reasoned sequential units.

Gospel Foundations: Beginnings and True Light (1:1–2:6)

John writes not as an academic theorist but as a pastoral leader troubled by error

---

▶ Irenaeus on Cerinthus

The second-century Christian leader Irenaeus wrote extensively about religious movements that mixed Christian language with unchristian convictions and practices. A leader of one of these movements, very likely gnostic in nature, was Cerinthus:

Cerinthus, again, a man who was educated in the wisdom of the Egyptians, taught that the world was not made by the primary God, but by a certain Power far separated from him, and at a distance from that Principality who is supreme over the universe, and ignorant of him who is above all. He represented Jesus as having not been born of a virgin, but as being the son of Joseph and Mary according to the ordinary course of human generation, while he was nevertheless more righteous, prudent, and wise than other men. Moreover, after his baptism, Christ descended upon him in the form of a dove from the Supreme Ruler, and that then he proclaimed the unknown Father, and performed miracles. But at last Christ departed from Jesus, and that then Jesus suffered and rose again, while Christ remained impassible [unaffected by suffering or feeling], inasmuch as he was a spiritual being.[A-2]

Structure of 1 John		
Opening Words	Verses	Statement of
"That which was from the beginning . . ."	1:1–2:6	Central burden: God is light
"My dear children . . ."	2:7–17	Central command: Heed the age-old message
"Dear children . . ."	2:18–3:8	Key counsel: Remain in his anointing and receive eternal life
"No one who is born of God will continue to sin . . ."	3:9–4:6	Central warning: Beware Cain's error and false prophets
"Dear friends . . ."	4:7–14	Foundational assurance: God's love
"If anyone acknowledges that Jesus is the Son of God . . ."	4:15–5:15	Necessary instruction: Believing in Jesus the Christ, the Son of God
"If anyone sees a brother commit a sin . . ."	5:16–21	Concluding admonition: The true God and the threat of impostors

and discord in Christ's churches. In this first section of his letter he touches on a number of key concerns: the genuineness of the Christian message, the validity of the apostles' witness, the nature of God, the weightiness of sin, the goals of his letter, the atoning ministry of Jesus Christ, the effect of God's love, and more. All of these relate to what John sees as original and therefore foundational because they relate to "that which was from the beginning"—Jesus Christ.

Having established these claims and concerns in the letter's opening lines, he will return to them repeatedly in subsequent sections.

From the beginning (1:1). In the modern West, newest is best—new ideas, new cars, new beliefs. But in John's world, for something to be true it must be shown to have an ancient heritage. This conviction lies behind the Gospel genealogies (Matt. 1; Luke 3). Jesus assumes it in his disputes with opponents: He is more ancient than their ancestor Abraham (John 8:58). Eusebius (ca. A.D. 300) commends his *Ecclesiastical History* because by it "the real antiquity and divine character of Christianity will be . . . demonstrated to those who suppose that it is recent and foreign, appearing no earlier than yesterday."[11] Even Moses, as he compiled Genesis, realized the importance of showing that his account connects with the world's primal beginnings (Gen. 1:1). As John addresses troubled churches, he

"IN THE BEGINNING..."

▼

grounds the basis for his remarks in the antiquity of what he has seen.

We (1:1). The "we" refers to the earliest disciples, especially the apostles—those who personally saw and lived with Jesus in his earthly days. Why are witnesses important? Jesus appointed the apostles to be his witnesses (Acts 1:8; cf. 1:2). He is in line here with Moses, who taught that testimony must be based on two or more witnesses (Deut. 19:15). This rule was observed in the early church (2 Cor. 13:1). It was likewise observed in Judaism, as reflected in the attempt to establish credible testimony at Jesus' trial (Matt. 26:60).[12] Like John, Luke claims that his Gospel is based on eyewitness testimony (Luke 1:2).

Heard . . . seen . . . looked at . . . touched (1:1). John's letter, he claims, is based on truth. That is, the things he will say about Jesus Christ correspond to the way Jesus actually appeared, lived, died, and rose. For John and others had heard, seen, and touched him. Ancient writers who spoke about historical matters—Jesus of Nazareth's coming *is* a historical and not just religious fact—were concerned that their reports be accurate.[13] Social stability was threatened when people no longer told the truth.[14] Those claiming to relate historical matters must adhere to the facts on which knowledge of history is based.[15] The historian Plutarch (ca. A.D. 100) distinguished between "conjecture" and "definite historical evidence" (*Fall of the Roman Republic, Gaius Marius* 11).[16] John had personal, extensive, and tangible proof—shared with others, so it could not be personal delusion—to back up his letter's teaching about Jesus.

Philo points out that some authorities in ancient times threw out evidence based on hearing alone, "on the ground that what is believed through the eyes is true but through hearing is false."[17] Seneca warns that "credulity is a source of very great mischief. . . . We should believe only what is thrust under our eyes and becomes unmistakable . . . and develop the habit of being slow to believe" (*On Anger* 2.24). Whether hearing, seeing, or touch is demanded for validation, John can vouch for the truth of what he claims (see comments on 1 John 5:9).

Eternal life (1:2). See comments on 2:25.

Fellowship . . . with the Father and with his Son (1:3). See comments on 1:7.

Joy (1:4). See comments on 2 John 4.

God is light (1:5). This, John says, is the core of his letter's message. By this he refers primarily to God's moral excellence,

---

R E F L E C T I O N S

NORTH AMERICAN CHURCH PUBLICITY OFTEN MAKES use of the phrase "food, fun, and fellowship." But for John and his readers "fellowship" is apparently something more profound than good food and good times. Judging from John's letter, fellowship involves commitment to a common body of belief (doctrine) and faithfulness in a dedicated life of obedience. It also involves that elusive thing called love—love for God as well as love for people and especially fellow believers.

So where do "food" and "fun" fit in? In the early church the Lord's Supper was probably observed weekly and involved a full meal. Recreational eating was not the goal, but the shared table was part of corporate worship. As for fun, in a social setting where the very survival of the church was an ongoing challenge, just being able to celebrate another week of life in Christ and shared ministry as God's people might have seemed cause enough to rejoice.

his separateness from all darkness and evil. (On God's character, see "God's Moral Perfection," below. On God as light, see "The True Light" at 2:9.)

The connection between "God" and "light" has little to do with either gnostic or Qumran thought.[18] It is rather from the Old Testament, first of all, that John would have first gained associations between God and light. God made the light of the physical world (Gen. 1:3). He gave his people visual light during their escape from Egypt (Ex. 13:21). David extolled God's spiritual light in prayer (2 Sam. 22:29); with his last words he praised the divine radiance: God "is like the light of morning at sunrise on a cloudless morning" (2 Sam. 23:4). Micah proclaimed, "Though I have fallen, I will rise. Though I sit in darkness, the LORD will be my light" (Mic. 7:8). Like Micah John underscores God's moral light. He knows that in the church age, as at other times in redemptive history, there are "those who call evil good and good evil, who put darkness for light and light for darkness" (Isa. 5:20). They are morally blinded.

Not only God but also Jesus is "light" in John's writings (John 8:12; 9:5). Jesus said, "I have come into the world as a light, so that no one who believes in me should stay in darkness" (12:46).

John's "God is light" stands in contrast with pagan religious systems whose gods or goddesses were associated with the heavenly bodies. Under Roman rule the Syrian Baal, for example, was associated with the sun; his female consort was the moon.[19] Well after New Testament times a cult arose that worshiped the sun.[20] But the true God is personal, not a distant gleam in the night darkness, or even the blazing fire of sunlight. He gives light, ethical direction, rather than condoning harmful or lawless acts. He creates the natural light but is in no way to be identified with it. We can all see the sun, but no one has ever seen God (John 1:18).

At the core of John's letter is the conviction that there is a light, peculiar to God the Father though shared with Christ the Son, which those who know God recognize. Those who do not know God will not recognize that intimate Father-Son connection but will define one apart from the other. Much of 1 John addresses the evils that arise when this occurs.

The truth (1:6, 8; 2:4). See comments on 2 John 1.

The blood of Jesus . . . purifies us from all sin (1:7). If God is perfectly pure and people are weighed down by sin, how can they be brought together? How can there be "fellowship . . . with the Father and with his Son" (1:3)? John's answer: through Jesus' death on the cross—his blood shed for sin.

Others in John's day would have completely disagreed. Philo (influenced by Stoic doctrine) writes that "reason is a priest."[21] Thinking the right thoughts and

▶ God's Moral Perfection in the Ancient World

John's claim that "God is light; in him there is no darkness at all" (1 John 1:5) expresses a widespread Jewish conviction grounded in many Old Testament passages. The Alexandrian Jewish writer Philo (ca. 20 B.C.–A.D. 50) writes most emphatically: "God is absolutely not the cause of any evil whatever of any kind."[A-3]	In traditional Greek religion, which was part of the seedbed of Gnosticism, the gods were not morally upright at all. Xenophanes (c. 570–488 B.C.) writes: "Both Homer and Hesiod have attributed to the gods all things that are shameful and a reproach among mankind: theft, adultery, and mutual deception."[A-4]

saying no to bodily pleasures will purify from sin: "The perfect man is always trying to attain to a complete emancipation from the power of the passions" (3.131). The notion of reason, or knowledge, being the key to salvation is foundational to Gnosticism. It is grounded in the older conviction of Greek religion that reason is the key to blessedness.

In contrast to this, John does not think the human mind can attain what is necessary for salvation. Only an act of God can provide this, and that act is the saving death of Jesus, which saves all who believe (John 1:12).

Without sin (1:8). Numerous Old Testament passages insist that everyone has sinned.[22] The Jewish writer Philo states, "To be aware of what one has done amiss, and to blame one's self, is the part of a righteous man."[23] Even more explicitly, he writes that "there is no man who self-sustained has run the course of life from birth to death without stumbling, but in every case his footsteps have slipped through errors, some voluntary, some involuntary."[24]

In pagan thinking clear moral standards were lacking. "In general the standard was public opinion and not a code of conduct."[25] But there was still an awareness of sin. For example, in the ancient Greek religion Orphism one could receive punishment for sins in the afterlife.[26] The Latin poet Horace (65–8 B.C.) decries the sins of individuals and society at some length.[27]

John writes to sharpen awareness that humans too easily digress from divine standards—and then deceive themselves into protesting their innocence (see "Philo on Sin and Self-Deception").

If anybody does sin (2:1). If sin is the problem, what is the solution? It is Jesus, "who speaks to the Father in our defense" (2:1). Other faith communities of John's day saw the matter differently. Jews at Qumran believed that no willful sin against Moses' law could be forgiven; even minor sins required lengthy periods of penance, and atonement for sin took place through human acts of prayer and complete obedience to the community's teaching.[28] Yet there was hope through God's mercy and pardon (11.11–15). But the basis for hope is frustratingly vague.

John's prescription for forgiveness is as definite as it is simple: "Jesus Christ, the Righteous One." Writing shortly after John's death, Ignatius warns the church at Smyrna against those who deny the atoning power (cf. 1 John 2:2) of Jesus' death: "Let no man be misled. Even the heavenly beings and the glory of the angels and the rulers, both visible and invisible, are also subject to judgment, if they do not believe in the blood of Christ."[29]

Atoning sacrifice (2:1). The Greek word is *hilasmos* (used also in 4:10), a word associated with the Hebrew *kpr* word group found extensively (112 times) in the Old Testament. In some contexts the word means "to remove or wipe away." But it can also refer to a death by one victim that satisfies the guilt before God of some other victim. That is, a *hilasmos* ("propitiation" or "propitiatory sacrifice") bears God's wrath toward sin so that the sinner who deserves wrath may escape. Paul describes this process in 2 Corinthians 5:21: "God made him who had no sin to be sin for us, so that in him we might become the righteousness of God." That is, "God presented him as a sacrifice of atonement" (*hilastērion*; Rom. 3:25). John's usage carries the same notion. In most world religions, people do things to

make themselves acceptable to God. For John, Jesus' death is the basis for forgiveness and salvation, not human merit.

The sins of the whole world (2:2). While John does not believe everyone will go to heaven, he states that Christ's saving

Roman Sculptures and Sarcoph

right ▶

ADVOCATE

Statue of a Roman lawyer in a toga.

▶ **Philo on Sin and Self-Deception**

John feels the need to warn readers about taking sin lightly. Philo elaborates on the human tendency toward flagrant sin and forgetfulness of both personal error and morality itself:

Therefore men in general, even if the slightest breeze of prosperity blows their way for only a moment, become puffed up and give themselves great airs, becoming insolent to all those who are in a lower condition than themselves, and calling them dregs of the earth, and annoyances, and sources of trouble, and burdens of the earth, and all sorts of names of that kind, as if they had been thoroughly able to establish the undeviating charac-

ter of their prosperity on a solid foundation, though, very likely, they will not remain in the same condition even till tomorrow, for there is nothing more inconstant than fortune, which tosses human affairs up and down like dice. Often has a single day thrown down the man who was previously placed on an eminence, and raised the lowly man on high. And while men see these events continually taking place, and though they are well assured of the fact, still they overlook their relations and friends, and transgress the laws according to which they were born and brought up ... no longer remembering a single one of their ancient usages.[A-5]

death has opened blessings to all persons. In keeping with the universal scope of Christ's blessing, not many years after John's death Ignatius writes to Christians in Asia Minor: "Pray continually for the rest of mankind as well, that they may find God, for there is in them a hope of repentance."[30] Many religions of antiquity were focused primarily on the people group that practiced them. The Christian gospel, rooted in the knowledge of the one true God who created heaven and earth, had a comprehensive saving scope.

God's love is truly made complete (2:5). John, probably writing from Ephesus, teaches that obeying God's Word is a mark of being perfected in God's love. Ignatius warns the Ephesian Christians against people who traffic in God's name but disobey his commands: "For there are some who maliciously and deceitfully are accustomed to carry about the Name while doing other things unworthy of God."[31] But he commends the Ephesians: "So you are all fellow pilgrims . . . adorned in every respect with the commandments of Jesus Christ."[32]

The fact is that for many religions of that time obedience to a moral standard was not important at all. Social morality was at a low ebb. Immoral sexual practice was widespread. Religion did little to check these trends. Sometimes it even encouraged them. "Cultus had little to do with morality except in cases of grave offence, and priests did not function as moral guides."[33] Part of the reason for this lay in the Greek belief that reason, not revelation, was the sole foundation for knowing how to live. Xenophanes (c. 570–488 B.C.) wrote: "Truly the gods have not revealed to mortals all things from the beginning, but mortals by long seeking discover what is better."[34]

In contrast, John announces what is "from the beginning" (1 John 1:1), a God who loves (see comments on 4:8) and who reveals his will in Scripture and then in human hearts. God's love is completed as his people "walk as Jesus did" (2:6).

Statement of the Letter's Central Command: Heed the Age-Old Message (2:7–17)

If the preceding section is a kaleidoscope of concerns and assertions, this section is a microscope focused on one issue: the imperative to love—and to direct love to the proper objects. This imperative is not some new message but has a distinguished pedigree. At the same time it is new indeed.

Not . . . a new command but an old one, which you have had since the beginning (2:7). By "command" in this section John most likely refers to the imperative to love. It is "old" in the sense that it goes back to Moses' time, as John would have learned from the synagogue as well as from Jesus. (It is even more ancient than Moses, of course, in that it is grounded in God's eternal character and existence.)

◀ *left*

MERCY SEAT

A representation of the high priest sprinkling blood on the mercy seat (or atonement cover) in the Most Holy Place on the Day of Atonement.

Jesus' teaching on love is not something he inaugurated but something he inherited from the Hebrew Scriptures: "All the Law and the Prophets hang on these two commandments," Jesus said (Matt. 22:37–40): "Love the LORD your God with all your heart and with all your soul and with all your strength" (Deut. 6:5); "love your neighbor as yourself" (Lev. 19:18). This twofold ancient command—for John grounds the love that people express in the love that God has revealed (1 John 4:10)—is the heart of the message Christians receive.

But old messages are easy to forget. The Old Testament reminds readers many times to remember God: "Remember the wonders he has done, his miracles, and the judgments he pronounced" (Ps. 105:5). And even when memory is active, response may be lacking. The Greek writer Xenophon (4th century B.C.) wrote that the very oldest laws of the Greeks were widely praised, but they were not heeded.[35] Nor did these laws center on love but on virtuous and gentlemanly character, in the thinking of the Spartan law-giver Lycurgus (9th century B.C.).[36]

Old messages may also be overlooked because they are out of step with the times. In the modern West a basic belief is "individualist realism."[37] In such an outlook "I" am the center of my life, not other people. Love for others becomes a secondary concern; self-love is primary. John does not share this cultural outlook because it is not the outlook endorsed by God and instilled by the Christian message. Rather, the age-old reality to which God's love calls us is love—for God and for others, especially brothers and sisters in the faith.

Yet I am writing you a new command (2:8). Often John writes in terms of black-white contrasts. But here he speaks not of "either-or" but of "both-and." The love command is very old, but it is also very new.

The command is new because Jesus reaffirmed and dramatized it in unprecedented ways. Jesus dramatized love by the way he experienced it from God:

▶ The True Light

God, his ways, and his word are associated with light in numerous ancient writings. An example would be the *Odes of Solomon*, a poetic book perhaps composed in Syriac and dating from around A.D. 100:

> The Lord has directed my mouth by his Word,
>   and has opened my heart by his Light. (10:1)
> And the Lord renewed me with his garment,
>   and possessed me by his light. . . .
> And the Lord (is) like the sun
>   upon the face of the land.
> My eyes were enlightened,
>   and my face received the dew. (11:11, 13–14)

> As the sun is the joy to them who seek its
>   daybreak,
>   so is my joy the Lord;
> because he is my sun,
>   and his rays have restored me;
>   and his light has dismissed all darkness from
>   my face. (15:1–2)
> Let not light be conquered by darkness,
>   nor let truth flee from falsehood. (18:6)
> A lamp you set for me both on my right and on
>   my left,
>   so that there might not be in me anything
>   that is not light. (25:7)

▶ Hating People

The same Qumran scroll that teaches hatred of "all the sons of darkness" paints a graphic picture of the struggle between good and evil in the world.[A-6] "Everlasting hatred" is part of the present world until the final age. This may be seen as justifying hatred of evil people:

The nature of all the children of men is ruled by these (two spirits), and during their life all the hosts of men have a portion in their divisions and walk in (both) their ways. And the whole reward for their deeds shall be, for everlasting ages, according to whether each man's portion in their two divisions is great or small. For God has established the spirits in equal measure until the final age, and has set everlasting hatred between their divisions. Truth abhors the works of falsehood, and falsehood hates all the ways of truth. And their struggle is fierce in all their arguments for they do not walk together.[A-7]

"The Father loves the Son and has placed everything in his hands" (John 3:35). "For the Father loves the Son and shows him all he does" (5:20). He reaffirmed love in the way he loved others, whether friends like Martha, Mary, and Lazarus (11:5); or lost souls like the rich young ruler (Mark 10:21); or his close disciples (John 13:1).

Jesus also taught his disciples to love others as he had loved them. He illustrated this by washing their feet (John 13:1–17). Jesus even termed his teaching a new command: "A new command I give you: Love one another. As I have loved you, so you must love one another" (13:34). The primary background for John's talk of a "new" command in 1 John may well be Jesus on the night he was betrayed.

Its truth (2:8). See comments on 2 John 1.

In the light (2:9). See "The True Light."

Hates his brother (2:11). Jesus cited popular opinion that honoring God and hating certain people were compatible: "You have heard that it was said, 'Love your neighbor and hate your enemy'" (Matt. 5:43). Jesus rejected this, and so does John. But not all religious teachers of the time thought that hatred was necessarily a bad thing. *The Community Rule* of the Qumran community (CD 1.9–11) teaches that community members are to "love all the sons of light, each one according to his lot in God's plan, and to detest all the sons of darkness, each one in accordance to his blame in God's vindication." This hatred could be seen as a reflection of God's own loathing of evil; since God abhors the wickedness of the world, his people would be justified in

"STILL IN THE DARKNESS..."

abhorring wicked people (see "Hating People," below). In contrast to this John's teaching focuses on love and leaves judgment in God's hands.

John's teaching is unique here in the way it is grounded in the love shown in the death of Jesus Christ. But the notion that one should love one's enemies, or at least be kind to them, was present in Judaism long before New Testament times. For example, the *Letter of Aristeas* (170 B.C.?) describes a (probably fictitious) banquet in which an Egyptian king poses difficult questions to Jewish scholars.[38] One of the questions is, "To whom must a man be generous?" The answer is, first, that one should be magnanimous to friends, which is called "the general opinion." But like Jesus, though for different reasons, the Jewish scholar takes the matter a step farther: "My belief is that we must also show liberal charity to our opponents so that in this manner we may convert them to what is proper and fitting to them."

To the question, "To whom must one show favor?" the same Jew replies, "To his parents, always, for God's very great commandment concerns the honor due to parents. Next (and closely connected) [God] reckons the honor due to friends, calling the friend an equal of one's own

self. You do well if you bring all men into friendship with yourself." If this is not identical to 1 John's appeal to love one's brother and not hate, it is at least consistent with John's thrust.

The evil one (2:13–14). This refers to the angelic being spoken of elsewhere in John as the devil, Satan, or "the prince of this world."[39] Jesus said that with his death and resurrection the power of the evil one is broken (12:31); he has "no hold" on Jesus (14:30). Yet until Christ returns, Satan makes trouble in the world and in the church by deceiving people and by spawning the lies and murderousness that are his trademarks. Satan is referred to in the Old Testament and frequently in Jewish literature of the New Testament era, often under the name Belial ("the worthless one") or Beliar, an evil being who orchestrates the workings of evil people. No wonder John's letter commends Christians who by faith in Christ "have overcome" this shadowy figure.

Do not love the world (2:15). Philo concurs: "It is impossible for love of the world to coexist with love for God, just as it is impossible for light and darkness to be present at the same time."[40] Philo traces the incessant wars of his age to one common source: "the desire of money, or fame, or pleasure. For the human race has its heart set on these things."[41] Many ancient authors speak of the evil in the world and how best to escape its consequences (see "Salvation from the World," below).

The world and its desires pass away (2:17). John's insight that the things of the world are not ultimate is important but far from unique. The third-century A.D. philosopher Porphyry commends a

▶ Salvation from the World

According to a Qumran document "The Wicked and the Holy" (4Q181), it is God who calls "sons of the world" into eternal life:

In accordance with the mercies of God, according to His goodness and wonderful glory, He caused some of the

sons of the world to draw near (Him) . . . to be counted with Him in the com[munity of the g]ods as a congregation of holiness in service for eternal life and (sharing) the lot of His holy ones . . . each man according to his lot which He has cast for . . . eternal life.[A-8]

life of self-contentment rather than pursuit of luxury, for riches and fame bring nothing but problems.[42] Other pagan thinkers voice the same conviction.[43] The Hellenistic Jewish writer Philo, reflecting Stoic values, writes, "One should practice being contented with a little, for this is being near God; but the contrary habit is being very far from him."[44]

More distinctive is John's view of time.[45] The world is passing away; things are not an endless cycle. History is moving toward a grand goal. John is convinced that with Christ's coming it is now "the last hour" (2:18). This is the sense in which the world is passing away. He is not saying that created reality, or existence itself, can somehow disappear. It is rather that with Christ's coming the redemption of the world, the dawn of the long-awaited age to come, has moved a quantum leap closer. What that means is one of the subjects of the next section.

Key Counsel: Remain in His Anointing and Receive Eternal Life (2:18–3:8)

Dear children (2:18). John has feelings of affection for those he addresses. The religion he champions is a personal relationship with God through Jesus Christ (see 1:3). This God is known personally

and intimately, cares for each of his worshipers, and unites them to other community members in a bond of love. Such a doctrine was virtually unknown in Greco-Roman religion. Albert A. Bell Jr. comments that the Egyptian goddess Isis "is virtually the only ancient divinity who displays any love or concern for her devotees."[46] But this did not translate into a community whose members' high calling was to love one another. The blessings of the mythological Isis pale in comparison to the promises of the real-world, incarnate Christ.

While John's language points to a stance of love for those he addresses, Stoic philosophy of the day reflected a different ideal. Life's goal was not to be united with others but to be free from the demands they might make. For the Roman moralist Seneca "not to be disturbed" was a high priority—to know "tranquillity of mind."[47] In Epictetus's teaching this called for maintaining distance from people and not being too attached to them—not even to wife and children.[48] Very different is the Christian mandate of loving others (as John evidently cares for his "dear children") and finding joy even in sacrifice for them.

Antichrist is coming (2:18). "Christ" means "Messiah," God's Anointed One, the deliverer of God's people. Among Jews and Christians of the first century was a wide range of messianic beliefs. Jesus warned his disciples about "false Christs" (Matt. 24:24). His disciples, who expected Christ himself to appear again to usher in the final age, taught that before he returned a sinister figure would arise, who would exalt himself against God and Christ's kingdom (2 Thess. 2:1–12). In all likelihood this is the shadowy "antichrist" of whom John speaks. In fact, he is already present in the form of "many antichrists," presumably enemies of the Jesus Christ preached by John and the other apostles.

Early Christian writers identified this antichrist in various ways. Polycarp (early 2d century) has a threefold description of such a figure.[49] He first quotes 1 John (cf. 1 John 4:2–3): "For every one who shall not confess that Jesus Christ is come in the flesh, is antichrist." He then issues two parallel warnings: "Whosoever shall not confess the testimony of the Cross, is of the devil; and whosoever shall pervert the oracles of the Lord to his own lusts and say that there is neither resurrection nor judgment, that man is the first-born of Satan." It is clear that early Christians kept their eyes open for opponents of Christ and the Christian message. The expectation of a satanic usurper of God's earthly kingdom is widespread in both ancient Christian (see "The Deceiver of the World," below) and Jewish apocalyptic writings.

They went out from us (2:19). Despite Jesus' stress on love and unity (e.g., John 13:34–35), the early church experienced frequent disagreement (e.g., Acts 15) and even open division. In the church at Ephesus (where the apostle John was active) late in the first century, there were "wicked men . . . who claim to be apostles but are not" (Rev. 2:2). False teachers also appear to have been a problem at the nearby churches of Pergamum (2:14–15) and Thyatira (2:20). As John writes 1 John, he is apparently aware that there has been schism in the congregation or congregations he addresses. This is lamentable.

But John sees it as evidence that those who have departed have never truly embraced the gospel to begin with: "If they had belonged to us, they would have remained with us" (1 John 2:19). Unity is a high priority, but even higher is fidelity to the apostolic message that "Jesus is the

---

▶ The Deceiver of the World

John's reference to the Antichrist seems to be paralleled by a (slightly later?) early Christian writing that issues the following warning (see *Didache* 16:3–5):

For in the last days the false prophets and corrupters will abound, and the sheep will be turned into wolves, and love will be turned into hate. For as lawlessness increases, they will hate and persecute and betray one another. And then the deceiver of the world will appear as a son of God and will "perform signs and wonders" [Mark 13:22], and the earth will be delivered into his hands, and he will commit abominations the likes of which have never happened before. Then all humankind will come to the fiery test, and "many will fall away" and perish; but "those who endure" in their faith "will be saved" [cf. Matt. 24:10, 13].

Christ" (2:22). It is likely that John sees the division that has occurred as necessary because those who have departed physically have already departed from the Christian message doctrinally and ethically.

You have an anointing (2:20). In the days of Moses fine olive oil was rubbed or poured on objects to mark them off for God's special use. Aaron and his sons were anointed in this fashion for their service in the Tent of Meeting. This designated them as "a priesthood that will continue for all generations to come" (Ex. 40:15). Later in the history of Israel, prophets like Samuel anointed men chosen by God to be king. David was honored in this way; on that occasion the Holy Spirit "came upon David in power" (1 Sam. 16:13). Still later, and in John's own lifetime, Jesus Christ, the Son of David, was viewed by the early Christians as God's Anointed One par excellence (Acts 4:26; cf. Ps. 2:2).

As John writes to believers who "have an anointing," he has in mind this heritage of blessing and setting apart for service dating back many centuries to God's people in Old Testament times. The climactic coming of the "Anointed One" (*christos* in Greek, from which we get the word "Christ") results in a whole community who revel in the "anointing" that faith in Christ bestows. While some have recently departed from the Christian community (1 John 2:19), John addresses those who remain. From "the Holy One" (which can refer to either God or Christ) they have been gifted with the saving gospel message, the Holy Spirit, and baptism. As they remain true to the apostolic teaching in which John's letter confirms them, their "anointing" will keep them pointed in the right direction.[50]

The truth (2:20–21). See comments on 2 John 1.

What you have heard from the beginning (2:24). See comments on 1:1.

He promised us . . . eternal life (2:25). Clearly John views "eternal life" as an incentive to remain faithful. The words suggest to Christians the promise of heaven, and rightly so. One of the New Testament's best-known verses promises "eternal life" to all who place full personal trust in Jesus Christ (John 3:16), and Christ himself promised to prepare a place for his followers where they would join him in the afterlife (14:1–3).

But eternal life is more than something for later, after we die. It is for now. In John's time—and here our world is hardly different—life is constantly overshadowed by the threat of death. Coping mechanisms have to be devised. One notable philosophical response was denial, or more precisely apathy—a posture of resolute indifference to the surrounding world. This is seen in Epictetus's strategy of pretending that death is not what troubles people; it is rather the idea of death (see "Dealing with Death"). At work here is the belief that all reality is interconnected and material; life is a never-ending cycle of recurrence, in which there is no transcendent good or evil or indeed eternal meaning of any kind. Seneca's description of people illustrates this: "Born from nothingness they go back to nothingness" (*On Tranquillity of Mind* 15.4). We must therefore simply live in accordance with this inexorable natural flow. Meanwhile, within ourselves we work to stay insulated from pain and grief. Insulation is necessary because "the future, either in this life or after it, is nothing to look forward to."[51]

John, however, proclaims "the eternal life, which was with the Father and has appeared to us" (1 John 1:2). There *is* hope for the future![52] Obviously John points to Jesus Christ, who spoke of himself as "the resurrection and the life" and stated that whoever believes in him "will live, even though he dies" (John 11:25). But eternal life denotes more than the excellence and longevity of life with God in the age to come. It involves a spiritual quality of life in the here and now, a personal relationship with the Lord through faith.

Jesus illustrated eternal life not merely by alluding to heaven but also by pointing back to Moses' day. Just as the children of Israel lived by looking in faith on the bronze serpent displayed on a pole, so hearers of the gospel message "have eternal life" by looking in faith upon "the Son of Man . . . lifted up" (John 3:14–15; see "[Eternal] Life in Old Testament"). While Old Testament believers did not have specific knowledge of all points of Christian doctrine, New Testament writers see the offer of salvation extended in Old Testament times as a precedent for the gospel message now being preached.

For this reason, the words "live" and "life" in certain Old Testament contexts reverberate with the promise of "eternal life" sounded by John in 1 John 2:25. Notable examples are found especially in Deuteronomy.[53] Most telling here is 30:6: "The LORD your God will circumcise your hearts and the hearts of your descendants, so that you may love him with all your heart and with all your soul, and *live*" (italics added). Talk of circumcised hearts and of loving God with all one's heart and soul is, of course, language familiar to New Testament believers. It is the language of eternal life, God's covenant blessing, in the here and now.

Although John's letters have few direct references to the Old Testament, John (who was himself a Jew) has been educated in the synagogue. He has heard Jesus teach extensively from the Old Testament. He has heard Jesus tell skeptical detractors, "If you believed Moses, you would believe me, for he wrote about me" (John 5:46). John's Gospel also records Jesus' words "salvation is from the Jews" (4:22). It is little surprise, then, that the primary background for understanding "life" as the eternal God bestows it in salvation through Christ, or "eternal life," is the Hebrew Scriptures and the history of Israel.

Anointing (2:27). See comments on 2:20.

▶ Dealing with Death

The gospel message promises eternal life, meaning a transformed "now" as well as a glorious "hereafter." Death has been defeated by Christ. Very different is the vision set forth by the Stoic writer Epictetus, which does not so much face death as deny it:[A-9]

When you see a person weeping in sorrow for a child gone abroad or dead, or for loss of his property, take care that the appearances do not carry you away, as if he were suffering in external things. Make a distinction in your own mind and say, "It is not what happened that afflicts this man, but it is the opinion about that thing that afflicts the man." So far as words, then, do not be unwilling to show him sympathy, and even to lament with him. But take care that you do not lament in your inner being also.

► **(Eternal) Life in the Old Testament**

Jesus taught Nicodemus about eternal life by reminding him of an incident that took place in Moses' day (John 3:10–15). There the people "lived"—were spared God's judgment and could enjoy covenant blessings—by heeding the message Moses proclaimed to them.

They traveled from Mount Hor along the route to the Red Sea, to go around Edom. But the people grew impatient on the way; they spoke against God and against Moses, and said, "Why have you brought us up out of Egypt to die in the desert? There is no bread! There is no water! And we detest this miserable food!" Then the LORD sent venomous snakes among them; they bit the people and many Israelites died. The people came to Moses and said, "We sinned when we spoke against the LORD and against you. Pray that the LORD will take the snakes away from us." So Moses prayed for the people. The LORD said to Moses, "Make a snake and put it up on a pole; anyone who is bitten can look at it and live." So Moses made a bronze snake and put it up on a pole. Then when anyone was bitten by a snake and looked at the bronze snake, he lived. (Num. 21:4–9)

Do not need anyone to teach you (2:27). In part this is a figure of speech; King Agrippa uses it in a letter to Josephus.[54] If his audience literally needed no instruction, John would not be writing.

Children of God (3:1–2). In broad terms all humankind are children of God in that God is their Maker (Isa. 45:11–12). More particularly, Israel has God as its Father (Deut. 32:6ff.; Isa. 43:6–7). But Christians are children of God in a still fuller sense: Christ has given to those who believe in him "the right to become children of God—children born not of natural descent, nor of human decision or a husband's will, but born of God" (John 1:12–13).

Human fathers in the Greco-Roman world had the power of life and death over children. They were not always affectionate or even equitable. Children were unwanted in many quarters of the classical world. When they were born, a father was free to order them to be "exposed"—that is, taken to an out-of-the-way place and left to die. The church father Tertullian notes that under the proconsulship of Tiberius in north Africa, children were sacrificed to Saturn; across the empire children were killed "by drowning, or by exposure to cold and hunger and dogs."[55] Childhood was by no means always a time of safety and nurture in such an age. Nor is it today, with child neglect a perennial problem and abortion on demand an international, and especially American, disgrace (see "Tertullian on Abortion," below).

How different from heartless human parents is the heavenly Father, who has "lavished" love on his children (3:1) both in this world and in the next, when "we shall be like him, for we shall see him as he is" (3:2). This sure hope moves God's children to purify themselves, "just as he is pure" (3:3). In this they are assured of success because Christ has been successful in his mission "to destroy the devil's work" (3:8).

Do not let anyone lead you astray (3:7). John writes to protect his readers against false teachers, teachings, and practices. In Old Testament times idolatry misled many (Deut. 13:6; 2 Kings 21:9). The subversion of God's people by evil angelic beings is a recurrent theme of later Jewish literature as well (*1 Enoch* 6–10, *Jub.* 5:1–10). *Testament of Levi* 10:2 and 16:1, in warning of end-time transgression, use a word related to John's "lead astray." John is warning of missteps that can have consequences of eschatological proportions.

Son of God (3:8). See also comments on "children of God" at 3:10. "Son of God" is the title for Jesus Christ that occurs most frequently in the Johannine letters.[56] Its shortened version "Son" is even more common.[57] It refers to Jesus' divinity, his unique oneness with God the Father. In Hellenistic religion there was talk of divine sonship via human cohabitation with a god; the offspring would be a "son of a god." Caesar Augustus was thought to have divine parentage as the result of his mother's impregnation by a snake in the temple of Apollo.[58] In a religious setting where the gods were both numerous and essentially human in their characteristics, the notion of a human attaining some semblance of divinity is hardly startling.

Very different is the idea of Jesus' divine sonship. He is the only Son (John 1:18: Gk. *monogenēs hyios*) of the "God" who is "holy"—utterly unique. His conception by the Holy Spirit was without male human agency. His relationship to God is unparalleled because he had been "with God" and "came from God" in a sense true of no other human being (1:1; 8:42). He was sinless. He fully shared our lot but at the same time transcended it. No wonder he (and only he) is able, as 1 John 3:8 says, "to destroy the devil's work."

The devil (3:8). See comments on 2:13–14.

Statement of the Letter's Central Warning: Beware Cain's Error and False Prophets (3:9–4:6)

In this section John uses the negative example of Cain to warn his readers of certain dangers they face—especially the danger of lovelessness. He then reminds them, once again, of the love command and urges them to scrutinize the beliefs,

---

REFLECTIONS

IT HAS BEEN NOTED THAT "CLEARLY WITHOUT BELIEF in God sin has no meaning."[A-10] For increasing numbers of people in postmodern society, the classical Christian idea of God is on the wane. The consciousness of sin likewise diminishes.

Even where sin is recognized, it may be rationalized as inhabiting only the most depraved few (Hitler, Stalin, serial killers, etc.), as being solely the product of social conditioning; or as being only a cultural perception when in fact there is no right or wrong. In some understandings sin is ignorance; therefore education is the answer to personal and social problems. Others believe that medicine, especially behavior-modifying drugs, hold the answer to "sin" (to the extent there is such a thing). One of the most popular responses to sin, in all ages, is denial, grounded in that most persistent of all human character traits: proud self-righteousness.

We all must admit that life has its gray areas. But if the Bible's commands articulate valid standards of God's character and prescriptions for people's attitudes and behavior, gray areas are the exception and not the rule. Christ came to take away our sin, not make us experts in self-justification or sin management. The power that raised him from the dead can fill our lives with the desire to move toward a higher plane on which Christ's commands become our goal and delight.

ideas, and practices they adopt. Such scrutiny is necessary because "many false prophets have gone out into the world" (4:1).

God's seed (3:9). Other writers recognize that what is true and noble within persons is the result of divine implantation (see "Saving Understanding" at 5:20, in which Philo speaks of God sowing virtues in humankind). Biblical writers tend to speak of the implantation of the divine word (see James 1:18, 21).

Cannot go on sinning (3:9). The Roman moralist Seneca attributes virtuous behavior to the power of human goodness. Virtuous action comes from within and by one's own volition. Seneca speaks of "the man of perfect wisdom," who is impervious to lapses of good judgment and behavior.[59] As an example he points to Horatius Cocles, a mythical one-eyed military leader of Rome's early history, who modeled consistency and was good, not by dint of conscious planning but simply because that was his character. "Moral perfection" was recognizable in him, Seneca concludes.[60]

John refers not to human virtue in the Greco-Roman sense but to compliance with God's law (3:4) and conformity to

Jesus' daily walk (2:6). This is possible only because of spiritual new birth, which John calls being "born of God" (3:9). It is unlikely that John has in mind absolute sinless perfection, since earlier he has denounced those who say they are without sin (1:8, 10). Rather, John has in mind the blatant sinning to which those who have left the community have fallen prey (2:19). In view of the letter as a whole, such sinning probably involves denial of Christ's human nature (4:2–3; theological lapse), flaunting of God's (or Christ's) commands (2:4; ethical lapse), failure to love (4:20; relational lapse), or some combination of these grave errors.

We know who the children of God are (3:10). See comments on 3:1–2. The first-century rhetorician Dio Chrysostom records a conversation between the Cynic philosopher Diogenes and Alexander the Great.[61] The latter asked the Cynic his opinion of the claim of some that Alexander was begotten by a god. Diogenes's reply was that if Alexander lived in a disciplined fashion and showed understanding of "the divine art of being king," then nothing prevented Alexander from being "a son of Zeus."[62]

Like Diogenes, John sees a connection between human behavior and divine

---

▶ **Tertullian on Abortion**

"Children of God" in Christ can count on faithful love and protection from their heavenly Father. In the ancient world Greco-Roman fathers sometimes set a very different family tone. Children were destroyed in the womb if they were unwanted or illegitimate. The early Christian leader Tertullian protested this and described the contrasting behavior of Christians:

In our case, murder being once for all forbidden, we may not destroy even the fetus in the womb, while as yet the human being derives blood from others parts of the body for its sustenance. To hinder a birth is merely a speedier man-killing; nor does it matter whether you take away a life that is born, or destroy one that is coming to the birth. That is a man which is going to be one; you have the fruit already in its seed.[A-11]

▶ Josephus on Cain

John's letter limits its criticism of Cain to the murder of Abel recorded in Genesis 4. Josephus extends the condemnation considerably:

> Even while Adam was alive, it came to pass that the posterity of Cain became exceeding wicked, every one succes-sively dying one after another more wicked than the former. They were intolerable in war, and vehement in robberies; and if anyone were slow to murder people, yet was he bold in his profligate behavior, in acting unjustly and doing injuries for gain.[A-12]

blessing. But "God" for John is not Zeus, part of the Greco-Roman pantheon of gods and goddesses. Consequently, John calls for doing "what is right"—that is, living in keeping with the nature and commandments of the God whom Jesus revealed. Likewise, John calls for love for others—something fundamentally characteristic of the Hebrew-Christian God but alien to the nature of the deities of the Greco-Roman religion. "Children of God" in John's sense and a "son of Zeus" in Diogenes's sense are actually two very different things.

Children of the devil (3:10). See comments on "the evil one" at 2:13–14; 5:19. Just as a child of God is someone who reflects his or her divine parentage by embodying the heavenly Father's goodness (see Eph. 5:1–2), a child of the devil is someone who practices Satan's deceit and ill will toward God and fellow humans.

Do not be like Cain (3:12). In the twentieth century names like Stalin, Pol Pot, and Hitler became synonymous with murderous intrigue and social chaos. In ancient Jewish literature Cain played a similar role. Why was he so despised? Philo thinks Cain's sin lay in his focus on "earthly and inanimate things," his love for himself, and his offhand attitude toward God's standards of acceptable sacrifices.[63] For Philo virtue lies in attention to the things of the soul, not of the earth. Josephus accuses Cain of greed and of impropriety in plowing the earth; this meant that the sacrifice he offered to God was "forced from nature by the ingenuity of grasping man."[64] He introduced great evil into the world by "rapine and violence"; further, he corrupted "that simplicity in which men lived before by the invention of weights and measures: the guileless and generous existence which they had enjoyed in ignorance of these things he converted into a life of craftiness."[65]

Genesis 4:1–16 relates the original story of Cain's slaughter of his brother Abel. John's critique of Cain is simple: He murdered Abel because of jealousy. Abel's sacrifice was acceptable to God, and Cain's sacrifice was rejected. Cain's behav-

SYNAGOGUE

The fourth-century A.D. Jewish synagogue at Sardis.

▼

▶Ben Sirach on Almsgiving

Christians should be exemplary in their love for each other, John teaches. This love must not be mere words but extend to deeds and physical goods (3:17). The second-century B.C. Jewish writing quoted below sounds similar notes. It is different from Christian writings in that it forbids giving alms to "the sinner." Also, it suggests that almsgiving atones for sin (Sir. 3:30). John presents Christian love as a response to God's grace, not a means of acquiring that grace.

If you do good, know to whom you
do it,
and you will be thanked for your
good deeds.
Do good to the devout, and you will
be repaid—
if not by them, certainly by the
Most High.

No good comes to the one who
persists in evil
or to one who does not give alms.
Give to the devout, but do not help
the sinner.
Do good to the humble, but do
not give to the ungodly;
hold back their bread, and do not
give it to them,
for by means of it they might
subdue you;
then you will receive twice as
much evil
for all the good you have done
to them.
For the Most High also hates sinners
and will inflict punishment on the
ungodly.
Give to the one who is good, but do
not help the sinner. (12:1–7)

ior and underlying attitude were the utter antithesis of love. John uses Cain, the epitome of treachery, as an example of how God's people must *not* regard each other. Christian faith generates active goodwill for others, not murderous impulses toward them. Christians know they "have passed from death to life" (1 John 3:14) because they love each other rather than despise each other or remain indifferent to a brother or sister in need.

Hates his brother (3:15). Seneca frankly points out how "hatred of the human race seizes us" because of the corruption and foolishness we see on every hand. But his strategy for coping with it is as flimsy as it is surprising: Laugh! Scoff and be cynical! "Therefore all things must be made light of and borne with a calm mind. It is more manlike to scoff at life

than to bewail it."[66] Seneca's frankness is admirable, but John points to a better solution in 3:16.

Eternal life (3:15). See comments on 2:25.

Jesus Christ laid down his life for us. And we ought ... (3:16). Whereas Seneca prescribed cynicism as an antidote for hatred of others (see comments on 3:15), John calls for attention to Christ's saving death. The cross, which is our only ground for salvation, summons those it saves to take up their cross in seeking the good of others. Just as Jesus prayed for his enemies and could therefore intercede for them even as they willed his death (Luke 23:34), so his followers can learn to walk in love where otherwise they might harbor malice.

▶Give to Needy Brothers

In language similar to that found in John's letter, the Old Testament calls on the people of God to extend physical aid to needy brethren.

If there is a poor man among your brothers in any of the towns of the land that the LORD your God is giving you, do not be hardhearted or tightfisted toward your poor brother. Rather be openhanded and freely lend him whatever he needs. . . . Give generously to him and do so without a grudging heart; then because of this the LORD your God will bless you in all your work and in everything you put your hand to. (Deut. 15:7–8, 10)

If anyone has material possessions . . . but has no pity (3:17). Jewish religion of the first century went to great lengths to care for the poor. Josephus boasted that "no Jew depended on outsiders for charitable support, since the Jews cared for all of their destitute and disabled brethren."[67] Writers like Ben Sirach extolled the virtues of giving to the needy (almsgiving). Yet only good people ought to receive charitable aid (see "Ben Sirach on Almsgiving").

This then is how we know that we belong to the truth (3:19). If "this then" refers back to preceding verses (esp. to 3:18), John seems to be linking Christian assurance to ethical behavior. If we love in deed and not word alone, our standing before God is confirmed. It is always tempting to think we are right with God when our hearts are in fact hardened toward him, as revealed by lack of compassion for others. An Old Testament background for John's teaching here is likely (see "Give to Needy Brothers").[68]

Truth (3:19). See comments on 2 John 1.

False prophets (4:1). In Greco-Roman religion of the time there was high interest in secret or privileged knowledge of supernatural mysteries. There was "proliferation of personal dream revelations, oracles and their interpretation, magic and astrology"; further, there were "numerous exclusive groups offering initiates higher knowledge for their personal weal and salvation."[69] A Roman military leader kept a Syrian prophetess named Martha with his army to furnish advice on important decisions; the Roman senate itself might settle an issue according to the prophetic pronouncement of a priest or priestess.[70] In Jewish settings both Philo and Josephus warn against false prophets.[71]

Jesus Christ has come in the flesh (4:2). On the rise of docetic views of Christ, see comments on Cerinthus and Gnosticism under "Challenges Confronting the Churches" in the introduction.

QUMRAN

Cave 4—the principal cave for the discovery of many of the Dead Sea Scrolls. ▼

Spirit of truth (4:6). See comments at 2 John 1.

Foundational Assurance: God's Love (4:7–14)

Thus far John has focused on statements of fact about God, on various commands and counsel, and on necessary warnings. In this section he repeats these themes but shifts the emphasis slightly to concentrate on the love of God shown in the sacrifice of Christ.

Let us love one another (4:7). See comments on 2:5, 7, 8, 11, 18.

God is love (4:8). He is not *only* love, of course; one listing arrives at 152 different "designations, descriptions, and figures of speech for God" in the Bible![72]

Yet a foundational tenet of Old Testament theology is that the God of Abraham, Isaac, and Jacob is a God who zealously loves his people. Moses composed a hymn to God that stated, "In your unfailing love you will lead the people you have redeemed" (Ex. 15:13). Although he punishes rebellion, God shows "love to a thousand generations of those" who turn to him in faith (20:6). When Moses was granted a glimpse of the distant edge of God's glory, the heavenly voice he heard affirmed: "The LORD, the LORD, the compassionate and gracious God, slow to anger, abounding in love and faithfulness, maintaining love to thousands, and forgiving wickedness, rebellion and sin" (34:6–7). The Psalms reverberate with affirmations of God's love. Prophets like Isaiah and Hosea repeatedly extol it.

The covenant love of God is one of the most prevalent themes of all three divisions of the Hebrew Bible—Law, Prophets, Writings. This same God "showed his love among us" (1 John 4:9) in Christ.

In Greco-Roman religion there were many gods, with diverse qualities, so one

---

▶ Seneca's Theology of Despair

John affirms that God is love. He has shown this by sending "his one and only Son into the world that we might live through him" (4:9). God, love, and life are closely linked.

Very different is the "god" of Seneca and of Stoic philosophy popular among many first-century intellectuals. This god admits that sometimes life is tough. But he advises suffering humans to respond to hardship with scornful indifference. And if this is not enough, why, die at your own hand! John's assurance regarding the God who knows us personally and loves us and gives us life, and Seneca's cold depiction of a god totally indifferent to whether people live or die, could not be more antithetical.

["God" says:] Yes . . . I have armed your minds to withstand [all sorrows]; endure with fortitude.

Scorn poverty; no one lives as poor as he was born. Scorn pain; it will either be relieved or relieve you. Scorn death, which either ends you or transfers you. . . . Above all, I have taken pains that nothing should keep you here against your will; the way out lies open. . . . Death lies near at hand. . . . Anywhere you wish, the way is open. Even that which we call dying, the moment when the breath forsakes the body, is so brief that its fleetness cannot come within the ken. Whether the throat is strangled by a knot, or water stops the breathing, or the hard ground crushes in the skull of one falling headlong to its surface, or flame inhaled cuts off the course of respiration—be it what it may, the end is swift. Do you not blush for shame? You dread so long what comes so quickly![A-13]

could not say that the gods were of any particular single quality (except maybe unpredictable). Moreover, where Stoicism held sway, even when "god" (Latin *deus*) is spoken of in the singular, he is subject to a force greater than he is: fate. Seneca writes, "Although the great creator and ruler of the universe himself wrote the decrees of Fate, yet he follows them. . . . It is impossible for the moulder to alter matter; to this law it [i.e., the god] has submitted."[73] No picture of God as being love, or even expressing love, can be glimpsed here. In fact, in one remarkable passage Seneca represents "god" as inviting people who encounter sorrows and hardships just to be tough and scorn it all; if that doesn't work, commit suicide! (see "Seneca's Theology of Despair").

He sent his . . . Son . . . that we might live (4:9). Christ brings life; Greco-Roman gods might encourage death (see "Seneca's Theology of Despair"). In any case no pagan gods came as a real human being (like Jesus of Nazareth), died a sacrifice for sin, and rose from the dead to ensure (eternal) life.

Not that we loved God (4:10). Many Jewish sources appear to portray God's love as the result of some merit on our part. Philo speaks of a sect called the

Therapeutae, whose "virtue . . . has procured [for] them his [i.e., God's] love as their most appropriate reward."[74] Another source states, "God loves nothing so much as the person who lives with wisdom."[75] God "will love you more than does your mother" if you are "like a father to orphans" (Sir. 4:10). It is important to visit the sick "because for such deeds you will be loved [by God]. In all you do, remember the end of your life, and then you will never sin" (Sir. 7:35–36).

But John grounds God's love not in human virtue or meritorious acts (as important as good works are for John), but in Christ's "atoning sacrifice for our sins" (1 John 4:10; see comments on 2:1). The background for John's understanding of atoning sacrifice is clearly the Old Testament sacrificial system as fulfilled in the crucifixion of Jesus.

Since God so loved us, we also ought to love one another (4:11). Since Old Testament times God has called on his people to reflect his character: "Be holy, because I am holy" (Lev. 11:45). The call to love is no less binding than the call to holiness. Here too is a noteworthy link between John and Paul, who wrote to the Ephesians (among whom John later served as pastor): "Be imitators of God, therefore, as dearly loved children and live a life of love, just as Christ loved us and gave himself up for us" (Eph. 5:1–2).

We have seen (4:14). See comments on 1:1.

Necessary Instruction: Believing in Jesus the Christ, the Son of God (4:15–5:15)

In the Greek text 80 percent of the occurrences of the words "believe" or

▶

ALTAR OF BURNT SACRIFICE

A model of the altar in the Court of Priests in the Jerusalem Temple.

"faith" in 1 John occur in this section of the letter. John moves to express in a more didactic way matters that he touched on in the form of commands, counsel, warnings, or assurance in previous sections.

Rely on the love God has for us (4:16). This can also be translated, "Believe the love that God has for us." God's love is of no saving effect if the sinner is not inclined to desire and reciprocate it. Numerous Old Testament passages lament that God's people, to whom he extended himself in love, would "not listen," much less return his affection.[76]

God is love (4:16). See comments on 4:8.

Confidence on the day of judgment (4:17). According to *1 Enoch*, judgment will be a horror for many: "But the Lord of the Spirits himself will cause them to be frantic, so that they shall rush and depart from his presence. Their faces shall be filled with shame, and their countenances shall be crowned with darkness."[77] Jesus warned of a time of "weeping and gnashing of teeth" (Matt. 8:12; 25:30).

But John holds forth confidence on the last day because of the work of God's love among his people, and because they have allowed themselves to be conformed to him (1 John 4:17: "In this world we are like him"; cf. 2:6). God's love is not just to be admired at a distance; it aims to transform the lives of those it touches and give them hope.

No fear in love (4:18). Pagan writers of antiquity recognized that servile fear of ruling authorities was an ineffective control measure. It was far better for rulers to cultivate the loyalty of love in their subjects. This would enhance attainment of both personal and societal goals, according to Cicero (first-century B.C.).[78] Another writer, Palladius of Alexandria (fourth century A.D.) recognizes that love involves trust, not anxiety and compulsion.[79] Love is free from fear in the sense of fawning insecurity or abject terror.

What is complex here is that there is both an *absence of fear* before God that "perfect love" for God casts out and an appropriate fear of God. An extreme example of the latter might be Uzzah's lack of fear in touching the ark of God, for which he was struck dead (2 Sam. 6:6–7).

John is apparently not speaking of that worshipful, awe-filled veneration of the God before whom the earth shakes, the positive "fear of the LORD" spoken of elsewhere in Scripture (e.g., Prov. 1:7; cf. Luke 12:5). A theologian of the Reformation era wrote, "The gist of true piety does not consist in a fear which would gladly flee the judgment of God, but . . . rather in a pure and true zeal which loves God altogether as Father, and reveres him

203

1 John

REFLECTIONS

DOES "WHOEVER LIVES IN LOVE, LIVES IN GOD" (4:16) perhaps imply that if a human being experiences love, he or she is experiencing God and therefore has no need to believe in Christ for salvation? For John the answer would seem to be no. "Love" in 1 John, as in John's Gospel, might be called "cruciform." That is, it is expressed in and defined by the cross of Jesus Christ. For John, to live in love means to believe in the crucified Christ for salvation, honoring his commands and learning to love his priorities in this world. Those without Christ may still experience the "love" of God's creation order. But they have not yet received the full measure of love that hearing and receiving the gospel bestows.

truly as Lord, embraces his justice and dreads to offend him more than to die."[80]

What John says here in no way rules out "fear of the Lord" defined as highest respect and worshipfulness in the presence of Almighty God.

Cannot love God, whom he has not seen (4:20). John's logic in this verse is profound, yet simple. Another first-century Jewish writer reflects a similar chain of thought: "And it is impossible that the invisible God can be piously worshipped by those people who behave with impiety toward those who are visible and near to them."[81] Plutarch wrote, regarding human relations in the family, that love among siblings is practically tantamount to love for parents.[82] This would imply that children of God, by loving one another, are already well on their way to showing the love for their Father that Scripture commands.

Children of God (5:2). See comments on 3:1–2.

This is love for God: to obey his commands (5:3). John proposes a two-way street between love and law. Love seeks to fulfill the law, while honoring the law is a means of expressing love (see "Love Instead of Law?"; see also comments on 2 John 6).

His commands are not burdensome (5:3). Even prior to Christ's coming there was awareness among God's people that relationship with the Lord is a matter of the heart and not just formal obedience to ponderous commands. For example, Tobit instructs his son Tobias, "So now, my child, remember these commandments, and do not let them be erased from your heart" (Tobit 4:19). Later Tobit affirms, "If you turn to him with all your heart and with all your soul, to do what is true before him, then he will turn to you and will no longer hide his face from you" (13:6). The touching Prayer of Manasseh (11–12) has the king of Judah praying, in view of his sins: "And now I bend the knee of my heart, imploring you for your kindness. I have sinned, O Lord, I have sinned, and I acknowledge my transgressions."

All of these accounts are fictitious, and none of them expresses the conviction and clarity of John's affirmation in 1 John 5:3. Yet all show an awareness of

---

▶ **Love Instead of Law?**

While John calls both for upholding the law and expressing love, a first-century writer under apparent Christian influence calls for meditation on God's love, not on the law (cf. Ps. 1:2). Other themes of 1 John that appear below: children of God, truth, faith, life, and light.

Let all the Lord's babes praise him,
  and let us receive the truth of his faith.
And his children shall be acknowledged by him,
  therefore let us sing of his love.

We live in the Lord by his grace,
  and life we receive by his Messiah.
For a great day has shined upon us,
  and wonderful is he who has given to us
    his glory.
Let us, therefore, all of us agree in the name of
    the Lord,
  and let us honor him in his goodness.
And let our faces shine in his light,
  and let our hearts meditate in his love,
  by night and by day.[A-14]

a similar hope—a hope awaiting fulfillment at the coming of Christ—that the God who expresses himself in his law redeems people in their hearts so as to love and fulfill his will.

Came by water and blood (5:6). Jesus' identity is gauged by both his baptism ("water") and crucifixion ("blood"). The false teacher Cerinthus, followed by others, denied Jesus' essential deity. In this view Jesus was a normal man who received a special spiritual gift at his baptism. But he remained fully and only mortal. As a result it was not really God the Son who died on the cross, just a man who exemplified God in many ways (see "Irenaeus on Cerinthus" in the introduction).

John disagrees. Jesus' divine status was not merely conferred from the outside at his baptism, a view called adoptionism. Rather, from his very conception his relationship with God and origin in God marked him as unique, though fully sharing in the human condition. Jesus therefore "came," embodied and revealed God's presence, not only at his baptism by the Spirit (as Cerinthus argued) but also in his death on the cross. In his Son, God himself (and not merely a representative human) bore the penalty of human sinfulness. This is the saving truth of the gospel to which "the Spirit ... testifies" (5:6).

The Spirit is the truth (5:6). See comments on "truth" at 2 John 1.

We accept man's testimony (5:9). See comments on 1:1. While ancient means of historical reporting sometimes lacked the precision of modern data collection, there was still concern for truth-telling in relating recollection of events. Josephus complains that some had written "histories" about the Roman war against

Jerusalem around A.D. 70, but those persons had "never visited the sites nor were anywhere near the actions described, but, having put together a few hearsay reports . . . with the gross impudence of drunken revellers, miscalled their productions by the name of history."[83] To the extent that Josephus is right, John's statement rings true that if we give credence to human testimony, we ought to heed God all the more.

God's testimony is greater (5:9). During Jesus' earthly days he pointed to a rich fourfold divine witness to himself: John the Baptist's testimony, the miraculous works that Jesus performed, the Father's own testimony (at Jesus' baptism?), and the Scriptures (John 5:31–40).

Eternal life (5:11, 13). See comments on 2:25.

Have the Son . . . . believe in the name of the Son (5:12, 13). What is the most important thing in the pursuit of knowing God? For John, having the Son is foremost a matter of believing, of exercising faith in the apostolic proclamation about Jesus Christ's life, death, and resurrection (1:1–4).

THE JORDAN RIVER

Other writers of the time saw things differently. Philo extolled four virtues: wisdom, courage, temperance, and justice. These flow from the word of God in the form of doctrines that increase and nourish the "souls that love God."[84] Philo cannot be said to reject the notion of faith, but neither does it play an explicit prominent role in his writings. The writer of 1 Maccabees calls for faithfulness like Abraham's (not "faith," as Paul describes it in Abraham; see Rom. 4), whose obedience when he was ordered to slay Isaac "was reckoned to him as righteousness" (1 Macc. 2:52). Abraham's greatness lay in his obedience to the law (Sir. 44:20), not in the trust he placed in God's promise when all visible possibilities of the promise's fulfillment had vanished

(cf. Paul's differing assessment in Rom. 4:20–22).

John does not criticize virtues and commands—far from it. But he grounds salvation in Christ's work, not human actions. That is why the Son is central as the source of eternal life, and that is why believing in him is presented as the primary characteristic of the true child of God.

Ask . . . according to his will (5:14). In the prayers of Greco-Roman religion, "the attitude was that of self-interest."[85] Central was the will of the worshiper, not the will of the god or goddess being petitioned. In the Old Testament Apocrypha prayer is portrayed as a means of gleaning secret information from God for personal and political gain (Judith 11:17)—though to be sure, in many other passages in the Apocrypha, more noble views of prayer are suggested. Whereas John implies that God is anxious to hear our prayers because he is the loving Father of his children, the book of Tobit sees human merit as the key to successful prayer (see "Prayer and Good Works").

If we know he hears . . . we have what we ask (5:15). John was present the night Jesus prayed in Gethsemane (Matt.

▶ Prayer and Good Works

In the Old Testament Apocrypha book of Tobit an angel gives the following instruction regarding prayer to Tobit and his son Tobias:

> Prayer is good when accompanied by fasting, almsgiving, and righteousness. A little with righteousness is better than much with wrongdoing. It is better to give alms than to treasure up gold. For almsgiving delivers from death, and it will purge away every sin. Those who perform deeds of charity and of righteousness will have fullness of life; but those who commit sin are the enemies of their own lives. (Tobit 12:8–10 RSV)

At the end of the book the aged and dying Tobit makes this observation: "See now, my children, consider what almsgiving accomplishes and how righteousness delivers" (14:11 RSV). In contrast to this, 1 John speaks of a confidence grounded in Christ's perfect sacrifice, not in our good works.

26:37). Jesus requested some way around "this cup"—the cross (26:39). Yet his highest desire was the Father's will, not his own (26:42). When we pray with that same confidence in the Father, and with abandonment of personal short-term gain, "we have what we asked from him" (1 John 5:15), which is the privilege of an audience with the Father, the confidence (5:14) of his listening ear, and the benefit of his all-wise decision. This decision may or may not correspond to what we in our human limitations would like to see happen.

Concluding Admonition: The True God and the Threat of Imposters (5:16–21)

In the letter's last six verses John touches in a summary way on themes he has already mentioned. These include love for others by praying for them (or not), the assurance of being children of God, and a final blanket imperative to avoid all God-substitutes.

A sin that does not lead to death (5:16). There is no one whose life is free of sin (see comments on 1:8). The only final remedy for sin is Jesus Christ (see comments on 2:1). But like his master Jesus, John believes in the power of prayer. Part of the ministry of prayer is supplication for others, even for their sins.

By "a sin that does not lead to death" John probably has in mind the full range of transgressions that even Christians may fall into. These can be serious. Note how Jesus prayed for Peter in advance of Peter's betrayal of him (Luke 22:32). He prayed for his persecutors at his crucifixion (23:34), a prayer that Stephen later echoed as he was being stoned to death (Acts 7:60). Paul prayed for the salvation of fellow Jews (Rom. 10:1). Yet if one scans the full range of New Testament prayers,[86] it is remarkable how few prayers are recorded for the forgiveness of sins of Christians. The assumption seems rather to be that Christians will be characterized by active obedience to God rather than chronic rebellion against him. Still, when Christians stumble, others should seek their restoration (Gal. 6:1). Prayer is an aspect of the ministry of restoration (Rom. 12:12: "Be . . . faithful in prayer"). We should also pray that we will not succumb to sin ourselves: "Pray that you will not fall into temptation" (Luke 22:40); "and lead us not into temptation" (Matt. 6:13).

Perhaps John would say that many sins that do not "lead to death" are to be dealt with in the daily course of confession and prayer by God's people, whether personally or together as the church (1 John 1:9). An example of Christians coming to grips with sin in their midst is found in 2 Corinthians 7:8–11. The Corinthians exercised the repentance (which implies prayer) "that leads to salvation." Their waywardness was serious, but it did not "lead to death" (i.e., irrevocable judgment at God's hand) in the end because they turned to God in prayer and adjusted their lives accordingly.

A sin that leads to death (5:16). John knew that even though Christ wept over Jerusalem (Luke 19:41) and in a sense died for all (1 John 2:2), not all will be saved. Even among those in the church, there are pretenders and deceivers (1 John 2:19; 4:1). John may be speaking here of sins that, if persisted in, will result in eternal judgment (see comments on 3:9; a biblical example is perhaps Esau; see Heb. 12:16–17). Those who "know him who is true" (5:20), by contrast, manifest signs of life rather than these symptoms of death.

I am not saying that he should pray about that (5:16). John does not forbid prayer for "sin that leads to death," but he does not command it. Perhaps this may be compared to God's command to Jeremiah not to pray for God's people who had so flagrantly turned aside from God's counsel (Jer. 7:16; 14:1). Apparently this was a temporary order, for God has to repeat it, and late in life Jeremiah is still interceding and receiving answer to his prayers (Jer. 42). But in times of spiritual deception, one may need to disengage emotionally from situations and relationships. Prayer involves an emotional engagement that can lead us past the point of legitimate intercession for others' forgiveness, to the dangerous point of sympathizing more with sinners in their rebellion than with God in his just enforcement of the terms of his promises.

Sometimes a situation has reached the point that the time for prayer has passed (Isa. 1:15; 16:12), even though that point may be tempered with God's rich mercy—as Abraham discovered when he pled for Sodom (Gen. 18:23–32) and as John himself discovered when he and his brother James wished to call down destroying fire from heaven (Luke 9:54–55). Jesus prayed before he chose Judas and later even washed his feet, but the time came when he had to let him go his own way (John 13:27).

In a word, as John addresses a church setting where some have fallen prey to the deception of the Antichrist, the evil one, he may be granting permission to commend the souls of some, whose separation from God seems to be terminal, into God's hands. This does not mean hate them. This does not mean that prayer cannot turn a sinner from his ways (James 5:16–20). But if one's spiritual rebellion leads him or her away from God and threatens to draw us away too, there may come a time to entrust such a person's soul to God and focus our worship and prayer on other matters, at least for a time.

Born of God (5:18). See comments on 3:1–2.

▶ Saving Understanding

For John the insight that mediates salvation comes from God and points to God's Son (5:20). Philo extols a different, philosophical understanding, praising that treasure-house

> in your own keeping, not where gold and silver, substances corruptible, are stored, but where lies that most beautiful of all possessions, the knowledge of the Cause and of virtue, and, besides these two, of the fruit which is engendered by them both.[A-15]

Philo agrees that this redemptive knowledge is from above—it is divinely implanted. But God's gift is not the gift of his Son but of virtues:

> A husband unites with his wife . . . in a union which tends to the generation of children, in strict accordance with and obedience to nature. But it is not lawful for virtues, which are the parents of many perfect things, to associate with a mortal husband. But they, without having received the power of generation from any other being, will never be able by themselves alone to conceive any thing. Who, then, is it who sows good seed in them, except the Father of the universe, the uncreated God, he who is the parent of all things?[A-16]

Under the control of the evil one (5:19). John has made it clear elsewhere that the Lord, not "the evil one," has ultimate control. By faith God's children are free from evil's dominion, "because the one who is in [believers] is greater than the one who is in the world" (4:4). Yet until Christ's return, the evil one (also called "antichrist" in 1 John) has a vast following (4:5). The world has the appearance of belonging to him, not to God and Christ (see comments on 2:13–14).

Given us understanding (5:20). Christians are not saved by "understanding" alone. But because salvation comes via Christ and the saving message that points to him, neither are Christians saved without "understanding." In contrast to this, another Jewish writer of the same era points to philosophical and speculative knowledge as what counts (see "Saving Understanding"). Plutarch likewise states that to live and die properly "we need a firm foundation based on reason and education."[87]

Eternal life (5:20). See comments on 2:25.

Keep yourselves from idols (5:21). Idols were a symbol of all that was wrong and evil in the pagan world; God had long ago condemned them through Moses in the second commandment (Ex. 20:4). Moreover, "the idea of making idols was the beginning of fornication, and the invention of them was the corruption of life" (Wisd. Sol. 14:12). People make them and use them because they "err about the knowledge of God" (14:22). John's readers are wonderfully spared the degrading fruit of false worship through the one who "is the true God and eternal life" (1 John 5:20).

ANNOTATED BIBLIOGRAPHY

Brown, Raymond. *The Epistles of John*. AB. Garden City, N.Y.: Doubleday, 1982.
　　Masterful and voluminous discussion of most background evidences and issues. Brown's stress on the polemical nature of 1 John may be overdone.
Burge, Gary. *The Epistles of John*. NIVAC. Grand Rapids: Zondervan, 1996.
　　Popular-level treatment with emphasis on application today.
Schlatter, Adolf. *The Theology of the Apostles*, trans. by Andreas Koestenberger. Grand Rapids: Baker, 1999, 108–85.
　　Insightful though not systematic treatment of the history and theology of John's letters.
Schnackenburg, Rudolf. *The Johannine Epistles*, trans. by Reginald and Ilse Fuller. New York: Crossroad, 1992.

In-depth analysis of the letters' message as well as their background. Good feel for elements of John's theology.
Strecker, Georg. *The Johannine Letters*, trans. by Linda M. Maloney, ed. by Harold Attridge. Philadelphia: Fortress, 1996.
　　Erudite rather than edifying. Reflects the critical, largely post-Christian outlook dominant in German universities. Notable as a barometer of late twentieth-century discussion. Valuable collection of background citations in footnotes.
Yarbrough, Robert. *1–3 John*. BECNT. Grand Rapids: Baker, forthcoming.
　　Pays close attention to the letters' grounding in the Old Testament and Jesus' teaching. Frequent allusions to Jewish, Greco-Roman, and patristic authors.

Main Text Notes

1. On Papias's date see R. Yarbrough, "The Date of Papias: A Reassessment," *JETS* 26 (1983): 181–91; Eusebius, *Eccl. Hist.* 3.39.17.
2. Eusebius, *Eccl. Hist.* 3.23.1.
3. Ephesus was by far the dominant city of the region. For information on its history and first-century status see L. F. DeVries, *Cities of the Biblical World* (Peabody, Mass.: Hendrickson, 1997), 372–79.
4. John evokes the memory of a famous Old Testament troublemaker; see 1 Kings 16:32–33; 18:4, 13; 19:1–2; 21.
5. John 14:15; 1 Thess. 1:3.
6. See, e.g., 1 John 1:6, 8, 10; 2:4, 6, 9, 11, 15, 24.
7. See Eusebius, *Eccl. Hist.* 3.27.
8. For a sample of a half dozen proposals see I. H. Marshall, *The Epistles of John* (Grand Rapids: Eerdmans, 1978), 22–27. Underscoring the unsatisfactory results of all outlines proposed thus far is Floyd V. Filson, "First John: Purpose and Message," *Int* 23 (1969): 261–63.
9. R. Schnackenburg, *The Johannine Epistles,* trans. Reginald and Ilse Fuller (New York: Crossroad, 1992), 12.
10. Denoted by small numerals in the inner margins of the modern Nestle-Aland Greek text.
11. Eusebius, *Eccl. Hist.* 1.2.1.
12. Josephus, *Ant.* 4.8.15 §219.
13. Philo, *Moses* 1.4.
14. Josephus, *Ant.* 16.11.4 §376.
15. Josephus, *Life* 65 §§336–339; cf. Josephus' concern for fact in *Life* 65 §363–366.
16. Plutarch cited here and elsewhere from *Fall of the Roman Republic,* trans. Rex Warner (New York: Penguin, 1972).
17. *Exodus,* Book 2.
18. Georg Strecker, *The Johannine Letters,* trans. Linda M. Maloney, ed. Harold Attridge (Minneapolis: Fortress, 1996), 26. The similarities between Qumran thought and John are "concerns common to all great religions" (Thomas A. Hoffman, "1 John and the Qumran Scrolls," *BTB* 8 [1978]: 122) and do not necessitate an assumption of either literary dependence or direct social contact.
19. Everett Ferguson, *Backgrounds of Early Christianity* (Grand Rapids: Eerdmans, 1987), 222.
20. Ibid., 252–53.
21. Citing the translation by C. D. Yonge, *The Works of Philo* (Peabody, Mass.: Hendrickson, 1993); Philo, *Alleg. Interp.* 3.82.
22. E.g., 1 Kings 8:46; Prov. 20:9; Eccl. 7:20.
23. Philo, *Fragments* in Yonge, *The Works of Philo* 885.
24. Philo, *God* 75.
25. Ferguson, *Backgrounds of Early Christianity,* 118.
26. Ibid., 124.
27. Horace, *Odes* 3.6.
28. *The Community Rule* 8.21–23; 9.
29. Ignatius, *To the Smyrnaens* 6.
30. Ignatius, *To the Ephesians* 10.
31. Ibid., 7.
32. Ibid., 9.
33. Ibid., 53.
34. Finegan, *Myth and Mystery,* 166.
35. Xenophon, *Respublica Laccdaemoniorum* 10:8; Georg Strecker and Udo Schnelle, eds., *Neuer Wettstein* (Berlin/New York: Walter de Gruyter, 1996), 2:1429–30.
36. Ibid.
37. John J. Pilch and Bruce J. Malina, eds., *Handbook of Biblical Social Values* (Peabody, Mass.: Hendrickson, 1998), xxxii.
38. *Let. Aris.* 227–28.
39. John 8:44; 13:2; 1 John 3:8, 10; John 13:27; John 12:31; 14:30; 16:11.
40. My translation of a Philo fragment cited in Strecker and Schnelle, *Neuer Wettstein,* 2:1431.
41. Ibid., 2:1321.
42. Ibid., 2:1433; Porphyry, *De abstinentia* 1.54.3–4.
43. Ibid., 2:1432.
44. Philo, *Fragments* as translated by Yonge in *The Works of Philo* 890.
45. See John Anderson, "Cultural Assumptions Behind the First Epistle of John," *Notes on Translation* 4 (1990): 41.
46. *A Guide to the New Testament World* (Scottdale, Pa.: Herald, 1994), 149.
47. Moses Hadas, ed., *Essential Works of Stoicism* (New York: Bantam, 1961), 58.
48. Ibid., 88–89.
49. Polycarp, *Phil.* 7.
50. For discussion of "anointing" in ancient Jewish and Greek religion see Strecker, *The Johannine Letters,* 65–66.
51. Albert J. Bell Jr., *Exploring the New Testament World* (Nashville: Nelson, 1998), 172.
52. For stinging rejection of the notion of hope, see Plutarch, *Fall of the Roman Republic, Gaius Marius* 46.
53. E.g., 4:1, 9, 10, 40; 5:16, 33; 8:1, 3; 11:9; 12:1, 10; 16:20; 17:19; 25:15; 30:15, 16, 19, 20; 32:39, 47.
54. Josephus, *Life* 65 §366.

55. Tertullian, *Apology* 9.
56. 1 John 4:15; 5:5, 10, 12, 13, 20.
57. 1 John 1:3, 7; 2:22, 23, 24; 3:23; 4:9, 10, 14; 5:9, 10, 20; 2 John 3, 9.
58. Suetonius, *Caesars* 94.
59. Seneca, *Ep.* 72.6.
60. Ibid., 120.10; Strecker and Schnelle, *Neuer Wettstein*, 2:1435–36.
61. Dio Chrysostom, *Orations* 4.21–23.
62. Ibid., 2:1437.
63. Philo, QG 1.59–60.
64. Josephus, *Ant.* 1.2.1 §54.
65. Ibid., 1.2.2 §61; see "Josephus on Cain."
66. Hadas, ed., *Essential Works of Stoicism*, 77.
67. Stephen M. Wylen, *The Jews in the Time of Jesus* (New York/Mahwah, N.J.: Paulist, 1996), 92.
68. J. M. Court, "Blessed Assurance?" *JTS* 33 (1982): 508–17.
69. Markus Bockmühl, *Revelation and Mystery in Ancient Judaism and Pauline Christianity* (WUNT 2/36; Tübingen: J. C. B. Mohr [Paul Siebeck], 1990), 20.
70. Plutarch, *Fall of the Roman Republic, Gaius Marius* 17.
71. Philo, *Spec. Laws* 1.315; Josephus, *J.W.* 6.5.2 §§285–88.
72. Walter A. Elwell, ed., *Topical Analysis of the Bible* (Grand Rapids: Baker, 1991), 24–34.
73. Seneca, *On Providence* 5.8–9.
74. Philo, *Contempl. Life* 90, Yonge trans..
75. Wisd. Sol. 7:28; cf. Sir. 4:14.
76. See, e.g., 2 Kings 17:14, 40; 2 Chron. 24:19; Ps. 81:11; Isa. 28:12; Jer. 6:17; Zech. 7:12.
77. *1 En.* 62:10.
78. Strecker and Schnelle, *Neuer Wettstein*, 2:1439; Cicero, *De Officiis* 2.23–24.
79. Ibid.
80. John T. McNeill, ed., *Calvin: Institutes of the Christian Religion*, trans. Ford Lewis Battles (Philadelphia: Westminster, 1960), 1:40.
81. Philo, *Decalogue* 120, Yonge trans.
82. Strecker and Schnelle, *Neuer Wettstein*, 2:1440; Plutarch, *Moralia* 480 d–f.
83. Josephus, *Ag. Ap.* 1.8 §46.
84. Philo, *Posterity* 128–29.
85. Ferguson, *Backgrounds of Early Christianity*, 149–50.
86. Conveniently accessible in Herbert Lockyer, *All the Prayers of the Bible* (Grand Rapids: Zondervan, 1979).
87. *Fall of the Roman Republic, Gaius Marius* 46.

Sidebar and Chart Notes

A-1. W. H. C. Frend, *Martyrdom and Persecution in the Early Church* (Grand Rapids: Baker, 1981), 213.
A-2. Cerinthus, *Against Heresies* 1.26.1.
A-3. Philo, *Providence* Fragment 2.53, Yonge translation, 754.
A-4. Jack Finegan, *Myth and Mystery* (Grand Rapids: Baker, 1989), 166.
A-5. Philo, *Moses* 1.30–31, Yonge translation.
A-6. *Community Rule* 1, cited here and below according to Geza Vermes, ed., *The Dead Sea Scrolls in English* (New York: Penguin, 1985), 72.
A-7. *Community Rule* IV, Vermes, *Dead Sea Scrolls*, 77.
A-8. Cited according to Geza Vermes, ed., *The Dead Sea Scrolls in English* (New York: Penguin, 1985), 251–52.
A-9. *The Manual* 16, in Moses Hadas, ed., *Essential Works of Stoicism* (New York: Bantam, 1961), 89.
A-10. Kenneth McLeish, ed., *Key Ideas in Human Thought* (Rocklin, Calif.: Prima, 1995), 681.
A-11. *Manual* 9.
A-12. Ibid., 1.2.2 §66, Whiston translation.
A-13. Ibid., 6.6, 7, 9.
A-14. *Odes Sol.* 41:1–6.
A-15. Philo, *Cherubim* 2, 48.
A-16. Ibid., 2, 43–44, Yonge translation.

2 JOHN

by Robert Yarbrough

The Setting of 2 John

Little is known outside of what the letter itself contains. Because the language and topics of 2 John are similar to those found in 1 John, and since both letters appear to have the same author, it is reasonable to conclude that they are addressing similar concerns. These include obeying what "the Father commanded" (4), resisting heresy (7–8), and contributing to the Christian joy that the apostolic message brings to the world by continuing an authentic embrace of the gospel (12).

For reflections on the possible setting, see "The Setting of 1 John" in the introduction to 1 John.

Structure of the Letter

The organization reflects the conventions of a Hellenistic letter:

EPHESUS

The remains of the first-century A.D. Basilica of Augustus.

2 John
IMPORTANT FACTS:

- **AUTHOR:** "The elder" (v. 1). All Greek manuscripts name "John" in the title. This is probably the same John who wrote 1 John (and 3 John).

- **DATE:** Perhaps the last third of the first century A.D., near the time when 1 John was written.

- **OCCASION:** John is coming to visit a local church soon (v. 12). Until then, he wants believers to be faithful to God's commands, especially the love command (v. 6). He also needs to pass on warnings regarding deceivers (v. 7).

- **KEY THEMES:**
  1. The truth of Christ.
  2. The command to love.
  3. The threat of antichristianity masquerading as gospel belief.
  4. Preparation for the elder's visit.

author's name and greetings (1–3), body of letter (4–11), final words and farewell (12–13). What is different from a Hellenistic letter is the content of each section. John expresses thoughts, concerns, and convictions (e.g., "Grace, mercy and peace from God the Father and from Jesus Christ," v. 3) that are foreign to normal Greco-Roman correspondence. (For samples of ancient letters see "Ancient Letters'" in the introduction to 3 John.)

Message of the Letter

The letter serves as a stopgap until a longer, personal visit is possible (v. 12). The writer assumes much more information than he actually conveys. But what he does convey may be summarized by taking note of the letter's commands:

- v. 5: love one another
- v. 8: watch out lest you lose your reward
- v. 10: do not support the travels and ministry of heretical Christian leaders
- v. 12: be prepared for an apostolic visit

Assumptions of the Letter

Among ancient churches 2 John seems to have struggled to find universal acceptance. But its underlying premises are consistent with apostolic Christianity as modeled in other New Testament letters. These premises include:

- the close identification of the true and living God with Jesus Christ his Son (3)
- the validity and redemptive power of the commands coming from this God (4–6)

- the importance of right belief concerning God's Son (7)
- the promise of heavenly reward, assuming believers' faithful perseverance (8)
- the responsibility of Christians to participate in the furthering of Christ's kingdom through (discerning) support of gospel messengers (10–11)
- the joy of knowing God in Christ (12)
- the communion of saints in churches everywhere (1, 13)

The elder (1). In early Christianity "elders" were the leaders or shepherds of local congregations—in other words, they were pastors.[1] But an apostle could also refer to himself as an elder, as Peter does: "To the elders among you, I appeal as a fellow elder" (1 Peter 5:1). In other words, the word "elder" could apply to an apostle and thus to the "elder" John, the apostle—especially in his pastoral capacity among Asia Minor congregations.[2] The apostles did not see themselves as social superiors to elders but as their coworkers in the gospel and as "brothers" to other Christians of all levels (Acts 15:23).

The chosen lady (1). The word translated "lady" is the Greek word *kyria*. Some have thought that John refers to a female person by the name Kyria or to an anonymous "select lady." But this Greek word was also used for a sociopolitical subdivision in Athens, a subdivision of the larger *ekklesia* (often translated in the New Testament as "church").[3] John appears to be using a word for a local congregation that is not attested elsewhere in early Christian writings. This word is chosen because of distinctive local social and linguistic conventions about which we have no additional information. "Chosen lady," then, simply means a local congregation who, as God's people, are by definition "elect" or "chosen" (a common term for Christians; see, e.g., Rom. 16:13; 1 Peter 1:1; 2:9).

All who know the truth (1; cf. 2, 3, 4). Among pagan writers "truth" was arrived at by rational contemplation or by observation of nature, or perhaps by both. There was no widespread agreement on what truth is, on how knowledge of it can be assured, or on what, if anything, ought to be done once truth has been determined.

For biblical writers there is a common conviction that truth relates closely to God; he is "the God of truth" (Ps. 31:5; cf. Isa. 65:16). Truth is God's possession. It is grounded in his nature just as love is (Ps. 40:11). God sends forth truth like light; this truth guides us to the place where God dwells (43:3). God's truth will be the basis for final judgment: "He will judge the world in righteousness and the peoples in his truth" (96:13). God always speaks the truth: "I, the LORD, speak the truth; I declare what is right" (Isa. 45:19). God commands his people to seek and love truth (Jer. 5:3; Zech. 8:16, 19). Truth is not rational knowledge alone but relates equally to "wisdom, discipline and understanding" (Prov. 23:23). Truth is found in God's word (Ps. 119:30).

Jesus claimed to speak the truth he had heard from God (John 8:40). He claimed to be "the truth" that leads to God (14:6) and equated truth with God's word (17:17). He told Pilate that he "came into the world, to testify to the truth," and added, "Everyone on the side of truth listens to me" (18:37).

Jesus' apostles saw truth as residing in Christ and the gospel message about him (Gal. 2:5, 14; Col. 1:5). Christians are "taught in [Christ] in accordance with the truth that is in Jesus" (Eph. 4:21). Truth is part of the Christian's armor: "Stand firm then, with the belt of truth buckled around your waist" (6:14). To reject the truth of the gospel is to be eternally lost (2 Thess. 2:12). Truth is not something merely known but is to be sought and loved (2:10). Belief in the truth is the way to be saved (2:13). The church is "the pillar and foundation of the truth" (1 Tim. 3:15). Gospel truth "leads to godliness" (Titus 1:1); it is not about abstract speculation but an honest and godly life. Obeying God's truth leads to love for others (1 Peter 1:22).

The Johannine letters contain numerous references to "truth."[4] No single definition explains every occurrence. The references seem to fit into the following categories:

(1) Truth is possessed and imparted by the Holy Spirit, who is truth.[5]

◄ *left*

CHOSEN LADY

Painted statue of a woman from Amphipolis.

(2) Truth refers to the ethical standards God has established for his people as expressed in his commandments.[6]

(3) Truth is God's sanctifying presence, which gives the believer the capacity to reflect God's character traits, such as love and aversion to sin.[7]

(4) Truth refers to the quality of conformity to the way things are in God's omniscient wisdom (2:8).

(5) Truth refers to the gospel of Jesus Christ, its implications, and the sphere of eternal life into which the gospel ushers those who embrace it.[8]

A famous ancient tale praises truth as the greatest of all powers on earth (see "The Greatness of Truth"). But "truth" in this story, while it may be defined as the expression and outworking of the perfect divine will, lacks the personal and living dimension of "truth" as portrayed in Scripture. Nor is truth primarily just a matter of not telling lies (as implied in *Let. Aris.* 206).

The Johannine letters are distinct in their clear, forceful, and diverse characterization of God—Father, Son, and Holy Spirit—as the God of truth. This truth is known particularly through the gospel and is mediated to believers by the Spirit. The test of truth is not intellectual brilliance or scientific accuracy (though these are not disparaged) but divinely imparted character traits, especially love and compassion for others and zeal for Christ's gospel and ways.

Great joy (4). For Stoic thinkers joy, like all strong emotions, was to be avoided. But joy had always accompanied news of Jesus: There was joy at his birth (Luke 1:14; 2:10); there was joy among his disciples as they ministered (10:17); there was joy in the presence of the Lord after his resurrection (24:41, 52). Jesus had promised abundant joy to his disciples (see John 15:11; 16:20, 24). Jesus prayed to the Father that his followers would have joy after he left them (17:13).

Joy is often associated with human celebration, but this is too simplistic: "Even in laughter the heart may ache,

---

▶ The Greatness of Truth

A Hellenistic understanding of truth is dramatized by the famous story of three youths who sought their king's approval by staging a debate to settle which is strongest: wine, the king, or women. The winner of the contest argued, "Women are strongest, but truth is victor over all things" (1 Esd. 3:12). To truth is ascribed "the power and majesty of the ages." In the Johannine letters, truth describes qualities of God's being, his work, and his revelation, but it is never receives the praise that belongs to God alone. In the story, the winning debater argues as follows (4:35–36, 38–40):

Truth is great, and stronger than all things. The whole earth calls upon truth, and heaven blesses it.... Truth endures and is strong forever, and lives and prevails forever and ever. With it there is no partiality or preference, but it does what is righteous instead of anything that is unrighteous or wicked.... To it belongs the strength and the kingship and the power and the majesty of all the ages. Blessed be the God of truth!

and joy may end in grief" (Prov. 14:13). True joy comes from participation in the kingdom of God, which is not a matter of partying, "of eating and drinking, but of righteousness, peace and joy in the Holy Spirit" (Rom. 14:17). Joy is a fruit of the Holy Spirit (Gal. 5:22).

The joy John expresses is closely related to the love he has for his readers. Shared labor for Christ's sake brings a sense of togetherness, appreciation for each other, and praise for the Lord because he forgives our sins and is redeeming our lives. Such work together often involves fervent prayer, sacrifice, and even suffering; these are powerful bonding agents in human relationships, especially when they are truly for Christ's sake. The result can be a profound shared sense of how great the message of the cross is and what a privilege it is to share in gospel ministry, benefits, and challenges. This is to say nothing of the indescribable joy of the presence of Christ himself through his Spirit. This is most likely the sort of joy of which John speaks.

Dear lady (5). John probably addresses the congregation as a whole; see comments on verse 1.

Not . . . a new command (5). See comments on 1 John 2:7 and 2:8.

From the beginning (5–6). See comments on 1 John 1:1.

This is love: that we walk in obedience to his commands (6). See comments on 1 John 5:3. Some religions seem obsessed with commands; Paul may have been addressing such a viewpoint in Colossians 2:20–23. Other religious perspectives seem intent on rejecting or flaunting the commands of Scripture (Titus 1:16; 2 Peter 2). Jesus warned of a time when disregard for God's law would be widespread (Matt. 24:12). John apparently feels the necessity of stressing that those who claim to know and love God must be diligent in seeking to obey Christ's commands and follow his example. This is exactly what Jesus taught during the last hours of his life on this earth.[9]

Deceivers (7). See comments on 1 John 3:7; 4:1; see also "Challenges Confronting the Churches" in the introduction to 1 John. Some scholars think that the warning against docetic doctrine in 1 John 4:2 is different from the warning in 2 John 7. In the 1 John passage the word translated "has come" is in the perfect tense. But in 2 John 7 the word translated "coming" is in the present tense. Accordingly, in 2 John the warning is perhaps against those who deny the "coming" appearance of Christ on earth, that is, his literal physical return in judgment and glory to inaugurate an earthly messianic era.

The antichrist (7). See comments on 1 John 2:18.

▶

ATHLETE WITH WREATHS

A stone relief from Isthmia depicting a victorious athlete with his crowns.

False teachers are no longer strangers once their identity becomes public knowledge! John has in mind the kind of hospitality that Jesus told his followers to look for in Luke 10:5–8. To open one's home to non- or quasi-Christian religious propagandists for the sake of their ministry is forbidden to Christians. An ancient Greek father warned his son, "The evil man wants the good man to turn bad so he will become like him."[10]

John's warning in no way questions philanthropic work by Christians on behalf of non-Christians—rescue missions, building projects, prison ministries, care for the homeless, medical missions, educational initiatives, disaster relief, and other outreaches too numerous to detail. It may call in question, however, the tendency of some in recent times to put the resources of Christian churches at the disposal of "interfaith" enterprises whose main effect seems to be the dethronement of Jesus Christ from his place as sole Lord and Savior and the replacement of evangelical Christianity with a "tolerant" humanitarianism bearing only negative resemblance to the gospel of Christ's death and resurrection (see also comments on 3 John 8).

Runs ahead (9). This unusual expression is probably explained by what follows: "does not continue in the teaching of Christ." While apostolic Christianity was richly creative, it was equally committed to a definite and sure foundation (see comments on 1 John 1:1). This means that sheer novelty was unwelcome if it was felt to be untrue and therefore destructive of the gospel message, which could not be tampered with (cf. Gal. 1:8–9; Jude 3).

Joy (12). See comments on verse 4.

Chosen sister (13). Since the author of 2 John refers to the congregation he addresses as "chosen lady [*kyria*]" in verse 1, he may be extending the metaphor in verse 13 in referring to a "sister" congregation, using language of the nuclear family.

Do not take him into your house (10). This is not a contradiction of Christian teaching elsewhere that commends hospitality to strangers (e.g., Heb. 13:2).

ANNOTATED BIBLIOGRAPHY

Brown, Raymond. *The Epistles of John.* AB. Garden City, N.Y.: Doubleday, 1982.

Masterful and voluminous discussion of most background evidences and issues. Brown's stress on the polemical nature of 1 John may be overdone.

Burge, Gary. *The Epistles of John.* NIVAC. Grand Rapids: Zondervan, 1996.

Popular-level treatment with emphasis on application today.

Schlatter, Adolf. *The Theology of the Apostles,* trans. by Andreas Koestenberger. Grand Rapids: Baker, 1999, 108–85.

Insightful though not systematic treatment of the history and theology of John's letters.

Schnackenburg, Rudolf. *The Johannine Epistles,* trans. by Reginald and Ilse Fuller. New York: Crossroad, 1992.

In-depth analysis of the letters' message as well as their background.

Good feel for elements of John's theology.

Strecker, Georg. *The Johannine Letters,* trans. by Linda M. Maloney, ed. by Harold Attridge. Philadelphia: Fortress, 1996.

Erudite rather than edifying. Reflects the critical, largely post-Christian outlook dominant in German universities. Notable as a barometer of late twentieth-century discussion. Valuable collection of background citations in footnotes.

Yarbrough, Robert. *1–3 John.* BECNT. Grand Rapids: Baker, forthcoming.

Pays close attention to the letters' grounding in the Old Testament and Jesus' teaching. Frequent allusions to Jewish, Greco-Roman, and patristic authors.

CHAPTER NOTES

Main Text Notes

1. Acts 14:23; 15:2, 4, 6, 22, 23; 16:4; 20:17; 21:18; 1 Tim. 5:17, 19; Titus 1:5; James 5:14.
2. Eusebius, *Eccl. Hist.* 3.23.1.
3. Strecker and Schnelle, *Neuer Wettstein,* 2:1442.
4. 1 John 1:6, 8; 2:4, 8, 20, 21; 3:18, 19; 4:6; 5:6; 2 John 1, 2, 3, 4; 3 John 1, 3, 4, 8, 12.
5. 1 John 2:20; 4:6; 5:6; 3 John 12.
6. 1 John 1:6; 2:21; 3:18; 2 John 4; 3 John 3, 4.
7. 1 John 1:8; 2:4, 21.
8. 1 John 3:19; 2 John 1, 2, 3; 3 John 1, 8.
9. John 13:17; 14:21, 23–24; 15:9, 10–12, 14, 17.
10. Strecker and Schnelle, *Neuer Wettstein,* 2:1443.

3 JOHN

by Robert Yarbrough

The Setting of 3 John

Like 2 John, there are few definite clues to a historical setting outside of what 3 John itself contains—and these are vague. Because the language of 3 John is so similar to that of 2 John and since both appear to share a common author, the setting of these little letters may be closely related. Words that both letters share include "truth," "children," and "love." Both speak of those who "went out" (v. 7), although in 3 John this is a positive movement while in 2 John it refers to the spread of false teaching. Both letters speak of the imminent coming of the writer, who calls himself "the elder." This elder rejoices that his readers "walk in the truth" in both letters. Some even feel that the letter referred to in 3 John 9 ("I wrote to the church") is 2 John.[1]

COUNTRYSIDE AROUND EPHESUS

This is near the traditional site of the prison of St. Paul.

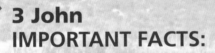

3 John
IMPORTANT FACTS:

- **AUTHOR:** "The elder" (v. 1). All Greek manuscripts name "John" in the title. This is probably the same John who wrote 1 John (and 2 John, judging from numerous close similarities of language).

- **DATE:** Perhaps the last third of the first century A.D., close to when 2 John was written.

- **OCCASION:** John will soon be visiting his dear friend Gaius (1, 14). Until then, he wishes Gaius well (2), commends his faithfulness (5), warns him regarding a troublemaker (9), exhorts him to do good (11), commends Demetrius (the letter carrier?), and promises a speedy arrival (14).

- **KEY THEMES:**
  1. The shared joy of perseverance in Christian faith.
  2. The importance of Christian hospitality.
  3. The existence of church division.
  4. The importance of ethics to legitimate Christian confession.

For broader reflections on the possible setting of the author, assuming that John wrote all three letters that bear his name, see "The Setting of 1 John" in the introduction to 1 John.

Structure of the Letter

Like 2 John, 3 John's organization reflects the conventions of a Hellenistic letter: author's name (or title) and greetings (1), prayer for and commendation of the reader (2–4), body of letter (5–12), and final words and farewell (13–14). One scholar notes, "Third John very much resembles a common papyrus letter as the writer commends certain travelers and censures a certain Diotrephes"[2] (see "Ancient Letters").

Message of the Letter

"The elder" plans to arrive soon (14). This short letter serves to:

- express the joy that the author shares with Gaius (3–4)

▶Ancient Letters

Short notes to friends and family did not begin with the invention of e-mail. Even in New Testament times people sent letters. Some of these letters, written on papyrus and dug up from the desert sands of Egypt, have features like those found in 2 and 3 John.

This letter from about A.D. 25 (Oxy. 292[A-1]) predates any possible Christian influence. But the length, organization, and certain concerns (commendation of a joint acquaintance, wishes for health) resemble similar features in 2 or 3 John.

> Theon to his esteemed Tyrannos, many greetings. Herakleides, the bearer of this letter, is my brother. I therefore entreat you with all my power to treat him as your protégé. I have also written to your brother Hermias, asking him to communicate with you about him. You will confer upon me a very great favor if Herakleides gains your notice. Before all else you have my good wishes for unbroken health and prosperity. Good-bye.

A second example[A-2] (third century A.D.) does show Christian influence. Like 3 John it mentions God, truth, and the reader's health and soul. "Comforter" is John's term for the Holy Spirit in the Fourth Gospel. A Christian boy named Besas writes to his mother:

> To my most precious mother, from Besas, many greetings in God. Before all I pray to our Father, the God of truth, and to the Spirit who is the Comforter that he may guard you in soul, body, and spirit, and give health to your body, cheerfulness to your spirit, and eternal life to your soul. If you find someone coming my direction, do not hesitate to write me a letter concerning your health so that I might hear and rejoice. Do not neglect to send my cloak for the Easter holiday and send my brother to me. I salute my father and my brothers. I pray that all of you might have continual good health.

- commend Gaius and his church for the support of itinerant missionaries (5–8)
- mention a problem that his arisen with a certain Diotrephes (9–10)
- convey advice, personal information, and the promise to visit soon (11–14)

A social-science reading interprets 3 John as a formal letter of recommendation.[3] In this view the letter should be understood primarily as a reflection of first-century Mediterranean social posturing: "The elder" has been challenged by Diotrephes, so "the elder" sends Demetrius, with a letter of commendation, to Gaius. Gaius (and others who receive John's words favorably) then becomes an ally for "the elder" in advance of his coming visit to put Diotrephes in his place. The letter is therefore not strictly private. It has a private addressee, Gaius, but is intended to serve a somewhat public function—the function of reestablishing the honor of "the elder" after Diotrephes has disparaged it.

The advantage of the social-science approach is that it brings important insights and considerations (like the values of honor and shame in that culture) to the discussion of 3 John's interpretation. Its drawback is that it may tend to reduce 3 John to no more than the sum total of social interrelations. However important honor and shame may have been for named players in the social drama, the transcendent realities denoted by the letter's language (truth, God, the Name, the church, good, evil, testimony, peace) should retain their central importance. Also, as an apostle who had seen and lived with the Lord (1 John 1:1–4), John's written counsel would not only relate to, but also tower above, the social categories of first-century Mediterranean culture, at least for those who received the gospel as the unique saving message of eternal life.

Features of the Letter

Like 2 John, 3 John seems to have struggled to find universal acceptance among ancient churches. But its content and tone are consistent with apostolic Christianity as modeled in other New Testament letters. Among distinctly Christian features are:

- John's and Gaius's mutual affection in the truth (of the gospel of Jesus Christ) (1–3; cf. 14, reciprocal greetings of "friends")
- the priority of Christian outreach for the whole church and of the support of those who go forth "for the sake of the Name" (5–8)
- a frank acknowledgment of tensions among early Christian leaders (9–10)
- the importance of good behavior as an expression of embracing true doctrine (11)

The elder (1). See comments on 2 John 1.

Love in the truth (1; cf. "truth" at 3, 4, 8, 12). The elder has a love for Gaius, a shared "group attraction and group bonding,"[4] because of their common life in the gospel of Jesus Christ. On "truth" see comments on 2 John 1.

Good health (2). Wishes for good health were typical in letter greetings, much like casual references to the weather in a modern English letter. But the wish could also be sincere. Life expectancy was half that of modern Western standards, and for most sickness and disease there was no sure cure. Seneca (*On the Shortness of Life* 1.1) voiced a common first-century perception that "the space that has been granted to us rushes by so speedily and so swiftly that all save a very few find life at an end just when they are getting ready to live." Antibiotics and effective medication for pain did not exist. Death could snatch away a loved one, or oneself, with little warning. So it is understandable that wishes for good health echo frequently in epistolary greetings.

What about the healing power of the gospel? Even though miraculous healings did take place in the early church, they were exceptional. Even an apostle like Paul could not perform them at will (1 Tim. 5:23; 2 Tim. 4:20). Sometimes physical ailments are God's will for his servants (2 Cor. 12:7–10).

Joy (4). See comments on 2 John 4.

Walking in the truth (4). See also "love in the truth" (1) and comments on

"truth" at 2 John 1. To walk in the truth means to live in the light of the gospel. It also involves honoring God's commands (see comments on 2 John 6). "Walking in the truth" is an expression that probably seemed natural to early Christians because of Old Testament phraseology.[5] In places this wording is retained in a modern translation like the NIV (Ps. 26:3; 86:11).

Your love (6). Gaius's love is not an emotional sensation but a concrete act of compassion on behalf of traveling Christians, probably missionaries, whom Gaius did not even know. Love here relates closely to obedience to God's commands regarding how to treat others (see comments on 1 John 2:5, 7, 8, 11, 18; 4:8, 11).

Send them on their way (6). The Greek verb used here (*propempō*) often connotes sending forth with necessary resources.[6] Churches were expected to support Christian missionaries and other Christian workers, financially and other-

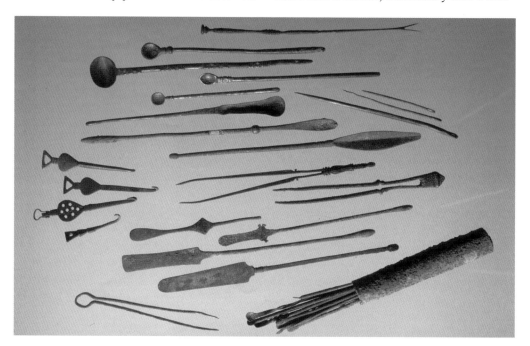

TOOLS OF A ROMAN DOCTOR

wise, as they carried out their ministries. This is most evident in Paul's words to Titus: "Do everything you can to help Zenas the lawyer and Apollos on their way and see that they have everything they need" (Titus 3:13). James warns against phony hospitality, the verbal blessing masking material stinginess (James 2:15–16).

Show hospitality (8). Opening one's home to other Christians, even if they were strangers (5), was important for the survival and spread of the gospel.[7] Inns were not found everywhere, and conditions in them could be marginal.[8] Often "sleeping quarters were filthy and insect and rodent infested, inn-keepers were extortionate, thieves were in wait, government spies were listening, and many [inns] were nothing more than brothels."[9]

The demands and risks of showing hospitality are acknowledged in a pre-Christian Jewish document that found its way into the Bible of many early churches because it was included in the Greek version of the Old Testament (see "Warning Against Showing Hospitality").

Loves to be first (9). Seneca noted that "no man is able to rule unless he can also submit to be ruled."[10] Apparently Diotrephes enjoyed wielding power but had little desire to defer to someone else's judgment. Among Jesus' followers highest honor is not supposed to attach to power but to humility and servant-hood (Matt. 18:3; 23:11). His disciples argued more than once about who was greatest, right under the nose of their master (Luke 9:46; 22:24). It is therefore no wonder that in later generations of the church the problem crops up regularly.

Will have nothing to do with us (9). The same word is translated "refuses to welcome" in verse 10.[11]

SHOW HOSPITALITY

Modern Samaritan men seated around a table at meal-time.

▶ Warning Against Showing Hospitality

While "the elder" commends an open-door policy toward traveling Christian workers, Sirach warns against receiving strangers into one's home (Sir. 11:29–34):

> Do not invite everyone into your home,
>   for many are the tricks of the crafty.
> Like a decoy partridge in a cage, so is the mind
>   of the proud,
> and like spies they observe your weakness;

> for they lie in wait, turning good into evil,
>   and to worthy actions they attach blame.
> From a spark many coals are kindled,
>   and a sinner lies in wait to shed blood.
> Beware of scoundrels, for they devise evil,
>   and may ruin your reputation forever.
> Receive strangers into your home and they will
>   stir up trouble for you,
> and will make you a stranger to your
>   own family.

Imitate . . . what is good (11). Gaius should not imitate the bad example of Diotrephes. He should rather respond to the capacity for love and the pursuit of God's goodness that the gospel makes possible. That is what "walking in the truth" (4) is all about. Different is a pagan writer's advice on how to subdue evil in the heart: "Yet nothing is so hard and difficult that it cannot be conquered by the human intellect and be brought through persistent study into intimate acquaintance, and there are no passions so fierce and self-willed that they cannot be subjugated by self-discipline."[12] John teaches we should look to Jesus Christ for salvation from evil, not to human reason and self-discipline.

Our testimony is true (12). See comments on 1 John 1:1. John refers to the apostolic eyewitness, not the generic testimony of Christian belief alone.

Peace to you (14). Philo is credited with writing, "Peace is the greatest blessing, which no man is able to afford, since this is a divine action."[13] "Peace" was the greeting of the risen Jesus Christ to John and the other disciples (John 20:19, 21, 26). As an apostle John passes on that greeting to other believers with particular assurance. With that same word "peace" Christians have greeted one another through the centuries.

REFLECTIONS

THE APOSTLE JOHN RECOGNIZES a sworn enemy of the gospel in Diotrephes. What was he up to that was so wrong?

The problem was apparently not a "big" sin like murder or flagrant moral lapse. It was rather a combination of "little" problems—some of them seemingly harmless. Diotrephes "loves to be first." Don't we all? And then he gossips some. It's pretty hard not to talk about people at all. And then he "refuses to welcome the brothers" and shows the door to people who disagree with his character judgments. Maybe he was zealous for the purity of the church. Isn't "purity" one of John's own concerns (1 John 3:3)? As for his defiance of John's leadership—didn't John teach that "perfect love drives out fear" (4:18)? Maybe Diotrephes was just exercising the bold confidence he inferred from John's pastoral teaching.

It is easy to make excuses for sub-Christian attitudes and behavior. But when what we say or do goes against apostolic counsel—which for us means Holy Scripture—we are near the edge of a precipice. It doesn't take many "little" willful missteps to move us a great distance from the mercy and grace of Christ.

ANNOTATED BIBLIOGRAPHY

Brown, Raymond. *The Epistles of John.* AB. Garden City, N.Y.: Doubleday, 1982.

Masterful and voluminous discussion of most background evidences and issues. Brown's stress on the polemical nature of 1 John may be overdone.

Burge, Gary. *The Epistles of John.* NIVAC. Grand Rapids: Zondervan, 1996.

Popular-level treatment with emphasis on application today.

Schlatter, Adolf. *The Theology of the Apostles,* trans. by Andreas Koestenberger. Grand Rapids: Baker, 1999, 108–85.

Insightful though not systematic treatment of the history and theology of John's letters.

Schnackenburg, Rudolf. *The Johannine Epistles,* trans. by Reginald and Ilse Fuller. New York: Crossroad, 1992.

In-depth analysis of the letters' message as well as their background.

Good feel for elements of John's theology.

Strecker, Georg. *The Johannine Letters,* trans. by Linda M. Maloney, ed. by Harold Attridge. Philadelphia: Fortress, 1996.

Erudite rather than edifying. Reflects the critical, largely post-Christian outlook dominant in German universities. Notable as a barometer of late twentieth-century discussion. Valuable collection of background citations in footnotes.

Yarbrough, Robert. *1–3 John.* BECNT. Grand Rapids: Baker, forthcoming.

Pays close attention to the letters' grounding in the Old Testament and Jesus' teaching. Frequent allusions to Jewish, Greco-Roman, and patristic authors.

CHAPTER NOTES

Main Text Notes

1. Strecker, *The Johannine Letters*, 253–54.
2. Stanley K. Stowers, *Letter Writing in Greco-Roman Antiquity* (Philadelphia: Westminster, 1986), 43.
3. Bruce J. Malina, "The Received View and What It Cannot Do: III John and Hospitality," *Semeia* 35 (1986): 171–94.
4. John J. Pilch and Bruce J. Malina, eds., *Handbook of Biblical Social Values* (Peabody, Mass.: Hendrickson, 1998), 127.
5. 1 Kings 2:4; 3:14; 2 Kings 20:3; Isa. 38:3.
6. Acts 15:3; Rom. 15:24; 1 Cor. 16:6, 11; 2 Cor. 1:16.
7. See Rom. 16:23; Heb. 13:2; 1 Peter 4:9; 2 John 10.
8. Abraham J. Malherbe, *Social Aspects of Early Christianity*, 2d ed. (Philadelphia: Fortress, 1985), 95.

9. Ferguson, *Backgrounds of Early Christianity*, 67.
10. Seneca, *On Anger* 2.15.4.
11. For discussion see Margaret M. Mitchell, "'Diotrephes Does Not Receive Us': The Lexicographical and Social Context of 3 John 9–10," *JBL* 117 (Summer 1998): 299–320.
12. Seneca, *On Anger* 2.12.3.
13. *Fragments Preserved by Antonius*, Ser. 56; Cited from Yonge, *The Works of Philo* 893.

Sidebar and Chart Notes

A-1. Adapted slightly from Adolf Deissmann, *Bible Studies*, trans. Alexander Grieve (Edinburgh: T. & T. Clark, 1901), 23.
A-2. Stowers, *Letter Writing in Greco-Roman Antiquity*, 74.

JUDE

by Douglas J. Moo

Jude

Most English translations use the name "Jude" only here in the New Testament. In fact, however, the Greek behind "Jude" is *Ioudas*, a name that occurs forty-three other times in the New Testament. It is usually translated "Judah," referring to the Old Testament patriarch or the territory within Israel named after him, or "Judas." The latter, of course, usually refers to Judas Iscariot, the betrayer of Jesus. But the name is also given to four other men who appear in the New Testament: (1) "Judas the Galilean," a revolutionary; (2) "Judas son of James," one of the Twelve; (3) "Judas, called Barsabbas," an early Christian prophet; and (4) a brother of Jesus named "Judas."[1]

JUDEAN FOOTHILLS
WEST OF
JERUSALEM

◀

Jude
IMPORTANT FACTS:

- **AUTHOR:** Jude, the brother of James and Jesus.
- **DATE:** Sometime between A.D. 40 and 80; perhaps in the middle 60s.
- **OCCASION:** False teachers have arisen in the church, and some Christians are attracted to their ideas.
- **PURPOSE:** To encourage Christians to stand fast in their faith by bringing them to recognize the dangerous doctrines and sinful lifestyle of the false teachers.

The author of this letter is almost certainly Judas, the brother of Jesus, for he identifies himself as a "brother of James." This James must be the famous James who led the Jerusalem church (cf. Acts 15:13–21; 21:18), "the Lord's brother" (Gal. 1:19). Like James in his letter, Jude refrains from claiming to be a brother of the Lord because the physical relationship was the basis neither for his own faith nor for his authority in the church. Jesus' brothers did not believe in his claims during his own lifetime (John 7:3). Only, apparently, after his resurrection did they recognize the truth of his messianic claims and become his followers (Acts 1:14).

With the growth of ascetic traditions of spirituality, Christians in the first centuries began to have difficulties with the idea that Mary did not remain a virgin after the birth of Jesus. They therefore stumbled over references in the New Testament to "brothers" of Jesus. Some, like Jerome, suggested that the word meant "cousins" in these contexts (this interpretation became known as the "Hieronymian" view). But New Testament evidence for this meaning of the word *adelphos* is lacking. Others claimed that Jesus' brothers were sons of Joseph and a wife before Mary (the so-called "Epiphanian" view). Still others see no difficulty in thinking that Mary may have had other children; they think that Jesus' brothers were born to Joseph and Mary after Jesus' birth (the "Helvidian" view).[2]

The Circumstances of the Letter

Jude never appears in any other New Testament book outside the brief mention in Mark 6:3; so we know nothing about his ministry. But Paul's brief allusion to the "Lord's brothers" in 1 Corinthians 9:5 suggests that he may have traveled rather extensively. The lack of specific information about Jude and the very general way he introduces the letter—"to those who are called, who are loved by God the Father and kept by Jesus Christ"—makes it difficult to pinpoint matters such as the date, occasion, or address of the letter

---

▶ **Apocalyptic**

An influential movement within Judaism in the time just before and during the New Testament was apocalyptic.[A-1] Scholars debate the exact nature and essence of this movement. But it is commonly agreed that it arose in response to the severe tribulations experienced by the Jewish people in the two centuries before Christ. No tribulation was more traumatic than the attempt of the Seleucid king Antiochus IV "Epiphanes" to eradicate the Jewish religion. His oppression and the resultant successful Jewish guerilla resistance (the Maccabees) took on legendary status among the Jews.

But difficult times did not end for the Jews, as they continued to be subjected to a series of governing powers. Thus, apocalyptic seers tried to make sense of this difficult situation by appealing to knowledge of what God was "really doing" behind the scenes. They claimed to have been given visionary evidence of his true plan and how it would work out in human history.

Apocalyptic literature therefore assured God's struggling people that he was still sovereign and that both judgment for the wicked and deliverance for the righteous would surely come. This message was especially pertinent to the situation Jude was addressing, as he sought to convince his readers of the eventual downfall of the false teachers and to encourage his readers to persevere in their faith in order to attain the final reward.

that he wrote. But the contents of the letter point to "Jewish-Christians living in a Gentile society."[3] Jude's constant reference both to the Old Testament and to Jewish noncanonical books strongly suggests a Jewish audience. But the sins he warns against are those that would typically arise in a Gentile environment. Further, Jude's frequent references to noncanonical Jewish apocalypses, such as *1 Enoch*, suggest that these Jewish-Christians were conversant with this kind of Jewish tradition.

The identity of the false teachers cannot be determined either. Jude's description of them is dominated by condemnation of their licentious lifestyle. They are scornful of authority, greedy, and sexually immoral. Claiming to be leaders of the community, they have nothing of substance to offer in their teaching. Jude's claim that they fulfill the prediction about "scoffers" to come in the last days (vv. 18–19) may suggest that, like the false teachers in 2 Peter, they were skeptical about the return of Christ in glory (see 2 Peter 3:1–7). The profile of the teachers in Jude is therefore so general that identification with any known heretical group in the first century is precarious.

One popular suggestion is that these teachers were gnostics, or (since Gnosticism did not really exist until the second century), "proto-gnostics." Some of the characteristics of the teachers do, indeed, fit what we know of these early gnostic-inclined groups, as we note in the commentary. But the same characteristics fit other groups as well, so we should probably avoid equating the teachers with gnostics. It is more useful to recognize that the false teachers whom Jude condemns represent a certain tendency within the early Christian church: the abuse of God's grace, and the temptation to turn the free offer of forgiveness in Christ into a cloak for sin and a libertine lifestyle (see v. 4).

One other literary matter may help pin down the background of Jude: its relationship to 2 Peter. As the accompanying chart shows, the two letters share common ideas and vocabulary.

Parallels Between Jude and 2 Peter		
Jude		**2 Peter**
4	the false teachers' "condemnation" from the past	2:3
4	they "deny" the "Sovereign [and] Lord"	2:1
6	angels confined for judgment; "gloomy" (2 Peter) and "darkness" (Jude) translate the same Greek word (*zophos*)	2:4
7	Sodom and Gomorrah as examples of judgment of gross evil	2:6
8	they "reject [Jude]/despise [2 Peter] authority" they "slander celestial beings"	2:10
9	angels do not bring "slanderous accusation[s]"	2:11
12	the false teachers are "blemishes"	2:13
12	Jude: "clouds without rain, blown along by the wind" Peter: "springs without water and mists driven by a storm"	2:17
18	"scoffers" following "their own evil [Peter]/ungodly [Jude] desires"	3:3

So close, indeed, are the parallels, that some form of literary relationship must be posited. But scholars disagree about the nature of that relationship. Most think that Peter has borrowed from Jude.[4] Others, however, think that it is just the reverse: Jude borrows from Peter.[5] And still others suggest that both Jude and Peter borrow from a lost common source.[6] We do not have enough evidence to decide the matter. But one intriguing bit of evidence is Jude's reference in vv. 17–18 to a warning from the "apostles" about scoffers that will arise in the last days. Could this be an allusion to 2 Peter 3:3–4?

> First of all, you must understand that in the last days scoffers will come, scoffing and following their own evil desires. They will say, "Where is this 'coming' he promised? Ever since our fathers died, everything goes on as it has since the beginning of creation."

Proof is certainly impossible. But it can be suggested that Jude, facing a similar outbreak of false teaching as did Peter, has borrowed extensively from

ANCIENT LETTER

A papyrus letter from a son to his father dated to A.D. 127 and found in Egypt.

Peter. Jude would then probably date from about the same time as, or shortly after, 2 Peter—for example, in the middle to late 60s.

Jude and Rhetoric

An influential force in ancient Greco-Roman society was the focus on *rhetoric*. We often use this term, or its derivatives, to connote an elaborate, or flowery, manner of speech. But rhetoric in the ancient world was the art of persuasion. Both the Greeks and Romans were fond of legal disputes, and techniques of persuasion were intensely studied and carefully categorized. Aristotle wrote an influential treatise, *The Art of Rhetoric*, on the topic.

F. Duane Watson has persuasively argued that the letter of Jude employs a traditional rhetorical structure.[7] He analyzes the rhetorical movement of the letter as follows, giving each unit the Latin name that had come to be associated with the specific argumentative stage:

- the *exordium* (v. 3): introducing the "case" that the "rhetor" is going to argue
- the *narratio* (v. 4): setting forth the concerns that require the rhetor to address the matter
- the *probatio* (vv. 5–16): seekings to persuade his audience by means of argument and illustration
- the *peroratio* (vv. 17–23): recapitulating the case and appealing to the emotions of the audience in a last-ditch attempt to persuade

Jude, therefore, adopts a strategy of persuasion that fits into the models his world knew. Whether he does so deliberately or unconsciously "echoes" the usual form of argument in his day is hard to determine.

Introduction (1–2)

Jude follows the convention of ancient letters, including New Testament ones, by introducing himself and his readers at the beginning. But he departs from custom in adding a prayer wish for "mercy, peace, and love." His is the only New Testament salutation that does not include a reference to "grace" and the only one to refer to "love."

A servant of Jesus Christ (1). The Greek word here is not *diakonos*, "household servant," but *doulos*, "(bond)-slave." The word, of course, connotes Jude's strong sense of Christ's lordship in his life. But it also implies that his position as Christ's "slave" is an honorable one and one that carries authority. The phrase "servant/slave" of God occurs often in the Old Testament to refer to such revered figures as Moses and David.[8] Note that "Jesus Christ" takes the place of "the Lord" in his honorific title.

A brother of James (1). Why refer to himself as "a brother of James" and *not* indicate that he was a brother of Jesus? We explained the latter in the introduction: Physical relationship to Jesus brought no spiritual benefit or special authority to Jude. But we still must explain why he refers to James. Presumably his readers know and respect James. This, in turn, suggests that Jude writes to Christians living in the areas where James ministered: Jerusalem and surrounding territories.

Those who have been called (1). To be "called" (*klētoi*) means to be summoned by God to enter into his people. The word is not applied to Israel in the Old Testament, but is used in the New Testament regularly to denote believers.

The Occasion and Theme of the Letter (3–4)

As we noted above, these verses correspond to the *narratio* in Jude's rhetorical strategy: the place where he introduces the background and purpose of his argument. Though wanting to write a positive letter of encouragement, Jude must instead mount a sustained attack on people who are abusing God's grace. His goal is to secure the spiritual safety of his readers.

To contend for the faith that was once for all entrusted to the saints (3). "Contend" translates a Greek word (*epagōnizomai*) that refers to athletic contests, such as a wrestling match. Paul reveals this notion in his use of a cognate verb in 1 Corinthians 9:25: "Everyone who *competes* in the games goes into strict training. They do it to get a crown that will not last; but we do it to get a crown that will last forever."[9] The ancient world was as "sports crazy" as ours, so the imagery of athletics would have been a natural one.

The New Testament normally uses the language of "faith" (*pistis*) to describe the subjective response of human beings to Christ: for example, "faith in Christ," "believing in Christ." But sometimes *pistis* refers not so much to the act of believing as that in which one believes. See, for instance, Galatians 1:23: "They only heard the report: 'The man who formerly persecuted us is now preaching the faith he once tried to destroy.'" Jude clearly uses the word in this sense, a meaning underscored by the phrase "once for all entrusted to the saints." The New Testament elsewhere speaks of the basic truth of what God had done in Christ as the "tradition" (*paradosis*, a cognate to the verb here translated "entrusted"). Paul uses the same verb as Jude uses here to talk about his role in "handing down" that tradition (1 Cor. 15:1–8):

Now, brothers, I want to remind you of the gospel I preached to you, which you received and on which you have taken your stand. By this gospel you are saved, if you hold firmly to the word I preached to you. Otherwise, you have believed in vain. For what I received I *passed on to* you as of first importance: that Christ died for our sins according to the Scriptures, that he was buried, that he was raised on the third day according to the Scriptures, and that he appeared to Peter, and then to the Twelve. After that, he appeared to more than five hundred of the brothers at the same time, most of whom are still living, though some have fallen asleep. Then he appeared to James, then to all the apostles, and last of all he appeared to me also, as to one abnormally born.

Paul makes similar references to this tradition (using other language) in 1 Timothy 1:10; 6:3; 2 Timothy 1:13; 4:3; Titus 1:9; 2:1. Jude claims to stand in a line of true teaching about Christ and his significance. Already, in the 60s, a clear notion of "apostolic" teaching had emerged as a standard against which to measure what could be genuinely called Christian and what could not.

Whose condemnation was written about long ago (4). Where exactly was this condemnation predicted? If, as we have suggested, Jude depends on 2 Peter, he may be thinking of Peter's own predictions (see 2 Peter 2:1–4). But "long ago" (*palai*) probably makes a reference to 2 Peter unlikely. Another possibility is that Jude refers to predictions about judgment in *1 Enoch*. He will quote a "prophecy" from this book in Jude 14–16 to document just this point. But we have no good reason, here at the beginning of the letter, to confine Jude's reference to one source. In the course of his argument, he refers to the Old Testament (vv. 5–8, 11), Jewish tradition (vv. 9, 14–16), and the teaching of the apostles (vv. 17–18). Jude has all these in mind in verse 4.

Godless men (4). "Godless" translates *asebeis*, a word that connotes a person who is "without religion," who "fails to worship."[10] A broad term, it can cover all kinds of sins, but Hellenistic Jews used it especially often of irreverence in an eth-

---

▶ *1 Enoch*

Jude is clearly fond of the book *1 Enoch*. He quotes it explicitly in Jude 14–15 and is influenced by its teaching at several other places. This book is found in the collection we call the "Pseudepigrapha," a diverse group of Jewish writings from the time just before and after Christ. Like many of the books in this collection, *1 Enoch* is an apocalypse. It purports to be the revelation that Enoch received from God about the spiritual realm and about God's plan for history. Many scholars have studied *1 Enoch* because of its extensive influence on both Jude and other parts of the New Testament. But little agreement has been reached about this book. Most think it was probably written in several stages, with at least some of the sections coming before the time of Christ.[A-2]

The Same Incidents in Jewish Sources		
Sirach 16:7–10	*Damascus Document* 2:17–3:12	*3 Maccabees* 2:4–7
"…ancient giants [= angels of Gen. 6] who revolted in their might. He [God] did not spare the neighbors of Lot.… He showed no pity on the doomed nation.…"	"The Watchers of the heavens [= angels of Gen. 6] fell … their males [of the people of God] were cut off in the wilderness."	"You destroyed … the giants.… You consumed with fire and sulfur the people of Sodom."
Testament of Naphtali 3:4–5	Mishnah, *Sanhedrin* 10:3	
"… so that you do not become like Sodom, which departed from the order of nature. Likewise the Watchers departed from nature's order.…"	"The men of Sodom have no share in the world to come.… The generation of the wilderness have no share in the world to come."	

ical sense: "not theoretical atheism, but practical godlessness."[11] This is probably Jude's intention too, since he says little about the false teachers' doctrinal errors and much about their aberrant lifestyle.

Certain men … secretly … godless … immorality (4). We should briefly note the way Jude uses strong negative and emotive language to introduce these false teachers. He is clearly already engaged in his argument to convince his Christian readers to have nothing to do with such people.

Condemnation of the False Teachers: Cycle 1 (5–10)

In verses 5–16, Jude runs through three "cycles" in his condemnation of the false teachers. In each (vv. 5–10, 11–13, 14–16), he cites Old Testament or early Christian creedal traditions and then applies them to the false teachers (using the word "these," vv. 8, 12, 16). Verses 5–10 focus on prominent Old Testament illustrations of judgment, but also include an allusion to a Jewish tradition. But Jude may be somewhat dependent on Jewish traditions even in his use of Old Testament material, for the same incidents that he cites in verses 5–7 are also found together in several Jewish sources (see table above).

I want to remind you (5). Ancient letter writers made the transition from the introduction to the body by means of a "disclosure formula," such as "But I want you to know," or "But let me remind you."

The Lord delivered his people out of Egypt (5). Jude, of course, alludes to one of the great formative events in Israel's history: God's rescuing his people from their slavery in Egypt in order to form them into his own special people (Ex. 6–14). An interesting variant reading in some manuscripts has "*Jesus* delivered his people out of Egypt" in place of "Lord." A few scholars think this may be original, reflecting the same tradition that Paul refers to in 1 Corinthians 10:4, where he identifies the "rock" that followed the Israelites in the desert with Christ. But the variant does not have sufficient support for it to be considered original.

Later destroyed those who did not believe (5). The generation God rescued from Egypt doubted God's power and promise in the desert. They were therefore sentenced to die in that desert and did not enter the Promised Land (e.g., Num. 14).

Angels who did not keep their positions of authority (6). Jude's first and third examples of judgment are well-known to any reader of the Old Testament. But who are these "angels" who sinned and were sentenced to hell? Some commentators think this refers to the primeval "fall" of Satan and his minions, a tradition that some think is alluded to in Isaiah 14 and Ezekiel 28. But, as we noted in the introduction to this section, Jude seems to be following here a pattern of references found elsewhere in Judaism, which included reference to a widespread Jewish tradition based on Genesis 6:1–4:

When men began to increase in number on the earth and daughters were born to them, the sons of God saw that the daughters of men were beautiful, and they married any of them they chose. Then the LORD said, "My Spirit will not contend with man forever, for he is mortal; his days will be a hundred and twenty years." The Nephilim were on the earth in those days—and also afterward—when the sons of God went to the daughters of men and had children by them. They were the heroes of old, men of renown.

Old Testament scholars debate over whether these "sons of God" were men or angels. But Jewish tradition seemed pretty clearly to come down on the side of angels. This text, in fact, became the basis for a common explanation of the origin of sin among Jewish apocalyptic writers in particular: The angels, often called "watchers," introduced evil into the world by cohabiting with human women. See, for instance, *1 Enoch* 6:1–2:[12]

In those days, when the children of man had multiplied, it happened that there were born unto them handsome and beautiful daughters. And the angels, the children of heaven, saw them and desired them, and they said to one another, "Come, let us choose wives for ourselves from among the daughters of man and beget us children."

Kept in darkness, bound with everlasting chains (6). Jude here uses common ancient images of divine judgment. "Darkness" was associated with the place of the dead in Greek thought in conjunction with the idea of the underworld. This language, along with reference to "chains," is picked up in what seems to have been a favorite Jewish book of Jude, *1 Enoch*. Note *1 Enoch* 10:4–6:

And secondly the Lord said to Raphael, "Bind Azazel hand and foot and throw him into the darkness!" And he made a hole in the desert which was in Dudael and cast him there; he threw on top of him rugged and sharp rocks. And he covered his face in order that he might not see the light; and in order that he might be sent into the fire on the great day of judgment.

Sodom and Gomorrah and the surrounding towns (7). See Genesis 19:20–22, Deuteronomy 29:23; where reference is made to Admah, Zeboiim, and Zoar.

Perversion (7). This is the NIV rendering of a difficult phrase in Greek, literally translated "going after other flesh." Since homosexuality figures prominently in the stories about Sodom and Gomorrah, most interpreters think that "other flesh" refers to the tendency to have sexual relationships with "flesh" other than that which God had ordained. But a few interpreters think that the reference may be to the "flesh" of angels. This view is not as far-fetched as it might at first appear, since Jewish tradition associated the sin of the angels (v. 6) with that of the people in Sodom and Gomorrah. As the angels sinned by yearning for human flesh, so the people in Sodom and Gomorrah erred by seeking angelic flesh. But it seems unlikely that Jude associates "flesh" with angels. Thus, the usual view, that Jude refers to homosexuality, is to be preferred.

They serve as an example of those who suffer the punishment of eternal fire (7). God's judgment on the cities was spectacular and final. According to Genesis 19:24, "the LORD rained down burning sulfur on Sodom and Gomorrah—from the LORD out of the heavens." Contemporaries of Jude saw in the barren topography of the area traditionally associated with the cities continuing reminders of the judgment of God. See, for example, Philo: "Even to this day there are seen in Syria monuments of the unprecedented destruction that fell upon them, in the ruins, and ashes, and sulphur, and smoke, and dusky flame which still is sent up from the ground as of a fire smouldering beneath" (Philo, *Moses* 2.56). "Fire" was a common metaphor for judgment.[13]

These dreamers (8). As Jude turns now to apply his illustrations to the false teachers, he first calls them "dreamers." This word refers to visionary experiences in its one other New Testament occurrence (Acts 2:17, quoting Joel 2:28). The same verb is used in the LXX to refer to the visions that false prophets claimed to receive (e.g., Deut. 13:2, 4, 6).

[They] reject authority (8). The word "authority" (*kyriotēs*) comes from the same word root as the word for "Lord" (*kyrios*). Jude probably means these false teachers are rejecting the lordship of Christ.

Slander celestial beings (8). "Celestial beings" is probably the correct interpretation of the Greek here, which has simply "glories" (*doxai*). Glory was frequently associated with angels in Jewish teaching. How were the false teachers "slandering" (or "blaspheming") angels? Some interpreters, who think that the false teachers had some kind of relationship to Gnosticism, cite evidence that gnostics spoke against angels by associating them with an inferior god. But the link to Gnosticism is not that clear. Thus, the connection may be with the false teachers' skepticism about future judgment. This skepticism is explicitly mentioned in the parallel 2 Peter 3 and may be hinted at in Jude 18 ("scoffers"). Jewish tradition saw the angels as having a critical role in the judgment. Another possibility is that Jude is referring to the false teachers' immorality. For angels were considered to be the guardians of the law (cf. Acts 7:38; Gal. 3:19–20), and by flaunting the law, the false teachers may also, effectively, have been slandering angels.

But perhaps we should look in a different direction entirely. The connection between Jude 8 and 9 suggests that the "celestial beings" may be evil rather than good angels. If this is the case, the false teachers may have been pooh-poohing any baneful influence from these evil angels.

The archangel Michael (9). Jews in the intertestamental period had a fascination with angels, speculating about their significance and constructing elaborate hierachies of relationships. The "arch-angel" was the highest rank. Jews some-times named four, sometimes seven, archangels. Michael, mentioned three times in the Old Testament (Dan. 10:13, 21; 12:1) and once in the New Testament (Rev. 12:7) is always included in this rank and is often singled out as the most prominent of the archangels.

When he was disputing with the devil about the body of Moses (9). This story appears neither in the Old Testament nor in any extant Jewish book. But several early Christian fathers claim that the story appeared in a book known to them, called variously *The Assumption of Moses* or *The Testament of Moses*.[14] In any case, the story seems to be based loosely on Zechariah 3:1–2 (see quotation of this passage in comments on Jude 23). We have no way of knowing what status Jude accorded this story about the body of Moses. Did he think that the incident actually took place? Or does he simply

view it as a well-known tradition that he can cite to make his point—similar to a contemporary preacher's citing an inci-dent from *The Chronicles of Narnia*?

Condemnation of the False Teachers: Cycle 2 (11–13)

In his second round of condemnations, Jude associates the false teachers with three notorious Old Testament sinners and then describes their immoral and reckless lifestyle.

Woe to them! (11). The English "woe" transliterates the Greek *ouai*, which in turn translates a Hebrew word used often by the prophets to warn about the pain and distress that the judgment would bring. See, for example, Isaiah 3:11: "Woe to the wicked! Disaster is upon them! They will be paid back for what their hands have done."

The way of Cain (11). In the Old Testa-ment Cain is known especially as the first murderer.[15] The false teachers may then, Jude implies, be "murdering" the souls of people through their destructive heresies. But Jewish tradition suggests other options. Some texts picture Cain as the classic example of an ungodly skeptic. The Jerusalem Targum, an Aramaic para-phrase of the Pentateuch, presents Cain as saying, "There is no judgment, no judge, no future life; no reward will be given to the righteous, and no judgment will be imposed on the wicked."[16] Other texts claim that Cain was a corrupter of humankind. Josephus, for instance, writes that Cain "incited to luxury and pillage all whom he met, and became their instructor in wicked practices."[17]

R E F L E C T I O N S

MOST PEOPLE LIKE TO FOCUS ON THE POSITIVE. Christians are no exception. We like to bask in the good news of all the blessings God has showered on us. This positive emphasis was what Jude had been hoping to convey in his letter (v. 3). But circumstances demanded otherwise. False teachers were such a threat that he felt compelled to warn his readers about them. Those of us in Christian ministry will often find ourselves in simi-lar situations. We would rather not dwell on the negative; and we do not want to be thought "unchristian" by criticizing others who claim the name of the Lord. But Jude's letter stands as an exam-ple of the need for negative preaching on occasion. God's people need to be warned about the dangerous heresies that pop up all over the place in our day. The faithful teacher of God's Word will need to help people discern truth from error.

Balaam's error (11). As Jude implies in this context, Balaam, the pagan prophet whom king Balak hired to curse Israel (Num. 22–24), was know above all for his greed.[18]

Korah's rebellion (11). Korah "became insolent and rose up against Moses" (Num. 16:1–2) and led two hundred other prominent Israelites in rebellion against Moses and the Lord. God reacted with a severe judgment, causing the earth to open up and swallow all the rebels along with their households. Numbers 16 also mentions judgment by fire, as does a later commentary on the incident (Ps. 106:16–18). Even in Moses' day, Korah became a warning example to those who might be tempted to resist the Lord and his appointed leaders (cf. Num. 26:9–10). The vivid nature of this incident captured the imagination of later Jews. Korah became the poster boy for the antinomian heretic.[19]

Blemishes (12). The word (*spilades*) should probably be translated "(hidden) reef" (see NASB). Jude pictures the false teachers as lying in wait, like reefs below the surface of the water, to bring destruction on believers.

Love feasts (12). Early Christians ate a festive meal together when they celebrated the Lord's Supper. The practice is attested in many ancient Christian texts and is assumed in 1 Corinthians 11:17–32.[20]

Shepherds who feed only themselves (12). "Shepherds" is not a metaphor here, as if Jude suggests the false teachers are like actual shepherds. He uses the word in the technical sense it gained in the Old Testament and Judaism, as a way of denoting the leaders of God's people. Jude may

be thinking here specifically of Ezekiel 34:2: "Son of man, prophesy against the shepherds of Israel; prophesy and say to them: 'This is what the Sovereign LORD says: Woe to the shepherds of Israel who only take care of themselves! Should not shepherds take care of the flock?'"

Clouds without rain (12). The image is a natural one for people who promise what they will not, or cannot, deliver. See Proverbs 25:14: "Like clouds and wind without rain is a man who boasts of gifts he does not give."

Autumn trees, without fruit and uprooted—twice dead (12). A tree without fruit in the autumn has not fulfilled its purpose in being. Jude's imagery in this context may again be dependent on a tradition preserved in *1 Enoch* 80:2–3:

In respect to their days, the sinners and the winter are cut short. Their seed shall lag behind in their lands and in their fertile fields, and in all their activities upon the earth. He will turn and appear in their time, and withhold rain; and the sky shall stand still at that time. Then the vegetable shall slacken and not grow in its season, and the fruit shall not be born in its proper season.

Wild waves of the sea (13). Jude may be thinking of Isaiah 57:20: "But the wicked are like the tossing sea, which cannot rest, whose waves cast up mire and mud."

Wandering stars (13). The Greek word for "wander" (*planaō*) is the word from which we get our word "planet." The ancients sought to find harmony and sense in the movement of the heavenly bodies and were therefore puzzled and offended at the arbitrary movements of the planets. They therefore sometimes attributed their movements to the influence of evil angels. Note *1 Enoch* 18:13–15:

> And I saw the seven stars (which) were like great, burning moutains. (Then) the angel said (to me), "This is the (ultimate) end of heaven and earth: it is the prison house for the stars and the powers of heaven. And the stars which roll over upon the fire, they are the ones which have transgressed the commandments of God from the beginning of their rising because they did not arrive punctually."

Whether by chance or not, the four images Jude uses in verses 12b–13—clouds, trees, waves, planets—correspond to the typical ancient division of the four "regions" of the earth: air, earth, sea, and the heavens.

Condemnation of the False Teachers: Cycle 3 (14–16)

Jude's final denunciation of the false teachers uses a long quotation from *1 Enoch*. He uses the quotation to confirm the pronouncement of judgment on these false teachers.

Enoch, the seventh from Adam (14). Enoch, an early descendant of Adam through the line of Seth, appears in the Old Testament only in genealogical lists (Gen. 5:18–24; 1 Chron. 1:3). But interest among Jews was focused on him because of the scriptural claim that he "walked with God; then he was no more, because God took him away" (Gen. 5:24). The text suggests that, like Elijah (2 Kings 2:1–13), Enoch did not die but was translated directly to heaven (see also Heb. 11:5). Enoch's enigmatic appearance in the Old Testament made him a natural figure for Jewish speculation; and

at least two books of apocalyptic visions were written in his name.

He can be called the "seventh" from Adam because Jews counted inclusively (i.e., including the first and last in a series): Adam, Seth, Enosh, Kenan, Mahalalel, Jared, Enoch. Jewish writers dwell on the same point (*Jub.* 7:39), presumably because seven was the number that symbolized perfection.

"See, the Lord is coming . . ." (14b–15). The quotation comes from *1 Enoch* 1:9:

> Behold, he will arrive with ten millions of the holy ones in order to execute judgment upon all. He will destroy the wicked ones and censure all flesh on account of everything that they have done, that which the sinners and the wicked ones committed against him.

Absent from this text is Jude's language about "harsh words ungodly sinners have spoken against" the Lord. Jude may add this reference from *1 Enoch*, 27:2: "This accursed valley is for those accursed forever; here will gather together all (those) accursed ones, those who speak with their mouth unbecoming words against the Lord and utter hard words concerning his glory."

Grumblers (16). This language occurs regularly in the Old Testament to depict Israelites who grumbled against God for bringing them out of Egypt into the barren desert.[21] So Jude may imply that the false teachers are also grumbling against God.

The Need to Persevere (17–23)

As we suggested in the introduction, this section of Jude's letter corresponds to the *peroratio* in a rhetorical arrangement: the appeal to the emotions to seal the orator's case. Typical of this rhetorical style,

Jude repeats some of the key ideas from the beginning of the argument:

- "love": vv. 1 and 2; cf. "beloved" in v. 3/"keep yourselves in God's love" (v. 21)
- "mercy": v. 2/"be merciful to those who doubt" (v. 22)
- "keep": "kept by Jesus Christ" (v. 1)/"keep yourselves in God's love" (v. 21)
- The need to adhere to apostolic tradition: "contend for the faith that was once for all entrusted to the saints" (v. 3)/"remember what the apostles of our Lord Jesus Christ foretold" (v. 17)
- Identification and negative characterization of the false teachers: v. 4/vv. 18–19.

Jude wants his readers to avoid the contagion of the false teaching by taking to heart the teaching of the apostles (vv. 17–19) and by striving to maintain their own spiritual vitality (vv. 20–21), and to minister to those who are affected by the false teaching (vv. 22–23).

Scoffers (18). If Jude is dependent on 2 Peter 3:3 (see the introduction), he is probably assuming that the scoffing is directed toward predictions of the Lord's coming back in glory. But it is also possible, especially considering the degree to which Jude faults the teachers for ethical lapses, that he is thinking of their scoffing at commandments that require them to lead righteous lives.

The men who divide you (19). The verb Jude uses here (*apodiorizō*) is rare. Because Aristotle uses the verb to mean "make logical distinctions," it has been supposed that Jude is referring to the gnostic tendency to divide believers into two distinct categories, based on their ability to apprehend esoteric spiritual truth. But we must again note that the association of the false teachers with gnostics is anything but certain. Perhaps

---

▶ *1 Enoch* and the Canon of Scripture

Jude's explicit quotation from a noncanonical book has naturally been the subject of much comment when it comes to the issue of the canon. Early Christians took three different positions on the significance of the quotation for the canon:

1. A few fathers argued on the basis of Jude that *1 Enoch* should be included in the canon (e.g., Clement of Alexandria, *Eccl. Proph.* 3; Tertullian, *De cultu fem.* 1.3).
2. Other fathers took the opposite tack: Because Jude quotes from *1 Enoch,* it should be excluded from the canon (Jerome refers to these in *De. vir. ill.* 4).
3. Augustine thought that Jude's quotation proved that *1 Enoch* was inspired at some points only (*City of God* 15.23).

Modern opinion is likewise divided. Some scholars think that Jude reveals that the canon of Scripture was still "open" at that time and that we should therefore be wary of the whole idea of canon. But most interpreters rightly note that Jude never calls *1 Enoch* "Scripture" (*graphē*). While using the book in his letter, he never accords it canonical status. It remains an open question just how Jude viewed the actual words that he quotes. He may have simply reported these words as a known tradition without implying anything about their divine origin or authority. But his use of the verb "prophesy" suggests perhaps that he did think that *1 Enoch* included at this point a genuine prophecy from Enoch.

Jude simply means that the false teachers, as false teachers usually do, are creating dissension in the community.

Keep yourselves in God's love (21). Jude may be thinking of the teaching of Jesus: "Now remain in my love" (John 15:9). The allusion would be particularly appropriate, since Jesus goes on to indicate that obeying his commandments is one key manifestation of love.

Be merciful to those who doubt (22). According to the NIV, Jude urges his readers to take specific action toward three different groups in verses 22–23. The NIV is probably right in this decision, but we should note that the text is complicated, both from a textual-critical standpoint and from a grammatical standpoint (note the different arrangement in KJV; TEV; RSV). "Those who doubt" likely refers to believers who are wavering in their commitment, somewhat attracted to the false teaching but not yet ready to follow it all the way.

Snatch others from the fire and save them (23). Other believers have gone much farther down the road of the false teaching; so far that they are in danger of eternal damnation ("fire"). Jude's imagery reflects Zechariah 3:1–4:

> Then he showed me Joshua the high priest standing before the angel of the LORD, and Satan standing at his right side to accuse him. The LORD said to Satan, "The LORD rebuke you, Satan! The LORD, who has chosen Jerusalem, rebuke you! Is not this man a burning stick snatched from the fire?" Now Joshua was dressed in filthy clothes as he stood before the angel. The angel said to those who were standing before him, "Take off his filthy clothes." Then he said to Joshua, "See, I have taken away your sin, and I will put rich garments on you."

To others show mercy, mixed with fear—hating even the clothing stained by corrupted flesh (23). Jude continues to use imagery from Zechariah 3. The word "stained" comes from the same verb (*spiloō*) that occurs in Zechariah 3:3 to describe the clothes ("filthy") that Joshua is to take off. Jude is probably now thinking of the false teachers themselves. They are to be shown mercy in the prayers of the community for them.

Doxology (24–25)

Jude concludes his letter with one of the greatest ascriptions of glory to God that we find in the Bible.

Without fault (24). The Greek word (*amōmos*) originally was applied to sacrifices (cf. Heb. 9:14; 1 Peter 1:19), but was transferred into the moral realm.

The only God (25). Pursuing the idea that Gnosticism may lurk in the background of Jude, some scholars think that Jude makes this point to counteract their typical emphasis on the existence of two or more competing gods. But the ascription is so common in Judaism that this particular background need not be considered.

ANNOTATED BIBLIOGRAPHY

Bauckham, Richard. *Jude, 2 Peter.* WBC. Waco, Tex.: Word, 1983.

The most important conservative commentary on these letters in decades; arguably the best technical commentary now available. Rich in references to extrabiblical materials and marred only by its assumption of pseudonymity for 2 Peter.

Bigg, Charles. *A Critical and Exegetical Commentary on the Epistles of St. Peter and St. Jude.* ICC. New York: Scribners, 1903.

Classic treatment, oriented to historical and grammatical issues.

Kelly, J. N. D. *A Commentary on the Epistles of Peter and of Jude.* HNTC. New York: Harper & Row, 1969.

Careful treatment of the text.

Mayor, Joseph B. *The Epistle of St. Jude and the Second Epistle of St. Peter: Greek Text with Introduction, Notes and Comments.* Grand Rapids: Baker, 1979 (= 1907).

Lengthy treatment, focusing especially on historical and linguistic matters.

Moo, Douglas J. *2 Peter and Jude.* NIVAC. Grand Rapids: Zondervan, 1996.

Exposition of the English text with focus on contemporary application.

Neyrey, Jerome H. *2 Peter, Jude: A New Translation with Introduction and Commentary.* AB. Garden City, N.Y.: Doubleday, 1993.

The most recent English language technical commentary, incorporating social-critical and literary approaches.

CHAPTER NOTES

Main Text Notes

1. Acts 5:37; Luke 6:16; Acts 1:13; Acts 15:22; cf. 15:27, 32; Mark 6:3.
2. For a recent survey of the whole matter, see esp. R. Bauckham, *Jude and the Relatives of Jesus in the Early Church* (Edinburgh: T. & T. Clark, 1990).
3. R. Bauckham, *Jude, 2 Peter* (WBC; Waco, Tex.: Word, 1983), 16.
4. E.g., Bauckham, *Jude, 2 Peter*, 141–43.
5. E.g., C. A. Bigg, *A Critical and Exegetical Commentary on the Epistles of St. Peter and St. Jude* (ICC; New York: Scribners, 1903), 216–24.
6. E. M. B. Green, *The Second Epistle of Peter and the Epistle of Jude* (TNTC; Grand Rapids: Eerdmans, 1968), 50–55.
7. F. D. Watson, *Invention, Arrangement, and Style: Rhetorical Criticism of Jude and 2 Peter* (SBLDS 104; Atlanta: Scholars, 1988).
8. Josh. 14:7; 2 Kings 18:12; Ps. 18:1; Ezek. 34:23.
9. See also Col. 1:29; 1 Tim. 4:10; 6:12; 2 Tim. 4:7.
10. See Rom. 5:6; 1 Tim. 1:9; 1 Peter 4:18; 2 Peter 2:5–6; 3:7.
11. Bauckham, *Jude, 2 Peter*, 35–36.
12. See also *Jub.* 5:1; 10:1–6; Josephus, *Ant.* 1.73; Philo, *Giants* 6; QG 1.92; CD 2:18.
13. See, e.g., Ps. 18:7–8; 1QS 2:8; 4:13.
14. Scholars dispute the relationship of these two books and/or titles (see discussion in Bauckham, *Jude, 2 Peter*, 65–76).
15. Gen. 4:1–16; cf. 1 John 3:12.
16. See *Targum Pseudo-Jonathan* on Num. 16:1–2.
17. Josephus, *Ant.* 1.2.2 §61; see also Philo, *Posterity* 38–39.
18. See Targum on Num. 22–24; Philo, *Moses* 1.266–28; *Migration* 114; Rev. 2:14.
19. See Josephus, *Ant.* 4.2.2–3 §§14–21.
20. See G. Wainwright, "Lord's Supper, Love Feast," *DLNT*, 686–94.
21. E.g., Ex. 16:7–12; 17:3; Num. 14:27–29; 17:5, 10.

Sidebar and Chart Notes

A-1. For further information on apocalyptic, see L. J. Kreitzer, "Apocalyptic, Apocalypticism," *DLNT*, 55–68; for more detail, P. D. Hanson, *The Dawn of Apocalyptic* (Philadelphia: Fortress, 1975); Christopher Rowland, *The Open Heaven: A Study of Apocalyptic in Judaism and Christianity* (New York: Crossroad, 1982); D. S. Russell, *The Method and Message of Jewish Apocalyptic* (Philadelphia: Westminster, 1964).

A-2. For further information on *1 En.*, see OTP, 1:5–12.

REVELATION

by Mark Wilson

Early Christianity and Ephesus

On his second ministry journey Paul attempted to preach in Asia but was prevented by the Holy Spirit (Acts 16:6). On his return to Jerusalem, he stopped briefly at the synagogue in Ephesus (18:19–21). Paul finally came to Asia during his third journey, making Ephesus his base for about two and a half years. Through his ministry the entire province was reached with the gospel (19:1–41, esp. v. 10). During his subsequent imprisonment in Rome, Paul wrote three letters to the Christians in Asia—Colossians, Philemon, and Ephesians. After his release he stopped briefly in Ephesus, leaving Timothy to deal with problems in the church there (1 Tim. 1:3). He later wrote two letters to Timothy in Ephesus.

ISLAND OF PATMOS

A view of the bay.

▶ Revelation
IMPORTANT FACTS:

- ■ **AUTHOR:** John.
- ■ **DATE:** c. 69 (early date) or 95 (late date).
- ■ **OCCASION:**
  - To prepare believers in Asia for the coming of Jesus.
  - To expose false teaching and ungodly behavior in the seven churches.
  - To reveal the divine judgments to fall on the unrepentant.
  - To exhort believers to persevere despite persecution and hardship.
- ■ **THEMES:**
  1. God, ruling from his divine throne, is the sovereign Lord of history.
  2. Jesus as the sacrificial Lamb is victorious over Satan and the world.
  3. The world system typified by Babylon and the two beasts is opposed to God and his people.
  4. The saints who overcome will receive eternal rewards in the new heaven and new earth.

How Peter developed a relationship with the church in Asia is unknown. Although the New Testament never states that Peter traveled through Asia Minor (also called Anatolia, modern Turkey), he most likely did on his way to Corinth (1 Cor. 1:12) and Rome (1 Peter 5:13). Peter later wrote to the church in Anatolia, with the province of Asia named specifically in his greeting (1 Peter 1:1).

The New Testament is also silent on how John came to reside in Asia. Church tradition relates that a community of Christians migrated to Asia from Judea in A.D. 66 at the beginning of the Jewish revolt. Philip and his daughters settled in Hierapolis, while John and his community located around Ephesus. The early church fathers, such as Polycrates and Irenaeus, provide the literary evidence for John's ministry in Asia. The book of Revelation, along with the Gospel and Letters of John, all have their provenance in and around Ephesus.[1]

Historical Background

The writing of Revelation has been placed either in the decade of the 60s or the 90s of the first century A.D. The later date is suggested in a statement by the church father Irenaeus (late second century) that Revelation was seen at the end of the reign of the emperor Domitian (A.D. 81–96).[2] Domitian's cruelty is well documented by Roman historians, and the church historian Eusebius calls him a second Nero because of his persecution of the church.[3] Revelation's portrait of mass martyrdom appears to link it historically to a persecution by Domitian. However, late twentieth-century historians have proven convincingly that no persecution of the church occurred under Domitian, only one limited to the Roman aristocracy in his immediate circle.[4]

The early date places the composition of Revelation between Nero's death in

MODERN PATMOS

Orthodox monastery of St. John with its massive fifteenth-century walls and seventeenth-century battlements.

A.D. 68 and the fall of Jerusalem in 70. The *Sitz im Leben* (life setting) depicted in Revelation better accords with the historical situation of the Roman empire during the 60s. After the fire in Rome in 64, Nero began to persecute the church. Many Christians, including Peter and Paul, lost their lives during this time. The late 60s was one of the most turbulent periods in Roman history. In 66 the Jews revolted in Judea, and over one million Jews died during Titus's siege of Jerusalem in 70.[5] Other revolts broke out in Gaul, Batavia, and Dacia. Most serious was the struggle among the Roman generals and their legions for control of Rome following Nero's suicide. In 68–69 the reigns of Galba, Otho, and Vitellius followed in quick succession. In July 69 Vespasian was proclaimed emperor by his supporters in Egypt and Judea, but not until December 20 were his troops able to occupy Rome and kill Vitellius. During the "Year of the Four Emperors" the Roman empire appeared to be self–destructing and its famed *Pax Romana* (Roman peace) lost.

How is this internal evidence to be reconciled with the explicit statement of Irenaeus that Revelation was seen during Domitian's reign? Like Eusebius, Irenaeus may have misunderstood his sources because, at the time he wrote, the identity of 666 was already forgotten. Since Domitian ruled in Rome for nearly a year in the absence of his father Vespasian, perhaps the historical tradition became confused.[6] Because I believe the evidence favors an early date, this commentary will presuppose a date of composition around 69.

Prophetic Background

A prophet named John receives this revelation while experiencing persecution because of his Christian witness. As John considers the present situation of the Asian churches in light of the history of God's people, many parallels present themselves. Moses, the first prophet, led Israel to her freedom after a series of ten plagues forced Pharaoh to free them. Isaiah prophesied during the exile of the northern kingdom (Israel) after its capital, Samaria, fell to the Assyrians in 722 B.C. Jeremiah, Ezekiel, and Daniel were all prophets of the Exile who experienced the capture of Jerusalem and the destruction of the temple by the Babylonians in 586 B.C. The prophet Zechariah saw the Jews return from the Exile and rebuild the temple in 516 B.C.

John sees himself standing in the line of these great prophets, who spoke to God's people during similar turbulent times. He reflects this by drawing much of his language and imagery from Old Testament prophetic literature. Revelation has approximately 150 allusions and near quotations of Old Testament texts, a literary phenomenon called intertextuality. These references are not prefaced with such typical introductions used in the New Testament as "It is written" or "The Scripture says." John presumes his

JOHN

An icon of St. John receiving his revelation on the island in the monastery at Patmos.

▼

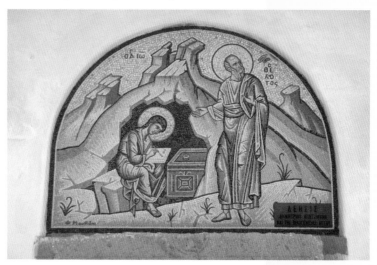

audience is familiar with the Old Testament and can recognize the historical and theological background for these allusions. This is why we should be familiar with the Old Testament, because New Testament books like Revelation cannot be understood apart from that background.

The prophetic situation of Revelation's initial audience is politically and spiritually precarious, and these early Christians need encouragement to persevere in the face of overwhelming odds. This has been the power of Revelation's message for Christians throughout church history. Each generation has faced its own unique prophetic situation that has tested its resolve to uphold the word of God. Because the church has entered the new millennium, it will see fresh challenges arise as it moves closer to that final generation that will not only see the rise of the Antichrist but will also witness the return of Christ.

Interpreting Revelation

As the last book of the New Testament and of the Bible, Revelation's position in the canon makes it one of the most important books in Scripture. Many biblical themes introduced in Genesis, such as the creation, garden, Fall, and promise of a Messiah, find their fulfillment in Revelation.

Besides the Gospels and Acts, Revelation is the only other place in the New Testament where Jesus speaks directly and extensively. Bibles that use red letters have Revelation 1:17b–3:22 all in red! Revelation is the only New Testament book where Jesus speaks to churches from heaven as the ascended Lord.

Many readers of the New Testament, however, approach the book of Revelation with great apprehension. Not only are its language and imagery difficult to understand, but its interpretation has generated much controversy. Prophecy teachers present various charts on Revelation that purport to hold the key to interpreting the book. Scholars often differ on how to understand the basic issues surrounding the book. How then is the average reader supposed to make any sense of this book? Certainly the original audience would have understood most of the book. Otherwise John would not have chosen this way to communicate to the seven churches.

Throughout church history Revelation has come to be the Bible's most abused book. Numerous sects and cults have had an unhealthy preoccupation with its contents and often claimed to be its only true interpreters. Often such claims have led to tragedy. An example is the Branch Davidian leader, David Koresh, who claimed to be the Lamb of God. His fanaticism led to the disastrous events at his compound, Ranch Apocalypse, at Waco, Texas, in April 1993. Many Christian leaders have used Revelation to speculate about the coming end of the world, particularly with the turn of the new millennium. Numerous popular books and movies have derived end-time themes from its contents. Unfortunately the historical background and audience of the book is often ignored or forgotten in the discussions. By discovering the meaning of John's revelation to the first churches, we will better understand its relevance for us as Christians today.

Prologue and Greeting (1:1–8)

The revelation of Jesus Christ (1:1). This opening phrase functions as the title of the book. The Gospels of Matthew and Mark begin with similar introductory titles. It also declares that this divine revelation is from Jesus (its source) and about him (its content). The Greek word *apokalypsis,* from which we derive the book's other name (the Apocalypse), means "unveiling" or "revelation." Today the word "apocalypse" has negative connotations and specifically suggests end-time cataclysmic events. However, in the early church, prophets commonly received revelations, which were then shared with others (1 Cor. 14:30–31). Paul himself received the gospel he preached through a revelation of Jesus Christ (Gal. 1:12, 16).

The phrase "revelation of Jesus Christ" already had end-time connotations in the Asian church John served. Both Paul (1 Cor. 1:7) and Peter (1 Peter 1:7, 13) used the phrase to speak of the future *parousia,* a Greek word often simply transliterated as Parousia, which means Christ's second coming. This is likewise an emphasis in Revelation, which repeatedly declares that Jesus is coming soon (cf. Rev. 1:1, 7; 22:7, 12, 20).

Sending his angel (1:1). Angels play a prominent role in mediating this revelation vision to John. Angelic mediation is frequently found in other prophetic and apocalyptic literature. In the Old Testament angels are sent to interpret the visions given to Ezekiel (Ezek. 40–48), Daniel (Dan. 7–12), and Zechariah (Zech. 1–6). Angelic intermediaries often appear in intertestamental apocalypses as well. Uriel, Raphael, Raguel, Michael, and Enoch are angels mentioned in *1 Enoch,* while Uriel and Ezra are named as mediators in *4 Ezra.* Angels were important to the religious life of the people in Asia Minor. Numerous Jewish and Christian inscriptions found in Turkey call on angels for protection and assistance. A

grave inscription from Eumena, northeast of Laodicea, declares, "If anyone inters another [here], he will have to reckon with God and the angel of God."[7] These angels were thought to serve as supernatural servants and messengers for God. However, these inscriptions provide no evidence that angels were called on in a mystical sense for visionary revelation.

His servant John (1:1). John identifies himself first as a "servant" (cf. 22:9), a designation used by such apostles as Paul (Rom. 1:1; Gal. 1:10), Peter (2 Peter 1:1), and James (James 1:1). "Servants" (used eleven times) and "saints" (used twelve times) are the two most frequent designations for Christians in Revelation. The author also identifies himself as John on three other occasions (Rev. 1:4, 9; 22:8). Which "John" he is has been debated throughout church history. The most prominent John in the Synoptics was the son of Zebedee and brother of James. John was a fisherman in Galilee when Jesus called him to become one of his first disciples (Mark 1:19–20). He was later named as one of the twelve apostles (Mark 3:17). John and Peter were frequent companions in ministry (Acts 4:1–23; 8:14–25). Justin Martyr, speaking to the Jew Trypho in Ephesus (c. A.D. 135), identified the author of Revelation as one of Christ's apostles. Irenaeus claimed that the beloved disciple who wrote the Gospel of John in Ephesus was the same John who authored Revelation.[8]

However, as early as the third century, Christian writers like Dionysius, bishop of Alexandria (190–264), began to deny that John the apostle wrote Revelation.[9] They noted its thematic and stylistic differences with the Gospel and the first letter, but these can be attributed to factors other than different authors. Papias (A.D.

60–135), also a disciple of John and bishop of Hierapolis, further confused the issue by appearing to mention a second John called "the elder." This seemed to confirm an early tradition of two tombs in Ephesus, each called John's. The early church historian Eusebius mistakenly used Papias's statement to identify this second John as the author of Revelation.[10]

Despite these objections, no explicit internal or external evidence exists to rule out John the apostle, author of the Gospel and 1, 2, and 3 John, from being the author of Revelation. Today in Ephesus there is only one grave site for John, found in the central section of the remains of the cross-shaped Basilica of St. John. This magnificent church was built by the emperor Justinian (527–65) over the site of an earlier church that also marked John's grave.

Blessed is (1:3). This is the first of seven unnumbered beatitudes in Revelation (cf. 14:13; 16:15; 19:9; 20:6; 22:7, 14). Their form resembles the beatitudes spoken by Jesus: "Blessed are the poor in spirit. . . . Blessed are those who mourn," and so on (Matt. 5:3–11). The beatitudes in Revelation are all eschatological; that is, they relate to Christ and his second coming and to the blessings promised to believers in the new heaven and new earth. Their predominance in the second half of the book suggests that the original Asian audience was in view throughout the book, not just in chapters 1–3.

The one who reads . . . those who hear (1:3). The lector of Revelation was undoubtedly John's close associate, who was entrusted with delivering the scroll to the churches. (This assumes that John was still on the island of Patmos when the document was circulated.) Reading

Scripture aloud by a lector was a common practice in the early church, as Paul wrote to Timothy: "Devote yourself to the public reading of Scripture" (1 Tim. 4:13). It followed an established custom in the Jewish synagogues, where Moses was read on every Sabbath (Acts 15:21; cf. 13:15).

There was a practical reason for reading aloud publicly: Only about fifteen percent of the general populace in cities such as Ephesus were literate. Scholars make this estimate based on the large number of extant inscriptions. A casual walk through the site of Ephesus today confirms this abundance of inscriptions. In fact, over 3,750 Greek inscriptions from Ephesus are catalogued, the largest number from any city in antiquity apart from Athens and Rome.[11] In the churches, however, the literacy percentage would likely be higher because of the presence of Jewish believers. The Jews of the Diaspora taught their children to read so they could read the Greek Old Testament, known as the Septuagint (abbreviated LXX). In the remote Galatian city of Lystra, Timothy was taught the Scriptures from infancy by his grandmother Lois and his mother Eunice (2 Tim. 1:5; 3:15).

This prophecy (1:3). Genre is the literary classification to which a particular document belongs. Revelation is an example of mixed genre because it shares characteristics with prophetic, apocalyptic, and epistolary literature. Like the Old Testament prophets, the author of Revelation identifies himself by name. He links himself to these prophets through shared prophetic experiences, commissions, acts, and curses (to be highlighted in the commentary). The Greek phrase *tade legei* ("These are . . ."), found at the beginning of each message in chapters 2–

3, is used over 300 times in the LXX to introduce prophetic declarations (e.g., Zech. 1:3). Its only other use in the New Testament occurs when the prophet Agabus addressed Paul (Acts 21:11).

Often Revelation is categorized as apocalyptic because it shares with other intertestamental literature such features as visions, cosmic dualism, symbolism, angelic mediation, transcendent reality, and imminence of time. Such similarities are readily apparent. But unlike other apocalypses, Revelation is not pseudonymous; that is, it does not claim its author to be a departed saint such as Enoch or Ezra, and it contains paraenesis, or words of exhortation. By calling his work a "prophecy" six times (1:3; 19:10; 22:7, 10, 18, 19), John clearly puts his work in the same literary stream as its Old Testament predecessors, particularly Ezekiel, Daniel, and Zechariah.

The province of Asia (1:4). When the New Testament uses the word "Asia," it does not mean the present continent that includes China. Rather it refers to a Roman province located across the western

---

REFLECTIONS

BIBLICAL ILLITERACY IS A PROBLEM NOT ONLY IN society at large but also in the church. Most Christians have never read the Old Testament in its entirety. Surveys indicate that few can name the Ten Commandments or the Beatitudes. Such lack of Bible knowledge produces believers who may be ignorant of God's will, dependent on feelings, and vulnerable to false teaching. Revelation's first audience was promised a blessing for reading and obeying its prophetic word. A similar blessing is likewise available for today's readers of the Bible. A renewed emphasis on Scripture reading, both public and private, has the potential to produce in our generation believers who are not only biblically literate but spiritually mature.

third of the peninsula called Asia Minor or Anatolia, the modern country of Turkey. The province was formed about 129 B.C. after the Attalid king Attalus III bestowed on the Romans his kingdom based in Pergamum. Asia included such former Greek regions as Mysia, Lydia, Phrygia, and Troas as well as the islands of Lesbos (Mitylene its chief city), Kios, Samos, and Cos—all places mentioned in Acts.

Asia was one of the richest provinces under Rome's hegemony, and Roman officials eagerly plundered its wealth. In 88 B.C. the Asians joined the revolt of Mithridates, the king of Pontus, and massacred in one day over 80,000 Italian residents of Asia. After order was restored and the Roman republic gave way to the principate in 27 B.C., the Asians became enthusiastic supporters of the first emperor Augustus and his policies. Because of its wealth and secure location, the province fell under the jurisdiction of the Roman Senate, which annually appointed a proconsul to govern Asia.

Grace and peace (1:4). This apostolic greeting is identical to that found in the letters that Peter and Paul wrote to the Asian churches (except 1 and 2 Tim.). When these believers heard Revelation's typical apostolic greeting, they would naturally associate it with the letters received earlier from these apostles. These letters were undoubtedly still being read in the congregations. Like other ancient letters, Revelation contains an opening (Rev. 1:4–5) and a closing (22:21) that frame the body of the letter.

From him who is, and who was, and who is to come (1:4). This unique phrase, alluding to the Septuagint reading of Exodus 3:14, focuses on God's eternal nature of past, present, and future (cf. Rev. 1:8; 4:8). As the sovereign God who controls the future, he now uses his knowledge to inform and encourage his people about their destiny on earth and in heaven. Part of this name, written on a carnelian gemstone, was apparently found in Ephesus. The Greek magical inscription includes the words, "for you are him who is," with the wording from Exodus 3:14 in Hebrew on the reverse.[12] The addressees learn that this prophetic writing is from God, who identifies himself in a unique trinitarian way.

From the seven spirits before his throne (1:4). Whether this imagery refers to the Holy Spirit is difficult to determine. However, the parallel prepositional construction with the Father and Son strongly points to such an identification. These seven spirits (or sevenfold Spirit; see NIV note) are seen in 4:5 before the throne blazing as lamps. In 3:1 Jesus says he holds the seven spirits of God along with the seven stars, or angels, the two being closely linked here. Later these seven spirits are described as the Lamb's seven eyes sent out into the earth (5:6).

ROMAN PROVINCE OF ASIA

▼

A possible Old Testament background for this striking image is Zechariah 4:1–10, where the seven lights on a gold lampstand seen by the prophet are said to be "the eyes of the LORD, which range throughout the earth" (4:10). Another possible source is the LXX reading of Isaiah 11:2, where a seventh attribute of the Spirit—the Spirit "of the fear of the LORD"—is added to the other six. The Holy Spirit in his sevenfold ministry is thus presented as the omniscient enabler for the omnipotent God. Since the plurals of Revelation 1—seven spirits, seven churches, and seven angels—all become singular in chapters 2–3, John's emphasis may also be on the distinctive ministry of the Holy Spirit to each church.

From Jesus Christ (1:5). Three phrases follow that describe Jesus: "faithful witness," "firstborn from the dead," and "ruler of the kings of the earth." Each title emphasizes a distinctive theme related to Christ's work and ministry—the cross, resurrection, and ascension—developed later in the book. The messianic king from the Davidic line promised in Psalm 89 is called "my firstborn" (Ps. 89:27) and "faithful witness" (89:37). Paul, writing to the Colossians, likewise calls Jesus "the firstborn from among the dead" (Col. 1:18). Colosse was located only eleven miles southeast of Laodicea, and Paul's letter was known to the Christians there (4:16). The Laodicean title describing Jesus as "the ruler of God's creation" (Rev. 3:14) also parallels language found in Colossians 1:15, "the firstborn over all creation." In Revelation the kings of the earth consistently oppose God (e.g., 16:14, 16; 19:19). The question whether Christ or Caesar is sovereign is answered immediately in the book: Christ is!

To him who loves us and has freed us from our sins by his blood, and has made us to be a kingdom and priests to serve his God and Father (1:5b–6). John erupts in praise as he recalls four things that Christ has done for the people of God. Jesus loves them and has redeemed them by his blood. As Jesus expressed it, "greater love has no one than this, that he lay down his life for his friends" (John 15:13). The promise to be a kingdom and priests recalls God's promise to the Israelites on Mount Sinai, "You will be for me a kingdom of priests and a holy nation" (Ex. 19:6). Peter saw that promise fulfilled in Christ for all believers, both Jew and Gentile, "But you are a chosen people, a royal priesthood, a holy nation" (1 Peter 2:9). The kingdom of God from an earthly perspective undoubtedly looked powerless in the face of the mighty Roman empire. Exclusion from both the Jewish priesthood and the priesthood of the pagan cults likewise brought religious separation. Yet God promises a ministry to the believers that guarantees rulership in an alternative kingdom and priesthood in a superior sanctuary. In Revelation the word "Father" is always used with a possessive pronoun, emphasizing God's relationship to Jesus Christ (cf. 2:27; 3:5, 21; 14:1).

Look, he is coming with the clouds (1:7). The manner and situation of Christ's coming is now vividly portrayed. Four things will characterize his Parousia: (1) It is with the clouds; (2) every eye will see him; (3) his pierced body will be seen especially by his executors; and (4) everyone on earth will mourn because of him. The language of this verse, set as poetry in the NIV, is drawn from Daniel 7:13 and Zechariah 12:10. Whereas Zechariah limits the looking and mourning to the house of David and the inhabitants of Jerusalem, Revelation universalizes the reference to include people from every tribe on earth. This text from Zechariah is also quoted in John 19:37, but the emphasis in the Fourth Gospel is on the historical witness of the Roman soldiers to Jesus' pierced body. Matthew's version of the Synoptic apocalypse likewise mentions the universal mourning that will break forth at the appearance of the Son of Man before the gathering of the elect (Matt. 24:30–31). Do the Christians participate in the mourning, or is this restricted to only unbelievers? Since only unbelievers are depicted as mourning in Revelation (cf. 18: 9, 11, 15, 19), they are the ones who become remorseful at Jesus' coming when they recognize him whom they have rejected.

I am the Alpha and the Omega ... the Almighty (1:8). "Alpha" (A) and "Omega" (Ω) are the first and last letters of the Greek alphabet. This title, first attributed to the Lord God (cf. 21:6), is later assumed by Jesus (22:13). Alpha and Omega, like "First and Last" (1:17) and "Beginning and End" (with which it is coupled in 21:6), is a figure of speech stating extreme opposites to emphasize all that lies in between. Here it highlights the eternal nature of God, who is now at work in human history. "Almighty" is a frequent designation for God in the Old Testament. Its Hebrew form (*šadday* or *ṣᵉbaʾôt*) is translated *pantokratōr* in the Greek Old Testament (cf. 2 Cor. 6:18). Nine out of its ten occurrences in the New Testament are in Revelation, where it emphasizes his sovereignty and dominion over creation.

MODERN PATMOS
▼

Almighty is always used in Revelation to speak of God, never of Jesus.

The Vision of the Son of Man (1:9–20)

There are four numbered septads, or series of sevens, in Revelation—churches, seals, trumpets, and bowls. The beginning and end of these septads serve as major structural markers in the book. The first septad is the seven messages to the churches in Asia. But before Jesus speaks these prophetic messages to the Asian churches, he reveals himself in a dramatic vision to John.

Companion in the suffering . . . on the island of Patmos (1:9). John's banishment to Patmos was not unique in the first century. The Romans often exiled political prisoners to islands in the Aegean Sea.[13] Two primary types of exiles occurred. The first, called *deportatio in insulam*, could be pronounced only by the emperor and was often given to important citizens who fell from favor. The banishment was permanent, and these Romans subsequently lost their civil rights and their property. The second, called *relegatio ad insulam*, could be imposed by a provincial governor. The sentence could be either temporary or permanent, but normally did not require the loss of Roman citizenship or property. John's exile to Patmos probably fell into the latter category.[14]

Because of the word of God and the testimony of Jesus (1:9). John attributes the cause of his exile to his obedience and witness. The expression (or its parts)—"the word of God and the testimony of Jesus"—is an important catch phrase in Revelation and found nine times. In 1:2 it signifies the content of John's vision, which he sees and records. The testimony of Jesus is, first of all, his own words (recorded primarily in chs. 1–3) and those of his angel, which are directed to the seven churches (22:16). This is the same message that Jesus himself preached during his earthly ministry. It is also what the early church proclaimed about Jesus. The central gospel message, commonly called the kerygma, focused especially on Jesus' death, burial, and resurrection. Because of this testimony, John and the saints are persecuted (cf. 6:9; 12:11; 20:4). The word of God is his commands to obey and to endure (12:17; 14:12), even as it is Jesus' (3:8, 10).

The Roman government, beginning with the emperor Nero, no longer considered Christianity as a sect of Judaism, which was a legal religion in the empire. Instead Rome began to view it as an undesirable foreign cult that was a menace to society. John's testimony about

▶ **The Island of Patmos**
IMPORTANT FACTS:[A-1]

- Population: over 50,000
- Volcanic and barren island comprising about 14 square miles
- Harbor at Skala lay thirty-seven miles off the coast of Asia Minor
- Under the jurisdiction of the port city of Miletus and guardian of its western sea boundary from the island fortress of Castelli
- Small Greek Orthodox church surrounds sacred grotto where John traditionally received his vision
- Home of Monastery of St. John the Theologian since 1088

Jesus Christ was viewed as a political crime and hence punishable under Roman law. His suffering was the price paid for obeying a different King and testifying to a different Lord.

On the Lord's Day I was in the Spirit (1:10). This is the earliest text designating Sunday, the first day of the week (cf. Acts 20:7; 1 Cor. 16:2), as "the Lord's Day." Two later Christian texts, *Didache* 14:1 and Ignatius's *Letter to the Magnesians* 9:1, confirm this understanding of the Lord's Day as Sunday.

This is the first of four times in Revelation when John finds himself "in the Spirit." On each occasion an angel summons John to see a vision, whether of the Son of Man (Rev. 1:10), the heavenly throne (4:2), the prostitute Babylon (17:3), or the new Jerusalem (21:10). Some commentators see these "in the Spirit" experiences as a structural key to the book. The content of each vision comprises the section that follows, with the four visionary blocks framed by an introduction and conclusion.[15] The weakness of this proposal is that the seventh trumpet concludes in chapter 11, and John then sees fresh visions in chapters 12–16 that are not introduced with the "in the Spirit" formula. Also, in chapter 21 the phrase occurs in the second vision of the new Jerusalem rather than in the first, where the section clearly begins. John's prophetic experiences resemble those of the prophet Ezekiel, who was taken in the Spirit to Babylon where he received a vision of the captivity (Ezek. 11:24). Ezekiel was later brought by the Spirit to a dry plain where he saw the vision of the valley of dry bones (37:1).

The seven churches (1:11). When John wrote to the Asian Christians, there were more churches in the province than just these seven. Seven other sites are certain locations of churches in the first century: Troas (Acts 16:8–11; 20:5–12), Assos (20:13–14), Miletus (20:15, 17), Colosse (Col. 1:2), Hierapolis (4:13), Tralles (Ignatius), and Magnesia on the Meander (Ignatius).

W. M. Ramsay conjectured that the order of the seven churches represents a circular postal route that a courier would usually follow along the existing Roman roads.[16] (The modern Turkish highways largely follow the same routes.) Such a route, although not proven, might well have existed. Official Roman correspondence would be distributed from Ephesus to the district, or conventus, centers in the province. The mention of only seven churches suggests that John's use of the number seven here is representative and symbolic. Therefore Revelation was to be circulated beyond its original addressees, even as Paul's letter to the Colossians was (4:12).

"Like a son of man" (1:13). In this opening vision John uses much figurative language to describe Jesus Christ. Similar imagery is found in the visions of a "son of man" figure seen by Daniel (Dan. 7:9–14; 10:5–19). While John's inclination is to identify this figure as an angel, his hair white as wool and snow links him to Daniel's "Ancient of Days." Many of the vivid descriptions and titles of Jesus presented in chapter 1 are found again at the beginning of each of the seven messages, although in largely reverse order.

Out of his mouth came a sharp double-edged sword (1:16). The striking image of the sharp sword proceeding from his mouth is used three other times in Revelation (cf. 2:16; 19:15, 21). In each of

▶ Knowing the Future

People seem to have an innate interest in knowing "what will take place later." Today many seek to know the future through horoscopes, seances, Ouija boards, and fortune tellers. The ancient residents of Asia likewise had an interest in knowing the future. Two of the most famous oracles in antiquity were located near the seven churches.

Claros was near Ephesus and drew inquirers from as far away as the Black Sea. The Roman historian Tacitus, himself once a governor of Asia, describes how the oracle was consulted: "Here it is not a prophetess, as at Delphi, but a male priest . . . who hears the number and the names of the consultants, but no more, then descends into a cavern, swallows a draught of water from a mysterious spring, and . . . delivers his response in set verses dealing with the subject each inquirer has in mind."[A-2] The oracle, in its typical cryptic fashion, apparently foretold the death of Germanicus, the adopted son of Tiberius, when he visited it. Five inscriptions have been found at Claros describing the visits of delegations from Laodicea who were apparently regular visitors to the oracle.[A-3]

The other oracle was located at Didyma, near Miletus, and also dedicated to the god Apollo. Its temple was the third largest structure in the Greek world. Visitors brought their questions to the sanctuary where a prophetess, after a ritual bath, drank from a sacred spring for inspiration. Her prophecy, in hexameter verse, was transcribed and delivered to the inquirer by the prophet of Apollo.[A-4] The Asian churches were thus situated in a place where oracles and prophecy were highly valued. The spread of Christianity spelled the doom for oracles, and by the fourth century the pool of potential clients inquiring at these sacred springs had dried up.

---

these texts the sword is a metaphor for the tongue that Jesus uses to speak words of judgment against his enemies. Most of these titles have their background in the Old Testament. (For the intertextual background of the Old Testament references in Revelation, consult the cross references in your NIV Bible or UBS Greek New Testament.)

I am the First and the Last (1:17). A title such as the First and the Last, first given to the Lord Almighty in Isaiah (Isa. 44:6; 48:12), is now assumed by Jesus. Such sharing of titles emphasizes the divinity of Jesus and his equality with the Father. The Greek word translated "Last" is *eschatos*, from which is derived the theological term *eschatology*. Eschatology is usually described as the teaching about last things. However, events are not at the center of eschatology; rather a person is—Jesus Christ, the Last One, the *Eschatos*.

I am the Living One. . . . And I hold the keys of death and Hades (1:18). The figure whom John is worshiping further identifies himself as the One who was dead but now lives forever. John now realizes that he is seeing another post-resurrection appearance of Jesus, who declared, "I am the resurrection and the life" (John 11:25). Following Jesus' resurrection, the angels at the tomb asked the women, "Why do you look for the living [One] among the dead?" (Luke 24:5).

"Death" and "Hades" are almost synonymous terms for the place of the dead in the Greek Old Testament (cf. Prov. 5:5), where Hades translates the Hebrew word *Sheol.* Peter quoted Psalm 16:10 as a prophetic word about Jesus' resurrection: "because you will not abandon me to the grave [*hadēs*]" (Acts 2:27).

"Keys" is a metaphor for authority in Revelation (cf. Rev. 1:18; 9:1; 20:1). The only other New Testament text to use "Hades" and "keys" together is Matthew 16:18–19. There Jesus affirmed that the powers of death cannot prevail against the church and that he has given the church, epitomized by Peter, the authority to allow or forbid entrance into the kingdom. Because of his resurrection, Jesus now has power over death and the grave.

Write, therefore, what you have seen, what is now and what will take place later (1:19). Some commentators regard this verse also as a structural key to the book. A threefold division based on this text states that chapter 1 is what has been

▶ The Structure of the Seven Messages

The so-called "letters" to the seven churches are probably the most familiar section of Revelation. Since the book's opening and closing (1:4; 22:21) exhibit distinctive letter forms absent in these chapters, it is preferable not to call them letters. Even a casual reading reveals a similar structure among them. These structural elements have parallels with ancient Near East covenants, imperial edicts, and rhetorical letter forms. However, given John's immersion in Old Testament literature, it seems best to describe them as prophetic messages influenced by such examples as Balaam's seven oracles (Num. 22–24), Amos's prophecies to the seven nations (Amos 1–2), and Ezekiel's oracles against the nations (Ezek. 25–32). Seven sections, or sayings, can be recognized in these prophetic messages to the seven churches:

Address—Command to write to the angel of each church

Epithet—Title of Jesus drawn largely from the opening vision in chapter 1

Praise—Commendation for each church's positive deeds

Blame—Rebuke for each church's negative deeds

Coming—Call to repent with imminent judgment for failing to do so

Hearing—Call to hear and obey what the Spirit is saying to the churches

Promise—Eschatological promises given to the victors who overcome

This structural pattern holds true except for several notable exceptions. The messages to Smyrna and Philadelphia—churches experiencing persecution from the Jews—contain no blame sayings. The final message to Laodicea—the lukewarm church—contains no praise saying. In the first three messages—to the three leading cities of Asia—the hearing saying precedes the promise saying. In the final four messages the order is reversed. Lastly, the middle letter to Thyatira is the longest—230 words in the Greek text—with the characteristic central emphasis of chiastic structure (see ch. 12). The spiritual struggle in the Thyatiran church epitomizes that faced by the other churches. The hearing sayings sound familiar because Jesus uses a similar expression in his parables, "He who has ears to hear, let him hear" (Mark 4:9, 23). Such hearing sayings serve as a wake-up call to his listeners, as he tries to grab their attention. Modified hearing sayings are found in Revelation 13:9 and 22:17, another indication that the original Asian audience is still being addressed in these later chapters.

seen, chapters 2 and 3 are what is now, and chapters 4–22 are what will take place later. However, a better translation of "what is now" is "what they are," that is, the explanation Jesus provides for the imagery. For the symbolic meaning of the stars and the lampstands is immediately given for John to write down. With the phrase "what will take place later," Jesus declares that he is Lord of the future. For the Asian Christians facing uncertain times ahead, this knowledge must have brought comfort and encouragement.

The mystery (1:20). Jesus now gives John the interpretation of two elements of the vision. He calls them a "mystery," even as God's divine plan and the identity of the prostitute/woman are likewise called mysteries (10:7; 17:5, 7). John, like Paul (cf. Eph. 1:4; 3:9; 5:32; Col. 1:26; 2:2), refers to mysteries not as hidden spiritual matters known only to a few initiates, as in ancient mystery religions, but as divine secrets now revealed to all believers.

The seven stars are the angels of the seven churches (1:20). These angels are addressed first in each of the seven messages. Actual angels rather than human pastors are the probable referent here. In the early church the presence of angels

was assumed at the assemblies (1 Cor. 11:10), and, as we saw in Revelation 1:1, angels were an integral part of worship in Asia.

The seven lampstands are the seven churches (1:20). The lampstand, or menorah, was a fixture found first in the desert tabernacle (Ex. 27:21; Lev. 24:2–4) and later in the first and second temples (2 Chron. 4:20; 1 Macc. 4:49–50). The lampstand in the temple was permanently extinguished when Titus destroyed Jerusalem in A.D. 70 and carried the lampstand to Rome as booty.[17] This lampstand is depicted on a panel on the triumphal Arch of Titus erected in Rome a decade later. A lampstand graffito on the steps of the Library of Celsus (c. A.D. 110) can still be seen in Ephesus today. It is one of the few evidences of a Jewish presence in the city. John transforms this traditional image of a single menorah with seven bowls to an image of seven individual lampstands. The Asian churches are thus depicted as holy vessels of spiritual light in their respective communities (cf. Matt. 5:14–16).

To the Church in Ephesus (2:1–7)

Holds the seven stars in his right hand and walks among the seven golden lampstands (2:1). Two attributes of deity are clearly suggested by these images—omnipotence and omnipresence. Jesus is especially present among his churches, knowing firsthand the situations in each. Similar imagery, probably traditional, was used by the emperor Domitian in A.D. 83 to celebrate the deification of his infant son following his death. Coins were issued showing the child seated on a globe surrounded by seven stars. This is

◀ *left*

LAMPSTAND GRAFFITO

This depiction of the *menorah* was inscribed on the pavement near the Library of Celsus in Ephesus.

▶

TEMPLE OF DOMITIAN

Remains of the temple in Ephesus.

▶ Ephesus

Ephesus (modern Selçuk) was the fourth largest city in the Roman empire after Rome, Syrian Antioch, and Alexandria. Its population numbered over 250,000 residents. An important port and commercial center, Ephesus was the western terminus of a road that ran eastward across Asia Minor. Inscriptions refer to the city as "First and Greatest Metropolis of Asia."

After the Romans created the province of Asia in 129 B.C., Ephesus became increasingly important as an administrative center. In the first century A.D., the city became the official residence of Roman proconsul of Asia. Although a temple for Roman residents to Dea Roma, the patron goddess of Rome, and Divus Julius, the deified Caesar, was built as early as 29 B.C., a temple for the imperial cult was not built in the city until A.D. 89/90. Some scholars who hold a late date for the book see the building of the cult temple by Domitian as the life

setting for the conflict with the state depicted in Revelation 13.[A-5]

Ephesus was known throughout the ancient world as the temple keeper (neōkoros; cf. Acts 19:35) of the goddess Artemis. The temple of Artemis was one of the seven wonders of the ancient world and its largest religious structure, measuring 220 by 425 feet. Thousands journeyed to Ephesus each spring for the annual Artemisia festival, recalling the Jewish pilgrimages to Jerusalem for the feasts. Although the worship of Artemis is not mentioned specifically in Revelation, it remained an opponent of Christianity in the city until the temple's destruction by the Goths in about A.D. 262. At least fourteen other deities have been identified with temples in first-century Ephesus. The Ephesian Christians therefore had an ongoing struggle with the pervasive paganism in their city.[A-6]

the first of a number of motifs in Revelation that are shared with the imperial cult, suggesting that the latter is a satanic parody of divine truth.

Those who claim to be apostles but are not (2:2). The Ephesians are commended for deeds of hard work and perseverance. Deeds are important to Jesus because he mentions them either explicitly or implicitly in each message. The teaching of Revelation is thus in harmony with that of James: Faith without deeds is dead (James 2:17, 26). One good deed was their intolerance of wickedness, particularly in those who purported to be Christian leaders.

The early church, particularly at Ephesus, was plagued by false apostles and teachers. At Miletus Paul prophesied that even some of the Ephesian elders would tragically betray the cause of Christ by distorting the truth and leading away disciples (Acts 20:29–30). Timothy's primary duty at Ephesus was to command certain persons to cease teaching false doctrine (1 Tim. 1:3). Hymenaeus, Alexander, and Philetus are even named as Ephesians who wandered from the truth (1:19–20; 2 Tim. 2:17–18). When John arrived in Ephesus, this church probably examined even his message. Found to be a true apostle, John now exercised apostolic authority over the church, even as Paul did. The criteria used to examine apostles and prophets became formalized in the *Didache*, a late first-century manual summarizing early church practice. One example is: "And when the apostle leaves, he is to take nothing except bread until he finds his next night's lodging. But if he asks for money, he is a false prophet" (*Did.* 11:6).

Forsaken your first love (2:4). In spite of hardships, the Ephesians have not grown weary in resisting evil. Yet the congregation has experienced a great spiritual fall: They have forsaken their first love. Years of vigilance concerning orthodoxy (correct doctrine) have perhaps dulled their sensitivity to orthopraxy (correct practice), both of which are necessary for a spiritually healthy congregation. Jesus' remedy for the church is repentance and a return to their first work—love. The message of love characterizes the teaching of Jesus (e.g., John 13:34–35). Love

▶ Local References

Does each of the seven messages contain facts and characteristics unique to its own city? W. M. Ramsay, who is perhaps the best-known advocate for local references, identified numerous features in the messages related to each city's geography and history.[A-7] Other scholars are more skeptical of such supposed links, viewing these associated ideas simply as literary devices devoid of historical connections.[A-8] Since John probably (and Jesus certainly) had a firsthand knowledge of the seven cities and their churches, the inclusion of local references is likely. Indeed the rhetorical situation of each church—suffering, persecution, false teaching, materialism—relates to the life setting of its host city. The vivid imagery often relates to known Asian backgrounds, so it is difficult to deny all local references. Local references are either generic or familiar enough that the audiences in the other churches can understand them. However, the repetition of such images as "crown" (2:10; 3:11), "white clothes" (3:4, 18) and "new name" (2:17; 3:12) suggests that caution must be used in limiting their relevance to localized associations.

for one another expressed in good deeds is likewise reiterated in 1 John 3:11–18.

I will come to you and remove your lampstand (2:5). This is the first of Jesus' warnings to come in judgment if each church does not repent or is not found faithful. With the Ephesian church, failure to repent seemingly means that Christ will close down the church. A less harsh, and perhaps better, reading is that Christ will move the Ephesian lampstand from its leadership position as an apostolic church among the Asian churches and pass its authority along to another congregation. Ephesus remained an important ecclesiastical center until Constantinople gained preeminence in the latter fourth century A.D. The Third Ecumenical Council, which dealt with the heresies of Nestorianism and Pelagianism, was held in Ephesus in 431 in the Double Church, whose ruins remain at the site.

The practices of the Nicolaitans (2:6). The Ephesians are commended for hating the practices of this obscure sect, mentioned again in the letter to Pergamum (2:15). An early tradition names Nicolaus, one of the first seven deacons in Jerusalem, as the founder of this sect (Acts 6:5). However, there is little evidence, apart from the similar name, that this proselyte from Antioch was connected with the group. The word Nicolaitan (literally, "victor over the people") is a wordplay on Revelation's key word *nikaō*, "to be victorious, conquer" and translated "overcome" in the victor sayings. Unlike the true victors, who were to overcome by resisting the existing political, social, and religious order, the Nicolaitans apparently advocated accommodation to pagan society by eating food sacrificed to idols and engaging in sexual immorality.[18]

Eat from the tree of life, which is in the paradise of God (2:7). The imagery of the promise is drawn primarily from the account of the primeval garden in Genesis 2–3. "Paradise" is the word used in the Septuagint for Eden. After the Fall, Adam and Eve were forever barred from eating of the tree of life in the Garden of Eden. The Ephesians who overcome will experience a reversal of the Fall and the restoration of eternal access to God. This promise of eternal life in God's presence is foundational to all the other promises. A possible local reference involves the grove Ortygia outside of Ephesus, thought to be the traditional birthplace of Artemis. This sacred grove, called a *paradeisos*, still

CULT TEMPLES

(left) Ruins of the temple of Apollo at Didyma.

(right) The scant remains of the temple of Artemis at Ephesus. The Byzantine-era church of St. John is in the background.

▼

drew pilgrims in the first century.[19] The paradise available to the worshipers of Artemis paled in comparison to the coming paradise of God.

To the Church in Smyrna (2:8–11)

I know your afflictions and your poverty (2:9). Jesus first assures the Christians in Smyrna that he knows what they are going through. Believers have apparently lost their jobs or their businesses are being boycotted, hence depriving them of material support. Such economic discrimination is well known in many parts of the world even today where Christians comprise a minority.

A synagogue of Satan (2:9). Certain Jews in Smyrna and Philadelphia (3:9) are called a synagogue of Satan. Satan, mentioned here only in passing before his formal introduction in Revelation 12:9, is opposing the church not only through false teachers but also through members of the Jewish community.

The denunciation of the Jews here is not anti-Semitic (Jesus and John were both Jews); rather it is directed at institutional Judaism of the period, which became a formidable opponent of the church. It was the rulers of the synagogue in various Roman cities who often persecuted Paul (e.g., Acts 13:50; 14:2, 19), and Jews from Asia were responsible for Paul's imprisonment in Jerusalem (Acts 21:27–36). In the Gospel of John, written to an

SYMRNA

The agora with Mount Pagus in the background.

▶ Smyrna

Smyrna (modern Izmir) was a major seaport on a gulf of the Aegean located forty miles northwest of Ephesus. It claimed to be the home of the great poet Homer. Smyrna was noted for its beauty in the ancient world. Some of its coins read "First of Asia in beauty and size"—a statement continually contested by its chief rivals, Ephesus and Pergamum. The Roman writer Cicero called Smyrna "the city of our most faithful and most ancient allies."[A-9] Her long-time alliance with Rome began in 195 B.C. when Smyrna became the first city anywhere to erect a temple to the goddess Roma.[A-10]

In A.D. 26 Tiberius chose Smyrna from eleven Asian applicants to become the keeper for the second imperial cult temple in Asia. No archaeological evidence of this temple has yet been discovered.[A-11] A disciple of John named Polycarp later served as the bishop of Smyrna. His confession shortly before his dramatic execution (c. A.D. 156) epitomizes that of martyrs throughout the centuries: "For eighty-six years I have been his servant, and he has done me no wrong. How can I blaspheme my King who saved me?" (*Mart. Poly.* 9:3).

audience around Ephesus, "the Jews" are repeatedly singled out as the enemies of Jesus (e.g., John 2:18; 5:18; 10:31). As F. F. Bruce notes, the Jews here are not the people as a whole but "the religious establishment in Jerusalem, whether the Sanhedrin or the temple authorities."[20] Later, at the martyrdom of Polycarp, the Jews played a prominent role in his execution (*Mart. Poly.* 12.2; 13.1; 17.2; 18.1). For John and the other Jewish believers, the doors of the synagogue have been closed to them, and its leaders are inciting the Roman authorities to persecute the church.

Suffer persecution for ten days (2:10). Jesus confirms that suffering is coming, but the Christians are encouraged not to be afraid. In fact, the period of persecu-tion will be short—only ten days. Ten days is symbolic for a brief period of time. Daniel and his three Hebrew friends refused to eat the defiled Babylonian food and were tested for ten days. When the period was over, they emerged vindicated (Dan. 1:12–15), as those in Smyrna are expected to be.

The crown of life (2:10). For those who die in the persecution, a crown of life is promised. The victor's crown, or wreath, was an established eschatological image in early Christian literature. Both Paul and Peter told their Anatolian audiences that they would receive a crown at the Lord's coming (2 Tim. 4:8; 1 Peter 5:4). This imagery has an interesting local reference related to Smyrna's topography. The acropolis Mount Pagus, which

---

▶ **Jews in Asia**

A community of Jews probably lived in each of the seven cities. Obadiah 20 mentions some exiles of Jerusalem who had settled in Sepharad, a likely reference to Sardis. About 210 B.C. the Seleucid ruler Antiochus III relocated 2,000 Jewish families from Mesopotamia to Phrygia and Lydia. Since Sardis was the capital of Lydia and Laodicea was an important city in Phrygia, both cities probably received Jewish settlers at this time.

As citizens in the Asian cities, these Jews could maintain civic associations and were allowed to practice their own laws. When the local civic administrators prevented the Jews from sending money to the temple in Jerusalem, the Jews appealed to Augustus, who confirmed their right.[A-12]

Sardis is the only city in Asia Minor where an ancient synagogue has been discovered. A synagogue, part of a Roman bath and gymnasium complex, has been excavated and restored by American archaeologists in recent years. Although the synagogue dates from the early third century A.D., its remarkable size and central location indicate the wealth and strength of a long-standing Jewish community.[A-13]

The presence of Jews in Ephesus is richly documented, particularly by the Jewish historian Josephus who makes ten references to that fact.[A-14] However, the synagogue mentioned in Acts 19:8 has never been located by archaeologists.

Similarly, little archaeological or literary evidence exists for the synagogues mentioned at Smyrna and Philadelphia. The small amount of gold confiscated from the Jews of Pergamum in 62 B.C. suggests the presence of only a small community there.[A-15] Lydia probably became a God-fearer through the influence of Jews in her native city of Thyatira (Acts 16:14). Twenty pounds of gold bound for Jerusalem was confiscated in Laodicea by the proconsul Flaccus (62 B.C.). This amount suggests a Jewish population of over 7,500 male adults plus women and children in the city at the time.[A-16]

▶ Nike Christians

Nike, the namesake of the well-known athletic company, was the Greek goddess of victory. She is usually represented as a winged maiden, alighting from flight, holding in each hand her most frequent attributes—a palm branch and a wreath. Numerous coin types that circulated in Asia depict Nike in this way. The Roman Senate installed Nike's statue in its chambers in 29 B.C. to commemorate the beginning of Augustus's rule and opened its sessions each morning with a sacrifice to her.[A-17]

Athletics in the Greco-Roman world were as popular as they are today. The *koinon,* or league, of Asia sponsored games in each of the seven cities except Thyatira. The larger festivals were held every five years in Ephesus, Pergamum, and Smyrna. The leader of the League of Asia, who also served as chief priest of the emperor cult, often presided as the judge of the festival. Major events at

such games included running and boxing (cf. 1 Cor. 9:24–27). The winners usually received symbolic crowns, or wreaths (*stephanoi*), made out of olive, pine, wild celery, or bay leaves. Palm branches (cf. Rev. 7:9) were also symbols of victory given to those victorious in the games. The Greek verb *nikaō* is found repeatedly on a well-known Greek inscription dating from 400–350 B.C., which lists the amphorae to be given to the victors at the Panathenaic games in Greece.[A-18]

Jesus exhorts the Asian believers to triumph spiritually over the internal and external enemies confronting them. Victory is assured because Jesus himself has been victorious (cf. 3:21; 5:5). For the Christians who overcome, participation in the future blessings of the new heaven and new earth is promised. These same blessings are promised to us today if we too will become Nike Christians.

---

loomed over the city, was described by ancient writers as its crown.[21]

The second death (2:11). A connection between death and Smyrna existed in the ancient world. Its name was identical to the Greek word for the sweet-smelling spice in which dead bodies were wrapped for embalming (e.g., that of Jesus; John 19:39). A number of mourning myths became associated with the city, particularly that of Niobe, the Greek mythological figure whose tear-stained face was thought to be etched in the marble of nearby Mount Sipylus.[22] A city associated with suffering produced a church known for its

suffering. Second death is not further defined until chapter 20.

To the Church in Pergamum (2:12–17)

Him who has the sharp, double-edged sword (2:12). Two types of swords are mentioned in Revelation—the long *rhomphaia* here, which was used for piercing and cutting (cf. 1:16; 2:16; 19:15, 21), and the short dagger-like *machaira*, which measured less than sixteen inches (6:4; 13:10, 14). The Roman governor of Asia exercised the *ius gladii,* or right of the sword, from his bench of judgment in Pergamum. In the province

▶

▶ Pergamum

Pergamum (modern Bergama) was situated fifteen miles inland from the Aegean coast about seventy miles north of Smyrna. It was the capital of the Attalid empire for over a century (263–133 B.C.). When Attalus III bequeathed his kingdom to the Romans in 133 B.C., the city became the first seat of the new province of Asia. Pliny the Elder calls the city "the most famous place of Asia."[A-19] Its four patron deities were Zeus, Athena, Dionysus, and Asclepius, all of whom appear on the city's coinage. The temple to Athena Nikephoros ("Victory-Bearer") was the most important in the city. These temples were situated on a spectacular acropolis that towered a thousand feet over the lower city. Also located on the acropolis was the city's famous library, which totaled over 200,000 volumes, the second largest in antiquity after Alexandria. After the Alexandrian library was partially destroyed by Julius Caesar in 47 B.C., Pergamum's library was plundered in 41 B.C. by Mark Antony, who presented it to his lover Cleopatra. Nevertheless, the city remained a center for learning. Population projections for Pergamum in the first century estimate over 150,000 residents.[A-20]

he represented the authority of the emperor, who himself carried a sword or dagger as a symbol of his office.[23] The governor's power to render capital punishment gave him the right of life and death in his jurisdiction. As Pilate, the governor of Judea, said to Jesus at his trial, "Don't you realize I have power either to free you or to crucify you?" (John 19:10). By using this epithet in the message to Pergamum, Jesus establishes his preeminence, even over the Roman governor. This image echoes his response to Pilate, "You would have no power over me if it were not given to you from above" (John 19:11).

Where Satan has his throne (2:13). The throne of Satan has been variously identified as the altar of Zeus, the temple of Asclepius, or the shape of the acropolis. However, the church's most pernicious enemy was Rome, who had its tentacles both in Asia's political and religious affairs. The first temple in Asia to be dedicated to the emperor cult was built in Pergamum in 29 B.C. by Augustus. A similar temple was also built then in Nicomedia (moder Izmit), the capital of the province of Bithynia. By the time Revelation was written, emperor worship had been established in Pergamum for over a century. Unfortunately, no archaeological evidence for this imperial cult temple, which is believed to have been built in the lower city, has been found yet. Because Satan was the underlying force in Rome's hostility to the church, Pergamum could be described as his throne.

Antipas, my faithful witness (2:13). Antipas is the only believer named in Revelation who had died for the faith. He was probably a leader of the church in Pergamum. The word "martyr" is derived from the Greek word *martys*, here translated as "witness." Jesus is the first faithful witness (1:5), who is also called the "true witness" in Revelation 3:14. James, the brother of Jesus and leader of the early Jerusalem church, is likewise called a true witness. He was executed in A.D. 62 during the high priesthood of Ananus II by being thrown down from the pinnacle of the temple, stoned, and beaten with a fuller's club.[24] Because the early Christian witnesses were sometimes put to death, "martyr" came to have the connotation of one who died for the faith. The theme of martyrdom is prominent in Revelation (cf. 6:9; 11:3; 12:11; 17:6).[25]

The teaching of Balaam (2:14). The seven prophecies of Balaam are among the most eloquent in the Old Testament (Num. 23–24). Because of his greed, however, Balaam disobeyed God and counseled the Moabite king Balak to seduce the Israelites away from God through sexual immorality and idolatry (25:1–3). In the New Testament, Balaam is portrayed as the prototypical false prophet (see 2 Peter 2:15; Jude 11). The teaching of Balaam was, in practice, probably the same as that of the Nicolaitans (see comments on Rev. 2:6).

Eating food sacrificed to idols (2:14). The issue of eating idol meat is mentioned explicitly in this message and in the one to Thyatira (2:20). Ramsay describes the situation: "In both Pergamum and Thyatira some of the Christians still clung to their membership of the pagan associations and shared in the fellowship of the ritual meal."[26] Eating food sacrificed to idols is one of the four practices from which the Jerusalem council asks Gentile believers to abstain

(Acts 15:29; 21:25). Paul addresses this issue from Ephesus in his first letter to Corinth (1 Cor. 8:1–13; 10:19–33). The raging conflict that tore apart congregations in the early decades of the Gentile churches later appears resolved. Around A.D. 100 the command, probably based on the teachings of Paul and John, is simply "keep strictly away from meat sacrificed to idols, for it involves the worship of dead gods" (*Did.* 6:3).

The hidden manna (2:17). The promise of hidden manna is very obscure. Manna, of course, is the supernatural sustenance provided by God during Israel's forty years in the desert (Num. 11:6–9; Deut. 8:3; Josh. 5:12). Aaron sets aside a golden jar of manna to be placed in the ark as a testimony for future generations (Ex. 16:32–34; cf. Heb. 9:4). When the temple is destroyed by the Babylonians in 586 B.C., its sacred objects are lost. One Jewish tradition claims that Jeremiah rescued the ark with its pot of manna and hid them in a cave on Mount Nebo until God should regather his people (2 Macc. 2:4–8). Another states that an angel hid these sacred temple objects in the earth and is to guard them until the end times (2 Bar. 6:8). Jesus uses the manna imagery in his teaching: He himself is the true bread of God and whoever eats of him will live forever in the age to come (John 6:30–58). During his earthly ministry, Jesus' teaching is largely hidden from the Jews (Matt. 13:34–35) and from his disciples (Luke 18:34). Another idea that was apparently current in the late first century is that the messianic age would be inaugurated by restoring the gift of manna (cf. 2 Bar. 29:8). Jesus now promises to give some of his manna, an image never used again in Revelation, to the victor. Apparently, manna is the spir-

itual sustenance of the future life and suggests eternal fellowship with Jesus himself, the bread of life.

A white stone with a new name written on it (2:17). A white stone had various uses in antiquity: a token of admission, a voting piece, a symbol of victory, a Christian amulet, or something used in an initiation into the service of Asclepius. White stones were also the writing surface for official edicts. One such relevant decree was issued in 9 B.C. by Paulus Fabius Maximus, the governor of Asia. This edict, confirmed by the provincial league, decreed that Augustus's birthday should be made an official holiday in Asia as well as to mark the beginning of the municipal new year. It was inscribed in Latin and Greek on a white stone and set up in the imperial cult temple in Pergamum. The decree was apparently distributed throughout the province because copies have been found in five Asian cities.[27] This was the best white stone that the province could give to its citizens; Jesus has an alternative stone to give to his overcomers.

To the Church in Thyatira (2:18–29)

The Son of God (2:18). This phrase is found nowhere else in Revelation. It anticipates the quotation in 2:27 of Psalm 2:9, a psalm in which the messianic Anointed One is twice called the "Son" (Ps. 2:7, 12). Son of God is the most important Christological title in the New Testament because it describes Jesus' relationship to God in terms of divine sonship. Although each of the Gospel writers uses the title, John gives it a distinctive emphasis in his Gospel and first letter (cf. John 20:31; 1 John 5:20).

Whose eyes are like blazing fire and whose feet are like burnished bronze (2:18). This portrayal of Jesus is apparently a polemic against the local deity Helius Pythius Tyrimnaeus Apollo, who was primarily a sun god syncretized from Lydian, Macedonian, and Greek deities.[28] Jesus is portrayed here as barefoot. Roman statuary occasionally depicted emperors and their families barefoot, an indication that the individual had entered the realm of the divine. Only here and in Revelation 1:15 is the Greek word *chalkolibanos* found in Greek literature. The term was certainly understood in Thyatira, perhaps as the product of a local metal trade guild. Although the KJV translates it as "brass" (an alloy of copper with zinc), it is better understood as "bronze" (an alloy of copper with tin).

That woman Jezebel, who calls herself a prophetess (2:20). Jezebel was the queen of Israel whose idolatrous worship of Baal was condemned by the prophet Elijah (1 Kings 16:31–21:25). Her spiritual counterpart in Thyatira is nicknamed after this notorious queen. Jesus rebukes her because of her message, not because of her gender or prophetic ministry. The daughters of Philip were well-known prophetesses (Acts 21:8–9) who had relocated to Asian Hierapolis with their father.[29]

To ease social and economic tension, Jezebel, like the Nicolaitans, advocates moral compromise with pagan neighbors by eating food sacrificed to idols and committing sexual immorality. Jesus promises to bring spiritual, maybe even physical, death upon her and her followers unless they repent. Some of the Corinthian Christians who had indulged in the same sins had also experienced premature deaths (1 Cor. 11:30). Unlike the Christians in Smyrna and Philadelphia, the suffering of the Thyatirans would not be *for* Christ but *because* of Christ.

So I will cast her on a bed of suffering (2:22). "To cast someone on a sickbed" is a Hebrew idiom meaning to punish a person with different kinds of illnesses (cf. Ex. 21:18; 1 Macc. 1:5; Judith 8:3). "Bed" (Gk. *klinē*) can also be translated as "couch." It is thus used ironically to describe Jezebel and her followers, who reclined on marble couches while dining in the banqueting hall of the pagan temples. Such couches were also used for sexual immorality, as

▶ Thyatira

Thyatira (modern Akhisar) was a major inland Asian city in the first century. Standing midway between Pergamum and Sardis on a broad fertile plain, its location made it an ideal commercial center. Many trade guilds were formed that grew to have an influential role in civic life. The city was particularly noted for its local purple dye derived from the madder root. As a result there was a prosperous guild of dyers. Lydia, the businesswoman Paul met in Philippi, was a purple dye seller from the city (Acts 16:14). Syncretism characterized the city's religious life. Outside the city in a sacred precinct of the Chaldeans, there was a shrine of the oriental Sibyl Sambathe. Sometime before 2 B.C. a locally organized civic cult of Rome and Augustus was dedicated.[A-21]

depicted in Greek vase paintings and described in Greek literature. Because Jezebel had used her freedom to lie on a couch of pleasure in the temples, God would instead make it a bed of sickness unless she repented.

All the churches (2:23). Apart from each hearing saying, this is the only direct mention of the other churches in the seven messages. Jezebel's message of accommodation must have appealed to believers throughout Asia, hence her correction served as an object lesson both to the church in Thyatira and to all the other Asian churches.

Satan's so-called deep secrets (2:24). Jezebel and her followers are involved in esoteric teachings that emphasize acquiring knowledge of divine mysteries, but whose source is Satan rather than God. Like their Corinthian counterparts, they believe that everything is permissible and that no sin committed in the body would harm them spiritually (cf. 1 Cor. 6:12–18). Such teaching has parallels among several second-century Gnostic groups, which likewise advocated eating meat sacrificed to idols and attending festivals in honor of the gods. Another early heresy believed that Jesus was not born the Christ, but became so when the Christ descended upon the human Jesus at his baptism (cf. 1 John 2:22; 5:1). Cerinthus was a prominent advocate of this teaching. When the apostle John spotted Cerinthus sitting in a bathhouse in Ephesus, he rushed back out without taking a bath and cried, "Let us get out of here, for fear the place falls in, now that Cerinthus, the enemy of truth, is inside!"[30] The opponents of Jezebel are to turn their focus instead on the deep things of God (cf. 1 Cor. 2:10).

Authority over the nations (2:26). This is the only letter to have a double promise to the victors who are to do his will to the end. Jesus first promises the same authority over the nations as he himself received from the Father. The nature of that rule is quoted from Psalm 2:9, the only certain quotation from the Old Testament in Revelation. It says of the Messiah, "You will rule them with an iron scepter; you will dash them to pieces like pottery." That rule is finally established when the rider on the white horse strikes down the nations with his iron scepter (Rev. 19:15). The victors, seen as the armies of heaven riding on white horses (19:14), will begin to exercise their rule during the thousand years (20:4).

The morning star (2:28). This striking metaphor is a probable allusion to Balaam's third oracle, "A star will come out of Jacob" (Num. 24:17). The next line, "a scepter will rise out of Israel," repeats the scepter imagery found in Psalm 2:9. The faithful in Thyatira are promised both rule and relationship with the Morning Star! The image of a star from Jacob became a stock messianic expression in intertestamental Judaism.[31] The messianic leader of the Jewish revolt in A.D. 132 was given the name Bar Kokhba, which is translated "son of the star." Second Peter 1:19 is another New Testament text that links Jesus with this metaphor: "And the morning star rises in your hearts." In antiquity, the planet Venus was linked to the morning star. From Babylonian times, it was a symbol of rule. The Roman legions carried Venus's zodiac sign, the bull, on their standards. Therefore, the church and the empire had conflicting notions about what the morning star heralded for the world.

To the Church in Sardis (3:1–6)

A reputation of being alive, but you are dead (3:1). The Greek historian Herodotus records that Croesus consulted the oracle at Delphi about his course of action regarding Cyrus and the Persians, who threatened from the east. The oracle counseled that Croesus would destroy a great empire if he crossed the Halys River into Persian territory. Thinking that the destruction of Cyrus's empire was prophesied, Croesus attacked. After an inconclusive campaign, Croesus retreated to Sardis whereupon Cyrus launched a surprise attack. The seemingly impregnable acropolis was taken through a security lapse, and Croesus and Sardis were captured by Cyrus in 547 B.C. The Lydian king had destroyed his own great empire.[32] Sardis had an illustrious history, but by the first century it was on the decline. The church likewise had a better past than present. Instead of moving forward, it was resting on its reputation, and for this reason Jesus calls it a dead church.

I will come like a thief (3:3). The metaphor of the thief, with its elements of surprise and unpreparedness, is a familiar one in New Testament eschatology. Jesus likens his return to that of a thief in one of his parables (Matt. 24:42–44). Both Paul (1 Thess. 5:2) and Peter (2 Peter 3:10) compare the day of the Lord to the unexpected coming of a thief. In this context, however, Jesus' promise refers not to his coming at the Parousia, but to an imminent coming in judgment. Unless the Christians in Sardis repent and demonstrate their faith through deeds

▶ Sardis

Sardis (modern Sart) is located in the fertile Hermus River valley approximately thirty-five miles southeast of Thyatira and sixty miles east of Smyrna. It was the capital of the Lydian empire (c. 680–547 B.C.) The wealth of the legendary King Croesus (c. 560–547 B.C.) came from the gold found in the Pactolus River, which flowed through the city. As the westernmost point on the Royal Road, the city also prospered greatly from trade. Following Alexander the Great's capture of the city from the Persians (334 B.C.), it served as the capital of the Seleucid empire (281–190 B.C.).

The Romans assumed control of Sardis following a period of rule by Pergamum (190–133 B.C.). In A.D.

17, Sardis was devastated by an earthquake. The emperor Tiberius promised ten million sesterces for rebuilding Sardis and remitted taxes for five years. Nine years later, the city lost its bid to become the home of the second imperial cult temple in Asia.[A-22]

A large Ionic temple to Artemis was built in Sardis, although it was never finished. The population during the Roman period numbered between 60,000 and 100,000 residents.[A-23] Melito was a prominent bishop of Sardis in the second century. He is remembered for his *Homily on the Passion* and for the letter he preserved from Antoninus Pius forbidding the league of Asia from continuing the persecution of Christians (A.D. 161).[A-24]

consistent with the gospel, Jesus will come at a time unknown to them.

Dressed in white (3:4, 5). White clothing is used in Revelation to depict moral and ritual purity. The metaphor is frequently used in other biblical and intertestamental literature. God on his throne is depicted as wearing white (Dan. 7:9), angels wear white clothing (e.g., Dan. 10:5; 2 Macc. 11:8; Acts 1:10), and Jesus appears in white garments at his transfiguration (Matt. 17:2). Those seated at the messianic feast are dressed in white (*4 Ezra* 2:38–40). In the *Shepherd of Hermas*, Hermas in his vision sees the faithful rewarded with white clothing (*Herm.* 68.3). On the other hand, soiled clothing indicates defilement. When Zechariah sees a vision of Satan accusing the high priest Joshua, the priest's sin is represented as dirty garments (Zech. 3:1–3). A minority of the believers in Sardis have remained faithful, and Jesus promises that they will be dressed in white as victors. The Laodiceans are later told by Jesus to buy white clothing to cover the shame of their spiritual nakedness (Rev. 3:18). The victorious martyrs who have been slain because of their faithful witness are also

depicted in heaven wearing white robes (6:11; 7:9, 13–14).

The book of life (3:5). In the Old Testament, the book of life represents a register of God's covenant people (Ex. 32:32–33; Isa. 4:3; Dan. 12:1). To be blotted out of his book meant to forfeit the privileges of covenant status. This perspective is likewise seen in *1 Enoch*: "the names of (the sinners) shall be blotted out from the Book of Life" (*1 Enoch* 108:3). Jesus tells the seventy-two to rejoice because their names are written in heaven (Luke 10:20). Likewise, Paul tells the Philippians to rejoice always because their names are written in the book of life (Phil. 4:3; cf. Heb. 12:23). Greek cities in the ancient world maintained a list of citizens in a public register. When someone committed a criminal action and was condemned, he lost his citizenship and his name was then erased from the register. This action, using the same Greek verb *exaleiphō*, is attested by

THE SYNAGOGUE AT SARDIS

The interior remains of the fourth-century A.D. synagogue; the Torah table is in the foreground.

▼ ▶

several ancient authors and inscriptions.[33] Those who overcome are promised that they will never lose their citizenship in the heavenly city.

Acknowledge his name before my Father and his angels (3:5). This promise closely resembles Jesus' statement to the twelve disciples in Matthew 10:32: "Whoever acknowledges me before men, I will also acknowledge him before my Father in heaven." The parallel in Luke 12:8 substitutes "the angels of God" for "my Father in heaven." The text in Revelation conflates, or combines, this word of Jesus, but it does not mention the aspect of denial found in both Synoptic sayings. Since a public forensic context is indicated in the earthly acknowledgment, some kind of heavenly courtroom scene is undoubtedly envisioned for the divine acknowledgment. The Christians in Sardis are thus warned that a relationship exists between their conduct on earth and their final sentence rendered before the heavenly Judge.

To the Church in Philadelphia (3:7–13)

Holds the key of David (3:7). In Revelation 1:18, Jesus declares that he holds "the keys of death and Hades." Jesus here describes his spiritual authority using language drawn from Isaiah. God had vowed to depose Shebna, the steward of the king's palace (and probable vizier over the land), for hewing a grave for himself in a place of prominence among the tombs of the kings (Isa. 22:15–19). God instead promises to give his authority to another named Eliakim (22:20–21). "The key of David"—a symbol of that authority—would be placed upon his shoulder. In Old Testament times, keys were often large and therefore carried over the shoulder. What Eliakim opened throughout Judah "no one can shut, and what he shuts no one can open" (22:22). As a type of the Messiah, Eliakim is to function as the godly administrator of the Old Testament theocratic kingdom ruled by the Davidic dynasty. Peter and the church likewise are appointed earthly stewards of the keys of the kingdom (Matt. 16:19). This same key of authority is to be exercised particularly in the areas of excommunication (18:18) and the forgiveness of sin (John 20:23). Jesus, who now reigns "on David's throne and over his kingdom," is

REFLECTIONS

WHAT WOULD JESUS SAY TO YOUR church today? His message would likely follow the pattern found in the seven letters. After greeting your church in _____, he would introduce himself with one of his divine names. Since most churches have positive features, he would first commend your church for the things it has done right. But most churches also have areas of weakness where improvement is needed. Jesus would lovingly, yet firmly, point out where repentance is required. For those churches living under persecution, Jesus' message would be singular—persevere through the testing and endure. Jesus is still speaking to every congregation today through the Holy Spirit. Each church must hear what the Spirit is saying to maintain an effective witness in its community. And each Christian must likewise obey Jesus' message to overcome in order to receive the same great promises of eternal life in the new heaven and new earth.

▶Philadelphia

Philadelphia (modern Alascehir) is located about thirty miles southeast of Sardis. Its acropolis rests on a spur of the Tmolus range, with the basin of the Cogamus River stretching below. The newest of the seven cities, Philadelphia was founded by the king of Pergamum, Eumenes II (197–159 B.C.), or perhaps by his brother, Attalus II (159–138 B.C.). When the Romans attempted to turn Attalus against his brother, he remained loyal and earned the nickname "Philadelphus."[A-25] The name of the city reflects the love between these brothers. The city was strategically situated at the junction of several major roads and became the gateway to Phrygia and points eastward.

Because of its newness, the city had few religious traditions. An inscription from around 100 B.C. documents the presence of cultic altars for at least ten gods and goddesses in the city.[A-26] The frequency of earthquakes caused the region around Philadelphia to be called the Catacecaumene, "the burnt land." Like its neighbor Sardis, Philadelphia was devastated by an earthquake in A.D. 17. The daily aftershocks forced the residents to abandon the city and live temporarily in the surrounding countryside.[A-27] The only crop that would produce in the volcanic soil was grapes, and vineyards dotted the countryside, even as they still do today.[A-28]

▲

PHILADELPHIA

The ruins of the ancient stadium.

the master Keyholder, carrying the government on his shoulders (cf. Isa. 9:6).

An open door that no one can shut (3:8). The Philadelphians have little strength to exercise their God-given key of authority, undoubtedly because of the opposition of the "synagogue of Satan." Therefore, Jesus intervenes and opens a

door for them that their opponents cannot shut. The shut door has been understood to refer to the excommunication of Christians from the synagogue according to the Twelfth Benediction issued by the Jews at the Council of Jamnia in A.D. 90. However, this benediction only formalizes the earlier practice of local synagogues, which excommunicated those who professed Jesus (cf. John 9:22; 12:42; 16:2).[34] The "open door" metaphor in the New Testament usually refers to an opportunity to evangelize. Paul wrote to the nearby church at Colosse, "And pray for us, too, that God may open a door for our message" (Col. 4:3). Evangelization, however, does not appear to be in mind here since Jesus admonishes the Philadelphians only to "hold on to what you have" (Rev. 3:11), which is not an encouragement for active outreach. Rather, the phrase looks forward to the open door to heaven, which

John is given in 4:1. This same open door to fellowship with God is likewise available to the Philadelphians, in spite of their exclusion from the synagogue.

Fall down at your feet and acknowledge that I have loved you (3:9). While the door of the synagogue may be closed to the Christians, the door to the church will soon be opened by the Jews in a surprising turnabout. Isaiah prophesied that the Gentiles would worship at the feet of Israel (Isa. 49:23; 60:14). In an ironic twist, the unbelieving Jews will worship at the feet of the true Israel (cf. Gal. 6:16). This dramatic acknowledgment that God's covenant love now rests on Jewish and Gentile believers is Jesus' sign to the Philadelphians that he holds the key.

The hour of trial (3:10). Because the Philadelphians have heeded the command to endure patiently, Jesus pledges to exempt them from the universal trial to come soon upon "those who live on the earth" (or "earth dwellers"; *katoikountes*). This distinctive participle is found here and in ten other texts. The earth dwellers consistently oppose God and his will on earth (13:8; 12, 14 [2x]; 17:2, 8). Within Revelation, this hour of trial unfolds through the seal, trumpet, and bowl judgments. Exemption from the hour of trial is not deliverance from persecution in the great tribulation, because those later depicted as slain are martyred at the hands of the earth dwellers (6:9–11; cf. 11:10 [2x]). The trial is God's wrath poured out on the rebellious earth dwellers (8:13), and only the Christians are spared divine judgment.

A pillar in the temple of my God (3:12). Every Greco-Roman city had temples that were supported by pillars capped with exquisite capitals of the Doric, Ionic, or Corinthian orders. Coins from the Asian cities often featured pictures of their civic temples. For example, the temple of Artemis appears on many coins of Ephesus, some showing the correct number of eight pillars that fronted the temple while other types are miniaturized, showing only four pillars. Asian temples were built to withstand earthquake damage. Their foundations were laid on beds of charcoal covered with fleeces, which caused the structure to "float" on the soil like a raft. Each block was joined to another by metal cramps, so the platform was a unity. The temples would be among the most secure structures in the city.[35] This promise of eternal security and safety would certainly comfort the Philadelphians always living with the threat of imminent destruction by an earthquake.

I will write on him the name of my God (3:12). Pillars with names inscribed on them are commonly seen at sites throughout western Turkey today. Two

◄

A PILLAR WITH NAMES

This pillar in the Ephesian city council building is inscribed with the names of the priests of Artemis.

inscribed Doric pillars found at the Prytaneion in the upper agora at Ephesus are of particular interest. In this important building burned the eternal flame of the city's hearth dedicated to the goddess Hestia. Some of the inscriptions found on these pillars list the names of the members of the League of Curetes, a class of priests affiliated with the temple of Artemis. During the reign of Augustus, these priests began to perform both religious and civic duties. Their main responsibility, however, was to oversee the celebration of the birth of Artemis in the Ortygian grove every year. So the imagery of pillars inscribed with names was familiar to the Asian believers. Upon the pillar/believer will be written three names—that of God, the heavenly new Jerusalem, and the new name of Jesus. The significance of these names is further developed in Revelation 19–22.

To the Church in Laodicea (3:14–22)

Lukewarm—neither hot nor cold (3:16). This statement probably refers to the city's water supply. The white travertine cliffs at Hierapolis, in view six miles north of Laodicea, were formed because of the nearby mineral hot springs. Colosse, about eleven miles to the east, was known for its cold pure waters. Laodicea, on the other hand, received its water supply through an aqueduct built by the Romans. Its source was an abundant spring five miles to the south. This water, which had a high mineral content, apparently arrived in the city lukewarm. Calcified pipes from the water system can still be seen near the city's water tower.[36] "Lukewarm" does not refer to believers who lack zeal or are half-hearted, but rather to those whose works

are barren and ineffective. Even as Jesus would spit out lukewarm water, he promises to spit out such Christians.

You say, "I am rich . . . ." But . . . you are wretched, pitiful, poor, blind, and naked (3:17). In A.D. 60, an earthquake devastated the Asian cities of the Catacecaumene, including Philadelphia and Laodicea. Laodicea had accepted aid from Rome following earlier earthquakes. However, after the earthquake in 60, only Laodicea among the Asian cities refused to accept Roman financial assistance and recovered using its own resources.[37] This indicates Laodicea's wealth and civic independence. The key word in the Laodicean letter is "rich" (3:17, 18), which reappears in chapter 18 (18:3, 15, 19). The Laodiceans prided themselves on their self-accomplishments and financial independence. This attitude seems to be reflected in the church, for the congregation apparently participated in the wealth of its host community. The socioeconomic situation of Laodicea was a microcosm of Rome's excessive materialism depicted in chapter 18.

Cover your shameful nakedness (3:18). The city was noted in antiquity for a breed of sheep that produced soft, raven-black wool.[38] This local wool presumably was the raw material for the textile factories that the Romans established here to manufacture the sleeved tunic and the hooded cloak.[39] This industry was another factor in the city's prosperity. A certain irony is found in this figure: Jesus finds his people naked despite the local looms that produced their own version of "designer" clothing. Nakedness is a symbol of shame in the Old Testament and results from God's judgment. Isaiah, speaking of the Virgin Daughter of Babylon, cries, "Your nakedness will be exposed; and your shame uncovered" (Isa. 47:3; cf. Nahum 3:5). Only the white garments of purity and righteousness given by Jesus can cover their spiritual nakedness (see also comments on Rev. 16:15).

▶ Laodicea

Laodicea (three miles north of modern Denizli) was situated forty miles southeast of Philadelphia along the Lycus River valley. It was one of several cities founded around 260 B.C. by the Seleucid ruler Antiochus II, which he named after his wife Laodice. Its location at the junction of the main road that ran westward one hundred miles through the Meander River valley to Ephesus and eastward across Anatolia to Syrian Antioch caused the city to thrive as a commercial and banking center.[A-29] Laodicea was the capital of the conventus of Cibyra, and in 50 B.C. Cicero resided in the city ten weeks conducting judicial business.[A-30] Paul's letter to the Colossians was to be read to the church in Laodicea (Col. 4:16). It is possible that the Laodicean letter mentioned in the same verse is the present letter of Ephesians. Although Paul lived in Ephesus for about two and a half years, the readers addressed in Ephesians 1:15 had never personally met him (cf. Col. 2:1). There is no evidence that Paul ever visited the Laodicean or Colossian churches.

LAODICEA

The ruins of the ancient city.

Salve to put on your eyes, so you can see (3:18). Laodicea was the home of a medical school in the first century.[40] One of its graduates was Demosthenes Philalethes, a renowned ophthalmologist who wrote an influential textbook on the eye. An ancient healing formula called Phrygian powder was also linked with the city. Zinc and alum were common in the area and formed the active elements in the popular eyesalves marketed by the city's merchants.[41] Thus, this image is also rich in irony: The Laodiceans live in a place noted for its treatment of the eye, yet they are spiritually blind.

I stand at the door and knock (3:20). Holman Hunt's famous painting, *The Light of the World*, shows Jesus standing at a door and knocking to enter. Who is to receive Jesus, according to his announcement here, is not unbelievers but Christians. The imagery is reminiscent of Jesus' parable of watchfulness (Luke 12:35–40). The master's servants are to be prepared for his knock on the door at any hour. In the ancient world, eating together was a sign of intimate friendship. Perhaps this is a reference to the Eucharist where a celebration of the bread and wine occurred. More likely, it is a general meal, much like the love feast celebrated in the early church (Jude 12).

The right to sit with me on my throne (3:21). Laodicea was a "throne city" because Zeno, one of its citizens, was elevated by the Romans to the kingship of Cilicia in 39 B.C. and of Pontus in 36. This was the city's reward for resisting the invader Labienus Parthicus.[42] Zeno's family continued to rule in some measure in Anatolia over the next century. The Zenoid family figures prominently on the city's coinage. The throne was the most visible symbol of the power of an earthly king. In ancient Israel, the king could share his throne with his son (2 Kings 21:1) or his mother (1 Kings 2:19), and such co-regencies were a common feature of the Davidic dynasty in Judah. Jesus thus promises to share his reign in the eternal kingdom with those who overcome.

The Throne in Heaven (4:1–11)

A door standing open in heaven (4:1). Doors play a prominent role in the final two messages to the churches. While

---

▶ **Interpreting the Seven Prophetic Messages**

How should these seven messages be interpreted for the church today? One popular approach has been to identify each church with a particular period in church history. Many Christians, particularly in the West, would see the present age as epitomized by the Laodicean church. The weakness of such a typological approach has been its subjectivity. Depending on the creativity of the interpreter, the churches could be linked to a variety of epochs and individuals. Although the seven messages were addressed to particular churches and life settings, each letter was meant to be read by the other churches. The seven churches were representative of all the Asian churches, with their strengths and weaknesses. Such a representative view is preferred for interpreting the letters today. Within the universal church, at all times and in all places, there are churches matching each of the seven churches. In the body of Christ today, churches still struggle with the issues of apathy, materialism, persecution, false teaching, and formalism.

Jesus himself provides the open door for the church in Philadelphia (3:8), the Laodiceans are required to open the door to fellowship with him (3:20). This image provides a thematic transition to the next section of the book. John's next vision shares many elements with Ezekiel's initial vision, which also begins with heaven being opened (Ezek. 1:1).

Come up here, and I will show you what must take place after this (4:1). John hears a familiar voice whose piercing timbre reminds him of a trumpet. This same voice, which earlier instructs him to write to the seven churches (1:10–11), now invites him to leave earth and enter into the heavenly realm. What John sees next is "what will take place later" (1:19). John's heavenly experience is a highly sensory one, filled with colorful sights, loud sounds, and exotic smells, which continue through the rest of the vision. Much of the imagery is drawn from God's appearance to Moses on Mount Sinai (Ex. 19) and the visions of Ezekiel.

A throne in heaven with someone sitting on it (4:2). While "in the Spirit" for the second time (cf. 1:10), John sees a heavenly throne occupied by an otherworldly figure. At his commission, Isaiah likewise "saw the Lord seated on a throne, high and exalted" (Isa. 6:1). Enoch, in his heavenly vision, also saw a throne with the Great Glory sitting on it (*1 Enoch* 14:18–25). John, like other Jewish authors, never describes him, because God declared, "You cannot see my face, for no one may see me and live" (Ex. 33:20).

The appearance of jasper and carnelian. A rainbow, resembling an emerald, encircled the throne (4:3). The divine figure

reminds John of two precious stones— jasper and carnelian. Jasper is usually an opaque red, brown, or yellow color, while carnelian is translucent red or yellowish-red. The Greeks and Romans highly valued carnelian, especially in jewelry-making. The rainbow encircling the throne is compared to a green emerald. The three stones are later used to describe the new Jerusalem (21:11, 19). In his heavenly vision, Ezekiel similarly compared the heavenly throne to a precious stone—in his case, a sapphire—and likened the radiance of the figure on it to "a rainbow in the clouds on a rainy day" (Ezek. 1:28). Jasper and emerald were two of the stones in the high priest's breastpiece (Ex. 28:18, 20).

Twenty–four elders (4:4). The appearance of these elders is striking: Their white garments, crowns, and thrones are eschatological rewards already promised to the victors (2:10; 3:5, 21). In Revelation 7:11, they are clearly distinguished from the angels. These elders with their golden incense bowls later serve as representative priests of the saints (5:8). They are also among the heavenly chorus giving thanks for the saints' vindication (11:16–18; 19:4). Twenty-four is a significant number in the temple ministry. Twenty–four divisions of priests rotate

◀

CARNELIAN
STONES

through their ministry (1 Chron. 24:3–19), and twenty-four groups of singers prophesy with harps, lyres, and cymbals (25:1–31). Revelation uses the number twelve and its multiples symbolically; in the heavenly city are the names of the twelve tribes and the twelve apostles (Rev. 21:12, 14). These twenty-four elders are probably to be understood as the heavenly representatives of the Old Testament and New Testament saints.

From the throne came flashes of lightning, rumblings and peals of thunder (4:5). Throughout Revelation, lightning and thunder accompany every heavenly proclamation as a kind of divine emphasis. These phenomena, accompanied by an earthquake, signal the conclusion of each sevenfold judgment—the seals (8:5), the trumpets (11:19), and the bowls (16:18). Thunder and lightning typically accompany divine theophanies, such as God's giving of the law on Mount Sinai (Ex. 19:16; 20:18). And when God spoke to Jesus on one occasion, the crowd nearby believed it had thundered (John 12:29). It is through the sevenfold Spirit around the throne that God executes his will on earth.

A sea of glass, clear as crystal (4:6). Before the throne John sees a transparent expanse that reminds him of a body of water so clear, one can see through it. He likens its clarity to crystal. When Moses, Aaron, and Israel's elders saw the Lord on Mount Sinai, "under his feet was something like a pavement made of sapphire, clear as the sky itself" (Ex. 24:10). Ezekiel likewise saw an expanse that sparkled like ice above the four living creatures (Ezek. 1:22). The Greek belief that crystals were formed like clear ice clearly underlies the Septuagint's translation of

crystal here in Ezekiel. In fact, crystals are an almost transparent quartz rock. Asia Minor was an important source for crystal. The Romans considered crystal a luxury, and a crystal drinking bowl reportedly sold for the exorbitant sum of 150,000 sesterces (approx. $1,800,000). Pliny the Elder recorded that the largest crystal he ever saw—weighing fifty pounds—was dedicated in the Capitol by Livia, wife of the emperor Augustus. When Nero smashed two crystal cups upon realizing that his political situation was lost, his anger was vented in a costly manner.[43] Heaven is presented, both here and in chapter 21, as a place of splendor and extravagance.

Four living creatures . . . covered with eyes, in front and in back (4:6). John now sees around the throne some otherworldly beings. Each has a different appearance—like a lion, an ox, a man, and a flying eagle. These four creatures, clearly patterned after the cherubim that Ezekiel had seen, are, as usual, transformed in Revelation. Such symbolic winged creatures figure prominently in the mythology and architecture of the ancient Near East. Winged creatures dating from 1200–800 B.C. have been discovered by archaeologists at such diverse sites as Carchemish, Aleppo, and Nimrud. At the Phoenician city of Gebal (Byblos), a carved representation of two cherubim supporting the throne of King Hiram (c. 1000 B.C.) have been found.[44] While Ezekiel's cherubim all have the same four faces—of a man, a lion, an ox (or cherub), and an eagle (Ezek. 1:10; 10:14)—each of John's visionary creatures has a single face. These creatures represent God's created order in a unique way. Humankind is the head of all creation and noted for his intelligence, the lion is the chief of the wild animals and noted for his ferocity, the ox is the chief of the domesticated animals and noted for his strength, and the eagle is the chief of the birds of the air and noted for his freedom. Another difference between the visionary figures is that Ezekiel's have four wings (1:6; 10:21) while John's have six. John's creatures resemble the six-winged seraphim that Isaiah saw around the throne (Isa. 6:2). Two of the wings are used for covering their face, two for covering their feet (perhaps a euphemism for genitals), and two for flying. Eyes cover the entire bodies of the cherubim seen both by Ezekiel (Ezek. 1:18; 10:12) and John. These eyes symbolize God's omniscience and probably function like the eyes of the sevenfold Spirit (Rev. 5:6).

Holy, holy, holy is the Lord God Almighty (4:8). Around the clock the living creatures lift up worship to the One who sits on the throne. Their expression of exaltation echoes the triasagion—holy, holy, holy—proclaimed by the seraphim in Isaiah 6:1. The use of this liturgical formula must have been common in the early church because Clement, in his letter to the Corinthians (c. A.D. 95), encourages them to cry out to God using the same words (*1 Clem.* 34:6). "Lord God Almighty" is declared by Amos (Amos 4:13 LXX) to be the name of the Creator of the natural world. While Almighty (*pantokratōr*; see comments on Rev. 1:8) suggests God's activity in creation, it speaks primarily of his supremacy over all things. Added is his unique name in Revelation: "who is, and who was, and who is to come" (cf. 1:4, 8), which in effect declares that he "lives forever and ever" (4:9). The living creatures begin the euphony of worship around the throne by celebrating God as the eternal One of all time.

The twenty-four elders fall down before him ... and worship him (4:10). The perpetual heavenly adoration inaugurated by the living creatures elicits a similar response from the elders. On three other occasions the elders are seen falling down and worshiping God (5:14; 7:11; 11:16). Worship in the ancient world was more than just vocal expression; it also involved physical action. One gesture

▶ The Living Creatures in Church History

The four living creatures have often been depicted in Christian paintings, drawings, and church decorations. This stems from a popular interpretation that associates them with the four Gospels. Which creature symbolizes a particular Gospel has varied among interpreters. Irenaeus linked the lion with John, the ox with Luke, the human face with Matthew, and the flying eagle with Mark.[A-31] Victorinus in his *Commentary on the Apocalypse*, the first known commentary on Revelation (4th century), made a different association—the lion with Mark, the man with Matthew, the ox with Luke, and the eagle with John. Augustine connected the lion with Matthew, the man with Mark, the ox with Luke, and the eagle with John. Augustine's interpretation has been adopted by many subsequent interpreters because the inner character of each Gospel seems to accord best with its related creature. Matthew presents Jesus as the messiah from the tribe of Judah, Mark as the servant, Luke as the Son of Man, and John as the Son of God. While such a symbolic interpretation has produced interesting Christian art, it is doubtful that the Asian audience understood the living creatures in such a symbolic way.

▶ Worship in Revelation

A key activity in Revelation is worship. Verbal expressions of praise in Revelation are presented in the NIV in poetic form. In fact, there is more poetry in Revelation than in any other New Testament book. The two poetic hymns in this chapter are the first of nineteen hymns and antiphonal responses found throughout the book.[A-32] Revelation's hymns incorporate many traditional Jewish and Christian liturgical elements: the language of hallelujah (19:1, 3), amen (5:14; 19:4), and holy (4:8); doxology (5:13; 7:12); thanksgiving (11:17–18); and acclamation (12:10–12; 19:1–2).

The heavenly worship portrayed in Revelation sharply contrasts with the reality faced by the Asian believers. At Pergamum, the emperor Augustus had organized an imperial choir to celebrate his birthday annually, with lesser birthday celebrations conducted monthly. Thirty-six members constituted the choir, which performed in the imperial cult temple. They were the cheerleaders, so to speak, for promoting imperial festivals. As one edict of the league of Asia decreed, "One should each year make clear display of one's piety and of all holy, fitting intentions towards the imperial house."[A-33]

The Christians were thus confronted with the ultimate choice: Do we worship God or Caesar? The frequent portrayal of true heavenly worship in Revelation reiterated to the believers caught in this epic struggle that God was the only true object of veneration.

was to bow down by kneeling. The psalmist invites Israel, "Come, let us bow down in worship, let us kneel before the LORD our Maker" (Ps. 95:6). Another action was to prostrate oneself. In the Old Testament this posture is described in relationship to human authorities as well as to pagan deities and the true God Yahweh. Once, after David addressed the assembly of Israel, "they bowed low and fell prostrate before the LORD and the king" (1 Chron. 29:20). The Jewish writer Philo describes how the barbaric custom of falling down in adoration before the emperor was introduced into Italy, which was contrary to native feelings of Roman liberty. When Philo led a Jewish delegation from Alexandria to Rome in A.D. 39/40, the Jews refused to prostrate themselves in worship before Gaius Caligula and thus offended the emperor.[45]

They lay their crowns before the throne (4:10). Crowns presented by a subject to a ruler was a typical act of subservience in antiquity. When Mark Antony visited Ephesus in 41 B.C., the Judean Jews sent an embassy to petition him regarding the injustice to their people. This delegation brought him a golden crown, the reception of which Antony acknowledged in his reply. Such a gift was common practice, for Josephus records the presentation of a crown from nearly every Jewish embassy to the Romans.[46] In A.D. 63 the Parthian royal prince Tiridates laid his crown before the effigy of Nero, signifying his submission to the emperor. In 65 Tiridates traveled to Rome to regain his crown, visiting the cities of Asia on his return to Parthia.[47]

You are worthy, our Lord and God, to receive glory and honor and power (4:11).

The elders now express their worship to God who is worthy to receive three things: glory, honor, and power. Two reasons are given for his worthiness. First, he has created everything. God is first introduced in Scripture as the Creator of the universe (Gen. 1–2). Second, not only did he bring the world into existence, but he also sustains his creation "by his powerful word," according to the author of Hebrews (Heb. 1:3). God's foundational witness to the world is through creation (cf. Acts 14:15–17). Early Christians acutely felt the tension when they were asked to acclaim the emperor as Lord and God (Lat. *dominus et deus*). Gaius Caligula was the first living emperor to claim divinity, calling himself "best and greatest," a title traditionally reserved for the chief Roman deity Jupiter. Nero accepted acclaim as *dominus*. However, it was Domitian who specifically adopted the twin titles Lord and God. Not only did he send out letters under these names, but also demanded that he be addressed by them.[48]

The Scroll and the Lamb (5:1–14)

A scroll with writing on both sides and sealed with seven seals (5:1). In the first century there were primarily two types of written documents—parchments (2 Tim. 4:13) and scrolls. Parchment was made from the skins of sheep and goats, and its name is derived from the Latin word *pergamena*. This refers to Pergamum, which was a center of parchment production and traditionally believed to be the place of its invention.[49] Parchment was more expensive than papyrus, but its greater durability and erasability caused it to become the predominant book material by the fourth century A.D.

Scrolls were made of papyrus from the Nile delta in Egypt and usually written on one side. This was the side on which the fibers ran horizontally, which made it easier to write on with a pointed reed pen dipped in black ink made from charcoal, gum, and water.[50] The scroll that John sees in God's hand is called an opisthograph because it has writing on both sides. In his initial vision Ezekiel also sees a two-sided scroll containing words of lament and mourning and woe (Ezek. 2:9–10). Prophets often recorded their visions on a scroll (cf. Jer. 36:1–32). However, when a scroll was sealed, its contents could not be read by unauthorized readers (cf. Isa. 29:11; Dan. 12:9). Thus, a scroll with its seals intact indicated that

A SCROLL WITH SEALS

A model of a papyrus document sealed with four *bulae*.

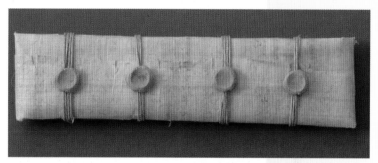

REFLECTIONS

REVELATION'S PORTRAYAL OF HEAVENLY WORSHIP suggests that worship should be an integral part of the Christian life. It is to be more than a weekly experience done as part of a "worship service." Rather, it is an ongoing activity based on our relationship with the living God. Revelation provides a vocabulary for our worship whether expressed through singing, crying out, or shouting. It also suggests various postures such as standing or falling prostrate. Jesus overcame the devil's temptation with this declaration, "Worship the Lord your God and serve him only" (Luke 4:5–8; cf. Deut. 6:13). By worshiping God and the Lamb, we as Christians, in essence, deny worship to the devil's "beasts," who arise in each generation.

▶ Archaeologists Find a Scroll With Seven Seals

In 1962, Ta'âmireh Bedouin tribesmen discovered a number of papyri in caves north of Jericho. The American School of Oriental Research purchased these papyri, which included parts of sealed scrolls. The least damaged among these was a papyrus roll sealed with seven seals. After these seals were cut, the papyrus was moistened carefully and the folds flattened. Much of the left side of the document was missing because it was unprotected by the sealings or by the tough fiber strings that bound the rolled papyrus in its sealings. Six turns of the roll revealed only a blank, so the archaeologists began to suspect a fraud. However, on the seventh turn twelve lines of Aramaic script appeared. The scroll was a legal document recording the sale of a slave named Yehohanan and was dated March 18, 335 B.C. All the papyri turned out to be legal or administrative documents.[A-34] When John saw a similar scroll with seven seals, he would immediately recognize that its contents were important heavenly business.

a document had not been tampered with and its contents were secure.

Who is worthy to break the seals and open the scrolls? (5:2). A mighty angel rhetorically asks who has the requisite spiritual authority to discover the scroll's contents. God himself is worthy as the Creator (4:11), but no created beings in heaven or earth have the rank or status to do so. The importance of such a document is indicated by who has the clearance to open and read it. John's reaction is profound weeping because he is distressed that the contents of this heavenly scroll may not be revealed.

The Lion of the tribe of Judah, the Root of David, has triumphed (5:5). Finally, an elder announces that someone qualified has been found to open the scroll. His identity is indicated by two messianic titles. "The Lion of the tribe of Judah" refers back to Jacob's prophetic blessing over his son: "You are a lion's cub, O Judah" (Gen. 49:9).[51] In the apocalyptic vision of Ezra, contemporaneous with Revelation, the lion is interpreted as the Messiah "who will arise from the offspring of David" (2 Esdras [*4 Ezra*] 12:31–32, NRSV). The second title is drawn from the Septuagint reading of Isaiah 11:1, "A scepter will come out from the root of Jesse." Paul interprets the parallel verse in Isaiah 11:10 in a messianic sense as well: "The root of Jesse will spring up, one who will arise to rule over the nations" (Rom. 15:12). The One who is the Lion and the Root is able to open the sealed scroll because of his triumph. Before his death, Jesus announces his triumph to the disciples, "But take heart! I have overcome the world" (John 16:33). In both sentences the word *nikaō* is used. The victory that Jesus has promised the Asian believers is predicated on his triumph as the Messiah, the basis of which is next depicted.

A Lamb, looking as if it had been slain (5:6). When John looks to see this heavenly Victor, he sees not a Lion but a Lamb in the center of the throne. However, the Lamb is not dead but standing alive in the midst of the living creatures and elders. This is a superb example of John's use of irony. Before God delivered the Israelites from Egyptian bondage, he commanded them, "Go at once . . . and slaughter the Passover lamb" (Ex. 12:21). Israel was to celebrate this festival each Passover to commemorate their deliverance (12:1–14). The unblemished lambs set apart for the Passover sacrifice were ritually slaughtered with their throats cut between the collarbones. This ritual slaughter mark on the neck allows John to identify the peculiar nature of this Lamb.[52] Lamb is the most common title for Jesus in Revelation and is used twenty-eight times.

He had seven horns and seven eyes (5:6). Juxtaposed on the Lamb in surreal fashion are seven horns and seven eyes. Horns are a biblical metaphor for power. Asaph exclaims, "I will cut off the horns of all the wicked, but the horns of the righteous will be lifted up" (Ps. 75:10). Seven, the biblical number of completeness or perfection, describes the absolute power and authority of the Lamb. The equality of the One on the throne (Rev. 4:5) and the Lamb is suggested because both possess the sevenfold Spirit.

Each one had a harp and they were holding golden bowls full of incense, which are the prayers of the saints (5:8). After the Lamb takes the scroll from the One who is sitting on the throne, the living creatures and the elders fall down in worship before him. In the left hand of each elder is a harp. The ancient harp was a stringed instrument apparently invented by Jubal (Gen. 4:21). Its portability and rich sound combined to make it Israel's favorite instrument. David was proficient on the harp (1 Sam. 16:15–23), and many of his psalms were to be sung to its accompaniment (e.g., Pss. 4, 6, 54, 55). The Levites prophesied and offered praise to God in the temple accompanied by harps, lyres, and cymbals (1 Chron. 25:1–8; 2 Chron. 5:11–13). As part of their worship, Paul encourages the Asian

▶ ## Sacrifices in the Ancient World

Animal sacrifice not only characterized the worship of the Jews, but also that of the Greeks and Romans. The Jews could only offer sacrifices at the temple in Jerusalem. Therefore, Jews from Asia and other parts of the Diaspora would travel to the Holy City for the annual feasts (e.g., Acts 2:1–11). Sacrifices to the pagan gods occurred in every Greco-Roman city with a temple. The Greek religious calendar (several of which still survive today) included a list of sacrifices, indicating which god or hero was to receive the offering on a given day. Most commonly, the thighbones of slaughtered animals, wrapped in fat, were burned on a raised altar for the gods. The meat was then cooked and eaten by the priests and priestesses and those sacrificing.[A-35]

Often the remainder of the carcass was sold at the public meat market, the macellum. This issue of meat sacrificed to idols was a problem in the churches at Ephesus, Pergamum, and Thyatira. Pliny the Younger reported in the early second century that Christianity had become so successful in Bithynia and Pontus that the sacred rites at temples had lapsed and no one would buy the flesh of the sacrificial victims. He pointed out to the emperor Trajan, however, that his policies had successfully reversed this trend and sacrifices were again being offered.[A-36]

Christians to "sing psalms, hymns and spiritual songs" (Col. 3:16). This singing was probably accompanied by a harp.

The elders hold golden bowls of incense in their right hands. These censers are designed to fit in the palm of the hand. Bowls similar to these have been found at archaeological sites throughout the Near East. Twelve golden censers, each weighing ten shekels (4 oz.), were given by the tribal leaders of Israel for worship in the tabernacle (Num. 7:14, 20). Solomon later made similar bowls for use in the temple (2 Chron. 4:22), and these were among the items taken by the Babylonians when they pillaged the temple (2 Kings 25:15). While the harps represent the praise of the saints, the golden incense bowls represent their prayers (cf. Rev. 8:3). David expressed their liturgical relationship, stating: "May my prayer be set before you like incense" (Ps. 141:2).

They sang a new song (5:9). New songs are sung before the throne three times in Revelation: here by the elders, in 14:3 by the 144,000, and in 15:3 by all the victors. This singing fulfills the prophecy in Isaiah 42:10 where the nations are exhorted to sing a new song because the Lord will make his servant "a covenant for the people and a light for the Gentiles" (42:6). Isaiah's servant songs (chaps. 42–53) provide a rich prophetic background for John's imagery.

You were slain, and with your blood you purchased men for God (5:9). "You are worthy," the same words addressed in Revelation 4:11 to the Lord God, are now sung to the Lamb by the elders. His death fulfills Isaiah's prophecy of the servant who "was led like a lamb to the slaughter" (Isa. 53:7). Jesus the Lamb was slain willingly and purchased people with his blood. The Greek word *agorazō*, translated "purchased," is a term of the public marketplace. Every Greco-Roman city had a marketplace called the agora, or forum, where slaves would be bought and sold. Here the metaphor of the slave auction is used to describe Christ's spiritual purchase of individuals for God (cf. Rev. 14:4). Peter used similar language when he addressed the Asian church, "It was not with perishable things such as silver or gold that you were redeemed . . . but with the precious blood of Christ, a lamb without blemish or defect" (1 Peter 1:18–19).

From every tribe and language and people and nation (5:9). In Revelation salvation is always portrayed as a gift for both Jews and Gentiles. The ethnocentrism of Judaism was superceded by the universal nature of the gospel. As Jesus commanded, "Therefore go and make disciples of all nations" (Matt. 28:19). Such universalism is marked with this inclusive terminology—tribe, language, people, and nation—used six other times in Revelation but always with variations (cf. 7:9; 10:11; 11:9; 13:7; 14:6; 17:15). Such language certainly has a background in Daniel who saw in his vision the Ancient of Days worshiped by "all peoples, nations and men of every language" (Dan. 7:14). The Table of Nations found in Genesis 10 documents the dispersion of the descendants of Noah according to clans, languages, territories, and nations (10:5, 20, 31). From the total of this list, the Jews deduced that there were seventy nations in the world.

You have made them to be a kingdom and priests (5:10). Christ's redemption made all believers "a kingdom and priests" (cf. 1:5–6). His people will reign on the earth as kings. Whether this reign is to be physical or spiritual, to be on the present earth or the new earth, is left unstated at this time. However, the priestly duties are now spiritual and to be performed through the ministry of praise and prayer. Because the early church had no temple or formal priesthood, the pagans regarded Christians as atheists. At his trial in Smyrna, Polycarp was asked by the Roman proconsul to repent by saying, "Away with the atheists!" meaning the Christians. Rather than renounce his congregation and his Lord, Polycarp instead looked at the lawless heathen gathered in the stadium and exclaimed, "Away with the atheists!" (*Mart. Poly.* 9.2–3). Shortly after he was burned at the stake.

The voice of many angels, numbering thousands upon thousands and ten thousand times ten thousand (5:11). John now gives his attention to a spectacle around the throne so extravagant that the number of its participants is incalculable. Similar descriptions of angels in heaven in Daniel 7:10 and Hebrews 12:22 suggest it is impossible to count them. Enoch in his vision of heaven saw tens of millions of angels around the throne (*1 Enoch* 14:22). The angels form a part of the ever-widening circle of worshipers around the throne beyond that of the living creatures and elders. Their song echoes that of the elders: The Lamb who is slain is worthy. Seven attributes are now named, which the Lamb is to receive: power, wealth, wisdom, strength, honor, glory, and praise. David lavished similar praise upon the God of Israel: "Yours, O LORD, is the greatness and the power and the glory and the majesty and the splendor, for everything in heaven and earth is yours" (1 Chron. 29:11).

Every creature in heaven and on earth and under the earth and on the sea . . . singing (5:13). In the Old Testament, the natural order is often depicted as participating in the praise of God (cf. Isa. 55:12). In Psalm 96 the psalmist exhorts, "Sing to the LORD a new song; sing to the LORD, all the earth." Here the created order is singing such a new song. Paul wrote that creation groans as it awaits its total freedom in the new created order (Rom. 8:19–22). Nevertheless, all creation is now seen rejoicing over its Creator who has made such final liberation possible. Their praise is directed both to God on the throne and to the Lamb. For the first time in Revelation, the two together become the focus of praise. Glory, honor, and power—prerogatives attributed to the Lord God in Revelation 4:11 and to the Lamb in 5:12—are now shared by both.

REFLECTIONS

CHRISTIANITY'S PRESENTATION OF a religious priesthood with no animal sacrifices must have been truly radical in the first century. The sacrificial demands of the new covenant are quite different. Our financial offerings are to be cheerful and heartfelt sacrifices, moving beyond a mandated tithe (2 Cor. 9:7; Phil. 4:18). Our ongoing prayer and praise is now to rise heavenward as spiritual offerings (Heb. 13:15; Rev. 5:8). Finally, our own bodies are to be offered sacrificially as a regular spiritual act of worship (Rom. 12:1–2). Through such spiritual sacrifices, our lives become acceptable, pleasing, and holy to God.

The four living creatures said, "Amen" (5:14). The living creatures and the twenty-four elders reappear one last time to close this great heavenly scene. The living creatures, caught up in worship, close with a simple "Amen," while the elders silently prostrate themselves again before the throne.

The First Six Seals (6:1–17)

The Lamb opened the first of the seven seals (6:1). Only one person is authorized to open the heavenly scroll, and the victorious Lamb now breaks each of its seals, one by one. The living creatures take turns inviting John to look at four horsemen who are released at the unfastening of the first four seals. The prophet Zechariah likewise saw riders on colored horses who were sent forth into the earth (Zech. 1:8–11). The color of each horse symbolizes the reality it represents: white for victory, red for blood, black for famine, and pale (gray) for death. While the scroll itself represents the broader destiny of humanity, the seals appear to represent a specific historical period, from the ascension of Jesus to the fall of Jerusalem (A.D. 30–70). This is suggested by the close correlation between the first six seals and Jesus' prediction of events to be fulfilled within a generation (see "False Christs"). By opening the first seal, Jesus precipitates the apocalyptic situation prophesied in the Synoptics and whose fulfillment is now seen in Revelation. The "birth pains" have indeed begun (Matt. 24:8).

▶ False Christs

False Christs have appeared periodically throughout history. Numerous false prophets appeared during the Jewish revolt. One named Jesus prophesied for seven and a half years in Jerusalem, crying, "Woe to Jerusalem!"[A-37] In recent years, Jerusalem has been the focal point for a "messiah syndrome." The Israeli police have a special unit to deal with individuals who appear claiming to be the Messiah. One of the most unusual incidents in the history of Messianism relates to Smyrna. Sabbatai Zevi was born there in 1626 to a prosperous Jewish broker. Sabbatai was a manic-depressive visionary who was expelled from the city by the other rabbis in the 1650s. He wandered around the east for a decade, but in the summer of 1665 returned to Smyrna where he became the center of a messianic frenzy. Hysterical scenes of mass repentance, which began in Smyrna's streets, soon spread throughout the entire Jewish world. When news of Sabbatai's messianic claims reached England, it heightened the expectations of Christians there that the year 1666 was to be apocalyptic. However, Sabbatai was arrested by the Turks and in September 1666 brought before the Sultan. Faced with the choice of death or conversion, Sabbatai became a Muslim. Many of his disciples followed him into Islam, while others refused to believe his apostasy.[A-38] The fact that Christians became involved in his movement shows the church's susceptibility to date-setting and to messianic claims, particularly Jewish ones.

There before me was a white horse! Its rider held a bow, and he was given a crown, and he rode out as a conqueror bent on conquest (6:2). Several interpretations for this seal have been proposed. Some identify the first rider with the Parthians, who were Rome's bitter rivals along its eastern frontier. However, Nero secured the peace with the Parthians in A.D. 63 and the Romans had no further trouble with the Parthians during the rest of the first century. If the rider cannot be identified with them, whom does he represent? His description as a crowned conqueror riding a white horse certainly has messianic overtones. In fact, Jesus is depicted similarly at his return (19:11–12). Some interpret the rider as Jesus himself, or closely related, as the spread of the gospel throughout the world. Given the judgment brought by the next three riders, it is problematic to view the first rider's mission as redemptive. What of the rider's bow? In Greek mythology, Apollo was the god who inspired prophecy, and he is often depicted carrying a bow. The bow probably represents false prophecy, whose effect has already been felt in the Asian churches. A comparison of the seven seals with the Synoptic apocalypses (see "The Seven Seals and the Synoptic Apocalypses") validates the interpretation that the rider is a false prophet, the first of many antichrists to come.

Then another horse came out, a fiery red one. Its rider was given power to take peace from the earth. . . . To him was given a large sword (6:4). The sword represents war that was to fall upon the earth, taking away the peace. Ezekiel 21 celebrates the sword as God's instrument of judgment, "I will draw my sword from its scabbard. . . . I have stationed the sword for slaughter" (Ezek. 21:3, 15). The troika of seals 2 through 4—war, famine, and death—is often portrayed together as instruments of divine judgment in the Prophets. For example, in Jeremiah 14:12 the Lord says, "I will destroy them with the sword, famine and plague" (cf. Ezek. 6:11–12; 12:16).

There before me was a black horse! Its rider was holding a pair of scales in his hand (6:5). The balance held by the third rider symbolizes divine judgment. Daniel declared to King Belshazzar, "You have been weighed on the scales and found wanting" (Dan. 5:27). Leviticus 26:26 describes the distribution of bread during times of famine: "They will dole out the bread by weight. You will eat, but you will not be satisfied" (cf. Ezek. 4:16). In the Old Testament period, the balance consisted of an equiarmed beam with two pans; however, in the Roman period the common balance was the steelyard type, which used only one pan and a counterpoise. Balances were normally used by merchants to weigh large quantities of coins, metal, and items such as spices (cf. John 19:39).

A quart of wheat . . . and three quarts of barley for a day's wages (6:6). Products

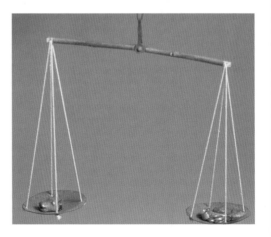

SCALE

A reconstruction of a Roman scale utilizing the the original parts.

such as grain were measured according to various dry measures. A quart (*choinix*, 1.081 of a quart) of wheat and three quarts of barley were being sold at the inflated price of a denarius—a day's wages. This price was eleven to sixteen times the price of wheat in Sicily during this period. Such overpricing of grain in a famine occurred during the latter years of Nero's reign.[53] A man normally consumed a quart of wheat each day. Because a family could no longer afford wheat, they were forced to survive by eating barley. Hence the famine indicated is only moderate and not life-threatening. Rome received most of her grain supply from Egypt; and when the giant grain ships failed to deliver their precious commodity, bread and circuses were put on hold. In A.D. 51, the emperor Claudius barely escaped a hostile crowd during a grain shortage and resulting famine that left Rome with only a fifteen-day supply of grain.[54] During their revolt, the Jews in Jerusalem experienced great famine. Thousands died as relatives fought over the smallest morsel of food. The most horrific example involved a young mother named Mary of Bethezuba who, because of her hunger, tore her baby from her breast and roasted it, devouring half the corpse. This abomination of infant cannibalism horrified both the Jewish rebels and the Romans.[55] Although this act was extreme, it illustrates how the ravages of hunger can overrule even the most basic instinct of mother to child.

Do not damage the oil and the wine! (6:6). In A.D. 92 Domitian issued an edict that half of the vineyards in the provinces should be cut down. The previous harvest had produced an abundance of wine but a lack of wheat, so the order was issued to correct a perceived imbalance in production. The order provoked outrage in Asia, and a delegation headed by the Smyrnean orator Scopelianus was sent to Rome to

---

▶ The Seven Seals and the Synoptic Apocalypses

The seven seals show a close correlation with the synoptic apocalypses found in Jesus' Olivet Discourse in Matthew 24, Mark 13, and Luke 21. They correspond not only in prophetic subject but also in order and in detail. The following chart compares the seals with Matthew's version. There are several minor differences between the accounts: Earthquakes are distinctively emphasized in the Synoptics, and, among the Synoptics, pestilence is mentioned only in Luke's account (Luke 21:11).

Seals–Revelation 6	Matthew 24
1. False Christ (2)	False Christs (4–5)
2. Wars (3–4)	Wars (6–7)
3. Famine (5–6)	Famines (7)
4. Pestilence (7–8)	Earthquakes (7)
5. Persecutions (9–11)	Persecutions (9–10)
6. Earthquake, solar eclipse, ensanguinal (blood-stained) moon, stars falling (12–13)	Solar & lunar eclipse, stars falling, heavenly bodies shaken (29)
7. Heavenly silence (8:1)	Son of Man appears (30)

The Synoptic apocalypses all conclude with the appearance of the Son of Man. With the fulfillment of these signs and the soon passing away of the forty-year generation (Matt. 24:34), it is no wonder that many Christians expected Jesus to return soon. However, the seventh seal is silent about such a coming, and this difference was perhaps intended to signal the churches that the Parousia was delayed and that any expectation of an imminent return needed to be adjusted.

protest the action. The order remained moot because the emperor failed to implement it. Some commentators see Domitian's edict behind this reference, and, in fact, it is one of the few pieces of internal evidence pointing to a late date. However, famines were frequent in the East (cf. Acts 11:28), and many of the cities in Asia Minor never could produce enough corn for their populace.[56]

And there before me was a pale horse! Its rider was named Death, and Hades was following close behind him (6:8). The pale-colored horse of the fourth seal suggests the appearance of sick persons and corpses. Its rider comes as a pair whose identity is personified. Death is the deadly agent while Hades becomes the domain for his victims. Although the two are here depicted as vital forces on earth, Jesus has already declared his spiritual authority over them (1:18). Death and Hades are authorized to kill a fourth of the earth using sword, famine, pestilence, and wild beasts. These same four dreadful judgments, once promised to idolatrous Jerusalem (Ezek. 14:21), are now coming upon the whole world. Wild beasts, although not mentioned before,

are the carnivorous scavengers who now move in to terrorize the decimated populace and to gorge themselves on the scattered corpses.

In the Septuagint, death is the frequent translation of the Hebrew word *debner* meaning "pestilence" (cf. Jer. 15:2–3). Pestilence was sent as divine judgment upon Israel when the covenant was broken. However, if his people repented, God promised to forgive their sins and heal the land of its pestilence (2 Chron. 7:13–14). Pestilence is the probable means of death promised to the followers of Jezebel (Rev. 2:23). The NIV reading, "I will strike her children dead," fails to specify how death will occur. This is explicit in the Greek text: "with death," that is, "with pestilence" (REB). Often pestilence accompanied the siege of cities. Poor sanitation in overcrowded conditions and contaminated water supplies provided the breeding ground for such diseases as typhoid and cholera. (These diseases threatened the survivors of the devastating earthquake in Turkey in 1999.) A plague and its effects on an ancient city were vividly described by the Greek historian Thucydides when Athens was devastated during the Peloponessian War in 430 B.C.: "Indeed the character of the disease proved such that it baffles description, the violence of the attack being in each case too great for human nature to endure."[57] During the summer of 65 when Nero was persecuting the church, a plague broke out in Rome killing 30,000 residents. Pestilence also broke out in Jerusalem due to overcrowding during the Roman siege in A.D. 70.[58]

I saw under the altar the souls of those who had been slain (6:9). With the opening of the fifth seal the perspective changes from earth to heaven. Beneath

the altar John sees a group of individuals who have been slain, even as the Lamb was (cf. 5:9). Because these saints are dead, they do not have bodies; yet they maintain an individual identity as eternal souls. Like John, they were persecuted because of the word of God and the testimony of Jesus Christ (cf. 1:9). Their loud petition echoes that of the psalmist who also asked, "How long, O Lord?" He then cried, "Before our eyes, make known among the nations that you avenge the outpoured blood of your servants" (Ps. 79:5, 10). The song of Moses declared God's willingness to "avenge the blood of his servants; he will take vengeance on his enemies" (Deut. 32:43). Because of God's promise to avenge his people, Paul counseled Christians never to seek revenge themselves (Rom. 12:19).

Each of them was given a white robe, and they were told to wait a little longer (6:11). Here the faithful are depicted in white robes, just as the victors are promised that they would be dressed in white (3:5). These white robes indicate the group's blessedness as they patiently await the time when God will avenge his enemies. The robes perhaps are individual honors of victory given in anticipation of the general rewards to be given at the Parousia. The seal closes with an ominous prediction: More martyrs still remain to be killed to complete the heavenly assembly. A famous early martyr was Ignatius, the bishop of Antioch. In A.D. 110, Ignatius was taken to Rome to be thrown to the beasts in the Colisseum. While passing through Asia, he wrote letters to five churches in the province—to Ephesus, Magnesia on the Meander, Tralles, Philadelphia, and Smyrna—as well as to Polycarp, the bishop of Smyrna. Ignatius

expressed his attitude toward martyrdom: "May I have the pleasure of the wild beasts that have been prepared for me. . . . Fire and cross and battles with wild beasts, mutilation, mangling, wrenching of bones, the hacking of limbs, the crushing of my whole body, cruel tortures of the devil—let these come upon me, only let me reach Jesus Christ!" (*Rom.* 5:2–3)

There was a great earthquake. The sun turned black like sackcloth made of goat hair (6:12). Various cosmological phenomena characterize the sixth seal. These are stock expressions commonly associated with divine judgment in the Old Testament. Isaiah predicted that before the day of the Lord, "The stars of heaven and their constellations will not show their light. The rising sun will be darkened and the moon will not give its light" (Isa. 13:10; cf. Joel 2:10–11). These Old Testament passages were cited by Jesus in his Olivet Discourse to describe the heavenly signs that would accompany his return (Matt. 24:29). Premature darkness and an earthquake were signs that accompanied Jesus' crucifixion (27:45, 51). The evangelists recognize in these cosmic occurrences a fulfillment of divine judgment upon Israel. Such prodigies (Lat. *prodigia*) were likewise understood by the Romans to be portents warning of divine wrath. Roman historians often listed the prodigies that were observed annually or those seen accompanying important historical events. During the reigns of Tiberius (A.D. 14–37) and Claudius (A.D. 41–54), Tacitus noted that few prodigies occurred; however, during Nero's reign (A.D. 54–68) prodigies multiplied. At the end of the tumultuous year A.D. 69, he observes that "there were prodigies in the sky and on the earth, warnings given by thunderbolts, and prophecies of the future, both joyful and gloomy, uncertain and clear."[59] The Jewish historian Josephus writing for a Roman audience, mentioned numerous prodigies that were seen around Jerusalem before its fall. A star resembling a sword hung over the city as well as a comet that lasted a year. One night in the temple a light illuminated the sanctuary and the altar for half an hour. Josephus concluded that the Jews imprudently ignored these warnings from God and hence were conquered.[60]

The whole moon turned blood red (6:12). This vivid image echoes Joel who declared that God would turn "the moon to blood before the coming of the great and dreadful day of the LORD" (Joel 2:31). This lunar phenomenon is called an ensanguinal moon and depicts the deep copper color that the moon assumes during a total eclipse. Such an eclipse occurred on October 18, 69. The historian K. Wellesley gives this vivid description of the prodigy: "The moon itself was turned to blood. Its eclipse, which entered its maximum phase of near totality at 9.50 p.m., four hours after dusk, gives it a sinister copper-coloured appearance as the light of the sun, drained of its blue component, was refracted round the earth by the latter's atmosphere, and fell dimly upon the almost full orb of the moon. This must surely be a portent of disaster and death."[61] Seven days later Vitellius' army

---

▶ Roman Society

Ancient Roman society was highly stratified and divided into legal groups. The seven groups mentioned in 6:15 approximately parallel the Roman social order. At the top was the emperor (*imperator* or *princeps*) and his household (*familia Caesaris*). Allied client kings, like Herod, ruled the frontiers of the empire not yet incorporated as provinces. The "princes" were the ruling elite of Roman society who filled the principal civic magistracies by serving as quaestors, praetors, and consuls. Highest were the senators (*senatores*) who numbered approximately six hundred and held property worth at least one million sesterces. During the first century wealthy individuals from provinces like Asia were gradually admitted into the Senate.

Next were the equestrians (*equites*) who numbered several thousand members. Membership came through birth or appointment by the emperor and property holdings of 400,000 sesterces. From these ranks came the generals (*tribuni militum*), who commanded Rome's twenty-eight legions stationed along the empire's frontier.[A-39] These generals had great influence over their troops, and it was four generals and governors—Galba, Otho, Vitellius, and Vespasian—who used their legions to vie for the principate following Nero's suicide.

In each city of the empire was a group of the one hundred most "mighty" men called *decuriones*. Some *decuriones* in the Roman cities were also citizens. Roman citizenship was a further important social distinction. In the first century, a minority of individuals outside of Italy were Roman citizens. Paul's status as a citizen (Acts 16:37; 22:25–29) was therefore unique, particularly in the eastern provinces. Following these groups were the freeborn urban plebs and the rural peasantry. The rest of the population was divided between the free persons and the slaves. Slaves were common throughout the empire because its economy was based on slave labor. At least one third of the residents of a major urban center like Ephesus would be slaves, suggesting around 100,000 slaves among its populace. The early church, reflecting the society at large, had great social diversity among its members—rich and poor, free and slave.[A-40]

was completely routed at the second Battle of Cremona, ensuring the accession of Vespasian as emperor.

Fall on us and hide us from the face of him who sits on the throne and from the wrath of the Lamb! (6:16). This is the desperate cry of the inhabitants of the earth, whom John classifies in a sevenfold manner (see "Roman Society"). Their retreat to caves is again a stock reaction to God's judgment: "Men will flee to caves in the rocks and to holes in the ground from dread of the LORD" (Isa. 2:19, cf. 2:10, 21). At last the earth dwellers recognize the source of their woes—the One on the throne and the Lamb. The day of divine wrath has finally arrived, and no one can resist God's purposes any longer. The Lamb who loved and shed his blood for the sins of his people (Rev. 1:5) is here described as the same Lamb whose wrath is so great that the wicked cannot stand against it.

The Sealing of the 144,000 (7:1–8)

Four angels standing at the four corners of the earth, holding back the four winds (7:1). The successive opening of the seals has fulfilled all the necessary earthly and heavenly signs. Yet the destructive winds that will initiate the day of the Lord are held back. In Jewish thought, four winds stood at each corner of the compass. These winds could either destroy a nation (Jer. 49:36) or bring new life (Ezek. 37:9). In Zechariah these winds are personified as chariots pulled by different colored teams of horses, which go out from the presence of the Lord throughout the earth (Zech. 6:5–7). At his second coming, Jesus taught that the angels "will gather his elect from the four

winds, from one end of the heavens to the other" (Matt. 24:31). Although that time is near, a divine pause is introduced in the tension.

A seal on the foreheads (7:3). Another angel commands the angels holding the four winds not to harm the earth until the seal of the living God is dispensed. A seal, which was used to authenticate the heavenly scroll, is now placed on the foreheads of God's servants. The Old Testament background for this sealing is found in Ezekiel 9, although its specific nature will not be discussed until Revelation 14:1. The seal functions similarly in Revelation, separating God's servants from the faithless earth dwellers and marking those who are to be exempted from the coming divine judgments. Because of such marking, a Jewish author who wrote after Pompey desolated the temple in Jerusalem (63 B.C.) declared that famine and sword and death "will retreat from the devout like those pursued by famine. But they shall pursue sinners and overtake them" (*Pss. Sol.* 15:7–8). In antiquity, foreheads were often marked to designate slaves or devotees of a deity (*3 Macc.* 2:29).

Sealing assumed a more symbolic interpretation in early Christian theology. Paul taught the Asian churches that "you were marked in him with a seal, the promised Holy Spirit" (Eph. 1:13; cf. 4:30). However, this seal of ownership is placed in the heart (2 Cor. 1:22). Paul spoke of another kind of seal that God places on the faithful in Ephesus to distinguish them from the false teachers and their wicked acts (2 Tim. 2:19).

Those who were sealed: 144,000 from all the tribes of Israel (7:4). The sealing that was announced is now described as a completed task. The number and identity of the sealed are given next: 12,000 (12 times 1,000) are sealed from each tribe of Israel. The twelve tribes of Israel are listed numerous times in the Bible (e.g., Gen. 35:23–26; 49:3–27; Deut. 33:6–25), and Reuben as the firstborn usually heads these lists. Revelation's list has several notable differences. Judah is listed first because from this tribe came the Lion of Judah, the firstborn from the dead (cf. Rev. 1:5; 5:5). John also includes Manasseh, the firstborn of Joseph, while omitting his younger brother Ephraim. Dan is also omitted, and it has been suggested that this omission occurred because of Dan's role as an apostate worship center in northern Israel (1 Kings 12:29–30). The church father Irenaeus postulated that Dan was omitted because the antichrist was to come from this tribe, a belief based on the Septuagint reading of Jeremiah 8:16: "From Dan we will hear the sound of swift horses."[62] Both are dubious suggestions since Dan is mentioned first among the tribes to receive land in the restored Israel (Ezek. 48:1). No satisfactory explanation arises from the text to account for these changes.

Although the 144,000 are spared the divine wrath poured out in seals 1–4, they are not spared the persecution of the earth dwellers. This leads to the conclusion that they are probably the martyrs under the altar seen in Revelation 6:9–11. This group representing all the tribes of Israel is most likely comprised of Jewish believers. "Twelve tribes" is used as a figure of speech for Jewish Christians in James 1:1. For over a decade (A.D. 30–45) the early church was predominantly Jewish. Acts 1–9 describes the expansion of the gospel among the Jews. Stephen was the church's first martyr (Acts 7:60), and following his death a great persecu-

tion broke out against believers (8:1). The church in Jerusalem experienced great hardship until it left the city before its destruction in A.D. 70.

Sectarian groups such as the Jehovah's Witnesses often interpret this number literally to define the number of "true believers." The expanded number of God's people that John sees in his next vision suggests that any attempt to restrict the number to be saved is misguided.

The Great Multitude in White Robes (7:9–17)

A great multitude that no one could count, from every nation, tribe, people and language, standing before the throne and in front of the Lamb (7:9). In this vision John's temporal perspective is fast forwarded to the time of the Parousia. There are several visions like this in Revelation that are proleptic, that is, they present a future event as if it has already happened. Many elements of this vision represent the heavenly perspective following Christ's coming elaborated in chapters 19–22. A dramatic transformation occurs in Revelation 5:6 when John turns to see a lion and instead sees a

NIKE HOLDING A PALM BRANCH

A relief of Nike in Ephesus along Curetes Street.

slaughtered lamb. Here the exclusive tribes of 144,000 Jews are similarly transformed into an inclusive multitude encompassing every race, ethnic group, and nation on earth. From this group Christ purchased individuals with his blood (5:9).

While a metropolis like Ephesus might have many ethnic groups among its population, only in Rome could the total ethnic population represented in the empire and beyond be found. Juvenal's tongue-in-cheek comment bears this out: "Long ago the Orontes has overflowed into the Tiber."[63] (The Orontes was the river flowing through Syrian Antioch, while the Tiber flowed through Rome.) Such ethnic diversity likewise characterized the early church. This picture fulfills numerous Old Testament prophecies that speak of the gospel going forth to all nations. These prophecies are all based on God's foundational covenant promise with Abraham: "All peoples on earth will be blessed through you" (Gen. 12:3).

The phrase "great multitude" has an interesting historical tie. Both the Roman historian Tacitus and the Roman presbyter Clement spoke of "great multitudes" of Christians who lost their lives under Nero.[64]

They were wearing white robes and were holding palm branches in their hands (7:9). Like the twenty-four elders, this multitude around the throne is also dressed in white robes, which identifies the group as victors (cf. 3:4, 18; 4:4). They are also holding palm branches (cf. 2 Esd. 2:45–46). The palm tree is indigenous to the warm Mediterranean climate, and to the ancient Greeks and Romans the palm served as a symbol of victory. The Greek author, Pausanius, provides the background: "But

at most games they use a wreath of palm, and everywhere the winner has a palm branch put in his right hand. The reason for the tradition is this: they say when Theseus came home from Crete he held games at Delos for Apollo, and crowned the winners with palm."[65] In the third century B.C., the Romans began to award palm branches to the winners at the games, a custom taken over from the Greeks. Palm branches are depicted on many coin types from Asia, and a particular favorite was a standing Nike with a wreath and palm.[66] The palm branch also became a symbol of victory for the Jews. After Simon captured Gaza in 141 B.C., he and his men entered the city rejoicing and carrying palm branches "because a great enemy had been crushed and removed from Israel" (1 Macc. 13:51 NRSV). When Jesus made his triumphal entry into Jerusalem shortly before his passion, the crowds heralded his arrival by waving palm branches (John 12:13). Understanding these Jewish and Greco-Roman backgrounds, the palm branches in the hands of the martyrs make a powerful statement of their triumph over the forces of evil. This multi-ethnic multitude now celebrates God and the Lamb for one primary benefit they have received—salvation.

All the angels … fell down on their faces before the throne and worshiped God (7:11). Space in heaven is obviously of a different dimension than on earth. For this great multitude is now joined around the throne by a myriad of angels. These angels again raise their voices in worship, this time to God and not the Lamb. As in Revelation 5:12, they ascribe seven attributes to him, which are the same except "thanks" is substituted for "wealth."

▶ The Church and the Tribulation

Revelation provides a mixed portrait regarding the subject of Christians and tribulation. John himself was suffering on Patmos, while Antipas had already been martyred in Pergamum. The believers in Smyrna and Philadelphia had been persecuted, and those in Smyrna were about to endure even more trials. The picture here in Revelation 7 shows many who had shed blood for their faith. However, the four other churches in Asia had yet to experience significant tribulation.

In the modern church three main views of the tribulation are currently taught. Pretribulationists believe that the rapture of the church will occur before the great tribulation. The catching up of John to heaven in Revelation 4:1 is seen as a type of the rapture. Because the church is not mentioned between chapters 4–18, it must therefore be absent when the seal, trumpet, and bowl judgments fall upon the earth.

Midtribulationalists hold that the church will be on earth during the first half of the great tribulation, but at its midpoint after three and a half years the church will be raptured. Thus, the church is spared the more severe judgments of divine wrath that will come upon the earth.

Posttribulationists believe that the rapture will not occur until the great tribulation is over. Christians will be on earth during the judgments described in Revelation but will be protected, even as Israel was during the plagues that came upon Egypt. Regardless of one's perspective, we must all heed the warning with which Jesus prepared his church: "In the world you have tribulation, but take courage; I have overcome the world" (John 16:33 NASB).[A-41]

These are they who have come out of the great tribulation (7:14). One of the elders engages in a question-and-answer exchange with John, who is asked to identify this group in white robes. Rather than guess, John defers to the elder who identifies the multitude as those who have come out of the great tribulation. This is the last explicit mention of tribulation in the book, although its reality continues to be described. Daniel spoke of a great tribulation to be endured by the saints when the end came (Dan. 12:1). Jesus also warned his disciples about those days, "For then there will be a great distress, unequaled from the beginning of the world until now" (Matt. 24:21). In his third vision, Hermas, an early Christian, was refused permission to sit at the right hand of the angel because this special place was reserved for those who had endured "scourgings, imprisonments, great tribulations, crosses, and wild beasts for the sake of the Name" (*Vis.* 3.2.1). The scale of such suffering described in this postapostolic document (ca. A.D. 95–100) accords with the historical facts of Nero's persecution. Finally, the Christian reviser of the *Ascension of Isaiah* (early 2d cent.) recalled that it was the king of iniquity, Nero, who persecuted the plant (i.e., the church), which the twelve apostles of the Beloved had planted (*Mart. Ascen. Isa.* 4:3).

They have washed their robes and made them white in the blood of the Lamb (7:14). This imagery related to the action of the tribulation saints seems paradoxical—clothing is reddened, not whitened, when dipped in blood. The symbolism is obviously spiritual and not literal. After the Exodus from Egypt when the law was given at Mount Sinai, the Israelites consecrated themselves by washing their clothes and abstaining from sexual relations (Ex. 19:14–15). While the victors in Sardis were commended for not defiling their garments (Rev. 3:4), here the commendation is for cleansing them. This portrait shows the victors as active, not passive, participants in their salvation. For this action, they are qualified to receive the benefits of heaven described in the following three verses.

Therefore, "they are before the throne of God and serve him day and night in his temple; and he who sits on the throne will spread his tent over them" (7:15). Serving God in his temple fulfills the promise to the victors in Philadelphia: That they would be pillars "in the temple of my God" (3:12). This temple in which they serve is not to be understood in any material sense like the temple in Jerusalem. Its spiritual reality is expressed well by the author of Hebrews: "For Christ did not enter a man-made sanctuary that was only a copy of the true one; he entered heaven itself" (Heb. 9:24). The promise that God would spread his tent over his people resonates throughout the Bible. In the desert his Shekinah presence manifested itself through the cloud by day and the fire by night (Ex. 13:21). Solomon built the temple as a place for God to tabernacle forever (1 Kings 8:12–13). Isaiah prophesied that a day will come when "the LORD will create over all of Mount Zion and over those who assemble there a cloud of smoke by day and a glow of flaming fire by night; over all the glory will be a canopy" (Isa. 4:5). This promise that God would dwell with his people was initially fulfilled with the coming of Jesus, who made his dwelling (literally, "tabernacled") among us (John 1:14). Here is a proleptic announcement that a day is coming when the tabernacle of God is with his people forever.

Never again will they hunger; never again will they thirst (7:16). The language of the heavenly benefits for those who endured the tribulation is drawn directly out of Isaiah 49:10. There the servant of the Lord promised to restore his people to the land, where he will care for them. The provisions for God's people in both passages include no hunger or thirst, no sun or scorching heat beating down, and springs of water. In Revelation the servant of Isaiah is identified as the Lamb who will shepherd his people. This same Lord, who was David's shepherd (Ps. 23:1), declared, "I am the good shepherd" (John 10:11, 14). Instead of a literal fulfillment of this Servant Song back to the physical land of Israel, John importantly sees a spiritual fulfillment of Isaiah's prophecy in heaven.

And God will wipe away every tear from their eyes (7:17). This final benefit is especially fitting for those who have shed so many tears in behalf of the kingdom of God because of their tribulation. It fulfills a promise that, at the time of the final messianic banquet, "the Sovereign LORD will wipe away the tears from all faces" (Isa. 25:8). This personal act of divine comfort will finally occur for all in the new Jerusalem after the old order of things, including death, has passed away (Rev. 21:4).

The Seventh Seal and the Golden Censer (8:1–5)

When he opened the seventh seal, there was silence in heaven for about half an hour (8:1). The Lamb's opening of the seventh seal does not bring the anticipated Parousia, but instead heavenly silence. Heaven has been full of sound up to this point with uninterrupted praise around the throne. In the Old Testament silence is frequently a precursor of judgment (cf. Isa. 41:1; Amos 8:3). During the final plague of the firstborn, the Israelites and their animals were commanded to remain silent (Ex. 11:7). After Babylon's judgment was determined by the Lord from his heavenly temple, "let all the earth be silent before him" (Hab. 2:20; cf. Zech. 2:13). With the opening of the last seal, the scroll is finally opened and its contents fully seen. The fury of the coming judgments has now moved even heaven to silence. Half an hour symbolizes a brief time and is the shortest period mentioned in Revelation.

The seven angels who stand before God . . . were given seven trumpets (8:2). The content of the seventh seal is another vision of seven angels who are given seven trumpets of judgment. This is the first mention of seven specific angels before the throne, who are probably not the angels of the seven churches. Jewish tradition identifies seven holy angels who offer up the prayers of the saints as they enter before the glory of the Holy One (Tobit 12:15). Seven other angels are responsible later for pouring out the seven bowls of God's wrath (Rev. 15:1).

Another angel, who had a golden censer, came and stood at the altar (8:3). A familiar sight in the ancient world was animal and incense sacrifices offered from altars dedicated to various deities. Such altars would be typically made of stone. Israel's worship at the tabernacle and temple required both an altar of burnt offering and an altar of incense. The altar of incense was made of acacia wood overlaid with pure gold. At each corner were four projections called horns (see 9:13). The priests of Israel were commanded in the law to burn incense on the altar every morning and evening. Zechariah the priest burnt incense in the temple for the evening offering (Luke 1:10–11). Once a year on the Day of Atonement, the high priest was to rub blood from the sin offering on its horns (Ex. 30:7–8). A glass bottle, probably used at the synagogue, has been discovered in Ephesus. It is inscribed with the Greek word for altar of incense and also depicts a seven-branched menorah.[67]

The Greeks originally worshiped before an altar and only later did these altars come to be associated with temples. The largest and most spectacular Greek altar was the altar of Zeus at Pergamum. Built during the reign of Eumenes II (197–159 B.C.), the altar sat in a horseshoe-shaped sanctuary that rose forty feet from a base measuring 112 by 120 feet. Its situation on the acropolis rising a thousand feet above the lower city has suggested to some interpreters that this altar is "the throne of Satan" mentioned in Revelation 2:13. The regular columns of dense smoke that billowed up from this altar would certainly suggest to an observer below what a heavenly incense offering might look like. Augustus built a monumental altar called the Ara Pacis in Rome in 13 B.C. and modeled it after the altar of Zeus. John sees only an altar of incense in heaven because the sacrifice of the Lamb made unnecessary any further sacrifices on the altar of burnt offering (cf. Heb. 7:27).

He was given much incense to offer, with the prayers of all the saints (8:3). The golden bowls full of incense in 5:8 represent the prayers of the saints. The heavy smoke from the incense suggests that many prayers are offered to God. The saints' prayer in part surely echoes the martyrs' cry in 6:10: "How long . . . until you judge the inhabitants of the earth and avenge our blood?" That moment of judgment has finally begun, for the angel now takes the censer filled with coals from the altar and hurls its contents to the earth (8:5). Incense was an integral part of worship in Israel's tabernacle and temple. It was prepared according to an exact formula given by God: "Take fragrant spices—gum resin, onycha and galbanum—and pure frankincense, all in equal amounts, and make a fragrant blend of incense" (Ex. 30:34–35). Incense was one of the gifts presented to the infant Jesus by the Magi from the east (Matt. 2:11). Spices like frankincense and myrrh came from southern Arabia along trade routes established as early as the mid-second millennium B.C. These were among the luxury trade goods imported by Roman merchants (Rev. 18:13). In the Roman world, incense was commonly used with animals as sacrifices to the gods and to the emperor. Coins from Ephesus (3d cent. A.D.) show worshipers standing before an imperial temple with their arms raised in acclamation. A garlanded altar topped by a burning flame stands in their midst with a bull standing ready for sacrifice. In the temple's pediment is the Greek transcription of the Latin word *vota* (vows). Such vows were made annually to the gods to protect the emperors in the coming year.[68] Pliny the Younger asked Christians to deny Christ by making offerings of wine and incense to the emperor Trajan's statue.[69]

Peals of thunder, rumblings, flashes of lightning and an earthquake (8:5). Each of the judgment cycles of seals, trumpets (11:19), and bowls (16:18) ends with these same cosmological phenomena. This similar language would alert early hearers of the book that a section had ended and a new one was beginning. The literary term for such recurring phrases that indicate sectional openings and closings is *inclusio*.

The First Six Trumpets (8:6–9:21)

The seven angels who had the seven trumpets (8:6). The trumpet used in ancient Israel was of two basic types—a

---

REFLECTIONS

SOME CHRISTIANS TODAY DO NOT think it is necessary to understand eschatological issues or to take a position on them. They call themselves pan-tribulationists and pan-millennialists because they believe everything will "pan out" in the end. However, what we believe influences how we live out our Christian lives. Those who believe in an imminent rapture may not get involved in politics or social change. Others who believe in future global catastrophic events might retreat to rural areas to establish self-sufficient communities. Christians should not be passive regarding these important eschatological issues, because in one way or another we will act out what we believe.

◀ *left*

SHOFAR

The ceremonial Jewish trumpet made of a ram's horn.

shofar made from a ram's horn and a metal trumpet made of bronze or silver. Because the Greek word *salpigx* is used for both types in the Septuagint, it is impossible to determine which is meant in Revelation. Trumpets played a role in Israel's religious calendar. The Jewish new year began with the Feast of Trumpets (Lev. 23:23–25), and the year of Jubilee was inaugurated by the shofar being blown throughout Israel (25:9). Trumpets played a major role in warfare as signaling instruments (Num. 10:8–9). The use of seven trumpets to defeat God's enemies is seen in the destruction of Jericho when seven priests blew seven trumpets for seven days before its walls collapsed (Josh. 6:4–20). Detailed instructions on the military use of trumpets can be found in one of the Dead Sea Scrolls, *The War of the Sons of Light against the Sons of Darkness* (1QM 3:1–11; 7:12–9:8). Trumpets are often depicted on Roman reliefs in association with civic ceremonies and military triumphs. Josephus mentions the importance of the trumpet to the Roman army: "The hours for sleep, sentinel-duty, and rising, are announced by the sound of the trumpet; nothing is done without a word of command."[70]

The trumpet call, which signaled judgment, came to have a special escha-tological association with the Day of the Lord (Joel 2:1; Zeph. 1:16). Both Jesus (Matt. 24:31) and Paul (1 Thess. 4:16) declared that a trumpet will sound at the Second Coming. The seven trumpets in Revelation 8–11 should not be confused with that last trumpet because they are preparatory and not final. Interestingly, trumpet imagery is not used in Revelation 19 to announce Christ's return. While only a fourth of the earth was affected by the seal judgments (Rev. 6:8), a third of the earth is now devastated by the trumpet judgments. A progression is thus seen in the intensity of the judgments. These judgments have many similarities with the plagues of Egypt (see "The Trumpet and Bowl Judgments and the Egyptian Plagues" at 15:6).

There came hail and fire mixed with blood, and it was hurled down upon the earth (8:7). The first trumpet brings an environmental disaster. Hail and lightning, perhaps triggering wildfires, consume whatever plants, trees, and grass are in their path. Such losses affect food supplies, fuel and building materials, as well as forage for livestock. Joel described the Day of the Lord similarly: "For fire has devoured the open pastures and flames have burned up all the trees of the field" (Joel 2:19). Famine would be the inevitable result of such a catastrophe.

Something like a huge mountain, all ablaze, was thrown into the sea (8:8). Whereas the first trumpet affects the land, the second wreaks havoc on the sea. The picture seems to describe the eruption of a volcano near the coastline. The fiery ash lights the sky. The seismic activity produces a tidal wave that destroys sea creatures and capsizes vessels caught in its path. The eruption of Mount

▶

MOUNT VESUVIUS

Vesuvius in A.D. 79 provides an interesting parallel. On August 24 the mountain exploded, burying the coastal cities of Pompeii and Stabiae under lava and ashes and Herculaneum under mud. The Roman naturalist Pliny the Elder, who also commanded the fleet at nearby Misenum, set sail across the Bay of Naples to rescue a friend at Stabiae. He became trapped by the rough surf once ashore and could not escape by sea. He choked to death through inhalation of the dense fumes. His nephew Pliny the Younger described his uncle's death and his own escape in two remarkable letters to the historian Tacitus. His description of the volcano's destructive effects provides an eerie parallel to our text: "We also saw the sea sucked away and apparently forced back by the earthquake: at any rate it receded from the shore so that quantities of sea creatures were left stranded on dry sand. On the landward side a fearful black cloud was rent by forked and quivering bursts of flame, and parted to reveal great tongues of fire, like flashes of lightning magnified in size."[71]

A great star, blazing like a torch, fell from the sky (8:10). The third trumpet brings forth a star resembling a meteor or comet that contaminates the earth's freshwater sources. Falling stars are an apocalyptic motif heralding disaster and death, and are mentioned four times in Revelation. Here and in 6:13 the stars represent cosmic phenomena; in 9:1 and 12:4 they are personified as angelic beings. At God's judgment of Edom "all the starry host will fall" (Isa. 34:4). Jesus alluded to this text in the Synoptic Apocalypse when he declared that, following the distress of the last days, "the stars will fall from the sky" (Matt. 24:9; Mark 13:25). The single destructive star mentioned here has a parallel in *Sibylline Oracle* 5.158–59: "a great star will come from heaven to the wondrous sea and will burn the deep sea and Babylon itself." However, the star seen by the Sibyl fell on saltwater, destroyed rather than poisoned, and was angelic rather than cosmic.

The name of the star is Wormwood (8:10). The star that poisons these drinking supplies is called Wormwood, or "Bitterwood" (*apsinthos*). The plant *Artemesia absinthium* is a perennial herb that produces small, yellow flowers and grows throughout the eastern Mediterranean. Dioscorides Pedanius, a military doctor and pharmacologist during the reigns of Claudius and Nero (A.D. 41–68), described three types of *absinthium* known to the Romans. The most bitter type grew in the Anatolian provinces of Pontus and Cappadocia. Because it harmed the stomach and caused headaches, it was administered primarily for external purposes.[72] A toxic agent found in wormwood is thujone, which causes intoxication, hallucinations, convulsions, and damage to the central nervous system. However, it is usually not lethal. In the Old Testament bitter water came to symbolize disobedience, and wormwood was linked with judgment. After the Exodus, the Israelites came to the spring of Marah and tried to drink its bitter water. Although the people grumbled against Moses, God provided a piece of wood to sweeten the water before testing them to see if they would keep his commands (Ex. 15:23–25). Twice in Jeremiah God made this declaration regarding Israel and its prophets: "I am feeding this people with wormwood, and giving them poisonous water to drink" (Jer. 9:15; 23:15 NRSV). Although one third of the drinking supply is affected, only a vague "many" die from these contaminated waters.

A third of the sun was struck, a third of the moon, and a third of the stars, so that a third of them turned dark (8:12). The final judgment on the natural world affects the heavens. Darkness on the sun, moon, and stars produces a blackout even during the daytime. Such darkness could be caused by smoke, dust, or volcanic ash—all products of the previous judgments. Solar or lunar eclipses could also cause such heavenly darkness. In Joel's day, a plague of locusts was sent as divine judgment. Their numbers were so great that at their approach the skies became darkened (Joel 2:10). Such darkness also characterized God's judgment of Pharaoh: "When I snuff you out, I will cover the heavens and darken their stars" (Ezek. 32:7). Like the other three trumpet judgments, the effect of the fourth is also just partial.

An eagle that was flying in midair call out in a loud voice, "Woe! Woe! Woe to the inhabitants of the earth" (8:13). Like the seal sequence, a break occurs between the fourth and fifth trumpets where three "Woes" are announced. Woe is typical prophetic language used to announce impending judgment: "Look! An eagle is swooping down, spreading its wings over Moab . . . Woe to you, O Moab! The people of Chemosh are destroyed" (Jer. 48:40, 46). Jesus issued seven Woes to the scribes and Pharisees (Matt. 23:13–32). The ominous tone of the eagle's declaration suggests that the final three trumpets will be even more devastating. This messenger is flying in midair, or middle heaven. Revelation portrays a typical Jewish cosmology with three heavens (cf. 2 Cor. 12:2). The upper heaven is revealed in Revelation 4:1 when John begins to see a series of visions around the divine throne. The celestial middle heaven is the home of the sun, moon, planets, and stars (cf. Rev. 14:6; 19:17). The lowest atmospheric heaven is mentioned as clouds in 1:7.

I saw a star that had fallen from the sky to the earth. The star was given the key to the shaft of the Abyss (9:1). The fifth trumpet shifts the divine wrath to a new region—that beneath the earth. This woe and the next are the lengthiest and most complex of the judgments seen in Revelation. The "star" that John sees is an angel, as in 20:1, who is given the key (i.e., authority; cf. 3:7) to open the Abyss.

▶

ENTRANCE TO THE PLUTONIUM AT HIERAPOLIS

The consequences are a plague unlike anything yet experienced on earth. The Abyss was believed to be the underworld prison of evil spirits. When the demons were cast out of the demoniac by Jesus, they pleaded with him not to send them to the Abyss (Luke 8:30–31). The Abyss was also considered the realm of the dead. Jesus, after his death, descended into the Abyss ("deep" NIV; Rom. 10:7 quoting Deut. 30:13 LXX). However, in Revelation the name Hades is used for the realm of the dead (cf. Rev. 1:18; 6:8; 20:13, 14), reflecting the Septuagint in which the Hebrew *Sheol* is translated by "Hades" rather than "Abyss."

Smoke rose from it like the smoke from a gigantic furnace (9:2). Large furnaces were used in antiquity to burn limestone into lime. Limestone was stacked in concentric layers to form a dome. At the bottom was an opening to supply fuel for the fire, while the top contained a hole for air and smoke to escape. Another type of furnace was used for smelting ore, mainly iron. Such furnaces required great and prolonged heat, and the fires produced

▶ The Plutonium: An Asian Abyss

An epitaph from Diogenes Laertius (3d cent. A.D.), which describes the underworld as "the black abyss of Pluto," suggests a possible local reference.[A-42] Just north of Laodicea was the city of Hierapolis (cf. Col. 4:13). The city was noted for its shaft to the underworld. The Sibyl—an ecstatic prophetess depicted as an aged woman—wrote from Egypt: "Hierapolis also, the only land that has mingled with Pluton."[A-43] The patron deity of Hierapolis was Apollo and beneath his temple was the Plutonium, the dwelling place of Pluto, the god of the dead in Greek mythology. Strabo described the Plutonium's entrance as "an opening of only moderate size,

large enough to admit a man, but it reaches a considerable depth."[A-44] Spewing from the shaft was a dense mist that brought immediate death to any living creature, such as livestock or birds, that happened into the opening. Only the local eunuch priests of Cybele were immune, but they survived only by holding their breath. In 1962, Italian archaeologists uncovered the entrance to the Plutonium during their excavations. Because a strong smelling gas continues to be emitted, a sign at the entrance of the shaft warns would-be explorers: DANGER POISONOUS GAS.

thick, dark columns of smoke. The destructive judgment of Sodom and Gomorrah produced a similar effect: "and he [Abraham] saw dense smoke rising from the land, like smoke from a furnace" (Gen. 19:28). Jesus' use of "fiery furnace" in his parables suggests that the image is synonymous with hell (Matt. 13:42, 50).

And out of the smoke locusts came down upon the earth (9:3). Locusts were a common plague in the ancient world, and total devastation was usually left in their wake. These insects were the eighth plague that God sent against Egypt: "Nothing green remained on tree or plant in all the land of Egypt" (Ex. 10:15). In Revelation, however, these locusts do not devour their usual fodder but instead attack humans. These locust/scorpions are empowered to sting anyone missing the seal of God on their foreheads (cf. Rev. 7:3). Thus, all the earth dwellers, not just a third, are affected.

And the agony they suffered was like that of the sting of a scorpion when it strikes a man (9:5). Numerous species of arachnids are found throughout the eastern Mediterranean region. Their poisonous venom kills the insects and spiders upon which they feed but, while painful to humans, rarely kills them. Sirach names scorpions as one of God's instruments of vengeance (Sir. 39:30). The venom of these locusts is sufficiently toxic to torture the victims for five months. This period of time again indicates incompleteness: God is not yet ready for his judgment to be terminal. The pain, however, is so great that everyone seeks death but cannot find it (cf. Job 3:21). There is no assisted suicide for these earth dwellers under divine judgment.

The locusts looked like horses prepared for battle (9:7). The uncanny resemblance of locusts to horses was proverbial in antiquity: "They have the appearance of horses; they gallop along like cavalry" (Joel 2:4). Hence their arrival was likened to that of an enemy army (Rev. 9:5). Joel is a key source for John's description of the locusts. An army of locusts "has the teeth of a lion" (Joel 1:6), and they make a noise "like that of chariots" (2:5).

The angel of the Abyss, whose name in Hebrew is Abaddōn, and in Greek, Apollyōn (9:11). The two names given the ruler here suggest that John and part of his audience were bilingual. In Old Testament Wisdom literature, *Abaddōn* ("Destruction") is closely linked with *Sheol* ("Death"; cf. Job 26:6; Prov. 15:11). In the LXX, *Abaddōn* is usually translated by the Greek word *apōleia*, with *Apollyōn* being its personal form. *Apollyōn* has also been understood to be a word play on the god Apollo in his role as destroyer. *Apollyōn* may also be another clue to identify Nero as the church's persecutor because Nero's patron deity was Apollo. This identification is likely, given John's only other use of *apōleian* in 17:8, 11, when the beast—the eighth emperor, Nero *redivivus*—is ready to go to his destruction. Nero's voice and appearance were compared to those of Apollo, and he was hailed as "our Apollo."[73] Nero also had a coin struck depicting himself in the guise of Apollo playing a lyre, while other coins from his reign show him with a hairstyle identical to Apollo's. It has been suggested that the reference is an indirect attack on Domitian, who apparently liked to be regarded as Apollo incarnate. However, no Roman sources link Domitian with Apollo, but instead record that Domitian revered the goddess Minerva the most.[74] This devotion was expressed by the consistent issuance of four coin types annually, the erection of temples, and the sponsorship of an annual festival in Minerva's honor. If the allusion in Revelation 9:11 is to Apollo, and it probably is, the reference is to Nero and not to Domitian.

Release the four angels who are bound at the great river Euphrates (9:13). A voice from the heavenly altar commands the sixth angel to issue the release order. Four angels were introduced in 7:1, who were to hold back the destructive four winds until God's servants were sealed. In contrast, four other angels, poised on the Euphrates River for their moment of divine judgment, are released to destroy a third of humanity. In Revelation the east is the direction from which both redemption (7:2) and destruction (9:14; 16:12) come. In the Old Testament Israel's eschatological enemy likewise came from the east (Isa. 41:2; 46:11) or from the north (Jer. 6:1, 22; Ezek. 38:6).

The Euphrates and the Tigris were the two great rivers of Mesopotamia. Both were headwaters into which the river in the garden of Eden flowed (Gen. 2:14). Today the source of the Euphrates is in eastern Turkey. The river drains a course of 1,780 miles before emptying

into the Persian Gulf. In the Old Testament, the Euphrates is also called "the great river" (Deut. 1:7; Josh. 1:4), and it formed the northeastern boundary of the Promised Land (Gen. 15:18; Deut. 1:7). In the first century the Euphrates River marked the eastern frontier of the Roman empire. The river, because of its limited number of fords, served as an effective barrier to the Parthians and Armenians to the east. The southernmost ford was at Zeugma ("bridge"; near Birecik, Turkey), where the Romans stationed a legion during the 60s. Here was the most likely place where an army from the east would be mobilized to cross.

The number of mounted troops was two hundred million (9:16). The size of this demonic army is literally a double myriad of myriads, 2 x 10,000 x 10,000. The numerical background for this huge number is Daniel 7:10: "ten thousand times ten thousand stood before him (God)." The number is probably to be understood figuratively as an innumerable host. The troops released at the Euphrates are compared to a deadly mounted cavalry. Armored cavalry developed in the Middle East in the 9th or 10th centuries B.C. The Parthians favored armored horses and riders (*kataphraktoi*) in warfare, and used them in 53 B.C. to defeat decisively the Romans near the Euphrates at Carrhae (Haran [Gen. 12:4–5]; Harran, Turkey). By the first century A.D., the Romans had their own mounted cavalry, and such troops were used in Judea during the Jewish revolt. The armored breastplates of the cataphracts consisted of either mail or scale shirts.[75]

The heads of the horses resembled the heads of lions, and out of their mouths

came fire, smoke and sulfur (9:17). The second woe brings death to a third of humanity. The horselike creatures are the instruments of death, and they accomplish their mission in a twofold way—with their mouths and their tails. The use of the snake simile in 9:19 suggests that the "horses" are demonic beings, whose purposes are to make life a hell on earth for the earth dwellers.

The rest of mankind . . . still did not repent of the works of their hands (9:20). This is the first of three vice lists found in Revelation (cf. 21:8; 22:15). Paul presents similar catalogs of sins in his writings (cf. Rom. 1:29–31; 1 Cor. 6:9–10). Such lists, developed by Hellenistic Jews to describe the sins of the pagan world, often regarded idolatry as the root sin (cf. Wisd. Sol. 14:22–29). The earth dwellers who survive the second woe still fail to acknowledge God. They persist in violating the first two of the Ten Commandments (Ex. 20:3–4) and in worshiping the demons who energize the idols (cf. Deut. 32:17; 1 Cor. 10:19–20). The prophets often chastised Israel for worshiping idols: "All who make idols are nothing, and the things they treasure are worthless. Those who speak up for them are blind; they are ignorant, to their own shame" (Isa. 44:9; cf. Jer. 10:3–9). Unlike the living God, these idols cannot see, hear, or walk (Dan. 5:23).

In Ephesus at least twenty-six other gods and goddesses besides Artemis were worshiped (cf. Athens; Acts 17:16). Gold statues of Artemis were carried in processions through Ephesus. The Greeks associated gold with divinity, equating its near indestructibility with the gods' immortality. During this period solid gold was used only for the statues of emperors and gods.[76] Smaller statuettes of bronze have also been discovered. Most of the cult statues, including three of Artemis found by excavators in the city, were made of quality marble. The gods are also represented in mosaics and frescos found in the upper-class homes in Ephesus. Such idolatry was found throughout the other cities of Asia.

The earth dwellers are likewise cited for continual disobedience of commandments 6–8: murder, adultery, and theft (Ex. 20:13–15). Here in Revelation is the first mention of repentance since chapters 2–3. The judgment on those who fail to repent is an explicit reminder both to the Nicolaitans and to Jezebel and her followers of their potential destiny. For idolatry and sexual immorality are the primary sins that Jesus identified in the Asian churches.

Their magic arts (9:21). Magical arts comes from the Greek word *pharmakon*, from which the English word pharmacy is derived. Except for Paul's inclusion of it among the works of the flesh ("witchcraft," NIV; Gal. 5:20), the *pharm-* word group is used exclusively in Revelation (cf. 18:23; 21:8; 22:15). To alter one's fate and to protect oneself against evil spirits, the Greeks and Romans employed magical practices. Ephesus was known for its magical arts and for its "Ephesian letters"—written magical spells believed to provide power to ward off evil spirits. Some in the Ephesian church had probably once practiced the magical arts and, following their conversion, were among those who had burned their occult scrolls publicly (Acts 19:19).

Although magic was officially disapproved in the Roman empire, it was still widely practiced. For example, a consul named Marcus Servilius Nonianus wore a piece of papyrus around his neck inscribed with the Greek letters *rho* and *alpha* to ward off eye inflammation. People would often curse their enemies by writing the victim's name on a lead tablet, consecrate him or her to the spirits of the underworld, and then stick a long nail through the name. In one such inscription, a chariot driver cursed his opponents, asking that both the horses and the drivers be killed.[77] Lovers used special charms to attract the object of their affection. Two popular forms of divination were augury, which is the interpretation of a divine message given by the flight pattern or eating habits of birds, and extispicium, which is the interpretation of signs found in the entrails of sacrificial animals. Divination was employed to undertake every activity of life, from getting married to going to war. This common practice, however, is repeatedly denounced in Revelation.[78]

The Angel and the Little Scroll (10:1–11)

Then I saw another mighty angel coming down from heaven . . . his face was like the sun, and his legs were like fiery pillars (10:1). The seventh trumpet and final two woes are delayed while John sees another vision of a mighty angel. His

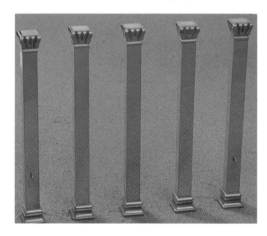

appearance with a cloud and a rainbow indicate that he is a special messenger from the heavenly throne (cf. 4:3). Like the son of man (1:16), this angel also has a face beaming like the sun. The remarkable appearance of this angel has suggested comparison with the Colossus of Rhodes, one of the seven wonders of the ancient world. Chares of Lindos cast this 110-foot statue from bronze around 282 B.C. It depicted the sun god Helios, whose rayed head is also seen on Rhodian coins of this period. In 227, fifty-six years after it was dedicated, an earthquake toppled the Colossus breaking it at its knees. An oracle advised the citizens not to rebuild the statue, so it was left lying next to its base for hundreds of years. The fame of the Colossus was still widely recognized in the first century A.D., as both Pliny the Elder and Strabo comment on its extraordinary size.[79] The exact appearance of the statue is unknown, but it certainly stood erect with perhaps a right hand extended upward. However, the medieval image of his legs spanning the entrance to the harbor is incorrect. Wherever this statue stood in Rhodes, its gleaming bronze legs, resembling fiery pillars, stood visible to land and sea.

He was holding a little scroll, which lay open in his hand (10:2). When the first mighty angel appears in 5:2, he asks John who is worthy to open the sealed scroll in God's right hand. Once the seventh seal is opened (8:1), that scroll is not mentioned again until now. A second mighty angel holds an opened "little" scroll in his right hand. Because the Greek form is a diminutive here, some scholars have suggested a second scroll is now revealed. However, the scroll's small size is only in relation to the angel's large hand, and "scroll" and "little scroll" are used interchangeably in the chapter (10:8, 9, 10). Thus, it is likely that only one scroll is seen throughout these visions.

He planted his right foot on the sea and his left foot on the land (10:2). The land and the sea are the primary foci of the first two trumpet judgments (8:7–9). The stance of this mighty angel suggests that he represents the Creator of the earth and the sea and that further judgment still awaits them both. His shout like a lion's roar suggests a possible link with the lion of Judah (5:5), but the simile is for comparison of sound, not for identification purposes.

Seal up what the seven thunders have said (10:4). To this point John is allowed to record the contents of his visions. However, an unknown voice from heaven now forbids him to write down the mysterious utterance of the seven thunders, who appear only here in Revelation. Perhaps their message concerns the final seven bowls of judgment, whose disclosure is premature at this time. Daniel was told to seal up his visions (Dan. 8:26; 12:4, 9). And Paul, after being taken up into the third heaven, was likewise forbidden to describe his revelation (2 Cor. 12:4). Following the final vision, John is commanded by the angel not to seal up the words of this prophecy (Rev. 22:10).

Then the angel . . . raised his right hand to heaven. And he swore by him who lives forever and ever (10:5–6). The angel takes an oath to add credence to his statements that follow. Such a practice is mentioned several times in the Old Testament. At the close of his visions, Daniel saw an angelic figure hovering above the water who "lifted his right hand and his left hand toward heaven, and I heard him swear by him who lives forever" (Dan. 12:7). The Song of Moses describes the oath of vengeance God takes against his adversaries: "I will lift up my hand to heaven, and I will swear with my right hand" (Deut. 32:40 LXX). Today witnesses in court likewise raise their right hand to swear that they will tell the truth.

There will be no more delay! (10:6). The angel literally declares to John that "time (*chronos*) will be no longer." This time reference links back to the fifth seal where the martyred servants are told to wait "a little longer" (literally, "a short time"; 6:11) for the rest of their brothers and sisters to be killed. Daniel praised God because "he changes times and seasons" (Dan. 2:21). Here in Revelation, God has now determined that the short time has run out.

The mystery of God will be accomplished, just as he announced to his servants the prophets (10:7). The angel next dramatically announces: When the seventh trumpet is sounded, God's purposes will be completed. God has always used his prophets to reveal his plans: "Surely the Sovereign LORD does nothing without revealing his plan to his servants the prophets" (Amos 3:7). As a New Testament prophet, John is commanded to prophesy later in verse 11. The mystery of God relates to his divine purposes in redemption and judgment on earth. Paul was also a prophet (Acts 13:1) who frequently declared the mysteries of God, particularly those related to the Parousia (1 Cor. 15:51; 2 Thess. 2:7). The angelic announcement here is again proleptic because John's prophecy does not immediately bring the consummation, but instead concerns the final period of tribulation and judgment on earth. Thus, John's new prophetic assignment is to warn his audience of its approach.

Take it and eat it. It will turn your stomach sour, but in your mouth it will be as sweet as honey (10:9). The command to take the open scroll from the right hand of the mighty angel and to eat it signals the beginning of a new period of ministry. At Ezekiel's prophetic commissioning, he was also commanded to eat a scroll (Ezek. 2:8; 3:1). Like Ezekiel's scroll (Ezek. 3:3), John's tasted sweet as honey in his mouth. However, it became sour after John swallowed it. The bitterness of the coming judgments apparently gives John an upset stomach.

You must prophesy again about many peoples, nations, languages and kings (10:11). The event is John's recommissioning as a prophet, and he is told the subject of his future prophecy. The mention of kings is a departure from John's fourfold formula, which usually mentions tribes (cf. 5:9; 7:9). As it relates to the Roman empire, the word "kings" is better translated as "emperors." This is particularly true in chapter 17 where seven emperors are mentioned in the context of the great prostitute Rome.

The Two Witnesses and the Seventh Trumpet (11:1–19)

I was given a reed like a measuring rod and was told, "Go and measure the temple of God and the altar, and count the worshipers there" (11:1). The 144,000 and the great multitude are introduced after the sixth seal (ch. 7) as God's servants and martyrs on earth. Now, after the sixth trumpet, these servants are presented as two new figures—worshipers and witnesses. John, like Ezekiel (Ezek. 8:1–11:25), receives a vision of worshipers in the temple in the "holy city" (cf. Isa. 52:1). While Ezekiel's worshipers are marked for destruction because of

MOUNT OF OLIVES IN JERUSALEM

their idolatry, John's are preserved because they measure up to the divine standard. Reeds were commonly used as measuring rods in biblical times. They grew along rivers and in marshy areas in Palestine and Egypt, often to heights of twenty feet with a stem up to three inches in diameter. For regular construction purposes, reeds were either three or six long cubits (approximately five or ten feet). Ezekiel used a rod six cubits long to measure the new temple that he saw in his vision (Ezek. 40:3, 5). John is now instructed to perform a similar prophetic act, but unlike Ezekiel's vision, few details are given.

The New Testament speaks of the temple in three dimensions—heavenly, physical, and spiritual—and in Revelation John refers to the temple similarly. The heavenly temple, first mentioned in Revelation 7:15 and again in 11:19, is the heavenly reality of which the earthly temple was only a copy (cf. Heb. 9:1–25). Paul, writing from Ephesus, addressed the subject of the church as the spiritual temple, "Don't you know that you yourselves are God's temple" (1 Cor. 3:16; cf. 6:19). Although the temple here in Revelation 11:1 is primarily a figure for the church, there appears to be a secondary reference to the temple still standing in Jerusalem. Historically, the only group eligible to worship at the temple in Jerusalem were Jewish believers, and these are numbered earlier as part of the 144,000 (Rev. 7:4–8).

But exclude the outer court; do not measure it, because it has been given to the Gentiles. They will trample on the holy city for 42 months (11:2). The outer court was the only area of the temple that Gentiles could enter. They were barred from the inner courts by a

WARNING INSCRIPTION

A first-century inscription from the balustrade around the Jerusalem temple warning Gentiles not to enter on the pain of death.

balustrade that contained thirteen inscribed stones that read in Greek and Latin: "No intruder is allowed in the courtyard and within the wall surrounding the temple. Those who enter will invite death for themselves." Two of these warning inscriptions are on display in the Istanbul Archaeological Museum and the Rockefeller Museum in Jerusalem. The trampling of the holy place by Israel's enemies was a common theme in Old

REEDS

Papyrus reeds growing along the bank of the Nile River in Egypt.

Testament apocalyptic texts (cf. Isa. 63:18; Dan. 8:13). Before the end, the Gentiles would lay siege to Jerusalem and trample it (Zech. 12:3 LXX). In his Olivet Discourse, Jesus prophesied using similar words: "Jerusalem will be trampled on by the Gentiles until the times of the Gentiles are fulfilled" (Luke 21:24). The Roman siege and destruction of Jerusalem in A.D. 70 is a fulfillment of these prophecies. The Jewish revolt began in the fall of 66 and concluded on September 26, 70 when Titus entered the city, a period of approximately forty-eight months. (Masada did not fall until May 73, however.) The time mentioned for the trampling in Revelation is forty-two months. While this period approximates the length of the Jewish revolt, its prophetic fulfillment lies in the time of the persecution of the spiritual temple—the church.

And I will give power to my two witnesses, and they will prophesy for 1,260 days, clothed in sackcloth (11:3). Nowhere does John identify the two witnesses who are divinely empowered. However, their prophetic activities mirror those of Moses and Elijah, whose spirit they clearly embody (cf. Mal. 4:4–5). At Jesus' transfiguration Moses and Elijah were the two witnesses, representing the Law and the Prophets respectively (Matt. 17:3–4). Their period of prophesying is given as 1,260 days, which equals forty-two months in the Jewish lunar calendar of thirty days each. It is also equivalent to three and a half years, the period of judgment that Elijah pronounced against Ahab and Israel (Luke 4:25; James 5:17). Whereas God's people in heaven are dressed in white clothing (Rev. 7:9, 14), the two witnesses wear sackcloth during their ministry on earth.

This sackcloth is black and made from goat's hair (cf. 6:12). The Israelites put on sackcloth on the day of judgment as a sign of lament while seeking to avert God's wrath (Isa. 3:24; Jer. 4:8; Ezek. 7:18). Conversely, Daniel expressed his true repentance by fasting and covering himself with sackcloth and ashes (Dan. 9:3). The sackcloth on the two witnesses symbolizes the message of judgment that they will proclaim to the earth dwellers.

The two olive trees and the two lampstands that stand before the Lord of the earth (11:4). Olive trees produced the oil used as fuel in ancient lamps (Matt. 25:3, 8). Olive oil was also a core ingredient for the special anointing oil used by the priests in worship (Ex. 30:22–33). The lampstand, or menorah, was not a typical household item, but rather was used ceremonially in Israel's worship (see comments on Rev. 1:20). Zechariah saw similar imagery in a vision and asked what the olive trees represented (Zech. 4:3, 11). An angel explained, "These are the two who are anointed to serve the Lord

of all the earth" (4:14). The two anointed men in Zechariah's day were Zerubbabel and Joshua, who represented Israel's kingship and priesthood respectively. This suggests that the two witnesses, while also being patterned after actual individuals, are likewise representative of New Testament spiritual realities.

Fire comes from their mouths and devours their enemies (11:5). Fire destroying a third of humanity comes from the mouths of the demonic horses in the sixth trumpet (9:17–18). Now a similar destructive fire is emitted from the mouths of the two witnesses against those attempting to harm them. However, such temporal judgment is not the final divine judgment of fire to be given to God's foes (cf. 20:10, 15). Fire from heaven played an important role in the ministries of Moses and Elijah. When the Israelites complained about their hardships, God sent fire among them that was only abated through Moses' prayers (Num. 11:1–3). And when Korah rebelled against Moses' authority, God sent fire that consumed 250 elders (16:35). The famous confrontation on Mount Carmel between Elijah and the prophets of Baal was resolved when God sent fire to consume the sacrifice and the altar (1 Kings 18:38). At Elijah's word fire twice fell from heaven to consume a captain and his fifty men sent by King Ahaziah (2 Kings 1:9–12). On one occasion the disciples sought to demonstrate their power by asking Jesus if they should call down fire on a village of inhospitable Samaritans (Luke 9:54). The prophetic activity of Moses and Elijah serves as a model for the ministry of the two witnesses.

These men have power to shut up the sky so that it will not rain . . . and they have power to turn the waters into blood **(11:6).** The two witnesses are empowered to perform miracles in the natural world like their prophetic forerunners. Elijah declared that it would not rain in Israel for a time; and when the drought was over, his prayer brought rain again (1 Kings 17:1; 18:41–42). Moses was given power to turn the Nile River into blood (Ex. 7:14–24). This was the first of ten plagues that God brought against Egypt through Moses.

The beast that comes up from the Abyss will attack them, and overpower and kill them (11:7). The beast is now introduced for the first time. His place of origin is the Abyss, where the demonic locusts of the fifth trumpet also originate (9:2–3). The beast is a malevolent character whose ultimate mission is to kill the two witnesses. By implication, he is the power behind the death of Antipas, the faithful witness in Pergamum (2:13).

REFLECTIONS

THE MARTYRDOM DESCRIBED IN REVELATION IS being repeated around the world today at an alarming rate. In fact, the 100 million martyrs who have died for their faith in the twentieth century are more than those martyred in the previous nineteen centuries of the church combined. This number is greater than the total of all those killed in war during the twentieth century. Researcher David C. Barrett estimates that 160,000 believers were martyred in 1996 alone. Persecution is common particularly in Africa, Asia, and the Middle East. However, shootings in schools and churches have recently produced young martyrs in the United States. Western Christians have a responsibility to be intercessors and public advocates on behalf of their brothers and sisters who are being persecuted and killed. Current information on the persecuted church can be found on the Internet at www.persecution.com.

Their bodies will lie in the street of the great city (11:8). A second type of city is now mentioned in this chapter. Whereas the holy city is the sacred domain of God's people (11:2), the great city is the dwelling place of the ungodly. This distinction is maintained throughout the rest of Revelation. Rome certainly represents the historical "great city" of the first century. During the Neronian persecution in 65, the Christians were martyred publicly. When Clement wrote to the Corinthian church several years later, he recalled two noble examples of his own generation, Peter and Paul, who "were persecuted and fought to the death" (*1 Clem.* 5:2).[80] The Christian addition of the *Ascension of Isaiah* mentions that "some of the twelve will be given into his hand," that is, Nero's, the one who murdered his mother Agrippina (*Mart. Ascen. Isa.* 4:3). Eusebius recorded an early tradition from the bishop of Corinth, Dionysius (A.D. 110–80), that Peter and Paul were martyred at the same time. However, it is more likely that Peter was martyred before Paul during the period 65–67. Eusebius also pointed out that the burial monuments of the two could be seen at the Vatican and on the Ostian Way.[81] The recent ministry and deaths of these two key apostolic witnesses, Peter to the Jews and Paul to the Gentiles, provides a compelling background for the imagery John uses here.

Which is figuratively called Sodom and Egypt, where also their Lord was crucified (11:8). Sodom was the city of wickedness that God destroyed with burning sulfur (Gen. 19:24), while Egypt was the country of Israel's oppression (Ex. 3:7–9). Ezekiel names both as places of godlessness which seduced Israel from following God (Ezek. 16:26, 46–56). The

great city is thus a place of wickedness, oppression, and seduction. The reference to Jesus' crucifixion seems to identify Jerusalem as this city. However, several things suggest otherwise. First, Jerusalem is never called the great city in Revelation, although it is called such elsewhere (e.g., Jer. 22:8). Second, John employs language that is figurative and spiritual, not literal, to describe the city. Third, the use of "also" points to somewhere else besides the historical Jerusalem.

An intriguing story related to Peter—the so-called "Quo Vadis?" tradition—dates to the late second century. When the Roman church learned of a conspiracy to kill Peter, they sent the apostle out of the city. As Peter was leaving Rome, he had a vision of Jesus entering the city. Peter asked him, " 'Lord, where are you going [*Quo vadis*]?' And the Lord said to him, 'I go to Rome to be crucified.' And Peter said to him, 'Lord, are you being crucified again?' And he said to him, 'Yes, Peter, again I shall be crucified.' " Peter soon came to himself and watched Jesus return to heaven. He then returned to Rome where he was arrested and later crucified (*Acts of Peter* 35). Although Jesus was crucified in Jerusalem at the behest of the Jews, the Romans bore equal culpability because it was their duly appointed governor Pilate who authorized the crucifixion. In that sense, Rome also played a role in crucifying Jesus.

For three and a half days men . . . will gaze on their bodies and refuse them burial (11:9). In the ancient world, the failure to receive a proper burial was the greatest insult at death (cf. Ps. 79:3–4; Jer. 22:18–19). When Pompey was assassinated in Egypt following his defeat by Julius Caesar, his body was abandoned and left unburied.[82] Roman funerary law normally forbade such care of corpses: "Whoever strips or exposes to the rays of the sun a body entrusted to permanent burial or left for a short period of time in some place, commits sacrilege."[83] Josephus called the Zealots barbarous and an outrage to humanity because they forbade the burial of the dead during the siege of Jerusalem and in fact killed those who attempted to bury their relatives.[84] The great anger of the earth dwellers against the two witnesses is expressed by this ultimate indignity. The deaths of the witnesses provoke a great celebration in which the residents from every nation rejoice over their release from torment (Rev. 11:10). A gift exchange often accompanied public festivals in the Greco-Roman world, and such an exchange now ensues.

But after the three and a half days a breath of life from God entered them (11:11). Even as the two witnesses prophesied for three and a half years (= 1260 days; cf. 11:3), their death lasted only three and a half days. At the conclusion of this brief period, the two witnesses come back to life. At creation the divine breath gave life to all humanity (Gen. 2:7). And when Ezekiel saw the valley of dry bones, God told him to prophesy to the bones: "I will put breath in you, and you will come to life" (Ezek. 37:6). The unexpected resurrection of the witnesses strikes terror in the onlookers, even as Jesus' resurrection brought great fear to the Roman guards at the tomb (Matt. 28:4).

Then they heard a loud voice from heaven saying to them, "Come up here" (11:12). The mighty angel, whose descent from heaven begins this vision (10:1–3), now invites the two witnesses to join him. His invitation is the same as that extended to John, although John's heavenly ascent is only visionary (4:1). The witnesses return to heaven in a cloud, even as Jesus did at his ascension (Acts 1:9).

Some midtribulationalists interpret the ascension of the two witnesses as representing the rapture of the church. (Other midtribulationists see the rapture occurring at Rev. 14:14.) Because their return to heaven occurs at the end of 1,260 days, it stands at the midpoint of the seven–year tribulation, but before the final outpouring of wrath in the final forty-two months. Two things in Revelation argue against this interpretation. First, this event concludes the sixth trumpet and the second woe, and, therefore, it is not midway in Revelation's sevenfold cycle. Rather, it occurs just before the final judgment announced in the seventh trumpet. Second, the translation of Enoch (Gen. 5:24) and Elijah (2 Kings 2:11) to heaven without experiencing death is a type of the New Testament rapture. But the two witnesses have died; and when they go up to heaven, it is as resurrected, not raptured, saints. The event seems to symbolize the resurrection of the dead saints, not the rapture of the living ones.

The survivors were terrified and gave glory to the God of heaven (11:13). The severe judgment that follows the resurrection of the two witnesses is still partial, as only a fraction of the city and its residents are affected. The survivors give the same response that the angel later calls for when he announces the eternal gospel: "Fear God and give him glory" (14:5). Since other earth dwellers later fail to glorify God (16:9), the response of the earthquake survivors suggests that they at last repent and acknowledge his lordship. Whether such repentance is voluntary is questionable. Nebuchadnezzar likewise glorified God, but only after he was judged for his pride and arrogance (Dan. 4:29–37). The continued worship of idols in the palace suggests that the king's conversion was temporary (5:4). This is the only passage in Revelation that *may* suggest a large-scale conversion before the Parousia. Every other text is pessimistic regarding the willingness of the earth dwellers to repent in the face of divine judgment (Rev. 9:21). The second woe, begun in 9:13, is at last over.

The seventh angel sounded his trumpet (11:15). Unidentified voices in heaven make an announcement following the seventh and final trumpet. God has at last established his rule on earth. The answer to the prayer of Jesus and the saints throughout church history—"your kingdom come, your will be done on earth as it is in heaven" (Matt. 6:10)—is now finally answered. This eternal kingdom is ruled by both the Lord and his Christ, who ascended to the throne following his victory over death (Rev. 3:21; 5:5).

And the twenty four elders ... fell on their faces and worshiped God (11:16). The elders, last seen in 7:13–17, are again heard in heaven thanking God that his reign on earth has begun. The familiar description of God as past, present, and future (1:8; 4:8) here assumes a new dimension. He is now acclaimed as the God only of the present and past. He is no longer the One who is to come because the future has now arrived forever.

The nations were angry; and your wrath has come (11:18). The language of the song echoes the messianic Psalm 2. There the angry nations are also described as God's enemies upon whom he pours his wrath (Ps. 2:1–5). The elders also announce proleptically the final judgment, which has two parts—rewarding the prophets and saints for their faithfulness, which Jesus does at his coming (Rev. 22:12), and destroying those who have opposed God's purposes on earth (20:11–15).

Then God's temple in heaven was opened, and within his temple was seen the ark of his covenant (11:19). The trumpet cycle ends with the characteristic eschatological earthquake that concludes each judgment cycle. This must complete the third woe; however, there is no explicit mention in this chapter of its completion. Although John sees the heavenly temple in several of his visions, this is the only occasion where he sees the ark of the covenant. The ark was the central fixture in the desert tabernacle as well as in Solomon's temple. After the destruction of the temple by the Babylonians in 586 B.C., the ark and its contents, including the jar of manna, were lost. One tradition states that Jeremiah rescued the ark and hid them in a cave on Mount Nebo until God should regather

▶ Chiasmus in Revelation

Chiasmus (or chiasm) is a structural device found in many types of ancient literature including the Bible. Its name is derived from a likeness to the Greek letter *chi* (X). Chiasmus provided a way to organize documents internally because ancient writings did not use paragraphs, punctuation, or capitalization. Because most people in the ancient world were illiterate, they got their information from oral performances. For such listeners, chiastic structure provided verbal clues to introduce and close sections of text, to signal emphasis, and to define argumentation. Chiasmus was used to organize a sequence of words or ideas in a sentence, a paragraph, or even a book. Two critical elements are involved—inversion and balance. A simple chiasmus is found in Jesus' saying in Mark 2:27: "The Sabbath was made for man, not man for the Sabbath." When the inversion has a middle element, the climax often occurs at the central crossing point. Chapter 12 is uniformly placed at this crossing point in all proposed chiastic structural models of Revelation.[A-45] Even the noted British novelist D. H. Lawrence, despite his unusual approach to the book, declared chapter 12 to be "the centre–piece of the Apocalypse" because it portrays the birth of the Messiah.[A-46] Although chapter 12 falls chronologically at the middle of Revelation, its content is a flashback to the beginning of the gospel story.

his people (cf. 2 Macc. 2:4–8). Another believed that an angel hid these sacred temple objects in the earth and is to guard them until the last days (*2 Bar.* 6:8). During the second temple period, it is probable that the ark was not in the Most Holy Place. John could never have seen it anyway since only the high priest was allowed to enter the Holy of Holies once a year. Yet John now recognizes the ark, to which he has access in the heavenly temple.

The Woman, the Male Child, and the Dragon (12:1–17)

A great and wondrous sign appeared in heaven (12:1). The ancients believed that heavenly signs signaled changes on earth. The magi followed a star a great distance to see the new king of the Jews. Because Herod knew the importance of such an omen, he gathered information about the star in order to kill his potential rival to the throne (Matt. 2:1–8). During Nero's reign a comet appeared, and its appearance was generally believed to foretell a change of emperor.[85] John's audience now awaits an explanation of the meaning of this astral sign.

A woman clothed with the sun, with the moon under her feet and a crown of twelve stars on her head. She was pregnant and cried out in pain (12:1–2). The incarnation of Jesus is now described using apocalyptic and mythological symbols. The woman, whose clothing depicts her character as with the other figures in Revelation (e.g., 4:4; 17:4), wears the sun, which symbolizes her heavenly nature (cf. 1:16; 10:1). The phrase "under her feet" signifies dominion and authority over creation (cf. Ps. 8:6; Mal. 4:3). She wears the victor's crown covered with twelve stars. In Revelation 1:20,

HOUSE OF MARY
AT EPHESUS
▼

seven stars represented the seven churches; here twelve stars represent the twelve tribes of Israel. This imagery was seen by Joseph in his dream of ruling his brothers (Gen. 37:9). Isaiah depicted eschatological Zion as pregnant and giving birth: "Before she goes into labor, she gives birth; before the pains come upon her, she delivers a son" (Isa. 66:7). Therefore, Israel is prophesied as the source of the promised Messiah, and the nation is personalized in a virgin daughter of

Judah named Mary who gives birth to Jesus Christ (Luke 1:27).

An enormous red dragon with seven heads and ten horns and seven crowns on his heads (12:3). The other heavenly sign that John sees is a menacing one. The imagery is borrowed from Daniel's vision of the fourth beast (Dan. 7:7). As the fourth and final one, this beast is commonly understood as the Roman empire, which is how it is interpreted in *4 Ezra* 4:10 (ca. A.D. 100). Unlike the Lamb who has seven horns (Rev. 5:6), the dragon has ten horns. His earthly representatives (to be introduced shortly)— the beast out of the sea (13:1) and the great prostitute (17:3, 7)—likewise have ten horns, which represent great satanic power. In Revelation, the number ten is used only regarding the opponents of God and their activities.

The dragon stood in front of the woman who was about to give birth, so that he might devour her child (12:4). Using tra-

▶ The House of Mary

In the hills above Ephesus stands a shrine called the House of Mary (Meryemana), which is visited by thousands of pilgrims each year. Here, according to one tradition, Mary lived until her death, after accompanying John to Ephesus. At his crucifixion, Jesus told John to care for his mother (John 19:25–27). Epiphanius (ca. A.D. 315–403) wrote that the Scriptures were silent, however, about John bringing Mary with him to Asia.[A-47] Later evidence from the fifth to the sixth centuries—church buildings dedicated to Mary, the *transitus Mariae* legends, and the *Euthymiac History*—located Mary's life and death specifically in Jerusalem.[A-48]

The modern claim of Mary's presence in Ephesus began with a German nun and mystic named

Catherine Emmerich. In a vision received between 1818–24, Emmerich saw a house in the mountains south of Ephesus in which the virgin mother Mary had lived. In 1890 the book containing this vision was read by some Roman Catholics in Smyrna, and the local priest journeyed to Ephesus to prove that such a house did not exist. However, on his third day of exploration, July 29, 1891, he discovered the house exactly as described in the vision. Roman Catholics gather there annually every August 15 to celebrate the Feast of the Assumption of the Virgin, and both Pope Paul VI in 1967 and Pope John Paul II in 1979 have celebrated mass at the sacred spot. Nevertheless, the better historical tradition locates Mary's death in Jerusalem.

ditional Jewish imagery from the Old Testament, Revelation appears to parody a familiar Hellenistic combat myth. The dragon Python pursued the goddess Leto, who was pregnant with Apollo. Leto fled to a distant island where she eventually gave birth to Apollo who, though just four days old, killed Python.[86] The converts from paganism in Asia would surely be familiar with this mythological account of cosmic struggle. To this myth is added features of the story of Artemis, who was the daughter of Leto and twin sister of Apollo. Artemis was traditionally born just outside Ephesus in the sacred grove Ortygia. She too was a virgin who protected women giving birth. A second century A.D. statue, now on display in the Ephesus Museum, portrays her as a queen of heaven, with the moon in the background of her three-tiered crown. This symbolism stems from her common identification as the moon goddess. Two other statues of the goddess in the museum show her wearing an extravagant necklace decorated with the twelve

signs of the zodiac, which some interpreters link to the twelve stars on the woman's head. Jews were forbidden to worship the stars (Deut. 4:19), yet later the zodiac was used decoratively in the mosaic floors of a number of synagogues (e.g., Hammath at Tiberias in Galilee; 4th–7th century A.D.). Although astral imagery figures prominently in Revelation, John does not use such images to promote astrological determinism, but rather to affirm God's sovereignty over his created order.

She gave birth to a son, a male child, who will rule all nations with an iron scepter. And her child was snatched up to God and to his throne (12:5). The language echoes the messianic promise in Isaiah 7:14 that a virgin would bear a son named Immanuel. Psalm 2:7–9 speaks of the anointed Son who would one day rule the

◀ *left*

ARTEMIS OF EPHESUS

This cultic statue depicts her with her three-tiered crown.

◀

ZODIAC ON THE FLOOR OF A SYNAGOGUE

The mosaic floor of the fourth-century synagogue in Tiberius (Galilee).

nations with an iron scepter. The male child is clearly Jesus the Messiah. The earthly life of Jesus is passed over in this apocalyptic description. Only his ascension is mentioned, an event described in Acts 1:9. Though the woman's flight is announced here, it is not described until verse 14. The reason for her flight is given next.

Michael and his angels fought against the dragon (12:7). Heaven, a place of worship and divine activity to this point, suddenly becomes a battlefield. Michael leads the other angels in expelling the dragon and his angels from heaven. Michael is the archangel who helps Daniel's heavenly messenger to prevail over the prince of Persia (Dan. 10:13, 21). He is also called the prince over the Jewish people who would protect those written in the book of life during a final time of distress (12:1–2). Jude 9, alluding to a lost document called the *Assumption of Moses*, identifies Michael as the archangel who disputed with the devil over the body of Moses. Michael is listed as one of the seven archangels in *1 Enoch* 20:1–7.

The great dragon was hurled down—that ancient serpent called the devil, or

▶ Snake Imagery in Asian Religions

Pergamum was home to the renowned healing sanctuary of Asclepius, the god of healing. Known to the Romans as Aesculapius, he was also called "Savior." After Epidaurus in Greece, Pergamum was the most famous sanctuary of Asclepius in the ancient world. Sick and infirmed people seeking to be healed daily filled the roads to the city. The noted second-century A.D. orator Aelius Aristides spent thirteen years as a patient at the Asclepium. Galen (c. A.D. 130–200), antiquity's most famous physician after Hippocrates, was a native of Pergamum and received his training at the Asclepium. Asclepius was always depicted with a serpent, usually holding a staff around which a serpent was coiled. Snakes associated with the god were a popular image on coins issued not only in Pergamum, but also in Laodicea, Thyatira, and Philadelphia. A column engraved with multiple snake images greeted visitors to the sanctuary. Real snakes were a part of the healing cure in an Asclepium:

A man had his toe healed by a serpent. He, suffering dreadfully from a malignant sore in his toe, during the daytime was taken outside by the servants of the Temple and set upon a seat. When sleep came upon him, then a snake issued from the Abaton and healed the toe with its tongue, and thereafter went back again to the Abaton. When the patient woke up and was healed he said that he had seen a vision: it seemed to him that a youth with a beautiful appearance had put a drug upon his toe.[A-49]

Other deities like Dionysus, Cybele, Zeus, and the Phrygian Sabazios likewise used snakes as part of their religious rites. Snakes were thus a popular image linked with pagan deities in Asia. However, John's association of the snake with Satan certainly positioned these cults as adversaries of Christ and the church. Today the snake encircling a staff—the symbol of Asclepius and healing—continues to serve as a symbol for medical associations.

Satan (12:9). The identity of the great dragon is now fully revealed. Although the names "devil" and "Satan" were mentioned in three of the messages to the churches (2:9, 10, 24; 3:9), his formal introduction is made here. In the Septuagint, the Greek word *diabolos* ("devil") is the usual translation of the Hebrew word *satan*. In the New Testament, both terms are frequently used—*diabolos*, 37 times and *satanas*, 36 times. The serpent imagery is derived primarily from the story of the Fall in Genesis 3. There the offspring of the woman was predicted to crush the serpent's head, while the serpent would only strike his heel (Gen. 3:15). During his earthly ministry Jesus saw a similar prophetic vision of Satan's fall after the seventy–two disciples told of their victory over demons (Luke 10:17–19; cf. John 12:31). These are the only two biblical texts that speak specifically of a fall of Satan. Early church commentators such as Tertullian and Gregory the Great saw in Isaiah's description of the "son of the dawn" (Lucifer) a prophetic description of the primeval fall of Satan (Isa. 14:12). However, this text describes the historical downfall and removal of the king of Babylon because he assumes the role of a god. (Ezekiel 28 likewise describes the fall of the king of Tyre.) In the Old Testament, there is no explicit mention of a fall of Satan, only a fall of humanity. The dragon's primary mission is now also disclosed—to deceive the whole world. Even as deception motivated the teaching of Jezebel (Rev. 2:20), it becomes the dragon's key tool to manipulate his human agents throughout the rest of the book.

Now have come the salvation and the power and the kingdom of our God, and the authority of his Christ (12:10). The successful expulsion of Satan and his angels from heaven elicits a hymn of triumph from a heavenly voice: Christ's incarnation has initiated a new kingdom on earth. The message of the kingdom characterized Jesus' earthly teaching: "The kingdom of God is near. Repent and believe the good news" (Mark 1:15). This was the same message the apostles announced: "Boldly and without hindrance he [Paul] preached the kingdom of God and taught about the Lord Jesus Christ" (Acts 28:31). This heavenly hymn continues through verse 12.

The accuser of our brothers . . . has been hurled down (12:10). In the Old Testament, Satan (meaning "adversary") is portrayed as the prosecuting attorney in several heavenly courtroom scenes. Satan came before the Lord and accused Job of serving God only for his blessings (Job 1:6–12). He likewise stood at the right side of Joshua the high priest, accusing him of unforgiven sin (Zech. 3:1–3). In both scenes Satan had access to God in heaven. A fundamental shift is described in Revelation. Since Satan has been cast from heaven forever, he can no longer accuse God's people. Paul captures this theological truth when he declares there is now no longer any condemnation to those in Christ Jesus (Rom. 8:1).

They overcame him by the blood of the Lamb and by the word of their testimony (12:11). Because Satan can no longer accuse God's people in heaven, he begins a campaign of terror against them on earth. The extent of his persecutions have already been shown proleptically in the visions of the martyrs (7:14) and the two witnesses (11:7). The formula for victory is now given: the blood of the Lamb coupled with their testimony

right ▶

EAGLE

An image of an eagle on a coin from the reign of the emperor Vespasian (A.D. 69–79).

about him. However, the testimony that overcomes Satan is the same action that provokes his rage and causes him to declare war on the church (11:17). Even as Jesus was ready to lay down his life (John 10:17), the saints are now prepared to lay down theirs. They do this in obedience to Jesus' command given in the context of his Parousia: "But whoever loses his life for me and for the gospel will save it" (Mark 8:35).

Therefore rejoice, you heavens .... But woe to the earth and the sea, because the devil has gone down to you! (12:12). Satan's expulsion produces two opposite reactions: joy in heaven and grief on earth. Rejoicing has characterized the scenes of heaven up to this point; however, the seal and trumpet judgments, especially the last three trumpets, have produced great woe upon the earth. Satan's reaction to his new spiritual situation is one of fury because he realizes the kingdom of darkness has only a short time left to exist. This is the short time of God's prophetic calendar that coincides with the forty-two months or 1260 days of the church's witness.

The woman ... might fly to the place prepared for her in the desert (12:14). Verse 13, which describes the dragon's pursuit of the birth mother, resumes the narrative interrupted in 12:6. The escape to the desert recalls an earlier work of divine deliverance—Israel's exodus from Egypt. God recalls this event to Moses on Mount Sinai: "You yourselves have seen what I did to Egypt, and how I carried you on eagles' wings and brought you to myself" (Ex. 19:4). A parallel likewise exists in the early history of the Jerusalem church. In his warning about the forthcoming destruction of Jeru-

salem, Jesus admonished the disciples to flee from the city to the mountains (Matt. 24:15–22). Church tradition recalls such a flight of the Jerusalem church in A.D. 66 to Pella (modern Tabaqat Fahil), a city in the Decapolis.[87] Although Pella was not in the Transjordanian mountains, it was situated in their foothills approximately twenty miles south of the Sea of Galilee. The dragon's attempt to destroy the Jewish Christians, first in the Zealot/Roman conflict and then while crossing the Jordan in the winter floods (cf. Mark 13:18), came to nothing. Instead, the Gentile churches of the Decapolis rescued and cared for the Jewish Christian refugees. Around this time John led a community from Palestine to Ephesus. Although the Jerusalem church was now safe, the dragon was making war against the saints in Rome and the province of Asia.

Where she would be taken care of for a time, times and half a time, out of the serpent's reach (12:14). When Daniel asked how long it would be before the astonishing things seen in his vision would be fulfilled, the angel replied, "It will be for a time, times and half a time" (Dan. 12:7). John adopts this prophetic time designation to encompass the period of the woman's protection. This is identical to the 1260 days mentioned earlier in 12:6, the same period that the two witnesses prophesy (Rev. 11:3). This period delineates a time for God's people involving both protection and witness in Revelation.

But the earth helped the woman by opening its mouth and swallowing the river that the dragon spewed out of his mouth (12:16). The woman is saved by the earth from the dragon's attempt to drown her. One of Israel's ancient myths concerned God's victory over a sea monster named Leviathan. Leviathan is often translated "dragon" in the Septuagint, particularly in Job 41:1–34, which gives the fullest description of this primeval beast. Asaph also exalted before God, "It was you who crushed the heads of Leviathan [dragon, LXX] and gave him as food to the creatures of the desert" (Ps. 74:14). Rahab is another probable name for this dragon. Isaiah compared God's destruction of Rahab to the deliverance of Israel from Egypt: "Was it not you who cut Rahab to pieces, who pierced that monster through? Was it not you who dried up the sea, the water of the great deep[?]" (Isa. 51:9–10). The victory that God has previously accomplished over Leviathan is the pattern for the woman's triumph over the dragon.

Then the dragon . . . went off to make war against the rest of her offspring—those who obey God's commandments (12:17). The use of the term "offspring" links directly back to the first messianic promise in Genesis 3:15: "And I will put enmity between you and the woman, and between your offspring and hers." While offspring, or seed, can be interpreted in the singular as a specific reference to the

Messiah Jesus, John uses it as a collective noun. Obeying (literally, keeping) God's commandments was a key theme in three of the messages to the churches (Rev. 2:26; 3:3, 8, 10). The relationship between obedience to Jesus and discipleship is likewise a theme in John 14:21: "Whoever has my commands and obeys them, he is the one who loves me." Reciprocally, whoever loves Jesus will obey his teaching, and both the Father and the Son will love such disciples (John 14:23). This theme, resumed now in Revelation, reminds the victors that obedience to Jesus identifies them as fellow offspring of the woman. This makes them vulnerable to the dragon's attacks.

REFLECTIONS

REVELATION PORTRAYS THE REALITY of spiritual warfare in the Christian life. The dragon has proclaimed a declaration of war against all of God's children, so we are now combatants in that struggle, willing or not. The present eschatological period between Christ's two comings is often compared to two decisive events in World War II—D day and V day. D day marked the landing of Allied troops in Europe. This decisive operation guaranteed the final defeat of Germany. D day is therefore like the first coming of Jesus portrayed in Revelation 12. However, the final surrender of the Axis forces did not occur until almost a year later on V day. Christ's second coming—the V day for the church—remains a future event. Christians now live in this interim period, called by God to overcome the dragon and his forces by putting on the spiritual armor that he has given us (cf. Eph. 6:10–18).

The Two Beasts (13:1–18)

And I saw a beast coming out of the sea (13:1). John's next vision discloses the dragon's two agents who will make war against the saints. Satan and his two beasts form a counter unholy trinity. While the beast in 11:7 came up from the Abyss, here his origin is from the sea. There is no difference, however, because John draws on an early Old Testament tradition that beneath the earth was a subterranean sea (Ex. 20:4). Job 41:31 equates the abyss and the sea as the home of the monster Leviathan: "He makes the depths [abyss, LXX] churn like a boiling cauldron and stirs up the sea like a pot of ointment."

Geographically the province of Asia was oriented westward toward the sea. Ephesus and Smyrna were both major seaports on the Aegean. When the governor would arrive in Asia from Rome, his port of "First Landing" was Ephesus. The legend of coins dating from the third century A.D. affirms this long-standing right.

The four beasts of Daniel's vision also arise from the sea, and John's beast is the prophetic ten–horned beast who has devoured the leopard, bear, and lion (Dan. 7:3–7). The traditional view of Daniel holds that these four kingdoms are Babylon, Medo-Persia, Greece, and Rome. (The main alternative view believes the kingdoms are Babylon, Media, Persia, and Greece.) *Fourth Ezra* (c. 2d cent. A.D.) similarly identifies the fourth beast coming out of the sea as an eagle—the Roman empire (*4 Ezra* 12:10).

Seven heads, with ten crowns on his horns, and on each head a blasphemous name (13:1). The seven heads symbolize the rulers of the beast's kingdom, while the ten horns symbolize their client kings. The crowns, probably of gold, symbolize the authority of the beast. Domitian wore a gold crown engraved with the images of Rome's chief deities Jupiter, Juno, and Minerva. His priests representing Jupiter and the deified Flavian family also wore similar golden crowns, which

▶

THE HARBOR OF EPHESUS

Only an outline of the harbor is visible today due to the Cayster River filling it with silt.

were decorated with Domitian's likeness.[88] Imperial cult priests in Asia Minor normally wore golden crowns that displayed busts of the emperor and his family. The blasphemous name on each head no doubt alludes to the divine names such as lord (*kyrios*), which the emperors adopted.

One of the heads of the beast seemed to have had a fatal wound, but the fatal wound had been healed (13:3). The death and resurrection of one of the heads parodies that of the Lamb (5:6) and the two witnesses (11:7–11). While the earth dwellers react to the two witnesses with contempt and then terror, they are astonished by the beast's reappearance and follow him. Instead of worshiping the resurrected Lamb, they worship the resurrected beast. This imagery bears a strong resemblance to the *Nero redivivus* myth (see "The *Nero Redivivus* Myth").

The beast was given a mouth to utter proud words and blasphemies and to exercise his authority for forty-two months (13:5). The beast's reign is forty-two months, the same period the Gentiles are given to trample the holy city (11:2). This time frame is used exclusively for the period in which God's enemies persecute and oppress his people. The beast's persecution is a trampling on God's temple, which is to be identified as his people and represented by the two

◀

THE *RES GESTAE* INSCRIPTION

A portion of the inscription found at Pisidian Antioch.

▶ The *Res Gestae*

One of the most important inscriptions preserved from Roman antiquity is the Monumentum Ancyranum. Before his death in A.D. 14, Augustus deposited four documents with the Vestal Virgins in Rome, one of which was an account of his deeds (*Res Gestae*). The original brass tablets upon which his deeds were engraved have never been found. But most of the document has been recovered from the Greek and Latin versions found on the walls of the imperial cult temple at Ancyra (modern Ankara), which was the capital of the province of Galatia. The lengthy inscription reads like political propaganda. One paragraph mentions the province of Asia: "After my victory I replaced in the temples of all the communities of the province of Asia the ornaments which my adversary (Mark Antony) in the war had, after despoiling the temples, taken into his own possession." Fragments of the Res Gestae have also been found in Pisidian Apollonia and on the propylon at the entrance of Augustus square in Pisidian Antioch. The account of Augustus' deeds was probably displayed in the imperial cult temple at Pergamum as well as distributed among Asia's other leading cities.[A-50]

witnesses. The arrogance of the beast causes him to blaspheme God and his name. Like the Jews who blasphemed ("slander," NIV) the believers in Smyrna (2:9), the beast now blasphemes God and those dwelling in heaven with him. Because the beast has killed the saints, he appears to have triumphed over the church. Yet the audience already knows that those in heaven have overcome the devil through the blood of the Lamb (7:15; 12:11–12).

All whose names have not been written in the book of life belonging to the Lamb that was slain from the creation of the world (13:8). The beast's universal authority elicits worship from all his subjects. Unlike the victors who are assured a place in the book of life (3:5), the earth dwellers are excluded from this heavenly registry. The book of life relates to the doctrine of election. The time when God decided that his Son should die for the sins of the world was from "the creation of the world." Peter used this same phrase to assure his Anatolian readers that their redemption was secured by the precious

▶

NERO

A statue of the emperor from the Corinth Museum.

▶ The *Nero Redivivus* Myth

An unusual "urban legend" arose in the middle of the first century after Nero's death. Some residents of the eastern provinces refused to believe that this despotic, though popular, emperor was really dead. Rumors began to circulate that Nero's enemies had conspired to stage the whole event and that, after escaping to the East, he would return (Nero redux). Such speculation was fueled when imperial edicts continued to be circulated in his name. Others accepted that Nero had died but believed he would return to life (Nero redivivus).

In July 69 (after Nero had died), Asia became terrified over a report of Nero's arrival. His look-alike soon gathered a mob around him. Forced to land on the Aegean island of Cythnus, this slave from Pontus (or freedman from Italy, as some said) was confronted shortly by Calpurnius Asprenas. Calpurnius was the newly appointed governor of Galatia and Pamphylia and was sailing to assume his new post. This Roman official quickly captured and killed the pretender, whose body was first taken to Ephesus before being transported to Rome.

A second pretender named Tarentius Maximus appeared in Asia in 80. Gathering supporters as he moved eastward, he received the backing of Artapanus IV, a pretender to the Parthian throne. The two tried to depose the emperor Titus, but his continued rule suggests they were unsuccessful.

A third pretender appeared during Domitian's reign (ca. A.D. 88/89) and received the support of the Parthian king Pacorus II. When the Romans demanded that the Parthians hand him over, they did so only with great reluctance.

Dio Chrysostom, a native of Prusa in Bithynia, summarized the popular expectations at the end of the first century: "Even now everyone wishes he (Nero) were alive, and most believe that he is."[A-51] We do not know when these Nero sightings ended, but the myth and its outworking is surely one of the most bizarre events in Roman imperial history.

▶ The Four *Hōde* Sayings

One popular view of Revelation believes that, since the church is never mentioned after chapter 3, it must be in heaven following the rapture.[A-52] The four *hōde* ("This calls . . .") sayings found in the second half of the book suggest otherwise. The first saying in 13:10 exhorts the saints to patient endurance and faithfulness, even though the beast is making war against them. The second saying in 13:18 calls for those with insight to calculate the meaning of the beast's name, 666. This and the fourth saying recall the parenthetical aside found in the Olivet Discourse—"let the reader understand" (Matt. 24:15). The third saying in 14:12 precedes the second beatitude and again encourages obedience and faithfulness. The persevering saints are to forgo the worship of the beast and his image, and to refuse his mark. The first three sayings also function as structural markers closing three of John's visions. The final saying in 17:9 invites the audience to have understanding about the symbolism of the seven heads and ten horns seen by John. More will be said about this complex imagery in chapter 17. Through these four *hōde* sayings, the Asian believers are exhorted to recognize and act on the spiritual implications of the present crisis. Therefore, Christians are still in view in these later chapters of Revelation.

blood of Christ the Lamb (1 Peter 1:20). Paul also used the phrase to assure his Gentile and Jewish audience concerning God's eternal plan of election for them (Eph. 1:4). The remarkable repetition of this theme is no doubt reassuring to the beleaguered Asian Christians, who were perhaps the same audience that received Ephesians. Christ's life, death, and resurrection on their behalf was no afterthought with God.

He who has an ear, let him hear (13:9). This modified hearing saying recalls the close of the seven prophetic messages (chaps. 2–3). The pronouncement of the unidentified speaker—"If anyone is to go into captivity . . . . If anyone is to be killed with the sword"—is drawn from a dirge in which God described the judgment of disobedient Judah at the hands of the Babylonians (Jer. 15:2; cf. 43:11). John's use of the saying is not deterministic, but a realistic warning for the saints to be prepared for future suffering. The beast's sword may appear to triumph, but only temporarily.

Then I saw another beast, coming out of the earth. He had two horns like a lamb, but he spoke like a dragon (13:11). John sees another beast, but this one comes

REFLECTIONS

WHAT DOES IT MEAN TO HAVE ENDURANCE AND faithfulness as believers today? This question is especially relevant for Christians living in countries where persecution exists. Survival may be a day-to-day matter, staying one step ahead of political and religious officials who are attempting to eliminate your faith or even your life. But what about those of us in the West, where freedom of religion exists and tolerance of Christianity prevails? Our beast is a subtle adversary who can work through culture, government, and false religion, all the while seeking to erode biblical faith and the eternal kingdom it represents. Both threats call for a mind of wisdom, which only the Holy Spirit can give.

from the earth, not the sea. Although its horns resemble those on the Lamb (5:6), when the beast speaks, his true colors are revealed. He is the mouthpiece of the dragon, a sheep in wolf's clothing (cf. Matt. 7:15). As the first provincial capital and the site of Asia's first imperial cult temple, Pergamum was also the seat of its league (*koinon*). Approximately 150 delegates—the leading citizens of the province—comprised the league. Because there was no separation of church and state in the Roman empire, the president of the league also served as the chief priest of the emperor cult. This was regarded as the most prestigious position in Asia. The high priest and league president is probably the individual represented as the second beast out of the earth.[89]

And he performed great and miraculous signs, even causing fire to come down from heaven to earth in full view of men (13:13). The second beast is the field representative for the dragon and the first beast, soliciting worship through deceptive signs and wonders. His activity fulfills Jesus' warning that false prophets would perform great signs and miracles (Matt. 24:24). Even as the two witnesses brought forth fire in the spirit of Elijah (see comments on 11:5), the second beast likewise produces fire. This power encounter is reminiscent of Moses' confrontation with the Egyptian magicians (Ex. 7:10–8:19). Trickery was commonly practiced by sorcerers in antiquity, and special-effects machines producing thunder and lightning were used in theatrical productions. In fact, the emperor Gaius had a device "by which he gave answering peals when it thundered and sent return flashes when it lightened."[90] Yet John seems to regard this supernatural

activity as genuine, although its source is demonic and not divine.

He ordered them to set up an image in honor of the beast (13:14). The Old Testament background is clearly Nebuchadnezzar's command to worship an image that he set up in Babylon. Because Shadrach, Meshach, and Abednego refused the order, they were thrown into the fiery furnace from which they were delivered (Dan. 3:1–17). People living in the Roman empire were quite accustomed to seeing images of the various Roman emperors.

He was given power to give breath to the image of the first beast, so that it could speak (13:15). Statues that spoke, typically in oracular utterances, were known in the Greco-Roman world. Plutarch noted that a particular statue spoke twice after it was erected in a temple. An omen pointing to Gaius's imminent murder occurred when a statue of Olympian Jupiter burst in laughter. Alexander of Abonuteichos (in Bithynia on the Black Sea coast) apparently erected an image of a serpent representing Glaucon-Asclepius that had a movable mouth and concealed speaking tubes.[91] Although no specific evidence of speech by imperial cult statues is extant, John again regards this activity as genuine since through it the nations were led astray (18:23).

No one could buy or sell unless he had the mark, which is the name of the beast or the number of his name (13:17). The mark given by the beast on the right hand and forehead is a parody of the seal received by the 144,000 (7:3). In order to buy and sell, the earth dwellers are forced to have the mark of the beast—his name or the number of his name (as grammatical appositives)—inscribed on their right hand or forehead. The position of this mark reflects that of the phylacteries worn by the Jews at the daily morning prayer. This Jewish practice reflects the divine command that God's word be bound on the hand and over the forehead (cf. Ex. 13:9; Deut. 6:8). The mark of the beast is a perversion of this custom, however, because the mark is on the right, not the left, hand and the mark on, not over, the forehead.[92] While the victors are promised that the name of God and the new name of Jesus will be inscribed on them (Rev. 3:12), the followers of the beast likewise have his name written on them. Two marks—one on the righteous and another on sin-ners—are likewise described in *Psalms of Solomon* 14:6, 9.

If anyone has insight, let him calculate the number of the beast, for it is man's number. His number is 666 (13:18). The use of codes in the Bible continues to provoke much interest, but there are

◀

IMAGES OF THE EMPEROR AUGUSTUS

Images of the emperor on Roman coins.

▶ Images of the Roman Emperor

The image (*eikōn*) of the emperor was a familiar sight in Asia. Such images were not necessarily realistic representations, but were standardized expressions of imperial ideology. About 250 portraits of Augustus survive from his forty-one year reign. Images of an emperor could be either busts or full statues. The imperial busts were set up in temples and could be so large that they were disproportionate to the size of the temple. The colossal head of Domitian (or Titus) in the Ephesus Museum gives the impression that this person was no ordinary human.

The full statues fell into three categories. First, cuirassed statues represented the emperor as a military conqueror. A coin from Pergamum shows Dea Roma crowning Augustus in his military dress inside the imperial cult temple. A second group of cult statues depicted the emperor naked, like the statues of Greek gods. This representation of the emperor suggested that he too was a divine being. An almost naked statue of Hadrian (A.D. 117–38), found in the imperial room of the Asclepium in Pergamum, had inscribed on its base the "god

Hadrian." The third category showed the emperor in civilian clothing, usually in a Roman toga but occasionally in Greek dress, the *himation*. The imperial cult temple in Smyrna contained a cult statue of Tiberius dressed in a toga.

Such images of the emperor were also placed in dedicated rooms in porticoes and gymnasiums. The north stoa of the agora in Ephesus' upper city had a basilica containing statues of Augustus and his wife Livia. There were also free-standing imperial buildings in the sanctuaries of other gods and goddesses. In Ephesus, within the sanctuary of the temple of Artemis stood a smaller building that served as an imperial shrine to Augustus. Approximately thirty temples, shrines, and porticoes containing images of the emperor stood in the province of Asia during the first century. Imperial images were also displayed publicly, being carried in processions that were part of imperial festivals and other important civic occasions. The emperor's image was well known to the early Christians in the seven churches.[A-53]

only a few clear examples where a code is used. Sheshach (Jer. 25:26; 51:41) and Leb Kamai (51:1) are atbash cryptograms used by Jeremiah to hide the name Babylon or its synonym Chaldea.[93] *Gematria* is the type of code used in Revelation. Hebrew and Greek lent themselves to *gematria* because the letters of their alphabets also represented numbers (a A = 1, b B = 2, g G = 3, etc.). In *gematria*, the name of a person is represented by a number whose sum is the numerical equivalent of its letters.

Examples of *gematria* have been found in graffiti at Pompeii (c. A.D. 79). One reads, "Amerimnus thought upon his lady Harmonia for good. The number of her honorable name is 45 (*me*)," while another states, "I love her whose number is 545 (*phme*)." After Nero murdered his mother in 59, a Greek verse circulated around Rome lampooning the emperor: "Nero, Orestes, Alcmeon their mothers slew/A calculation new. Nero his mother slew." The name Nero is the numerical equivalent of 1005 in Greek, the same as the phrase "his mother slew."[94] The *Sibylline Oracles* provide two examples of *gematria*. The emperors from Julius Caesar to Trajan are alluded to by the

gematria of their initials, and in a Christian passage Jesus is referred to by his number 888.[95] It is evident such a practice was well known in the ancient world.

The solution of the 666 riddle has puzzled Christians for centuries. By the time of Irenaeus (2d cent.), the exact identity of the beast was lost. His best guesses were "Teitan," the mythological Titans who rebelled against the gods, or "Lateinos," the Roman empire. Irenaeus records that a variant, 616, was already known in some versions.[96] Of the various solutions proposed for this cryptic cipher, Nero is the only first-century emperor whose name can be calculated to equal 666. Nero's Greek name *NERON KAISAR* was inscribed on the obverse of coins from Ephesus, Sardis, and Laodicea during this period.[97] John used this name to calculate the number of the beast in Hebrew (cf. Rev 16:16). Could John's audience have known the identity of the beast? Probably so, otherwise John would not have encouraged the Asian believers to calculate the beast's number. The Hebrew and Greek *gematria* associated with the calculation of the names of Nero and Jesus are shown in the chart below.

The Hebrew and Greek *Gematria* Associated with the Calculation of the Names of Nero and Jesus		
Neron Kaisar	**Nero Kaisar**	**Jesus**
נ = 50 N	נ = 50 N	
ר = 200 R	ר = 200 R	I = 10 I
ו = 6 O	ו = 6 O	η = 8 E
נ = 50 N		σ = 200 S
ק = 100 K	ק = 100 K	o = 70 O
ס = 60 S	ס = 60 S	υ = 400 U
ר = 200 R	ר = 200 R	ς = 200 S
666	616	888

IN OUR DAY, ATTEMPTS HAVE BEEN made to link public figures with the number 666. Identifying persons like Henry Kissinger and Mikhail Gorbachev as 666 has proven embarrassingly futile. Because the English alphabet is not used to represent cardinal numbers, it is impracticable to calculate a name using gematria. The prophetic significance of 666 is to understand the political reality it represents—despotic individuals who use their power to persecute the church and oppress humanity. Rulers such as Adolph Hitler, Joseph Stalin, and Idi Amin are examples from the twentieth century.

The 144,000 and the Two Harvests (14:1–20)

Then I looked, and there before me was the Lamb, standing on Mount Zion (14:1). A threefold series of visions, which begin in heaven and move to earth, comprises chapter 14. The 144,000, introduced in chapter 7, now reappear with the Lamb around the heavenly Mount Zion. The earthly Zion was the mount in Jerusalem upon which the temple was built. This was the dwelling place of God: "Sing praises to the LORD, enthroned in Zion" (Ps. 9:11; cf. 132:13–14). Zion later became a synonym for the entire city of Jerusalem (cf. Isa. 4:3–4; 52:1–2). In Hebrews, Zion is viewed not as an earthly reality but as a heavenly city where God, the angels, and the church reside (Heb. 12:22–23; cf. 2 Esd. 2:42). Heavenly Zion has become the meeting point for the saints, even as earthly Zion was the meeting point for the tribes of Israel. John views Zion as the center of the eschatological kingdom, for Christ has been installed here to begin his messianic reign (cf. Ps. 2:6).

And with him 144,00 who had his name and his Father's name written on their foreheads (14:1). The names written on the foreheads of the 144,000 fulfills the promise given to the victors (3:12). These names are evidently the content of the seal mentioned in 7:3, whose nature has long been debated. Its Old Testament background is found in Ezekiel 9:3–11 where an angel is told to put a mark on the foreheads of Jerusalem's residents who grieve over evil. The angel is to slaughter those who do not receive the mark (Heb. *taw*; Ezek. 9:5). Taw is the last letter of the Hebrew alphabet, and in the Old Hebrew script used during Ezekiel's day until the New Testament period taw was written in the form of a cross (X). The Greek letter chi (C) was recognized as an equivalent to taw. Chi, the first letter of Χριστός, was a common abbreviation for this Greek word meaning Christ, or Anointed One. The *Damascus Document*, quoting Ezekiel, states that at the time of the Messiah's coming, the only ones to be spared the sword are those marked by the taw (CD 19.12).[98] A Jewish Christian told the third-century church father Origen that "the form of the Taw in the old [Hebrew] script resembles the cross, and it predicts the mark which is to be placed on the foreheads of the Christians."[99] The mark therefore signifies possession and protection because God's presence is with his people.

And they sang a new song before the throne and before the four living creatures and the elders (14:3). The elders sing a new song around the throne in 5:8; now the 144,000 sing their new song. Although its words are unstated, their quality is suggested through several metaphors: the roar of rushing waters, a loud peal of thunder, and harpists playing their harp. None of the heavenly creatures can learn this song because participation is restricted to those redeemed from the earth. Their praise undoubtedly centers on redemption by the Lamb and deliverance from the beast.

These are those who do did not defile themselves with women, for they kept themselves pure (14:4). Before going into battle, Israelite soldiers were required to maintain ritual purity including abstinence from sex (cf. Deut. 23:9–10; 1 Sam. 21:5; 2 Sam. 11:11). The Lamb's followers, literally called virgins (*parthenoi*), have kept themselves pure for the spiritual holy war. To interpret their continence literally is problematic, because the New Testament affirms the role of sex in Christian marriage (cf. 1 Cor. 7:2–5). A figurative interpretation is preferred: The virgins are believers of either sex, who have not defiled themselves through spiritual fornication. Some at Sardis had not defiled their white garments (Rev. 3:4). Two women—Jezebel and the great prostitute—are the primary adversaries of the church. In Thyatira, the woman Jezebel threatened the churches with her false prophecy (2:20). And later Babylon/ Rome is described as a woman who is the mother of all prostitutes (17:3, 4, 6, 7, 9, 18). Believers who have contact with either woman, Babylon or Jezebel, will soil their garments or, to change metaphors, lose their virginity.

They were purchased from among men and offered as firstfruits to God and the Lamb (14:4). Israel was the firstfruits of God's spiritual harvest (Jer. 2:3). Although firstfruits is used to describe a variety of spiritual blessings in the New Testament, Paul used the term to speak specifically of Israel as the spiritual root of the church (Rom. 11:16). Jewish believers in the Messiah comprised the firstfruits of God's new kingdom community (cf. James 1:18). The use of the term here helps to confirm the identification of the 144,000 as Jewish believers. This group that does not lie about the Lamb contrasts with those in the synagogue of Satan who are liars (Rev. 3:9).

Another angel . . . had the eternal gospel to proclaim to those who live on the earth (14:6). John's vision changes abruptly, and he next sees three angels flying in the middle heaven who have messages to deliver. The first angelic message is directed to individuals from every people group, who seem to be earthly

▶ The Emperor's "Gospel"

The white stone stele discussed in 2:17 was inscribed with an edict issued by the proconsul Fabius and approved by the assembly of Asia. It too contained a "gospel" message, which served as political propaganda celebrating the victories of the emperor Augustus and his generous benefactions to his subjects. The edict's language has several parallels in the New Testament. Providence sent Caesar as a savior that he might bring peace (cf. Titus 1:4). His coming is described as an appearing (cf. 2 Tim. 1:10). His birth is also said to be the beginning of life and breath (cf. Rev. 3:14). Likewise, the honor of Augustus is to remain forever (cf. 4:9; 5:13; 7:12). The decree closes by declaring that the birthday of the god Augustus "was the beginning for the world of the good tidings (*euangelion;* gospel) that came by reason of him."[A-54] When Paul and John proclaimed the gospel of Jesus Christ in Asia, it is no wonder that their message faced conflict with the imperial gospel. Jesus was both a political and a religious rival to the emperor in Rome and his ambassadors in the provinces.

---

representatives of the heavenly multitude seen in 7:9. This composite group living on the earth is specifically distinguished from the earth dwellers. The angel's announcement repeats that of the elders: The hour of judgment has come, bringing the positive rewards for the saints and the negative destruction of the wicked (cf. 11:18). The message of the eternal gospel is to fear and to worship God, something that only the saints do (cf. 15:4). This is the only use of the word "gospel" in Revelation.

A second angel followed and said, "Fallen! Fallen is Babylon the Great" (14:8). The second angel's announcement about Babylon's fall is proleptic because the city's actual destruction is not seen until chapter 18. From a heavenly perspective, Babylon's fall has already occurred. This is the first of six uses of the code name Babylon in Revelation (cf. 16:19; 17:5; 18:2, 10, 21). Babylon is used as a cipher in other contemporaneous Jewish literature (*4 Ezra* 15:46; *2 Bar.* 11:1; *Sib. Or.* 5.143). This dirge resembles similar pronouncements over Babylon spoken by Isaiah (Isa. 21:9) and Jeremiah (Jer. 51:8). Babylon was the capital of the Near Eastern empire that captured Jerusalem in 586 B.C. Jeremiah prophesied during this period of Judah's political instability, and twice he spoke judgment oracles against Babylon (25:12–38; 50:1–51:64). Babylon made the whole world of its day drunk when the nations drank her wine (51:7). Which first-century city does John refer to? Peter's use of Babylon (1 Peter 5:13) provides a clue. His probable referent is Rome, the place from which he is writing. Historical tradition dates Peter's martyrdom to the Neronic persecution of 65–66.[100] This would place the writing of 1 Peter before A.D. 70 and thereby attest to the use of Babylon for Rome before the destruction of the temple. Because of Rome's persecution, the early church named their adversary Babylon, a city opposed to God and his people.

A third angel followed them and said . . . "he, too, will drink of the wine of God's

fury, which has been poured full strength into the cup of his wrath" (14:9, 10). In the ancient world, wine was usually mixed with water before it was drunk. The typical ratio was one part wine to three parts water, depending on the type of wine. To drink wine full strength was considered a sign of debauchery and revelry. A cup of unmixed wine became a metaphor for God's unmitigated judgment. God told Jeremiah: "Take from my hand this cup filled with the wine of my wrath and make all the nations to whom I send you drink it" (Jer. 25:15; cf. Ps. 75:8). Because Babylon destroyed Jerusalem, Jeremiah prophesied that it would be the primary nation to drink of God's wrath (Jer. 25:26–28). Even as Babylon fell to the Persians in 539 B.C., so too Rome would one day be destroyed.

He will be tormented with burning sulfur in the presence of the holy angels and of the Lamb (14:10). Sulfur is a nonmetallic yellowish element that burns with a blue flame while emitting a noxious, suffocating sulfur dioxide gas. The punishment of the wicked with burning sulfur is a common eschatological motif.

SULPHUR

▼

David wrote, "On the wicked he will rain fiery coals and burning sulfur" (Ps. 11:6). This is because the breath of the Lord is "like a stream of burning sulfur" (Isa. 30:33). God's destruction of Sodom and Gomorrah with burning sulfur is a paradigm of the final judgment (Gen. 19:24). For when Jesus returns, fire and sulfur will rain down from heaven as in the days of Lot (Luke 17:29–30). Burning sulfur is associated four times with punishment in Revelation (cf. 19:20; 20:10; 21:8).

"Blessed are the dead who die in the Lord from now on." "Yes," says the Spirit, "they will rest from their labor, for their deeds will follow them" (14:13). No beatitudes have been spoken since 1:3, so this is the first of the final six that occur in the second half of the book. The Asian audience is pulled from visions of the future back to their present situation, with those who will die being promised a special blessing. The Spirit who speaks to the seven churches in chapters 2–3 now speaks again. He promises the same rest ("wait," NIV) as that which is promised to the martyrs in 6:11. Unlike the idolatrous worshipers who receive no rest from their torments (9:4; 14:11), the saints receive rest from their work of testifying for the Lamb.

There before me was a white cloud, and seated on the cloud was one "like a son of man" (14:14). In his initial vision, John sees someone called "a son of man" whose identity is clearly Jesus (1:13). Because the figure seen here receives orders and then acts as a harvester, he seems more angelic than divine. In 14:14–20 two harvests are announced and completed—of grain and of grapes. In the parable of the weeds, Jesus compared the end of the age to a harvest in which the angels are the harvesters. The angels will separate the weeds, representing the devil's sons, from the good seed, representing the sons of the kingdom (Matt. 13:30, 37–43).

Take your sickle and reap, because the time to reap has come, for the harvest of the earth is ripe (14:15). Sickle can refer to two types of curved knives used for agricultural purposes. Grain was harvested with a short-handled hand scythe, while the sickle used by vintagers was a small knife that could cut grape clusters from the vine. The time of ripeness depended on the crop. The wheat harvest occurred in June, while the harvest of grapes for wine production occurred in September. This agricultural analogy suggests that two groups are to be harvested—the righteous and the wicked. Two things in chapter 14 suggest that the grain harvest is of the righteous. The 144,000 are identified as firstfruits, an agricultural metaphor (14:4; cf. Lev. 2:14), and the audience addressed with the eternal gospel both fear and worship God (Rev. 14:7). Jesus likewise described the ingathering of the righteous as reaping the harvest (John 4:35–38).[101]

Take your sharp sickle and gather the cluster of grapes from the earth's vine, because its grape are ripe (14:18). The angel in charge of the fire on the heavenly incense altar commands another angel to gather the people like grapes. This second harvest is not for blessing but for judgment. Revelation's imagery follows that of Joel 3:13: "Swing the sickle, for the harvest is ripe. Come, trample the grapes for the winepress is full." The fullness of the winepress and its overflowing vats is not because of the abundance of the harvest, but because of the overwhelming wickedness of the nations.

They were trampled in the winepress outside the city (14:20). Archaeologists have discovered many winepresses in excavations throughout the Mediterranean world. Winepresses were square or circular pits, hewn out of rock or holes dug in the ground and then lined with rocks and sealed with plaster. The grapes would be placed in the press and then trampled by several individuals. The juice then flowed through a channel to a lower vessel called a winevat. Here the grape juice was collected and allowed to ferment. During his judgment of the nations, God is asked about his appearance: "Why are your garments red, like those of one treading the winepress?" (Isa. 63:2). This graphic description portrays the slaughter that will accompany the harvest of the unrighteous.

Joel located this final judgment in the valley of Jehoshaphat (Joel 3:2). The church historian Eusebius identified this valley as the Hinnom, which lies south of Jerusalem. This was the traditional valley of judgment in the Old Testament (Jer. 7:31–32; 19:5–6), and became the prototype for the concept of Gehenna seen in Jewish intertestamental literature (cf. 2 Esdras 7:36, NRSV note) and the New Testament (Matt. 5:22). Later Jewish,

WINEPRESS

The surface of a winepress in a village near Hebron.

Christian, and Muslim traditions came to identify the valley as the Kidron, east of Jerusalem. To secure a place in the resurrection, Muslims buried their dead on Kidron's western slope beneath the Golden Gate, while Jews buried their dead on the east beneath the Mount of Olives. John seems to delocalize purposely the valley from a Palestinian context by placing it outside the city—here Babylon—which is martyring the saints.

The Song of Moses and the Seven Last Plagues (15:1–8)

I saw in heaven another great and marvelous sign: seven angels with the seven last plagues (15:1). John's next series of visions, which run through chapter 18, replays through the final events that usher in the two harvests. The seven plagues are called last because with them God's wrath reaches its full measure. Before these plagues are revealed, John sees another vision of the victors in heaven.

Standing beside the sea, those who had been victorious over the beast and his image and over the number of his name (15:2). The clear sea of glass that John saw before the throne in 4:6 now has a fiery red hue. The color is ominous, foreboding the coming judgments of fire that will complete God's wrath (16:8; 18:8; 20:15). The victors find their ultimate deliverance at the sea of glass, just as Israel was delivered through the Red Sea. They have triumphed over the beast, the historical equivalent of the pharaoh.

They . . . sang the song of Moses the servant of God and the song of the Lamb (15:3). Like the 144,000 who sing a new song before the heavenly throne (14:1–3), the rest of the victors also sing a song of triumph. Their song imitates the heavenly song celebrating the triumph of the Lamb through his blood (cf. 5:5, 9–10). It has parallels with two songs of Moses recorded in the Old Testament. The first song celebrates God's triumph over the Egyptians (Ex. 15:1–18), while the second promises judgment to his enemies and reward to his servants (Deut. 32:1–43). The words of the song reflect a number of Old Testament texts including "Great are the works of the LORD" (Ps.

111:2) and "all his ways are just" (Deut. 32:4). This worship language carefully balances God's miraculous works with his moral attributes, both essential aspects of his nature. The question in verse 4 is drawn directly from Jeremiah 10:7: "Who should not revere you, O King of the nations?" There Jeremiah is contrasting the worship of God with idols, concluding that idolatry was foolishness. By refusing to worship the beast's image and receive his number, the victors have likewise rejected the temptation to idolatry.

For you alone are holy (15:4). Here and in 16:5 are the only occurrences of the distinctive Greek word *hosios*, translated "holy," which indicates the close relationship between the two songs. The language is drawn directly from the second Song of Moses: "just (*dikaios*) and holy (*hosios*) is the Lord" (Deut. 32:4 LXX). The linkage of these divine attributes is also found in these words of David: "The Lord is just in all his ways, and holy in all his works" (Ps. 145:17 LXX). The most unique gods worshiped in the Phrygian and Lydian regions of Asia (around Laodicea, Philadelphia, and Sardis) were called *Hosion kai Dikaion*, "Holy and Just." A funerary inscription from the area invokes Holy and Just to take vengeance on an individual if she does not return to the family some personal possessions left for safe keeping by the deceased. A limestone stele found in northeastern Asia depicts Holy and Just, one holding the scales of justice and the other the staff of authority.[102] John's insistence on the Lord as the only holy and just God would serve as a polemic against these popular indigenous deities.

All nations will come and worship before you (15:4). The universal worship of

God is the great prophetic hope of the Old Testament. David cried, "All the nations you have made will come and worship before you, O LORD" (Ps. 86:9). In the new heavens and new earth "all mankind will come and bow down before me [God]" (Isa. 66:23; cf. Mal. 1:11). The victors echo this longing. However, there is no idea of mass conversion present in this language. Such worship is based on obedience to God's revealed righteousness and excludes the rebellious (Isa. 66:24). Representatives of all nations who have triumphed over the beast are among these worshipers (cf. Rev. 7:9; 14:6).

Out of the temple came the seven angels with the seven plagues (15:6). The visionary sign introduced in verse 1 is now fully revealed. After the seventh trumpet, John sees the ark of the covenant in the open temple (11:19). Again John sees the temple opened in heaven. This temple is also called the tabernacle of Testimony, a name that recalls the portable tabernacle that accompanied Israel in the desert (Ex. 38:21; cf. Acts 7:44). The Testimony refers to the two tablets of stone containing the ten commandments that were

THE TABERNACLE

A model of the tabernacle showing the entrance.

▼

inscribed by the finger of God (Ex. 31:18). These stones were housed in the ark of the covenant along with the gold jar of manna and Aaron's staff that had budded (Heb. 9:4).

Then one of the four living creatures gave to the seven angels seven golden bowls filled with the wrath of God (15:7). The golden bowls seen in 5:8 and 8:3–5 are full of incense, which represent the prayers of the saints. This second set of golden bowls has a different function in both the earthly and the heavenly temple ritual. The use of the verb "pour out" in chapter 16 suggests that they are not censers but libation bowls. Moses made such sprinkling bowls for use at the altar of burnt offering (Ex. 27:3; Num. 4:14). For worship in the temple, Solomon had a hundred gold sprinkling bowls made for holding wine, which often accompanied sacrifices to God (2 Chron. 4:8; Hos. 9:4). These libation bowls now function as cups containing the wine of God's wrath (Rev. 14:10; 16:19).

And the temple was filled with smoke from the glory of God and from his power, and no one could enter the temple (15:8). On several occasions in the Old Testament, the glory of God was also heavy. After the tabernacle was erected,

Moses could not enter it because the divine cloud had settled upon it, and the glory of God had filled the tabernacle (Ex. 40:35). When Solomon brought the ark of the covenant into the temple, the cloud of God's glory so filled it that the priests could not perform their service (1 Kings 8:10–12; 2 Chron. 5:13–14). When Ezekiel saw the glory of the Lord filling the temple, he fell face down (Ezek. 44:4). The temple's closure until the plagues of the seven bowls are complete suggests that God's mercy is exhausted and that only his wrath remains for the earth dwellers.

The Seven Bowls of God's Wrath (16:1–21)

Ugly and painful sores broke out on the people who had the mark of the beast and worshiped his image (16:2). The outpouring of the seven bowls upon the worshipers of the beast completes the fullness of God's wrath announced in 14:10. The first bowl replicates the sixth Egyptian plague. Moses initiated the plague of boils by throwing soot from a furnace into the air. That soot spread as fine dust over Egypt to produce festering boils on both people and animals (Ex. 9:8–11). No medium like soot is mentioned in Revelation. Once the bowl is

▶ The Trumpet and Bowl Judgments and the Egyptian Plagues

The Exodus tradition is an important background for Revelation. The Passover typology was initially introduced in 5:6 when John sees a slain Lamb. The two witnesses, like Moses, were empowered to turn the waters into blood and to smite the earth with plagues (11:6). The song of Moses also became the song of the Lamb (15:3). The plagues against Egypt provide a prophetic background for the serial judgments of the seven trumpets and the seven bowls, with six of the ten being replicated in Revelation. Like Exodus, John arranges his judgments in increasing degrees of intensity. Like the pharaoh whose heart became hardened (Ex. 7–14 passim), the inhabitants of the earth refuse to repent (Rev. 9:20–21; 16:9, 11).

poured on the land, sores break out only on the earth dwellers. God warned Israel that one of the curses for disobedience would be painful boils covering the entire body (Deut. 28:35). Although it is impossible to determine medically the nature of the sores in Revelation, their appearance is repulsive and their festering pustules are extremely painful.

The sea . . . turned into blood like that of a dead man, and every living thing in the sea died. The third angel poured out his bowl on the rivers and springs of water . . . became blood (16:3, 4). The content of bowls two through four is comparable to that of the first three trumpets. Whereas only a third of the people are affected by the trumpet judgments, the destruction is total with the bowls. The sea turns to blood in the third bowl, while freshwater sources become blood in the fourth bowl. This parallels the first Egyptian plague; however, only the Nile River and freshwater sources were affected, not the sea (Ex. 7:17–21). From the perspective of John and his audience, the sea was the Mediterranean. The Old Testament frequently calls the Mediterranean "the sea" (e.g., Num. 34:5). Variations are "the Great Sea" (Num. 34:6) or "the western sea" (Deut. 11:24). The Romans, like the Greeks, called it "the inner sea" (Lat. *Mare Internum*). Several of the Asian cities were near the major rivers or their tributaries that drained western Anatolia: the Caicus River at Pergamum, the Hermus River at Sardis, the Cayster River at Ephesus, and the Lycus branch of the Meander River at Laodicea. These rivers provided valuable water resources for domestic and agricultural uses. Ephesus and Miletus were at the mouths of the Cayster and the Meander, but the ongoing deposit of silt from these rivers required regular dredging to keep the navigational channels of these great harbors open.

You have given them blood to drink as they deserve (16:6). Because the earth dwellers have shed innocent blood (cf. 17:6), God now pours out two blood judgments. Revelation's imagery is probably drawn from Isaiah 49:26: "They [your oppressors] will be drunk on their own blood, as with wine." This principle of juridical reciprocity is called *lex talionis*. It forms the foundation for the administration of biblical law: "You are to take life for life, eye for eye, tooth for tooth, hand for hand, foot for foot, burn for burn, wound for wound, bruise for bruise" (Ex. 21:23–25). Jesus' teaching in the Sermon on the Mount appears to overturn this concept that the punishment should fit the crime (Matt. 5:38). However, serious injury is not involved with any of the three examples he gives. Jesus is espousing the ethics of the citizens of the kingdom of God—a lifestyle demonstrated by the martyrs—and is not addressing the punishment of the wicked either by divine or secular justice.

And I heard the altar respond (16:7). John is not implying that an article of furniture now speaks. Rather, the sentence is better translated, "And I heard someone from the altar respond." The angel's declaration of God's justice elicits a response from a representative of those most affected—the martyrs themselves. These same saints under the altar cry out for justice in 6:10 and declare God's judgments true and just in 15:3.

The sun was given power to scorch people with fire (16:8). In the fourth bowl, the sun sears all people with unrelenting and oppressive heat (cf. 8:7). The earth dwellers for the first time now blaspheme ("cursed," 16:19 NIV) God, following the example of the beast (13:5–6). The earth dwellers' failure to repent and their blasphemy against God likewise serve as refrains to close the fifth and seventh bowls (16:11, 21).

His kingdom was plunged into darkness. Men gnawed their tongues in agony and cursed the God of heaven (16:10–11). With the outpouring of the fifth seal, total darkness descends on the beast's kingdom and his throne (cf. 8:12). The beast's seat of power in the first century was at Rome, while his localized throne in Asia was at Pergamum (2:13). The ninth plague on Egypt similarly covered the entire land in darkness for three days. Yet the Israelites had light where they lived (Ex. 10:21–23). Jesus often used a similar eschatological motif in his parables: "And throw that worthless servant outside, into the darkness, where there will be weeping and gnashing of teeth" (Matt. 25:30; cf. 22:13). Like the gnashing of teeth, gnawing the tongue represents the despair of the wicked.

The great river Euphrates . . . was dried up to prepare for the kings from the East (16:12). Babylon was captured in 539 B.C. when the Persians diverted the Euphrates River and marched into the city on the dried-up river bed.[103] In 9:14, the army gather at a ford on the Euphrates prepared for battle. Now that the river is dried up, perhaps because of drought, the crossing of the kings can occur anywhere. These kings are often identified with the Parthians who lived east of the Euphrates.

Then I saw three evil spirits that looked like frogs (16:13). The second plague on the Egyptians was a plague of frogs that covered the land. By using their magic arts, the Egyptian magicians were able to duplicate this miracle (Ex. 8:1–14). The same demonic deception employed by the magicians is now operating out of the mouths of the unholy trinity. The second

---

▶ Parthia and "The Kings from the East"

After Augustus became emperor in 27 B.C., the Romans began to vie with the Parthians for control of Armenia. Finally, Nero initiated a military campaign to secure Rome's eastern frontier. General Corbulo's conquest of Armenia (A.D. 59) and victory over the Parthians was total. Only through the folly of the Roman client king Tigranes in 60 and the ineptitude of Corbulo's replacement Paetus were the Parthians able to regroup and defeat the Romans at Rhandeia in 62. Once Corbulo reestablished the Roman position in 63, the Parthians again become suppliants with Tiridates and he was forced to travel to Rome in 65 to receive his crown. This new client king was treated as visiting royalty by Nero, and the emperor was hailed for restoring peace to the empire. Tiridates visited the cities of Asia on his return to Parthia. The civil war in 68–69 would have been an ideal time for the Parthians to strike against their longtime enemy. This was because Mucianus, the governor of Syria, had left the eastern frontier vulnerable when he led the sixth legion westward to depose Vitellius. However, neither Vologeses nor his brother Tiridates in Armenia desired to break the accord recently secured by Nero. In fact, Vologeses offered Vespasian 40,000 Parthian cavalry to help him secure the principate. The Flavian dynasty was therefore indebted to the Parthians for their cooperation during this tumultuous transition, and these kings in the east ceased to be a threat to Rome in the first century.[A-55]

beast is henceforth called the false prophet (cf. Rev. 19:20; 20:10). According to 1 John 4:1, "many false prophets have gone out into the world," whose false message about Jesus is "the spirit of the antichrist" (4:3). Although the word antichrist is not used in Revelation, the deceptive activity of the false prophet and the prophetess Jezebel (cf. 2:20) both have the demonic spirit of antichrist as their source. In the Old Testament, the prophet Micaiah saw a vision as to why the other prophets were prophesying falsely to the kings Ahab and Jehoshaphat. The Lord was enticing Ahab to die in battle by putting a lying spirit in the mouths of all the court prophets (1 Kings 22:1–28). God Almighty similarly allows the three evil spirits to deceive his opponents into believing they are prepared to fight him in battle.

They go out to the kings of the whole world (16:14). Through miraculous signs, these demonic spirits gather the kings of the whole world (*oikoumenē*; cf. 12:9). From a Roman perspective the *oikoumenē* was not only a geographical concept, but also a political and cultural one. The world consisted of its inhabited and civilized empire. The decree of Caesar Augustus that a census should be taken of the world is rightly translated in the NIV as "the entire Roman world" (Luke 2:1). Thus, Josephus could call Caesar "the lord of the universe," that is, of the *oikoumenē*.[104] The concept became idealized through the goddess Oikoumene. Her statues, sometimes used as lighthouses, served as useful propaganda symbols throughout the empire of Rome's global domination.[105]

The battle on the great day of God Almighty (16:14). Western Anatolia was the site of several important battles of the Greco-Roman period. Alexander the Great, the Macedonian leopard in Daniel's vision of four beasts (Dan. 6:6) who is also described as a one-horned goat (8:5–8), defeated the Persians for the first time in 334 B.C. at Granicus River. The battle site is just south of the Sea of Marmara near Biga in northwestern Turkey. Following Alexander's death, his successors fought one another at the "Battle of the Kings" at Ipsus (near modern Çay) in 301 B.C.; Antigonus and his son Demetrius confronted their rivals Lysimachus and Seleucus. The latter prevailed, and Alexander's great empire was broken up and divided among four successor states (cf. 11:4). In 190 B.C., the Romans defeated the Greek army near Smyrna at Magnesia and Sipylum (modern Manisa). Lucius Scipio Asiaticus was the Roman commander who gained control of the coastlands of western Anatolia and put an end to the insolence of Antiochus III (cf. 11:17–18). Such great historic battles will pale in comparison to the final battle of the Lord.

Behold, I come like a thief! Blessed is he who stays awake and keeps his clothes with him, so that he may not go naked and be shamefully exposed (16:15). Jesus suddenly speaks again in the midst of the sixth bowl, encouraging the Asian believers to persevere. Jesus uses imagery already introduced in the messages to Sardis and Laodicea. The believers were to remain watchful lest his coming be like a thief in the night (3:2–3) and to dress in white clothes to cover their shameful nakedness (3:18; see comments). Although the clothing/nakedness imagery is largely figurative here, it suggests an ancient cultural practice whereby people slept nude. There were varying opinions about nakedness in the ancient world. Greek athletes competed nude and introduced the gymnasium (from *gymnos*, "naked") to the Romans and Jews. The Romans were more conservative than the Greeks about public nudity. Males portrayed in Roman statues were usually clothed while their Greek counterparts were not.[106] When a gymnasium was established in Jerusalem and Jewish youth began to practice Greek customs such as nudity, traditional Jewish sensibilities were greatly offended (2 Macc. 4:9–15). This grievance was a background to the Maccabean rebellion.

Then they gathered the kings together to the place that in Hebrew is called Armageddon (16:16). Armageddon is popularly recognized as the place where the last battle between the forces of good and evil will take place. John appears to give a clue to its geographical location. Unlike 9:11 where John translates the Hebrew name *Abaddōn* into the approximate Greek form *Apollyōn*, here he simply provides the transliterated Hebrew word *Harmagedōn*. The closest Hebrew equivalent is *Har Megiddo*, meaning

"mountain of Megiddo." However, no such name exists in the Old Testament, although the plain of Megiddo is mentioned twice (2 Chron. 35:22; Zech. 12:11). Megiddo was a city in the Jezreel valley in lower Galilee that sat on the international highway connecting Egypt with Mesopotamia. It was the site of several major battles (cf. Judg. 5:19), including the one in 609 B.C. between the armies of Judah and Egypt. Pharaoh Neco, on his way to Carchemish on the Euphrates to reinforce the Assyrians, was engaged by King Josiah at Megiddo. Judah was defeated and her last good king was killed in the battle (2 Kings 23:29–30). Ezekiel locates the defeat of Gog in the final eschatological battle on the mountains of Israel (Ezek. 39:4). John combines these Old Testament battlefield traditions and delocalizes the future battle site by naming it *Harmagedōn* (Eng. "Armageddon"), a place without geographical reality. John has already done something similar in Revelation 1:7. There he takes Zechariah's comparison of Jerusalem's weeping at the coming of the pierced one with the weeping at Megiddo (Zech. 12:10–11) and universalizes that mourning to all the peoples of the earth.

Out of the temple came a loud voice from the throne, saying, "It is done!" (16:17). With the outpouring of the seventh bowl comes the completion of the bowl judgments. An *inclusio* involving cosmic phenomena occurs here as in the seal and bowl judgments (cf. 8:5; 11:19). However, the earthquake is unprecedented, splitting the great city into three parts and leveling all other cities. Babylon's demise through the cup of the Lord's wrath fulfills the angelic announcement in 14:8. Although the

REFLECTIONS

JESUS OFTEN LIKENS HIS COMING TO THAT OF A THIEF in the night. His use of this simile suggests several attitudes for Christian living. The first is expectation. Since we know Jesus will return, meeting him at death or at the rapture should not be a surprise to us. Next is spiritual preparation. By living with a heart of repentance and faith, we will not be caught spiritually undressed but instead always be clothed with robes of righteousness. Finally, we are to be vigilant, "staying awake" to the voice of the Holy Spirit as he seeks to guide us through the spiritual hazards of life. Adopting such attitudes is the Christian's "security system" to avoid a surprise visit from the Lord.

MEGIDDO

An aerial view of
the tel at Megiddo.

earthquake's damage is tremendous, it is not the final plague. A plague of large hailstones weighing a hundred pounds each falls on people (cf. 11:19). Hail was the seventh plague that fell upon Egypt (Ex. 9:22–26). For the earth dwellers, this is the third time in the chapter that they curse God because of the plagues. Because the plagues are done, their destiny at the judgment seat is finalized because they do not repent.

The Woman on the Beast (17:1–18)

Come, I will show you the punishment of the great prostitute, who sits on many waters (17:1). One of the seven angels who pours out the bowl judgments now shows John a detailed vision of the judgment against the church's foe personified as a prostitute. Although the great prostitute is not initially identified, her activities suggest she is a first-century Babylon. The angelic interpretation in verse 18 states that she symbolizes the

great city that rules over the kings of the earth. Jerusalem (Isa. 1:21), Tyre (Isa. 23:16–17), and Nineveh (Nah. 3:4) were cities in the Old Testament called prostitutes because of their godlessness. Historical Babylon was a city of many waters because the Euphrates River flowed through the city from north to south (Jer. 51:13 [28:13 LXX]). Rome was similarly situated, with the Tiber River flowing through the city. It is not these literal waters, however, that the angel is talking about. They are interpreted in Revelation 17:15 as "peoples, multitudes, nations and languages," that is, her subjects throughout the empire. Such interpretive clues suggest that the imagery in this chapter is highly symbolic.

There I saw a woman sitting on a scarlet beast (17:3). For the third time, John finds himself "in the Spirit" (cf. 1:10; 4:2). In the desert he sees a second woman whose appearance (i.e., character) is the opposite of the woman he saw in the desert in 12:14. She sits on the same beast that was revealed in 13:1. Rome was named after Roma, the daughter of the site's first settler, Evander. Roma came to personify the city and was worshiped as a goddess. In 195 B.C., Smyrna became the first city anywhere to establish a cult to Rome by building a temple for the deity Roma.[107] By the time of Augustus, about twenty cults of Roma existed in Asia Minor. When Augustus visited Ephesus in 30 B.C., he gave permission for a temple to Dea Roma and Divus Julius to be built for the city's Roman residents.[108] Archaeologists have located this temple between the Boule-

terion and the Prytaneion, two important civic structures in the upper city. The original imperial cult temple to Augustus built in Pergamum in 29 B.C. was jointly dedicated to Roma. Most of the seven cities had active cults to Roma in them. A coin issued in Asia during the reign of Vespasian (A.D. 69–79) shows his image on the obverse and that of Dea Roma seated on seven hills on the reverse. In her left hand is a small sword whose tip rests on her left knee, symbolizing Rome's military might. At the feet of the goddess is a representation of the river god Tiber, while beneath her is a she-wolf suckling Romulus and Remus. Since imperial coin engravers normally copied real statues and structures, it is likely that this portrait of Roma is a copy of an actual marble or bronze relief.[109] Therefore, John sees an image probably known to him.

The woman was dressed in purple and scarlet (17:4). The woman dressed in bright, expensive clothing and adorned with precious jewels is a stock descrip-

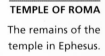

▶

THE GODDESS ROMA

An image of the goddess on a Roman coin.

▶

TEMPLE OF ROMA

The remains of the temple in Ephesus.

tion of a prostitute in antiquity. God asked wayward Jerusalem: "Why dress yourself in scarlet and put on jewels of gold? . . . You adorn yourself in vain. Your lovers despise you" (Jer. 4:30). Purple also signified wealth and nobility in the ancient world. Daniel was awarded the right to wear purple by King Belshazzar (Dan. 5:16, 29). Purple was a color associated with Thyatira (cf. Acts 16:14). A number of inscriptions attest to the presence of a guild of purple dyers in the city.[110] The purple dye used there was derived from the madder root and of lesser quality than that derived from several types of mollusks found in the eastern Mediterranean. This superior dye, known as Tyrian purple, was extracted from the throat of the shellfish with each one producing a single drop. The resulting colors fell in the violet-scarlet range. Because such dyes were expensive, purple came to represent social status on the togas worn by all male Roman citizens. Senators displayed a broad purple stripe on their togas and equestrians a narrow purple stripe. Emperors wore togas entirely of purple. The woman's purple dress symbolizes her connection to Rome and its political elite.[111]

She held a golden cup in her hand, filled with abominable things (17:4). First-century Jews well understood the meaning of abominations, for this unusual word (*bdelygma*) had a rich history in second-temple Judaism. Daniel prophesied about an abomination that would be set up and desolate the temple (Dan. 9:27; 11:31; 12:11).

In 167 B.C., the Seleucid ruler Antiochus IV Epiphanes erected the abomination of desolation—an altar to the Greek god Zeus Olympius—in the Jerusalem temple (1 Macc. 1:54). This and other sacrileges against the Jews sparked the Maccabean rebellion. When Jerusalem was recaptured in 164 B.C., the abomination in the temple was immediately destroyed (1 Macc. 6:7). The cleansing and rededication of the temple was celebrated annually at the Feast of Hanukkah (cf. John 10:22).

Jewish freedom ended in 61 B.C. when the Roman army under Pompey captured Judea and Jerusalem. Pompey desolated the temple by entering the Holy of Holies, forbidden to everyone but the high priest. Pompey's defeat by Julius Caesar and subsequent assassination fifteen years later was attributed by one Jewish writer to his insolence and contempt in despising God (*Pss. Sol.* 2:26–27).

Augustus and the emperors that followed largely respected the sacred status of Jerusalem. Roman military standards, which bore the imperial image, were banned from the city to avoid breaking the second commandment against graven images. In A.D. 40, however, the megalomaniac Caligula provoked the Jews by issuing an order that his image be erected in the temple. Only the persuasive intervention of King Agrippa prevented an insurrection against Rome.[112]

Jesus prophesied that the abomination causing desolation would appear before the destruction of Jerusalem. In Luke's version that desolation is related to Jerusalem's encirclement by Roman armies (Luke 21:20). The Jerusalem church took this as a sign to flee the city in A.D. 66. Matthew's version locates the abomination as standing in the holy place of the temple (Matt. 24:15; cf. Mark 13:14).

Josephus attributed the defilement of the temple to the Zealots who first shed their blood in it and later stopped its daily sacrifice. After the Roman general Titus led his troops into Jerusalem, a confrontation broke out between the Jews and the Romans in the temple area. On August 30, A.D. 70 Roman soldiers set the temple on fire. When Titus entered the temple and saw the splendor of the holy place, he attempted to put out the flames. However, the fire was too far advanced to be extinguished.[113] The desolation of the temple was complete and it was never rebuilt.

Certain Jewish and Christian activists today are mobilizing resources to rebuild the temple in Jerusalem. However, the el-Aksa Mosque and the Dome of the Rock now stand on the temple mount, and any attempt to remove these Muslim holy places would provoke a holy war.

This title was written on her forehead (17:5). The mark of the beast worn by the earth dwellers on their foreheads (cf. 13:16) reflects what the woman herself has on her forehead. The word "mystery" is probably not part of the title, as in the NIV, but rather describes the nature of the name that follows (see 17:7). This is the third and final mystery revealed in the book (cf. 1:20; 10:7). This woman, finally identified as Babylon the Great, is the mother of prostitutes and source of the earth's idolatrous abominations. Again, she stands in contrast to the woman who bore the male child and the other offspring who followed him (12:13, 17). It is inevitable that the descendants of these two lineages would clash. John sees that this woman for the moment has the upper hand in the struggle, for she is intoxicated not with wine, but with the blood of the saints.

The beast, which you saw, once was, now is not, and will come up out of the Abyss (17:8). John's reaction to seeing the woman on the beast is astonishment. For the rest of the chapter, the angel explains the vision he has shown John. The span of the beast's finite rule parodies that of the eternal Father who is and was and is to come (cf. 1:4, 8). When the earth dwellers finally realize his true nature, they too will be astonished, for their names are not written in the book of life. This language is nearly identical to 13:8, except the stress here is on God's eternal election of a people rather than his eternal redemption through the Lamb.

The seven heads are seven hills (17:9). The angel's explanation continues with this final *hōde* saying directed to the original audience. These believers are to discern two things related to the significance of the beast's seven heads. First, they represent seven hills. Rome was known throughout the ancient world as the city of seven hills, whose names are: Capitoline, Aventine, Caelian, Esquiline, Quirinal, Viminal, and Palantine. Numerous Roman writers used the phrase "seven hills" as a locution for Rome.[114] The names of the seven hills are inscribed on the base of a second-century A.D. statue found in Corinth. The statue apparently depicted Dea Roma sitting or standing on Rome's seven hills.[115]

They are also seven kings (17:10). The heads also represent seven emperors, whose identity is problematic. Some scholars have questioned whether John is even referring to actual individuals. While the number seven undoubtedly symbolizes the full sequence of Roman emperors, to interpret it as exclusively symbolic is problematic, since both the seven churches and the seven hills represent literal realities. If it is a historical reference, which emperor is the first?

The Roman historian Suetonius began his *The Twelve Caesars* with Julius Caesar. However, his contemporary Tacitus started his *Annals* with Augustus. From a Roman historiographical tradition, the evidence is inconclusive.

For John and the Asian churches, Augustus, called Octavian until 27 B.C., seems the better starting point. Augustus had a strong link to Asia through his slave Zoilos. In 39 B.C., Octavian influenced the Senate to grant special status to Zoilos's native town Aphrodisias, near Laodicea. Around 35 B.C., Octavian guaranteed the right of the Asian Jews to send the temple tax to Jerusalem. He was the ruler who introduced imperial cult worship to the province in 29 B.C.

Augustus made a personal visit to Asia in 20 B.C. during a tour of Asia Minor. In 9 B.C. the Asian calendar was changed to begin on Augustus's birthday. Jesus was born during the reign of Augustus (Luke 2:1; ca. 4 B.C.). The epigraphical record shows that Augustus still had a pervasive influence over the lives of the Ephesians at the end of the first century A.D.[116]

During Julius's lifetime, the only provincial cities to issue coinage with his portrait were the Anatolian cities of Nicea and Lampsacus. However, the coming of the principate brought a major change to this pattern. Suddenly the portrait of Augustus began to dominate the obverse of provincial coinage. During his reign, seventy-three Asian mints (out of the ninety-seven for the Anatolian peninsula) issued Augustan bronze coins. Augustus' face was as familiar in Asia as the portrait of Atatürk, the founder of the Turkish republic, is today in the region. Because Suetonius called the brief reigns of Galba, Otho, and Vitellius a rebellion,[117] some interpreters omit these three from the sequence of seven. Such lists ignore the ancient literary evidence because the three are recognized as legitimate emperors by Suetonius, the *Sibylline Oracles* (5:12–51), and *4 Ezra* (chs. 11–12). Numismatic evidence demonstrates that the three were recognized as legitimate emperors in the provinces. Galba's representation on Asian coinage shows specifically that his rule was recognized there.[118] Therefore, any identification that omits the three ignores that evidence. Interpreters who date Revelation to Domitian's reign must begin with an emperor later than either Julius or Augustus to make Domitian the current emperor. Or they must develop

---

▶ The Eight Emperors

Revelation presents the eight emperors in a distinctive numerical pattern: 5 + 1 + 1 = 7 + 1 = 8. Five have died, one is currently reigning, another is yet to come. The eighth is the beast, an emperor *redivivus* or *redux*, who will go to his destruction. Nero was the likely head with the mortal wound who was and now is not (see comments on 13:3). Since he would be dead, Nero could not be the reigning emperor ("one is"). Numerous interpretations of the eight emperors have been proposed, but the Principate view that begins with Augustus is now presented:

Five Fallen—1. Augustus, 2. Tiberius, 3. Gaius, 4. Claudius, 5. Nero
One is—6. Galba
One not yet—7. Otho
Beast or Nero redivivus—8.

Revelation would date approximately to the early months of 69, if this model were correct.

an alternate criterion for the list, such as emperors who were deified or died violently.

The ten horns you saw are ten kings (17:12). Rome was the temporary home of many foreign notables who awaited appointments as rulers over client kingdoms throughout the empire. Herod the Great received his appointment as King of Judea there from Antony, Octavian, and the Senate in 40 B.C. Herod's descendants—Archelaus, Antipas, Philip, Agrippa I, and Agrippa II—who ruled various kingdoms in Palestine after Herod's death in 4 B.C. either were reared in Rome or were appointed to their rule there. The ten kings receive authority to rule for one hour. During this brief period they mobilize their kingdoms to join the beast in fighting one final battle.

The Lamb will overcome them because he is Lord of lords and King of kings (17:14). The allied forces of the beast and the kings take the offensive against the Lamb by crossing the Euphrates and gathering at Armageddon (16:12, 16). However, they cannot prevail against the Lamb "because he is Lord of lords and King of kings." While God is called "God of gods and Lord of lords" in the Old Testament (Deut. 10:17; Dan. 2:47), the singular title "King of kings" does not occur until the intertestamental period (2 Macc. 13:4; 3 *Macc.* 5:35). Paul is the only other New Testament writer to use this dual title. Mentioning the Parousia, he writes that "God will bring [it] about in his own time—God, the blessed and only Ruler, the King of kings and Lord of lords" (1 Tim. 6:15). The allies of the Lamb in this last battle are his followers said to be called, chosen, and faithful.

This is the only place in Revelation where believers are described as called and chosen, both familiar designations in the New Testament (cf. Rom. 8:28; Col. 3:12; 2 Tim. 2:10). Faithfulness, commanded to the Christians in Smyrna about to suffer (Rev. 2:10), is rewarded by association with the Lamb at the end.

The Fall of Babylon (18:1–24)

Fallen! Fallen is Babylon the Great! (18:2). Like the angel's announcement in 14:8, this one also speaks of Babylon's fall as if it had already occurred. In fact, for the six different voices heard in this chapter, either lamenting or celebrating the city's demise, Babylon's fall is still future. Jeremiah's prophetic description of the fall of historical Babylon (Jer. 50–51) provides an important backdrop for this chapter. There are at least twelve allusions to Jeremiah in its language and imagery. The angel's opening lament in verses 2–3 mentions several reasons for Babylon's devastation.

A haunt for every evil spirit, a haunt for every unclean and detestable bird (18:2). The Jewish belief that evil spirits lived in desolate places is reflected in the teaching of Jesus (Luke 11:24). He healed a demoniac who lived in the hill country southeast of the Sea of Galilee (Mark 5:5). Jerusalem is described as a ruined city that had become a habitation for unclean spirits (Bar. 4:35). The levitical law identifies twenty different species of birds as unclean (Lev. 11:13–19). The majority of these are birds of prey that drink blood and whose diet consists mainly of carrion or flesh. Isaiah (Isa. 13:21) and Jeremiah (Jer. 50:39) both prophesied that Babylon would be devastated and that owls—an unclean bird—would inhabit the site. Unclean birds, probably carnivorous vultures, are again mentioned in Revelation 19:21.

The merchants of the earth grew rich from her excessive luxuries (18:3). The potential for great profits enticed many merchants to bring their commodities to Rome. However, the risks were also enormous. Storms on the Mediterranean caused many ships to sink, bankrupting the merchants who had laid out a life's savings for the cargo. The business interests of Asian merchants in Rome are attested through an inscription found on the tomb of T. Flavius Zeuxis in Hierapolis. Dating from the first century, the inscription in part reads: "a merchant had rounded Cape Malea [the tip of Greece] seventy-two times on voyages to Italy."[119] To complete such an ambitious itinerary,

Flavius Zeuxis must have averaged two trips a year from Asia to Rome. This merchant probably dealt in the textiles for which the Lycus valley was famous.

Revelation 18 is the only New Testament text to use the Greek word group that speaks of living in luxury and sensuality (18:3, 7, 9). One scholar calls the economic critique in this chapter "one of the fiercest attacks on Rome and one of the most effective pieces of political

◀

DENARIUS

A Tyrian silver denarius with the image of Alexander the Great.

▶ Roman Money

The common unit of Roman money was the sesterce. Calculating the exchange rate of the sesterce to modern currencies, such as the dollar, is difficult because of inflation and the differences in buying power between ancient and modern society. However, such equivalencies can be approximated. During Julius Caesar's time (50 B.C.), foot soldiers received 900 sesterces a year and day laborers earned about 1000 sesterces. Around A.D. 100, Roman soldiers received 1200 sesterces a year, and day laborers, given the same percentage increase, would receive approximately 1333 sesterces. Since four sesterces equaled a denarius, laborers in Rome would receive approximately one denarius a day, the salary of a day laborer in Palestine (Matt. 20:2).

Today the salary of a person receiving a wage of $6 would be $48 a day (approximately $12,500 a year). A denarius would therefore equal approximately $48, and a sesterce $12. Such wages were barely subsistence level in first-century Rome, even as they are at the poverty line in America today. The Roman lower class received monthly grain handouts to supplement their meager wages. The disparity between the rich and poor becomes apparent when we read that Pliny the Younger purchased one piece of property for 3 million sesterces, Cicero paid 500,000 sesterces for a single table, or Vitellius, during his brief reign from May to December 69, spent approximately 900 million sesterces on banquets.[A-56]

resistance literature from the period of the early empire."[120] The wanton luxury of several Caesars is well known. Both Tacitus and Suetonius document the licentious living of Nero and record all manner of his debaucheries. Roman writers during the Neronian period, such as Lucan, Petronius, and Seneca, routinely issued diatribes against wanton luxury.[121] The extravagances of the emperor Vitellius were notable. The menu for one banquet was 2000 fish and 7000 birds.[122] The list of edibles procured from every corner of the empire for the banquet resembles remarkably the cargoes mentioned in this chapter. To feed Rome's appetites generated great riches, and her destruction would be particularly sobering to the Laodicean church, which was flush with wealth (3:17–18). That church is again reminded to desist from its false prosperity, lest the judgment pronounced on Rome's economic system would also come upon it.

Come out of her, my people, so that you will not share in her sins (18:4). The readers are jarred from the prophetic future to present reality by another voice, probably that of God. For this is the only place in the book where the saints are called "my people" (contrast "his people" in 21:3). God frequently calls Israel "my people" in the Old Testament, particularly in the Prophets. Jeremiah issued a similar exhortation to the Jews living in exile to flee Babylon before it was destroyed (Jer. 51:6). In Revelation, however, to come out is not so much to have physical separation, but to be separate spiritually from Rome's sins. The plagues, already poured out prophetically in chapter 16, have only been received in part by Babylon as judgment. Those believers who have failed to repent still

have time to spare themselves from the remaining plagues.

The kings of the earth . . . will stand far off and cry: "Woe! Woe, O great city" (18:9–10). Three groups of Babylon's allies—the kings, the merchants, and the seafarers—now recognize her inevitable doom and cry over her fate. Their mourning is not in repentance, but over lost revenues. Each of their laments begins with "Woe! Woe, O great city" and ends with a declaration of the suddenness of her end. The client kings, who have shared Babylon's power, are now terrified at her fate. As co-conspirators against the Almighty, their doom is likewise imminent. Although they stand apart still hoping to escape, soon the evil trinity will deceive them into joining the great battle at Armageddon (16:12–16).

The smoke of her burning (18:9, 18). Rome, the city on seven hills (17:9), was

REFLECTIONS

WHAT DOES JOHN'S INCISIVE CRI-tique of Roman luxury say to Christians today, particularly those in the West? With household debt and personal bankruptcies rising and personal savings and charitable giving on the decline among Christians, perhaps the "good life" has become an idol to many. The situation of the Laodicean church demonstrates that financial prosperity does not necessarily mean spiritual prosperity. What is our responsibility to our brothers and sisters who are living in poverty conditions? Given the excessive materialism in Western culture, maybe the Holy Spirit is now speaking to the church, "Come out of it, my people."

accessible to the sea through its port Ostia at the mouth of the Tiber. A repeated image in this chapter is a city being destroyed by fire whose smoke is seen miles away by sea captains (17:17–19). This description of an apocalyptic conflagration has a historical antecedent in the fire at Rome in A.D. 64. Rumored to have been started by Nero himself, it was certainly of the massive scale described in this chapter. After burning for six days and seven nights, the fire left only four of Rome's fourteen districts still standing.[123] During Titus' reign (A.D. 79–81), a smaller fire in Rome burned three days and nights, consuming the area from the Capitol to the Pantheon.[124] There is no record of any destructive fire in Rome during Domitian's reign.

The merchants of the earth will weep and mourn over her because no one buys their cargoes any more (18:11). John provides a detailed list of the cargoes carried from the emporia of the world to Rome by ship. Such products were very costly and affordable only to the wealthy of Roman society. The list resembles that of the merchandise brought to Tyre by merchants before its destruction (Ezek. 27:12–24). Of the twenty-eight trade

items listed in Revelation, seventeen are found in Ezekiel. Unlike Ezekiel, John does not give the products' origination point or its middleman to market. Asia was one of the richest provinces in the empire and exported many of its products to Rome. It was noted for its wine, marble, olive oil, textiles, and parchment.

Bodies and souls of men (18:13). The final, and only human, commodity on the list is slaves. The Greek word for bodies (*sōma*) is an idiom meaning slaves. Slaves played an important role in the Roman economic system. In the first century A.D., slaves, most of whom were men, numbered about ten million, approximately twenty percent of the population of the empire. People became slaves for various reasons—sale by parents, indebtedness, self-sale for economic stability, and kidnapping by slave traders. Another important source was prisoners of war. During the Jewish revolt, 97,000 Jewish captives were sent into slavery.[125] Perhaps the most unusual and important source was foundlings—those children who were unwanted and left exposed by their parents. The interior of Asia Minor was an important source of slaves, and many of these would pass through the slave markets in Ephesus before being shipped to Rome. Many slaves were numbered among the members of the early church. Of the twenty-six Roman Christians greeted by Paul (Rom. 16:3–16), it is estimated that two-thirds were of slave origin. Unlike race-based slavery in the antebellum South, the Roman slaves were from every race, nationality, economic class, and educational background. And most slaves had the expectation of manumission by age thirty. Roman slavery was a temporary process, not a permanent condition.[126]

◀ *left*

MERCHANT SHIP

A coin from the reign of Nero depicting a galley ship from Alexandria, Egypt.

Every sea captain . . . and all who earn their living from the sea, will stand far off (18:17). The final group of profiteers is the mariners. Aelius Aristides, the Greek rhetorician from Mysia in Asia, described the scene in Rome: "So many merchant ships arrive here, conveying every kind of goods from every people every hour and every day, so that the city is like a factory common to the whole earth. . . . The arrivals and departures of the ships never stop, so that one would express admiration for the harbor, but even the sea."[127] What John describes is a total disruption of such frenetic activity.

They will throw dust on their heads (18:19). Throwing dust on your head was a sign of mourning in the ancient world. After thirty-six Israelites were killed by the men of Ai, the elders of Israel sprinkled dust on their heads (Josh. 7:6). When the mariners and seamen saw the destruction of Tyre, they sprinkled dust on their heads and rolled in ashes (Ezek. 27:30). The seafarers similarly show their grief.

Rejoice over her, O heaven! (18:20). The speaker, whose identity is probably the same as that in verses 1–4, abruptly changes (not brought out in the NIV). He exhorts those in heaven and on earth to rejoice over Babylon's judgment. Three groups of believers are singled out— saints, apostles, and prophets. In the parallel verse 24, the reference to apostles is omitted. This is the first mention of true apostles in the book (cf. 2:20).

Then a mighty angel picked up a boulder the size of a large millstone and threw it into the sea (18:21). An angel now seals the fate of Babylon by performing the symbolic act of hurling a boulder into the sea. The violence of the act symbolizes the violence with which Babylon would be destroyed. Jeremiah performed a similar act by tying a stone to a scroll of judgment oracles against Babylon and throwing it into the Euphrates. He then declared, "So will Babylon sink to rise no more because of the disaster I will bring upon her. And her people will fall" (Jer. 51:64). Such is Babylon's fate here as well.

Will never be heard in you again . . . will be found in you again (18:22–23). This refrain, with the variation "will never shine in you again," is echoed six times in these verses. The normal activities of life—music, work, and marriage—will forever disappear from the streets of Babylon. However, Babylon's dark under-

ROME AND ITALY

▼

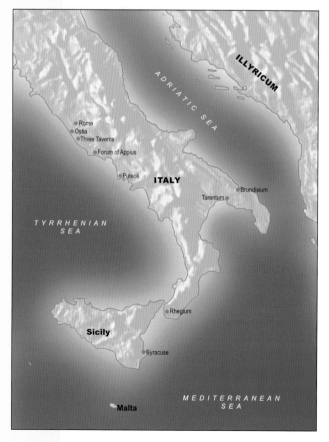

belly is also exposed—her economic exploitation and political control through deceptive magic. The language and imagery again resemble that in the judgment oracles against Tyre in Isaiah 23 (v. 8) and Ezekiel 26 (vv. 13, 21). There is an eeriness to this picture, like the modern visitor to Pompeii who sees time frozen upon streets that one day vibrated with life and the next were sepulchers of ash from Mount Vesuvius.

In her was found the blood of prophets and of the saints (18:24). The shift from the second to the third person in this closing verse suggests that again a direct address to believers is spoken. Its explanatory nature clarifies and complements verse 20. The refrain in verses 22–23 says there is no longer life "in you" (Babylon) because the blood of Christians was found "in her." Babylon's persecution of the church is the primary cause of her downfall. "All who have been killed on the earth" does not refer to a group distinct from the prophets and saints, but simply explains where their blood was shed. These martyrs are identical to the slain seen earlier who also had shed their blood (6:9–10).

The Hallelujah Chorus (19:1–10)

The roar of a great multitude in heaven shouting: "Hallelujah!" (19:1). With the destruction of Babylon, a hallelujah chorus is heard in heaven. The great multitude reappears for the first time by name since 7:9. Responding to the exhortation to "Rejoice" in 18:20, this multitude shouts its praise to God for two mighty acts of judgment: the condemnation of the great prostitute and his avenging the blood of the saints. This chapter records the only four uses in the New Testament

of *hallelujah*, a Hebrew word meaning "Praise the Lord!" that is found frequently in the book of Psalms. David likewise rejoices over divine judgment: "But may sinners vanish from the earth and the wicked be no more. . . . Hallelujah" (Ps. 104:35; see NIV note). Tobit 13:17 states that in the eternal Jerusalem the houses of the holy city will cry, "Hallelujah!"

The smoke from her goes up for ever and ever (19:3). The great multitude's second hallelujah focuses on the eternal nature of Babylon's judgment. The phrase "for ever and ever" is used a number of times in Revelation both positively and negatively. God (15:7) and Jesus (1:18) are both eternal, and praise to them is everlasting (5:13). The reign of Jesus (11:15) and the saints (22:5) is forever. Conversely, fallen Babylon, those who worshiped the beast (14:11), and the devil, the beast, and the false prophet (20:10) must suffer the smoke of eternal torment. This continued emphasis on the kingdom's eternal nature serves to shift the audience's attention from the temporary trials being experienced in this life to the blessings they will enjoy forever.

The twenty–four elders and the four living creatures . . . cried: "Amen, Hallelujah!" (19:4). The response given by the elders and living creatures resembles that given in 5:14 and 7:12, to which is added hallelujah. The focus of their worship is still God seated on his heavenly throne. Their amen concludes the heavenly response concerning Babylon's judgment.

Then a voice came from the throne, saying: "Praise our God" (19:5). This unidentified voice enjoins God's servants to praise God. The focus of praise shifts from Babylon's judgment to the long-anticipated rewards of the saints. The twenty-four elders offer similar praise proleptically in 11:18 because the time has come for the saints to be rewarded.

For the wedding of the Lamb has come, and his bride has made herself ready (19:7). The great multitude shouts the final hallelujah hymn. The focus of their joy is that God's eternal reign has begun and the moment of the Lamb's wedding to his bride has arrived. The Greek word translated "bride" here is literally "wife" (cf. Eph. 5:23). It reflects the Jewish custom in which the formal wedding is preceded by a legally binding betrothal. During this period, which normally lasted no longer than a year, the pair were called husband and wife. To dissolve the betrothal required a formal divorce, which Joseph briefly considered doing with Mary (Matt. 1:18–20). As part of the betrothal, gifts were exchanged between the families. The bridegroom paid a bride-price to the family of the bride (Ex. 22:16–17), while the bride's father presented a dowry to his daughter (Judg. 1:14–15). When the wedding day arrived, the bride prepared herself by dressing in finery, such as an embroidered garment (Ps. 45:13–14), jewels (Isa. 61:10), ornaments (Jer. 2:32), and a veil (Gen. 24:65).[128] The wedding is a familiar metaphor used in Scripture to describe God's relationship with his people. God likened Israel to a bride in the Prophets (Isa. 49:18; Jer. 2:2). In the Gospels, John the Baptist compared Jesus to a bridegroom (John 3:29) as does Jesus himself (Luke 5:35). In the eschatological parable of the ten virgins, the bridegroom (unnamed but surely Jesus) found only five virgins prepared to attend the wedding banquet (Matt. 25:1–13). Paul explicitly identified the church as the bride (2 Cor. 11:2). Revelation's four references to the church as the bride of Christ are the most in the New Testament (cf. Rev. 21:2, 9; 22:17).

Fine linen, bright and clean, was given her to wear (19:8). The bride's garment, which she receives for her wedding with the Lamb, is clean shining linen. Her apparel contrasts with the purple and scarlet linen in which the harlot was dressed (17:4; 18:16). The victors are likewise promised to be dressed in white if they were worthy (3:4–5). John adds an explanatory note interpreting the spiritual meaning of fine linen: It represents the righteous acts of the saints. The plural "acts" suggests that those who overcame had a lifestyle of worthy deeds. These worthy deeds flow out of justification, that is, washing one's robes in the blood of the Lamb (7:14). The antonym of righteous acts is used in 18:5. Because of the volume of Babylon's sins, God has remembered her unrighteous acts ("crimes," NIV). As the day of the Lord's return draws near, the behavior of the saints and the sinners becomes set. As 22:11 declares, the wicked are to continue in their wickedness while the righteous (i.e., the justified) are to continue to do righteous deeds.

Blessed are those invited to the wedding supper of the Lamb (19:9). An angel announces the fourth beatitude, which gives a blessing to those participating in the messianic banquet. The Laodiceans who repented and opened the door to eat with Jesus are now eligible to participate in this wedding supper (3:20). The idea of an end-time feast is found in Isaiah 25:6, where the menu is aged wines and fine meats and the invitation list includes guests from all peoples. The location of this banquet—Mount Zion—is seen in 14:1 with the Lamb and the 144,000 already gathered on it. Before he went to the cross, Jesus had a last supper with his disciples. He announced at the meal's conclusion, "I will not drink of this fruit of the vine from now on until that day when I drink it anew with you in my Father's kingdom" (Matt. 26:29). The church's ongoing celebration of the Eucharist, or communion, is an eschatological event looking forward to that time. As Paul wrote, "For whenever you eat this bread and drink this cup, you proclaim the Lord's death until he comes" (1 Cor. 11:26). The wedding supper thus becomes a reunion dinner when for the first time his bride can drink the cup and break bread together with him.

At this I fell at his feet to worship him (19:10). John's reaction is to prostrate himself before the angel whom he believes is divine. The angel, however, rebukes him and identifies himself as a fellow servant with John and the Asian believers. Angels similarly forbid worship and focus attention on God in other apocalyptic literature (cf. Tobit 12:16–22; *Mart. Ascen. Isa.* 7:21). The worship of angels was a problem in the Asian churches, and Paul condemns the practice in Colossians 2:18. A similar incident of attempted angel worship occurs in Revelation 22:8–9, where again John is rebuked. Rather than attribute John's strange behavior to memory loss, the double rebuke perhaps serves as a strong repudiation of angel worship and a reminder that only God is to be worshiped.

For the testimony of Jesus is the spirit of prophecy (19:10). The phrase, "the testimony of Jesus," was discussed in 1:9 and is common in Revelation. The interpretation of "the spirit of prophecy" is difficult. The NIV translation suggests that the testimony of Jesus is the spirit (uncapitalized), or essence, of all prophetic utterance. While this is true generally for all Christian prophecy, it fails to account for the context in Revelation. By capitalizing Spirit and inserting the untranslated article "the" from the Greek text—"For the testimony of Jesus is the Spirit of the prophecy"—a more viable interpretation can emerge. The seven messages (chaps. 2–3) strongly link the words of Jesus with "what the Spirit says to the churches." Although the Spirit is clearly referred to only nine times in Revelation (the adjective Holy is never added), this text is probably another reference. To paraphrase, the testimony that Jesus is speaking to the churches is the same message that the Holy Spirit is speaking through the rest of the prophecy in Revelation.[129]

The Battle with the Rider on the White Horse (19:11–21)

Before me was a white horse, whose rider is called Faithful and True (19:11). For the second time, John sees heaven opened. The first occasion in 4:1 forms a major transition in the book. There John is caught up to heaven to see God on his heavenly throne and to view the opening of the scroll of destiny. Now John sees another divine figure poised to descend to earth for the final judgment of its inhabitants. The great battle of Armageddon, announced in 16:12–16, finally occurs. The rider is presented using imagery that is introduced earlier in Revelation. His appearance shares aspects with a Roman general returning from a successful triumph over his enemies. White was a color of victory in the ancient world, and the appearance of four snow-white horses was viewed as an omen of victory.[130] The Roman Senate granted Julius Caesar permission to drive a chariot drawn by white horses through Rome to celebrate his victory in north Africa.[131] During such triumphs, Rome became a *candida urbs*, a "city in white," which Juvenal describes as "the imposing procession of white-robed citizens marching."[132] The conquering horseman of the first seal—the false messiah—also rode a white horse (6:1–2).

And on his head are many crowns (19:12). Many diadems ("crowns," NIV) sit upon the Rider's head. Isaiah associated the diadem with royalty (Isa. 62:3), and Esther received a diadem when she became queen of Persia (Est. 2:17). The Greeks and Romans adopted the diadem as a regal badge from the Persians, distinguishing it from the wreath, or crown (cf. Rev. 2:10). Diadem appears two other times in the Greek text. The dragon had a diadem on each of his seven heads (Rev. 12:3), and the beast had a diadem on each of his ten horns (Rev. 13:1), which represent ten kings (Rev. 17:12). After Ptolemy VI Philometer conquered Antioch around 169 B.C., he wore two diadems on his head, one representing his sovereignty over Egypt and the other over Asia (1 Macc. 11:13). Upon the rider's diadem is a name known only to himself. Israel's high priest wore a diadem upon which was inscribed the phrase, "Holy to the LORD" (Ex. 39:30). The many diadems on the rider's head suggest his superior strength, and contrast with the finite number belonging to the dragon and the beast. The diadems visually validate his claim to be King of kings and Lords of lords.

His name is the Word of God (19:13). Of the three names mentioned in this section, only "Word of God" is new to the audience. "Faithful and True" and "King of kings and Lords of lords" have already been named (cf. 1:5; 3:7, 14; 17:14). Although the phrase "word of God" is found in 1:2 and 9, it is not used as a personal name there. The personified Word (*logos*) of God is likewise used as a name for Jesus in the Gospel of John (John 1:1, 14). Word as a title coupled with the imagery of the sword out of his mouth emphasizes the authority by which he declares that the nations are destroyed. The Wisdom of Solomon portrays a similar image, describing the all-powerful word leaping from the heavenly throne as "a stern warrior, carrying the sharp sword of your authentic command" (Wisd. Sol. 18:15–16 NRSV). In Hebraic thought, the concept of word conveys both idea and action (cf. Heb. 4:12), and now the eternal Word moves into action as the divine warrior.

The armies of heaven were following him (19:14). Several clues suggest the identity of this heavenly army. In the preview of this battle in 17:14, the Lamb was accompanied by his faithful followers. And the uniform of these mounted troops—clean white linen—is the same apparel worn by the saints at the messianic banquet (19:8). The army is thus to be identified as the bride, the saints, and not as an angelic host. Their white horses indicate that they are the victors who have triumphed over the beast.

"He will rule them with an iron scepter." He treads the winepress (19:15). The destiny of the male child is to rule all nations with an iron scepter (12:5). Now that time has come when the messianic prophecy of Psalm 2:9 is fulfilled. Not only will Jesus rule the nations, but the victors will rule with him, as the Thyatirans were promised (Rev. 2:26–27). The winepress imagery depicting the harvest of wrath for the earth is first introduced in 14:17–20. There the vintner is unnamed; here Jesus himself is identified as the one who treads the winepress.

On his robe and on his thigh he has this name written: KING OF KINGS AND LORD OF LORDS (19:16). This is the name written on him that no one knows but he himself (19:12), and it is probably the new name that Jesus promises he would write upon the victors (3:12). It is introduced in 17:14, although in reverse order, in a brief preview of the battle. While the image is perplexing, it cannot be interpreted as a body tattoo because the Jews prohibited permanent body markings (Lev. 19:28). Inscriptions were sometimes placed on the thighs of statues that stood in the Greco-Roman cities. Cicero mentions a statue of Apollo that had a name written on it in small silver letters. At Altis, the sacred precinct of Zeus at Olympia, Pausanius saw a statue with this couplet written on its thigh: "To Zeus, king of the gods, as first-fruits I placed here, by the Mendeans / who reduced Sipte by might of hand."[133] The portrait of the Rider contrasts with that of the beast, who is covered with blasphemous names, and the woman sitting upon it, who has various titles on her forehead (Rev. 17:3–5). This title emphatically declares that the beast is not the ultimate head of the kings of the earth, but that Jesus is.

Come, gather together for the great supper of God (19:17). Two banquets are presented in this chapter and implicitly contrasted. The first banquet is the wedding supper of the Lamb and serves as a blessing for the saints. The second is the great supper of God and results from the outpouring of his wrath. The slaughter that occurs is complete and excludes no one who has taken the mark of the beast (cf. 6:15; 13:16). The guests are the carnivorous birds who are invited to feast on the carcasses of the victims. These birds are probably not eagles (cf. 8:13), because the Greek word can also be translated to "vulture." It is translated this way in Jesus' proverb which describes his coming: "Wherever there is a carcass, there the vultures will gather" (Matt. 24:28). That proverb is literally fulfilled in the devastation portrayed here.

But the beast was captured, and with him the false prophet (19:20). The armies of the beast and the kings are gathered at Armageddon to battle the rider of the white horse and his army. Interestingly, no battle is described, for the struggle is over before it begins. Only two prisoners are taken alive—the beast and the false prophet. The false prophet is particularly singled out for his role in working false miracles to delude the earth dwellers. The two are then thrown alive into the lake of burning sulfur. This is the first mention of this fiery lake, composed of burning sulfur or brimstone. In the Olivet Discourse, Jesus made a curious statement about the last judgment: The King will ask the cursed to depart from him into the eternal fire prepared for the devil and his angels (Matt. 25:41). Whereas God was forced to provide a place of punishment for Satan and his rebellious angels, that abode was never intended for man and woman who were created for fellowship in the eternal kingdom. But after the Fall, those who choose to rebel likewise find themselves destined for the eternal fire.

All the birds gorged themselves on their flesh (19:21). The earth dwellers are killed en masse by the Rider's sword, that is, his word of judgment. The resulting carnage resembles Ezekiel's graphic description of the slaughter associated with Gog's destruction. There God also issued an invitation to carnivorous birds: "At my table you will eat your fill of horses and riders, mighty men and soldiers of every kind" (Ezek. 39:20). The defeat of Gog's army serves as a prophetic antecedent to the battle of Armageddon.

The Thousand Years and the First Resurrection (20:1–6)

And I saw an angel coming down out of heaven, having the key to the Abyss and holding in his hand a great chain (20:1). This is the second time that the Abyss is opened with a key. In 9:1, a "star" opens the Abyss to release a plague of demonic locusts. Here an angel is dispatched from heaven, not to release, but to imprison. Fallen angels are likewise bound with chains as they await the day of judgment (Jude 6; cf. 2 Peter 2:4). Chains binding Satan and his fallen angels is a motif found in other apocalyptic literature (cf.

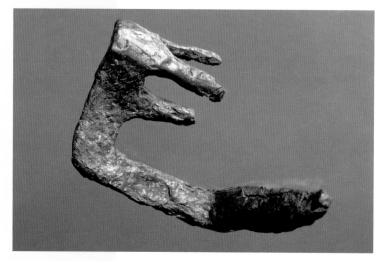

1 En. 54:3–6; *2 Bar.* 13; *Sib. Or.* 2.289). That such a large chain is required suggests the great demonic power of the one being bound.

He seized the dragon . . . and bound him for a thousand years (20:2). The visions from chapters 13–19 trace the activities of the beast and the false prophet. Except for four brief references (13:2, 4, 11; 16:13), the dragon has been out of the picture since his introduction in chapter 12. The relationship between chapters 12 and 20 is apparent. His names are in the same order—dragon, ancient serpent, devil, and Satan (12:9; 20:2), his activity is deceiving (or not) the nations of the world (12:9, 12; 20:3), and the heavenly action either casts him to earth (12:13–17) or into the abyss (20:3). Six times in 20:2–7 a thousand years is mentioned. During this period, the devil is bound and prevented from deceiving the nations (vv. 2, 3), the martyrs live again and reign with Christ (vv. 4, 6), and the unbelieving dead wait in their graves (v. 5).

A thousand years is mentioned in two familiar verses—Psalm 90:4 and 2 Peter 3:8—in which a thousand years is compared to a day, a brief period from a divine perspective. Jewish rabbis speculated about the length of the messianic age, and Eliezer ben Hyrcanus (ca. A.D. 90) estimated the period to be a thousand years.[134] The book of *Jubilees* (ca. 150 B.C.) mentions a thousand years, but this is said to be the life span of persons in the messianic age (*Jub.* 24:15, 27). An early Christian document, the *Epistle of Barnabas*, allegorizes the Genesis account of a six-day creation to signify that there are six thousand years of human history. The Sabbath day signifies the seventh and final thousand-year period when the Son comes and judges the ungodly (*Barn.* 15:4–5). Barnabas's use of a thousand years comes closest to that in Revelation, where John likewise uses the number as a cipher to describe the final period of divine activity.

He threw him into the Abyss . . . to keep him from deceiving the nations anymore until the thousand years were ended (20:3). The dragon's mission is described in 12:9 as leading astray the whole world. He accomplishes this through the great signs and miracles performed by the false prophet. However, "if those days had not been cut short, no one would survive, but for the sake of the elect those days will be shortened" (Matt. 24:22, 24). The binding of Satan suspends his deceptive activity so that the saints might be preserved. The chronicle of Satan's demise is resumed in verse 7.

I saw thrones on which were seated those who had been given authority to judge (20:4). John's vision abruptly changes from the Abyss to heaven, where he sees the martyred souls depicted in 6:4. The martyrs are rewarded with thrones and given authority to judge, fulfilling the promises given to the victors (2:26; 3:21). Judgment by the saints is a familiar theme in the New Testament. Jesus promised the apostles that they would "sit on thrones, judging the twelve tribes of Israel" (Luke 22:30). And Paul reminded the Corinthians, "Do you not know that the saints will judge the world? . . . Do you not know that we will judge angels?" (1 Cor. 6:2–3). While the martyrs are given authority to judge, they are never shown judging. No judgment actually occurs until that of the great white throne when the dead are judged (Rev. 20:11–12). The scene serves to encourage the Asian Christians that one day the power to judge will no longer be in the hands of their oppressors.

And I saw the souls of those who had been beheaded (20:4). Roman law provided two forms of capital punishment. The first was vindictive and involved crucifixion, exposure to wild animals, or burning at the stake. Such punishment was meted out to persons of low social

▶ The Meaning of the Millennium

The thousand years of Revelation 20 is often called the millennium (Lat. *mille* = thousand, and *annus* = year). Chiliasm, from the Greek word *chilia* meaning a thousand, is the belief in a literal thousand-year reign on earth. Three basic understandings of the millennium are current. Premillennialism is the belief that Jesus will return before the millennium; and after Satan is bound, the saints will then reign on this earth with Christ for a thousand years. Amillennialists believe that the millennium is a present spiritual reality instituted by Christ at his first coming, at which time Satan was bound. The thousand-year reign is now occurring as the souls of deceased believers rule with Christ in heaven. Postmillennialism is the belief that the church with its evangelistic outreach has a direct role in bringing in the millennium. As the nations become progressively more Christian and the kingdom of God is established more fully on earth, the millennial period is ushered in. After the thousand years of peace and prosperity on earth, Jesus will then return. There are, of course, variations on these three positions, which have been held by Christians throughout church history. Each position has its strengths and weaknesses, as its advocates attempt to understand this difficult concept of the thousand years.

status. Jesus, of course, died by crucifixion (John 19:18) as did Peter, according to tradition (*Acts of Peter* 37–38). Some Christians killed during Nero's persecution were dressed in wild animal skins and torn to pieces by dogs at the Roman Circus. Others were crucified along the public streets or wrapped in tunics soaked with oil to be lit as human torches in Nero's private gardens.[135] John's disciple Polycarp was burned at the stake in Smyrna. The death penalty was uncommon for persons of the upper classes. Their punishment usually involved exile or deportation. John's exile to Patmos suggests that his social influence was considerable (Rev. 1:9). However, when capital punishment was proscribed for them, it took a second form—beheading either with a sword or an axe. The governor of Asia could execute only with the sword (cf. 2:12). Probably Antipas had been killed this way in Pergamum, and Paul traditionally died by beheading in Rome (*Acts of Paul* 11.5). Christians who died by beheading were either Roman citizens or persons of social status. This vision probably preserves a memory of John's own brother James, who was the first apostolic martyr and beheaded with the sword by Herod Antipas I in the early 40s (Acts 12:2). Beheading is the only method for the death of the saints mentioned in Revelation.

They came to life and reigned with Christ a thousand years. . . . This is the first resurrection (20:4–5). Jesus is the first to die and come to life again (2:8). The testimony of the angels to the women in Gethsemane was: "Why do you look for the living [One] among the dead?" (Luke 24:5). Through his death and return to life, Jesus became the Lord and Judge, before whose judgment seat all believers will stand one day (Rom. 14:9–12). The beast's power to deceive results from his counterfeit resurrection that occurs following his fatal wound (13:14). Such scriptures suggest that this resurrection should be interpreted as physical, not spiritual, as amillennialists suggest. While the martyrs who epitomize the righteous dead are included in the first resurrection, another group does not come back to life until after the thousand years. This implied "second resurrection" is for the unrighteous dead, who are not the recipients of the beatitude that follows, but whose fate is the second death. This is the third pair of images that contrast the destiny of the righteous and unrighteous—two harvests, two banquets, and two resurrections.

Blessed and holy are those who have part in the first resurrection (20:6). This is the fifth beatitude directed to all of the Asian believers. Sin's juridical authority to produce death is now broken for those who participate in the first resurrection. Here the second death is contrasted with the first resurrection. The implied "first death" is universal, except for those raptured at Christ's coming. The time of the first resurrection is neither the believer's spiritual resurrection following a decision of faith (John 11:25–26), nor the intermediate state with Christ after death (Phil. 1:23). Rather, the first resurrection occurs at Christ's return during the "thousand years." This perspective accords with Paul's teaching on the resurrection of the saints (1 Thess. 4:16–17; 1 Cor. 15:51–52).

They will be priests of God and of Christ and will reign with him for a thousand years (20:6). The reign of the saints was prophesied by Daniel: "Then the sovereignty, power and greatness of the king-

REFLECTIONS

FOR JOHN AND THE OTHER NEW Testament writers, the threat of persecution and martyrdom was constant. Yet many Christians today live free of tribulation and die peaceful deaths. How do we maintain our spiritual edge when life is relatively easy and our faith goes largely unchallenged? Jesus calls us as his disciples to deny ourselves and take up his cross daily and follow him (Luke 9:23). In principle, every Christian must be a living martyr, ready to lay down his or her life for the faith. Martyrdom then is an attitude rather than an act for Christians in safe countries.

doms under the whole heaven will be handed over to the saints" (Dan. 7:27). The identity of those who reign is sometimes questioned. Are they only the martyrs or all the righteous dead? Two things suggest the latter. First, the beatitudes are addressed to all Asian believers, and John never suggests that everyone will be martyred. Second, this priestly reign of the saints fulfills the new song of the elders that people from every language and nation would be a kingdom and priests (Rev. 5:10; cf. 1:6). This group is a universal, not a select, one. The inclusive nature of this beatitude is echoed in one of Paul's trustworthy sayings: "If we died with him, we will also live with him; if we endure, we will also reign with him" (2 Tim. 2:11–12).

The Judgment of Satan and the Dead (20:7–15).

Satan ... will go out to deceive the nations in the four corners of the earth—

Gog and Magog (20:7, 8). After Satan's release, he resumes his deception of the nations, which is described in 16:13–16 as leading to the battle of Armageddon. Here that last battle is called Gog and Magog. "The sand of the seashore" is a figure of speech used to describe a large army (cf. Josh. 11:4; 2 Sam. 17:11). The background of the language and sequence here lies in the eschatological restoration and battle described in Ezekiel 37–39. First, there is the resurrection of the dry bones and the return of Israel to the land (Ezek. 37:1–14; cf. the first resurrection). The covenantal restoration that follows in 37:15–28 is not portrayed by John until chapters 21–22. Next, Israel is attacked from the north by the armies of Gog and Magog (Ezek. 38:1–16). The early Lydian king Gyges of Sardis (ca. 700 B.C.) is thought to be the historical figure behind the Jewish tradition of Gog, a tradition undoubtedly familiar to the Asian Christians. Known in Assyrian inscriptions as Gugu, Gog came to personify the evil forces that would come against Israel in the last days. Gyges is buried in a conspicuous necropolis of tumuli, or burial mounds, called Bin Tepe ("a thousand mounds") about five miles north of Sardis. Gyges' mound is set on the highest point of the bedrock and is one of three mounds that rises higher than the other hundred tumuli. Gog's attack against Israel arouses God's anger, and he sends judgments of sword, plague, and hailstones against the nations mobilized against his people (Ezek. 38:17–39:6). That judgment culminates when God sends fire on Magog (39:6). The clean-up of Gog's armies is accomplished by the carnivores, birds and beasts who feed on the rotting corpses (39:4, 17–20), a scene already depicted in Revelation 19:17–21.

The shared tradition in Ezekiel that underlies these scenes in Revelation 19 and 20 shows that the battles are one and the same.

They . . . surrounded the camp of God's people, the city he loves (20:9). "Camp" refers to a fortified military facility, such as the Roman barracks in which Paul was incarcerated in Jerusalem (cf. Acts 21:34). Using a related word, Jesus warned that Jerusalem would be surrounded by army camps before its desolation (cf. Luke 19:43; 21:20). The Romans established several camps around the city to quarter the four legions that besieged Jerusalem and brought its fall. "Camp" can also be translated as "army" (cf. Judg. 8:11 LXX). God's people as an army are portrayed in Revelation 19:14 where they are seen accompanying the Rider. While the Rider's sword (i.e., word) causes the destruction of the armies in chapter 19, here heavenly fire devours them. The link between the two is seen in God's question to Jeremiah, "Is not my word like fire?" (Jer. 23:29; cf. 5:14). God's army of saints is also compared to a beloved city, whose nature is fully revealed in chapter 21.

And the devil . . . was thrown into the lake of burning sulfur (20:10). The source of the lake of fire imagery is obscure. Gehenna, the usual biblical expression for hell (cf. Matt. 5:29–30; Mark 9:43–49), is missing in Revelation. The linkage with brimstone/sulfur suggests the destruction of Sodom and Gomorrah (Gen. 19:24; cf. Luke 17:29) by a God who will rain fire and brimstone upon sinners (Ps. 11:6). The final verse of Isaiah 1 (v. 31) and the book's final verse (Isa. 66:24) both state that the fate of the wicked is to burn, and no one can quench the fire (cf. 34:9; Mark 9:48). Burning sulfur was one of the elements God used to destroy Gog and his armies (Ezek. 38:22). Similar themes are found in the intertestamental book of *1 Enoch*. The unrighteous burn and die for eternity as their punishment on the great day of judgment (*1 En.* 10:12–13; cf. 103:8), while suffering in the presence of the righteous (48:9). The lake of burning sulfur—the end of the beast and the false prophet following the great battle (Rev. 19:20)—is likewise the fate of the devil. Eternal torment is the final destiny of this unholy trinity, who never appear again in Revelation. Their judgment occurs before that of the unrighteous dead, which follows.

The Judgment of the Dead (20:11–15)

Then I saw a great white throne and him who was seated on it (20:11). The judgment scene that follows resembles that in Daniel 7:9–10. There the Ancient of Days, seated on his throne, executes judgment as the heavenly books are opened. Although John sees the heavenly throne many times, only here does he describe it as large and white. The color white suggests the triumph of God's righteousness, and the large throne suggests the great task of final judgment. The judgment of the great and small, announced in Revelation 11:18, involves all those in the second resurrection. The dead are judged according to their individual deeds as recorded in the books. *Second Baruch* 24:1 likewise speaks of books that will be opened "in which are written the sins of all those who have sinned." In Revelation, salvation is never based on good works, but always related to the blood of the Lamb.[136] Jesus spoke of a judgment of the nations at the Parousia (Matt. 25:31–46). As the nations are gathered before his throne, Jesus will separate the righteous from the unrighteous, as a shepherd separates sheep from goats. Although the people are first gathered collectively in nations, they are judged individually. The wicked receive eternal punishment, while the righteous go to eternal life (v. 46). The disappearance of the earth and sky signals the passing away of the first heaven and earth (cf. Rev. 21:1).

Another book was opened, which is the book of life (20:12). Daniel prophesied that "everyone whose name is found written in the book—will be delivered" (Dan. 12:1). The deliverance promised to the righteous dead is everlasting life (12:2). The victors in Sardis are promised that their names would not be erased from the book of life (Rev. 3:5). The primary act disqualifying the earth dwellers from inclusion in the book of life is worshiping the beast rather than the Lamb (cf. 13:8; 17:8). The consequence of

omission from the book of life is being thrown into the lake of fire. An angel has earlier warned those who worship the beast that eternal torment with burning sulfur would be their fate (14:10–11). That moment has finally arrived.

Then death and Hades were thrown into the lake of fire. The lake of fire is the second death (20:14). The second death is eternal, and to suggest it is annihilation introduces a theological concept absent from the text. The language of eternity here forbids thinking of a dissolution into nothingness. Whatever its specific outworking in the divine plan, for John's audience the lake of fire was meant to be a hard saying to dissuade false teachers and to frighten potential apostates. The dead, who are excluded from the first resurrection, are the multitudes spoken of by Daniel who will awaken to shame and eternal contempt (Dan. 12:2). Upon hearing the voice of the Son of Man, those practicing evil will come out of their graves to be condemned to the resurrection of judgment (John 5:28–29). The second death is the punishment Jesus warned about: "Rather, be afraid of the One who can destroy both soul and body in hell" (Matt. 10:28). Death and Hades are the last to be thrown into the lake of fire. He who holds the keys of death and Hades has finally turned the lock (cf. Rev. 1:18). This picture accords with Paul's statement, "The last enemy to be destroyed is death" (1 Cor. 15:26).

The New Jerusalem (21:1–22:6a)

Then I saw a new heaven and a new earth (21:1). The transformation of the universe was prophesied by Isaiah: "Behold, I will create new heavens and a

◀ *left*

CENSUS DOCUMENT

A first-century A.D. papyrus census list from Egypt.

new earth" (Isa. 65:17; cf. 66:22). Its inhabitants would be the nations from the far corners of the earth, including Lydia and Javan ("Greece," NIV; 66:19). Ionia, a region on Anatolia's western coast, is the Greek equivalent of Javan. Ephesus and Smyrna were geographically located in ancient Ionia; Sardis and Philadelphia in Lydia. This Old Testament prophecy was being fulfilled through the believers in these churches. Following the day of God, the early church was "looking forward to a new heaven and a new earth" (2 Peter 3:13). "New" (*kainos*) is an eschatological catchword in Revelation that speaks of the kingdom of God and the coming age when all things become new (Rev. 21:5). Other "new" spiritual realities include a new name (2:17; 3:12) and the new Jerusalem (3:12; 21:2). Irenaeus likened the new order to the resurrection body,[137] an apt analogy since John deals with it

first in Revelation 20:5–6. The spiritual body has both continuity and discontinuity with the natural body, according to Paul (1 Cor. 15:42–44). The spiritual body necessarily follows the natural body (15:46), but they are of two different worlds—the first heavenly, the second earthly (15:48). Heaven and earth will undergo a similar transformation when the new order arrives.

I saw the Holy City, the new Jerusalem, coming down out of heaven from God (21:2). From the new heaven the Holy City descends. The descent of the new Jerusalem is described twice in this chapter. Here it is compared to a bride, while verse 10 begins its full description as a city. The bridal imagery resumes from 19:7–9, where the wedding of the Lamb and his bride is announced. The use of this image suggests that the new Jerusalem is a people, the church. In 11:2, God's people are portrayed using the figure of a holy city that was trampled; here "Holy City" describes their heavenly destination where safety and security are assured (cf. 21:10; 22:19). The participation of the saints in this city fulfills the promise to be a part of the new Jerusalem (3:12). The coming of a new, second Jerusalem thus implies the passing away of an old, first Jerusalem. This newness suggests more than renewal or renovation, but, in fact, replacement.

Now the dwelling of God is with men, and he will live with them (21:3). God's desire to live with his people in covenant relationship is first stated in Leviticus 26:11–12. This hope, unrealized because of Israel's disobedience, was again expressed in the Prophets. "My dwelling place will be with them; I will be their God, and they will be my people" (Ezek.

R E F L E C T I O N S

PROPHETIC MOVEMENTS HAVE OFTEN SOUGHT TO locate the site where the new Jerusalem will descend from heaven. The Montanist movement, which began around A.D. 170, had its origins fifteen miles east of Philadelphia at Ardabav. Its founder Montanus, with his two prophetesses Prisca and Maximilla, taught that the Paraclete (Holy Spirit) would come just before the second advent. The Montanists believed that the new Jerusalem would descend at Pepuza, also near Philadelphia.[A-57] Recently a Korean prophet moved his followers to the Dallas, Texas area, where he believed Jesus would return and establish his eternal kingdom. Needless to say, his prediction was never fulfilled. Such attempts throughout church history to locate the site of the new Jerusalem have proven futile. Even relocation to Jerusalem to be present at the supposed site of Christ's return is misguided. For his return will be seen globally before his kingdom is established on the new earth (1:7).

37:27) and "Many nations . . . will become my people. I will live among you" (Zech. 2:11). The announcement in Revelation, given prophetically in the Old Testament and proleptically to the martyrs in Revelation 7:15–17, is now fully realized. God's transcendence, which was part of the old heaven and earth, has given way to his immanence as he now lives with his people. He is a personal comforter, particularly to those who have endured much hardship for their faith. Death, mourning, crying, and pain—all associated with the old order—have passed away for the saints. Just as salvation is assured for the saints with Jesus' declaration, "It is finished" (John 19:30), here their glorification is accomplished with God's pronouncement, "It is done" (Rev. 21:6).

To him who is thirsty I will give to drink without cost from the spring of the water of life (21:6). A final promise saying resembling those in Revelation 2–3 is now presented. This eighth saying completes and summarizes the rest. It is introduced by the epithets, "I am the Alpha and the Omega, the Beginning and the End" (cf. 1:8). The Lord God Almighty is the speaker here, not Jesus who addressed the seven churches. The victors are promised three things: the water of life, an inheritance, and adoption as children. Several of the beatitudes given by Jesus reflect these same themes: Those who thirst will be filled, the pure will see God, and the peacemakers will be called sons of God (Matt. 5:6, 8, 9). Water and thirst are familiar metaphors for spiritual life. The psalmist declares that all the righteous will drink from God's river, because with him is the fountain of life (Ps. 36:8–9). Enoch saw a fountain of righteousness that never becomes depleted: "All the thirsty ones drink (of the water) and become filled with wisdom" (*1 En.* 48:1). The promise of the water of life complements the earlier "life" promises—tree of life (Rev. 2:7), crown of life (Rev. 2:10), and book of life (3:5). Such metaphors emphasize that a high quality of life will be a hallmark of the new Jerusalem.

He who overcomes will inherit all this (21:7). Inheritance was an important matter in ancient society. In Israel, the father's inheritance was passed on to the sons, although daughters could obtain the inheritance if there was no male heir (Num. 27:4–11). Such social legislation protected a family's inheritance. The firstborn son, as the first sign of his father's strength, was given twice as much property as the other sons (Deut. 21:15–17). Greek society did not practice primogeniture; rather, the father's estate was divided equally among the surviving sons by lot. In Roman society, the father was the undisputed family head and retained full legal authority over his male children of any age until his death. A father could make his will as he determined, so the fear of disinheritance was a great motivation to filial obedience. Only with the father's death could full manhood be attained and one's inheritance enjoyed. This is the only reference to inheritance and sonship in Revelation. Paul developed the theme similarly: "And since you are a son, God has made you also an heir" (Gal. 4:7) and "Now if we are children, then we are heirs—heirs of God and co-heirs with Christ" (Rom. 8:17). The victors' inheritance—the sum of all the promises—relates directly to the promise of adoption as sons.

And I will be his God and he will be my son (21:7). This promise closely parallels

Nathan's promise to David that God would raise up his offspring to reign forever (2 Sam. 7:14). A similar covenant promise was made by God to Israel: "They will be my people, and I will be their God" (Jer. 32:38). Paul quotes these texts from 2 Samuel and Jeremiah to convince the Corinthian believers that they are now God's temple (2 Cor. 6:16, 18). This adoption formula also resembles the legal language of the covenants that God made with Abraham (Gen. 17:7–8) and Solomon (2 Chron. 7:18). There are varied traditions of adoptions in the ancient world. The Old Testament records three cases of adoption in Egypt and Persia—Moses (Ex. 2:10), Genubath (1 Kings 11:20), and Esther (Est. 2:7, 15). No specific examples of adoption are found in Israel, although the frequent use of such adoption language in the Old Testament suggests that such an institution existed.

A Greek man, either while he was alive or by will after his death, could adopt any male citizen as a son. The only condition was that the adopted son fulfill his legal and religious obligations. The Roman situation was basically the same for males who were fatherless. At age four, Augustus lost his father. Following the assassination of his great uncle Julius Caesar, he was designated the heir in Julius's will and adopted into the Caesar family.[138] However, when a father was still living, given his unique role in Roman society, adoption was more complicated. The natural father, using an adoption agreement, transferred his legal rights to the adoptive father. It was unlawful for the adoptive father ever to disinherit his new son or to reduce him to slavery. The use of adoption language here emphasizes the special relationship the victors will enjoy with God in the new Jerusalem.

But the cowardly, the unbelieving, the vile, the murderers, the sexually immoral, those who practice magic arts, the idolaters and all liars (21:8). This is the first, and most complete, of the vice lists found in the final two chapters (cf. 9:20–21). The parallel list in 22:15 omits only cowardice, unbelief, and vileness, while 21:27 mentions two sins—vileness and lying ("shameful or deceitful," NIV). Many of the sins denounced relate to the situation of the Asian churches. Cowardice and faithlessness were temptations to those facing persecution and possible death (cf. 2:10; 3:11); sexual immorality and idolatry were apparently advocated by the Nicolaitans and Jezebel (cf. 2:14, 20–21). To preserve their lives, some Christians had compromised by resuming the evil practices of their unbelieving friends. However, the warning is clear: Do this and you will experience the second death in the lake of burning fire and brimstone.

"Come, I will show you the bride, the wife of the Lamb." And he carried me away in the Spirit to a mountain great and high, and showed me the Holy City, Jerusalem (21:9–10). John now sees another vision of the heavenly city. However, the order of the images is reversed. John first sees the new Jerusalem prepared as a bride; here the bride is announced before John sees the holy city descending from God. Such a reversal of images suggests that for John, the New Jerusalem is both a people and a place (cf. John 14:2–4). This picture of a renewed city fulfills numerous Old Testament prophecies where Zion is now the "City of the LORD" (Isa. 60:14) and the "City No Longer Deserted" (62:12). Much of its imagery is specifically drawn from Ezekiel's vision of the renewed temple, land, and city in Ezekiel 40–48. This vision is contrasted deliberately with the vision of Babylon, the mother of prostitutes. Both are introduced by one of the seven angels who holds the seven bowls (Rev. 17:1; 21:9) who then takes John up in the Spirit to see the visions (17:3; 21:10). The earthly city Babylon is a prostitute while the heavenly Jerusalem, also called the "holy city" (21:2, 10), is a bride and wife. A similar connection between city, bride, and wife is found in *Joseph and Aseneth*. Aseneth is renamed the City of Refuge because many nations will find refuge in her (*Jos. Asen.* 15:7). She is promised as a bride for Joseph (15:9; 18:11) and later becomes his wife after Pharaoh blesses their union and stages a seven-day wedding feast in their behalf (21:4–9). Imagery related to a city now predominates in John's vision.

It had a great, high wall (21:12). Of the approximate one thousand cities in the Roman empire, most were founded as Hellenistic cities. Greek cities were usually walled for defensive purposes. The wall around Ephesus, part of which can still be seen on Mounts Koressos and Pion, was constructed by Lysimachus (3d cent. B.C.). Pergamum, Smyrna, and Sardis each had an acropolis surrounded by a wall. After Laodicea was ravaged by multiple earthquakes in the first century, it is doubtful that its wall was restored. Cities built during the Roman period often lacked defensive walls because of Rome's military might. The defensive walls found in Philadelphia today date to the later Byzantine period. Herodian Jerusalem was surrounded by three defensive walls; and after Titus captured the city in A.D. 70, he ordered that the walls be razed. He allowed the towers of Hippicus, Mariamne, and Phasael to remain,[139] and the lower portion of Phasael forms part of the Jaffa Gate today. The present walls around the old city were constructed by the Ottoman sultan Suleyman the Magnificent in 1537–40. The image of a walled city thus suggests safety and security for those allowed inside.

On the gates were written the names of the twelve tribes of Israel (21:12). This is the first use of the number twelve, used repeatedly in chapter 21 to speak of gates (vv. 12, 21), angels and tribes (v. 12), foundations and apostles (v. 14), and pearls (v. 21). Twelve signifies completion and perfection and is the product of the sacred numbers three and four. The gates were the only means of entrance to an ancient city. Ancient Babylon had eight massive gates, while Jerusalem in the time of Jesus had four gates through its outer defensive walls. Ephesus also had four outer gates—Magnesian, Harbor, Koressos, and Agora. The visionary city seen by Ezekiel likewise had twelve gates, three on each side, which were named after the twelve tribes (Ezek. 48:31–34). These twelve sons of Jacob differ from the list in Revelation 7:4–8 where Manasseh is mentioned and Dan omitted. The more general nature of John's description suggests that it is symbolic. Entrance through these gates guarded by angels is not based on Israelite lineage but through moral purity (cf. Rev. 21:27; 22:14). Gates were closed at night for protection but, because there is no night in the Holy City, its gates are forever open (21:25). The twelve open gates suggest unlimited access to God and the Lamb for the victors/kings who will forever offer up their glorious praise (21:24; cf. Isa. 60:11).

Twelve foundations, and on them were the names of the twelve apostles of the Lamb (21:14). The names of the twelve apostles are given in the Synoptics (Matt. 10:2–4; Mark 3:16–18; Luke 6:14–16). John—son of Zebedee, brother of James, a Son of Thunder—is named among the first four apostles in all three lists. Judas Iscariot is also named, but after Judas's betrayal and death, Matthias was chosen by lot to be added to the eleven apostles (Acts 1:15–26). Paul also considered himself an apostolic builder who laid the foundation of Jesus Christ (1 Cor. 3:10), but because he had not walked with Jesus during his earthly ministry, he could never be considered one of the Twelve (cf. Acts. 1:21–22). The church was the finished structure to be "built on the foundation of the apostles and prophets, with Christ Jesus himself as the chief cornerstone" (Eph. 2:20). The twelve tribes and the twelve apostles represent the collective people of God (see comments on Rev. 4:4).

The city was laid out like a square (21:16). In 11:2, John measures the temple of God; here an angel uses a golden rod to measure the city. The square was an important shape in Judaism. The breastplate of the high priest was square (Ex. 28:16), as was the Most Holy Place in Solomon's temple (2 Chron. 3:8). The angelic figure who measured the inner court of the eschatological temple found it to be a square of 500 cubits per side (Ezek. 42:16–20). Many hellenistic cities had square agoras. The lower agora in Ephesus is called the Square (*tetragona*) Agora, measuring approximately 365 feet per side. The length of each side of the heavenly Jerusalem measures 12,000 stadia (12 x 1000), while the walls are 144 (12 x 12) cubits thick. The previous use of the numbers 12, 144, and 1000 in Revelation plus the unreality of the precise measurements—1400 miles for the city and 200 feet for the walls—point to a figurative understanding of these numbers. The city is further given an identical height measurement of 12,000 cubits, making it a perfect cube. The description of the Most Holy Place in the temple is also of a cube (1 Kings 6:20). This portrayal of the eternal dwelling place of God and his people suggests perfection and completeness.

The wall was made of jasper, and the city of pure gold, as pure as glass (21:18). Jasper is a precious stone previously associated with God (cf. 4:3). The purity of the city and its streets is compared to two other precious commodities—gold and glass. Gold in antiquity was typically alloyed with another mineral such as silver, hence pure gold was especially valuable. The use of glass proliferated after the discovery of glassblowing near Sidon around 50 B.C. Glass tableware and vessels soon became common in households around the Roman empire. Impurities in the ingredients or air bubbles left during production commonly produced glass that was colored or translucent. Pure glass was thus highly valued. Sardis was a center both for the production of gold and glass. The gold deposits found along the Pactolus River valley provided the raw material for the gold refineries that archaeologists have discovered at the site. Although these date to the Lydian period of Croesus (6th century B.C.), inscriptions that speak of goldsmiths and gold gilding on public buildings suggest that the tradition of "Golden Sardis" continued into the Roman period. Sardis also emerged as a center of glass production in Asia, particularly in late Roman times (ca. A.D. 400). The Asian believers would associate wealth and splendor with this description of the new Jerusalem's building materials.

The foundations of the city walls were decorated with every kind of precious stone (21:19). Isaiah described the future Zion as a city whose foundations, walls, and gates are composed of precious stones (Isa. 54:11–12). Tobit likewise portrayed the restored Jerusalem as built with precious stones (Tobit 13:16–18). The square breastplate worn by the high priest contained twelve precious stones, each engraved with the names of one of the twelve tribes (Ex. 28:17–20; 39:10–13). The Septuagint reading of Ezekiel 28:13 gives a virtually identical list as that of the breastplate's twelve stones. However, these stones adorned the king of Tyre in the garden of paradise. As John does with other Old Testament borrowings, he adapts this list for his own purposes. His order is different than these other Old Testament lists, and he changes three stones: Chalcedony, chrysophase, and jacinth are substituted for carbuncle, ligurion, and agate, although these may be semantic equivalents. The colors of the stones represent different shades of yellow, red, blue, and green. The stones represent a city not only of majestic beauty and glory, but also one of great value to be desired by its future residents.

I did not see a temple in the city, because the Lord God Almighty and the Lamb are its temple (21:22). The activity in the heavenly city is described in the closing verses of this section using two divine metaphors—temple and throne (22:3). The temple symbolizes the eternal worship of God. The nations of redeemed peoples both worship and reign in the heavenly city. The transformed nations coming into a new Jerusalem is a popular prophetic theme. Isaiah wrote, "And they will bring all your brothers, from all the nations, to my holy mountain in Jerusalem as an offering to the Lord" (Isa. 66:20; cf. Zech. 14:16–19; Tobit 14:6–7). The destruction of the second temple in Jerusalem by the Romans in A.D. 70 was prophesied by Jesus (Matt. 24:1–2). For almost two thousand years, the Jews have not had a central sanctuary for worship and sacrifice. While many prophecy teachers believe that the temple must be rebuilt before the return of Christ, the New Testament never explicitly states that. Instead, the Gospel of John teaches that when the Word became flesh, the divine tabernacle was now with humanity (John 1:14). Because his own body was now the temple (2:19–22), Jesus taught that true worship would be spiritual rather than located at a physical temple either in Samaria or Jerusalem (4:21–24). The temple imagery suggests that

eternal worship will center on God and the Lamb.

The city does not need the sun or the moon to shine on it, for the glory of God gives it light, and the Lamb is its lamp (21:23). Heaven is portrayed here and in 22:5 as a place of perpetual light generated by God and the Lamb. The ongoing activity of the redeemed—worshiping and reigning—takes place in such an environment. The association of God with light is common in Scripture. God manifested his glory as a pillar of fiery light throughout Israel's travels in the desert (Ex. 40:38). David declared, "The LORD is my light and my salvation" (Ps. 27:1). In one of his "I am" sayings, Jesus declared, "I am the light of the world" (John 8:12). And John wrote, "God is light; in him there is no darkness at all" (1 John 1:5). Because of this constant light in the city, no evil or impurity can ever enter its gates.

The river of the water of life (22:1). The new heaven is a restored and renovated Eden, and several images from the original paradise now appear. A river flowed from Eden that watered the garden (Gen. 2:10). After Eden was barred to humanity after the Fall, renewed access to its blessings formed part of Israel's prophetic hope. Joel declared that on the Day of the Lord a fountain would flow out of the Lord's house (Joel 3:18). Both Ezekiel and Zechariah saw waters of life flowing out of the eschatological Jerusalem (Ezek. 47:1–10; Zech. 14:8). The source of these living waters changed from a place to a person with the Incarnation. At the Feast of Tabernacles, Jesus named himself as the source of the streams of living water and identified the Holy Spirit as the spiritual reality, for

which living water was a metaphor (John 7:37–39). The coming of the Spirit at Pentecost was the deposit guaranteeing the church's future eschatological inheritance (cf. Eph. 1:13–14), which in Revelation is the restored Eden. That the source of the river is the throne of God and the Lamb suggests that "water of life" is also used as a metaphor for the Holy Spirit. *Epistle of Barnabas* 6:13 summarizes the imagery found here: "He made a second creation in the last days. And the Lord says: 'Behold, I make the last things as the first.'"

On each side of the river stood the tree of life . . . . No longer will there be any curse (22:2–3). When Eve ate the fruit from the tree of life, a curse came upon humanity and the created order (Gen. 3:1–19). The effects of that curse are at last reversed, and the victors are permitted unlimited access to the tree. John's imagery comes directly from Ezekiel, who saw fruit trees lining the banks of the river flowing from the temple. These trees produced fruit monthly for food, and their leaves were for healing (Ezek. 47:12). In *4 Ezra* 2:18, the single tree of life likewise becomes twelve trees, each loaded with various fruits. The perpetual fruitbearing in the new order epitomizes the transformation of the normal seasonal cycles of seedtime and harvest (Eccl. 3:2). It also symbolizes the ongoing renewal that exists in the eternal city. The healing provided for the nations takes away the mourning, crying, and pain experienced under the curse in the old earth (Rev. 21:4). The abundant fruit and medicinal leaves symbolize the completeness of Christ's salvation for the victors.

The throne of God and of the Lamb will be in the city, and his servants will serve him (22:3). The second eternal activity of the redeemed besides worship (21:22) is service around the heavenly throne, which symbolizes God's eternal rule. Because the effects of sin are reversed, the saints are now free to reign eternally. To see God's face is an idiom suggesting personal contact and fellowship. Although Jesus' time on earth was brief, he promised that in heaven his disciples would be with him forever (John 14:2–3). God's servants continue to be identified as those marked with his name on their foreheads (Rev. 7:3; 14:1). The reign begun by the martyrs during the thousand years (20:4–6) now continues for eternity.

These words are trustworthy and true (22:6a). The angel mediating the heavenly vision affirms its truthfulness for a third time in the closing chapters (cf. 19:9; 21:5). Jesus likewise concluded his Olivet Discourse with an oath: "I tell you the truth . . . . Heaven and earth will pass away, but my words will never pass away" (Mark 13:30–31). Greco-Roman divinatory charms also emphasized the truthfulness of their revelation. This oath formula serves to validate the content of John's revelation to his audience.

The Coming of Christ (22:6b–21)

The Lord, the God of the spirits of the prophets, sent his angel (22:6b). The closing, or epilogue, of Revelation begins with the reintroduction of the angel who first appears in 1:1 and interprets the visions in the book. Since God superintends the spirits of the prophets, the readers are assured of the divine authority behind John's prophecy. Likewise, 2 Peter 1:21 affirms this: "For prophecy never had its origin in the will of man,

but men spoke from God as they were carried along by the Holy Spirit." It is God's intention to show his servants in the seven churches what was soon to take place (cf. Rev. 1:1). "Soon" is used four times as a catchword in these closing verses, signaling prophetic, not chronological, time.

Behold, I am coming soon! (22:7). Jesus has not spoken since 3:22, but now speaks three times in closing (cf. 22:12–16, 20). The final two beatitudes are also spoken by Jesus at this time. Like the threefold oath formula spoken by the angel, Jesus' three statements epitomize the principle that all testimony must be validated by two or three witnesses (cf.

REFLECTIONS

MANY PROPHECY TEACHERS TODAY HAVE LINKED events in Israel with Jesus' words about a generation passing away (Matt. 24:34). In 1988, a number of books appeared predicting the return of Christ, because forty years had elapsed since the founding of the state of Israel in 1948. Of course, Jesus never returned but speculation next turned to the change of the millennium, particularly with the Y2K crisis. Again apocalyptic hopes were disappointed. The next major date on the prophetic calendar is 2007, forty years from the Six-Day War when Israel captured the West Bank and the Jews gained control of Jerusalem for the first time since A.D. 70. Given the track record of previous date-setting, it is doubtful that Christ's return will occur then either.

Why do Christians spend so much time and money on prophetic speculation? It must be due to the fact that we do not believe Jesus' words that no one knows the day or hour of his return except the Father (24:36). Perhaps it is a diversion of Satan to keep the church from accomplishing its assigned task before the Parousia. For Jesus said that before the end will come, "this gospel of the kingdom will be preached in the whole world as a testimony to all nations" (24:14). Before Christ's return, the church must concentrate on completing the Great Commission.

Deut. 19:15; Matt. 18:16). Each begins with the declaration that he is coming soon. For the Asian believers who have not repented, his coming in judgment is imminent (cf. Rev. 2–3).

Blessed is he who keeps the words of the prophecy in this book (22:7). The sixth beatitude blesses those who keep the words of the prophecy, that is, the book of Revelation. This essentially repeats the first beatitude (1:3), which blesses those who keep ("take to heart," NIV) what is written in this prophecy. Keep is a key word in Revelation and means to trust and obey God and his commandments. Each of its eleven uses refers directly to the believers in the seven churches who must keep the word in order to overcome.

Your brothers the prophets (22:9). Here the angel calls the prophets John's brothers. John clearly regards himself as a prophet, for six times he calls his book a prophecy. In 10:11, he is told to prophesy in a ministry like other New Testament prophets (cf. 1 Cor. 14:29–32). Apostles and prophets were closely linked in the early church, since ministry was charismatic and functional (cf. Eph. 2:20; 3:5). Paul himself functioned in both offices during his ministry (Acts 13:1; 1 Cor 1:1; Eph. 1:1). John likewise ministered among the seven churches as both an apostle and a prophet.

Do not seal up the words of the prophecy of this book (22:10). The scroll that John sees in 5:1 has seven seals, which need divine authorization to be broken. In 10:4, John is told to seal up what the seven thunders said to him. Since the contents of the scroll and the words of the thunders have been revealed to John, the angel now

commands John to reveal them also to the churches. The only extrabiblical Jewish apocalypse to have a similar command to conceal and reveal is *4 Ezra.* Ezra is told to write what he has seen in a book and hide it, but he is to teach its contents to those who are wise and able to keep its secrets (*4 Ezra* 12:37–38; cf. 14:5–6, 45–46). John's prophecy must be communicated to all believers because the time of its fulfillment is near.

Let him who does wrong continue to do wrong . . . and let him who is holy continue to be holy (22:11). Four parallel commands follow, the first two to sinners, and the last two to the victors. This contrast between the righteous and unrighteous is likewise depicted at the conclusion of Daniel: "Many will be purified, made spotless and are refined, but the wicked will continue to be wicked" (Dan. 12:10). *Didache* 10:6 gives a similar exhortation to early Christians: "If anyone is holy, let him come; if anyone is not, let him repent." This and the hearing saying that follows in Revelation 22:17 are designed to stir the churches from their spiritual lethargy and to sharpen the divide between the faithful and the apostate in their midst.

I am the Alpha and the Omega, the First and the Last, the Beginning and the End (22:13). Jesus promises that the reward for the victors for their faithful deeds will be distributed at his coming. He affirms his declarations here and in verse 16 by describing himself by five epithets, all previously introduced in the book. "Alpha and Omega" and "Beginning and End" are used as epithets of the Lord God (cf. 1:8; 21:6). Jesus can claim these same titles because he shares God's nature. The meaning of the three epithets in verse 13 is synonymous: Jesus is the eternal One who spans all time. As "the Root and Offspring of David" (cf. 3:7; 5:5), Jesus is the king whose reign will never end; he is likewise the "bright Morning Star" promised to the victors in Thyatira (cf. 2:28).

Blessed are those who wash their robes (22:14). The final beatitude commends those washing their robes, which is the positive aspect of those who have not defiled their garments (3:4; 14:4). This is another version of Jesus' beatitude, "Blessed are the pure in heart, for they will see God" (Matt. 5:8). Meeting this condition is a prerequisite for realizing two other promises—partaking of the tree of life and entering the holy city, the new Jerusalem. This exhortation is a final reminder to the Asian believers to purify themselves, lest they defile themselves with those practicing the sins that follow.

Outside are the dogs (22:15). Dogs is a pejorative term based on the contemptible attitude of ancient Jews towards dogs (1 Sam. 17:43). Jesus, tongue in

---

▶ The Alpha and Omega Puzzle

In A.D. 79, the city of Pompeii was buried by the ash of nearby Mount Vesuvius. When archaeologists excavated the city, many fascinating discoveries were made including what some scholars believe is an early Christian puzzle. In the form of a square it reads in Latin:

```
R O T A S
O P E R A
T E N E T
A R E P O
S A T O R
```

The translation of these five words is: "Arepo the reaper holds the wheels with care." Those who have studied the puzzle observe that its simple meaning must go beyond the obvious. First, note that the words read the same no matter from which corner one begins. Second, the letters of the square spell out the opening words of the Lord's prayer, Pater Noster, if the letter N is used twice. Third, with the double use of N the letters must be spelled out in the form of a cross, which leaves four letters left over—two As and two Os. The diagram reads as shown below.

Back to the square, observe next that the central letter in each side is the letter T. Early Christian tradition saw significance in this shape: "And because the cross, which is shaped like the T, was destined to convey grace" (*Barn.* 9:8). Also note that the T is flanked on all sides by the A and O, the letters representing alpha and omega in Latin. The remarkable nature of the square suggests that these relationships are not merely coincidental, although some scholars question whether this Christian interpretation is viable. But if it is, G. R. Beasley-Murray is right to observe that "the significance of the square lies in its embodiment of the faith that he who is the Alpha and Omega of all things has been revealed as 'our Father' in the Christ who died on the cross."[A-58]

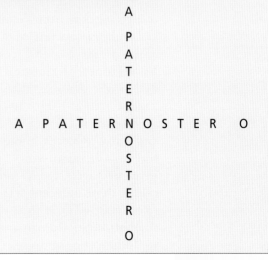

cheek, used the euphemism for Gentiles in general (Matt. 15:26–27).[140] It is also used to denigrate specific individuals: Paul called his Judaizing opponents dogs (Phil. 3:2) and Ignatius called false teachers mad dogs (*Eph.* 7:1). Deuteronomy 23:18 (see NIV note) uses dog as a euphemism for a male temple prostitute. The link with fornicators (NRSV) in this vice list suggests that sexual sin is being denounced. Pederasty was common in the Greek world, and older men routinely took boys as their lovers. The poetess Sappho, from the Aegean island of Lesbos (hence lesbianism), celebrated the beauty of her female students. Although Plato regarded homosexuality as unnatural,[141] intellectuals like Sophocles and Socrates had male lovers even in old age.

The Roman experience with homosexuality accelerated with Greek acculturation in the second century B.C. To describe these new sexual practices, the Romans had to adopt many Greek terms. A law passed in Rome in 149 B.C. made pederasty illegal. The Roman orator and statesman Cicero (d. 43 B.C.) provides two vignettes related to the sexual practices in Asia. Cicero discredited the character of a litigant from Pergamum by using as evidence his virtual kidnapping of a young man from Temnos. And while in Laodicea, a young man named Hortensius propositioned Cicero to have sexual relations.[142] Plutarch was a Roman author who denounced homosexuality as against nature.[143] His fellow critics used such terms as vile (cf. Rev. 21:8; 22:11) and filthy to attack homosexuality. Paul was a Christian voice that likewise inveighed against such "shameful lusts," calling these indecent acts a "perversion" (Rom. 1:26–27). In spite of negative cultural attitudes, Roman aristocrats began to indulge in same-sex relationships.

Julius Caesar's reputation was tarnished because of an affair with Nicomedes, king of Bithynia.[144] Of the eleven emperors in the first century, most were bisexual. The Roman historians Suetonius and Tacitus recorded numerous accounts of the sexual deviancy of these Caesars, particularly Nero who "married" young men on two occasions.[145] Homosexuality was a prevailing vice of Rome and its rulers.

The sexually immoral (22:15). Promiscuous heterosexual activity was even more common in antiquity. The orator Demosthenes, in summarizing the Greek view of sexuality, stated that men should have "mistresses for our enjoyment, concubines to serve our person, and wives for the bearing of legitimate offspring."[146] The mistresses, or *hetairai*, were a regular feature of the male-only Greek banquets and provided sexual pleasures on the dining couches following the meal. Among the Roman aristocracy, adultery was considered an illegal act, not because it broke a divine law but because it violated property rights (wives were considered property). Infidelity also worked against one's self-interest by compromising familial loyalty (Lat. *fides*). Marital sex was primarily for producing children and not for pleasure. Hence slaves were often used for sexual gratification both by the master and the mistress of the household. For the general population sexual intercourse was indulged in freely because it was regarded as a bodily function like eating and drinking (cf. 1 Cor. 6:12–13).[147] Few physical consequences, such as AIDS or sexually transmitted diseases, existed for promiscuous behavior in antiquity. Syphilis was first introduced to Europe in 1494 following Columbus's voyage to America. Jesus' warning of exclusion from the heavenly city because of immorality therefore flew in the face of the prevailing societal mores about sex.

I, Jesus, have sent my angel to give you this testimony for the churches (22:16). This is the only place in Revelation where Jesus identifies himself using the first person. He attests that he is the One who has sent the angel to give this prophetic witness to the churches. This is also the first explicit reference to the seven churches since chapters 2–3, although the original audience has been in view throughout the prophecy.

The Spirit and the bride say, "Come!" (22:17). For the second time, the Holy Spirit speaks directly (cf. 14:13). He is joined by the church presented again as the bride. Responding to Jesus' threefold announcement that he is coming soon, the church now answers three times in a crescendo that builds until the end of the book (22:20). The first invitation to "Come" begins with that of the Spirit and the bride. The Spirit, echoing the words of Jesus, speaks to the churches in the hearing sayings in Revelation 2–3 (cf. Ezek. 3:27). The second "Come" issues from those who are hearing in the seven churches. This same group is now itself invited to come and partake of the spiritual blessing of the water of life.

Whoever is thirsty, let him come; and whoever wishes, let him take the free gift of the water of life (22:17). Isaiah's water metaphor (Isa. 55:1) is now used to symbolize God's restored covenant with the victors, who are the new remnant Israel. This metaphor is likewise found in the invitation in *Odes of Solomon* 30:1–2, "Fill for yourselves water from the living spring of the Lord, because it has been opened for you. And come all you thirsty and take a drink, and rest beside the spring of the Lord." The divine promise to quench the thirst of the saints (Rev. 7:16; 21:6) is finally realized. This saying echoes a familiar word of Jesus in John 7:37: "If anyone is thirsty, let him come to me and drink" (cf. John 6:35). For the Laodiceans who were spiritually parched but did not know it, this final promise to quench their thirst would have been especially significant.

I warn everyone who hears the words of the prophecy of this book (22:18). The warning formula that closes the book is given to protect the integrity of the document. Such formulas, common in ancient sacred texts, acted in lieu of modern copyright laws. A similar injunction concerning God's commandments is found in Deuteronomy 4:2: "Do not add to what I command you and do not subtract from it" (cf. Deut. 12:32). The translators of the Pentateuch into Greek "commanded that a curse should be laid, as was their custom, on anyone who should alter the version by any addition or change to any part of the written text, or any deletion either" (*Let. Aris.* 311). The

REFLECTIONS

CHRISTIANS ARE AGAIN SURROUNDED BY A SOCIETY that has abandoned biblical teaching on sexuality and promotes a promiscuous lifestyle. How do we maintain purity of thought and body when we are constantly confronted by salacious images on television and the Internet, and in movies and magazines? This assault is already negatively impacting the church. The percentage of divorces among Christians approximates that of non-Christians. And several denominations are allowing homosexuals to serve in ministry. Revelation speaks prophetically against such moral compromise and warns that the failure to overcome sexual sin risks exclusion from the heavenly new Jerusalem.

translators of the Pentateuch into Greek "commanded that a curse should be laid, as was their custom, on anyone who should alter the version by any addition or change to any part of the written text, or any deletion either" (*Let. Aris.* 311).[148] And Barnabas warned his readers: "You shall guard what you have received, neither adding nor subtracting anything" (*Barn.* 19:11). This warning is addressed particularly to the Nicolaitans and the followers of Jezebel. Those who add or subtract, that is, distort or minimize, the words of this prophecy, God will add plagues or remove participation in the tree of life and in the holy city. The opposition parties in the seven churches are warned a final time that failure to heed John's prophetic word will result in eternal exclusion from the new Jerusalem.

Amen. Come, Lord Jesus. The grace of the Lord Jesus be with God's people. Amen (22:20–21). This invitation is the equivalent of the Aramaic words *marana tha* meaning "Our Lord, come!" That this word came into the vocabulary of the Greek-speaking churches shows its early use among Palestinian Christians. Paul closed 1 Corinthians with a curse upon those who did not love the Lord followed by the cry *Marana tha*, "Come, O Lord!" (1 Cor. 16:22). This language suggests that the Apocalypse was perhaps later

▶ The Seven Churches Today

Pilgrimages to the sites of the seven churches have been popular for over three centuries. In 1678, Tho. Smith wrote an account of his visit in A Survey of the Seven Churches of Asia, as they now lye in their ruines. Alexander Svoboda provided one of the earliest photographic records during his visit in 1869. Through the years, other famous travelers, such as Mark Twain, Lord Kinross, and Freya Stark, have recorded their impressions of the seven churches.[A-59]

What is the state of these sites today? For over a century, the Austrian Archaeological Institute has been excavating in Ephesus. Its team of archaeologists has completed extensive restoration to the city, making it the premier archaeological site in Turkey today. The site of ancient Smyrna is now occupied by Izmir, Turkey's third largest city. A two-story state agora with a vaulted basement is well preserved in the city center, and Roman ruins remain on the acropolis called the Kadifekale, which overlooks the city. Pergamum attracts many visitors because of its archaeological treasures. Although the altar of Zeus has been removed to the Staatliche Museum in Berlin, the Germans have done extensive restorations to the other remains on the acropolis. The theater that appears to hang from its hillside is one of the most spectacular in the ancient world. The Asclepium there has also been restored.

Thyatira has only a few ruins to see near the city center. Important inscriptions from the city must be viewed at the nearby regional museum at Manisa. At Sardis, an American archaeological team has done extensive restoration, most notably at the gymnasium complex. Its restored synagogue is the most elaborate outside of Israel. Columns from a temple of Artemis still stand below the acropolis. At Philadelphia, visitors can see the pillars of a Byzantine church and sections of a Roman wall running through the modern city of Alasehir. The ruins of a theater and a stadium on the acropolis are unexcavated. Laodicea's large, deserted site is normally bypassed today for the popular hot springs at Pamukkale and its nearby ruins of Hierapolis. However, Laodicea does offer the extensive remains of Greek and Roman theaters, a stadium, an aqueduct system, and the Ephesian gate.

read in the Asian churches when they celebrated the Eucharist. In *Didache* 9–10, the liturgy for communion closes with a prayer of thanksgiving that ends similarly, "Maranatha! Amen" (*Did.* 10:6). Revelation ends with a typical letter closing, "The grace . . . ," a phrase that concludes most of Paul's letters (e.g., Rom. 16:20; Gal. 6:18). The final word "Amen" in the NIV is not found in some manuscripts of Revelation and may be a scribal addition. If original, it would also be the last word in the New Testament and in the Bible, and stand like a divine punctuation mark underscoring the extraordinary revelation that precedes it.

ANNOTATED BIBLIOGRAPHY

Ekrem Akurgal. *Ancient Civilizations and Ruins of Turkey.* 8th ed. Istanbul, 1993.

This is the most complete work on the historical background and archaeological excavations for many of the biblical sites in Turkey. Numerous photographs and diagrams are included.

David E. Aune. *Revelation.* 3 volumes. WBC 52A. B. C. Dallas: Word; and Nashville: Thomas Nelson, 1997–1998.

Aune is one of the foremost interpreters of Revelation today and provides invaluable historical background, although the amount of information may be overwhelming.

Richard J. Bauckham. *The Theology of the Book of Revelation.* Cambridge: Cambridge University Press, 1993.

Bauckham, another outstanding interpreter of Revelation, carefully examines the book's theological themes in this volume. His collected essays on Revelation are found in *The Climax of Prophecy* (Edinburgh: T. & T. Clark, 1993).

G. K. Beale. *The Book of Revelation.* NIGTC. Grand Rapids: Eerdmans, 1999.

Based on the Greek text, this large commentary provides a thorough, up-to-date discussion of Revelation's theological issues as well as its background in Old Testament literature.

Colin J. Hemer. *The Letters to the Seven Churches of Asia in their Local Setting.* Grand Rapids: Eerdmans, 2000 repr.

W. M. Ramsay's foundational work is updated in this study, which surveys literary, epigraphical, archaeological, and numismatic sources.

J. Ramsey Michaels. *Interpreting the Book of Revelation.* Grand Rapids: Baker, 1992.

This incisive guide introduces readers to the various issues involved in interpreting Revelation. Michaels's volume *Revelation* (Downers Grove, Ill.: InterVarsity, 1997) is an insightful and readable commentary for lay readers.

S. R. F. Price. *Rituals and Power: The Roman Imperial Cult in Asia Minor.* Cambridge University Press, 1986.

This definitive and richly illustrated work thoroughly surveys the background and influence of emperor worship in Asia Minor.

William M. Ramsay. *The Letters to the Seven Churches.* Edited by Mark Wilson. Peabody, Mass.: Hendrickson, 1993.

Written by a pioneer epigrapher and archaeologist in Turkey, this is the classic work on the seven churches, particularly in his development of local references.

Main Text Notes

1. For an excellent overview of the development of Christianity in Asia Minor, see R. E. Oster Jr., "Christianity in Asia Minor," *ABD*, 1:938–54.
2. Irenaeus, *Haer.* 5.30.3.
3. Suetonius, *Dom.* 10; Eusebius, *Eccl. Hist.* 3.17–20.
4. See L. L. Thompson, *The Book of Revelation: Apocalypse and Empire* (New York: Oxford, 1990), 103–4; B. W. Jones, *The Emperor Domitian* (London: Routledge, 1992), 117.
5. Josephus, *J.W.* 6.9.3 §420.
6. The Roman poets Statius, *Theb.* 1.22–22; *Silv.* 1.1.79–81, and Martial, 5.5.7, describe Domitian's role during this period. Statius claims that it was Domitian who ended Jupiter's war (the battle for the Capitol) and other hostilities; Martial states that Domitian for a time held the reins formerly held by the Julians and then handed them to his father and brother to be third in the world. Suetonius, *Dom.* 13.1, likewise states that Domitian had "given" the empire to his father.
7. Cited in C. E. Arnold, *The Colossian Syncretism* (Grand Rapids: Baker, 1996), 80; see 61–89 for a full discussion of angel texts with numerous examples; cf. S. Mitchell, *Anatolia: Land, Men, and Gods in Asia Minor* (Oxford: Clarendon, 1993), 2:45–46.
8. Justin Martyr, *Dial.* 81.4; Irenaeus, *Haer.* 3.1.1; 4.20.11; 4.30.4; 5.35.2.
9. Eusebius, *Eccl. Hist.* 7.25.
10. Ibid., 3.39.2–4.
11. W. V. Harris, *Ancient Literacy* (Cambridge, Mass.: Harvard Univ. Press, 1989), 272–74; for the inscriptional evidence see G. H. R. Horsley, "The Inscriptions of Ephesos and the New Testament," in *NovT* 34 (1992): 105–68.
12. Horsley, "Inscriptions of Ephesos," 125.
13. Tacitus, *An.* 14.50; 15:71; cf. Eusebius, *Eccl. Hist.* 3.18.
14. This is the view held by Tertullian, *Praescr. Haer.* 36; cf. G. B. Caird, *The Revelation of St. John the Divine* (New York: Harper & Row, 1966), 21–23.
15. J. R. Michaels, *Revelation* (Downers Grove, Ill.: InterVarsity, 1997), 26–32.
16. W. M. Ramsay, *The Letters to the Seven Churches* (Peabody, Mass.: Hendrickson, 1994), 134. Ramsay's classic study of the seven churches along with C. J. Hemer's updated discussion in *The Letters to the Seven Churches of Asia in their Local Setting* (Grand Rapids: Eerdmans, repr. 2000) provide a comprehensive introduction to each church. Therefore, these foundational secondary sources will not be cited as references for the churches individually.
17. Josephus, *J.W.* 7.5.5 §§148–49.
18. See D. F. Watson, "Nicolaitans," *ABD*, 4:1106–7; D. E. Aune, *Revelation 1–5* (WBC; Dallas: Word, 1997), 1:148–49; Hemer, *Letters to the Seven Churches of Asia*, 87–94.
19. Strabo, *Geog.* 14.1.5, 20.
20. F. F. Bruce, *The Gospel of John* (Grand Rapids: Eerdmans, 1983), 46.
21. Philo, *Vit. Apoll.* 4.7; Aristides, *Or.* 15.20–22; cf. Aune, *Revelation*, 1:171–75.
22. Homer, *Iliad* 24.602–17; Ovid, *Met.* 6.310–12; Pausanius 1.21.3; Quintus of Smyrna 1.292–306. See J. R. March, "Niobe," *OCD*[3], 1045.
23. Tacitus, *Hist.* 3.68; Suetonius, *Galb.* 11; Dio Cassius, 42.37.
24. Eusebius, *Eccl. Hist.* 2.23.11–18.
25. For a full discussion of this important word, see L. Coenen and A. A. Trites, "Witness, Testimony" in *NIDNTT*, ed. Brown (Grand Rapids: Zondervan, 1978): 3:1038–51.
26. W. M. Ramsay, *Historical Commentary on First Corinthians*, ed. M. Wilson (Grand Rapids: Kregel, 1996), 119.
27. The text of this decree, *OGIS* 458, is published in A. C. Johnson, P. R. Coleman–Norton, and F. C. Bourne, *Ancient Roman Statutes* (Austin: University of Texas Press, 1961), §142.
28. *CIG* 300. See Hemer, *Letters to the Seven Churches*, 110–11; G. K. Beale, *The Book of Revelation* (NIGTC; Grand Rapids: Eerdmans, 1999), 259–60.
29. Eusebius, *Eccl. Hist.* 3.31; cf. 5.17. The tradition is confused as to whether Philip the apostle or the deacon is meant or perhaps both.
30. For the Gnostics, see Irenaeus, *Haer.* 1.24.5; Justin, *Dial.* 35; Eusebius, *Eccl. Hist.* 4.7; for Cerinthus, see Eusebius, *Eccl. Hist.* 4.14.6; cf. 3.28.6.
31. See *T. Levi* 18:3; *T. Jud.* 24:1; 1QM 11:6–7; 4QTestim. 9–13; CD 7:18–20.
32. Herodotus, *Hist.* 1.47–49, 71–91.
33. Dio Chrysostom, *Or.* 31.84; Xenophon, *Hell.* 2.3.51.
34. J. A. T. Robinson, *The Priority of John* (Oak Park, Ill.: Meyer-Stone, 1987), 72–81. See also W. Horbury, "The Benediciton of the *Minim* and the Early Jewish-Christian Controversy," *JTS* 33 (1982): 19–61.
35. Pliny, *Nat. Hist.* 36.95; cf. B. Ashmole, *Architect and Sculptor in Classical Greece* (New York: New York Univ., 1972), 7.

36. See Hemer, *Letters to the Seven Churches of Asia*, 186–91; M. J. S. Rudwick and E. M. B. Green, "The Laodicean Lukewarmness," *ET* 69 (1957–58): 263–64.

37. Strabo, *Geog.* 12.8.18; Suetonius, *Tib.* 8; Tacitus, *Ann.* 14.27.1.

38. Strabo, *Geog.* 12.8.16; Vitruvius, 8.3.14.

39. Pliny, *Nat. Hist.* 8.73.190.

40. Strabo, *Geog.* 12.8.20.

41. Pliny, *Nat. Hist.* 36.36.145ff.; Celsus, 5.2; see Hemer, *Letters to the Seven Churches*, 196–99.

42. Strabo, *Geog.* 14.2.24; Appian, *Bell. Civ.* 5.75; Dio Cassius, 49.25.4; Plutarch, *Ant.* 38.3.

43. Pliny, *Nat. Hist.* 37.9–10.

44. R. K. Harrison, "Cherubim," *ISBE*, 642–43. See also J. E. Pritchard, *The Ancient Near East in Pictures* (Princeton: Princeton Univ. Press, 1969), Plates 128, 456, 458, 644–56.

45. Philo, *Alleg. Interp.* 114–16.

46. Josephus, *Ant.* 14.3.1 §35; 14.12.2 §304; 14.12.3 §313; 16.9.4 §296.

47. Josephus, *J.W.* 7.5.2 §§105–6.

48. For Gaius, Philo, *Alleg. Interp.* 353; Suetonius, *Cal.* 22.2; Dio Cassius, 59.28.5; for Nero, Martial, 7.45.7; Suetonius, *Nero* 11.2; for Domitian, Martial, 5.8.1; 7.34.8; 9.66.3; Statius, 1.1.62; 3.3.103, 110; 4.2.6; 5.1.42, 112, 261; Suetonius, *Dom.*13.2; cf. Dio Cassius, 67.5.7; 67.13.4; Dio Chrysostom, *Or.* 45.1.

49. Pliny, *Nat. Hist.* 13.21–22.

50. See E. J. Goodspeed and I. A. Sparks, "Papyrus," *ISBE*, 3:651–55; I. A. Sparks, "Parchment," *ISBE*, 3:663; F. G. Kenyon, *Books and Readers in Ancient Rome and Greece* (Oxford: Clarendon, 1932); H. Y. Gamble, *Books and Readers in the Early Church* (New Haven, Conn.: Yale Univ. Press, 1995), 42–81.

51. Interestingly the *Testament of Judah* (2d cent. B.C.), which purports to be the last words of that patriarch, omits mentions of the lion in its eschatological imagery and instead focuses on the Shoot of God and scepter images (*T. Judah* 24:5; cf. Isa. 11:1, 10).

52. O. Michel, "σφάζω," *TDNT*, 7:934–35.

53. Cicero, *In Verr.* 3.81; Suetonius, *Nero* 45.

54. Tacitus, *Ann.* 12.43.

55. Josephus, *J.W.* 6.3.3–5 §§193–219.

56. Suetonius, *Dom.* 7.2; Philo, *Vit. Apoll.* 6.42; M. Rostovtzeff, *The Social and Economic History of the Roman Empire*, 2 vols. (Oxford: Clarendon, 1957), 1:201, 147.

57. Thucydides, *Hist.* 2.50.1; for the plague, see 2.47–55.

58. For Rome, Suetonius, *Nero* 38; for Jerusalem, Josephus, *J.W.* 6.9.3 §421.

59. For Nero, Tacitus, *Ann.* 12.64; 14.12; 15.47.; for A.D. 69, Tacitus, *Hist.* 1.3.3.

60. Josephus, *J.W.* 6.5.3 §§289–90; see also Tacitus, *Hist.* 5.11.

61. K. Wellesley, *The Long Year AD 69*, 2d ed. (Bristol: Bristol Classical Press, 1989), 140–41.

62. Irenaeus, *Haer.* 5.30.2.

63. Juvenal, *Sat.* 3.62; see also M. Reasoner, "Rome and Roman Christianity," *DPL*, 851.

64. Tacitus, *An.* 15.44; Clement, *1 Clem.* 6:1.

65. Pausanius, 8.48.2–3.

66. A. Burnett, M. Amandry, and P. P. Ripollès, *Roman Provincial Coinage* (London: British Museum/Paris: Bibliothèque Nationale, 1992). Examples from Asia are Smyrna (left 2465/1; right 2473), Sardis (left 3010), Laodicea (left 4403A–14), and Colossae (right 2891). In fact, Burnett et al. list thirty-seven coin issues of Nike that include a palm branch.

67. ΤΟ ΘΥΧΙΑΤΗΡΙΟΝ; see C. Foss, *Ephesus in Antiquity* (Cambridge: Cambridge Univ. Press, 1979), 45.

68. S. R. F. Price, *Rituals and Power: The Roman Imperial Cult in Asia Minor* (Cambridge: Cambridge Univ. Press, 1986), 214–15, Plate 3a.

69. Pliny, *Ep.* 10.96.

70. Josephus, *J.W.* 3.5.3 §86

71. Pliny, *Ep.* 6.16, 20.

72. Dioscorides Pedanius, *Mat. Med.* 3.23.1–4.

73. Seneca, *Apol.* 4.1.22–23; Suetonius, *Nero* 53; Cassius Dio, 61.20.5; 62.20.5.

74. Suetonius, *Dom.* 4.4; 15.3; Cassius Dio, 67:1.2; 67.16.2 [Athena]. For a coin type of Domitian showing a sacrifice to Minerva, see M. Grant, *Roman History from Coins* (New York: Barnes & Noble, 1968), Pl 4, #2.

75. P. Connolly, *Greece and Rome at War* (Englewood Cliffs, N.J.: Prentice Hall, 1981), 259.

76. Guy M. Rogers, *The Sacred Identity of Ephesos* (London: Routledge, 1991), 110–11.

77. For eye healing, see Pliny, *Nat. Hist.* 28.5.28–29; for the chariot curse, *ILS* 8753.

78. On magic, see C. E. Arnold, "Magic and Astrology," *DLNT*, 701–5; F. Graf, *Magic in the Ancient World* (Cambridge, Mass.: Harvard Univ. Press, 1997); H. D. Betz, ed., *The Greek Magical Papyri in Translation* (Chicago: University of Chicago Press, 1999); J. G. Gager, *Curse Tablets and Binding Spells from the Ancient World* (New York: Oxford Univ. Press, 1992).

79. Pliny, *Nat. Hist.* 34.41; Strabo, *Geog.* 14.2.5.

80. The early date of 70 is adopted rather than the traditional one of 96; cf. J. A. T. Robinson, *Redating the New Testament* (London: SCM, 1976), 327–34.

81. Eusebius, *Eccl. Hist.* 2.25.7–8

82. Plutarch, *Pomp.* 80; cf. *Pss. Sol.* 2:27.

83. From Paulus' *Opinions*, J. Shelton, *As the Romans Did* (Oxford: Oxford Univ. Press, 1988), 97.

84. Josephus, *J.W.* 4.6.3 §§381–83.

85. Tacitus, *Ann.* 14.21.

86. See F. Graf, "Apollo," *OCD*³, 122–23; F. Graf, "Leto," *OCD*³, 845–46; "Python," *DCM*, 343.

87. Eusebius, *Eccl. Hist.* 3.5.3; Epiphanius, *Haer.* 29.7; 30.2. Although Josephus does not specifically mention the Christians, he does state that many distinguished Jews abandoned Jerusalem at this time (*J.W.* 2.13.3 §556).

88. Suetonius, *Dom.* 4.4.

89. See D. E. Aune, "The Provincial League (Koinon) of Asia," *Revelation*, 2:773–75; R. A. Kearsley, "Asiarchs," *ABD*, 1:495–97; D. Magie, *Roman Rule in Asia Minor* (Princeton: Princeton Univ. Press, 1950), 1:447–52, 2:1295–1301.

90. Dio Cassius, 59.28.6.

91. Plutarch, *Cor.* 37.3; Suetonius, *Gaius* 57.1; Lucian, *Alex.* 12–26.

92. J. Finnegan, *The Archaeology of the New Testament* (Princeton: Princeton Univ. Press, 1992), 346.

93. The *Atbash* system of encipherment substitutes the last letter of the Hebrew alphabet for the first, the next to the last for the second, and so on through all the Hebrew alphabet. The three Hebrew consonants in Sheshach are decoded in this manner: sh=b (2x) and ch (or k)=l, hence bbl or Babel, the Hebrew word for Babylon. Cf. Charles L. Feinberg, *EBC*, 6:534–35.

94. For the Pompeii graffiti, see A. F. Johnson, "Revelation," *EBC*, 12:533; for the Nero verse see Suetonius, *Nero* 39.2.

95. *Sib. Or.* 5.12–42.

96. Irenaeus, *Haer.* 5.28.2.

97. Burnett et al., *Roman Provincial Coinage*, Nos. 2626, 3011, and 2917.

98. Finnegan, *Archaeology of the New Testament*, 344.

99. Origen, *Sel. Ezek.* 9.13.801.

100. Eusebius, *Eccl. Hist.* 2.25.5–7; cf. F. H. Chase, *HDB*, 3:769.

101. Many commentators believe both harvests are of the unrighteous. For a discussion of the arguments pro and con, see David E. Aune, *Revelation 6–16* (WBC; Nashville: Nelson, 1998), 2:801–3.

102. Mitchell, *Anatolia*, 2:25–26.

103. Herodotus, *Hist.* 1.191.

104. Josephus, *J.W.* 1.32.3 §633.

105. For examples, see Cornelius C. Vermeule, *Roman Imperial Art in Greece and Asia Minor* (Cambridge, Mass.: Belknap/Harvard Univ. Press, 1968), 35–37.

106. Pliny, *Nat. Hist.* 34.18.

107. Tacitus, *Ann.* 4.56.

108. Cassius Dio, 51.20.6–7.

109. For a full description of this figure, see Aune, *Revelation 17–22*, 3:920–23.

110. E.g., *CIG* 3496–98.

111. Pliny (*Nat. Hist.* 9.61–64) gives a description of the purple-dyeing process; see also L. A. Moritz, "Purple," *OCD*³, 1280.

112. Josephus, *Ant.* 18.8.2 §§261–3

113. Josephus, *J.W.* 4.3.12 §202; 4.6.3 §388; 6.2.1 §95; 6.4.5–7 §§250–66.

114. Juvenal, *Sat.* 9.130; Horace, *Carm. Saec.* 5; Ovid, *Trist.* 1.5.69; Pliny, *Nat. Hist.* 3.66–67.

115. H. S. Robinson, "A Monument of Roma in Corinth," *Hesperia* 43 (1974): 470–84.

116. Rogers, *Ephesos*, 94.

117. Suetonius, *Vesp.* 1.

118. A. Burnett et al., *Roman Imperial Coinage*, 1:386, 392, 518; 2:735.

119. *IGRR*, 4:841.

120. R. Bauckham, *The Climax of Prophecy* (Edinburgh: T. & T. Clark, 1993), 338.

121. Lucan, 10.110–21; Petronius, *Sat.* 55, 119; Seneca, *Ep.* 60.2; 89.22.

122. Suetonius, *Vit.* 13.

123. Tacitus, *Ann.* 15.40.

124. Suetonius, *Tit.* 11.8.

125. Josephus, *J.W.* 6.9.3 §420.

126. See K. R. Bradley, "Slavery," *OCD*³, 1415–17; E. Ferguson, *Background of Early Christianity*², 56–59; S. S. Bartchy, "Slavery," *ABD*, 6:65–73; T. Wiedemann, *Greek and Roman Slavery* (Baltimore: Johns Hopkins, 1981).

127. Aelius Aristides, *Or.* 26.11, 12.

128. See A. Edersheim, *Sketches of Jewish Social Life* (London: James Clarke, repr. 1961), 147–55; P. Trutza, "Marriage," *ZPEB*, 4:92–97.

129. This interpretation differs from the one I expressed earlier in "Revelation 19.10 and Contemporary Interpretation," in *Spirit and Renewal*, ed. Mark W. Wilson (Sheffield: Sheffield Academic Press, 1994), 191–202.

130. Virgil, *Aen.* 3.537.

131. Cassius Dio 43.14.3; the Roman poet Tibullus writes similarly: "The Fates sang true, and today Rome celebrates new triumphs,/ while the shackled Gallic chiefs pass, pair by pair./ In an ivory chariot drawn by matched and milk-white horses,/ Messalla wears the laurel that victors wear" (1.7.5–8).

132. Juvenal, *Sat.* 10.45.

133. Cicero, *Verr.* 4.43; Pausanius, 5.27.12.

134. *Midr. Ps.* 90.17

135. Tacitus, *An.* 15.43.

136. Contrarily, in the *T. Abr.* 13:9–14, two angels weigh the righteous deeds against the sins of each individual. Those whose deeds are burned up by fire are consigned to punishment with other sinners, while those whose works survive are placed with the other righteous.

137. Irenaeus, *Haer.* 5.36.1.

138. Suetonius, *Jul.* 83; *Aug.* 8.

139. Josephus, *J.W.* 7.1.1 §1.

140. For other examples in Jewish literature, see W. L. Lane, *Mark* (Grand Rapids: Eerdmans, 1974), 262 n. 63.

141. Plato, *Phaed.* 251a; *Leg.* 1.6363b–d; 8.841d–e.

142. Cicero, *Flac.* 21.51; 29.70; *Att.* 6.3.9; 10.4.6.

143. Plutarch, *Am.* 751c–d.

144. Suetonius, *Jul.* 49.

145. Suetonius, *Nero* 28, 29.

146. Demosthenes, *Or.* 59.118–22.

147. See A. Richlin, "Sexuality," *OCD*[3], 1399; P. Veyne, "The Roman Empire," P. Veyne, ed., *A History of Private Life* (Cambridge: Belknap, 1987), 33–49, 202–5; Shelton, *As the Romans Did*, 37–58; A. A. Bell, Jr., *Exploring the New Testament World* (Nashville: Nelson, 1998), 221–38.

148. Similar curses have been found on Jewish gravestones found in Phrygia dating from around A.D. 250. One example reads: "And if anyone after their burial, if anyone shall inter another corpse or do injury in the way of purchase, there shall be on him the curses which are written in Deuteronomy"; see W. M. Ramsay, "The Old Testament in Roman Phrygia," in *The Bearing of Recent Discovery on the Trustworthiness of the New Testament* (London: Hodder & Stoughton, 1915), 358.

Sidebar and Chart Notes

A-1. See S. T. Carroll, "Patmos," *ABD*, 5:178–79; O. F. A. Meinardus, *St. John of Patmos* (New Rochelle, N.Y.: Caratzas, 1979), 7–22; S. A. Papadopoulos, *The Monastery of Saint John the Theologian* (Patmos: Monastery of St. John the Theologian, 1993), 4–8.

A-2. Tacitus, *An.* 2.54.

A-3. For the translation of one of these inscriptions, see Arnold, *The Colossian Syncretism*, 12–13, 118–19.

A-4. For a fascinating discussion of how oracles at Claros and Didyma functioned, see R. L. Fox, *Pagans and Christians* (New York: Alfred A. Knopf, 1988), 200–61; cf. G. E. Bean, *Aegean Turkey* (London: John Murray, 1989), 155–60, 192–201; H. W. Parke, *The Oracles of Apollo in Asia* (London: Croom Helm, 1985).

A-5. S. Friesen, *Twice Neokorus* (Leiden: Brill, 1993), 25ff.

A-6. See R. E. Oster, Jr., "Ephesus," *ABD*, 2:542–49; C. E. Arnold, "Ephesus," *DPL*, 249–53; P. Trebilco, "Asia," in D. W. J. Gill and C. Gempf, eds., *The Book of Acts in its First Century Setting: Greco-Roman Setting* (Grand Rapids: Eerdmans, 1994), 302–57; H. Koester, ed., *Ephesos, Metropolis of Asia* (Valley Forge, Pa.: Trinity, 1995).

A-7. Ramsay, *Letters* 29–33.

A-8. D. L. Barr, "The Apocalypse of John as Oral Enactment," *Int* 40 (1986): 245–46 n. 9.

A-9. Cicero, *Phil.* 11.2.5.

A-10. Tacitus, *An.* 4.56; cf. R. Mellor, QEA RWMHÇ: *The Worship of the Goddess Roma in the Greek World* (Göttingen: Vandenhoeck & Ruprecht, 1975), 16.

A-11. See D. S. Potter, "Smyrna," *ABD*, 6:73–75; E. M. Yamauchi, *New Testament Cities in Western Asia Minor* (Grand Rapids: Baker, 1980), 55–62; C. J. Cadoux, *Ancient Smyrna* (Oxford: Oxford Univ. Press, 1938).

A-12. Josephus, *Ant.* 12.3.4 §149; 14.10.17 §235; 16.6.6 §171.

A-13. See A. R. Seager and A. T. Kraabel, "The Synagogue and the Jewish Community," in G. M. A. Hanfmann, *Sardis from Prehistoric to Roman Times* (Cambridge, Mass.: Harvard Univ. Press, 1983), 168–90.

A-14. Josephus, *Ant.* 14.10.11–12, 13, 16, 19, 25 §§223–27, 228–29, 230, 234, 238–40, 262–64; 14.12.2–3, 4 §§301–13, 314–17; 16.2.3 §§427–65; *Ag. Ap.* 2.4 §39.

A-15. Cicero, *Flac.* 28.68; cf. Josephus, *Ant.* 14.10.22 §§247–55.

A-16. For further information on the Jews in Asia Minor, see Aune, *Revelation*, 1:168–72; Mitchell, *Anatolia*, 2:30–37; P. Trebilco, *Jewish Communities in Asia Minor* (Cambridge: Cambridge Univ. Press, 1991).

A-17. See K. W. Arafat, "Nike" in *OCD*[3], 1044; Jenny March, *Dictionary of Classical Mythology* (London: Cassell, 1998), s.v.

A-18. *IG*[2], 2311.

A-19. Pliny, *Nat. Hist.* 5.126.

A-20. See M. Grant, "Pergamum," in *A Guide to the Ancient World* (New York: Barnes & Noble, repr. 1997), 484–86; R. North, "Pergamum," *ISBE*, 3:768–70; D. S. Potter, "Pergamum," *ABD*, 5:228–30; H. Koester, ed., *Pergamon: Citadel of the Gods* (Harrisburg: Trinity, 1998).

A-21. See E. M. Blaiklock, "Thyatira," *ZPEB*, 5:743–44; R. North, "Thyatira," *ISBE*, 4:846; E. C. Blake and A. G. Edmonds, *Biblical Sites in Turkey* (Istanbul: Redhouse, 1996), 131–33.

A-22. Tacitus, *An.* 2.37; 4.56.

A-23. See J. G. Pedley, "Sardis," *ABD*, 5:982–84; J. G. Pedley, *Ancient Literary Sources on Sardis* (Cambridge, Mass.: Harvard Univ. Press, 1972); G. M. A. Hanfmann et al., *Sardis from Prehistoric to Roman Times* (Cambridge, Mass.: Harvard Univ. Press, 1975).

A-24. Eusebius, *Eccl. Hist.* 4.13.1–8.

A-25. Polybius, 30:1–3; 31.1; 32.1.

A-26. M. E. Boring, K. Berger, and C. Colpe, *Hellenistic Commentary to the New Testament* (Nashville: Abingdon, 1995), §771.

A-27. Strabo, *Geog.* 12.8.18; 13.4.10.

A-28. See W. W. Gasque, "Philadelphia," *ABD*, 5:304–5; M. J. S. Rudwick and C. J. Hemer, "Philadelphia," *IBD*, 3:1210–11; Magie, *Roman Rule*, 1:124–25; 2:982–83.

A-29. See F. F. Bruce, "Laodicea," *ABD*, 4:229–31; G. E. Bean, *Turkey Beyond the Maeander* (London: John Murray, 1989), 213–21; E. M. Yamauchi, *New Testament Cities*, 134–46.

A-30. Cicero, *Att.* 5.15; *Fam.* 3.5.

A-31. Irenaeus, *Haer.* 3.11.8.

A-32. The others are found in 5:9, 12, 13, 14; 7:10, 12; 11:15, 17–18; 12:10–12; 15:3–4; 16:5–6, 7; 19:1–2, 3, 4, 5, 6.

A-33. Price, *Rituals and Power*, 61, 90, 105, 118.

A-34. F. M. Cross, Jr., "The Discovery of the Samaria Papyri," *BA* 26:4 (1963): 110–21.

A-35. T. T. Packer, "Greek Religion," in J. Boardman, J. Griffin, O. Murray, eds., *The Oxford History of the Classical World* (New York: Oxford, 1986), 262–63.

A-36. Pliny, *Ep.* 10.96.

A-37. Josephus, *J.W.* 6.5.3 §§300–309.

A-38. Paul Rycaut, the British consul at Smyrna (1667–78) who rediscovered the site of Thyatira, provided an early account of the Sabbatai affair in an anonymous contribution to John Evelyn's *History of the Three Late Famous Impostors* published in 1669. Later in 1679, Rycaut incorporated this account into his *The History of the Turkish Empire from the Year 1623 to 1677*. The story of Sabbatai Zevi and other messianic movements is recounted in M. O. Wise's *The First Messiah* (San Francisco: HarperSanFrancisco, 1999).

A-39. Shelton, *As the Romans Did*, 6–17, 206–31; E. Ferguson, *BEC*, 45–60.

A-40. See Bell, *Exploring the New Testament World*, 185–219; J. Matthews, "Roman Life and Society," 748–70; Veyne, *A History of Private Life*, 51–159; F. Dupont, *Daily Life in Ancient Rome* (Oxford: Blackwell, 1992).

A-41. On the principal views regarding the Tribulation, see W. H. Baker, "Tribulation," *EDT*, 1110–11; R. H. Gundry, *The Church and Tribulation* (Grand Rapids: Zondervan, 1987); G. A. Archer, Jr., P. D. Feinberg, D. J. Moo, R. R. Reiter, *The Rapture: Pre-, Mid-, or Post-Tribulational* (Grand Rapids: Zondervan, 1984).

A-42. Diogenes Laertius, 4.5.27.

A-43. *Sib. Or.*, 5.3.18.

A-44. Strabo, *Geog.* 13.4.14; cf. Dio Cassius, 68.27.3.

A-45. See N. W. Lund, *Chiasmus in the New Testament* (Peabody, Mass.: Hendrickson, repr. 1992 and its updated "Preface" by D. M. Scholer and K. R. Snodgrass). See also M. W. Wilson, "The Structure of Revelation and the Seven Letters," *A Pie in a Very Bleak Sky?* (University of South Africa: D.Litt. et Phil. thesis, 1996), 102–28.

A-46. D. H. Lawrence, *Apocalypse* (New York: Penguin, [1931] 1976), 85.

A-47. Epiphanius, *Pan* 3.78.11.

A-48. W. M. Ramsay, "The Worship of the Virgin Mary at Ephesus," in *Pauline and Other Studies* (London: Hodder and Stoughton, 1906), 125–59; G. E. Bean, *Aegean Turkey*, 146–48; V. Limberis, "The Council of Ephesos," H. Koester, ed., *Ephesos*, 321–40.

A-49. This inscription comes from the Asclepium at Epidaurus; E. J. Edelstein & L. Edelstein, *Asclepius* (Baltimore: Johns Hopkins Univ. Press, 1945), 1.§423.17; cf. Hippocrates, *Ep.* 15.

A-50. For the complete text, see C. K. Barrett, *The New Testament Background*, rev. ed. (San Francisco: HarperSanFrancisco, 1989), 1–5.

A-51. The sources for this myth are Tacitus, *Hist.* 2.8–9; John of Antioch, Fr. 104; Suetonius, *Nero* 57; Dio Chrysostom, *Or.* 21.10.

A-52. For example, H. Lindsay, *There's a New World Coming* (Santa Ana, Calif.: Vision House, 1973), 78.

A-53. This paragraph summarizes information drawn from the chapter "Images," in Price, *Rituals and Power*, 170–206.

A-54. Boring et al., *Hellenistic Commentary to the New Testament*, 225.

A-55. See B. W. Henderson, *The Life and Principate of the Emperor Nero* (London: Macmillan, 1903), 153–95; D. E. Aune, "Rome and Parthia," *Revelation*, 2:891–94; cf. F. Millar, *The Roman Near East 31 BC–AD 337* (Cambridge, Mass.: Harvard Univ. Press, 1993), 66–68.

A-56. Shelton, *As the Romans Did*, 129–37, 459; cf. Aune, *Revelation*, 3:1000.

A-57. See W. Tabbernee, *Montanist Inscriptions and Testimonia* (Macon, Ga.: Mercer Univ. Press, 1997).

A-58. G. R. Beasley-Murray, *Revelation* (NCBC; Grand Rapids: Eerdmans, 1978), 62. Other examples of the Rota-Sator square have been found in Cirencester, England and in Dura Europos on the Euphrates; see F. F. Bruce, *The Spreading Flame* (Grand Rapids: Eerdmans, 1958), 356–57; D. Fishwick, "On the Origin of the Rotas-Sator Square," *HThR* 57 (1974): 39–53.

A-59. These impressions are found in Mark Twain's *Innocents Abroad*, Freya Stark's *Ionia: A Quest*, and Lord Kinross's *Europa Minor*.

CREDITS FOR PHOTOS AND MAPS

Arnold, Clinton E. . . . . pp. 8, 132, 178, 180, 206, 248, 262, 266(3), 277, 324
Bredow, Dennis . . . . p. 179
Claycombe, Hugh . . . . p. 56
Dunn, Cheryl (for Talbot Bible Lands) . . . . pp. 22, 52, 215, 218, 304, 320, 344
Franz, Gordon . . . . pp. 36, 318, 351
Haradine, Jane (public domain photos) . . . . pp. 148, 182, 189, 279, 334
Isachar, Hanan . . . . pp. 58, 94, 225
King, Jay . . . . pp. 18, 29, 135, 291, 305, 322, 344
Kohlenberger, John R. III . . . . pp. 5, 89, 90–91, 122, 124, 154, 178, 252, 352
Konstas, Ioannis . . . . pp. 74, 141, 166, 186, 217, 319
McRay, John . . . . p. 302
Radovan, Zev . . . . pp. 4(2), 7, 8, 12, 15, 16, 20, 28, 42, 62, 70, 80,
96, 98, 104, 116, 134, 136, 190, 198, 224, 272, 283,
288, 289, 301, 311(2), 319, 329, 335, 336, 349, 358, 369
Ritmeyer, Leen . . . . pp. 49, 61, 202
Tabernacle . . . . pp. 31, 45, 51, 53(2), 54, 55, 59, 64, 187, 308, 316, 337
University of Michigan . . . . pp. 21, 34, 102, 232, 363
Wilson, Mark . . . . pp. 120–121, 123, 125, 259, 262, 263,
271, 272, 274, 275, 276, 295, 325
Zondervan Image Archive (Neal Bierling) . . . . pp. 2–3, 6(2), 9, 24, 39, 51,
77, 86–87, 105(2), 110, 114, 127, 147, 152–153,
156, 160, 162(2), 164(2), 176–177, 184, 200,
205, 212–213, 220–221, 228–229, 244–245,
246, 247, 248, 249, 254, 260, 310, 312, 326, 343